Kevin Myers

D0456362

Teaching Composition

Background Readings

Third Edition

p. 292-304
p. 163-71

T. R. Johnson

Tulane University

Bedford/St. Martin's Boston ◆ New York

For Bedford/St. Martin's
Senior Editor: Beth Castrodale
Associate Editor: Christina Gerogiannis
Developmental Editor: Stephanie Naudin
Senior Production Supervisor: Joe Ford
Senior Marketing Manager: Karita dos Santos
Project Management: DeMasi Design and Publishing Service
Text Design: Claire Seng-Niemoeller
Cover Design: Donna L. Dennison
Composition: LinMark Design
Printing and Binding: RR Donnelley & Sons Company

President: Joan E. Feinberg
Editorial Director: Denise B. Wydra
Executive Editor: Karen S. Henry
Director of Marketing: Karen Melton Soeltz
Director of Editing, Design, and Production: Marcia Cohen
Manager, Publishing Services: Emily Berleth

Library of Congress Control Number: 2007925241

Copyright © 2008 by Bedford/St. Martin's

All rights reserved. No part of this book may be reproduced, stored in a retrieval system, or transmitted in any form or by any means, electronic, mechanical, photocopying, recording, or otherwise, except as may be expressly permitted by the applicable copyright statutes or in writing by the Publisher.

Manufactured in the United States of America.

2 1 0 9 8
f e d c b

For information, write: Bedford/St. Martin's, 75 Arlington Street, Boston, MA 02116 (617-399-4000)

ISBN-10: 0-312-46933-0
ISBN-13: 978-0-312-46933-7

Acknowledgments
Acknowledgments and copyrights are continued at the back of the book on pages 578–579, which constitute a continuation of the copyright page.

Guy Allen, "Language, Power, and Consciousness: A Writing Experiment at the University of Toronto," from *Writing and Healing: Toward an Informed Practice*, edited by Charles M. Anderson and Marian MacCurdy. Copyright © 2000 by the National Council of Teachers of English. Reprinted with permission.

David Bartholomae, "Inventing the University," from *When a Writer Can't Write: Studies in Writer's Block and Other Composing-Process Problems*, edited by Mike Rose. Copyright © 1985. Reprinted with the permission of The Guilford Press.

Preface

This selection of readings is designed to help you acquire or broaden a theoretical and practical background for teaching college-level composition. Both first-time and veteran instructors in community colleges and four-year institutions will find here helpful perspectives, important ideas, and practical suggestions for teaching and adapting to this ever-changing discipline.

The thirty readings in *Teaching Composition: Background Readings* (ten of them new to this edition) address major concerns of composition theory and practice. Chapter 1, "Teaching Writing: Key Concepts, Philosophies, Frameworks, and Experiences," examines, describes, and reflects on the beliefs, assumptions, and experiences that inform writing pedagogies. The readings in Chapter 2, "Thinking about the Writing Process," discuss ways that writers shape thought into words when they explore ideas, plan, draft, design, consider (or ignore) audiences, reuse, and revise. This chapter also contains additional, updated subsections on the increasingly important topics of integrating technology and visual literacy into the writing classroom, including new sections on plagiarism and blogging. Chapter 3, "Responding to and Evaluating Student Writing," focuses on teachers' strategies for responding to writers' needs and engaging student drafts at different levels, from very specific issues of grammar to the broadest, most subjective forms of response. Chapter 4, "Issues in Writing Pedagogy: Institutional Politics and the Other," focuses on classroom and faculty diversity. Throughout this volume, many of the readings include helpful citations, and at the end of the volume, an annotated bibliography lists other relevant and important articles for further reflection and research.

You can, of course, jump in anywhere and read the article that best suits your needs at the moment. Know, however, that there are rich interconnections among the readings that build coherence into the collection. The articles by Peter Elbow and Nancy Sommers, for example, are referenced frequently in other readings in this collection; in "The Erasure of the Sentence," Robert J. Connors examines and evaluates the sentence-level rhetoric that Francis Christensen sets forth in "A Generative Rhetoric of the Sentence." So you may find yourself stopping in the middle of one reading to refer to another one. The readings have been carefully organized so as to explore important concepts in a logical fashion.

Because teachers are the primary audience for each writer in this collection, you will find very practical recommendations about teaching strategies. A headnote to each reading focuses on the writer's key assumptions and consistent themes. Two kinds of reflective question sets follow each selection: "The Writer's Insights as a Resource for Your Reflections" and "The Writer's Insights as a Resource for Your Writing Classroom." I wrote the first set of recommendations to prompt your reflection as a writing teacher. I based these recommendations on my experience working with writers, my training and supervision of novice writing instructors, and my work with colleagues across the curriculum. The second set of suggestions describes strategies that have worked for professors and graduate writing instructors alike as they apply the insights of a reading to their actual practice in the classroom.

Our discipline's conversations have always been spirited, whether about philosophical issues, specific theories of teaching, learning, and writing, or actual practices that guide our daily interaction with student writers. From such conversations — public and private, in scholarly journals, faculty lounges, listservs, and blogs — and from our own classroom experience and reflection, we gain confidence and clarity in our vision of what we do. I hope your "conversation" with these readings will help you in your work as a teacher of writing.

I would like to extend warmest thanks to the staff at Bedford/St. Martin's, especially to Joan Feinberg, president; Denise Wydra, editorial director; and Karen Henry, editor in chief, for their sincere dedication to offering teachers and students the best possible tools for teaching and learning. I am also grateful to Beth Castrodale and Christina Gerogiannis for their valued help as we shaped this revision; to Stephanie Naudin, developmental editor for the third edition, for her hard work and management of the project; to Emily Berleth, for her meticulous attention to detail and handling of the book's production; and to Cathy Jewel, for her thorough copyediting. Permissions were skillfully arranged by Bookworm Permissions' Douglas Hernandez, Barbara Hernandez, and Rick Lanford, under the direction of Sandy Schechter.

I am also grateful to two graduate students, Aleksandra Hajduczek and Nat Schmidt, whose research led me to include two articles in this edition that, otherwise, might have escaped my notice.

And, above all, I dedicate this new edition of the book to the memory of James F. Slevin (1945–2006), who first set me — and so many others — on this course.

T. R. Johnson
Tulane University

Contents

Preface iii

Other Bedford/St. Martin's Professional Resources xii

1 Teaching Writing: Key Concepts, Philosophies, Frameworks, and Experiences 1

David Bartholomae
Inventing the University 2
"[The student] has to invent the university by assembling and mimicking its language while finding some compromise between idiosyncrasy, a personal history, on the one hand, and the requirements of convention, the history of a discipline, on the other hand."

Gerald Graff
***From* Clueless in Academe** 32
"[A]cademia reinforces cluelessness by making its ideas, problems, and ways of thinking *look* more opaque, narrowly specialized, and beyond normal learning capacities than they are or need to be. As I see it, my academic intellectual culture is not at all irrelevant to my students' needs and interests, but we do a very good job of making it appear as if it is."

James Slevin
A Letter to Maggie 59
"Although we tell students that theses and topic sentences and transitions and clear (even elegant) sentences are important (because they *are*), what really matters is how what I am calling (with my usual intellectual sophistication and precision) 'stuff' becomes evidence."

Guy Allen
Language, Power, and Consciousness: A Writing Experiment at the University of Toronto 65
"The point is that unexpected results have shown me how important it is to examine and test what we do, especially in a field like the

teaching of writing where most practitioners adopt conventional procedures passed down from predecessors. Practices and truisms that we take for granted as common sense sometimes prove invalid when we examine them systematically. The best knowledge often comes out of the collapse of cherished ritual practices."

Dawn Skorczewski
From Playing the Role to Being Yourself: Becoming the Teacher in the Writing Classroom 99
"Becoming yourself as a teacher involves, more than anything, telling yourself who you are and who you are not in the classroom. Although we might have trouble remembering who we are not at the most difficult times, we are not the fearful daughters, sons, and students that we once might have been. . . . When we become ourselves in the writing classroom, we offer students opportunities rather than accusations. We channel our fears into productive comments."

James A. Berlin
Rhetoric and Ideology in the Writing Class 117
"[S]ince language is a social phenomenon that is a product of a particular historical moment, our notions of the observing self, the communities in which the self functions, and the very structures of the material world are social constructions — all specific to a particular time and culture. These social constructions are thus inscribed in the very language we are given to inhabit in responding to our experience."

2 Thinking about the Writing Process 139

GENERATING A DRAFT 140

Sondra Perl
Understanding Composing 140
"All the writers I have observed, skilled and unskilled alike, use the process of retrospective structuring while writing. Yet the degree to which they do so varies and seems, in fact, to depend upon the model of the writing process that they have internalized. Those who realize that writing can be a recursive process have an easier time with waiting, looking, and discovering."

Nancy Welch
Toward an Excess-ive Theory of Revision 207
"[I]ntentions are shaped by the community the writer wants to make his or her way into, and the revision process is not a simple matter of making text 'better' or 'clearer.' Revision is instead the very complicated matter of struggle between a full, excess-ive life and the seemingly strict limits of what can be written and understood within a particular discourse community."

CRAFTING SENTENCES 247

Robert J. Connors
The Erasure of the Sentence 247
"The sentence itself as an element of composition pedagogy is hardly mentioned today outside of textbooks. But we can learn as much from watching the working out of Darwinian intellectual failures as from participating in the self-congratulatory normal science of the current winners, and so I offer this history of syntactic methods since 1960 in the spirit of the old New England gravestone: 'As you are now, so once was I; as I am now, so you shall be.' "

Francis Christensen
A Generative Rhetoric of the Sentence 276
"We need a rhetoric of the sentence that will do more than combine the ideas of primer sentences. We need one that will *generate* ideas."

Ann E. Berthoff
***From* The Making of Meaning** 292
"Students can learn to write by learning the uses of chaos, which is to say, rediscovering the power of language to generate the sources of meaning. Our job is to design sequences of assignments that let our students discover what language can do, what they can do with language."

TEACHING WRITING WITH COMPUTERS 305

James P. Purdy
Calling off the Hounds: Technology and the Visibility of Plagiarism 305
"[T]hese new technologies increase the visibility of plagiarism, allowing interested parties to quickly and easily trace documents to those using similar language. As a result, writing teachers are more aware of plagiarism. In other words, if plagiarism is easier to commit because of the Internet, it is also easier to catch because of the Internet. We in English studies must, therefore, now think about plagiarism in light of technology."

Steven D. Krause
When Blogging Goes Bad: A Cautionary Tale about Blogs, Email Lists, Discussion, and Interaction 325
"As Walker puts it in her 'Talk at Brown' notes, 'How empowering is it to be forced to blog?' And yet, that is ultimately the power and even charm of web logs: it is very easy to master technology and interface in which just about anyone who *wants* to *can* post their writings and thoughts about anything. However, like the paper diaries and journals that web logs are so often compared, the writer has to have a reason — and generally, a personal reason — to write in the first place."

TEACHING VISUAL LITERACY 337

Mary E. Hocks
Understanding Visual Rhetoric in Digital Writing Environments 337
"Recognizing the hybrid literacies our students now bring to our classrooms, we need a better understanding of the increasingly visual and interactive rhetorical features of digital documents. As writing technologies change, they require changes in our understanding of writing and rhetoric and, ultimately, in our writing pedagogy."

John Trimbur
Delivering the Message: Typography and the Materiality of Writing 363
"From a typographical perspective, however, the visual design of writing figures prominently as the material form in which the message is delivered. That is, typography offers a way to think of writing not just in terms of the moment of composing but also in terms of its circulation, as messages take on cultural value and worldly force, moving through the Marxian dialectic of production, distribution, exchange, and consumption."

3 Responding to and Evaluating Student Writing 377

Nancy Sommers
Responding to Student Writing 377
"Instead of finding errors or showing students how to patch up parts of their texts, we need to sabotage our students' conviction that the drafts they have written are complete and coherent. Our comments need to

Other Bedford/St. Martin's Professional Resources

The Bedford / St. Martin's Series in Rhetoric and Composition

Assessing Writing: A Critical Sourcebook, by Brian Huot and Peggy O'Neill

Computers in the Composition Classroom: A Critical Sourcebook, by Michelle Sidler, Richard Morris, and Elizabeth Overman-Smith

Disability and the Teaching of Writing: A Critical Sourcebook, by Cynthia Lewiecki-Wilson and Brenda Jo Brueggemann

Second-Language Writing in the Composition Classroom: A Critical Sourcebook, by Paul Kei Matsuda, Michelle Cox, Jay Jordan, and Christina Ortmeier-Hooper

Visual Rhetoric in a Digital World: A Critical Sourcebook, by Carolyn Handa

Literacy: A Critical Sourcebook, by Ellen Cushman, Eugene R. Kintgen, Barry Kroll, and Mike Rose

Background Readings

Teaching Developmental Writing: Background Readings, Third Edition, by Susan Naomi Bernstein

Teaching Technical Communication: Critical Issues for the Classroom, by James Dubinsky

Teaching Developmental Reading: Historical, Theoretical, and Practical Background Readings, by Norman A. Stahl and Hunter Boylan

Teaching Argument in the Composition Course: Background Readings, by Timothy Barnett

Bibliographies

The Bedford Bibliography for Teachers of Basic Writing, Second Edition, by Linda Adler-Kassner and Gregory R. Glau

The Bedford Bibliography for Teachers of Writing, Sixth Edition, by Patricia Bizzell, Bruce Herzberg, and Nedra Reynolds

Teaching Advice

Take 20: Teaching Writing (DVD), by Todd Taylor

The St. Martin's Guide to Teaching Writing, Sixth Edition, by Cheryl Glenn and Robert Connors

Assigning, Responding, Evaluating: A Writing Teacher's Guide, Fourth Edition, by Edward M. White

Portfolio Teaching: A Guide for Instructors, Second Edition, by Nedra Reynolds and Rich Rice

The Elements of Teaching Writing: A Resource for Instructors in All Disciplines, by Katherine Gottschalk and Keith Hjortshoj

For more information, contact your local sales representative, e-mail us at sales_support@bfwpub.com, or visit Teaching Central at <bedfordstmartins.com/english>.

CHAPTER

1

Teaching Writing: Key Concepts, Philosophies, Frameworks, and Experiences

Every choice you make as a writing instructor is informed by some philosophy of composition and of teaching composition, even if you're not fully aware of the philosophy you hold. The more aware you become of your assumptions and premises, the more you can rethink and improve your teaching. Each of the writers in this chapter challenges us to examine the assumptions that govern the ways we teach. To begin this process of reflection, we recommend that — before you start to teach a writing course or early in the semester — you sit down and freewrite or brainstorm for about fifteen minutes, listing your "I believes" about writing and about the teaching of writing. Periodically shape those beliefs into a coherent format that you can refer to as you plan assignments, structure sequences of assignments, build or redesign a syllabus, ponder a writing curriculum, propose support services for writers across the curriculum, or discuss your pedagogy with colleagues.

After each of the readings in this text, you will find questions and suggestions that help link the piece to your professional development and classroom practice. You may find it useful to reflect on these prompts in a reflective teaching journal. Many first-year instructors keep a journal in which they log and reflect on what occurs in class and how students respond to assignments. Those instructors use the journal to describe their own reactions and responses to the class dynamic, to the process of building a writing community, and to the connections they are making between what they are reading outside the classroom and actual events within their classroom. Two or three times a semester they read over their entries and chart their own learning and growth as instructors. By the end of the first semester, most new instructors can see some dramatic changes in confidence, attitudes about writing communities and student writing, use of teaching strategies, and understanding of how the parts of the syllabus or the course connect. The journal is a very useful resource for writing about teaching, for developing a final draft of a philosophy for teaching writing, and for designing syllabi for second-semester or second-year courses. It could be an important part of a teaching portfolio, a collection of products that demonstrates your practice and improvement as an instructor. Such reflection must be ongoing, for no theory is ever quite complete, no concept will operate in your classroom as a magic formula that guarantees perfect teaching every time, and no framework for thinking about what you do will exhaustively cover every conceivable classroom situation. And so you should always consider your own philosophy of composition to be a work-in-progress, and try to build into your ideas a degree of flexibility that will allow them to evolve and grow over time. In fact, in this first set of readings, you'll encounter concepts that emerge, more or less explicitly, out of challenging contexts that the authors have been pondering and discussing with colleagues for quite a long time and that, moreover, are often engaged with the question of how challenges can serve as springboards for growth. And that, perhaps, is the only dimension of your own theory that must not be open to ongoing revision: the notion that you'll sometimes encounter that which doesn't fit smoothly with your expectations, and that only through a habit of careful, ongoing reflection, guided and steered by some useful and open-ended concepts, can you turn that challenge into a positive force for teaching or learning.

Inventing the University

David Bartholomae

What should writing teachers actually teach? First published in 1985, David Bartholomae argues, in what is now considered to be a classic statement about the overall aims of the composition classroom, that we must, above all, enable our students to participate in the discourses of the academy. These discourses embody the "conventional" ideals of skepticism and critique and require those who participate in them to move beyond what have traditionally been considered, by comparison, naïve clichés and commonplaces that more often characterize personal writing. Bartholomae is chiefly interested in bringing students to share in the authority that the academic institution makes available; in order to do so, he argues, we must teach students to acquire those particular habits of mind that are the mark of that authority. Bartholomae's argument here, though sometimes read as a manifesto, has remained controversial and perhaps raises as many questions as it answers—such as, what, finally, is academic discourse? What about the world outside the academy? And, if our supreme goal is to produce students who have academic authority (of a sort), what other dimensions of our mission have we perhaps neglected?

> Education may well be, as of right, the instrument whereby every individual, in a society like our own, can gain access to any kind of discourse. But we well know that in its distribution, in what it permits and in what it prevents, it follows the well-trodden battle-lines of social conflict. Every educational system is a political means of maintaining or of modifying the appropriation of discourse, with the knowledge and the powers it carries with it.
>
> —Foucault, *The Discourse on Language*

> . . . the text is the form of the social relationships made visible, palpable, material.
>
> —Bernstein, *Codes, Modalities and the Process of Cultural Reproduction: A Model*

I

Every time a student sits down to write for us, he has to invent the university for the occasion—invent the university, that is, or a branch of it, like history or anthropology or economics or English. The student has to learn to speak our language, to speak as we do, to try on the peculiar ways of knowing, selecting, evaluating, reporting, concluding, and arguing that define the discourse of our community. Or perhaps I should say the *various* discourses of our community, since it is in the nature of a liberal arts education that a student, after the first year or two, must learn to try on a variety of voices and interpretive schemes—to write, for example, as a literary critic one day and as an experimental psychologist the next; to work within fields where the rules governing the presentation of examples or the development of an argument are both distinct and, even to a professional, mysterious.

The student has to appropriate (or be appropriated by) a specialized discourse, and he has to do this as though he were easily and comfortably one with his audience, as though he were a member of the academy or an historian or an anthropologist or an economist; he has to invent the university by assembling and mimicking its language while finding some compromise between idiosyncrasy, a personal history, on the one hand, and the requirements of convention, the history of a discipline, on the other hand. He must learn to speak our language. Or he must dare to speak it or to carry off the bluff, since speaking and writing will most certainly be required long before the skill is "learned." And this, understandably, causes problems.

Let me look quickly at an example. Here is an essay written by a college freshman.

> In the past time I thought that an incident was creative was when I had to make a clay model of the earth, but not of the classical or your everyday model of the earth which consists of the two cores, the mantle and the crust. I thought of these things in a dimension of which it would be unique, but easy to comprehend. Of course, your materials to work with were basic and limited at the same time, but thought help to put this limit into a right attitude or frame of mind to work with the clay.
>
> In the beginning of the clay model, I had to research and learn the different dimensions of the earth (in magnitude, quantity, state of matter, etc.). After this, I learned how to put this into the clay and come up with something different than any other person in my class at the time. In my opinion, color coordination and shape was the key to my creativity of the clay model of the earth.
>
> Creativity is the venture of the mind at work with the mechanics relay to the limbs from the cranium, which stores and triggers this action. It can be a burst of energy released at a precise time a thought is being transmitted. This can cause a frenzy of the human body, but it depends on the characteristics of the individual and how they can relay the message clearly enough through mechanics of the body to us as an observer. Then we must determine if it is creative or a learned process varied by the individuals thought process. Creativity is indeed a tool which has to exist, or our world will not succeed into the future and progress like it should.

I am continually impressed by the patience and goodwill of our students. This student was writing a placement essay during freshman orientation. (The problem set to him was: "Describe a time when you did something you felt to be creative. Then, on the basis of the incident you have described, go on to draw some general conclusions about 'creativity.'") He knew that university faculty would be reading and evaluating his essay, and so he wrote for them.

In some ways it is a remarkable performance. He is trying on the discourse even though he doesn't have the knowledge that would make the discourse more than a routine, a set of conventional rituals and gestures. And he is doing this, I think, even though he *knows* he doesn't have the knowledge that would make the discourse more than a routine. He defines himself as a researcher working systematically, and not as a kid in a high school class: "I thought of these things in a dimension of . . ."; "I had to research and learn the different dimensions of the earth (in magnitude, quantity, state of matter, etc.)." He moves quickly into a specialized language (his approximation of our jargon) and draws both a general, textbook-like conclusion — "Creativity is the venture of the mind at work . . ." — and a resounding peroration — "Creativity is indeed a tool which has to exist, or our world will not succeed into the future and progress like it should." The writer has even picked up the rhythm of our prose with that last "indeed" and with the qualifications and the parenthetical expressions of the opening paragraphs. And through it all he speaks with an impressive air of authority.

There is an elaborate but, I will argue, a necessary and enabling fiction at work here as the student dramatizes his experience in a "setting"—the setting required by the discourse—where he can speak to us as a companion, a fellow researcher. As I read the essay, there is only one moment when the fiction is broken, when we are addressed differently. The student says, "Of course, your materials to work with were basic and limited at the same time, but thought help to put this limit into a right attitude or frame of mind to work with the clay." At this point, I think, we become students and he the teacher giving us a lesson (as in, "You take your pencil in your right hand and put your paper in front of you"). This is, however, one of the most characteristic slips of basic writers. (I use the term "basic writers" to refer to university students traditionally placed in remedial composition courses.) It is very hard for them to take on the role—the voice, the persona—of an authority whose authority is rooted in scholarship, analysis, or research. They slip, then, into a more immediately available and realizable voice of authority, the voice of a teacher giving a lesson or the voice of a parent lecturing at the dinner table. They offer advice or homilies rather than "academic" conclusions. There is a similar break in the final paragraph, where the conclusion that pushes for a definition ("Creativity is the venture of the mind at work with the mechanics relay to the limbs from the cranium") is replaced by a conclusion that speaks in the voice of an elder ("Creativity is indeed a tool which has to exist, or our world will not succeed into the future and progress like it should").

It is not uncommon, then, to find such breaks in the concluding sections of essays written by basic writers. Here is the concluding section of an essay written by a student about his work as a mechanic. He had been asked to generalize about work after reviewing an on-the-job experience or incident that "stuck in his mind" as somehow significant.

> How could two repairmen miss a leak? Lack of pride? No incentive? Lazy? I don't know.

At this point the writer is in a perfect position to speculate, to move from the problem to an analysis of the problem. Here is how the paragraph continues, however (and notice the change in pronoun reference).

> From this point on, I take *my* time, do it right, and don't let customers get under *your* skin. If they have a complaint, tell them to call your boss and he'll be more than glad to handle it. Most important, worry about yourself, and keep a clear eye on everyone, for there's always someone trying to take advantage of you, anytime and anyplace. (Emphasis added)

We get neither a technical discussion nor an "academic" discussion but a Lesson on Life.[1] This is the language he uses to address the general question, "How could two repairmen miss a leak?" The other brand of conclusion, the more academic one, would have required him to speak of his experience in our terms; it would, that is, have required a special vocabulary, a special system of presentation, and an interpretive scheme (or a set of commonplaces) he could have used to identify and talk about the mystery of human error. The writer certainly had access to the range of acceptable commonplaces for such an explanation: "lack of pride," "no incentive," "lazy." Each commonplace would dictate its own set of phrases, examples, and conclusions; and we, his teachers, would know how to write out each argument, just as we know how to write out more specialized arguments of our own. A "commonplace," then, is a culturally or institutionally authorized concept or statement that carries with it its own necessary elaboration. We all use commonplaces to orient ourselves in the world; they provide points of reference and a set of "prearticulated" explanations that are readily available to organize and interpret experience. The phrase "lack of pride" carries with it its own account of the repairman's error, just as at another point in time a reference to "original sin" would have provided an explanation, or just as in certain university classrooms a reference to "alienation" would enable writers to continue and complete the discussion. While there is a way in which these terms are interchangeable, they are not all permissible: A student in a composition class would most likely be turned away from a discussion of original sin. Commonplaces are the "controlling ideas" of our composition textbooks, textbooks that not only insist on a set form for expository writing but a set view of public life.[2]

When the writer says, "I don't know," then, he is not saying that he has nothing to say. He is saying that he is not in a position to carry on this discussion. And so we are addressed as apprentices rather than as teachers or scholars. In order to speak as a person of status or privilege, the writer can either speak to us in our terms—in the privileged language of university discourse—or, in default (or in defiance) of that, he can speak to us as though we were children, offering us the wisdom of experience.

I think it is possible to say that the language of the "Clay Model" paper has come *through* the writer and not from the writer. The writer has located himself (more precisely, he has located the self that is represented by the "I" on the page) in a context that is finally beyond him, not his own and not available to his immediate procedures for inventing and arranging text. I would not, that is, call this essay an example of "writer-based" prose. I would not say that it is egocentric or that it represents the "interior monologue or a writer thinking and talking to himself" (Flower, 1981, p. 63). It is, rather, the record of a writer who has lost himself in the discourse of his readers. There is a context beyond the intended reader that is not the world but a way of talking about the world, a way of talking that determines the use of examples, the possible conclusions, acceptable commonplaces, and key words for an essay on the construction of a clay model of the earth. This writer has entered the discourse without successfully approximating it.

Linda Flower (1981) has argued that the difficulty inexperienced writers have with writing can be understood as a difficulty in negotiating the transition between "writer-based" and "reader-based" prose. Expert writers, in other words, can better imagine how a reader will respond to a text and can transform or restructure what they have to say around a goal shared with a reader. Teaching students to revise for readers, then, will better prepare them to write initially with a reader in mind. The success of this pedagogy depends on the degree to which a writer can imagine and conform to a reader's goals. The difficulty of this act of imagination and the burden of such conformity are so much at the heart of the problem that a teacher must pause and take stock before offering revision as a solution. A student like the one who wrote the "Clay Model" paper is not so much trapped in a private language as he is shut out from one of the privileged languages of public life, a language he is aware of but cannot control.

II

Our students, I've said, have to appropriate (or be appropriated by) a specialized discourse, and they have to do this as though they were easily or comfortably one with their audience. If you look at the situation this way, suddenly the problem of audience awareness becomes enormously complicated. One of the common assumptions of both composition research and composition teaching is that at some "stage" in the process of composing an essay a writer's ideas or his motives must be tailored to the needs and expectations of his audience. Writers have to "build bridges" between their point of view and the reader's. They have to anticipate and acknowledge the reader's assumptions and biases. They must begin with "common points of departure" before introducing new or controversial arguments. Here is what one of the most popular college textbooks says to students.

> Once you have your purpose clearly in mind, your next task is to define and analyze your audience. A sure sense of your audience—knowing who it is and what assumptions you can reasonably make about it—is crucial to the success of your rhetoric. (Hairston, 1978, p. 107)

It is difficult to imagine, however, how writers can have a purpose before they are located in a discourse, since it is the discourse with its projects and agendas that determines what writers can and will do. The writer who can successfully manipulate an audience (or, to use a less pointed language, the writer who can accommodate her motives to her reader's expectations) is a writer who can both imagine and write from a position of privilege. She must, that is, see herself within a privileged discourse, one that already includes and excludes groups of readers. She must be either equal to or more powerful than those she would address. The writing, then, must somehow transform the political and social relationships between students and teachers.

If my students are going to write for me by knowing who I am—and if this means more than knowing my prejudices, psyching me out—it means knowing what I know; it means having the knowledge of a professor of English. They have, then, to know what I know and how I know what I know (the interpretive schemes that define the way I would work out the problems I set for them); they have to learn to write what I would write or to offer up some approximation of that discourse. The problem of audience awareness, then, is a problem of power and finesse. It cannot be addressed, as it is in most classroom exercises, by giving students privilege and denying the situation of the classroom—usually, that is, by having students write to an outsider, someone excluded from their privileged circle: "Write about 'To His Coy Mistress,' not for your teacher but for the students in your class"; "Describe Pittsburgh to someone who has never been there"; "Explain to a high school senior how best to prepare for college"; "Describe baseball to an Eskimo." Exercises such as these allow students to imagine the needs and goals of a reader, and they bring those needs and goals forward as a dominant constraint in the construction of an essay. And they argue, implicitly, what is generally true about writing—that it is an act of aggression disguised as an act of charity. What these assignments fail to address is the central problem of academic writing, where a student must assume the right of speaking to someone who knows more about baseball or "To His Coy Mistress" than the student does, a reader for whom the general commonplaces and the readily available utterances about a subject are inadequate.

Linda Flower and John Hayes, in an often quoted article (1981), reported on a study of a protocol of an expert writer (an English teacher) writing about his job for readers of *Seventeen* magazine. The key moment for this writer, who seems to have been having trouble getting started, came when he decided that teenage girls read *Seventeen*; that some teenage girls like English because it is tidy ("some of them will have wrong reasons in that English is good because it's tidy—can be a neat tidy little girl"); that some don't like it because it is "prim" and that, "By God, I can change that notion for them." Flower and Hayes's conclusion is that this effort of "exploration and consolidation" gave the writer "a new, relatively complex, rhetorically sophisticated working goal, one which encompasses plans for topic, a persona, and the audience" (p. 383).[3]

Flower and Hayes give us a picture of a writer solving a problem, and the problem as they present it is a cognitive one. It is rooted in the way the writer's knowledge is represented in the writer's mind. The problem resides there, not in the nature of knowledge or in the nature of discourse but in a mental state prior to writing. It is possible, however, to see the problem as (perhaps simultaneously) a problem in the way subjects are located in a field of discourse.

Flower and Hayes divide up the composing process into three distinct activities: "planning or goal-setting," "translating," and "reviewing." The last of these, reviewing (which is further divided into two subprocesses, "evaluating" and "revising"), is particularly powerful, for as a writer continually generates new goals, plans, and text, he is engaging in a process of learning and discovery. Let me quote Flower and Hayes's conclusion at length.

> If one studies the process by which a writer uses a goal to generate ideas, then consolidates those ideas and uses them to revise or regenerate new, more complex goals, one can see this learning process in action. Furthermore, one sees why the process of revising and clarifying goals has such a broad effect, since it is through setting these new goals that the fruits of discovery come back to inform the continuing process of writing. In this instance, some of our most complex and imaginative acts can depend on the elegant simplicity of a few powerful thinking processes. We feel that a cognitive process explanation of discovery, toward which this theory is only a start, will have another special strength. By placing emphasis on the inventive power of the writer, who is able to explore ideas, to develop, act on, test, and regenerate his or her own goals, we are putting an important part of creativity where it belongs — in the hands of the working, thinking writer. (1981, p. 386)

While this conclusion is inspiring, the references to invention and creativity seem to refer to something other than an act of writing — if writing is, finally, words on a page. Flower and Hayes locate the act of writing solely within the mind of the writer. The act of writing, here, has a personal, cognitive history but not a history as a text, as a text that is made possible by prior texts. When located in the perspective afforded by prior texts, writing is seen to exist separate from the writer and his intentions; it is seen in the context of other articles in *Seventeen*, of all articles written for or about women, of all articles written about English teaching, and so on. Reading research has made it possible to say that these prior texts, or a reader's experience with these prior texts, have bearing on how the text is read. Intentions, then, are part of the history of the language itself. I am arguing that these prior texts determine not only how a text like the *Seventeen* article will be read but also how it will be written. Flower and Hayes show us what happens in the writer's mind but not what happens to the writer as his motives are located within our language, a language with its own requirements and agendas, a language that limits what we might say and that makes us write and sound, finally, also like someone else. If you think of other accounts of the composing process — and I'm thinking of accounts as diverse as Richard Rodriguez's *Hunger of Memory* (1983) and Edward Said's *Beginnings* (1975) — you get a very different account of what happens when private motive enters into public discourse, when a personal history becomes a public account. These accounts place the writer in a history that is not of the writer's own invention; and they are chronicles of loss, violence, and compromise.

It is one thing to see the *Seventeen* writer making and revising his plans for a topic, a persona, and an audience; it is another thing to talk about discovery, invention, and creativity. Whatever plans the writer had must finally have been located in language and, it is possible to argue, in a language that is persistently conventional and formulaic. We do not, after all, get to see the *Seventeen* article. We see only the elaborate mental procedures that accompanied the writing of the essay. We see a writer's plans for a persona; we don't see that persona in action. If writing is a process, it is also a product; and it is the product, and not the plan for writing, that locates a writer on the page, that locates him in a text and a style and the codes or conventions that make both of them readable.

Contemporary rhetorical theory has been concerned with the "codes" that constitute discourse (or specialized forms of discourse). These codes determine not only what might be said but also who might be speaking or reading. Barthes (1974), for example, has argued that the moment of writing, where private goals and plans become subject to a public language, is the moment when the writer becomes subject to a language he can neither command nor control. A text, he says, in being written passes through the codes that govern writing and becomes "'de-originated,' becomes a fragment of something that has always been *already* read, seen, done, experienced" (p. 21). Alongside a text we have always the presence of "off-stage voices," the oversound of all that has been said (e.g., about girls, about English). These voices, the presence of the "already written," stand in defiance of a writer's desire for originality and determine what might be said. A writer does not write (and this is Barthes's famous paradox) but is, himself, written by the languages available to him.

It is possible to see the writer of the *Seventeen* article solving his problem of where to begin by appropriating an available discourse. Perhaps what enabled that writer to write was the moment he located himself as a writer in a familiar field of stereotypes: Readers of *Seventeen* are teenage girls; teenage girls think of English (and English teachers) as "tidy" and "prim," and, "By God, I can change that notion for them." The moment of eureka was not simply a moment of breaking through a cognitive jumble in that individual writer's mind but a moment of breaking into a familiar and established territory — one with insiders and outsiders; one with set phrases, examples, and conclusions.

I'm not offering a criticism of the morals or manners of the teacher who wrote the *Seventeen* article. I think that all writers, in order to write, must imagine for themselves the privilege of being "insiders"—that is, the privilege both of being inside an established and powerful discourse and of being granted a special right to speak. But I think that right to speak is seldom conferred on us—on any of us, teachers or students—by virtue of the fact that we have invented or discovered an original idea. Leading students to believe that they are responsible for something new or original, unless they understand what those words mean with regard to writing, is a dangerous and counterproductive practice. We do have the right to expect students to be active and engaged, but that is a matter of continually and stylistically working against the inevitable presence of conventional language; it is not a matter of inventing a language that is new.

When a student is writing for a teacher, writing becomes more problematic than it was for the *Seventeen* writer (who was writing a version of the "Describe baseball to an Eskimo" exercise). The student, in effect, has to assume privilege without having any. And since students assume privilege by locating themselves within the discourse of a particular community—within a set of specifically acceptable gestures and commonplaces—learning, at least as it is defined in the liberal arts curriculum, becomes more a matter of imitation or parody than a matter of invention and discovery.

To argue that writing problems are also social and political problems is not to break faith with the enterprise of cognitive science. In a recent paper reviewing the tremendous range of research directed at identifying general cognitive skills, David Perkins (1985) has argued that "the higher the level of competence concerned," as in the case of adult learning, "the fewer *general* cognitive control strategies there are." There comes a point, that is, where "field-specific" or "domain-specific" schemata (what I have called "interpretive strategies") become more important than general problem-solving processes. Thinking, learning, writing—all these become bound to the context of a particular discourse. And Perkins concludes:

> Instruction in cognitive control strategies tends to be organized around problem-solving tasks. However, the isolated problem is a creature largely of the classroom. The nonstudent, whether operating in scholarly or more everyday contexts, is likely to find himself or herself involved in what might be called "projects"—which might be anything from writing a novel to designing a shoe to starting a business.

It is interesting to note that Perkins defines the classroom as the place of artificial tasks and, as a consequence, has to place scholarly projects outside the classroom, where they are carried out by the "nonstudent." It is true, I think, that education has failed to involve students in scholarly projects, projects that allow students to act as though they were colleagues in an academic enterprise. Much of the written work that students do is test-taking, report, or summary—work that places them outside the official discourse of the academic community, where they are expected to admire and report on what we do, rather than inside that discourse, where they can do its work and participate in a common enterprise.[4] This, however, is a failure of teachers and curriculum designers, who speak of writing as a mode of learning but all too often represent writing as a "tool" to be used by an (hopefully) educated mind.

It could be said, then, that there is a bastard discourse peculiar to the writing most often required of students. Carl Bereiter and Marlene Scardamalia (1985) have written about this discourse (they call it "knowledge-telling"; students who are good at it have learned to cope with academic tasks by developing a "knowledge-telling strategy"), and they have argued that insistence on knowledge-telling discourse undermines educational efforts to extend the variety of discourse schemata available to students.[5] What they actually say is this:

> When we think of knowledge stored in memory we tend these days to think of it as situated in three-dimensional space, with vertical and horizontal connections between sites. Learning is thought to add not only new elements to memory but also new connections, and it is the richness and structure of these connections that would seem . . . to spell the difference between inert and usable knowledge. On this account, the knowledge-telling strategy is educationally faulty because it specifically avoids the forming of connections between previously separated knowledge sites.

It should be clear by now that when I think of "knowledge" I think of it as situated in the discourse that constitutes "knowledge" in a particular discourse community, rather than as situated in mental "knowledge sites." One can remember a discourse, just as one can remember an essay or the movement of a professor's lecture; but this discourse, in effect, also has a memory of its own, its own rich network of structures and connections beyond the deliberate control of any individual imagination.

There is, to be sure, an important distinction to be made between learning history, say, and learning to write as an historian. A student can learn to command and reproduce a set of names, dates, places, and canonical interpretations (to "tell" somebody else's knowledge); but this is not the same thing as learning to "think" (by learning to write) as an historian. The former requires efforts of memory; the latter requires a student to compose a text out of the texts that represent the primary materials of history and in accordance with the texts that define history as an act of report and interpretation.

Let me draw on an example from my own teaching. I don't expect my students to *be* literary critics when they write about *Bleak House*. If a literary critic is a person who wins publication in a professional journal (or if he or she is one who could), the students aren't critics. I do, however, expect my students to be, themselves, invented as literary critics by approximating the language of a literary critic writing about *Bleak House*. My students, then, don't invent the language of literary criticism (they don't, that is, act on their own) but they are, themselves, invented by it. Their papers don't begin with a moment of insight, a "by God" moment that is outside of language. They begin with a moment of appropriation, a moment when they can offer up a sentence that is not theirs as though it were their own. (I can remember when, as a graduate student, I would begin papers by sitting down to write literally in the voice — with the syntax and the key words — of the strongest teacher I had met.)

What I am saying about my students' essays is that they are approximate, not that they are wrong or invalid. They are evidence of a discourse that lies between what I might call the students' primary discourse (what the students might write about *Bleak House* were they not in my class or in any class, and were they not imagining that they were in my class or in any class — if you can imagine any student doing any such thing) and standard, official literary criticism (which is imaginable but impossible to find). The students' essays are evidence of a discourse that lies between these two hypothetical poles. The writing is limited as much by a student's ability to imagine "what might be said" as it is by cognitive control strategies.[6] The act of writing takes the student away from where he is and what he knows and allows him to imagine something else. The approximate discourse, therefore, is evidence of a change, a change that, because we are teachers, we call "development." What our beginning students need to learn is to extend themselves, by successive approximations, into the commonplaces, set phrases, rituals and gestures, habits of mind, tricks of persuasion, obligatory conclusions and necessary connections that determine the "what might be said" and constitute knowledge within the various branches of our academic community.[7]

Pat Bizzell is, I think, one of the most important scholars writing now on "basic writers" (and this is the common name we use for students who are refused unrestrained access to the academic community) and on the special characteristics of academic discourse. In a recent essay, "Cognition, Convention, and Certainty: What We Need to Know about Writing" (1982a), she looks at two schools of composition research and the way they represent the problems that writing poses for writers.[8] For one group, the "inner-directed theorists," the problems are internal, cognitive, rooted in the way the mind represents knowledge to itself. These researchers are concerned with discovering the "universal, fundamental structures of thought and language" and with developing pedagogies to teach or facilitate both basic, general cognitive skills and specific cognitive strategies, or heuristics, directed to serve more specialized needs. Of the second group, the "outer-directed theorists," she says that they are "more interested in the social processes whereby language-learning and thinking capacities are shaped and used in particular communities."

> The staple activity of outer-directed writing instruction will be analysis of the conventions of particular discourse communities. For example, a main focus of writing-across-the-curriculum programs is to demystify the conventions of the academic discourse community. (1982a, p. 218)

The essay offers a detailed analysis of the way the two theoretical camps can best serve the general enterprise of composition research and composition teaching. Its agenda, however, seems to be to counter the influence of the cognitivists and to provide bibliography and encouragement to those interested in the social dimension of language learning.

As far as basic writers are concerned, Bizzell argues that the cognitivists' failure to acknowledge the primary, shaping role of convention in the act of composing makes them "particularly insensitive to the problems of poor writers." She argues that some of those problems, like the problem of establishing and monitoring overall goals for a piece of writing, can be

> better understood in terms of the unfamiliarity with the academic discourse community, combined, perhaps, with such limited experience outside their native discourse communities that they are unaware that there is such a thing as a discourse community with conventions to be mastered. What is underdeveloped is their knowledge both of the ways experience is constituted and interpreted in the academic discourse community and of the fact that all discourse communities constitute and interpret experience. (1982a, p. 230)

One response to the problems of basic writers, then, would be to determine just what the community's conventions are, so that those conventions could be written out, "demystified" and taught in our classrooms. Teachers, as a result, could be more precise and helpful when they ask students to "think," "argue," "describe," or "define." Another response would be to examine the essays written by basic writers — their approximations of academic discourse — to determine more clearly where the problems lie. If we look at their writing, and if we look at it in the context of other student writing, we can better see the points of discord that arise when students try to write their way into the university.

The purpose of the remainder of this chapter will be to examine some of the most striking and characteristic of these problems as they are presented in the expository essays of first-year college students. I will be concerned, then, with university discourse in its most generalized form — as it is represented by introductory courses — and not with the special conventions required by advanced work in the various disciplines. And I will be concerned with the difficult, and often violent accommodations that occur when students locate themselves in a discourse that is not "naturally" or immediately theirs.

III

I have reviewed 500 essays written, as the "Clay Model" essay was, in response to a question used during one of our placement exams at the University of Pittsburgh: "Describe a time when you did something you felt to be creative. Then, on the basis of the incident you have described, go on to draw some general conclusions about 'creativity.'" Some of the essays were written by basic writers (or, more properly, those essays led readers to identify the writers as basic writers); some were written by students who "passed" (who were granted immediate access to the community of writers at the university). As I read these essays, I was looking to determine the stylistic resources that enabled writers to locate themselves within an "academic" discourse. My bias as a reader should be clear by now. I was not looking to see how a writer might represent the skills demanded by a neutral language (a language whose key features were paragraphs, topic sentences, transitions, and the like—features of a clear and orderly mind). I was looking to see what happened when a writer entered into a language to locate himself (a textual self) and his subject; and I was looking to see how, once entered, that language made or unmade the writer.

Here is one essay. Its writer was classified as a basic writer and, since the essay is relatively free of sentence-level errors, that decision must have been rooted in some perceived failure of the discourse itself.

> I am very interested in music, and I try to be creative in my interpretation of music. While in high school, I was a member of a jazz ensemble. The members of the ensemble were given chances to improvise and be creative in various songs. I feel that this was a great experience for me, as well as the other members. I was proud to know that I could use my imagination and feelings to create music other than what was written.
>
> Creativity to me, means being free to express yourself in a way that is unique to you, not having to conform to certain rules and guidelines. Music is only one of the many areas in which people are given opportunities to show their creativity. Sculpting, carving, building, art, and acting are just a few more areas where people can show their creativity.
>
> Through my music I conveyed feelings and thoughts which were important to me. Music was my means of showing creativity. In whatever form creativity takes, whether it be music, art, or science, it is an important aspect of our lives because it enables us to be individuals.

Notice the key gesture in this essay, one that appears in all but a few of the essays I read. The student defines as his own that which is a commonplace. "Creativity *to me*, means being free to express yourself in a way that is unique to you, not having to conform to certain rules and guidelines." This act of appropriation constitutes his authority; it constitutes his authority as a writer and not just as a musician (that is, as someone with a story to tell). There were many essays in the set that told only a story—where the writer established his presence as a musician or a skier or someone who painted designs on a van, but not as a person at a remove from that experience interpreting it, treating it as a metaphor for something else (creativity). Unless those stories were long, detailed, and very well told—unless the writer was doing more than saying, "I am a skier" or a musician or a van-painter—those writers were all given low ratings.

Notice also that the writer of the "Jazz" paper locates himself and his experience in relation to the commonplace (creativity is unique expression; it is not having to conform to rules or guidelines) regardless of whether the commonplace is true or not. Anyone who improvises "knows" that improvisation follows rules and guidelines. It is the power of the commonplace—its truth as a recognizable and, the writer believes, as a final statement—that justifies the example and completes the essay. The example, in other words, has value because it stands within the field of the commonplace.[9] It is not the occasion for what one might call an "objective" analysis or a "close" reading. It could also be said that the essay stops with the articulation of the commonplace. The following sections speak only to the power of that statement. The reference to "sculpting, carving, building, art, and acting" attests to the universality of the commonplace (and it attests the writer's nervousness with the status he has appropriated for himself—he is saying, "Now, I'm not the only one here who has done something unique"). The commonplace stands by itself. For this writer, it does not need to be elaborated. By virtue of having written it, he has completed the essay and established the contract by which we may be spoken to as equals: "In whatever form creativity takes, whether it be music, art, or science, it is an important aspect of *our* lives because it enables *us* to be individuals." (For me to break that contract, to argue that *my* life is not represented in that essay, is one way for me to begin as a teacher with that student in that essay.)

All of the papers I read were built around one of three commonplaces: (1) creativity is self-expression, (2) creativity is doing something new or unique, and (3) creativity is using old things in new ways. These are clearly, then, key phrases from the storehouse of things to say about creativity. I've listed them in the order of the students' ratings: A student with the highest rating was more likely to use number three than number one, although each commonplace ran across the range of possible ratings. One could argue that some standard assertions are more powerful than others, but I think the ranking simply represents the power of assertions within our community of readers. Every student was able to offer up an experience that was meant as an example of "creativity"; the lowest range of writers, then, was not represented by students who could not imagine themselves as creative people.[10]

I said that the writer of the "Jazz" paper offered up a commonplace regardless of whether it was true or not; and this, I said, was an instance of the power of a commonplace to determine the meaning of an example. A commonplace determines a system of interpretation that can be used to "place" an example within a standard system of belief. You can see a similar process at work in this essay.

> During the football season, the team was supposed to wear the same type of cleats and the same type socks, I figured that I would change this a little by wearing my white shoes instead of black and to cover up the team socks with a pair of my own white ones. I thought that this looked better than what we were wearing, and I told a few of the other people on the team to change too. They agreed that it did look better and they changed their combination to go along with mine. After the game people came up to us and said that it looked very good the way we wore our socks, and they wanted to know why we changed from the rest of the team.
>
> I feel that creativity comes from when a person lets his imagination come up with ideas and he is not afraid to express them. Once you create something to do it will be original and unique because it came about from your own imagination and if any one else tries to copy it, it won't be the same because you thought of it first from your own ideas.

This is not an elegant paper, but it seems seamless, tidy. If the paper on the clay model of the earth showed an ill fit between the writer and his project, here the discourse seems natural, smooth. You could reproduce this paper and hand it out to a class, and it would take a lot of prompting before the students sensed something fishy and one of the more aggressive ones said something like, "Sure he came up with the idea of wearing white shoes and white socks. Him and Billy 'White-Shoes' Johnson. Come on. He copied the very thing he said was his own idea, 'original and unique.'"

The "I" of this text—the "I" who "figured," "thought," and "felt"—is located in a conventional rhetoric of the self that turns imagination into origination (I made it), that argues an ethic of production (I made it and it is mine), and that argues a tight scheme of intention (I made it because I decided to make it). The rhetoric seems invisible because it is so common. This "I" (the maker) is also located in a version of history that dominates classrooms, the "great man" theory: History is rolling along (the English novel is dominated by a central, intrusive narrative presence; America is in the throes of a Great Depression; during football season the team was supposed to wear the same kind of cleats and socks) until a figure appears, one who can shape history (Henry James, FDR, the writer of the "White Shoes" paper), and everything is changed. In the argument of the "White Shoes" paper, the history goes "I figured . . .

I thought . . . I told . . . They agreed . . ." and, as a consequence, "I feel that creativity *comes from when* a person lets his imagination come up with ideas and he is not afraid to express them." The act of appropriation becomes a narrative of courage and conquest. The writer was able to write that story when he was able to imagine himself in that discourse. Getting him out of it will be a difficult matter indeed.

There are ways, I think, that a writer can shape history in the very act of writing it. Some students are able to enter into a discourse but, by stylistic maneuvers, to take possession of it at the same time. They don't originate a discourse, but they locate themselves within it aggressively, self-consciously. Here is another essay on jazz, which for sake of convenience I've shortened. It received a higher rating than the first essay on jazz.

> Jazz has always been thought of as a very original creative field in music. Improvisation, the spontaneous creation of original melodies in a piece of music, makes up a large part of jazz as a musical style. I had the opportunity to be a member of my high school's jazz ensemble for three years, and became an improvisation soloist this year. Throughout the years, I have seen and heard many jazz players, both professional and amateur. The solos performed by these artists were each flavored with that particular individual's style and ideas, along with some of the conventional premises behind improvisation. This particular type of solo work is creative because it is done on the spur of the moment and blends the performer's ideas with basic guidelines.
>
> I realized my own creative potential when I began soloing. . . .
>
> My solos, just as all the solos generated by others, were original because I combined and shaped other's ideas with mine to create something completely new. Creativity is combining the practical knowledge and guidelines of a discipline with one's original ideas to bring about a new, original end result, one that is different from everyone else's. Creativity is based on the individual. Two artists can interpret the same scene differently. Each person who creates something does so by bringing out something individual in himself.

The essay is different in some important ways from the first essay on jazz. The writer of the second is more easily able to place himself in the context of an "academic" discussion. The second essay contains an "I" who realized his "creative potential" by soloing; the first contained an "I" who had "a great experience." In the second essay, before the phrase, "I had the opportunity to be a member of my high school's jazz ensemble," there is an introduction that offers a general definition of improvisation and an acknowledgment that other people have thought about jazz and creativity. In fact, throughout the essay the writer offers definitions and counterdefinitions. He is placing himself in the context of what has been said and what might be said. In the first paper, before a similar statement about being a member of a jazz ensemble, there was an introduction that locates jazz solely in the context of this individual's experience: "I am very interested in music." The writer of this first paper was authorized by who he is, a musician, rather than by what he can say about music in the context of what is generally said. The writer of the second essay uses a more specialized vocabulary; he talks about "conventional premises," "creative potential," "musical style," and "practical knowledge." And this is not just a matter of using bigger words, since these terms locate the experience in the context of a recognizable interpretive scheme — on the one hand there is tradition and, on the other, individual talent.

It could be said, then, that this essay is also framed and completed by a commonplace: "Creativity is combining the practical knowledge and guidelines of a discipline with one's original ideas to bring about a new, original end result, one that is different from everyone else's." Here, however, the argument is a more powerful one; and I mean "powerful" in the political sense, since it is an argument that complicates a "naïve" assumption (it makes scholarly work possible, in other words), and it does so in terms that come close to those used in current academic debates (over the relation between convention and idiosyncrasy or between rules and creativity). The assertion is almost consumed by the pleas for originality at the end of the sentence; but the point remains that the terms "original" and "different," as they are used at the end of the essay, are problematic, since they must be thought of in the context of "practical knowledge and guidelines of a discipline."

The key distinguishing gesture of this essay, that which makes it "better" than the other, is the way the writer works against a conventional point of view, one that is represented within the essay by conventional phrases that the writer must then work against. In his practice he demonstrates that a writer, and not just a musician, works within "conventional premises." The "I" who comments in this paper (not the "I" of the narrative about a time when he soloed) places himself self-consciously within the context of a conventional discourse about the subject, even as he struggles against the language of that conventional discourse. The opening definition of improvisation, where improvisation is defined as spontaneous creation, is rejected when the writer begins talking about "the conventional premises behind improvisation." The earlier definition is part of the conventional language of those who "have always thought" of jazz as a "very original creative field in music." The paper begins with what "has been said" and then works itself out against the force and logic of what has been said, of what is not only an argument but also a collection of phrases, examples, and definitions.

I had a teacher who once told us that whenever we were stuck for something to say, we should use the following as a "machine" for producing a paper: "While most readers of ______ have said ______, a close and careful reading shows that ______." The writer of the second paper on jazz is using a standard opening gambit, even if it is not announced with flourish. The essay becomes possible when he sets himself against what must become a "naïve" assumption — what "most people think." He has defined a closed circle for himself. In fact, you could say that he has laid the groundwork for a discipline with its own key terms ("practical knowledge," "disciplinary guidelines," and "original ideas"), with its own agenda and with its own investigative procedures (looking for common features in the work of individual soloists).

The history represented by this student's essay, then, is not the history of a musician and it is not the history of a thought being worked out within an individual mind; it is the history of work being done within and against conventional systems.

In general, as I reviewed essays for this study, I found that the more successful writers set themselves in their essays against what they defined as some more naïve way of talking about their subject — against "those who think that . . ." — or against earlier, more naïve versions of themselves — "once I thought that. . . ." By trading in one set of commonplaces at the expense of another, they could win themselves status as members of what is taken to be some more privileged group. The ability to imagine privilege enabled writing. Here is one particularly successful essay. Notice the specialized vocabulary, but notice also the way in which the text continually refers to its own language and to the language of others.

> Throughout my life, I have been interested and intrigued by music. My mother has often told me of the time, before I went to school, when I would "conduct" the orchestra on her records. I continued to listen to music and eventually started to play the guitar and the clarinet. Finally, at about the age of twelve, I started to sit down and to try to write songs. Even though my instrumental skills were far from my own high standards, I would spend much of my spare time during the day with a guitar around my neck, trying to produce a piece of music.
>
> Each of these sessions, as I remember them, had a rather set format. I would sit in my bedroom, strumming different combinations of the five or six chords I could play, until I heard a series of which sounded particularly good to me. After this, I set the music to a suitable rhythm, (usually dependent on my mood at the time), and ran through the tune until I could play it fairly easily. Only after this section was complete did I go on to writing lyrics, which generally followed along the lines of the current popular songs on the radio.
>
> At the time of the writing, I felt that my songs were, in themselves, an original creation of my own; that is, I, alone, made them. However, I now see that, in this sense of the word, I was not creative. The songs themselves seem to be an oversimplified form of the music I listened to at the time.
>
> In a more fitting sense, however, I *was* being creative. Since I did not purposely copy my favorite songs, I was, effectively, originating my songs from my own "process of creativity." To achieve my goal, I needed what a composer would call "inspiration" for my piece. In this case the inspiration was the current hit on the radio. Perhaps, with my present point of

> view, I feel that I used too much "inspiration" in my songs, but, at that time, I did not.
>
> Creativity, therefore, is a process which, in my case, involved a certain series of "small creations" if you like. As well, it is something, the appreciation of which varies with one's point of view, that point of view being set by the person's experience, tastes, and his own personal view of creativity. The less experienced tend to allow for less originality, while the more experienced demand real originality to classify something a "creation." Either way, a term as abstract as this is perfectly correct and open to interpretation.

This writer is consistently and dramatically conscious of herself forming something to say out of what has been said *and* out of what she has been saying in the act of writing this paper. "Creativity" begins in this paper as "original creation." What she thought was "creativity," however, she now says was imitation; and, as she says, "in a sense of the word" she was not "creative." In another sense, however, she says that she *was* creative, since she didn't purposefully copy the songs but used them as "inspiration."

While the elaborate stylistic display — the pauses, qualifications, and the use of quotation marks — is in part a performance for our benefit, at a more obvious level we as readers are directly addressed in the first sentence of the last paragraph: "Creativity, therefore, is a process which, in my case, involved a certain series of 'small creations' if you like." We are addressed here as adults who can share her perspective on what she has said and who can be expected to understand her terms. If she gets into trouble after this sentence, and I think she does, it is because she doesn't have the courage to generalize from her assertion. Since she has rhetorically separated herself from her younger "self," and since she argues that she has gotten smarter, she assumes that there is some developmental sequence at work here and that, in the world of adults (which must be more complete than the world of children) there must be something like "real creativity." If her world is imperfect (if she can only talk about creation by putting the word in quotation marks), it must be because she is young. When she looks beyond herself to us, she cannot see our work as an extension of her project. She cannot assume that we too will be concerned with the problem of creativity and originality. At least she is not willing to challenge us on those grounds, to generalize her argument, and to argue that even for adults creations are really only "small creations." The sense of privilege that has allowed her to expose her own language cannot be extended to expose ours.

The writing in this piece — that is, the work of the writer within the essay — goes on in spite of, or against, the language that keeps pressing to give another name to her experience as a songwriter and to bring the discussion to closure. (In comparison, think of the quick closure of the "White Shoes" paper.) Its style is difficult, highly qualified. It relies on quotation marks and parody to set off the language and attitudes that belong to the discourse (or the discourses) that it would reject, that it would not take as its own proper location.

David Olson (1981) has argued that the key difference between oral language and written language is that written language separates both the producer and the receiver from the text. For my student writers, this means that they had to learn that what they said (the code) was more important than what they meant (the intention). A writer, in other words, loses his primacy at the moment of writing and must begin to attend to his and his words' conventional, even physical presence on the page. And, Olson says, the writer must learn that his authority is not established through his presence but through his absence — through his ability, that is, to speak as a god-like source behind the limitations of any particular social or historical moment; to speak by means of the wisdom of convention, through the oversounds of official or authoritative utterance, as the voice of logic or the voice of the community. He concludes:

> The child's growing competence with this distinctive register of language in which both the meaning and the authority are displaced from the intentions of the speaker and lodged "in the text" may contribute to the similarly specialized and distinctive mode of thought we have come to associate with literacy and formal education. (1981, p. 110)

Olson is writing about children. His generalizations, I think I've shown, can be extended to students writing their way into the academic community. These are educated and literate individuals, to be sure, but they are individuals still outside the peculiar boundaries of the academic community. In the papers I've examined in this chapter, the writers have shown an increasing awareness of the codes (or the competing codes) that operate within a discourse. To speak with authority they have to speak not only in another's voice but through another's code; and they not only have to do this, they have to speak in the voice and through the codes of those of us with power and wisdom; and they not only have to do this, they have to do it before they know what they are doing, before they have a project to participate in, and before, at least in terms of our disciplines, they have anything to say. Our students may be able to enter into a conventional discourse and speak, not as themselves, but through the voice of the community; the university, however, is the place where "common" wisdom is only of negative values — it is something to work against. The movement toward a more specialized discourse begins (or, perhaps, best begins) both when a student can define a position of privilege, a position that sets him against a "common" discourse, and when he or she can work self-consciously, critically, against not only the "common" code but his or her own.

IV

Pat Bizzell, you will recall, argues that the problems of poor writers can be attributed both to their unfamiliarity with the conventions of academic discourse and to their ignorance that there are such things as discourse communities with conventions to be mastered. If the latter is true, I think it is true only in rare cases. All the student writers I've discussed (and, in fact, most of the student writers whose work I've seen) have shown an awareness that something special or something different is required when one writes for an academic classroom. The essays that I have presented in this chapter all, I think, give evidence of writers trying to write their way into a new community. To some degree, however, all of them can be said to be unfamiliar with the conventions of academic discourse.

Problems of convention are both problems of finish and problems of substance. The most substantial academic tasks for students, learning history or sociology or literary criticism, are matters of many courses, much reading and writing, and several years of education. Our students, however, must have a place to begin. They cannot sit through lectures and read textbooks and, as a consequence, write as sociologists or write literary criticism. There must be steps along the way. Some of these steps will be marked by drafts and revisions. Some will be marked by courses, and in an ideal curriculum the preliminary courses would be writing courses, whether housed in an English department or not. For some students, students we call "basic writers," these courses will be in a sense the most basic introduction to the language and methods of academic writing.

Our students, as I've said, must have a place to begin. If the problem of a beginning is the problem of establishing authority, of defining rhetorically or stylistically a position from which one may speak, then the papers I have examined show characteristic student responses to that problem and show levels of approximation or stages in the development of writers who are writing their way into a position of privilege.

As I look over the papers I've discussed, I would arrange them in the following order: the "White Shoes" paper; the first "Jazz" essay; the "Clay Model" paper; the second "Jazz" essay; and, as the most successful paper, the essay on "Composing Songs." The more advanced essays for me, then, are those that are set against the "naïve" codes of "everyday" life. (I put the terms "naïve" and "everyday" in quotation marks because they are, of course, arbitrary terms.) In the advanced essays one can see a writer claiming an "inside" position of privilege by rejecting the language and commonplaces of a "naïve" discourse, the language of "outsiders." The "I" of those essays locates itself against the specialized language of what is presumed to be a more powerful and more privileged community. There are two gestures present then — one imitative and one critical. The writer continually audits and pushes against a language that would render him "like everyone else" and mimics the language and interpretive systems of the privileged community.

At a first level, then, a student might establish his authority by simply stating his own presence within the field of a subject. A student, for example, writes about creativity by telling a story about a time he went skiing. Nothing more. The "I" on the page is a skier, and skiing stands as a representation of a creative act. Neither the skier nor skiing are available for interpretation; they cannot be located in an essay that is not a narrative essay (where skiing might serve metaphorically as an example of, say, a sport where set movements also allow for a personal style). Or a student, as did the one who wrote the "White Shoes" paper, locates a narrative in an unconnected rehearsal of commonplaces about creativity. In both cases, the writers have finessed the requirement to set themselves against the available utterances of the world outside the closed world of the academy. And, again, in the first "Jazz" paper, we have the example of a writer who locates himself within an available commonplace and carries out only rudimentary procedures for elaboration, procedures driven by the commonplace itself and not set against it. Elaboration, in this latter case, is not the opening up of a system but a justification of it.

At a next level I would place student writers who establish their authority by mimicking the rhythm and texture, the "sound," of academic prose, without there being any recognizable interpretive or academic project under way. I'm thinking, here, of the "Clay Model" essay. At an advanced stage, I would place students who establish their authority as *writers*; they claim their authority, not by simply claiming that they are skiers or that they have done something creative, but by placing themselves both within and against a discourse, or within and against competing discourses, and working self-consciously to claim an interpretive project of their own, one that grants them their privilege to speak. This is true, I think, in the case of the second "Jazz" paper and, to a greater degree, in the case of the "Composing Songs" paper.

The levels of development that I've suggested are not marked by corresponding levels in the type or frequency of error, at least not by the type or frequency of sentence-level error. I am arguing, then, that a basic writer is not necessarily a writer who makes a lot of mistakes. In fact, one of the problems with curricula designed to aid basic writers is that they too often begin with the assumption that the key distinguishing feature of a basic writer is the presence of sentence-level error. Students are placed in courses because their placement essays show a high frequency of such errors, and those courses are designed with the goal of making those errors go away. This approach to the problems of the basic writer ignores the degree to which error is less often a constant feature than a marker in the development of a writer. A student who can write a reasonably correct narrative may fall to pieces when faced with a more unfamiliar assignment. More important, however, such courses fail to serve the rest of the curriculum. On every campus there is a significant number of college freshmen who require a course to introduce them to the kinds of writing that are required for a university education. Some of these students can write correct sentences and some cannot; but, as a group, they lack the facility other freshmen possess when they are faced with an academic writing task.

The "White Shoes" essay, for example, shows fewer sentence-level errors than the "Clay Model" paper. This may well be due to the fact that the writer of the "White Shoes" paper stayed well within safe, familiar territory. He kept himself out of trouble by doing what he could easily do. The tortuous syntax of the more advanced papers on my list is a syntax that represents a writer's struggle with a difficult and unfamiliar language, and it is a syntax that can quickly lead an inexperienced writer into trouble. The syntax and punctuation of the "Composing Songs" essay, for example, shows the effort that is required when a writer works against the pressure of conventional discourse. If the prose is inelegant (although I confess I admire those dense sentences) it is still correct. This writer has a command of the linguistic and stylistic resources — the highly embedded sentences, the use of parentheses and quotation marks — required to complete the act of writing. It is easy to imagine the possible pitfalls for a writer working without this facility.

There was no camera trained on the "Clay Model" writer while he was writing, and I have no protocol of what was going through his mind, but it is possible to speculate on the syntactic difficulties of sentences like these: "In the past time I thought that an incident was creative was when I had to make a clay model of the earth, but not of the classical or your everyday model of the earth which consists of the two cores, the mantle and the crust. I thought of these things in a dimension of which it would be unique, but easy to comprehend." The syntactic difficulties appear to be the result of the writer's attempt to use an unusual vocabulary and to extend his sentences beyond the boundaries of what would have been "normal" in his speech or writing. There is reason to believe, that is, that the problem was with *this* kind of sentence, in this context. If the problem of the last sentence is that of holding together the units "I thought," "dimension," "unique," and "easy to comprehend," then the linguistic problem was not a simple matter of sentence construction. I am arguing, then, that such sentences fall apart not because the writer lacked the necessary syntax to glue the pieces together but because he lacked the full statement within which these key words were already operating. While writing, and in the thrust of his need to complete the sentence, he had the key words but not the utterance. (And to recover the utterance, I suspect, he would need to do more than revise the sentence.) The invisible conventions, the prepared phrases remained too distant for the statement to be completed. The writer would have needed to get inside of a discourse that he could in fact only partially imagine. The act of constructing a sentence, then, became something like an act of transcription in which the voice on the tape unexpectedly faded away and became inaudible.

Shaughnessy (1977) speaks of the advanced writer as one who often has a more facile but still incomplete possession of this prior discourse. In the case of the advanced writer, the evidence of a problem is the presence of dissonant, redundant, or imprecise language, as in a sentence such as this: "No education can be *total*, it must be *continuous*."

Such a student, Shaughnessy says, could be said to hear the "melody of formal English" while still unable to make precise or exact distinctions. And, she says,

> the pre-packaging feature of language, the possibility of taking over phrases and whole sentences without much thought about them, threatens the writer now as before. The writer, as we have said, inherits the language out of which he must fabricate his own messages. He is therefore in a constant tangle with the language, obliged to recognize its public, communal nature and yet driven to invent out of this language his own statements. (1977, pp. 207–08)

For the unskilled writer, the problem is different in degree and not in kind. The inexperienced writer is left with a more fragmentary record of the comings and goings of academic discourse. Or, as I said above, he or she often has the key words without the complete statements within which they are already operating.

Let me provide one final example of this kind of syntactic difficulty in another piece of student writing. The writer of this paper seems to be able to sustain a discussion only by continually repeating his first step, producing a litany of strong, general, authoritative assertions that trail quickly into confusion. Notice how the writer seems to stabilize his movement through the paper by returning again and again to recognizable and available commonplace utterances. When he has to move away from them, however, away from the familiar to statements that would extend those utterances, where he, too, must speak, the writing—that is, both the syntax and the structure of the discourse—falls to pieces.

> Many times the times drives a person's life depends on how he uses it. I would like to think about if time is twenty-five hours a day rather than twenty-four hours. Some people think it's the boaring or some people might say it's the pleasure to take one more hour for their life. But I think the time is passing and coming, still we are standing on same position. We should use time as best as we can use about the good way in our life. Everything we do, such as sleep, eat, study, play and doing something for ourselves. These take the time to do and we could find the individual ability and may process own. It is the important for us and our society. As time going on the world changes therefor we are changing, too. When

> these situation changes we should follow the suitable case of own. But many times we should decide what's the better way to do so by using time. Sometimes like this kind of situation can cause the success of our lives or ruin. I think every individual of his own thought drive how to use time. These affect are done from environmental causes. So we should work on the better way of our life recognizing the importance of time.

There is a general pattern of disintegration when the writer moves off from standard phrases. This sentence, for example, starts out coherently and then falls apart: "*We should use time as best as we can* use about the good way in our life." The difficulty seems to be one of extending those standard phrases or of connecting them to the main subject reference, "time" (or "the time," a construction that causes many of the problems in the paper). Here is an example of a sentence that shows, in miniature, this problem of connection: "*I think every individual* of his own thought drive how to use *time*."

One of the remarkable things about this paper is that, in spite of all the syntactic confusion, there is the hint of an academic project here. The writer sets out to discuss how to creatively use one's time. The text seems to allude to examples and to stages in an argument, even if in the end it is all pretty incoherent. The gestures of academic authority, however, are clearly present, and present in a form that echoes the procedures in other, more successful papers. The writer sets himself against what "some people think"; he speaks with the air of authority: "But I think. . . . Everything we do. . . . When these situation changes. . . ." And he speaks as though there were a project underway, one where he proposes what he thinks, turns to evidence, and offers a conclusion: "These affect are done from environmental causes. So we should work. . . ." This is the case of a student with the ability to imagine the general outline and rhythm of academic prose but without the ability to carry it out, to complete the sentences. And when he gets lost in the new, in the unknown, in the responsibility of his own commitment to speak, he returns again to the familiar ground of the commonplace.

The challenge to researchers, it seems to me, is to turn their attention again to products, to student writing, since the drama in a student's essay, as he or she struggles with and against the languages of our contemporary life, is as intense and telling as the drama of an essay's mental preparation or physical production. A written text, too, can be a compelling model of the "composing process" once we conceive of a writer as at work within a text and simultaneously, then, within a society, a history, and a culture.

It may very well be that some students will need to learn to crudely mimic the "distinctive register" of academic discourse before they are prepared to actually and legitimately do the work of the discourse, and before they are sophisticated enough with the refinements of tone and gesture to do it with grace or elegance. To say this, however, is to say that our students must be our students. Their initial progress will be marked by their abilities to take on the role of privilege, by their abilities to establish authority. From this point of view, the student who wrote about constructing the clay model of the earth is better prepared for his education than the student who wrote about playing football in white shoes, even though the "White Shoes" paper is relatively error-free and the "Clay Model" paper is not. It will be hard to pry loose the writer of the "White Shoes" paper from the tidy, pat discourse that allows him to dispose of the question of creativity in such a quick and efficient manner. He will have to be convinced that it is better to write sentences he might not so easily control, and he will have to be convinced that it is better to write muddier and more confusing prose (in order that it may sound like ours), and this will be harder than convincing the "Clay Model" writer to continue what he has already begun.

Acknowledgments

Preparation of this chapter was supported by the Learning Research and Development Center of the University of Pittsburgh, which is supported in part by the National Institute of Education.

Notes

1. David Olson (1981) has made a similar observation about school-related problems of language learning in younger children. Here is his conclusion: "Hence, depending upon whether children assumed language was primarily suitable for making assertions and conjectures or primarily for making direct or indirect commands, they will either find school texts easy or difficult" (p. 107).
2. For Aristotle, there were both general and specific commonplaces. A speaker, says Aristotle, has a "stock of arguments to which he may turn for a particular need."

   > If he knows the *topoi* (regions, places, lines of argument)—and a skilled speaker will know them—he will know where to find what he wants for a special case. The general topics, or *common*places, are regions containing arguments that are common to all branches of knowledge. . . . But there are also special topics (regions, places, *loci*) in which one looks for arguments appertaining to particular branches of knowledge, special sciences, such as ethics or politics. (1932, pp. 154–55)

   And, he says, "the topics or places, then, may be indifferently thought of as in the science that is concerned, or in the mind of the speaker." But the question of location is "indifferent" *only* if the mind of the speaker is in line with set opinion, general assumption. For the speaker (or writer) who is not situated so comfortably in the privileged public realm, this is indeed not an indifferent matter at all. If he does not have the commonplace at hand, he will not, in Aristotle's terms, know where to go at all.

3. Pat Bizzell has argued that the *Seventeen* writer's process of goal-setting

> can be better understood if we see it in terms of writing for a discourse community. His initial problem . . . is to find a way to include these readers in a discourse community for which he is comfortable writing. He places them in the academic discourse community by imagining the girls as students. . . . Once he has included them in a familiar discourse community, he can find a way to address them that is common in the community: he will argue with them, putting a new interpretation on information they possess in order to correct misconceptions. (1982a, p. 228)

4. See Bartholomae (1979, 1983) and Rose (1983) for articles on curricula designed to move students into university discourse. The movement to extend writing "across the curriculum" is evidence of a general concern for locating students within the work of the university; see Bizzell (1982a) and Maimon et al. (1981). For longer works directed specifically at basic writing, see Ponsot and Deen (1982) and Shaughnessy (1977). For a book describing a course for more advanced students, see Coles (1978).
5. In spite of my misgivings about Bereiter and Scardamalia's interpretation of the cognitive nature of the problem of "inert knowledge," this is an essay I regularly recommend to teachers. It has much to say about the dangers of what seem to be "neutral" forms of classroom discourse and provides, in its final section, a set of recommendations on how a teacher might undo discourse conventions that have become part of the institution of teaching.
6. Stanley Fish (1980) argues that the basis for distinguishing novice from expert readings is the persuasiveness of the discourse used to present and defend a given reading. In particular, see the chapter, "Demonstration vs. Persuasion: Two Models of Critical Activity" (pp. 356–73).
7. Some students, when they come to the university, can do this better than others. When Jonathan Culler says, "the possibility of bringing someone to see that a particular interpretation is a good one assumes shared points of departure and common notions of how to read," he is acknowledging that teaching, at least in English classes, has had to assume that students, to be students, were already to some degree participating in the structures of reading and writing that constitute English studies (quoted in Fish, 1980, p. 366).

   Stanley Fish tells us "not to worry" that students will violate our enterprise by offering idiosyncratic readings of standard texts:

> The fear of solipsism, of the imposition by the unconstrained self of its own prejudices, is unfounded because the self does not exist apart from the communal or conventional categories of thought that enable its operations (of thinking, seeing, reading). Once we realize that the conceptions that fill consciousness, including any conception of its own status, are culturally derived, the very notion of an unconstrained self, of a consciousness wholly and dangerously free, becomes incomprehensible. (1980, p. 335)

   He, too, is assuming that students, to be students (and not "dangerously free"), must be members in good standing of the community whose immediate head is the English teacher. It is interesting that his parenthetical catalogue of the "operations" of thought, "thinking, seeing, reading," excludes writing, since it is only through written records that we have any real indication of how a student thinks, sees, and reads. (Perhaps "real" is an inappropriate word to use here, since there is certainly a "real" intellectual life that goes on, independent of writing. Let me say that thinking, seeing, and reading are valued in the academic community *only* as they are represented by extended, elaborated written records.) Writing, I presume, is a given for Fish. It is the card of entry into this closed community that constrains and excludes dangerous characters. Students who are excluded from this community are students who do poorly on written placement exams or in freshman composition. They do not, that is, move easily into the privileged discourse of the community, represented by the English literature class.

8. My debt to Bizzell's work should be evident everywhere in this essay. See also Bizzell (1978, 1982b) and Bizzell and Herzberg (1980).
9. Fish says the following about the relationship between student and an object under study:

> we are not to imagine a moment when my students "simply see" a physical configuration of atoms and *then* assign that configuration a significance, according to the situation they happen to be in. To be in the situation (this or any other) is to "see" with the eyes of its interests, its goals, its understood practices, values, and norms, and so to be conferring significance *by* seeing, not after it. The categories of my students' vision are the categories by which they understand themselves to be functioning as students . . . and objects will appear to them in forms related to that way of functioning rather than in some objective or preinterpretive form. (1980, p. 334)

10. I am aware that the papers given the highest rankings offer arguments about creativity and originality similar to my own. If there is a conspiracy here, that is one of the points of my chapter. I should add that my reading of the "content" of basic writers' essays is quite different from Lunsford's (1980).

References

Aristotle. (1932). *The rhetoric of Aristotle* (L. Cooper, Trans.). Englewood Cliffs, NJ: Prentice-Hall.

Barthes, R. (1974). *S/Z* (R. Howard, Trans.). New York: Hill & Wang.

Bartholomae, D. (1979). Teaching basic writing: An alternative to basic skills. *Journal of Basic Writing*, 2, 85–109.

Bartholomae, D. (1983). Writing assignments: Where writing begins. In P. Stock (Ed.), *Forum* (pp. 300–12). Montclair, NJ: Boynton/Cook.

Bereiter, C., & Scardamalia, M. (1985). Cognitive coping strategies and the problem of "inert knowledge." In S. S. Chipman, J. W. Segal, & R. Glaser (Eds.), *Thinking and learning skills: Research and open questions* (Vol. 2). Hillsdale, NJ: Erlbaum.

Bizzell, P. (1978). The ethos of academic discourse. *College Composition and Communication*, 29, 351–55.

Bizzell, P. (1982a). Cognition, convention, and certainty: What we need to know about writing. *Pre/text*, 3, 213–44.

Bizzell, P. (1982b). College composition: Initiation into the academic discourse community. *Curriculum Inquiry*, 12, 191–207.

Bizzell, P., & Herzberg, B. (1980). "Inherent" ideology, "universal" history, "empirical" evidence, and "context-free" writing: Some problems with E. D. Hirsch's *The Philosophy of Composition. Modern Language Notes*, 95, 1181–1202.

Coles, W. E., Jr. (1978). *The plural I.* New York: Holt, Rinehart & Winston.

Fish, S. (1980). *Is there a text in this class? The authority of interpretive communities.* Cambridge, MA: Harvard University Press.

Flower, L. S. (1981). Revising writer-based prose. *Journal of Basic Writing*, 3, 62–74.

Flower, L., & Hayes, J. (1981). A cognitive process theory of writing. *College Composition and Communication*, 32, 365–87.

Hairston, M. (1978). *A contemporary rhetoric.* Boston: Houghton Mifflin.

Lunsford, A. A. (1980). The content of basic writers' essays. *College Composition and Communication*, 31, 278–90.

Maimon, E. P., Belcher, G. L., Hearn, G. W., Nodine, B. F., & O'Conner, F. X. (1981). *Writing in the arts and sciences.* Cambridge, MA: Winthrop.

Olson, D. R. (1981). Writing: The divorce of the author from the text. In B. M. Kroll & R. J. Vann (Eds.), *Exploring speaking–writing relationships: Connections and contrasts.* Urbana, IL: National Council of Teachers of English.

Perkins, D. N. (1985). General cognitive skills: Why not? In S. S. Chipman, J. W. Segal, & R. Glaser (Eds.), *Thinking and learning skills: Research and open questions* (Vol. 2). Hillsdale, NJ: Erlbaum.

Ponsot, M., & Deen, R. (1982). *Beat not the poor desk.* Montclair, NJ: Boynton/Cook.

Rodriguez, R. (1983). *Hunger of memory.* New York: Bantam.

Rose, M. (1983). Remedial writing courses: A critique and a proposal. *College English*, 45, 109–28.

Said, E. W. (1975). *Beginnings: Intention and method.* Baltimore: The Johns Hopkins University Press.

Shaughnessy, M. (1977). *Errors and expectations.* New York: Oxford University Press.

Bartholomae's Insights as a Resource for Your Reflections

1. Make a brief list of the particular features of academic discourse. How does academic discourse differ from the sorts of mental and verbal habits that characterize students who are new to the university?

2. Consider the social and political implications of Bartholomae's argument. Will some students be at a distinct advantage or disadvantage in terms of appropriating "authoritative discourse" because of their social or cultural backgrounds? How might you level the playing field for your students?

Bartholomae's Insights as a Resource for Your Writing Classroom

1. Share with your students the student essays that Bartholomae uses as examples. After they have had time to think and form their own opinions about the essays, share with them Bartholomae's ideas about the essays. Ask students to compare and contrast their own sense of what's interesting about this student work with Bartholomae's ideas. What do they like or dislike about Bartholomae's vision of the composition classroom?
2. Have students explore the social implications of Bartholomae's theory. Will certain groups be excluded from appropriating this discourse, or at least face significant barriers to doing so? Ask students whether they feel that Bartholomae's views of helping students master this academic discourse are pragmatic, laden with cultural values, or both. What do they feel should be standards for valid discourse? Valued discourse?

From Clueless in Academe

Gerald Graff

Can you remember your first experiences in a college classroom, and how strange and remote some aspects of it seemed? Graff's goal, throughout the book from which these excerpts are taken, is to demystify the work of the university, to distill its discourse to a rather simple, even commonsensical set of moves — moves that readily form the core of a writing course. As he explains, teachers often take certain things for granted that students don't. This gap is a source of enormous confusion that wastes a great deal of time in classrooms. Ultimately, some students tune out, and teachers grow exasperated. But, if we can better understand the way newcomers to the university experience our teaching, we can go a long way toward minimizing that counterproductive gap.

Introduction: In the Dark All Eggheads Are Gray

This book is an attempt by an academic to look at academia from the perspective of those who don't get it. Its subject is cluelessness, the bafflement, usually accompanied by shame and resentment, felt by students, the general public, and even many academics in the face of the impenetrability of the academic world. It examines some overlooked ways in which schools and colleges themselves reinforce cluelessness and thus perpetuate the misconception that the life of the mind is a secret society for which only an elite few qualify.

Given the inherent difficulty of academic intellectual work, some degree of cluelessness is a natural stage in the process of education. If cluelessness did not exist, there would be no need for schooling at all. My argument in this book, however, is that academia reinforces cluelessness by making its ideas, problems, and ways of thinking *look* more opaque, narrowly specialized, and beyond normal learning capacities than they are or need to be. As I see it, my academic intellectual culture is not at all irrelevant to my students' needs and interests, but we do a very good job of making it appear as if it is.

One way we do so is by obscuring the convergence between academia and the popular media. Too often schools and colleges take intellectual conversations that resemble the ones students engage in or encounter in the popular media, and make them seem unrecognizable, as well as no fun. To put it another way, schooling takes students who are perfectly street-smart and exposes them to the life of the mind in ways that make them feel dumb. Why is this? Why in many cases do street smarts not only fail to evolve naturally into academic smarts, but end up seeming opposed to academic smarts, as if the two can't coexist inside the same head? Part of the reason has to do with the legacy of American anti-intellectualism, which elevates hardheaded common sense over supposedly impractical academic navel gazing. But educational institutions themselves contribute to the problem by making the culture of ideas and arguments look opaque and therefore more remote than it actually is from the wisdom of the street.

How this happens, "how schooling obscures the life of the mind," is my central concern. Jargon and specialized terminology, the most frequently blamed culprits, are only the tip of the institutional iceberg. I too am amused by the satires on opaque academic jargon produced by journalists, stand-up comics, and disaffected academics. But blaming the unintelligibility of academia exclusively on jargon and obscure writing prevents us from recognizing deeper sources of obfuscation that are rooted in the way academia organizes and thinks about itself. To appreciate these deeper causes, we need to go beyond spoofs of jargon to the way schools and colleges represent the culture of ideas and arguments.

By the culture of ideas and arguments, I refer to that admittedly blurry entity that spans the academic and intellectual worlds on the one hand and the arena of journalistic public discourse on the other. Not all "academics" are "intellectuals," and intellectuals come in many different types, including academic scholars, journalistic public intellectuals, policy wonks, information managers, media pundits, and legal and government professionals. What these different types have in common, from the research professor to the newspaper editorialist to the mythical educated layperson on the street, is a commitment to articulating ideas in public. Whatever the differences between their specialized jargons, they have all learned to play the following game: listen closely to others, summarize them in a recognizable way, and make your own relevant argument. This argument literacy, the ability to listen, summarize, and respond, is rightly viewed as central to being educated.

For American students to do better — all of them, not just twenty percent — they need to know that summarizing and making arguments is the name of the game in academia. But it's precisely this game that academia obscures, generally by hiding it in plain view amidst a vast disconnected clutter of subjects, disciplines, and courses. The sheer cognitive overload represented by the American curriculum prevents most students from detecting and then learning the moves of the underlying argument game that gives coherence to it all.

The college curriculum says to students, in effect, "Come and get it, but you're on your own as to what to make of it all." As John Gardner has rightly observed, American colleges "operate under the assumption that students know how to do it — or if they don't they'll flunk out and it's their problem."[1] And colleges play hard to get not only with their undergraduates, but with the lower schools. The schools are easy to blame for failing to prepare students for college, and it is indeed a scandal that, aside from a few "star" schools that resemble good colleges,[2] American high schools still don't see it as their mission to prepare all their students for college, even though everybody now agrees that college is a virtual prerequisite for success and a decent life. But it is the failure of higher education to clarify its culture of ideas and arguments that leaves the schools unable to prepare their students for college. The mystification of academic culture trickles down from the top.

Some readers will object that in claiming to know what students have to do to succeed in academia — enter the culture of ideas and arguments — I am really only revealing what they have to do to pass my course. They will say that there's more to being educated than learning to argue, and they are right. In giving priority to ideas and arguments, however, I don't minimize the importance of qualities that can't be reduced to pure rationality — emotional intelligence, moral character, visual and aesthetic sensitivity, and creativity in storytelling and personal narrative. What I do claim is that training in these qualities will be incomplete if students are unable to translate them into persuasive public discourse. To call attention to the educational importance of visual literacy and the body you have to make arguments, not just wave pictures, do a dance, or give hugs.

Argumentation need not be a joyless, bloodless activity, and there is no necessary quarrel between arguments and narratives. Good stories make an argumentative point, and arguments gain punch from imbedded stories. Nor does privileging argumentation in the curriculum necessarily represent the ethnocentric or racist bias that some make it out to be. On the contrary, since effective argument starts with attentive listening, training in argument is central to multicultural understanding and respect for otherness. Respecting cultures different from your own means summarizing others' arguments accurately, putting yourself in their shoes. After September 11 it is all the more crucial that Americans learn to understand the arguments of those who would destroy us, and that the world learn to fight with words rather than with guns and bombs.

I like to think I have first-class credentials for writing a book about cluelessness, having been a university professor for forty years, thereby encountering a great variety of students and others who were often puzzled by things I said and even more by why I said them at all. I have met my own share of incomprehensible academic utterances, which I duly pretended to understand in order to avoid humiliation. Given the genius-worship that runs through our culture, academics are often admired for speaking above other people's heads, but knowing this fact somehow doesn't save me from embarrassment when I fumble painfully to explain what I do to nonacademic relatives and friends.

My experience over the years playing both the baffler and bafflee has made me increasingly curious about the incomprehension, anxiety, and alienation that my academic intellectual world provokes. Finding that no study exists of the root causes of academic befuddlement, at some point I began contemplating a book-length analysis, a kind of notes toward a field of clueless studies. I had been unscientifically collecting data on attitudes toward "intellectualism" and what one of my students once called "life of the mind stuff,"[3] data that included notes on classes and office conferences, copies of student papers, and specimens, good and bad, of academic and journalistic writing. I began interviewing—and getting my students to interview—college undergraduates and high school students, probing how they felt about intellectualism and its forms of talk, and I plunged into the extensive scholarly literature on academic literacy and students' problems with it. I also thought back on my own cluelessness as an awkward college student, before the intellectual world had become so familiar to me that I forgot how strange and alienating it had once seemed. I reflected on the divided feelings I still harbor as someone who often feels most like an academic when I am around nonacademics and most like a nonacademic when I am with colleagues.

Since professors are supposed to be smart, sophisticated, and on the cutting edge, making a study of incomprehension can seem oddly retrograde—like giving up an endowed chair in order to reenroll in kindergarten. Professors are trained to think of cluelessness as an uninteresting negative condition, a lack or a blank space to be filled in by superior knowledge. This incuriosity, which helps explain why teaching has been so notoriously undervalued in universities, takes different forms: for some progressive educators, to speak of cluelessness at all is inherently snobbish, elitist, and undemocratic, as if acknowledging students' deficiencies necessarily denigrated their abilities. For some traditionalists, on the other hand, who see cluelessness as a distasteful symptom of cultural vulgarity and a dumbed-down popular culture, the clueless, like the poor, will always be with us, and there is nothing much anybody can do about it except to teach to the best students and let the rest fend for themselves.

These attitudes may explain why the opaque nature of academic intellectual culture, though a common target of jokes, is not a more prominent topic in debates over what ails American education. Though we all now claim to believe in democratic education, as a culture we have never been sure if we think everyone is cut out for the life of the mind or not. Then, too, the topic of academic cluelessness is so fraught with anxieties about class snobbery and inferiority that it is hard to have a frank discussion of it. On the other hand, the topic can often be discerned lurking in the background of discussions of other educational issues, particularly in growing concerns about the achievement gap between high- and low-income students. Recent debates about standardized testing, for example, are really a symptom of the murkiness about what it is that intellectuals do. It's as if standardized tests fill a gap left by our failure to clarify what real intellectual prowess is all about.

But attention to academia's opacity has been further diverted in recent years by the polarized politics of educational debate. In the curricular wars that have raged since the eighties and nineties, we have become so caught up in battles between rival lists of books — the traditional classics versus multicultural and minority texts — that we forget that the chronic problem for the vast majority of American high school and college students has always been *the culture of books and ideas as such*, regardless of which faction gets to draw up the reading list. We become so enmeshed in rivalries between traditional and progressive *versions* of intellectual culture that we overlook the fact that to most students intellectual culture of any kind, whatever its political leanings, is all the same old "school stuff."

This is not to minimize the importance of ideological differences or to avoid taking a stand in the canon wars. It is simply to point out that in order to understand or articulate a political stand you already have to belong to the culture of ideas and arguments, and wield its lingo of "whereas x argues ______, I claim ______." The point was rudely brought home to me in a course I taught at Northwestern in the late eighties: I had asked my class to write responses to essays by traditionalist Allan Bloom and radical black feminist bell hooks. In reading the papers I realized that some students saw little difference between Bloom and hooks. To their eyes, these two writers, who seem ideologically on different planets to me and my colleagues, were just a couple of professors conversing in arcane language about nonproblems. And many of the students who did discern the differences were not able to formulate them articulately or enter the debate. It was not that they lacked interest, but that the language of public controversy that Bloom and hooks commanded eluded them. I concluded that it wouldn't matter much whether Bloom's or hooks's side won the debate if these students remained excluded from the discourse in which it was carried on.

Call it the Law of Relative Invisibility of Intellectual Differences: to the non-egghead, any two eggheads, no matter how far apart, are virtually indistinguishable.[4] With apologies to cartoonist Gary Larson's *The Far Side*, we can picture the situation as follows:

G. Graff

In the dark all intellectual disagreements are gray.

On the other hand, being "in the dark" enables you to notice things that get overlooked by those supposedly in the know. If from a clueless eye view opposing intellectuals look the same, it is because they *are* the same in a crucial way. They share a public language of ideas and arguments that transcends their ideological differences and separates them from many students and other Americans.

As for the battle of the books, my argument cuts both ways in the skirmishes between traditionalists and progressives. Traditionalists are right to insist that not all texts are equal in value and that students should study a significant selection of the world's classics. But what does it profit them to keep the syllabus safe for Plato and Shakespeare if many students need the Cliffs Notes to get a clue about what such authors are up to? Progressives are right that students who are turned off by *Hamlet* may be turned on by Alice Walker's *The Color Purple* (though such results don't necessarily follow predictable racial, ethnic, or class lines). It's foolish not to assign Walker or a popular magazine or film if doing so inspires students to read and study who otherwise would not. Progressives are also right that since every reading list makes a statement about how the experience of particular groups is or is not valued, questions of cultural representation have a legitimate place in decisions about what texts to teach. But what does it profit progressives to get minority writers like Walker and Black Elk into the syllabus if many students need the Cliffs Notes to gain an articulate grasp of either?

In fact, works by Walker and other multicultural writers are now prominently displayed in the Cliffs Notes rack, perhaps the ultimate sign that multiculturalism has made it, but hardly in the way its advocates hoped. Again, then, our intense debates over course reading lists will be academic in the worst sense if students remain outside the academic conversation about books.

But who gives a fig, you ask, about "the academic conversation," which is often a bad conversation, boring, self-important, and dominated by insider orthodoxies? Academic conversations are often all these things, to be sure, but at their best moments they are more valuable and pertinent to students' lives than academic-bashers give them credit for. Even so, you persist, isn't the point of education to produce good citizens, not more academics? Surely it is, but these goals are compatible, for the issues and problems addressed by academic research and teaching are increasingly indistinguishable from the issues we wrestle with as public citizens. The point is not to turn students into clones of professors but to give them access to forms of intellectual capital that have a lot of power in the world.

Those who charge that academic discourse is itself the problem fail to see that *talk about* books and subjects is as important educationally as are the books and subjects themselves. For the way we talk about a subject becomes part of the subject, a fact that explains why we have book-discussion groups to supplement solitary reading, why Trekkies form clubs and hold conferences as well as privately enjoying *Star Trek*, and why sports talk call-in shows and sports journalism have arisen alongside the games themselves. Students must not only read texts, but find things to *say* about them, and no text tells you what to say about it. So our habit of elevating books and subjects over the secondary talk about them only helps keep students tongue-tied.

Seeing academia, then, as these struggling students see it, is a key prerequisite for improved teaching. It is also a key to improving the quality of professorial writing. The sociologist Howard Becker has observed that there is something unfairly circular about the common view that sociologists write badly, since sociological work that is well written is not considered sociology.[5] Becker's witticism holds for academic writing generally: people assume that if they understand it, it must not be academic. Though I have a good deal to say about why academic writing is often bad, I argue against the popular belief that academic writing generally turns its back on nonacademic outsiders or that to make it as a professor you have to envelop your ideas in a cloud of smoke.

The view that academic writing is necessarily insular and obscure props up the overdrawn opposition between research and teaching. We are so used to opposing research and teaching that we overlook the fact that good research is itself pedagogical, often drawing on skills of explanation, clarification, and problem-posing — of asking, "So what?" and "Who cares?" — that are central to good teaching. Indeed, as many academics testify, teaching often helps us sharpen our research writing and thereby advance our careers, a fact that refutes the renunciatory view of teaching that sees it as necessarily sacrificing professional self-interest.

I myself seem to have the most impact on professional audiences when I write in ways that are accessible to lay readers and take their outsider's perspective into account. As I see it, having to explain myself to freshmen or high school students forces me not to dumb my ideas down, but to formulate them more pointedly than I do when I address only my colleagues and graduate students. I agree with the linguist Steven Pinker that "having to explain an idea in plain English to someone with no stake in the matter is an excellent screen for incoherent or contradictory ideas that somehow have entrenched themselves in a field."[6] For again, those outsiders' questions that at first sight seem clueless — "So what?" "What's your point?" "What does it have to do with me?" and "Why does any of this matter?" — often turn out to be the smartest and most clarifying.

It is by making us feel that asking such questions would expose us as naive or foolish that academia gets away with its mystifications. As a recent college graduate put it when asked how well her English major had clarified the issues in her discipline, "The assumption seemed to be that if I was any good I *already* knew what those issues were and why they mattered. I couldn't ask, since I didn't want to look dumb." Academia has its own unspoken policy of "don't ask, don't tell" that prevents clarification from breaking out.

Much of the problem lies in the belief that to *simplify* academic inquiry is to vulgarize it, whereas simplification is a necessary feature of even the most complex kinds of work. Nothing inhibits clarification — and good teaching — more than the professorial fear and loathing of any formulation that seems reductive. In fact, reductions can be harmful or useful, and failing to make the distinction leads us to justify obfuscation and exclusion ("It's just too complicated to explain; if only you were in the field you'd understand what I'm talking about"). Reductive moments are central not only to teaching but to intramural communication between scholars as well. I am not urging professors, as Gregory Jay recently has, to "complement" our work "with essays and books that translate our fields for the public," though this is certainly a good thing to do.[7] I am arguing that translating academic ideas into nonacademic terms is already *internal* to successful academic communication itself. "Dare to be reductive" is one of my maxims for academics.

In addition to analyzing structures of academic obfuscation, this book suggests ways in which teachers and programs can cut through the curricular clutter to show students how the argument world works. The book draws on strategies I have developed in my own teaching or have borrowed from others that simplify the basic "moves" of public argument for students who have difficulty making them on their own. These include Argument Templates, which I use as training wheels that enable students to get on the argument bike and ride (example: "In the discussion that has followed the September 11 attacks, a controversial issue has been . . ."). Some will object to the formulaic nature of such templates, but all communication is partly formulaic. Formulas can enable creativity and complication as often as they can stifle them. If we refuse to provide such formulas on the grounds that they are too prescriptive or that everything has to come from the students themselves, we just end up hiding the tools of success.

Since it is freshman composition that has been assigned the job of teaching the basic moves of persuasive argument, this book amounts to a plea for making composition and writing across the curriculum programs far more central than they have ever been in high school and college curricula. The low status of composition in universities illustrates the "Law of Academic Prestige" that has been formulated by Deirdre N. McCloskey: "the more useful a field, the lower its prestige. The freshman English course, which is one of the most important things colleges do, is in academic prestige many notches below algebraic topology or medieval philosophy."[8] These priorities are particularly self-defeating for departments of English, which exalt literary studies over writing even though the quality of students' literary experience is registered only through what they say and write. The spread of college "first year experience" courses and "freshman success seminars" is a step in the right direction, but such courses generally stop short of providing intellectual socialization. They need to go beyond teaching study skills, time-management, using computers, and test-taking to give students more help in entering the academic culture of arguments and ideas.

Lastly, a word about the relation of this book to my previous work. In my educational writing, I am best known for the argument that the wisest response we can make to the philosophical and social conflicts that have disrupted education is to "teach the conflicts" themselves, to bring controversy to the center of the academic curriculum. The situation that called forth this argument was the culture wars of the eighties and nineties, which led me to conclude that if disagreements over what should be taught and how are inevitable, the sensible course would be to quit trying to hide these disagreements and start making productive use of them in classrooms so as to bring students in on them. Because my examples of conflicts to be taught were often the debates over the canon and politics in literary studies, some readers have assumed that teaching the conflicts for me focuses only on those debates, whereas teaching the conflicts can be done in any discipline or subject area.

But an even more important point that some readers of my work have missed is that the ultimate motivation of my argument for teaching the conflicts is the need to clarify academic culture, not just to resolve spats among academics or cultural factions. My assumption is that an institution as rife with conflicts as the American school and college can clarify itself only by making its ideological differences coherent. But even if our cultural and educational scene were a less contentious place than it is, the centrality of controversy to learning would still need to be stressed. For there exists a deep cognitive connection between controversy and intelligibility. John Stuart Mill pointed up the connection when he observed that we do not understand our own ideas until we know what can be said against them. In Mill's words, those who "have never thrown themselves into the mental position of those who think differently from them . . . do not, in any proper sense of the word, know the doctrine which they themselves profess."[9] In other words, our very ability to think depends on contrast — on asking "as opposed to what?"

This "dialogical" or contrastive character of human cognition has long been a given of modern thought, but the academic curriculum with its self-isolated courses has yet to reflect it. When schooling is bad or dull, it is often because the curriculum effaces this element of contrast or as-opposed-to-whatness from students' view. Thus the academic habit of evading conflict helps obscure the life of the mind.

The problem, however, is that simply throwing inexperienced students headlong into intellectual debates doesn't work. Students won't become engaged in academic debates about ideas unless they have a reason to be interested in them and can gain the rudiments of the public discourse in which these debates are conducted. Whereas my last book, *Beyond the Culture Wars*, was subtitled *How Teaching the Conflicts Can Revitalize American Education*, the present book might be subtitled "How Teaching the Conflicts — or Any Other Educational Approach — *Won't* Revitalize Education as Long as the Culture of Public Argument Remains Opaque to Many Students and Other Citizens."

To put it another way, the most fundamental conflict that needs to be taught in classrooms is the conflict between Intellectualspeak and Studentspeak. I argue that teachers need to be explicit about this conflict and even to sharpen the contrast between academic and student discourse, though their ultimate goal should be to help students discover that these forms of discourse are not as far apart as they seem. My students and I need to meet each other halfway, as they learn the kind of talk that I speak and write and I learn theirs, for the combination of these registers is more powerful than either alone.

This book extends my "teach the conflicts" argument in one further way by seeing conflicts as an internal principle of writing and the teaching of writing. We throw ourselves, as Mill put it, "into the mental position of those who think differently from" us by writing the voices of others into our texts, even trying them on for size. When students are asked to complete a sentence that starts, "At this point you will probably object that . . . ," they begin to move beyond the undivided, one-dimensional voice that is a surer mark of weak student writing than incorrect grammar. And it's by writing the voices of others into their texts that students start learning to produce a public voice.

There are those who argue that the academic obfuscation I examine in this book is no accident. They say that when schooling keeps students mystified it is not failing at all, but working all too well at doing exactly what our culture asks it to, sorting students into cognitive haves and have-nots and therefore into society's winners and losers. As this argument has it, our winner-take-all economy has to find some way to maintain high levels of social inequality, so academic institutions must keep the cultural capital of literate public discourse out of the grubby hands of the riffraff.[10] We academics, then, deliberately withhold our mysteries from the many in order to prop up the power of the cultural elite as well as the fiction that society needs our mumbo-jumbo. I have never accepted this cynical view of education, but I'm afraid we will go on giving it credibility until we change our practices. . . .

The Problem Problem and Other Oddities of Academic Discourse

As teachers we often proceed as if the rationale of our most basic academic practices is understood and shared by our students, even when we get plenty of signs that it is not. We take for granted, for example, that reflecting in a self-conscious way about experience—"intellectualizing"—is something our students naturally see the point of and want to learn to do better. If they don't, after all, why are they in school? At the same time, we cannot help noticing that many students are skeptical about the value of such intellectualizing. When students do poorly, the reasons often have less to do with their lack of ability than with their reluctance to become the introspective type of people who relish and excel at such tasks.

Aversion to the apparent pretentiousness of intellectual ways of communicating is often central to this reluctance. In *The Unschooled Mind* Howard Gardner observes that the problems students have in comprehending texts are often magnified by their "insensitivity . . . to the vocabulary of argument—'contend,' 'hypothesize,' 'refute,' 'contradict'. . . ."[11] Gardner is right about the connection between poor reading comprehension and students' lack of a "vocabulary of argument." The problem, however, often lies not in the students' "insensitivity" to this vocabulary but their disinclination to acquire it. In some high schools and colleges, students would risk ostracism if they use expressions like "hypothesize" or "I contend." As the saying goes, nobody likes a smart-ass.

Hillel Crandus, a teacher of eleventh-grade English, asked his class to write short papers (which Crandus shared with me) expressing how they felt about analysis, especially the kind of close interpretative reading of texts that's the staple of literature courses. One student, call her Karen, wrote, "Personally, I don't like analyzing everything that happens to me. Some of it would be a big waste of time. I sometimes find myself analyzing dreams that I've had, but it's usually pretty pointless. To me a lot of things happen for a very obvious reason that does not need a lot of discussion or insight." Another stated flatly that "the only thing that overanalyzing leads to is boredom."

In my experience, the distaste Karen feels for "analyzing everything that happens" to you, and the belief that some things "happen for a very obvious reason" and therefore need no further inquiry, don't necessarily disappear once students move on to college, though by then students have become more guarded about betraying such views in the presence of their teachers. As a University of Chicago undergraduate put it, "'Academic' type people take life too seriously and don't let themselves read for enjoyment. There's more to life than intellect . . . you can read for fun." A UIC freshman told his composition instructor that "I don't want to dig deeper into the meaning of something. What I say is what I mean." Whenever I survey students on the question, many admit they have a problem with academia's tendency to turn everything it touches into grist for the analytic mill, almost as if teachers were deliberately trying to spoil everybody's fun.

In this chapter, I look at some standard academic practices that often seem second nature to teachers and A-students but come across to many students as bizarre, counterintuitive, or downright nonsensical. These perceptions of the absurd nature of intellectual practices underlie the familiar stereotypes of the educated: eggheads, nerds, sissies, snobs, braniacs, know-it-alls, brown-nosers, control freaks, ideologues, and manipulative propagandists. These characterizations may be rooted in misperceptions of the life of the mind, but ones that are unlikely to be dispelled unless teachers flush them out and address them.

1. The Problem Problem

Nothing better exemplifies the apparently counterintuitive nature of intellectual practices than their preoccupation with what often appear to be bogus "problems." Academic assignments ask students not only to become aggressive know-it-alls, but to cultivate problems to an extent that seems perverse or bizarre. I call this syndrome the "problem problem."

One reason why students often resist the academic fixation with problems is suggested by Wayne Booth, Gregory Colomb, and Joseph Williams in their valuable primer on academic writing, *The Craft of Research*. Booth, Colomb, and Williams discuss the difficulties inexperienced students have with the conventions used to set up the problems that form the starting point of most expository essays.[12] Yet the difficulties students have in constructing the kind of problem that launches an essay stem not only from their unfamiliarity with the conventions of problem-posing, but from deeper uncertainties about the "problematizing" role itself.

Booth, Colomb, and Williams do not mention these uncertainties, but they provide a clue to them when they distinguish between problems that are recognized to be such and those that are not.[13] Problems of the first kind, such as earning a living, finding a mate, curing heart diseases, preventing air pollution, or eliminating poverty and homelessness come to us with an apparently *pre-given* quality. These problems are already so widely acknowledged that writers can take them up without having to make an argument for seeing them as problems, though there are situations in which they might have to (for example, talking about poverty with an audience of social Darwinists). Many of the problems with which academics deal, however, lack this pre-given quality, as when they concern the meanings of words, abstract concepts, and texts, or the actions of people long dead. In such cases, where we can't assume that others will see the problem we are taking up *as* a problem, we have to work to sell them on its reality and importance. Academics not only cultivate problems that are unrecognized as such, they like to *invent* problems that most people are unaware of, or look for new ways to describe already recognized problems.

In this penchant for problematizing, academic research scholars resemble avant-garde artists who "defamiliarize" previously familiar subjects, using alienation effects to make what seems obvious and unproblematic look strange. But despite the lip service given to Socrates' maxim that the unexamined life is not worth living, searching out new problems can seem profoundly counterintuitive: are there not already enough problems in the world without our straining to invent new ones? From a certain commonsense point of view, academia's cultivation of problems looks manufactured, perverse, and silly, and academic problem-posers resemble the dotty scientists on the island of Laputa in Jonathan Swift's *Gulliver's Travels*, who grapple earnestly, for instance, with the problem of turning excrement back into its original food.

A good example of the perceived absurdity of many of the problems addressed by academics is reported by Vivian Gornick in her memoir, *Fierce Attachments*, in which Gornick describes how her immersion in the intellectual life as a student at New York's City College alienated her from her mother in the Bronx. Gornick relates how her sentences "got longer within a month of [my] first classes. Longer, more complicated, formed by words whose meaning she did not know, . . . It made [my mother] crazy. . . . 'What are you talking about?' she would shout at me. 'What *are* you talking about? Speak English, please! We all understand English in this house, Speak it.'"[14] When Gornick tried to explain the thesis of the book she was reading, "a comparative history of the idea of love over the last three hundred years," her mother would have none of it: "That's ridiculous," she said slowly. "Love is love. It's the same everywhere, all the time. What's to compare?"[15]

The academic faith in the singular virtue of finding problems in subjects — love, in Gornick's case — generally thought to be unproblematic seems especially bizarre and forced when the problems have to do with the meanings of texts. The idea that, below their apparent surface, texts harbor deep meanings that cry out for interpretation, analysis, and debate is one of those assumptions that seems so normal once we are socialized into academia that we forget how counterintuitive it can be. In fact, this assumption has probably never been comprehensible, much less convincing, to much of the general population or even to some academics. (A certain college Dean is said to have wondered aloud why entire departments are needed to study the books he has no trouble reading on the train to work every day.) An exception might seem to be scriptural texts, whose meanings have been picked apart and debated for so many centuries that the practice does not seem odd — except to sects that see even scriptural interpretation and theological debate as coming between the believer and God.

In their written responses, many of Crandus's eleventh-graders confess that most classroom analysis of texts and interpretations seems tedious and pointless, an infinite regress that goes nowhere. As one student, Elaina, put it, "A student will make a comment that, maybe to me, seems straightforward, yet we still seem to dig deeper into just what that comment meant." Karen, the student whose reservations toward "analyzing everything that happens to me" I quoted above, wrote as follows about a class discussion of Richard Wright's autobiography, *Black Boy*:

> [I]t seems to me that we analyzed things that didn't seem to have much to analyze. For instance, the fire episode in the beginning of the book. In my opinion, Richard started the fire out of curiosity and boredom. The discussion we had in class got into things like it symbolizes his imagination or internal impulses, or even how he feels about his racial impression. I'm not saying that these aren't good ideas, but I think it's making something out of nothing. . . .
>
> Another reason I do not like [to] analyze, though this might sound arrogant, is because it is not important to me. I don't care what the fire in *Black Boy* symbolizes. It doesn't really make [any] difference to me. To some people, it does make a difference, and that's fine with me. But I don't really see how this helps me out in my life, the past, the present, or the future. It could end up helping me a lot, you never really know. I know it will help me out in college English classes.

Karen suspects that the symbolism attributed to works like *Black Boy* is simply not *there* in the text—in any case, she can't see it. Just as for her "a lot of things happen for a very obvious reason that does not need a lot of discussion or insight," what a text means is apparent on the surface and therefore needs no analysis. But even if deeper meanings are indeed present in the text, Karen adds, she doesn't care, though she acknowledges that such things do matter to some people and might some day to her, if only to help her get through college English courses.

Another student, Eileen, complains that

> during our classroom discussions, we tend to pick and pick at every single aspect of a paragraph until there is nothing left. I don't even remember half the time what the discussion started off about. . . . That is why I think that when we have our classroom discussions, they need not to be SO in-depth. . . . In my past, I have never really enjoyed reading, so that I am sure may be a factor in this. But I still feel that I am not alone on this one. Many students have agreed with me on my thoughts. In one paper a student described our classroom discussions as, ". . . beating a dead horse. . . ." I think that we have a great class that is a lot of fun, but sometimes, things just get way too deep for me.

A third student, Laura, who also dislikes being forced to analyze, writes that "I have talked to some students that I know feel this way. They dislike the thought of being forced to pick apart why things went a certain way. One, they don't see the point, two, they sometimes have no clue what's going on, and three, they could care less why it happened."

Again, from these three students' commonsense perspective, asking what texts mean is superfluous since texts are self-interpreting. Either they mean what they say or they are obscure, but either way there is little point trying to decode them. It is tempting to ascribe these beliefs to adolescent naivete, but their view is probably shared by most adults in our culture. Indeed, the belief that texts and other things speak for themselves and therefore do not require interpretation has deep roots in Western philosophy, as Jacques Derrida shows in a commentary on Plato's *Phaedrus*, a dialogue in which Socrates indicts writing for undermining the self-evident meaning that presumably becomes immune to misunderstanding in face-to-face oral communication.[16] From this Platonic point of view, the meaning of a text, say, on the nature of love is simply whatever the text itself says. To find out what the text has to say about love, you read the text. To make a *problem* out of what the text means, then, as teachers do in discussing the text in class, is to make a mountain out of a molehill. After all, if the author had really intended the hidden meaning ascribed to him by one or another interpreters, why didn't he come out and say it? In short, what's the big deal?

The problem is exacerbated by uncertainties about *intention*—a concept that has itself been endlessly debated by aestheticians and philosophers of language. Jay, another of Crandus's eleventh-graders, finds classroom analysis of textual intentions "not interesting": "Like when we are asked to think about the way an author would respond to our responses, how are we supposed to know? As far as I know most of us are not close personal friends with any of the authors we have read so far. So why would we know what the author would think?"

Laura writes that, when asked why something happens the way it does in a text, "I would have trouble analyzing why it happened because I wasn't there, I have never personally talked to the author. . . ." A tenth-grader at another school expressed a view similar to Jay's and Laura's in a symposium on Shakespeare's *The Tempest*, when I asked her if she thought Shakespeare shared the preference she had expressed for Caliban over Prospero: "I wouldn't know," she replied. "I never met the man." As these students see it, either a text's intention is obvious on the face of it or it isn't. If it isn't, we can phone the author and ask what his or her intention was, but if the author is dead or otherwise unavailable, there is nothing much to be done. So again, where's the problem?

If what authors intend does not seem a genuine problem, then making a problem of *unintended* psychological or social meanings in texts seems all the more patently a waste of time. A college teacher reports the following exchange between a freshman student on Mark Twain's *Adventures of Huckleberry Finn*. The teacher, hoping to get her class to see the ambivalent treatment of racial injustice in the novel, called attention to the apparent discrepancy between the novel's satire on slavery and racism and the many passages in which the slave Jim is made a comic butt of Huck and Tom Sawyer's pranks. One student, however, offered an explanation of the discrepancy that seemed more plausible to him than the presence of cultural contradictions.

> Teacher: So what do you all make of the apparent contradiction here?
>
> Student: Hey, maybe Mark Twain was having a bad day. Or maybe he just didn't care.
>
> Teacher: How's that?
>
> Student: I mean, maybe he was just lazy, or he had to make a deadline?

The teacher retorted that even if we assume that Twain was lazy, indifferent, or in a hurry, that would not explain why these qualities expressed themselves in such a racially coded way. She realized, however, that her response was not convincing the student nor many of his classmates. They resisted entertaining the kind of richly symptomatic reading that she, as a good intellectual, was angling for, one in which textual anomalies betray deeper, more interesting problems.

The instructor reflected that she had not prepared the class for looking at contradictions in texts, or even mentioned the topic. She also reflected that it had only been in graduate school that she had discovered that texts might be all the more interesting and valuable for the contradictions they contained. In both her high school and college she had been taught that great works of art are unified, and she had learned to write papers that discovered the principle of unity in the works' themes, language, or symbolism. If there were contradictions in a work, it presumably was second-rate. In her future classes, she resolved to introduce the issue of textual contradictions and discuss it with students rather than expect them to watch for such contradictions or to know what to say about them.

If it seems dubious to make a problem out of the meanings even of canonical writers like Shakespeare, Plato, and Twain, it has to seem doubly preposterous to find problems in the meanings of popular romances, films, and TV shows, not to mention events like the O. J. Simpson trial. (Teachers have long complained about students who, when asked to interpret popular culture, respond with the comment, "Hey, it's just a movie.") At the symposium I just mentioned on *The Tempest*, some college as well as high school students rolled their eyes conspicuously when a college student unpacked the assumptions about the nuclear family in an episode of the TV series *Home Improvement*. The students could grant the possibility of hidden depths in Shakespeare, but in a TV sitcom—give me a break!

Again, such doubts about intellectual overreading would not be so pervasive among students if they were not widely shared by educated adults. The view that popular culture productions either have no meaning or none that is worth discussing is pervasive among academics as well as journalists, who periodically issue derisive editorials whenever an academic is caught attributing gender attitudes, say, to a performance of popular music star Madonna or to an episode of the TV series *Friends*. To be sure, the elaborate allegories academic critics claim to find in popular or high culture do sometimes stretch the reasonable limits of credibility. Nevertheless, analysts of popular culture seem to me right that such works influence our beliefs and behavior all the more powerfully because they come imbedded in seemingly innocuous entertainment that is not thought worthy of close scrutiny. There is a difference, in other words, between legitimate critical skepticism toward over-the-top symbolic readings that fail to justify themselves with reasons and evidence, and the anti-intellectual dismissal of any reading that challenges the received understanding of a text or event. That said, however, it is important that teachers not dismiss students' skepticism of the academic obsession with the problem of hidden meanings. Unless those doubts are respected and fairly aired and discussed, students will feel they have no choice but to play along with an interpretative game whose validity they do not accept.

When this happens, students repress their anxiety and alienation and some end up resorting to Cliffs Notes — or increasingly nowadays to the Internet. In his recent book, *The Crafty Reader*, Robert Scholes quotes a sampling of recent Internet postings by desperate students who have been asked to produce accounts of what something in a text means:

1. Subject: Huck Finn symbolism of river.
   I am writing a paper on the symbolism of the Mississippi River in Huck Finn. How is the river a symbolic mother to Huck? I need examples from the book too. Please help fast.

2. Subject: Oedipus Rex — Irony
   I need help finding Irony in Oedipus Rex. There's supposedly a lot in there but I've been assigned Scene II and there's only so much.

3. Subject: symbolism: gardens
   what do gardens symbolize? are there any sexual innuendos? anything one could dig up on the symbolism of gardens would be of great help. Thanks.[17]

What is striking here is that the writers of these posts see interpretation as an occult process rather than one that might be mastered by learning disciplined reading. As they see it, rivers and gardens in themselves have some fixed but secret meaning that you either get or don't get; if you're one of those who doesn't, you can only get on the Web and try to find one of those who do.

Some, of course, would argue that this kind of student desperation only shows what a serious mistake it has been to put the interpretation of hidden meaning at the center of the academic humanities, thereby turning texts into crossword puzzles and trivializing reading. To me, however, these student postings demonstrate not the folly of asking students to search for deep meanings in texts, but the failure to give students the help they need to conduct that search well, with a sense of how and why it can be useful. As Scholes comments, "These students are crying for help."[18] Students who run to the Web to find out what gardens and rivers symbolize have no other recourse when their teachers treat such questions as self-evident. The practice of searching out and inventing "problems," whether posed by texts or other objects of study, needs to be discussed with students, with an open invitation to air their doubts about the practice and its value.

2. Negativism and Oppositionality

For many students, academia's fixation on seemingly superfluous problems seems linked with another off-putting trait, its relentless negativism and oppositionality. In *Errors and Expectations*, her classic book on the problems of basic-writing students, Mina P. Shaughnessy touches on this trait in describing the problems novice writers have when they are "expected to make 'new' or arguable statements and then develop a case for them."[19] To make "a case" for yourself, to make statements that are "arguable," you must be oppositional and defensive, if not cantankerous. Furthermore, the value academia places on making "arguable" statements can seem not only needlessly embattled, but flatly illogical. Why would any sane person go out of his or her way to say things that are "arguable"? Just as common sense suggests that it is foolish to invent problems that did not previously exist, it also suggests that the point of writing and speaking is to make statements that *nobody* is likely to dispute, so that provoking disagreement is a sign that the writer has failed. A sound essay, according to this way of thinking, consists of uncontroversially true statements. In fact, this way of thinking once dominated the academic disciplines, where knowledge was seen not as a conversation or debate but an accumulation of positivist truths, a sort of pyramid of discrete facts built up brick by isolated brick.

As often, however, common sense has things wrong, which explains why we do not find many essays with titles like "Human Beings Have Elbows," "Breathing Is Possible," and "Washington Is the Nation's Capital," though all these propositions are perfectly true. As Booth, Colomb, and Williams point out, "Readers think a claim significant to the degree that it is contestable,"[20] or, in Shaughnessy's term, "arguable." Precisely because nobody disputes them, uncontroversially true statements are by definition inarguable and therefore not worth making, at least not as an essay's main thesis. The reason why official prose sounds notoriously banal is that it goes out of its way to be uncontroversial. A college of education mission statement I have seen declares, "We are committed to preparing individuals to become outstanding teachers, who understand and teach students in thoughtful, caring, and intelligent ways." The College here takes a courageous stand against those who would prepare teachers to be thoughtless, uncaring, and unintelligent.

Paradoxically, claims that are arguable and solicit disagreement are a sign of an argument's viability, not its failure. A completely uncontroversial proposition does not even qualify as an "argument"—we would never say, "The man argued that Washington, D.C., is the nation's capital." Unless this paradox is explicitly addressed, however, many students will labor under the misapprehension that the goal of an essay is to string together a series of uncontroversially true statements. A student who turns in such an essay will—and should—draw an instructor's comment of "So?" or "Who disputes it?"

On the other hand, imagine such a student, chastened by such comments, trying to do as he or she is told. Instead of making an uncontroversial and therefore negligible claim, our student goes to the other extreme and offers a claim that is outrageously controversial. Now the instructor's response shifts from "Who disputes it?" to "Surely not," or "What's your evidence for that?" Clearly, formulating a tenable point is a tightrope act in which students have to court controversy, but only as much as they can anticipate and deal with. Here is why finding a makable "point," as Shaughnessy points out, can be harder than it looks.

Expert players of the game of public discourse know that the easiest way to set yourself up to make a tenable point is to contest a point somebody else has made or, even better, has taken for granted. Such experts have acquired an inventory of formulaic templates for this kind of contestation. In *Lives on the Boundary* Mike Rose cites fellow compositionist David Bartholomae's suggestion that "when stuck, student writers should try the following 'machine': 'While most readers of ______ have said ______, a close and careful reading shows that ______.'"[21] According to a walker's guide to the city of Chicago, freshmen at the University of Chicago are given the following advice: "If someone asserts it, deny it; if someone denies it, assert it."

Rose observes that this reflexive negativity "perfectly expresses the ethos of the university," though "university professors have for so long been socialized into this critical stance, that they don't realize how unsettling it can be to students who don't share their unusual background."[22] Rose is right, but it also needs to be added that some professors find this contentious ethos as "unsettling" as students do and perhaps for that reason fail to call students' attention to it. As students go from teacher to teacher and from subject to subject, they often receive confusingly mixed signals about the value of controversy: Mr. B the physicist regards it as a distraction from the uncontroversial truths of science, whereas for Ms. J the chemist the clash and warfare of competing hypotheses is at the center of science; Mr. R the embattled moralist philosopher and Ms. C the feminist political scientist love to stir up debate and they reward contentious students, but Ms. A the feminist art historian regards debate as an unfortunate expression of macho agonism.

To the confusion created by these mixed messages add the fact that what counts as a wildly controversial statement in one course or discipline may be seen as uncontroversial or old hat in another. As a consequence, students are often left unsure whether controversy is to be courted or avoided, and since their teachers' different views on the question are screened from one another in courses that do not communicate, the question is rarely posed in an overt way. No wonder, then, that many students end up opting for docility. Whereas high-achieving students intuit the conventional templates of contestation and contravention ("While most think X, I argue Y . . .") from their reading, others won't acquire them unless such templates are explicitly supplied. When this doesn't happen, students are forced to play the academic game with one hand tied behind their backs.

3. Persuasion as Aggression

When the academic penchant for problematizing and negativity goes unexplained, the intellectual energy expended on academic tasks tends naturally to look like mere aggression rather than reasonable behavior. There is thus a connection between the impenetrability of intellectual practices and the tendency to associate intellectualism with bullying and other unattractive personal qualities, especially those that involve persuasion. To argue persuasively, you have to have an axe to grind, to want others to do something they are not already doing, if only to think differently about something than they do. Such an attitude will seem at best presumptuous, and at worst arrogant and coercive.

In her autobiography, *A Life in School*, Jane Tompkins gives a vivid description of how it feels to be this sort of person, so bursting with the passion to persuade that it hurts: "There are situations that set going in me an electric current that has to discharge itself in words. I sit in meetings, and before I know it, I've spoken, passionately, sure there's some point that *has* to be made, which no one can see but me. If the meeting lasts long enough, I have to speak twice, three times. It's got nothing to do with the topic, or very little; the dynamic is almost physical; if I don't talk I'll explode. . . . When talking is being, and being is being listened to, not talking drains your life away."[23] Though Tompkins writes lyrically in passages like this one about her passion for argument, she fears that such a passion may have more to do with showing off, exerting control, and gratifying her ego than with a commitment to truth. Tompkins here expresses vividly the reasons why many students are ambivalent about their persuasive abilities.

For many students, the very word "argument" (like "criticism") conjures up an image not of spirited conversational give and take, but of acrimonious warfare in which competitors revile each other and make enemies yet rarely change each other's minds. Disputes end up producing winners and losers or a stalemate that frustrates all parties; either way they are useless except for stirring up bad blood.

This tendency to equate persuasion with aggression is especially rife among students who grow up in liberal pluralist surroundings, where "Live and let live" is a ruling maxim and "whatever" the popular mantra. As students often put it, "You have your opinions, I have mine, so what's the point of either of us trying to persuade each other? Everybody's an individual, so nobody has the right to tell anybody else what to do or think." There seems little value in becoming the type of person solicited by academic writing assignments — in other words, those who seem guided by the arrogant premise that everyone should think the way you do or that you have the right to generalize about or speak for others.

On the other hand, students from more traditional backgrounds often share their liberal classmates' dim view of persuasion. To Christian fundamentalists, the surrounding secularized society may seem too far gone to be open to persuasion, just as the culture of persuasion and argument seems in league with a Godless secular humanism that views moral issues as endlessly subject to debate. Whether from secular or religious backgrounds, then, American students are often trained to regard persuasion as a waste of time at best and asking for trouble at worst.

This student attitude toward persuasion is tied up with a deeper refusal to become the sort of *public* self that schooling assumes we all naturally want to be. Often when I am struggling unsuccessfully to help students master sentence structure or paragraphing, I realize that what I'm up against is not the students' inability to perform these operations, but their aversion to the role of public spokesperson that formal writing presupposes. It's as if such students can't imagine any rewards for being a public actor or even imagine themselves in such a role.

This lack of interest in entering the public sphere may in turn reflect a loss of confidence in the possibility that the arguments we make in public will have an effect on the world. Today's students' lack of faith in the power of persuasion reflects the waning of the ideal of civic participation that led educators for centuries to place rhetorical and argumentative training at the center of the school and college curriculum. Underlying the centrality of this training was a classical conception of public citizenship that has come to seem unreal as the small town has given way to urban massification and as the ideal of the citizen has been displaced by that of the consumer. If even successful adults find it hard to imagine themselves influencing public policy through their rhetorical and argumentative skills, students figure to find it all the harder to visualize themselves in such public roles.

The standard theme assignment that asks students to take a stand on public issues like homelessness, poverty or abortion rests on the increasingly hollow pretence that what we think and say about such issues can actually make a difference. Given the notoriously widespread cynicism about the chances that our opinions (or votes) will influence public policy, it is hardly surprising if students are fatalistic too. These doubts about the payoff of persuasion underlie much of the student relativism that has been so widely deplored for half a century now. When students say that value judgments are merely matters of subjective opinion, what looks like philosophical relativism may actually be an inability to imagine a world in which one's arguments might have consequences.

The emergence of the Internet, the electronic town meeting, and talk-back radio hold out some promise that this cynical fatalism can be reversed. We may also be witnessing a revival of student idealism and activism, qualities that may not have completely disappeared. The same student who claims at one moment that all beliefs are subjective can often be found a moment later arguing passionately for a cause. Adolescent cynicism and fatalism often mask uncertainty, as if students were challenging their elders to talk them out of it. Again, these are important issues to be raised in class.

4. Elaborated Codes

Another counterintuitive feature of academic intellectual discourse is its seemingly superfluous degree of self-explanation and elaboration, especially when we compare that discourse with casual conversation. Shaughnessy observes that conversation accustoms students to feeling "free to express opinions without a display of evidence or [to] recount experiences without explaining what they 'mean.'" Students so trained, according to Shaughnessy, tend to assume that "the reader understands what is going on in the writer's mind and needs therefore no introductions or transitions or explanations."[24] Instructors' comments like "needs further explanation," or "what's the context here?" seem simply obtuse, since to the student the explanation and the context seem self-evident. Novice writers often have trouble generating much quantity of text, since to unpack and elaborate on their points would make them feel they are laboring the obvious.

Shaughnessy's point is reinforced by the work of British sociolinguist Basil Bernstein, who argues that expository writing and other forms of public communication make up an "elaborated code," in which assumptions and arguments are explicitly unpacked for anonymous audiences who cannot be assumed to already know them, in contrast to the "restricted code" of conversation between intimates, where many things can go without saying. According to Bernstein, elaborated codes characterize the more abstract and distanced interactions of middle class and professional life, whereas restricted codes are characteristic of the face-to-face communication of working class culture.[25] Shirley Brice Heath cites Bernstein in her comparative analysis of working class and middle class cultures in *Ways With Words*, showing how restricted codes prevent working class students from entering the distancing—and often alienating—conventions of written discourse.[26]

Linguists like Rosina Lippi-Green and William Labov have challenged Bernstein's distinction, especially his overly neat identification of working class culture with restricted codes, when the same codes can often be found among middle class speakers and writers as well.[27] Labov rightly points out that what Bernstein regards as the superior elaborated code of middle class communication may simply be "turgid, redundant, bombastic and empty."[28] Though these criticisms do point up blind spots in Bernstein's view, Bernstein's distinction between restricted and elaborated codes seems to me to shed useful light on many problems students have with public discourse.

For example, the concept of restricted code helps account for students' difficulties with the convention of summarizing others' views before responding to them and that of anticipating and formulating possible objections to one's arguments, conventions that can seem pedantic and affected. I stumbled on this problem in the project to which I referred earlier that involved teaching Shakespeare's *The Tempest* to college and high school students: I noticed that though the eleventh-graders in the project often stated their interpretations of the play very forcefully, they almost never mentioned, much less summarized, the opposing interpretations of classmates or teachers, even when they were responding directly to those interpretations. Asked to take sides in the play's conflict between Caliban and Prospero, here is how two students, Dorothy and Chris, responded:

> Dorothy: We believe that Prospero's actions [against Caliban] were justified because Caliban attempted to rape Prospero's daughter. Caliban feels absolutely no remorse for attempting to "violate the honor" of Miranda. When Caliban was confronted by Prospero, he says, "O ho, O ho! Would't have been done!"
>
> Chris: Prospero is an evil, manipulative, racist, slaver, a murderer, a liar, and a tyrant. Caliban is an innocent, a victim of Prospero's cruel manipulations.

Dorothy and Chris express themselves with passion and force, and they have read the text with admirable closeness, but since they make no mention of what those who oppose them say or might say, they sound as if they are merely making counterassertions rather than engaging others in debate. They state their ideas in a vacuum rather than grapple with ones that are different from theirs.

Dorothy and Chris are apparently used to the restricted code of conversation, in which the physical presence of interlocutors relieves you of the need to summarize their views. Since in conversation their classmates are present to them and surely know what they have just said, why bother to summarize them? As for their teacher's views, it would seem even more superfluous, if not presumptuous, to restate them, since if anyone knows what he or she thinks it is your teacher. Nobody has told Dorothy and Chris that in the more distanced conditions of writing (and of rigorous oral argumentation), we often need to summarize others (even when they are physically present) in order to make sure we are on the same page, to establish the degree of common ground necessary for advancing the discussion.

Theorists of psychological development, like the influential William Perry, might see the self-centered quality of Dorothy and Chris's thinking as a reflection of the developmental stage typical of twelve-year-old minds.[29] This kind of developmental theory can readily become a self-fulfilling prophecy, however. Dorothy and Chris may fail to restate opposing views not because they have yet to reach the developmental stage for recognizing opposing views, but because nobody has ever suggested to them that they need to make such restatements, why they need to do it, and how they could do it. Even at their ages they can probably do better, but we won't find out unless they are challenged to do so and given help. I would start by asking them to complete the following template: "In response to my defense of Prospero [Caliban], Dorothy [Chris] would object that . . ."

In this chapter I have inventoried some of the main features of academic discourse that seem odd or counterintuitive when left unexplained. I have suggested that the best way to deal with these apparent oddities is not to duck them, but to build classroom discussions and writing assignments around the questions they pose and to let students debate these questions. What is the point of looking for hidden meanings in everything you read? Why must expository writers have a "point" all the time? How do you know if the meanings a reader ascribes to a text are really there or not, and how can you debate the issue? Do works of entertainment have hidden meanings as the acknowledged classics do? Why summarize and restate other people's views even when those people are present? Does academia reward or punish students who are aggressively argumentative? Is it in fact arrogant to try to persuade other people that you are right? Is debate about ideas a form of warfare or a way of getting beyond warfare? Do you want to intellectualize, and why or why not? All these challenging questions are central to education, yet they have been allowed to fall through the cracks between courses and disciplines.

Whatever side students come down on over these questions—and students will divide on them as much as most of us do—opening these questions for discussion has the educationally desirable effect of positioning students as anthropologists, intellectual analysts, of their own academic lives. Even if some students end up rejecting academic roles, they at least may discover that their rejection will be more powerfully expressed if they draw on the resources of academic discourse to formulate it. This tactic may not eliminate student anti-intellectualism, but it can give it a more intellectual cast, and for teachers this is more than half the battle.

Notes

1. John Gardner, quoted in Ellie McGrath, "Welcome Freshmen," *Time* (September 10, 2001): 64.
2. On star high schools, see Jay Matthews, *Class Struggle: What's Wrong (and Right) with America's Best Public High Schools* (New York: Times Books, 1998).
3. See Gerald Graff, "Life of the Mind Stuff," in *Beyond the Culture Wars: How Teaching the Conflicts Can Revitalize American Education* (New York: W. W. Norton, 1992), 86–104.
4. I am indebted to Michael Bérubé for this formulation.
5. Howard Becker, in conversation. Becker's own work and career refute the belief that social science writing has to obfuscate in order to make an impact. See Becker's useful guide, *Writing for Social Scientists: How to Start and Finish Your Thesis, Book, or Article* (Chicago: University of Chicago Press, 1986).
6. Steven Pinker, "Some Remarks on Becoming a 'Public Intellectual.'" Paper presented at the MIT Communications Forum "Public Intellectuals and the Academy," December 2, 1999. Posted January 5, 2000: http://media-in-transition.mit.edu/articles/pinker.html.
7. Gregory Jay, unpublished talk delivered at session on "Academic Criticism and the Public Media," Modern Language Association Annual Convention, December 1991.
8. Donald (now Deirdre) McCloskey, "The Neglected Economics of Talk," *Planning for Higher Education* (Summer 1994): 12.
9. John Stuart Mill, "On Liberty," in *Utilitarianism, Liberty, Representative Government* (London: Dent & Sons, 1951), 129. The internal connection between controversy and thought is well developed by Michael Billig, in *Arguing and Thinking: A Rhetorical Approach to Social Psychology*, rev. ed. (New York: Cambridge University Press, 1996).
10. See the arguments, for example, of Pierre Bourdieu, Jean-Claude Passeron, Monique de Saint Martin et al., in *Academic Discourse*, trans. Richard Teese (New York: Oxford University Press, 1994), and Samuel Bowles and Herbert Gintis, in *Schooling in Capitalist America: Educational Reform and the Contradictions of Economic Life* (New York: Basic Books, 1976).
11. Howard Gardner, *The Unschooled Mind: How Children Think and How Schools Should Teach* (New York: Basic Books, 1991), 172.
12. Wayne C. Booth, Gregory G. Colomb, and Joseph M. Williams, *The Craft of Research* (Chicago: University of Chicago Press, 1995), 59–63.
13. Booth, Colomb, and Williams, 48–60.

14. Vivian Gornick, *Fierce Attachments: A Memoir* (New York: Farrar Straus & Giroux, 1987), 108. Gornick's book was called to my attention by Ann Merle Feldman.
15. Gornick, 109.
16. Plato, *Phaedrus and the Seventh and Eighth Letters*, trans, Walter Hamilton (London: Penguin Books, 1973), 95–103; Jacques Derrida, "Plato's Pharmacy," in *Dissemination*, trans. Barbara Johnson (Chicago: University of Chicago Press, 1981), 102–12.
17. Robert Scholes, *The Crafty Reader* (New Haven: Yale University Press, 2000), 22–24.
18. Scholes, 25.
19. Mina P. Shaughuessy, *Errors and Expectations, A Guide for the Teacher of Basic Writing* (New York: Oxford University Press, 1977), 240.
20. Booth, Colomb, and Williams, *The Craft of Research*, 95.
21. David Bartholomae, as quoted by Mike Rose, *Lives on the Boundary: A Moving Account of the Struggles and Achievements of America's Educational Underclass* (New York: Penguin Books, 1989), 189. Bartholomae's comment is in "Inventing the University," *Cross-Talk in Comp Theory: A Reader*, ed. Victor Villanueva, Jr. (Urbana, Ill.: NCTH, 1997), 607. "Inventing the University" was first published in 1985.
22. Rose, *Lives on the Boundary*, 189.
23. Jane Tompkins, *A Life in School: What the Teacher Learned* (New York: Addison-Wesley, 1996), 65.
24. Shaughnessy, *Errors and Expectations*, 240–41.
25. Basil Bernstein, *The Structuring of Pedagogic Discourse*. Vol. IV. *Class, Codes and Control*, 2d ed. (London: Routledge & Kegan Paul, 1990), 94–130.
26. Shirley Brice Heath, *Ways With Words: Language, Life, and Work in Communities and Classrooms* (New York: Cambridge University Press, 1983), 398.
27. Rosina Lippi-Green, *English With an Accent: Language, Ideology, and Discrimination in the United States* (New York: Routledge, 1997), 111–2.
28. William Labov, "The Logic of Nonstandard English," in *The Politics of Literature: Dissenting Essays on the Teaching of English*, eds. Louis Kampf and Paul Lauter (New York: Random House, 1972), 208.
29. William Graves Perry, *Forms of Intellectual and Ethical Development* (New York: Holt, Rinehart and Winston, 1970).

Graff's Insights as a Resource for Your Reflections

1. Consider how the discourse of the academy can articulate itself in ways that are distasteful or off-putting, beyond the ways that Graff notes. Also consider how you might acknowledge and circumvent each of them.

2. How might you think of Graff's position here as an explicit response to the ideas in the selection from David Bartholomae? How does Graff differ?

Graff's Insights as a Resource for Your Writing Classroom

1. Graff suggests that we devise questions for students that allow them to study, academically, their own lives, perhaps even their own experience of being students. Try to write some discussion questions for use with your students, tailored to fit with the other topics about which they are reading and writing for your class, and then aim toward Graff's goal of self-reflection about life in school.
2. Ask your students to tell stories about classes they've taken in which they felt most lost or out of sync with the demands of the course. Then, on the basis of a handful of such stories, ask the class to generalize about what is engendering these feelings of cluelessness. Try to open up at least two different perspectives on how, as Graff puts it, "schooling obscures the life of the mind," and then have your students debate the relative merits of these two perspectives.

A Letter to Maggie

James F. Slevin

What's the difference between having a point and making a point? James Slevin would likely suggest, at least in the context of our classrooms, that the answer is simply all the difference in the world. Just as the preceding selections from Gerald Graff complicated, extended, and perhaps even corrected the essay by David Bartholomae that preceded it, the letter that follows, which Slevin wrote to a former student who has now become a teacher herself, extends and complicates this thread yet further. Slevin ultimately comes to suggest that the essential material of a good writing course belongs to the category of "evidence"—what counts as evidence, what does the evidence mean, what points can it support? These are the questions we should live with—and teach our students to live with—as the central element of our intellectual work.

Here is a letter to a former student of mine, in response to one from her. Her letter asked me a very common question—one I received at least a hundred times as department chair and director of the writing program: what should she do to prepare her students for writing in college.

I have always found the request somewhat exasperating—as the issue is so complex. After all, I asked myself, would anyone write to the chemistry department to find out in a nutshell what prospective students need to learn in high school? Well, I found out, people do write to our chemistry department, and our chemistry department writes them back. My colleagues in chemistry found my reluctance to do so just another sign that the humanities, and especially English, had become such a muddle that we couldn't even explain our dilemma to sympathetic colleagues.

So I decided to respond to Maggie's letter. Here it is.

Dear Maggie,

I can't speak for your students, but I can try to speak about mine—what I hope they had learned and what they need to unlearn, or at least complicate. What matters in college writing, more than any writing they have done before and perhaps more than any writing or speaking they will do later, what matters is *evidence*. The excitement of the academic life—of academic writing broadly conceived—is in the making of *stuff* (data, events, passages from a text, the work of other writers) into evidence. This is true of all disciplines, and it is as true of personal writing as it is of professional writing. Making stuff mean something is at the heart of the writing that gets admired at the university.

Although we tell students that these and topic sentences and transitions and clear (even elegant) sentences are important (because they *are*), what really matters is how what I am calling (with my usual intellectual sophistication and precision) "stuff" becomes evidence. Now my students think that assertions are what matter. Theses. Topic sentences. Big ideas. Even small ideas well expressed. I believe they think that because they have been taught to think so—by their teachers in high school, and by mass culture (ranging from the most serious public-affairs television to advertising). Struggling with 135 students a semester in five classes, teachers have been delighted to find meaning asserted coherently and cohesively in their students' papers. Sometimes a paper just *having* a thesis that is connected to its several unfolding paragraphs is a rare delight to behold. Politicians, pundits, advertisers have in common a studied commitment to assertion, often at the level of the sound bite. Neither evidence nor competing assertions make any difference, except as part of a staged drama. One notices with a kind of ghastly respect how politicians manage to turn serious questions into occasions for saying whatever it is they want to say; how they ignore counterarguments and just say whatever it is they want to say; in short, how they just keep saying whatever it is they want to say. So, while it is often said that our students don't have theses, I would counter that they have thousands of theses, that their minds are cluttered with theses, that simply accumulating theses is the lifeblood of their everyday lives.

Now, I recognize that delivering a *simulacrum* of support for their theses has become a feature of successful high school writing (just as such a simulacrum is a feature of political discourse and advertising). I am not equating the three (I respect the work of high school teachers and the ingenuity of advertising), but that all three share this feature marks the pervasiveness of the problem. Thanks in part then to admen and political hacks, most of my students come to college with an aesthetics of the essay form (or formula), a sense of its features as if they were literary or public-relations exercises and not forms of demanding and exciting intellectual labor.

September 4 was the thirtieth anniversary of the first college class I ever taught. I taught that class in an open-admissions program at Lincoln University, the oldest historically black college in the U.S., where my students came with serious "writing problems" that required (though the term was and is suspect) "remedial" help. They had not been prepared to spell, or compose and arrange sentences, or organize paragraphs in ways that matched the requirements of standard written English. They lacked, in other words, the training provided my students today. But nearly all of them possessed an awareness of evidence and were quite alert to the slippages between assertion and support. And they were particularly adept, as I remember, at locating and expressing the slippages in my own thinking. Those were the days.

We too easily think of those students as "remedial" but have a harder time thinking of today's "mainstream" students as "remedial." Yet they are. My students at Georgetown don't care about ideas (if they care about ideas at all) *in the way* faculty members do, though they can place ideas in papers. The students I am talking about today are remedial students in a much deeper sense than my students thirty years ago because, despite the surface correctness of their prose (maybe because of it) they are much further away from the intellectual culture of the academy, at least as this is professed in the liberal arts and sciences.

They lack a sense of the importance of evidence. What I mean by evidence is the intersection and interpenetration, perhaps better expressed as the dialectic, of thesis and development (elaboration, exemplification, illustration). There is no evidence without a thesis; but, more important, there is no thesis that isn't constructed and made possible by the evidence and penetrated by the evidence.

I wish my students could distinguish between having a point (or having a thesis) and making a point (or a thesis). (It is curious that the phrase, "making a thesis," is not idiomatic, and yet it is the heart of academic work.) We all *have* points but don't often *make* them. The distinction is important because most of my students believe that the goal of a paper is to express a point you have, rather than to make a point through the marshaling of reasons, explanations, clarifications, and supporting details. In short, I think we get ourselves into trouble whenever we tell students that a paper should "have" a thesis: it makes the thesis seem like a property of the paper rather than the goal of the work that *is* the paper.

The possibility that this was the defining difference between mass culture and academic culture, the main thing my students needed to know to be prepared for college, dawned on me while channel surfing some weeks ago. I was, as it were, participating in mass culture in one of its most compelling possibilities, and I came upon a re-run of *Columbo*. I was reminded that while in graduate school, this was the show with which academics most regularly "made an appointment." ("Making an appointment" is a popular concept in Media Crit. to identify those shows we make a special point to see, around which we might be said to build our schedules and so our lives. *Homicide* now has this status in our family, as does *Sesame Street*, the two high-quality urban dramas on TV.) As I say, *Columbo* had this status some generations ago, and may still have it for those free in the afternoons and having access to cable. What was innovative and seductive about this show was its format, which began with the dramatization of a murder in plain view of the TV audience, long before Columbo's character made an appearance. We therefore began with the facts of the case, and through careful but predictable direction, we were able to focus in on the evidence that would give the murderer away. Closeups of a glove left behind at the scene of the crime, for instance; an answering or videotape machine tape left running. The drama of *Columbo*, then, was not learning who murdered whom but watching Columbo learn that — watching him attend to the clues that combined to form the evidence for his (and the show's) conclusion. What the audience did, more exactly, was watch Columbo watch; we looked at him looking, and we did so from the superior, omniscient position that is every academic's fantasy (such is the state of our fantasy life). We observed his observing from the most fantastic of situations: because we knew all, we could focus on how he came to know. Observing and knowing really mattered (there was a killer on the loose); and there was always a right answer, always something to be found that brought closure. Precisely because academic culture is never like that — we are never omniscient, our work is almost never a matter of life and death, our conclusions never entirely conclusive, never closing on exactly the right answer that will effectively eliminate the need for any further work in our fields — because of all that, we found Columbo a weekly delight.

Academic culture is all about looking and looking for. It is about the hunt for a conclusion, not about conclusions; it's about the making of meaning, not the meaning. While we tell students more than they need to know about theses and the formats of our writing, about organization and lucidity and clarity (that is, about the form in which we make public our conclusions), what we value is something other than all that, though not unrelated to all that. The values of academic culture are not the conclusions we draw but the drawing of conclusions from the evidence before us — more exactly, the drawing of conclusions from the *possibilities* of evidence before us that we make into evidence enabling something worth saying.

In an age of academic professionalization, I think we have come to exaggerate the importance of exchange (and particularly the importance of undoing others' unsatisfactory explanations) and to minimize the importance of discovery and the dialectical process of arriving at satisfactory generalizations. We talk a great deal about examining the assumptions behind a thesis, looking at the bias of the author we are reading or the work we are composing. That is an important thing to do, but it doesn't necessarily clarify what is at stake in undertaking this critique. The point is not simply to identify bias but to explain what that particular bias does with the evidence to hand—how it misinterprets or inadequately explains the evidence, occasionally even distorting it. What is important is not that this thesis differs from my thesis, or this thesis is wrong because it depends on an ideology we do not like (academics spend their lives surrounded by different theses and unfriendly/unpalatable ideologies). What is important is that the thesis does not account for the poem, the historical event, the chemical reaction, the urban problem, the election result, etc. The data incorporated into the essay is not adequately explained by the thesis that constructs that data as evidence. So it is not evidence, and lacking evidence, the argument fails.

All this concern with evidence applies to class discussion, which becomes a discussion when folks attend to evidence (and not just the assertion of theses). In fact, most real discussions are about what we would ordinarily call evidence, and here theses are what get contested in the face of competing accounts of the evidence or (more interesting this) competing determinations of what constitutes evidence. We all want students to respond to one another so that we as teachers don't become the mediator of every comment. But if the comment is only the assertion of a thesis, then the teacher's mediation is all that's available by way of affirmation or dissent. There's nothing to talk *about*. It is desirable but not sufficient to create a class culture in which diversity of views is celebrated and disagreement encouraged. If there is to be something like a dialogue among views and not just an exchange of views, we have to enable students to make their points, not just have points.

And this concern applies to examining carefully the documents we ask students to read. To read for the thesis is another way of saying to read for understanding, something which is of course useful. But it is not sufficient because our challenge to students that they "read critically" is thus understood as simply reading to determine whether one agrees or disagrees with the thesis. What gets shortchanged in this process is reading for evidence: attending to the ways in which support is provided such that it makes the thesis possible in an evident way.

Now it has not escaped my notice that by all appearances nobody believes the positions I am articulating; I draw this conclusion based on all that I have read in composition textbooks, in course syllabi, in explanations to students about what it means to "write well" in a discipline (or at least in this or that particular course). Based on all the obvious evidence available to me, I have clearly gotten it all mixed up. This is particularly embarrassing for me since I am arguing both that this is what is most important and that this is precisely what *everyone* believes, though I admit it is what we rarely say. When we teach writing we rarely say that we teach evidence, the process of supporting, testing, and complicating conclusions. We assume the importance of this work but we don't teach it. Taking it too much for granted, and so neglecting it, could be the source of the problem because what students have to learn to do well in our courses is to find out what to look for that counts as evidence for their assertions. Sadly, they usually have to learn these crucial skills on their own because everyone is so occupied with rhetorical formalities that substitute for the substance of intellectual work at the university. In other words, theses are in fact subordinate to support; hypotheses to experiments; conclusions to the process of grappling with details and particulars to make them meaningful. While the heart of the essay may in its form appear to be the thesis, the heart of the work (and so of writing in the academy) is the support. I should rephrase that and say that the heart of academic writing is the process of *supporting, testing*, and *complicating* theses, not just *having* them. If we could teach students to do this work — and like their teachers love it — we would really be preparing them for writing in college.

Yours sincerely,
Jim

Slevin's Insights as a Resource for Your Reflections

1. How would you answer the question that Slevin receives from his student — what should high school English teachers do to prepare their students for college?
2. As you prepare to read the next selection by Guy Allen, consider what role accounts of personal experience play in the discourse of the university — do they count as evidence? What might Bartholomae say? What about Graff? Slevin?

Slevin's Insights as a Resource for Your Writing Classroom

1. Develop a sequence of assignments that follows Slevin's advice and foregrounds questions of what constitutes evidence. You might, for example, choose a hotly contested issue in a recent

editorial page of the newspaper and ask your students to identify the ways the arguments are playing out as essentially arguments over what evidence counts and what it means.

2. Ask your students, at the end of the semester, what they think their high schools should have emphasized to prepare them for their college writing classes. And what, incidentally, would they identify as the essential questions the first-year writing course teaches them to ask and answer.

Language, Power, and Consciousness: A Writing Experiment at the University of Toronto

Guy Allen

Though Allen's title might lead you to expect otherwise, he offers in this article a richly detailed story about his own work in the classroom, one that dramatizes quite powerfully the potentials of ongoing reflection about teaching, for Allen arrives at a breakthrough that has far-reaching implications for how he—and, for that matter, all teachers of writing—might conceive their mission. Allen's story is, in fact, about stories themselves, personal stories of the very sort he tells here, and the ways they can serve a writing classroom and even the wider goals of the university. Given the claims of earlier pieces in this chapter on behalf of the role of political, critical, and argumentative discourse in the academy, what might be the role of storytelling and of sharing personal experience?

In 1979, the dean of humanities at the western campus of the University of Toronto asked me if I would take over from him a half-course (one semester) he had been teaching called "Effective Writing." The college calendar listed the course in a catch-all non-department called Interdisciplinary Studies: The University's English Department wanted nothing to do with teaching writing skills because, it was felt, serious scholars did not teach writing and worthy students should know how to write by the time they get to university. The dean, himself a member of the English Department and a respected English Renaissance drama scholar, did not share the view that teaching writing fell beneath the concerns of a serious language department. He had decided to teach this course himself and had done so for several years.

The dean came to me because I believed writing belonged in the university curriculum and because he felt discouraged by his own efforts in the course. "I haven't been able to do much with this," he told me. "One or two students produce some interesting work, but I don't think many students improve much. It's a hard course for me to teach because there isn't a subject matter in the usual sense. Do what you can with it," the dean said. "There's nothing to lose."

I didn't know how to teach writing, so I adopted the dean's syllabus and book list: a grammar workbook and the *Norton Reader*, a collection of classic nonfiction essays by Plato, Jonathan Swift, George Orwell, Joan Didion, Martin Luther King Jr., and Art Buchwald, among others. These procedures reflected North American writing and rhetoric course orthodoxy: have students read and discuss model prose, teach them about the errors that afflict student writing, and assign essays on topics based on the readings: "Respond to Jean-Paul Sartre's claim that we invent God to evade responsibility for our lives."

I used the dean's procedures. I taught grammar, structure, and style. I assigned topics based on the readings. I graded the students' papers and returned them with comments.

I suffered icy silences as I coaxed class discussion about the readings. George Orwell's "Politics and the English Language" intimidated most students. They didn't know what to say. They wanted me to tell them what to say, and I found myself cooking something up before class so that I would not stand as mute as they did before these splendid essays. It was my job to know what to say.

The essays in the *Norton Reader* were real writing, the students thought, unlike the writing they did for me. The students were right. Their work lacked authenticity. They had no idea how to engage meaning around the kinds of topics they found in the *Norton Reader*.

They did know how to project engagement, how to playact it. Their writing was all make-believe. The teacher wants engagement; show the teacher engagement. Unlike the masterpiece writers, the students had no sense of a style that expressed their personalities and experience. They focused on "not making mistakes." Writing brought them into a dangerous, uncharted swamp. Even if they didn't die there, they knew they would feel lost and scared, and they knew the passage would be tough and unpleasant.

After two years and four sections of teaching this way, I felt sure that this course did not teach students how to write. In fact, the course, for all my positive intentions, confirmed the students' belief that they could not write. I felt shame as I walked into and out of those classrooms: This charade wasted public money, squandered the students' time, and insulted my image of myself as someone doing useful work.

Much of what the students wrote was acceptable in a university—that is, their writing was correct and in required form—but outside of the academic setting, the writing they did would have interested no one. Their writing fulfilled requirements, but it did not do what good writing should do. It did not engage a reader's interest—no one who was not being well paid to do so would read it—and, worst of all, it made no original meaning. Essay after essay repeated the tedium. The students had no idea that writing could be part of life. Life for them resumed *after* they got their essays in. I felt ashamed of my job. I didn't know what to do. The students gave this sad enterprise positive ratings—they didn't know any better.

I used the dean's procedures. I got the dean's results.

Luck; Or, the Students Teach the Teacher

I wanted change, but I had no idea what I wanted to change or how to bring it about. Then something happened in one of my classes. A new wave (this was 1982) orange-and-purple-haired, high-spirited student broke rank. Catherine Johnson ignored, or improvised upon, the topic I had assigned: "With reference to John Kenneth Galbraith's essay on inflation and government intervention in the economy, write an essay in which you defend or question the role of government in regulating the workplace."

Johnson handed in a piece about her job in a mice-infested bakery. The bakery failed to pass a health inspection. The incompetent owners blamed her and her co-workers for the mice that skittered over cakes and breads and into the flour sacks. This writing expressed meaning. I read Johnson's piece to the class, not to teach anything but to escape the embarrassing emptiness of my *Norton Reader* teaching.

The following week, another student handed in a well-written (and now published in one of my collections of peer models) piece about teenage shoplifting, about "the ultimate heist," "stealing the little silver bells that hung on the back of the heavy wooden doors of Mr. Bong's Variety . . . , the very small store behind our house where I went . . . after school [and] . . . spent the thirty-five cents my mother gave me for milk on a licorice twist and six pieces of Mr. Chuckle's Bubble Gum":

> Four of us swarmed into Bong's Variety wearing dirty red and white uniforms with Burlington Midget Bears stenciled across the front. The four silver bells tinkled, and Mr. Bong assumed his usual position. His eyes darted back and forth from one intruder to the next.
>
> I watched Mike Fass, the skinny center fielder, reach in the refrigerator for a Coke. Mr. Bong's eyes took in Mike's reaching hand, and I grabbed the four silver bells. Within minutes, the outfielders had their drinks, and the heavy wooden doors closed silently behind us.
>
> The next day, Mrs. Ellis caught me taking two packs of Smarties from the candy counter at Zellers.[1]

I read "Mr. Bong's Variety" to the class. Someone said, "That's brave to write about something like that." Someone else said, "This really tells me something because it's so honest, but I didn't know we could write like this."

Why did this writing make meaning that we cared about? How did it do it? We talked about the simple, direct style and the detailing. One student said, "I like 'licorice twist and Mr. Chuckle's Bubble Gum' because that's what we all used to buy and I can really picture it and it sticks in my mind. I can remember it."

"So," I asked, "if the writer just said 'candy' instead of 'licorice twist and Mr. Chuckle's Bubble Gum,' the piece wouldn't mean as much to you?" People agreed that the writer's detail animated the piece.

"I don't like the conclusion," someone said. The conclusion, not the conclusion in the excerpt above, moralized. "The conclusion's a cop-out. If you're going to write about stealing then write about stealing. Don't tell me it's bad."

Another student said, "Yeah. Don't tell us what to think. You've trusted us so far with your honesty. Don't blow it at the end."

Someone else said, "A lot of writing ends with a moral." "Because a lot of writing does that, doesn't mean it's good to do that." The students talked for fifteen minutes about how to end the piece.

"So, what do I do?" the writer asked me about the conclusion after class. "Should I change it?"

"I don't know," I said. "There's no right-and-wrong answer on writing issues like this. You've heard what people have to say. I guess you'll have to make up your mind. Think about what you've heard and decide what meaning you want to make."

A week later, Glen Ricketts, the writer, came with a revised version of "Mr. Bong's Variety." I asked him to read it to the class. He had produced a new conclusion, the one in the excerpt I have reproduced here. This conclusion refuses to moralize but still shows how the world meets the shoplifter's hubris. The class approved.

Students felt engaged by this piece and its writer because its subject and its setting came out of a world they knew about and felt qualified to comment on. Ricketts used language that was right for the experience he described. The students activated. They became a board of editors. The writer acted like a real writer, and the students acted like real editors. This was the real world of writers and editors come into the classroom.

Their discussion of the piece reminded me of the way I talked with other writers and artists in the performance art work I was doing after my academic workday. In the following weeks I received more assignments that expressed something and that had fine writing qualities. But, like the bakery piece and like "Mr. Bong's Variety," the best writing stepped outside usual expectations of what students in an academic setting should write.

Innovations: Getting Students to Work Like Writers

The next time I taught the course, I maintained the orthodox frame the dean had passed on to me, with some changes. I set up assignments designed to encourage the students to work and think like writers rather than like students—assignments that I hoped would lead to more of the kind of work Ricketts and others had done.

"Write about a job you have had," one assignment read. "Choose one incident or a series of incidents to present details that will show the reader what your job was like. Don't tell your reader what the job was like. Show it. Use detail that will allow readers to come to their own conclusions about the job. Make your readers participants in your piece." Another assignment read: "Present a short, detailed account of an experience you had as a child. Use details of setting, dialogue, and incident to show what happened. Present scenes and events. Do not tell us how to interpret the events you present." Along with these assignments, I read and passed out photocopied examples of what others at the same experience level had done with these topics. These peer models demonstrated originality, craft, a range of different voices and experiences, and freedom. These models made it clear to my students that they were, as *real* writers are, "condemned to be free."[2]

I parked these innovations—they felt naughty at the time—into one corner of my course. The orthodox paradigm remained predominant. Even so, I felt like I was breaking rules and doing something that I shouldn't tell anybody about. The students loved the innovative assignments, and I liked reading the vibrant personal essays that I was beginning to see. I edited these essays and returned them to the students for revising. Sometimes we revised the same piece as many as ten times. This exchange between writer and editor resembled writing as I had come to know it outside of the academic setting. Students were acting like writers, and I like an editor, more ally than judge.

The more I put good models of personal essays in front of my classes, the more quality writing I received. After about three years I had shifted the balance of work in my courses to about 50 percent traditional expository essays and 50 percent personal essays. In the personal essay assignments students used their own experience as subject matter.

I realized as I was doing this that all writing roots somehow in experience and observation. The research essay, for example, documents the controlled experience the writer creates with the research object. The lab report documents a precisely defined experience designed to yield specific information. My students' personal essays, I realized, were not really so different from the other writing they were expected to do in university. Yet in this form and working with their own experience, the students seemed so much better able to take on the issues of craft that every writer faces. The personal essays solved a problem that dogs university writing courses: the absence of real content. Under the new format students became directly responsible for content. Students reflected on themselves and their experience. Students came to recognize that their lives and the lives of their families contained meaning that could be the subject of writing.

The work I received during the personal essay segment of the course stood out in technical quality, honesty, vividness, and originality from the work they did in the traditional expository essay format. In the one form, students seemed engaged, ready to learn and take on the writer's craft. In the other, they seemed frozen, detached, fixated on not making mistakes (and therefore prone to mistakes), indifferent to meaning.

The expository essays improved slowly, I observed, but seemingly as a result of their work in the personal essays. I did not know what to make of it. I thought each class was a fluke that defied reasonable expectations. Then something else, something very mysterious, happened. Students reported again and again that the personal essay work they did in these classes improved their performance in other courses. Even more mysterious, students credited their writing work for better performance in courses like math and science. The more I deviated from orthodox procedure, the keener the results seemed. I felt baffled, confused, and suspicious. How did I know that the writing quality was really that good? Perhaps I saw what I wanted to see. How could I trust what the students were telling me? What do students know?

One more odd event occurred. Two professors, both academically conservative and notoriously tough on writing issues, referred many of their students to my course because, so they told the students, they had realized by observing the work of previous students that my course was the surest way for the students to bring their writing up to standard. This was strange: If these faculty members had known about the procedures I used in my course they would not have approved. Yet they endorsed the result, a result they observed in the writing they received in their courses, philosophy and survey law.

I felt excited. I felt afraid. Somebody, I thought, is going to call me a charlatan. I also thought that perhaps I had stumbled onto something important. I felt isolated; it didn't feel safe to talk about things I saw happening in my course. On the one hand, I was getting results that committed teachers dream about. On the other hand, I used procedures that many academics would dismiss as bogus and unprofessional. I needed evidence to deal with my own doubts and to confront the skepticism of colleagues.

Collecting Evidence: Do I See What I Think I See?

My teaching became research. I set out to devise qualitative and quantitative measures that might yield some rational perspective on what felt to me like almost mystical events. Here is what I came up with:

1. I interviewed students before their first exposure to my personal essay system. I recorded their answers to these questions:
   a. What do you think about yourself as a writer?
   b. What have teachers told you about your writing?
   c. Why are you taking a course in writing?

2. I surveyed students at the end of my course and asked for written answers to these questions:
   a. What do you think about yourself as a writer?
   b. What have others told you about your writing and any changes in it since you have been in this course?
   c. What, if anything, did you get out of this course? [Students provided this information on anonymous forms collected by a student volunteer who gave me the forms after I had assigned grades.]
3. I tracked grades and comments received by students on their written work in other courses in the university before, during, and after their writing course with me.

Finally, I needed some way of validating writing quality, some way to confirm that much of the writing I saw in my classes was as good as I thought it was. One standard measure is publication. I made submitting work for publication a regular part of my teaching. I encouraged and helped students to submit their best assignments to the same places where new writers publish their short prose work: magazines, newspapers, prose collections.

I introduced one innovation at a time and maintained other aspects of the course as constants. This way I could isolate and identify the effect, if any, of the innovation. For example, I set out to determine optimal assignment frequency. I taught two sections with an essay to be handed in every two weeks, and I taught two sections with one essay to be handed in every week. Here there was a clear result: Frequency improves learning in a writing course. However, another set of experiments showed that two essays per week, when students are taking a full load of other courses, reduces learning.

I have conducted a wide variety of experiments, and some of what I have learned has violated not only widely held beliefs about teaching writing, but even my own common sense. One such experiment, which I have repeated several times, has shown that direct attention to the expository essay does not improve students' performance on the expository essay. I will say more about this later. Another experiment has shown an unexpected way to help students whose first language is not English or else is some dialect of English that is considered unacceptable in the Western university. My experiments show that these students master the English usage demanded by the academy far more quickly and effectively when they are encouraged in various writing assignments to mix their home languages with the academy's "standard English."[3] I would have felt skeptical about this relationship if someone had told me about it, but repeated tests show that this procedure produces positive results whether the student's home language is a foreign tongue or working-class English. Why and how this procedure works, I do not know. It deserves investigation; many students and faculty members report frustration around the work of students who struggle with academy English.

The point is that unexpected results have shown me how important it is to examine and test what we do, especially in a field like the teaching of writing where most practitioners adopt conventional procedures passed down from predecessors. Practices and truisms that we take for granted as common sense sometimes prove invalid when we examine them systematically. The best knowledge often comes out of the collapse of cherished ritual practices.

Over a period of ten or fifteen years, a careful process of innovation, observation, and measurement has produced grounded knowledge about what enhances learning and what does not. The course I have experimented with is a half-course that I taught as many as five times a year on two different campuses of the university. Frequent repetition of the same course created optimal conditions for controlled experiments.

How Students See Writing before the Course

Here is a summary of student responses to my surveys about their sense of writing before they have any experience with the course I teach:

1. More than 95 percent of students entering my course have a negative view of their abilities as writers and a negative view of the experience of writing in a school setting. This astonishing statistic has varied almost not at all from year to year for fifteen years. The one in twenty who report a positive view of themselves as writers always trace that view back to a parent or a teacher who taught them that they have something important to say. This statistic becomes more dramatic when we consider that the sample is limited to students in a university with high standards. These are successful students.

2. More than 70 percent of incoming students report that they take the writing course to reduce the number of "mistakes" they make in their writing. The focus on mistakes comes from their previous experience with teachers. Most students expect teachers to criticize their work and to focus on formal errors. Even those with positive images of themselves as writers almost never say anything about the content of their work. They often say, "I don't make many errors" or "My teachers told me my grammar was basically okay." The students think of good writing as mistake-free writing. Almost none show any awareness of an editing process.

3. More than 85 percent report their dread of writing in an academic setting. They expect to perform poorly and to be criticized for violations of rules that they experience as a mysterious labyrinth of half-visible tripwires.

4. More than 70 percent of entering students believe they must adopt an artificial voice to write in an academic setting. This voice, they feel, must project sophistication through reliance on unfamiliar vocabulary, bloated phrasing, long sentences, and complicated syntax. When I teach them to simplify, they often tell me that they had not realized that simplicity is acceptable. Some object. "But that's how I got my A's," they say when I cut verbiage. Few have experience producing simple prose.

5. More than 65 percent of entering students feel that they must keep themselves out of their writing. When asked about writers who write about themselves and their lives, about 85 percent feel that this kind of writing can be done only by writers who are "gifted" with extraordinary talent. About 50 percent of students feel that they should avoid the first person in serious writing. More than 70 percent of entering students feel that the passive voice sounds more sophisticated and authoritative than the subjective "I." Most feel that writing should sound "objective."

6. Even with the cluster of negativity surrounding writing and the dread of stern judgments, the students feel writing will be important to them academically, professionally, and personally. Despite previous bad experiences, they want to try again. The students who come to my course are a select sample: These are students who have gone out of their way to choose a writing course. There must be many who have given up, who go through life avoiding situations where they might have to write. There must be those who believe that because they "don't make many mistakes," they have nothing more to learn.

How Students Regard Writing after the Course: Attitudes and Results

The course requires students to produce one original piece of writing each week for ten weeks as well as continuous revisions of their original work. Alongside the writing of these assignments, students attend weekly lectures and workshops on prose basics, a prose boot camp that I will outline later. They also attend three one-on-one sessions with the course instructor, in which the instructor, working as an editor, recommends edits and revisions for their original work. Here is what students have reported after exposure to one course of three-and-a-half months with at least two months of intensive work in personal essays:

1. Most students who have courses where written work is required report improved grade results that they trace directly to their experience in the writing course. Seventy-two percent of these students report improved grade results in written work in other university courses. Thirty-one percent of the students reporting improved results report an average one letter-grade (i.e., C to B, or B− to A−) rise in evaluated

written work such as essays and lab reports; 69 percent of these report a fractional letter-grade rise (for example, B− to B+, or C+ to B−, or B to A−). Of those reporting improved results, 21 percent reported that other instructors commented explicitly on the improvement in their writing. Students attribute their improved results mainly to three circumstances: increased confidence, knowledge of editing principles, and simplified style.

2. Some students have reported improvement in courses which require no writing, courses where, for example, they have only multiple-choice or short-answer tests. They attribute the change to increased personal confidence and sharpened awareness of language.

3. Most students report relief from the tension and trauma associated with writing. They attribute the change to intensive experience with writing, increased confidence, and better knowledge about writing process, especially editing. A typical observation: "Writing used to be a torment; now it is a strength for me. My friends always ask me to edit their work."

4. Seventy-four percent of the students report feeling more positive about themselves as a result of writing personal history. Many report positive life effects that reach beyond the academy. Increased confidence, self-awareness, and assertiveness are the commonest. Some report breakthroughs with issues they feel have interfered with their ability to realize their potential. Some comment on the redemptive power of writing. For example, a number report that their engagement with personal essays has helped them achieve perspective on personal shame resulting from racism, family breakup, physical and psychological abuse, relationship failures, cultural alienation, academic and job failures, and sickness: "After I wrote about that, it didn't bother me anymore" or "I used to try to hide that from people, but now I feel I can talk about it as part of who I am." Many report simply that they had never before thought of their lives as containing subject matter of interest. "I never thought there was anything in my life worth writing about" is a typical comment. "I have learned that being myself is good enough — and interesting" is another. Some come to a new appreciation of family members: "I never realized what an amazing thing my father had done until I interviewed him about his escape from Uganda."

5. Some students have reported that their engagement with personal essays has shown them how to bring aspects of their own lives into their academic work. One student, the daughter of a woman who immigrated from China in 1950, interviewed her mother, a peasant farmer from an isolated area in southern China, for several of her essays in my course. Later, in a Chinese history course, she again interviewed her mother about how her mother survived the Japanese invasion of China in the Second World War and used the things her mother told her as evidence in the essay (her professor, noting the fresh-

ness of her primary research, gave the essay an A+). Many students could supplement library research with material from their lives or the lives of people they know, but few realize this is possible or desirable. They see the academic universe as not welcoming original material found outside of the library.

6. Of the 451 students who have contributed responses to my surveys, more than 100 have published or read in public readings personal essays they wrote as assignments for my beginning prose course. In exceptional cases, they have published independently of any help from me in newspapers, magazines, and campus publications. In most cases, they achieve public exposure in venues I have helped them to contact. I have myself published much student work, and I use collections of personal essays by students as my course texts. Students who publish or read for the public report that public exposure and acceptance have provided validation and confidence-building recognition. For many, forms of public acceptance confirm that their experience in the writing course amounts to more than "just one professor's opinion." Well-written personal essays can attract readers. The purpose of writing is to communicate; public interest suggests success.

7. More than 90 percent of the students who took part in classes where I offered instruction in both the personal essay and in the expository essay felt that the work with personal essays accounted for their positive experience in the course. In almost all cases, it is the work with personal essays that students remember most about the course. Students also identify the personal essay work as the part of the course that helped them improve results in their other academic writing.

8. A few students, less than 3 percent, have found the course and the personal essay instruction unhelpful and frustrating. All of these have been students who came to the course looking for an anything-goes creative writing course. These students have found my prose boot camp "uncreative and formulaic." The instructor's insistence on nonfiction prose essays, coupled with assurance that students are free to select their own subject matter, seems to them "narrow-minded." Some wanted to write poetry or science fiction.

I have one observation to add. The student surveys have suggested that the personal essay work teaches them more than work with expository prose. I tested this notion. I taught sections of the course with 30 percent of the course devoted expressly to expository essays. I taught other sections purely on the personal essay with no attention to expository prose. What I found surprised me. Direct attention to the expository essay did not enhance students' ability to produce good expository essays. The students have it right: They learn most about writing through instruction and work on personal essays. And what they learned in their work with personal essays transferred to other genres, such as the expository essay, the lab report, and the book review. This result surprised and puzzled me. Teaching X enhances the ability to handle Y. This result suggests irrational processes and connections. We have mystery here.

The Prose Boot Camp

Colleagues who feel threatened by my questions about orthodoxy have often insulted my procedures as a soft, anything-is-okay-here anarchy that does not belong in a formal academic enterprise. Anarchy does not yield writing people want to read, at least not often. I teach students to write prose that makes meaning and attracts readers. That is not a soft enterprise.

I do teach about the value of unstructured free association in the "Twenty-Minute Journal" exercise:

> Sit down every day and write about anything as fast as you can for twenty minutes. Write as much as you can. Don't worry about quality. Do not think. Just write. Write as many words as you can in twenty minutes. I want to see that you do this, but I am, of course, not going to read your twenty-minute journals. This is a standard writer's warmup. You may get ideas doing this, but this is not real writing. This warms the writing engine. Almost all writers keep journals. Unless the writers become objects of public curiosity, these journals never see the light of day. Still, the unself-conscious journals help their writing.

But unstructured free association is only a first step in producing a crafted piece of writing. As Richard Rhodes puts it,

> Writing is a craft. Its primary function is communication. I mean "craft" strictly: like carpentry or pottery, writing is handmade. Like other crafts as well, writing can sometimes be organized to the special depth and resonance people call art (Rhodes 15).

Students learn the craft of writing by learning editing. Students must learn to be editors of their own and other people's writing. Through editing, writing attains clarity, shape, precision — the power to communicate the message the writer intends. Teaching editing requires what I call *boot camp*, tough basic training in prose essentials.

In a thirteen-week course, students must hand in one original assignment per week for ten weeks. Here is a sample assignment schedule.

Assignment 1: Write a short, detailed narrative about something that you experienced or observed as a child.

Assignment 2: Write a short, detailed narrative about something that you experienced or observed in school.

Assignment 3: Write a narrative designed to show us a place you know. Do not describe the place. Depict the place by showing what happens in it. Your place may be a room, a town, a store, someone's living room, anywhere.

Assignment 4: Write about a person. Use dialogue, setting, action, and other details to show this person to your reader.

Assignment 5: Write about a job you have held. Detail one incident, a series of incidents, or a period of time to present your experience of the job.

Assignment 6: Write about something you have observed or experienced about relations between women and men. Do not generalize. Detail particular incidents to make your points.

Assignment 7: Present a picture of life in a family. Detail an event or chain of events you have experienced or observed.

Assignment 8: Write an evaluation of some event or of some person such as a teacher in a position of responsibility. Do not tell your reader what to think. Guide your reader's response through your selection of details.

Assignment 9: Interview someone about something that interests you. Write a piece based on the material you collect in your interview.

Assignment 10: Write an argument, a piece designed to change someone's mind about something. Address a specific difference you have with someone in your life right now. Your objective is to get your addressee to see an old issue in a new way. Use details to show the issue as you see it.

Students may edit and revise assignments as many times as they like. During the course I review their work as editor, not judge. Most produce three or four versions of some assignments. Some revise one or two of their pieces as many as ten times. Revision is not a process of correction. I encourage students to edit their finest pieces and to forget about their duds. The best five pieces of writing in their file at the end of the course determine their grades. Because they have the opportunity to revise and because only their best work counts, I set high standards for final submissions.

Alongside the stream of assignments and revisions, I assign exercises, sometimes as many as four a week. Basic training exercises include collecting and revising examples of wordiness and clichés, replacing passives and forms of "to be" with active, specific verbs, replacing vagueness with detail, building parallel phrases, sentences, and paragraphs, and transforming weak writing into strong writing. At the end of thirteen weeks, students' files are four or five inches thick with writings, revisions, and exercises. One faculty member who read my syllabus said, "Well, anybody could learn to write under a system like that." That's my philosophy: Writers are made, not born. To make writers, we must stimulate students to do what good writers do — to sharpen their language skills, to write and write and edit and edit, and to use these skills to explore themselves and their world.

Repeatability: What Happens in Different Settings?

My experiments have shown me that the more I abandoned orthodox practice for new procedures which my experiments validated, the better the outcomes. Doubts persisted, however. The results I observed made a travesty of common wisdom about teaching writing in universities and colleges — that students' skills are so weak that they cannot be expected to behave like writers, that they need to be taught what they should have been taught a long time ago, mainly grammar and form.

I felt insecure about whether or not the results I was seeing could be repeated by other instructors. Were these procedures tied somehow to my personality? I enlisted teachers of writing at several universities and colleges to try these procedures and to report results. Five reported, with pleasure and amazement, results like those I have seen. One reported disappointment and said, "This system scared me, and I felt I was losing control."

One feature of personal essay work is its adaptability to individual cases. Writers use personal essays to explore aspects of self and life that arise as they sit alone before the blank page. Most often the writers at this stage do not see themselves as exploring themselves or as approaching significant issues. Their concerns are practical and immediate: They have a deadline to meet, and they need a topic. New writers often apologize for their topic choices: "I couldn't think of what to write, and I don't think this is very good, but I couldn't think of anything else." Yet, the first few essays, where students may experience their topics as desperation choices, contain the kernel of issues that lie at the heart of their lives. Later, as they come to recognize the importance of these subjects, they direct their writing with more confidence.

Survey results tell only so much about this process. Individual cases will tell us more. I will put before you a detailed case, Martha Kofie, that includes two of her essays and describes her experience with personal essay work. I highlight this case because it shows with particular clarity the healing potential of personal essay work. I will follow the long case with two brief case summaries to show how students adapt this process to their individual situations.

The Long Case: Martha Kofie

Martha Kofie took my course in the fall of 1990 when she was twenty-one. She came upon the course "just looking through the calendar":

> I had given up on English. I never did well in English, and I tried really hard. I got C's and low B's. I wasn't sure what the teachers wanted. I tried to follow the rules, I would put everything I had into a piece, and in the end usually got a nonresponse from teachers. I took this course at the university because it sounded like I could try again. Writing had always been a part of my life. It was something that interested me. But I needed someone to say it was okay before I could do it on my own. I was shocked when I found a course like yours at the University of Toronto. I remember an instant feeling of relief. Halfway through the first class, I felt I was going to get another chance. I felt a lot of freedom. You said to the class, "Nothing you write will surprise me." I had suspicions about that. I took it as a dare. I thought, "Let's get clear exactly what I can write about in here."

Kofie sat in the back of the room and spoke so softly that I strained to understand what she said. She radiated fragility. I avoided calling on her in class. I came to know her through her writing.

The daughter of middle-class professional parents, an African father and a white Canadian mother, Kofie wrote about growing up amid the racism in a nearly all-white Ontario city. She wrote about the child's terror in the house of angry, warring parents. Her first story documents both the racism she experienced in her community and the combat she experienced at home. "Kwame," the title of the story, is her brother's name.

*Kwame**

An imaginary but enforced line drawn through the yard of St. Bernadette Elementary School divides the big kids' side for Grades Four to Eight from the little kids' side for Junior Kindergarten to Grade Three. The swing set on the side for older students is the most popular attraction on the playground. Every lunch hour, Nicole and I wolf down peanut butter sandwiches so we can be the first ones on the swings.

Nicole digs the toe of her blue sneaker into the sand under her swing. "It doesn't matter if your Dad had him," she says. "Kwame can't be your real brother if your Mom adopted him."

I lean back and straighten my legs as I swing past Nicole.

"Kwame *is* my real brother," I say.

"He can't be. You two aren't even the same colour. He's dark like your Dad, but you're light brown, in between them and your Mom."

*© 1993 Martha Kofie

"So?" I see Sister Joanne walk out the rusted back doors for playground duty.

"So my Dad says your Mom is a nigger-lover, and he says Kwame is only your half-brother."

I drag my feet through the sand and jump off the swing. "Kwame's my brother. Okay? Kwame's my brother."

"Thirteen-zip," says Kwame. "Ready?"

The green ping-pong table spreads through half of the brown-paneled basement. Behind Kwame is a TV and a brown plaid chesterfield with grey stuffing sticking out the side where Tipper sharpens his claws. The staircase to my side of the table leads out to the back door, then up into the dining room and kitchen. Brown and yellow circles pattern the wallpapered wall that borders the left side of the staircase. On the right side, a beige wall rises half the height of the left wall to meet the dining room floor.

Kwame smacks the ping-pong ball with his red, rubber-lined paddle. The white ball top-spins low over the net and slips past my paddle as I swing.

"I can't get those ones, Kwame. Don't serve like that. It's not fair because you're way older."

"A game's a game, Martha," Kwame chuckles.

"Why can't we pretend I'm winning sometimes?"

"Fourteen-zip. Ready?" Kwame lifts his paddle.

The crash on the staircase wall shakes me to the floor. I peek over my end of the ping-pong table. Kwame looks at me, frozen in the serving position.

"What was that?" Kwame asks.

"Well, I don't care either!" Mommy yells from upstairs.

I look up the stairs and see the next dish before it hits the wall.

Kwame drops his ball and paddle. He runs over to me in time to see two halves of a dinner plate thump and tumble down the carpeted stairs.

"What are Mommy and Papa fighting about now, Kwame?"

"Beats me, but they must be throwing the dishes right from the kitchen cupboards. Mommy's got a good arm."

Two more dinner plates smash the wall. A pie-shaped chunk of one plate ricochets off the wall and clanks against the metal banister before it thuds to the floor.

Kwame drops his paddle on the table. "I can't stand to hear them fight anymore. Come on, let's try and get outside without them seeing us."

We make it to the fifth step. Plates, two at a time, fly over our heads, slam into the wall and pelt our backs as we duck. Kwame quickly leads me around the plate fragments on two more steps. Two coffee cups and saucers split and shatter against the wall. I scream and curl onto the stairs.

"Come on," Kwame yells. He leaps up the last three steps. "Hurry!" Kwame runs out the back door.

I try to stand. A soup bowl hits the wall and throws splinters against my back. I scream again.

"Did a dish hit you?" Papa calls from the kitchen.

"No, but it . . ."

Four more coffee cups smash the wall and spray my back. I cover my head with my hands and cry into my skirt.

• • •

Kwame shakes my shoulder. "Are you all right? Don't move. I've got shoes on. I'll go get some for you too."

Kwame and I go back down into the basement. He sits beside me on the couch and picks splinters out of my afro. "Why didn't you come outside with me?"

"I was too scared."

"I didn't mean to leave you like that. I stuck my head in the back door to see if I could make it down to you. I almost got a dish in the face."

I play with the loose thread on the hem of my skirt.

"What if I had to explain that one to my basketball coach, Martha? What would I say? 'Hey, Coach, I can't play in the city finals this weekend. Got hit by a flying saucer.' He'd lock me up."

I can't smile.

"It's over now, Martha. It's okay."

"But Kwame, what are we supposed to eat lunch on?"

Kwame leans toward me when he sees my tears. "Don't worry," he whispers. He looks down at the splinters of glass in his palm. "I'll fix us something good. Something real good."

Kofie's second story tells about pre-adolescent shenanigans and the horrific parental response. Like "Kwame," this story takes us between school and home. Here the writer probably suggests more than she knows: Her story emphasizes both the disconnection and the connection between school and home. What happens at home clearly sets the tone of the inner life of the child who goes to school, and yet the classroom on test day goes through its prescribed motions as the teacher tells the narrator to "stop talking." School requires silence; the narrator needs talk. The split between the inner and outer life of the child is one the personal essay can address. Here is "Testing, Testing":

*Testing, Testing**

"No. No. No. If it *sticks* it's done, if it *falls down* it needs to cook some more." Mandy whips a spaghetti noodle at the kitchen wall. The noodle slaps, peels and falls, curling with the others on the floor, just in front of the orange-and-blue flowered wall. Mandy and I stand behind strings of spaghetti marking the throw line on the beige linoleum. Pots of spaghetti and sauce sit on pot holders on the counter. Math books lie open on the kitchen table. Mandy and I celebrate the first PD (Professional Development) day of Grade Six at my house. On PD days, teachers work and students get the day off.

Mandy takes the bowl of drained spaghetti from me.

"Are you sure, Mandy?" I ask. I pick the last noodle out of the bowl and throw. "I thought it was the other way around." My noodle joins the heap of white swirls on the floor.

*© 1993 Martha Kofie

"No, it's not. Lisa told me and she's Italian."

"I know that. Lisa taught me how to swear in Italian in Grade Two."

"And besides," Mandy says, "these walls don't work. You're not supposed to test spaghetti on wallpaper. Lisa told me that too. Let's try it in your room."

"Okay."

Mandy holds the strainer while I pour more spaghetti out of the pot. Inside the door of my bedroom, I place the bowl of spaghetti on the purple-speckled carpet between us. I throw the first noodle over my pink-flowered bedspread at the mauve wall. The noodle sticks.

"See?" Mandy says. "I told you it doesn't work on wallpaper. My turn." Mandy throws a noodle. Her white squiggle clings to the wall above mine. "I wonder if it will stick to the ceiling," Mandy says. She bends her knees and like a cheerleader tossing a pom-pom throws a noodle at the ceiling. "Hey," Mandy says, hands on hips and looking up, "this spaghetti is really ready."

"Maybe it sticks to glass," I say. I whip a noodle at my mirror.

"That's a great idea. We can try it on your window too."

The bowl of noodles empties as strings of white slap and stick to the ceiling, mirror, window and walls.

"Hey, let's see if the meatballs are ready." Mandy runs to the kitchen.

"What?" The noodle I was about to throw falls to the rug. I run after Mandy.

"You gotta be . . ." I flatten myself against the kitchen wall, afraid Mandy might spill the jiggling pot of spaghetti sauce she carries as she runs back past me.

Mandy puts the pot on the carpet and dips her hand into the sauce. "Ow. I forgot this was still hot." Mandy scoops out a meatball and throws it at the wall. The meatball flattens to a semi-circle and slides to the carpet. "Nope," says Mandy. "This stuff ain't ready yet."

"You didn't throw hard enough. Here, I'll show you how to throw a meatball." I sweep my hand through the sauce and pull out another meatball. Winding up, I swing my arm behind my head. The meatball slips out of my hand and splatters against the wall behind us.

Mandy and I turn to look at the bits of hamburger forming a dripping red circle on the wall. "That is one ready meatball," I say.

Mandy doesn't laugh. "When are your parents coming back?" she asks.

I look at Mandy. Her eyes widen. Two car doors shut outside.

"Oh, my God. Oh, my God." Mandy dances on the spot, shaking her arms. She runs out ahead of me toward the kitchen window. "What are we going to do? I mean, we only got about ten seconds to pick up the spaghetti, wash the walls and the ceiling and the mirror and the window and the light — did you know I got a noodle to stick to your light? — and then we gotta put all the food away and make like we're studying for our test tomorrow."

I reach the window. Mandy grabs both my arms. She jerks me toward her. "It's just the Keshleys coming home next door, Marth."

Mandy collapses laughing. She smacks the kitchen floor. I laugh too, leaning against a kitchen wall and holding my stomach.

"Got ya that time," Mandy says, one hand on the floor, the other pointing at me.

I kneel and reach over to tickle Mandy's waist.

"I'm not ticklish," she says. She hugs me and laughs over my shoulder. Our bodies jiggle against each other. The shaking slows to a quiver and an occasional spasm. Mandy sniffs hard.

I flatten my palms against the sides of my face. "My cheeks hurt."

"Mine too," Mandy says. "Seriously now, we better clean up. I'll get the bleach and you get the rags. My mom says bleach will clean anything."

I lie on the edge of my double bed farthest from the bedroom door. I stare at patches of yellow paint showing through my mauve wall.

I hear Papa's steps coming toward my room. He pushes open my door. The door bangs against the wall. I shut my eyes and squeeze. The weight of his knee on my bed makes me slide toward him as he reaches across. With a finger, he pokes my bum. "Get up."

He stands beside my bed. I fake a slow stretch.

"I said 'Get up.'"

I sit on the edge of my bed, facing away from him.

"I want to see you in the kitchen."

"Okay."

"Look at me when I speak to you."

I stand slowly and turn. "Okay," I say. "I'm coming to the kitchen."

Before he leaves, Papa looks through my nightshirt at my breasts.

I walk to the kitchen. Papa pulls out a chair from the table. "Sit down."

I grasp the edge of the table and ease into the chair.

"Maybe Martha shouldn't go to school today." Mommy walks toward the table, tying the belt of her blue, terry-cloth housecoat.

"She's okay. Now stand up and sit down properly."

I stand, close my eyes and sit down quickly.

"That's better. Get ready to go to school."

In my room, I bend and look behind me at the mirror. Pink and puffy, the long, horizontal welts are still there. I touch one gently. The sting sucks air in through my closed teeth. I reach for my red-and-blue dotted underwear and pull them up.

Mandy watches me sit in my desk behind hers. "You got in shit, didn't you."

I force a smile.

"I'm sorry, Marth. I mean, I was the one who . . ."

"We both did it, Mandy. So forget it. We had fun."

Mr. O'Donnell hands out our math tests. "Stop talking and put your books away. You have until recess to finish the test."

Addressing the Split: Kofie's Experience with Personal Essays

Plain words and terse understatement lend Kofie's stories power and grace: low-key language portrays high-key events. Ominous multiple meanings of "testing" suggest more than is said. The indirect revelation of the parental violence that precedes the breakfast table scene shocks. Restraint sets cruelty in relief. Style, ironically cool and controlled, leaves horror to the reader. With dignified reserve, the writer reports; the reader feels. This, I saw, was a writer doing what writers do — very well.

Events have confirmed my sense of Kofie as writer. She went on to publish most of the work she wrote in the two courses she took from me, including "Kwame" and "Testing, Testing."[4] Kofie read some of her work on a Toronto radio program. Listeners phoned and wrote to say that her stories had helped them understand their own experiences of racism and family violence. Writing became central in Kofie's life. After she graduated, a publisher dedicated to women's writing hired Kofie as managing editor. Kofie attended international conferences where, despite shyness, she made speeches to publishers and prodded them to search out writing about people and lives that rarely make it into print. Kofie knew about the healing power of writing and urged publishers to make this available to as many different kinds of voices as possible. While she worked as managing editor, Kofie earned a master's degree in philosophy.

Kofie is a talented student, and her exposure to the writing process can claim limited credit for her academic successes. However, this case offers good evidence for the power of the writing process to release latent capacity. In Kofie's case, her writing appears to have catalyzed the healing of wounds that, unhealed, impeded performance. According to Kofie, the first writing course provided a pivot point for her. She had been in therapy since a suicide attempt six years before, when she was fifteen. Here is her account of her experience in that course:

> When I worked on my stories for the course, I started crying and I cried every day for two years after that. I delayed taking your second course for a year. I cried every day, and it was all about my dad. I remember feeling really driven to put to paper the scenes that were the most painful. I saw those scenes in my head. They never left me. Those were the scenes I wrote in my stories. Those were the scenes I had to put down.

What was my role during Kofie's confrontation with her trauma? I did not know about the crying. I did not discuss any of the psychological implications of Kofie's writing with her. That is not my role. As editor and teacher, my role is to guide students in issues of writing and language. Kofie wrote personal essays to confront and redeem damage suffered at the hands of heedless caregivers. That was her project. Mine was helping her to find her way to a clear, original, expressive language that would allow her to communicate clearly to herself and others. The process is self-regulating. Students take on what they are ready to take on. I have never seen writing students use their writing to wander into issues they could not manage.

Four years after her last course with me, I asked Kofie what made this writing process work for her.

> I'm not sure I totally understand. It's something about having a witness. But for years, I had had witnesses — counselors and therapists. Something about putting it on paper took the witnessing to another level. I became my own witness. Emotional damage is so hard to articulate in a story. It takes so much work to show in a story that something had the impact it had. Through all that labor, I relived those scenes. It was the first time I realized I had really been harmed — even though I already had the labels: I had heard of physical abuse; I had even heard of emotional abuse.
>
> For me, writing those stories stopped all the circling that goes on in the head. Yet, before I wrote them, that's what these thoughts did. They circled around and around in my head. Now, they're out of my head, and I can always go pick up the book and read those stories if want to.
>
> Before I wrote those stories, I needed to think about those scenes to remember them — even though I don't know why I would want to remember them. Now I have forgotten them. Just recently I read the stories in the book where they're published. I was shocked. I had forgotten.

I asked Kofie how the technical training around language, the prose boot camp, had contributed to her changes:

> The technical direction was like an anchor. There's such potential to drown in emotional stuff. The writing technology meant I was *en route* to something else. There was more than pain. I remember especially the lessons about sound patterns. I liked the softer vowels and the hard consonants — very different effects. For some reason, work with these sounds gave me a way to contact really sad places in me.

Kofie has not always enjoyed success. After her first year, when she received one A−, failed two courses, dropped another and received a D− in another, the university put Kofie on academic probation. By her fourth year, when she took the first of two writing courses with me, she had brought herself to a B− average. The year she took the writing course she received one A+, five A's (one for writing) and one B+. In her fifth and final year, she received six A's, one A+, one A−, and graduated with a major in philosophy. Kofie found herself as a student during her university years, and the personal essays played a role. "Formal essays became a lot easier for me," Kofie reports. "And learning about editing helped. I started to pretend I was the editor of the books and articles I was reading for my courses. This way, I could get quickly to the meaning of the piece."

Kofie's writing experience enabled her to take her life experience into her academic work. Before she wrote her stories, she says, "academic" and "life" were artificially split, and yet one intruded on the other. Her writing led to integration:

> Before my experience in your writing course, I didn't take chances with my courses. I did what was expected. After, I learned to see my experience as having meaning that could be used in analyzing ideas, I took chances. I brought my experiences into essays in my philosophy courses. As a graduate student I included a journal entry in an essay. I always got good responses.
>
> When I heard generalizations about people, I tested them by asking: "Does my experience fit here?"
>
> In one presentation to students and faculty in the Philosophy Department, I talked about my father. I talked about how I suffered abuse from him if I did not do well in school. Race was such an important factor. I inherited my father's fears about what would happen if I weren't a superior performer. "You have to listen to the teacher," my father said. But what about teaching that denies the place of my and my father's race in the history of thought? Racial bias in the curriculum puts me in a contradiction between listening to the teacher and accepting myself as a black woman. I explained this to [philosophy faculty members] to help them understand my reactivity to the subtlest hints of racism in the philosophy curriculum. My ability to connect my life to the theories I study has amounted to breakthrough for me. Theories and assumptions can be measured against experience.

Kofie, the writer, has put the abuse stories behind her. Still a fine stylist and still an acute observer of people in family settings, Kofie is now writing a series about unconventional human relationships that work well. Compassion, humor, and understanding distinguish Kofie's stories. Kofie reports that she is now in her fourth year of a new course of psychotherapy. She has applied to medical school, where, if accepted, she wants to qualify herself as a psychiatrist. Her writing forms an important part of the evidence she has presented to the medical school admissions committee.

Kofie's testimony suggests the catalytic potential of students developing writers' voices and using those voices to discover and develop themselves. Students choose the issues and incidents they want to explore, and as they write they learn how to use language that makes meaning. Students select the truth they want to tell and by telling come to know. They work to set their truth in language that expresses their personalities and experiences and that has the power to earn credibility with a reader.

A Short Case: Addressing a Cultural Split

June Irwin immigrated to Canada from Trinidad when she was eighteen, with her mother and sisters. In Trinidad, Irwin's mother, extremely poor, washed clothes by hand to support five children in a tiny rural village. In Canada, Irwin worked in a factory for ten years and took educational upgrading. In her late twenties, she gained entrance to the University of Toronto through a special access program. In her first year, Irwin dropped three courses, failed one, and passed one that her English professor told her was "a gift."

Irwin spoke tentatively in a beautiful Trinidadian accent. Professors, she told me, complained about her grammar and her writing. She had been told she "did not belong" in university. She had been told, "You live in Canada now and must leave your past behind." Irwin came to my course in distress.

Irwin's first essay told about an accident she witnessed as a six-year-old: A truck passing through her village hit and decapitated one of her playmates. The first version of this piece reported the incident in bare outline form and contained sentence fragments, run-ons, and faulty verb agreements. Irwin had not set the scene. The village, its people, and the way they speak were all absent. Irwin had tried to write about her past while leaving her past behind. I interrogated Irwin through another four versions of this piece: "What would we see if we could see the village? What did the people say? What did your mother do? Show me the place and the people, and show me what happened. I've never seen that village or anything like it. I want to see and hear it in your essay."

After three weeks and several drafts, Irwin produced details of setting and dialogue in the local tongue to produce a fine journalistic piece with a fascinating portrait of life in her town. Formal sentence problems disappeared. "You can write," I told her. Irwin eventually produced twenty essays for me in two courses. She set nineteen of these in the village of her childhood and mixed dialogue in the local tongue with the "standard English" of the narrator's voice. Her work presented a precise, unsentimental picture of the poverty her mother faced as she raised five children. Irwin's classmates felt educated by her picture of poverty and village life. Irwin had been determined at the beginning to keep the poverty of her childhood secret; she told me she felt ashamed of it.

Irwin went on to publish and receive extensive recognition for her work. She showed her stories to her professors. Her past, including her mother tongue, became a source of esteem rather than shame. And her problems in producing academy English withered. The year Irwin took the writing courses she received two A's and two B's and came off probation. She became an excellent student and has now applied to law school. Irwin claims that the work on personal essays enabled her academic transformation. She feels more confident, more decisive, and happier. Irwin used the personal essay to integrate her two lives, her life in university in Canada and her life in the village in Trinidad. Her mother tongue has helped her to produce rich literature and, it turns out, is an asset, not a liability. Irwin used her personal essay work to address and mend a cultural split that alienated her from a part of herself, her origins.

A Short Case: Addressing the Split between the Self and the Writing Self

Mike Demarco, a twenty-one-year-old commerce major, is the son of Italian immigrant parents. His father worked the assembly line at a Ford plant. Demarco, the first in his family to attend university, announced that he would never read his work aloud in the class editing sessions. His fear was phobic. "Flunk me if you have to," he said, "but I'll never read" — this from a student preoccupied with grades. Demarco wrote his first assignments in a stiff, this-is-how-you-write-for-a-professor style: turgid, bureaucratic, formally correct, dead. Yet Mike Demarco the person radiated informality, honesty, and self-mocking humor. When he sat down to write, Demarco encountered a split that divided him from the confidence that informed his actions on other occasions. Writing required a contrived self — a dry, dull, self that denied his origins.

Relations between us remained tense until he turned up with an essay about his family, whom, he had told me earlier, he could not write about because "there's really nothing interesting about them — and they're not educated." This essay presented an anarchic, funny, touching family dinner scene. The piece used dialogue, including the mixture of Italian and English spoken in his house, sharp detail, and a spare, informal style. "This is it," I said. "You are doing it." Demarco had fused his writing life with the rest of his life. Even in essays that had nothing to do with family, Demarco's family now made cameo appearances. The family was indeed "something special," he realized, and made a good subject. One day Demarco came in with an essay, "The Calculus Test," that presented a scene after a test where many students realized they would have to give up dreams and plans because they could not pass calculus, a prerequisite for many programs. "The Calculus Test," as good literature often does, evokes an ambivalent response; the scene is both comic and terrifying. I praised the piece. "This may seem funny to you, sir," he said, "but, if you want me to, I'll read it in class." He read not only in class but later before an audience of 200 university faculty members at a conference where I spoke about personal essays. The Math Department requested a copy of "The Calculus Test" to post on its bulletin board. Demarco has since given a public reading of one of his essays. Demarco reported other developments. His grades in written work for commerce assignments rose by 25 percent. He also reported that he became "chief editor" of his friends' writing, and, as Demarco put it, "I must be doing okay because they keep coming back." Demarco used his personal essay work to address the split between the person he is and the person he thought he had to be to succeed in the academy. Because of this split, he had left some of the most compelling aspects of himself out of his academy life. The fusion strengthened the person and his academic work.

Explaining Change: How Does the Personal Essay Work?

The evidence I have seen shows that work with personal essays produces better outcomes in expository writing than work directly on expository writing does. There is substantial qualitative evidence that work with expressive narrative enhances performance in courses where there is no writing, in courses where, for example, performance is measured only in multiple-choice tests. Academic results offer one kind of evidence of personal growth, of the person's ability to operate effectively in a setting the person has chosen as a kind of test. What do these results mean? Probably that something about the writing process releases or catalyzes potential otherwise trapped in the psyche. In other words, the expression of the self and its experience through language somehow develops the whole person, so that the evidence of development appears in the various things people do with their lives. Most students report not only improved academic results but improved confidence—better mental health.

How do we account for the capacity of this engagement with language and the self to catalyze positive change?

Bill Buford has written recently in *The New Yorker* about the revival of interest in storytelling. Stories, Buford writes, "protect us from chaos, and maybe that's what we, unblinkered at the end of the twentieth century, find ourselves craving." Buford goes on: "Implicit in the extraordinary revival of storytelling is the possibility that we need stories—that they are a fundamental unit of knowledge, the foundation of memory, essential to the way we make sense of our lives. . . . We have returned to narratives—in many fields of knowledge—because it is impossible to live without them" (Buford 11–12). For Alamatea Usuelli, "Story-telling creates the illusion that subject and object, the inner and the outer world, correspond, and that the subject's experience has meaning and is preserved from chaos." This view sees storytelling as a defense against the loss of the illusion of "a completed universe . . . in which we may stroll in relative safety." For the reader, according to Usuelli, the narrative may arouse "a play of identifications which enable [a person] to overcome the usual limits of . . . ego" (Usuelli 183–84). The illusion of "protection from chaos" creates an artificially safe place for development just as the illusion of safety created by caring parents does. The world is not a safe place, but the temporary illusion of security offers a time-out, an opportunity to gather real strength in preparation for the unsafe world.[5]

Beyond the possibility of this illusion, how does the making of stories in this blend of the academic and the personal stimulate development? The answer cannot be easy because the elements—self, expression, development — are complex and elusive. I suggest that the results I report here arise from three kinds of relatedness encouraged, or permitted, by the process I have described: the relation of the self to meaning, the relation of the self to the self, and the relation of the self to language.

Meaning

"I see," William Kerrigan writes about life in North America today, "careerism gone totally out of control, generating new jargons that seem to exist only to supply a place of dignity (lucrative dignity) for a priesthood able to manipulate them" (Kerrigan 23). Knowledge of the priestly codes signifies belonging. Students want to belong; that's why most come to university. For many, success means learning to reproduce mechanistic imitations of the specialized dialects of the academic disciplines (Saul 38–71). These dialects simulate seriousness and authority. They often substitute for and prevent genuine communication. They serve as membership cards, a way of telling who belongs and who does not belong in the narrow corridors of expertise our university departments stake out and defend. The empowering capacity of language to make meaning is lost. Writing becomes an act of subservience.

The "writing problem" we hear so much about in the university is really the "meaning problem." Students learn to fake meaning. Competent students, even when they have not read assigned material, know how to reproduce the dialect that will earn them the right to stay in the corridor. Students, who honor this survival strategy with terms like "bullshitting," do not confuse it with making meaning. They feel sure it has no meaning.

Complainers about the "writing problem" commonly see this problem as a deficiency of learned form: grammar, sentence structure, paragraphing, and so on. These are symptoms only, I believe. The real problem lies in the students' habit of generating language that fakes a relationship to meaning.

Writing in the academic setting easily becomes a negation of meaning, correct form filled with very nearly nothing. This writing expresses, clearly and unintentionally, the students' alienation from meaning. Most students feel the academic setting does not offer a safe place to make meaning that they can take responsibility for. Their alienated discourse derives from and reinforces not humility, but self-loathing. Most of the students I meet — and these include some of "the best" in our system — do not consider themselves worthy or capable of making a meaning that could matter to anyone, including themselves. Most think they have no meaning to make.

The personal essay system I have outlined confronts writers with responsibility for making meaning. Form follows substance. Jean-Paul Sartre's understanding of reflective consciousness has influenced my understanding of the writer's relationship to meaning. According to Sartre, we are "condemned to be free" (Sartre 707). We face a void, and we alone must fill it. We choose meaning and are responsible for the meaning we make, or decide upon.

The act of filling the page with the meaning the writer chooses to put into the world alters the writer's relationship to self and world: The writer becomes conscious of consciousness and at once defines and transcends a situation. The writer acts upon the world, and in so doing produces a changed world and a changed self in the world, a self that takes responsibility for deciding what meaning is. As R. D. Laing writes, "In so far as I put myself 'into' what I do, I become myself through this doing." The converse, Laing says, is to "go round in a circle, in a whirl, going everywhere and getting nowhere" (Laing 109). Laing's circle describes the world of the faker of meaning.

Personal essays confront students with the void because they encourage the putting of the self *into* their writing, into the academy, into the world. They must search themselves and their experience for meaning. Most resist. "What do you want me to write?" they ask. "What do you want to write?" I reply. Peer models, collections of writing by other writers at their level, make clear that they are indeed free *and* responsible for what they produce. This is tough practice, but when students learn to take responsibility for meaning, they become better writers of standard-form writing, like research reports, business letters, or the academic expository essay. Many move decisively in the direction of the free and responsible citizens that we talk about so much in Western universities. The responsible maker of meaning becomes a more responsible receiver of meaning.

Their confrontation with meaning yields a product: writing that contributes original meaning to the writer's world. The world desires and honors fresh meanings. Martha Kofie's stories are now taught in university courses. The self moves into the world and changes it. The self becomes partly responsible for the world it inhabits.

Self

Personal essays provoke reflections: Who am I? What is my experience? And, finally, what is its meaning? The writer creates a reality, "some vision of the subject in the world" (Schafer 361). Most new writers make a story or a series of stories that represents a decision about who they are and how they got that way.

Martha Kofie represented herself as the child of a father who suffered racist scorn and who poured his own scorn onto his imperfect daughter. She, isolated by the father's anger, fought her own race battles on the playground. Before she wrote her stories, Kofie told me, she had never thought about the problems her African father had living in a white Canadian town. They had more in common than she had realized.

Freud articulated a "talking cure," a system that creates a safe place to piece together a narrative, to find and make meaning from seemingly scattered pieces. Freud and his theoretical descendants, even those who challenge his system, agree that expression, and its opposite, repression, operate as powerful invisible agents in human health. A new wave of psychologists and researchers such as James Pennebaker now study the relationship between writing and healing.[6]

Jeremy Holmes, a British National Health Service psychotherapist, describes successful psychotherapy in these terms: The patient makes a story, "a model of the world as it was, transmuted into a form which can be stored, used, and, when necessary, updated." The desired outcome to psychotherapy, according to Holmes, is "autobiographical competence"—"to become a person is to know one's own story." There is a connection between the ability to build a coherent story, "and the sense of self-esteem and effectiveness which underlie a strong sense of identity. In order to know who you are, you need to know where you have come from, to be able to *own* your origins" (Holmes 13–17). Another psychiatrist, Rex Kay, puts the point succinctly: "When we are being creative, we are bringing order to chaos," "forming islands of consistency," "giving birth to the self." Partly this happens through allowing "disorganization to emerge" (Kay).

The successful writer of personal narrative must brainstorm, must free associate, must court the whirl of unassociated particulars to produce the patterns of detail that make a narrative thrive. Writers report that they had not realized just how much they have stored in their memories, that the search for detail and the shaping of that detail in a narrative changes the way they see themselves.

Psychoanalytic theorists point to the "therapeutic frame," a place where ordinary rules of "logic, common sense and taste" are temporarily suspended so that the analysand may go through "disorganization and reorganization" (Skura 376). A writing course that includes personal essays facilitates a similar process. The classroom, the course, the assignment—these are frames that set up a time and a space where the work of free exploration can happen. Controls are set aside so that the writer may discover the pieces that make up the story. The final produce is shaped and organized, but the process requires a suspension of the usual controls. The writing derives urgency from the risks the writer has taken. The writer's care becomes the reader's care. The writer's risk draws the reader's attention and respect. The self in transition is an arresting subject.

In this way of looking at personal essays, the process operates in what Donald Winnicott calls a "transitional space," an area of creative and spontaneous "play" and discovery, and the writing becomes a "transitional object," an object that mediates between the writer's inner self and the world the self inhabits. This is the process Kofie seems to describe when she says that her personal essay writing linked her inner

itated healing and much more
in the other world of the acad-
inner self is neglected because
lieve occurs when students feel
resence of the self, there devel-
True [inner] Self and the False
ıere is found a poor capacity for
living." In place of cultural pur-
people poor concentration, anx-
ctions to avoid the threatening

be, a therapist. However, the
ıvironment" (Winnicott's term),
to carry on their work, a work
ıe space and time within this
o many use this space, as Kofie
ɔetween their inner and outer
d, a substantial percentage will
and personally.

and revealing meaning brings
creativity of language because
ıething they have never said"
s new meanings, and the writer
itself and into the service of the
ıy the self. Here the writer be-
acted-upon object.
ed to give conscientious and expert attention to language. When we teach writers we teach the tough discipline and openness and creativity that close attention to language involves. Too often, though, students get only a sense of restriction and hazard from language instruction in schools. Our educational system too often fails to communicate that language is a living system of endless creation. Rather many students experience language as a system of menacing, mysterious, and fixed rules.

Grammar is not a dress code. Grammar, as Chomsky and other linguists have pointed out, is the internal system that allows us to generate and understand infinite new meanings from finite vocabulary. "The normal use of language is . . . free and undetermined but yet appropriate to situations, and it is recognized as appropriate by other participants in the discourse situation" (Chomsky 56–59). The academic addiction to rigid, formal discourse situations is like putting on a tuxedo every time we step out of the house. Language is amazingly flexible and able to address varying degrees of formality. Students learn how to use language by confronting its creativity and its flexibility, its capacity to meet and express a range of life situations.

Merleau-Ponty asserts that language *is* meaning, that our thoughts are not really thoughts until we express them in words. Language, endlessly creative, "like a wave, gathers and poises itself to hurtle beyond its own limits" (Merleau-Ponty 197). When we speak, when we write, we inevitably re-make, re-create the language. Language changes through usage, despite the efforts of many educators to pin the language down to something right or wrong. Within the past twenty years in North America, creative and influential changes in the English language have come from people who have opted out of education, kids in the streets of the poorest neighborhoods of the United States' big cities. Street-based rap culture has added much to the vocabulary and syntax of our language as we use it today, perhaps as much as the stream of new words and phrases from science and technology.

The personal essay, with its requirement that students find styles appropriate to the situations presented by their content, forces students to confront their potential to shape language. The meaning-making capacity of language becomes primary. Students must ask: Does this language express the meaning I intent? I know my teaching goes well when I hear my students echo the traditional writer's complaint: I can't get the language to say what I want it to say. That shows me that the students are working to stretch the language, to make it do more than it wants to do, as writers everywhere do.

Jacques Lacan was surely right when he sharpened the psychoanalytic focus on language. Lacan distinguished "*parole vide*"—Empty Speech from "*parole pleine*"—Full Speech (Lacan 61). The psychoanalytic interchange has as its goal, according to Lacan, the movement from Empty Speech to Full Speech. Full Speech makes meaning. Empty Speech evades meaning. "What determines whether or not [speech] is called 'empty' or 'full'? Precisely the extent to which it impedes or facilitates the realization of the truth of the subject [the speaker, or, in this case, the writer]" (Muller and Richardson 70). For Lacan, the successful analytic process leads to Full Speech. The same is true of the writing process. Full Speech means "'the birth of truth in speech'" (Lacan qtd. in Muller and Richardson 71). This leads to a full engagement of language that "renders the past *present*" (Muller and Richardson 72). Empty Speech avoids change because, as James DiCenso puts it, Empty Speech "confirms antecedently given perspectives and opinions; it is narcissistic in the sense that one always finds one's ego intact and unchanged." Full speech, on the other hand, "may be described as 'performative' because it acts on and effects changes in the ego's orientation . . . [by opening] the ego to repressed and unseen dimensions of meaning" (DiCenso 49).

For Lacan, the laws of language govern human interchange. Thus full and unrestricted engagement with language facilitates the student's ability to make original meaning and to incorporate the past within the present (represented in the act of writing). The instructor enables this process by guiding the student on language issues. The instructor points the student away from degenerate language, Empty Speech, alienated discourse, and toward the difficult process of finding language suitable to the meaning to be expressed. The instructor does not guide with regard to *meaning* and *self* but does guide with language. Here the instructor guides students toward precise, original, concrete, economical, and direct language. My linguistic boot camp jolts students who have become accustomed to filling out their essays with Empty Speech — and who have become accustomed to being rewarded for it. Many resist, at first, but persistent, supporting editing roots out concealing clichés and hollow phrases. As students move toward Full Speech, their language sharpens and their writing engages, rather than evades, life issues.

The work with language leads inevitably to work with the self and its life among other selves. The self uses sharpened language skills in a free and undetermined way to speak to itself and to speak to others. Stephen Marcus points out that once a "narrative account has been rendered in language, in conscious speech," it "no longer exists in the deformed language of symptoms. At the end, at the successful end, one has come into possession of one's own story. It is the final act of self-appropriation, the appropriation by oneself of one's own history. This is in part so because one's own story is in so large a measure a phenomenon of language" (Marcus 56). I add: For most university students, this process includes their appropriation of the language that will express *their* situations. This often means moving out of academy dialect, if only to return to it with more confidence, skill, and a heightened awareness of its strengths and weaknesses.

The Humanities Problem

The "writing problem" in our universities is really a humanism problem. We teach humanism and dodge its practice. We ask our students to study and understand meaning at the same time that we offer little opportunity for them to make original meaning. Only the person who has attempted to make original meaning can understand how difficult that is. We tell our students through the messages of Greek philosophy, of Aquinas and Augustine, of Freud and Jung, that "Know thyself" represents the most important knowledge, the necessary base for other knowledge. Yet we offer scant occasion for them to include this kind of knowledge in their education, except by accident.

We report to our students about the release of creativity and knowledge that accompanied the use of vernacular by Boccaccio, Chaucer, and Dante and other writers as part of the European Renaissance. We make little provision for vital new language in our institutions of higher learning, where self-perpetuating, archaic, and stifling dialects prevail. We make artificial distinctions between academic and creative writing, and we press these distinctions on our students. The personal essay process I have outlined in this chapter allows a parallel discourse, one that traverses the artificial chasm between the creative and the academic, between the subject and the object, between the self and the society.

The "writing problem" roots in our students' alienated discourse. My experiments with writing point to people's natural drive to make original meaning, to get beyond the idiot's tale that signifies nothing more than belonging. People want to make meaning even though it involves risk and makes intense demands of the maker. My experiments show that, given opportunity and knowledgeable support, writing students move toward using language, the language appropriate to their situation, to make meaning that appears to catalyze positive change in their relationships with themselves and with the world around them. As John Ralston Saul has put it, "the best hope for a regeneration of language lies not in academic analysis but in citizen participation" (Saul 173). Language is the tool of the human mind, whatever the mind's enterprise. Language can help us to live unconsciously, or it can help us to live consciously. Students who live consciously in language inform themselves and their fellow students and the society in which they seek a role. They become citizen participants in learning, citizens who come not only to learn, but to teach us and change us.

Notes

1. G. F. Ricketts, "Mr. Bong's Variety," in Allen 22–23.
2. For a published collection of peer models, see Guy Allen et al., *No More Masterpieces: Short Prose by New Writers* (Toronto: Canadian Scholars' Press, 1989).
3. I have learned to encourage students to use their home languages in appropriate situations — for example, in narratives where they quote the speech of someone who uses their language or where they use expressions from their home languages that do not translate well. Sometimes phrases from their home language will contribute to the understanding or atmosphere of the piece they are writing. I first tried this procedure when I came across awkward passages in essays where it was obvious that the student had tried to translate expressions that have no equivalency in academy English. When students use dialects or other languages, they provide translations in parentheses or footnotes.
4. Twelve of Kofie's stories are published in Nancy Chong, Martha Kofie, and Kwanza Msingwana, *Only Mountains Never Meet: A Collection of Stories by Three New Writers* (Toronto: Well Versed Publications, 1993), 57–116.

5. The illusion of security may be what Charles Anderson means by "sense of self." Certainly, it functions in the same way.
6. Marian MacCurdy offers a fuller discussion of writing and healing.

Works Cited

Allen, Guy, et al., ed., *No More Masterpieces: Short Prose by New Writers*, Toronto: Canadian Scholars' Press, 1989.

Anderson, Charles, and Marian MacCurdy. "Introduction." *Writing and Healing: Toward an Informed Practice*. Eds. Charles Anderson and Marian MacCurdy. Urbana, IL: National Council of Teachers of English, 2000.

Buford, Bill. "The Seductions of Storytelling." *The New Yorker* (24 June 1996): 11–12.

Chomsky, Noam. *Aspects of a Theory of Syntax*. Cambridge: MIT P, 1965.

Chong, Nancy, Martha Kofie, and Kwanza Msingwana. *Only Mountains Never Meet: A Collection of Stories by Three New Writers*. Toronto: Well Versed Publications, 1993.

DiCenso, James. "Symbolism and Subjectivity: A Lacanian Approach to Religion." *The Journal of Religion* 74 (1994): 45–64.

Holmes, Jeremy. *Between Art and Science: Essays in Psychotherapy and Psychiatry*. London: Routledge, 1993.

Kay, Rex. "The Meaning of Creativity in Psychoanalytic Process." Mt. Sinai Hospital, Toronto, Ontario, Canada: unpublished, 1996.

Kerrigan, William. "*Macbeth* and the History of Ambition." *Freud and the Passions*. Ed. John O'Neill. University Park, PA: Pennsylvania State UP, 1996. 13–24.

Lacan, Jacques. *Le Séminaire: Livre 1: Les Écrits techniques de Freud, 1953–1954*. Paris: Éditions de Seuil, 1953–54.

Laing, R. D. *Self and Others*. 2nd ed. New York: Pantheon, 1969.

MacCurdy, Marian. "From Trauma to Writing: A Theoretical Model for Practice Use." *Writing and Healing: Toward an Informed Practice*. Eds. Charles Anderson and Marian MacCurdy. Urbana, IL: National Council of Teachers of English, 2000.

Marcus, Steven. "Freud and Dora: Story, History, Case History." *Essential Papers on Literature and Psychoanalysis*. Ed. Emanuel Berman. New York: New York UP, 1993. 36–80.

Merleau-Ponty, Maurice. "On the Phenomenology of Language." *Signs*. Trans. Richard C. McCleary. Evanston: Northwestern UP, 1964.

Muller, John P., and William J. Richardson. *Lacan and Language: A Reader's Guide to Écrits*. Madison, CT: International Universities P, 1982.

Rhodes, Richard. *How to Write: Advice and Reflections*. New York: Morrow, 1995.

Sartre, Jean-Paul. *Being and Nothingness*. Trans. Hazel E. Barnes. New York: Washington Square, 1956.

Saul, John Ralston. *The Unconscious Civilization*. Concord, Ontario: House of Anansi Press, 1995.

Schafer, Roy. "Narration in the Psychoanalytic Dialogue." *Essential Papers on Literature and Psychoanalysis*. Ed. Emanuel Berman. New York: New York UP, 1993. 341–68.

Skura, Meredith Ann. "Literature as Psychoanalytic Process: Surprise and Self-Consciousness." *Essential Papers on Literature and Psychoanalysis*. Ed. Emanuel Berman. New York: New York UP, 1993. 374–402.

Usuelli, Alamatea Kluzer. "The Significance of Illusion in the Work of Freud and Winnicott: A Controversial Issue." *International Review of Psycho-Analysis* 19 (1992): 179–87.

Winnicott, Donald W. *The Maturational Processes and the Facilitating Environment: Studies in the Theory of Emotional Development*. 1965. Rpt. Madison, CT: International Universities P, 1988.

Allen's Insights as a Resource for Your Reflections

1. What do you make of the information Allen uncovers in his surveys? Do your writing students seem equally alienated? What are the chief sources of this alienation and how does it inform their writing?

2. Consider the case of Kofie: how would you define the changes she goes through and how might such changes be articulated in ways appropriate to the general goals of a writing course?

Allen's Insights as a Resource for Your Writing Classroom

1. Consider asking your students to read Allen's essay, and, in particular, the sorts of questions you would ask them about it. Would you use it to open up debates or might you use it to explore, in ever greater depth, what certain abstract concepts like those in his title — "self" and "power" and "consciousness" — have the potential to mean?

2. Follow Allen's example and start using student texts as the assigned reading for the course. What might be some appropriate guidelines for discussing this reading and writing about it?

3. Develop your own version of what Allen calls "the prose boot camp." What will it feature, in what order, and why?

From Playing the Role to Being Yourself: Becoming the Teacher in the Writing Classroom

Dawn Skorczewski

To be a good teacher partly means remaining open to reflection about one's teaching, remaining open to change, and this openness can sometimes manifest itself as anxiety about how best to comport one's self, especially when a class or even just a few students pose a significant challenge. How do we juggle the impulse toward authoritarian control over difficult classrooms with the opposite ideal? In this powerful blend of anecdote and theory, Skorczewski provides a framework for coming to terms with one's own version of this struggle to balance our institutional role with our sense of ourselves as human beings, and, as such, she implicitly invites you to begin to synthesize, in your own terms, the variety of possibilities afoot in readings by Allen, Bartholomae, and Spellmeyer.

> The situation most pregnant with the possibility for change is a system poised on the edge of chaos.
>
> —Esther Thelen and Linda B. Smith, *A Dynamic Systems Approach to the Development of Cognition and Action*

It was the end of her third day of teaching, and she could not wait to leave the campus. Although she had settled into the idea of being a teacher in a classroom on the first day and had led what she thought was a productive class discussion on the second, the next part of the task, to keep it going, was not working. She was unable to move the discussion forward. There were uncomfortable silences into which she inserted seemingly inconsequential information. A sea of blank faces stared at her in response to more than half the questions she asked. In addition, she found herself asserting authority over her students in the most banal ways: almost shouting at them as she told them they needed to speak if they were to have a productive discussion, irritated that one of the students was late for the second day in a row, and anxious that her mentor teacher would come visit the class and see her as the fraud that she knew she was. Her deepest fears about herself were surging to the surface. The worst part was that she could not talk about it with anyone she knew because they would then see that she was not qualified to teach the class.

When I first had these experiences eighteen years ago, I thought that I was alone in my fears of being an impostor rather than the teacher in a writing classroom. In the intervening years, as I moved from the position of writing instructor to director of composition, my fears have been echoed by dozens of teachers I have supervised. In my conversations with these teachers, I have tried to help them find ways of being themselves while maintaining authority in the classroom. As we shape a teaching self, we are in almost continual conversation with the internalized voices of people from our past: former teachers, teachers represented in popular culture and literature, family members, and peers. But this conversation is often unconscious and terribly messy. In the midst of this internal conversation, we may criticize ourselves for the profound disparity between what we imagine to be required of us in this role and what we are actually doing.

Like many new instructors confronting the problem of who to be in the writing classroom, I tried to imitate the good teachers I had had in the past. I imagined my first-year writing instructor, who would walk back and forth in the front of the classroom, reading a poem, cracking a joke, or telling a story about his granddaughter. He had seemed so at ease and confident in his directing of the class. I thought of other teachers as well, teachers who made me want to go home and write or stay up all night reading poetry. These teachers lived their subjects; they radiated excitement about the material and the students, and they never seemed afraid. But images of my former teachers did little to help me figure out how to conduct myself as a teacher in my classroom, to work productively with *my* 101 students. In fact, they underlined my self-doubt.

The problem with imagining myself as a teacher like my previous, almost-heroic instructors went beyond the fact that we were different people, teaching in different decades, with different students. Trying to be one of my former instructors, or some combination of them, meant somehow abandoning parts of myself. In my new role as teacher, I felt that I had to leave myself at the door, inject my former teachers' sensibilities into me, and go into class. I knew I couldn't do this. But I also knew that whoever I was in the classroom was not quite right yet, that the subjectivity of Dawn as teacher felt incommensurate to the job. I had heard that teachers become more comfortable with students over time, but I had no time to spare. I was losing my class.

In this chapter I examine how a new writing instructor negotiates the conflict between what a teacher should be and what we might call a "teaching self." Rather than providing a generic recipe for inventing a teaching self, I explore specific situations in which new instructors struggle to play the role of writing teacher as they connect with, feel disconnected from, and attempt to reconnect with students over and over again. I argue that important clues to fashioning a teaching self can be found in teachers' emotional responses to students and in what they can discern about students' emotional responses to them, particularly at the most difficult moments. The next step, I would suggest, is to try to identify, embrace, and make explicit use of our feelings, so that we can be more fully present to our students and invite them into more genuine interactions with us.

What I experienced in the classroom with my students on the third day of teaching evoked some of my most unwelcome feelings: fear, shame, and anger. Studies of new instructors invariably find that they express similar fears: of showing themselves as powerless, out of control, or unable to maintain their professional authority, fears that they do not really know who they are supposed to be in the classroom (Rankin). Jane Tompkins argues that one reason new teachers experience so much fear is that the model of teaching they are accustomed to is very much based on hierarchical models of achievement and performance: "Fear is the driving force behind the performance model. Fear of being shown up for what you are: a fraud, stupid, ignorant, a clod, a dolt, a sap, a weakling, someone who can't cut the mustard. In graduate school especially, fear is prevalent. Thinking about these things, I became aware recently that my own fear of being shown up for what I really am must transmit itself to my students, and insofar as I was afraid to be exposed, they too would be afraid" (17). Tompkins suggests that teachers' fears can create or increase students' anxieties and that teachers who are in graduate school are especially vulnerable, by virtue of their institutional positions. Rankin's study would support Tompkins's claim, for all the teachers she studied expressed anxieties about being judged.

Tompkins and Rankin might easily be describing Lucy (all names are pseudonyms), a beginning teacher at Emerson College. After her second class, she was euphoric. "It was great," she said. "They were all talking, and the text seemed to be opening up all over the place." But after her third class she was devastated. She said it was as if they had discussed it all previously and had only one thing to say about the text, which was what they had already said in the previous class. It was like those high school essays with a thesis statement plus three paragraphs, she said, the ones in which students solve the problems of the world in three steps and then remind us of what they've done.

There were other difficulties. She wrote me an e-mail about them later. "It's as if I can't really be myself with them," she wrote:

> I know that students like a strict teacher, but I am not really a strict person. I don't like imposing on anybody. I don't like to think of myself as an authority or expert in the classroom. I am not. I know I'm not, and I don't know how to pretend like I am. What's more, I do not want to pretend. I see what a teaching persona is with my sister, and frankly, I think it's false and unnecessary. But then how do I be myself as the teacher? I don't care if they like me; they don't need to like me. I don't need to be their friend. I think I'm just a lot more easygoing than they need me to be. I'm not sure what I need to do or say in order to seem less easygoing without feeling like a phony. Tomorrow is only the fourth class, but I feel that if I don't cement the policies now, or at least understandings, then I won't be able to later on. So how do I do it? What do I say?

Lucy's message reverberates with uncertainty and questions. Who should she be? Who do they want her to be? I suggested to Lucy that, like teachers, students bring their most difficult feelings into the classroom, especially fear. Suddenly, as we began to discuss what her students might be afraid of, she seemed less frightened about her class having ground to a halt. I reminded her of her observations about the essay and suggested that she address students' fears about the difficulties of writing their first college essay. Their essays were not to follow the template that many of them were accustomed to using in high school, and no formula existed for what they were to be. She might remind them that writing is really hard work and makes her anxious—ready to clean the bathroom, raid the refrigerator, or call a friend.

Just as I could not think of how to act in front of my silenced students, Lucy could not offer her students a story of her own struggles because she was paralyzed by fear. And she could not retreat to the safety of what she knew because she had so little experience as a teacher. Her course in the theories and practices of teaching had given her no method for figuring out how to regain a firm footing in a moment of utter chaos in the classroom. In particular, she had no clue about how to calm the internal storm that this moment caused so that she could handle the external challenge.

Over the years, I have discovered the value of paying careful attention to what I am calling the "inner storm" that new instructors experience in their attempts to use authority productively in the classroom. This storm is an internal response to a mixture of things, including our institutional positions and the social categories that we are subject to both inside and outside the class: race, class, gender, ethnicity, sexuality, and religion, for example, but there are many more. Most personally, perhaps, the storm responds to students' interactions with us in the here and now.

Lucy's attention to her own inner storm relates to the concepts of self- and interactive regulation from infant research (Beebe and Lachmann 224). She actively compares what she is observing in herself to what she believes is happening in her students' minds. This process of checking in, which is very subtle, verifies whether Lucy is correct in assuming that students are bored or restless or confused. Lucy is learning to compare these observations with what she is feeling inside, to gauge where to take the group next or how to respond to a particular question or challenge.

The inner storm that Lucy experiences also harkens back to what we might call the "there and then," interactions from the past that somehow get rekindled in difficult moments (Herzog 31). Often, these interactions relate to times when we learned something about how people behave in positions of authority while we played the role of the less powerful figure in relation to that person. We might call these people, real and symbolic, the "ghosts of authority" in our classrooms. Lucy's ghosts include her sister, who is older and also a teacher and who has, in Lucy's words, bullied her since she was a small child. Lucy was afraid of becoming her sister in the classroom. But her ghosts also included people who know more than she about all kinds of things, especially teaching. They included men who had also asserted authority over her, as well as people who had criticized her for her religious devotion. Sorting out the threads of her strong reactions, those based in the here and now and those which reflect the there and then, offered one way for Lucy to identify her implicit ways of being in the classroom: of interacting with students, creating space for them or closing it down. She inherited these ways of being from the ghosts in her past and from the more general social institutions that haunt us all. Identifying these ghosts would make it easier for her to teach without being overwhelmed by their presence.

When Lucy and I next spoke, we discussed her fear from a different perspective. She said again, "I don't want to be like my sister." I asked her to tell me what that would look like. Lucy elaborated: "Well, I would be bossy and controlling. I would tell them what to do, how to do it, when to do it, and when to hand it in. I would not let them be themselves but would insist that they conform to my ideas about who they should be. I would talk a lot and listen not at all." I agreed with Lucy that this persona did not sound like a very good one for a teacher. And yet, the setting of boundaries was a necessary part of the job. I deliberated about how to proceed.

"I wonder if there is anything that is useful in what you just described," I mused. "Although I have to admit your sister sounds awful, I wonder if it might be bad for a teacher to be a bully, but also not great to be a pushover?"

Lucy nodded, commenting, "I do think I am a bit of a pushover right now."

"And I have been a bully," I said. "Like in the days when I taught at an urban middle school, and I didn't know how to keep the kids calm, so I made them each stand on a square of the classroom floor when they entered the room until they were quiet."

"Yuck," said Lucy. I nodded. We laughed.

"Well," Lucy thought out loud, "I think I might need to be a little more like a bully and a little less like a pushover. Maybe I need to set the same boundaries that my sister might, but in a different way, like the way my college writing instructor used to. He would tell us that it was our responsibility to ourselves, to him, and to the class to be on time, to have our work done, and to be ready to participate in our discussion. He was really calm, but he didn't take any crap." She also mentioned an English teacher in high school who said "you are taking advantage of my goodwill" when students started coming to class late. As a result, she allowed no students in the door if they appeared even five minutes after the class was to begin. "But nobody was late, either," said Lucy.

We discussed how "not taking any crap" could be very different from giving students crap just because we are the ones who hand out the grades, how it could be a way of setting the boundaries within which students work. When Lucy left my office, she had a more commanding gait; she seemed ready to take charge of her class. Her sense of what it meant to be a good teacher had been challenged, or disrupted, and had now been transformed into something else. And the class, as she told me later, was now prepared to meet the expectations she had for them. By the end of the term, her anxiety about holding power had become a challenge rather than an obstacle, something she thought about how to handle rather than fought as the enemy.

Deborah Britzman uses the term "personal practical knowledge" to explain that "knowledge made from the stuff of lived experience is so intimately a part of teachers' enactments that its appearance as skills becomes taken for granted. Taken for granted as well are how their discursive practices come to express something about the structure of institutional life, and the ways in which power and authority are experienced there" (*Practice Makes Practice* 4–5). Britzman describes the intersection of the personal and the institutional stories that inform our responses to students from moment to moment in the classroom. Lucy's "enactments" reflect her own "personal practical knowledge." They informed her internalized understanding of power and authority that was learned from her own familial and educational experiences, and her application of that understanding in interactions with her class. Once she became aware of not one but several internalized personae who were exerting authority within her, she seemed more willing to negotiate between them as she fashioned her own teaching self. Rather than simply resisting the strongest internalized authority figure of her sister, in a battle of two, Lucy had entered a conversation of many about how to hold power in a group.

Students are always accommodating to the interpersonal reality of the teacher's character and institutional positioning, and their accommodations, invisible to us, both reflect back to us our ways of teaching and help us to perpetuate them. This was the experience of Simon, an instructor who came to my office during the fourth week of the semester with an anxious expression on his usually serene face. "What am I going to do about Valerie?" he asked. Valerie? I repeated her name to try to get the situation back into my head. "Well, in class today, she offered another one of her zingers. She said that she didn't see the point of responding to a stupid question about some obscure readings that were arbitrarily chosen by her instructor." "And what did you say?" I asked. "Well, nothing really," he replied. "That's why I am here."

At Emerson College, undergraduates seem to feel particularly free to make comments like Valerie's. But these students will not be unfamiliar to teachers anywhere. They question their instructors about why they are writing the papers, why they are reading these readings, and why they have to take the course at all. They constitute a minority in that usually only one student per class tends to ask such questions,

There are behavorial mavericks in most every classroom.

but a majority in the sense that every teacher has one. And for every teacher, these students seem to provoke intense anxiety about the teacher's authority and how to use it.

Students like Valerie present an extreme position, but they will be familiar to instructors who think carefully about how to assert authority in classrooms. In a classroom in which the teacher holds the answers to the student's every question, Valerie's challenge to the teacher's authority might be met by an answer like, "Because you are learning something about what it means to learn to write, which is something that I know about and you do not." But in what Paulo Freire terms a problem-posing classroom, the kind of classroom Simon said he was trying to create, "the teacher is no longer the one who teaches, but one who is himself taught in dialogue with the students, who in turn while being taught also teach" (67). In this kind of classroom, students and teachers together create what we call a "class." Student challenges might be heard as comments on what is happening in the classroom already, between the people in that room, rather than as simple affronts to the authority of the instructor.

Valerie's challenge provoked Simon to figure how to hold authority in a way that was both real and purposeful in the classroom. He needed to talk about reading and writing at the same time that he actually engaged his students as human beings. Simon needed to find ways to bring his whole self to the process of teaching if he was to engage his students' whole selves. He also needed to realize that his students, including Valerie, were struggling with their own demons. Like their teachers, they can sometimes feel overwhelmed and powerless, and therefore they too shut down.

Or they erupt. When Simon talked about Valerie, I had an image of an erupting volcano. I did not share this with him, in part because I wasn't sure who was the volcano: Simon, Valerie, or the pair. I also wondered if I could be the volcano, given my concern that the class was slipping away from Simon. Keeping these thoughts to myself, I asked him what was going through *his* head as Valerie spoke.

"I was terrified," he said. "I figured there was no way I could justify myself. I mean, I've only been teaching for four weeks. What do I know?" I wondered to myself if Valerie had an inkling that this was how Simon felt; perhaps she had launched the question to articulate just that.

But I also wondered if Valerie had made Simon angry. I wondered this because of the volcano image in my head, but also because it seemed so likely. Angry students provoke our anger. I told Simon that I had had students like Valerie myself and that they made me angry, because they were questioning everything about the course, and not just what was happening at the moment. They took me away from what I was trying to accomplish with students and focused me on global issues that were not foremost in my mind. They also questioned my presence in the room as the teacher, and I already questioned that about myself. And I told him that I did not need a student to amplify my self-doubt.

But what to do, I asked aloud? I placed the question between us. I wondered what a really good teacher would do at that moment, underlining the fact that this would be our fantasy about both of us as the failed instructors trying to find our way. Simon and I began to talk about what it means to be a really good teacher, and to him, it meant being a person who *knows* something he can share with others. He described a teacher in his undergraduate institution who knew all about southern literature. Implicit in his description was a theory of knowledge as expert, factual, and book driven, as well as embodied in a person who is older, with a Ph.D. Simon knew that he should have something to say about writing, because he was the teacher, but he also knew that he could not be the teacher because he did not fit with the image—we might say, the ghost—of a knowledgeable person in a classroom that he had imagined. As he spoke, I was imagining a man with a beard and a tweed jacket: a contrast to the slim figure in khakis and a button-down shirt in front of me. I was struck by how the image in Simon's mind was much less interesting to me than Simon himself. He was a witty, playful, and creative conversationalist. He was also very mature and offered insights to other teachers in our meetings. He was reflective and calm.

I decided that we should discuss something in which Simon did feel like an expert, because it might restore his sense of safety before we continued. I asked him what he knew about his own writing process. He began to talk about discipline and difficulty, about how writing takes time, about the importance of reading to learn about style and to expand one's consciousness. These seemed to me to be very important ideas to present to a writing class, I offered. I noticed that Simon seemed different as he talked about this. He seemed to sit up straighter in his chair, to become thoughtful, probing, and relaxed. I wondered aloud if it might be useful for him to share with his students these aspects of what it means to learn to write, and he said that he hadn't really considered it. He seemed relieved to have found something he might say to Valerie and her classmates. What he had found was almost a cliché to him, knowledge close to his understanding of what it means to write, even to be alive.

I believe that Simon did not consider talking about his sense of what it means to be a writer because assuming the role of teacher can prompt us to lose sight of ourselves as struggling human beings who have limited power in the world and make us feel that we need to sound like people who know what we are doing. As part of this, we leave behind our student selves and try to sound like teaching selves. But there are students in the room with us, and we need to find ways to connect with them as individuals and as a group. To this day, this aspect of teaching remains implicit, almost magical, and is rarely discussed in our literature in any detail. And no matter how many techniques we hear about from our collegues and from teaching manuals, it is not a static process. In *First Day to Final Grade: A Graduate Student's Guide to Teaching*, Anne Curzan and Lisa Damour point out the conflict between playing

Teachers are also students & can use this 'inner student' to connect with the students in the classroom.

a role and feeling authentic: "New teachers often need to rely on 'the rules' (guidelines, due dates, syllabi) and on established teacher-student roles to create a feeling of authority. For example, many teaching assistants start by imitating favorite teachers of their own. As you get more experience and confidence, you will be able to act more natural in your role as an instructor. You will then be able to be more yourself while being a teacher" (121). Although patience and time present crucial factors in teacher development, I think that ways exist to help a new teacher be herself and act naturally other than simply waiting for the feeling to take hold. What is "natural" for a new teacher, in other words, is not teaching. But even time and doing it will not necessarily make teaching come naturally to us. We all know plenty of teachers who do not seem comfortable in the classroom after years of teaching.

For Parker Palmer, a teacher's self-knowledge is essential to this sense of confidence. In *The Courage to Teach*, Palmer argues that a teacher who learns to pay careful attention to her or his inner life produces a classroom presence that feels real to students. Wondering "who is the self that teaches?" Palmer notes that "technique" is what teachers employ until the real teacher arrives (7). He contends that we need to reclaim ourselves for the sake of our students. Stephen Brookfield, in *The Skillful Teacher*, underlines the value of developing an "inner voice": "Until you begin to trust your inner voice, until you accept the possibility that your instincts, intuitions, and insights often possess as much validity as those of the experts in the field, and until you recognize that in the contexts in which you work *you* are the expert, there is a real danger that a profoundly debilitating sense of inadequacy may settle on you" (14). Brookfield and Palmer are echoed by many theorists who underline the emotional state of the instructor as essential to teaching success.

In their emphasis on the teacher's inner life, however, these theorists do not entirely take into account the dynamic and constantly-influx relationships between teachers and those in their environment. These relationships call on and alter a teacher's inner life in innumerable ways. Moreover, they call into question the usefulness of speaking about the teacher's inner life without simultaneously addressing the life of the classroom — daily interactions with students. Britzman advises that "the unitary, noncontradictory humanist discourse of the completed self" of a teacher should be replaced by "a provisional, contradictory, and multiple understanding of subjectivity as both individual and social" (*Practice Makes Practice* 56–57). Britzman's postmodern definition of the self complicates linear understandings of a teacher's development as a confident and authoritative presence in the classroom. Maxine Greene offers a similar discussion of the teacher's self: "One's 'reality,' rather than being fixed and predefined, is a perpetual emergent, becoming increasingly multiplex, as more perspectives are taken, more texts are opened, more friendships are made" (23).

I am particularly interested in Greene's use of the term "emergent," because it represents the teacher interacting in his or her environment in an ongoing way and being shaped by those interactions. Simon does this as he becomes more curious about what his students are evoking in him and more uncertain about where they might be heading together. At the same time, he needs to be able to articulate what he, the instructor, is trying to accomplish with this particular group of students. These two aims, open-ended curiosity and certainty about the goals of the group, are indeed at cross-purposes. Still, somehow they must work together. It is as if we need to go into ourselves and out again; a successful relationship with ourselves as teachers and with a particular group of students involves negotiation and conflict as well as tremendous self-awareness. And it requires a very close attention to what can often seem like business as usual.

The concept of "emergence" is also central to nonlinear dynamic systems theory, a theory to which I have turned in my efforts to conceptualize how the interactions between a teacher and her students facilitate the development of what I term a "teaching self." Nonlinear dynamic systems theory, which originated from principles developed in physics, chemistry, and mathematics, "concern[s] problems of emergent order and complexity: how structure and patterns arise from the cooperation of many individual parts" (Thelen and Smith xiv). Nonlinear systems theory offers a view of how systems develop over time that is based on unpredictability. In dynamic systems theory, the self consists of two conflicting impulses: one, "the sense and experience of cohesiveness and continuity across time," and two, "the experience . . . of self states which can be described as multiple, shifting, nonlinear, and discontinuous" (Beebe and Lachmann 232). In other words, the developing self seeks coherence and continuity even as it is in motion, changing over time. The constant flux in our classrooms is obvious to us, and yet its implications for the teaching self, particularly the motion back and forth from what is stable to what is not, are less obvious.

First, classroom interactions take place in what we might call the "split-second world," a term coined by infant researcher Daniel Stern that describes how babies respond to their mothers as active agents, from moment to moment, almost from birth (*Interpersonal World of the Infant* 10). Although Stern uses the term to capture interactions between mother and infant and trace the infant's participation in the process of making meaning, it is useful as a way to understand any human interaction. Stern and other infant researchers make use of dynamic systems theory as they attempt to understand how infants and mothers transform from moment to moment in their interactions. In the classroom, interactions happen in a group rather than a dyad, and they are terribly subjective and fast-paced, especially for the new teacher.

Second, our capacity for organizing ourselves in front of a class is at its most precarious when we first begin to teach. In fact, in nonlinear systems theory "the transformation from the old state to the new state takes place when the system is maximally vibrating and in its least predictable condition" (Stechler 77). The new teacher might be considered, in this sense, a maximally vibrating system, as might the class of students he is trying to work with, and the inner storm that Simon described would be an indicator of the internal ramifications for the new teacher. Systems theory suggests that the "local system" may be "maximally influencing the environment" at a moment of transformation. Thus, our students provide maximal influences in our first year as a teacher, which means that dealing with them in productive ways is essential to our development as instructors. It also means that our earliest students have an influence on us that our later students will find in their classrooms. We can trust students' responses, in other words, to show us some way of becoming ourselves in the classroom.

The idea that Valerie could be helpful to Simon was exactly the opposite of what Simon thought was happening, and yet I asked him to consider it as an enabling fiction in order to facilitate the repair that I believed the two needed to achieve. But first I urged Simon to get in touch with his rage at Valerie. I asked him if he was not trusting his reactions to her because he felt that they were inappropriate: that a good teacher should never be angry at a student, and perhaps even that an older male teacher should not be angry at a female student. But being angry and acting angrily, I told him, are different. If he could trust his anger, he might find a way to make use of it and then to make a decision about what he wanted to have happen. He could, for example, use his anger to gain intensity in the classroom. He could also use his anger to make a connection with his angry student. He could embrace his anger by jumping into the room with both feet, taking hold of Valerie's question, and turning it into an issue for the class rather than a problem between him and his student. In other words, he might find a new way to connect with his student and his entire class as a result of a frightening interaction with one student.

Whatever he decided, I was trying to help Simon make use of what he was feeling rather than abandoning himself as a teacher and retreating to a position of the failed teacher who is waiting for the expert to arrive. I was crafting a theory of expertise with Simon that related to paying close attention to his feelings and responses to students in a single moment and then making explicit use of them. Simon's internal storm of anger and frustration signaled his unconscious participation in a maximally vibrating classroom system, a system ripe for change, on the brink of chaos. By attending to the part that he played in that system and by thinking carefully about the components of his own internal storm, he could ideally find a way to connect with his students and bring them all into a new understanding of what they were trying to achieve together.

One of the primary ways in which I found my own response to Simon was through the volcano image, which I took to reflect the storminess of his internal world as a teacher, the storminess of his student's internal world, and the storm of my own response to the teacher's distress. I was a maximally vibrating administrator who worried that the writing program was without a purpose. Searching for a story from my experience to calm myself, I recalled a moment from the earliest days of my teaching career, when another teacher told me how she handled a crush she had developed on a student. At first she was mortified, imagining they knew that she was not qualified to teach, that she was immature and lascivious, the female version of the lecherous male professor. Once she calmed down and realized that she would never act on her response to the student, she decided to try to find a different use for her feelings. Rather than banishing them from the room, she decided to bring her loving feelings to the entire class — in her words, to have a love affair with her class. The teacher said that she decided to pay more attention to the way she looked, to dress up for her class, as a way to let them know that they mattered to her. She prepared very carefully, with these particular students in mind. Her crush on one student turned into a new interest in teaching. In other words, her idea worked. Her desire for them seemed to feed theirs for the material they were working on together.

This teacher's ability to transform a potential disaster into a productive classroom has been of use to me in numerous interactions with teachers who are developing their teaching selves. My former colleague's example of energy being freed up and fired up has been helpful to keep in mind. It is also useful to think that students, like their teachers, want to be authentic participants in the educational process. And like their teachers, they fail at this all the time. A teacher who is herself in the classroom offers the gift of authenticity to her students. Students know when we are faking it, and they know when we are not owning our role in the story. They know, for example, when we are expressing enthusiasm for a comment or a paper that we do not actually love all that much. Students want honesty, although they may resist it, and they want permission to be themselves. Like their teachers, they know what they can voice in a certain situation and what the consequences are. Seen in this way, teaching is not like building a model airplane, getting the right part in the right order. It is dealing with real people rather than the roles to which they are assigned, and reaching inside to figure out what feels right about that.

Matthew, a confident, brilliant man and an already published writer, came to see me in despair after his second week of teaching. He felt that his students were walking all over him. They were so lively in the discussions that they almost shouted over each other to speak. One student insisted on having conversations with the people next to him throughout the class; others waltzed in fifteen minutes late. Matthew's warnings about the late policy seemed to be ignored, as did the discussions he held about listening carefully to each other and waiting for one's turn to speak. I knew Matthew to be a very successful horse trainer, and I asked what he did with unruly horses. "Oh, I know how to handle them," he said. "But these are people, and there are many of them, not just one. I am sure they know that I am new at this, and they are taking full advantage."

I offered to visit Matthew's classroom, to see the group for myself, and to offer the students a quick introduction to the college writing program, which I do every year in every class. When I arrived, the students and the instructor were in a heated discussion of a Susan Bordo essay about the female body. Each student had an advertisement on his or her desk. Questions about Bordo's theories and their relationship to the advertisements covered the board. The atmosphere was lively and engaging. But it did seem as if some of the students were talking at the same time, and one student appeared to be conducting his own class in the corner of the circle. Matthew was in the front of the room, but he seemed nervous. His arms hugged his chest, and his body was turned slightly away from his students. It was almost as if he were trying to hide in plain sight.

After Matthew introduced me, I spoke to the students about the program, detailing the requirements, the sequence of writing courses, and the portfolio grading specifications. As I spoke, the lively student in the corner spoke to his neighbor. I noticed that I was feeling irritated with him and nervous that he was attempting to derail the class. I decided to be polite, because I was feeling that he was most impolite. "Oh, I'm sorry," I said. "I didn't know you wanted to speak."

"No, it was nothing," he said, smiling at me and the students around him.

"Oh, okay." I said. "Now back to the portfolio."

After a couple of minutes he had begun to talk to his neighbors again. This time I found myself feeling less anxious, more ready to handle the situation. I looked him in the eye with an expression that might be described as quizzical and asked him if he had wanted to say something. When he said no, I said, "I'm sorry, I just got confused. It looked as if you had something you wanted to ask or say." He said no, and smiled again. I smiled. I was having fun with him, and everyone knew it. But he was having some fun too, I gathered, and no harm had yet been done.

When this sequence was repeated for a third time, I tried a different tactic. After asking him if he wanted to speak, and being told no, I laughed, and said, "You'll have to forgive me. I am getting so old that I can't speak and listen at the same time." I was making fun of myself, exaggerating my weaknesses even as I made it clear that I was older and very much in charge. I was also clarifying what was happening—the student was talking over me. Everyone laughed, including Matthew.

But I was worrying that this student was hinting at some discontent in the class as a whole. I decided to play around with this by posing and answering some devil's advocate questions of my own design. I raised questions to the class, saying: "Let's play devil's advocate. What if this portfolio is a waste of time? Why write so many essays?" A number of students hypothesized that I could be correct; they were, after all, seasoned writers. What did they need to learn? I said that they were unlike me at their age, because I had lacked confidence in myself as a writer. In fact, I noted, I still had trouble writing. I struggled to figure out what it was I was trying to say, and I asked my peers to help me define and refine my arguments. A couple of students raised their hands to say that they were more like me. They struggled with writing and worried that they were not ready to write college essays. Several others nodded. I said that perhaps there were some lessons to be learned in 101, but that if they had doubts, they were always welcome to take up their concerns with their teacher and with me. Let's give it a little time, I said, and then see where you are.

My conversation with the students is difficult to characterize, because it is so firmly based in the particulars of these students, their teacher, and me. I would not have made some of the statements I did in the way that I did in a different classroom. I developed a sense of where these students were, and I went with it. It is also very much based on eye contact and the way we held our bodies, the space we occupied, and the movements we made as we spoke and listened. When they laughed and seemed to be enjoying themselves, for example, I kept going in the direction I was heading in, because it looked like it was working. When they grew quiet, I withdrew a bit to assess the situation. But even as I responded to this group, I drew from what I knew about students' doubts concerning composition courses over the years. I pursued students' uncertainties, which I might at one time have determined as stemming from my own inadequacies as a teacher. In a way, I attempted to make use of John Keats's concept of "negative capability," which I had learned about when I was their age: "That is when man is capable of being in uncertainties, mysteries, doubt, without any irritable reaching after fact and reason" (Keats 43). What I once might have tried to hide, I now shaped into material for the class to discuss.

It is important to identify how the unruly student played a part in this dynamic and how I found a way to work with him and his classmates despite the irritation that he provoked. At first, his comments distracted me, and I looked over at him, wanting him to stop so that I could continue speaking. As he ignored my gaze and continued to speak, I became more irritated. He seemed to become louder, although this may have been my imagination. The longer he spoke and the more he tried to speak (this must in reality have been a matter of minutes), the more distracted and irritated I became. I was aware that I was beginning to feel angry and that I wanted to tell him to be quiet, that he was rude. I knew that this would not work, however. First, I was a visitor in his class; second, if I were to attack him this way, both he and his classmates would lose respect for me.

I then tried to make use of my anger by transforming it into something different: curiosity. When that did not work, and my anger increased, I tried another option: playful but subdued banter. Finally, I moved to more pronounced banter. With each step, I checked the reactions of the class and the student as I proceeded. If they had seemed provoked or angered or insulted, I might have backed off and waited a bit before pursuing the difficulty. If it were my own class, I would have considered a pedagogical tool such as the one-minute essay or a quick, directed group exercise to change the energy in the room. Changing the energy in the room was directly related, of course, to changing the energy in myself—from anger to something more useful. The energy in myself might also be termed "countertransference."

This movement from the inside to the outside is essential to the work of a successful teacher who is authoritative and authentic in the classroom, and expert teachers make such a move unconsciously. When we slow down the process, as I did above, we can see that there is a constant shifting from recognizing our own feelings to attempting to perceive the feelings of our students, to using our feelings as we respond to what we believe is happening with our students. All of this occurs in the background as we are talking about something quite different: the reading for the day, an aspect of writing, a sample paper, or a grammatical issue. In the example above, I tried to respond without anger, fear, or self-doubt; these are unproductive emotions for an authority figure to voice toward students most of the time, but they are certainly useful when transformed into something else.

We might imagine that the balance between our internal experiences and our external actions involves a balance between self and other. But psychoanalytic theory and infant research provide another way of understanding this movement: "What is in balance is not self and other, but, rather, the processes of self- and interactive regulation. Each person is always sensing and modulating her own state, while simultaneously sensing how she affects and is affected by her partner. What is in balance is the degree to which one can flexibly go back and forth, in foreground-background fashion, between both processes" (Beebe and Lachmann 244). Improvisational theater offers the same point from a different perspective: "Practice in improvisational theatre . . . enhance[s] the teacher's ability to be 'in the moment,' to be flexible, to temporarily suspend their teaching strategies or their rules about their relationship with their student in order to enter into an authentic, personal interaction" (Tiberius and Tipping 11).

My effort to be authentic with the student concluded when he came up after class to chat a bit about the course. His first words were that he was dyslexic. He said that he had never done well in a writing class before, and he was sure he wouldn't this time. His teacher, he, and I discussed the Learning Assistance Center. He agreed that he would go there and that he would visit my office to discuss what, if anything, the Composition Program could do to help him. It seemed to me that, as is often the case, this student disrupted the class because of his own self-doubts. He was afraid he did not belong in this class, that he could not do the work required. He spoke to his classmate while I was speaking as a way of participating in the class by exerting some control, perhaps, or to distract himself from the enormous anxieties provoked by his presence there.

The teacher came to visit me after the class and looked enormously relieved. "That was weird," he said. "Watching you in class, I remembered having you as a teacher. It felt like you were just being yourself with them, and they responded to that. At the same time, they got that you meant business. I think I have been struggling with how to be myself and also mean business, and I thought that it was impossible to do both at the same time."

The question is how a teacher becomes confident in his work, a teacher who "means business," even as he "is himself" in the classroom. In the story above, that involved trying to figure out where the students were while keeping sight of where the teacher wanted them to be. The difficult student in the corner, I had mused, wanted attention, but he also wanted to invent a new class over in the corner to substitute for the one I was leading. I wanted us to be one class, working on the problem of writing successful research papers together, and so I had to harness the student's energy and move it in a different direction. But whether we moved in such a direction depended very much on the student's willingness to go there. In our dialogue, I implicitly asked his permission to join me in this new venture.

My friend Barrie, a teacher whom I have known for almost twenty years, recently showed me her first teaching notebook. It contained page after page of color-coded charts. Some of the charts denoted sample quotations from the text; others, possible questions; and others, possible answers. If a student answered A on question 1 about line 3 of the poem, then she'd proceed to the orange question 2, which went deeper into that line. But if the student answered B, then she'd try question 4, which headed to another part of the poem. And so on. We laughed and laughed as we looked at this notebook, imagining ourselves trying to use such a complex script now, so many years after we had begun teaching. And yet, my friend said rather seriously, she would have felt completely lost without it then.

Barrie's system, bizarre as it may sound, gave her a feeling of control over the direction of the class. But unlike a lecture, it had options. So she felt that she could give her students room to explore many directions rather than simply one. Students could produce many interpretations of a poem, for example, and many essays about it. Now, she does not need the chart because she has learned how to be open to students' ideas in a classroom without losing sight of a direction in which the class can move.

Becoming yourself as a teacher involves, more than anything, telling yourself who you are and who you are not in the classroom. Although we might have trouble remembering who we are not at the most difficult times, we are not the fearful daughters, sons, and students that we once might have been. We are not the students who, like my friend Marie, had a famous professor in graduate school who wrote on her evaluation, "Very poorly trained when she got here, she gets nearly everything wrong. She should not be allowed to remain in a graduate program in English." Yet we sometimes react as if we were still in these roles. We defensively make statements as I did in my first week of teaching: "It's not my job to keep the discussion going."

When we become ourselves in the writing classroom, we offer students opportunities rather than accusations. We channel our fears into productive comments. During a silence, we might ask them to find a quote and share it with the class. Or when a student seems to need attention, we might direct attention to the context of the classroom, for example, or use the needy student as a volunteer for a writing workshop. We work with our students and attempt to clear a space for everyone to speak. We call on students to invite them into the conversation and work to link one student's comments to another's.

In addition to all this, the teacher acts as the living memory for the class. We hold the class up to the class in front of our students, to show them who we are and what we are making together. We remind the class of where we have been together and where we are heading. In this way, we bring the outside world into the classroom to be transformed into knowledge. We remind our students that we are thinking about them when we are not in the classroom, that conversations we've had in class have influenced our understanding of events that have happened outside class. In the process, we initiate our students into an intellectual world in which school and the outside are part of the same continuum, a world in which reading and writing are real and in which real change can happen from the knowledge that we construct together.

Most of us would admit that fear poses a challenge in our lives. But can we move beyond fear, or embrace our fear, in order to create beauty in the classroom? When the classroom becomes a place where students can feel their fear, and any other feeling that they experience as forbidden, they no longer need to separate the process of learning from the process of being human. And when teachers do the same, however silently, we join students in the effort to achieve deeper understanding. Teaching and learning involve being in the moment in a total way, as a whole person. When there is a disruption, such as those I described above, a teacher can embrace the experience rather than trying to send it out of the room. If we accept fear as part of who we are, we can be fully present in the moment and open to the experience of a changing classroom that is part of a changing world.

Works Cited

Beebe, Beatrice, and Frank M. Lachmann. *Infant Research and Adult Treatment: Coconstructing Interactions*. Hillsdale, N.J.: Analytic Press, 2002.

Bordo, Susan. "Hunger as Ideology." In *Unbearable Weight: Feminism, Western Culture, and the Body*, 99–134. Berkeley: University of California Press, 1993.

Britzman, Deborah. *Practice Makes Practice: A Critical Study of Learning to Teach*. Albany: State University of New York Press, 1991.

Brookfield, Stephen. *The Skillful Teacher*. San Francisco: Jossey-Bass, 1990.

Curzan, Anne, and Lisa Damour. *First Day to Final Grade: A Graduate Student's Guide to Teaching*. Ann Arbor: University of Michigan Press, 2000.

Freire, Paulo. *Pedagogy of the Oppressed*. New York: Seabury Press, 1973.

Greene, Maxine. *Releasing the Imagination: Essays on Education, the Arts, and Social Change*. San Francisco: Jossey-Bass, 2000.

Herzog, James M. *Father Hunger: Explorations with Adults and Children*. Hillsdale, N.J.: Analytic Press, 2001.

Keats, John. *Letters of John Keats*. Edited by Robert Gittings. Oxford: Oxford University Press, 1970.

Palmer, Parker. *The Courage to Teach*. San Francisco: Jossey-Bass, 1998.

Rankin, Elizabeth Deane. *Seeing Yourself as Teacher: Conversations with Five New Teachers in a University Writing Program*. Urbana, Ill.: National Council of Teachers of English, 1994.

Stechler, Gerald. "Louis W. Sander and the Question of Affective Presence." *Infant Mental Health* 21 (2000): 75–84.

Stern, Daniel. *The Interpersonal World of the Infant*. New York: Basic, 1985.

Thelen, Esther, and Linda B. Smith. *A Dynamic Systems Approach to the Development of Cognition and Action*. Cambridge: MIT Press, 1994.

Tiberius, Richard G., and Jane Tipping. "The Discussion Leader: Fostering Student Learning in Groups." In *Teaching Alone, Teaching Together: Transforming the Structure of Teams for Teaching*, edited by James L. Bess and associates, 108–30. San Francisco: Jossey-Bass, 2000.

Tompkins, Jane. *A Life in School: What the Teacher Learned*. Reading, Mass.: Addison-Wesley, 1996.

Skorczewski's Insights as a Resource for Your Reflections

1. Some have suggested that, depending upon one's race, gender, and institutional position, one might either automatically have authority until one does something significant to lose it, or never

have authority until one does something significant to earn it. How might this notion add to your thinking about the cases Skorczewski examines? How might it add to your thinking about your own situation as a teacher?

2. Skorczewski uses systems theory and ideas about chaos as well as ideas about early childhood development to explore classroom dynamics, and the insights she thereby generates have far-reaching implications for all of us. Consider, in particular, one instance of the classroom interaction — either as described by Skorczewski or from your own experience — and use her concepts to map what might be happening in that instance and what alternatives, ideally, might happen next.

Skorczewski's Insights as a Resource for Your Writing Classroom

1. Discuss with your students the very concepts that Skorczewski sketches here. How might these ideas, as applied to teaching, also apply to the writing process? How might students describe the value of chaos within the larger goal of growth?
2. Ask your students to discuss the issue of intellectual authority, how it works both inside and outside of school. What are the differences, and what are the sources of these differences?

Rhetoric and Ideology in the Writing Class

James A. Berlin

What are the larger traditions of thought that organize the teaching of writing in modern times? This classic essay provides an introduction to the theories that Berlin developed fully in his 1987 book Rhetoric and Reality: Writing Instruction in American Colleges, 1900–1985. *According to Berlin, an ideology addresses three questions: What exists? What is good? What is possible? Berlin suggests that there are three competing ideologies of writing instruction in our time: (1) cognitivist, (2) expressionist, and (3) social-epistemic. Each of these three ideologies carries its own notion of what writing is, what good writing and teaching are, and what we should aspire to accomplish with our students. Each of the three also represents a political stance, a take on the power relations that exist among author, audience, and text, as well as between teacher and student. This valuable essay can be used as a bibliography for further reading about these different approaches. Given the variety of pieces about teaching composition that you've read in this unit so far, consider using Berlin's taxonomy to link or oppose them to each other in ways that open up a greater and greater sense in their implications.*

The question of ideology has never been far from discussions of writing instruction in the modern American college. It is true that some rhetorics have denied their imbrication in ideology, doing so in the name of a disinterested scientism — as seen, for example, in various manifestations of current-traditional rhetoric. Most, however, have acknowledged the role of rhetoric in addressing competing discursive claims of value in the social, political, and cultural. This was particularly evident during the sixties and seventies, for example, as the writing classroom became one of the public areas for considering such strongly contested issues as Vietnam, civil rights, and economic equality. More recently the discussion of the relation between ideology and rhetoric has taken a new turn. Ideology is here foregrounded and problematized in a way that situates rhetoric within ideology, rather than ideology within rhetoric. In other words, instead of rhetoric acting as the transcendental recorder or arbiter of competing ideological claims, rhetoric is regarded as always already ideological. This position means that any examination of a rhetoric must first consider the ways its very discursive structure can be read so as to favor one version of economic, social, and political arrangements over other versions. A rhetoric then considers competing claims in these three realms from an ideological perspective made possible both by its constitution and by its application — the dialectical interaction between the rhetoric as text and the interpretive practices brought to it. A rhetoric can never be innocent, can never be a disinterested arbiter of the ideological claims of others because it is always already serving certain ideological claims. This perspective on ideology and rhetoric will be discussed in greater detail later. Here I merely wish to note that it has been forwarded most recently by such figures as Patricia Bizzell, David Bartholomae, Greg Myers, Victor Vitanza, and John Clifford and John Schilb. I have also called upon it in my monograph on writing instruction in twentieth-century American colleges. I would like to bring the discussion I began there up to date, focusing on ideology in the three rhetorics that have emerged as most conspicuous in classroom practices today: the rhetorics of cognitive psychology, of expressionism, and of a category I will call social-epistemic.

Each of these rhetorics occupies a distinct position in its relation to ideology. From the perspective offered here, the rhetoric of cognitive psychology refuses the ideological question altogether, claiming for itself the transcendent neutrality of science. This rhetoric is nonetheless easily preempted by a particular ideological position now in ascendancy because it encourages discursive practices that are compatible with dominant economic, social, and political formations. Expressionistic rhetoric, on the other hand, has always openly admitted its ideological predilections, opposing itself in no uncertain terms to the scientism of current-traditional rhetoric and the ideology it encourages. This rhetoric is, however, open to appropriation by the very forces it opposes in contradiction to its best intentions. Social-epistemic rhetoric is an alternative that is self-consciously aware of its ideological stand, making the very question of ideology the center of classroom activities, and in so doing providing itself a defense against preemption and a strategy for self-criticism and self-correction. This third rhetoric is the one I am forwarding here, and it provides the ground of my critique of its alternatives. In other words, I am arguing from ideology, contending that no other kind of argument is possible — a position that must first be explained.

Ideology is a term of great instability. This is true whether it is taken up by the Left or Right — as demonstrated, for example, by Raymond Williams in *Keywords* and *Marxism and Literature* and by Jorge Larrain in *The Concept of Ideology*. It is thus necessary to indicate at the outset the formulation that will be followed in a given discussion. Here I will rely on Göran Therborn's usage in *The Ideology of Power and the Power of Ideology*. Therborn, a Marxist sociologist at the University of Lund, Sweden, calls on the discussion of ideology found in Louis Althusser and on the discussion of power in Michel Foucault. I have chosen Therborn's adaptation of Althusser rather than Althusser himself because Therborn so effectively counters the ideology-science distinction of his source, a stance in which ideology is always false consciousness while a particular version of Marxism is defined as its scientific alternative in possession of objective truth. For Therborn, no position can lay claim to absolute, timeless truth, because finally all formulations are historically specific, arising out of the material conditions of a particular time and place. Choices in the economic, social, political, and cultural are thus always based on discursive practices that are interpretations, not mere transcriptions of some external, verifiable certainty. The choice for Therborn then is never between scientific truth and ideology, but between competing ideologies, competing discursive interpretations. Finally, Therborn calls upon Foucault's "micropolitics of power" (7) without placing subjects within a seamless web of inescapable, wholly determinative power relations. For Therborn, power can be identified and resisted in a meaningful way.

Therborn offers an especially valuable discussion for rhetoricians because of his emphasis on the discursive and dialogic nature of ideology.

In other words, Therborn insists that ideology is transmitted through language practices that are always the center of conflict and contest:

> The operation of ideology in human life basically involves the constitution and patterning of how human beings live their lives as conscious, reflecting initiators of acts in a structured, meaningful world. Ideology operates as discourse, addressing or, as Althusser puts it, interpellating human beings as subjects. (15)

Conceived from the perspective of rhetoric, ideology provides the language to define the subject (the self), other subjects, the material world, and the relation of all of these to each other. Ideology is thus inscribed in language practices, entering all features of our experience.

Ideology for Therborn addresses three questions: "What exists? What is good? What is possible?" The first deals with epistemology, as Therborn explains: "what exists, and its corollary, what does not exist: that is, who we are, what the world is, what nature, society, men and women are like. In this way we acquire a sense of identity, becoming conscious of what is real and true; the visibility of the world is thereby structured by the distribution of spotlights, shadows, and darkness." Ideology thus interpellates the subject in a manner that determines what is real and what is illusory, and, most important, what is experienced and what remains outside the field of phenomenological experience, regardless of its actual material existence. Ideology also provides the subject with standards for making ethical and aesthetic decisions: "*what is good*, right, just, beautiful, attractive, enjoyable, and its opposites. In this way our desires become structured and normalized." Ideology provides the structure of desire, indicating what we will long for and pursue. Finally, ideology defines the limits of expectation: "*what is possible* and impossible; our sense of the mutability of our being-in-the-world and the consequences of change are hereby patterned, and our hopes, ambitions, and fears given shape" (18). This last is especially important since recognition of the existence of a condition (poverty, for example) and the desire for its change will go for nothing if ideology indicates that a change is simply not possible (the poor we have always with us). In other words, this last mode of interpellation is especially implicated in power relationships in a group or society, in deciding who has power and in determining what power can be expected to achieve.

Ideology always carries with it strong social endorsement, so that what we take to exist, to have value, and to be possible seems necessary, normal, and inevitable — in the nature of things. Ideology also, as we have seen, always includes conceptions of how power should — again, in the nature of things — be distributed in a society. Power here means political force but covers as well social forces in everyday contacts. Power is an intrinsic part of ideology, defined and reinforced by it, determining, once again, who can act and what can be accomplished. These power relationships, furthermore, are inscribed in the discursive practices of daily experience — in the ways we use language and are used (interpellated) by it in ordinary parlance. Finally, it should be noted that ideology is always pluralistic, a given historical moment displaying a variety of competing ideologies and a given individual reflecting one or another permutation of these conflicts, although the overall effect of these permutations tends to support the hegemony of the dominant class.

Cognitive Rhetoric

Cognitive rhetoric might be considered the heir apparent of current-traditional rhetoric, the rhetoric that appeared in conjunction with the new American university system during the final quarter of the last century. As Richard Ohmann has recently reminded us, this university was a response to the vagaries of competitive capitalism, the recurrent cycles of boom and bust that characterized the nineteenth-century economy. The university was an important part of the strategy to control this economic instability. Its role was to provide a center for experts engaging in "scientific" research designed to establish a body of knowledge that would rationalize all features of production, making it more efficient, more manageable, and, of course, more profitable. These experts were also charged with preparing the managers who were to take this new body of practical knowledge into the marketplace. The old nineteenth-century college had prepared an elite to assume its rightful place of leadership in church and state. The economic ideal outside the college was entirely separate, finding its fulfillment in the self-made, upwardly mobile entrepreneur who strikes it rich. The academic and the economic remained divided and discrete. In the new university, the two were joined as the path to success became a university degree in one of the new scientific specialities proven to be profitable in the world of industry and commerce. The new middle class of certified meritocrats had arrived. As I have indicated in my monograph on the nineteenth century, current-traditional rhetoric with its positivistic epistemology, its pretensions to scientific precision, and its managerial orientation was thoroughly compatible with the mission of this university.

Cognitive rhetoric has made similar claims to being scientific, although the method called upon is usually grounded in cognitive psychology. Janet Emig's *The Composing Process of Twelfth Graders* (1971), for example, attempted an empirical examination of the way students compose, calling on the developmental psychology of Jean Piaget in guiding her observations. In studying the cognitive skills observed in the composing behavior of twelve high school students, Emig was convinced that she could arrive at an understanding of the entire rhetorical context—the role of reality, audience, purpose, and even language in the composing act. Richard Larson was equally ambitious as throughout the seventies he called upon the developmental scheme of Jerome Bruner (as well as other psychologists) in proposing a problem-solving approach to writing, once again focusing on cognitive structures in arriving at an understanding of how college students compose. James Moffett and James Britton used a similar approach in dealing with the writing of students in grade school. For cognitive rhetoric, the structures of the mind correspond in perfect harmony with the structures of the material world, the minds of the audience, and the units of language (see my *Rhetoric and Reality* for a fuller discussion of this history). This school has been the strongest proponent of addressing the "process" rather than the "product" of writing in the classroom—although other theories have also supported this position even as they put forward a different process. Today the cognitivists continue to be a strong force in composition studies. The leading experimental research in this area is found in the work of Linda Flower and John Hayes, and I would like to focus the discussion of the relation of ideology and cognitive rhetoric on their contribution.

There is no question that Flower considers her work to fall within the domain of science, admitting her debt to cognitive psychology (Hayes's area of specialization), which she describes as "a young field—a reaction, in part, against assumptions of behaviorism" (vii). Her statements about the composing process of writing, furthermore, are based on empirical findings, on "data-based" study, specifically the analysis of protocols recording the writing choices of both experienced and inexperienced writers. This empirical study has revealed to Flower and Hayes—as reported in "A Cognitive Process Theory of Writing"—that there are three elements involved in composing: the task environment, including such external constraints as the rhetorical problem and the text so far produced; the writer's long-term memory, that is, the knowledge of the subject considered and the knowledge of how to write; and the writing processes that go on in the writer's mind. This last is, of course, of central importance to them, based as it is on the invariable structures of the mind that operate in a rational, although not totally predictable, way.

The mental processes of writing fall into three stages: the planning stage, further divided into generating, organizing, and goal setting; the translating stage, the point at which thoughts are put into words; and the reviewing stage, made up of evaluating and revising. This process is hierarchical, meaning that "components of the process [are] imbedded within other components" (Flower and Hayes 375), and it is recursive, the stages repeating themselves, although in no predetermined order. In other words, the elements of the process can be identified and their functions described, but the order of their operation will vary from task to task and from individual to individual, even though the practices of good writers will be very similar to each other (for a rich critique, see Bizzell). The "keystone" of the cognitive process theory, Flower and Hayes explain, is the discovery that writing is a goal-directed process: "In the act of composing, writers create a hierarchical network of goals and these in turn guide the writing process." Because of this goal-directedness, the protocols of good writers examined consistently "reveal a coherent underlying structure" (377).

It is clear from this brief description that Flower and Hayes focus on the individual mind, finding in the protocol reports evidence of cognitive structures in operation. Writing becomes, as Flower's textbook indicates, just another instance of "problem-solving processes people use every day," most importantly the processes of experts, such as "master chess players, inventors, successful scientists, business managers, and artists" (Flower 2–3). Flower's textbook says little about artists, however, focusing instead on "real-world" writing. She has accordingly called upon the help of a colleague from the School of Industrial Management (vi), and she includes a concern for consulting reports and proposals as well as ordinary academic research reports — "the real world of college and work" (4). This focus on the professional activity of experts is always conceived in personal and managerial terms: "In brief, the goal of this book is to help you gain more control of your own composing process: to become more efficient as a writer and more effective with your readers" (2). And the emphasis is on self-made goals, "on your own goals as a writer, on what you want to do and say" (3).

As I said at the outset, the rhetoric of cognitive psychology refuses the ideological question, resting secure instead in its scientific examination of the composing process. It is possible, however, to see this rhetoric as being eminently suited to appropriation by the proponents of a particular ideological stance, a stance consistent with the modern college's commitment to preparing students for the world of corporate capitalism. And as we have seen above, the professional orientation of *Problem-Solving Strategies for Writing* — its preoccupation with "analytical writing" (4) in the "real world" of experts — renders it especially open to this appropriation.

For cognitive rhetoric, the real is the rational. As we observed above, for Flower and Hayes the most important features of composing are those which can be analyzed into discrete units and expressed in linear, hierarchical terms, however unpredictably recursive these terms may be. The mind is regarded as a set of structures that performs in a rational manner, adjusting and reordering functions in the service of the goals of the individual. The goals themselves are considered unexceptionally apparent in the very nature of things, immediately identifiable as worthy of pursuit. Nowhere, for example, do Flower and Hayes question the worth of the goals pursued by the manager, scientist, or writer. The business of cognitive psychology is to enable us to learn to think in a way that will realize goals, not deliberate about their value: "I have assumed that, whatever your goals, you are interested in discovering better ways to achieve them" (Flower and Hayes 1). The world is correspondingly structured to foreground goals inherently worth pursuing — whether these are private or professional, in writing or in work. And the mind is happily structured to perceive these goals and, thanks to the proper cognitive development of the observer — usually an expert — to attain them. Obstacles to achieving these goals are labelled "problems," disruptions in the natural order, impediments that must be removed. The strategies to resolve these problems are called "heuristics," discovery procedures that "are the heart of problem solving" (36). Significantly, these heuristics are not themselves rational, are not linear and predictable — "they do not come with a guarantee" (37). They appear normally as unconscious, intuitive processes that problem solvers use without realizing it, but even when formulated for conscious application they are never foolproof. Heuristics are only as good or bad as the person using them, so that problem solving is finally the act of an individual performing in isolation, solitary and alone (see Brodkey). As Flower explains: "Good writers not only have a large repertory of powerful strategies, but they have sufficient self-awareness of their own process to draw on these alternative techniques as they need them. In other words, they guide their own creative process" (37). The community addressed enters the process only after problems are analyzed and solved, at which time the concern is "adapting your writing to the needs of the reader" (1). Furthermore, although the heuristics used in problem solving are not themselves rational, the discoveries made through them always conform to the mensurable nature of reality, displaying "an underlying hierarchical organization" (10) that reflects the rationality of the world. Finally, language is regarded as a system of rational signs that is compatible with the mind and the external world, enabling the "translating" or "transforming" of the non-verbal intellectual operations into the verbal. There is thus a beneficent correspondence between the structures of the mind, the structures of the world, the structures of the minds of the audience, and the structures of language.

This entire scheme can be seen as analogous to the instrumental method of the modern corporation, the place where members of the meritocratic middle class, the 20 percent or so of the work force of certified college graduates, make a handsome living managing a capitalist economy (see Braverman ch. 18). Their work life is designed to turn goal-seeking and problem-solving behavior into profits. As we have seen in Flower, the rationalization of the writing process is specifically designated an extension of the rationalization of economic activity. The pursuit of self-evident and unquestioned goals in the composing process parallels the pursuit of self-evident and unquestioned profit-making goals in the corporate marketplace: "whatever your goals are, you are interested in achieving better ways to achieve them" (Flower 12). The purpose of writing is to create a commodified text (see Clines) that belongs to the individual and has exchange value — "problem solving turns composing into a goal-directed journey — writing my way to where I want to be" (4) — just as the end of corporate activity is to create a privately-owned profit. Furthermore, while all problem solvers use heuristic procedures — whether in solving hierarchically conceived writing problems or hierarchically conceived management problems — some are better at using them than are others. These individuals inevitably distinguish themselves, rise up the corporate ladder, and leave the less competent and less competitive behind. The class system is thus validated since it is clear that the rationality of the universe is more readily detected by a certain group of individuals. Cognitive psychologists specializing in childhood development can even isolate the environmental features of the children who will become excellent problem solvers, those destined to earn the highest grades in school, the highest college entrance scores, and, finally, the highest salaries. Middle-class parents are thus led to begin the cultivation of their children's cognitive skills as soon as possible — even in utero — and of course there are no shortage of expert-designed commodities that can be purchased to aid in the activity. That the cognitive skills leading to success may be the product of the experiences of a particular social class rather than the perfecting of inherent mental structures, skills encouraged because they serve the interests of a ruling economic elite, is never considered in the "scientific" investigation of the mind.

Cognitive rhetoric can be seen from this perspective as compatible with the ideology of the meritocratic university described in Bowles and Gintis's *Schooling in Capitalist America*. Power in this system is relegated to university-certified experts, those individuals who have the cognitive skills and the training for problem solving. Since social, political, and cultural problems are, like the economic, the result of failures in rational goal-seeking behavior, these same experts are the best prepared to address these matters as well. Furthermore, the agreement of experts in addressing commonly shared problems in the economic and political arenas is additional confirmation of their claim to power: all trained observers, after all, come to the same conclusions. Once again, the possibility that this consensus about what is good and possible is a product of class interest and class experience is never seriously entertained. Cognitive rhetoric, then, in its refusal of the ideological question leaves itself open to association with the reification of technocratic science characteristic of late capitalism, as discussed, for example, by Georg Lukács, Herbert Marcuse, and Jürgen Habermas (see Larrain ch. 6). Certain structures of the material world, the mind, and language, and their correspondence with certain goals, problem-solving heuristics, and solutions in the economic, social, and political are regarded as inherent features of the universe, existing apart from human social intervention. The existent, the good, and the possible are inscribed in the very nature of things as indisputable scientific facts, rather than being seen as humanly devised social constructions always remaining open to discussion.

Expressionistic Rhetoric

Expressionistic rhetoric developed during the first two decades of the twentieth century and was especially prominent after World War I. Its earliest predecessor was the elitist rhetoric of liberal culture, a scheme arguing for writing as a gift of genius, an art accessible only to a few, and then requiring years of literary study. In expressionistic rhetoric, this gift is democratized, writing becoming an art of which all are capable. This rhetoric has usually been closely allied with theories of psychology that argued for the inherent goodness of the individual, a goodness distorted by excessive contact with others in groups and institutions. In this it is the descendant of Rousseau on the one hand and of the romantic recoil from the urban horrors created by nineteenth-century capitalism on the other. Left to our own devices, this position maintains, each of us would grow and mature in harmony. Unfortunately, hardly anyone is allowed this uninhibited development, and so the fallen state of society is both the cause and the effect of its own distortion, as well as the corrupter of its individual members. In the twenties, a bowdlerized version of Freud was called upon in support of this conception of human nature. More recently — during the sixties and after — the theories of such figures as Carl Rogers, Abraham Maslow, Eric Fromm, and even Carl Jung have been invoked in its support. (For a fuller discussion of the history and character of expressionistic rhetoric offered here, see my "Contemporary Composition," and *Rhetoric and Reality* 43–46, 73–81, 159–65.)

For this rhetoric, the existent is located within the individual subject. While the reality of the material, the social, and the linguistic are never denied, they are considered significant only insofar as they serve the needs of the individual. All fulfill their true function only when being exploited in the interests of locating the individual's authentic nature. Writing can be seen as a paradigmatic instance of this activity. It is an art, a creative act in which the process — the discovery of the true self — is as important as the product — the self discovered and expressed. The individual's use of the not-self in discovering the self takes place in a specific way. The material world provides sensory images that can be used in order to explore the self, the sensations leading to the apprehending-source of all experience. More important, these sense impressions can be coupled with language to provide metaphors to express the experience of the self, an experience which transcends ordinary nonmetaphoric language but can be suggested through original figures and tropes. This original language in turn can be studied by others to understand the self and can even awaken in readers the experience of their selves. Authentic self-expression can thus lead to authentic self-experience for both the writer and the reader. The most important measure of authenticity, of genuine self-discovery and self-revelation, furthermore, is the presence of originality in expression; and this is the case whether the writer is creating poetry or writing a business report. Discovering the true self in writing will simultaneously enable the individual to discover the truth of the situation which evoked the writing, a situation that, needless to say, must always be compatible with the development of the self, and this leads to the ideological dimension of the scheme.

Most proponents of expressionistic rhetoric during the sixties and seventies were unsparingly critical of the dominant social, political, and cultural practices of the time. The most extreme of these critics demanded that the writing classroom work explicitly toward liberating students from the shackles of a corrupt society. This is seen most vividly in the effort known as "composition as happening." From this perspective, the alienating and fragmenting experience of the authoritarian institutional setting can be resisted by providing students with concrete experiences that alter political consciousness through challenging official versions of reality. Writing in response to such activities as making collages and sculptures, listening to the same piece of music in different settings, and engaging in random and irrational acts in the classroom was to enable students to experience "structure in unstructure; a random series of ordered events; order in chaos; the logical illogicality of dreams" (Lutz 35). The aim was to encourage students to resist the "interpretations of experience embodied in the language of others [so as] to order their own experience" (Paull and Kligerman). This more extreme form of political activism in the classroom was harshly criticized by the moderate wing of the expressionist camp, and it is this group that eventually became dominant. The names of Ken Macrorie, Walker Gibson, William Coles, Jr., Donald Murray, and Peter Elbow were the most visible in this counter effort. Significantly, these figures continued the ideological critique of the dominant culture while avoiding the overt politicizing of the classroom. In discussing the ideological position they encouraged, a position that continues to characterize them today, I will focus on the work of Murray and Elbow, both of whom explicitly address the political in their work.

From this perspective, power within society ought always to be vested in the individual. In Elbow, for example, power is an abiding concern — apparent in the title to his recent textbook (*Writing with Power*), as well as in the opening pledge of his first to help students become "less helpless, both personally and politically" by enabling them to get "control over words" (*Writing without Teachers* vii). This power is consistently defined in personal terms: "power comes from the words somehow fitting the *writer* (not necessarily the reader) . . . power comes from the words somehow fitting *what they are about*" (*Writing with Power* 280).

Power is a product of a configuration involving the individual and her encounter with the world, and for both Murray and Elbow this is a function of realizing one's unique voice. Murray's discussion of the place of politics in the classroom is appropriately titled "Finding Your Own Voice: Teaching Composition in an Age of Dissent," and Elbow emphasizes, "If I want power, I've got to use *my* voice" (*Embracing Contraries* 202). This focus on the individual does not mean that no community is to be encouraged, as expressionists repeatedly acknowledge that communal arrangements must be made, that, in Elbow's words, "the less acceptable hunger for participation and merging is met" (98). The community's right to exist, however, stands only insofar as it serves all of its members as individuals. It is, after all, only the individual, acting alone and apart from others, who can determine the existent, the good, and the possible. For Murray, the student "must hear the contradictory counsel of his readers, so that he learns when to ignore his teachers and his peers, listening to himself after evaluating what has been said about his writing and considering what he can do to make it work" ("Finding Your Own Voice"). For Elbow, the audience can be used to help improve our writing, but "the goal should be to move toward the condition where we don't necessarily need it in order to speak or write well." Since audiences can also inhibit us, Elbow continues, "we need to learn to write what is true and what needs saying even if the whole world is scandalized. We need to learn eventually to find in *ourselves* the support which—perhaps for a long time—we must seek openly from others" (*Writing with Power* 190).

Thus, political change can only be considered by individuals and in individual terms. Elbow, for example, praises Freire's focus on the individual in seeking the contradictions of experience in the classroom but refuses to take into account the social dimension of this pedagogy, finally using Freire's thought as an occasion for arriving at a personal realization of a "psychological contradiction, not an economic one or political one," at the core of our culture (*Embracing Contraries* 98). The underlying conviction of expressionists is that when individuals are spared the distorting effects of a repressive social order, their privately determined truths will correspond to the privately determined truths of all others: my best and deepest vision supports the same universal and eternal laws as everyone else's best and deepest vision. Thus, in *Writing without Teachers* Elbow admits that his knowledge about writing was gathered primarily from personal experience, and that he has no reservations about "making universal generalizations upon a sample of one" (16). Murray is even more explicit in his first edition of *A Writer Teaches Writing*: "the writer is on a search for himself. If he finds himself he will find an audience, because all of us have the same common core. And when he digs deeply into himself and is able to define himself, he will find others who will read with a shock of recognition what he has written" (4).

This rhetoric thus includes a denunciation of economic, political, and social pressures to conform—to engage in various forms of corporate-sponsored thought, feeling, and behavior. In indirectly but unmistakably decrying the dehumanizing effects of industrial capitalism, expressionistic rhetoric insists on defamiliarizing experience, on getting beyond the corruptions of the individual authorized by the language of commodified culture in order to re-experience the self and through it the external world, finding in this activity possibilities for a new order. For expressionistic rhetoric, the correct response to the imposition of current economic, political, and social arrangements is thus resistance, but a resistance that is always construed in individual terms. Collective retaliation poses as much of a threat to individual integrity as do the collective forces being resisted, and so is itself suspect. The only hope in a society working to destroy the uniqueness of the individual is for each of us to assert our individuality against the tyranny of the authoritarian corporation, state, and society. Strategies for doing so must of course be left to the individual, each lighting one small candle in order to create a brighter world.

Expressionistic rhetoric continues to thrive in high schools and at a number of colleges and universities. At first glance, this is surprising, unexpected of a rhetoric that is openly opposed to establishment practices. This subversiveness, however, is more apparent than real. In the first place, expressionistic rhetoric is inherently and debilitatingly divisive of political protest, suggesting that effective resistance can only be offered by individuals, each acting alone. Given the isolation and incoherence of such protest, gestures genuinely threatening to the establishment are difficult to accomplish. Beyond this, expressionistic rhetoric is easily co-opted by the very capitalist forces it opposes. After all, this rhetoric can be used to reinforce the entrepreneurial virtues capitalism most values: individualism, private initiative, the confidence for risk taking, the right to be contentious with authority (especially the state). It is indeed not too much to say that the ruling elites in business, industry, and government are those most likely to nod in assent to the ideology inscribed in expressionistic rhetoric. The members of this class see their lives as embodying the creative realization of the self, exploiting the material, social, and political conditions of the world in order to assert a private vision, a vision which, despite its uniqueness, finally represents humankind's best nature. (That this vision in fact represents the interests of a particular class, not all classes, is of course not acknowledged.) Those who have not attained the positions which enable them to exert this freedom have been prevented from doing so, this ideology argues, not by economic and class constraints, but by their own unwillingness to pursue a private vision, and this interpretation is often embraced by those excluded from the ruling elite as well as by the ruling elite itself. In other words, even those most constrained by their positions in the class structure may support the ideology found in expressionistic rhetoric in some form. This is most commonly done by divorcing the self from the alienation of work, separating work experience from other experience so that self-discovery and -fulfillment take place away from the job. For some this may lead to the pursuit of self-expression in intellectual or aesthetic pursuits. For most this quest results in a variety of forms of consumer behavior, identifying individual self-expression with the consumption of some commodity. This separation of work from authentic human activity is likewise reinforced in expressionistic rhetoric, as a glance at any of the textbooks it has inspired will reveal.

Social-Epistemic Rhetoric

The last rhetoric to be considered I will call social-epistemic rhetoric, in so doing distinguishing it from the psychological-epistemic rhetoric that I am convinced is a form of expressionism. (The latter is found in Kenneth Dowst and in Cyril Knoblauch and Lil Brannon, although Knoblauch's recent *College English* essay displays him moving into the social camp. I have discussed the notion of epistemic rhetoric and these two varieties of it in *Rhetoric and Reality* 145–55, 165–77, and 184–85.) There have been a number of spokespersons for social-epistemic rhetoric over the last twenty years: Kenneth Burke, Richard Ohmann, the team of Richard Young, Alton Becker, and Kenneth Pike, Kenneth Bruffee, W. Ross Winterowd, Ann Berthoff, Janice Lauer, and, more recently, Karen Burke Lefevre, Lester Faigley, David Bartholomae, Greg Myers, Patricia Bizzell, and others. In grouping these figures together I do not intend to deny their obvious disagreements with each other. For example, Myers, a Leftist, has offered a lengthy critique of Bruffee, who — along with Winterowd and Young, Becker and Pike — is certainly of the Center politically. There are indeed as many conflicts among the members of this group as there are harmonies. They are brought together here, however, because they share a notion of rhetoric as a political act involving a dialectical interaction engaging the material, the social, and the individual writer, with language as the agency of mediation. Their positions, furthermore, include an historicist orientation, the realization that a rhetoric is an historically specific social formation that must perforce change over time; and this feature in turn makes possible reflexiveness and revision as the inherently ideological nature of rhetoric is continually acknowledged. The most complete realization of this rhetoric for the classroom is to be found in Ira Shor's *Critical Teaching and Everyday Life*. Before considering it, I would like to discuss the distinguishing features of a fully articulated social-epistemic rhetoric.

For social-epistemic rhetoric, the real is located in a relationship that involves the dialectical interaction of the observer, the discourse community (social group) in which the observer is functioning, and the material conditions of existence. Knowledge is never found in any one of these but can only be posited as a product of the dialectic in which all three come together. (More of this in a moment.) Most important, this dialectic is grounded in language: the observer, the discourse community, and the material conditions of existence are all verbal constructs. This does not mean that the three do not exist apart from language: they do. This does mean that we cannot talk and write about them—indeed, we cannot know them—apart from language. Furthermore, since language is a social phenomenon that is a product of a particular historical moment, our notions of the observing self, the communities in which the self functions, and the very structures of the material world are social constructions—all specific to a particular time and culture. These social constructions are thus inscribed in the very language we are given to inhabit in responding to our experience. Language, as Raymond Williams explains in an application of Bakhtin (*Marxism and Literature* 21–44), is one of the material and social conditions involved in producing a culture. This means that in studying rhetoric—the ways discourse is generated—we are studying the ways in which knowledge comes into existence. Knowledge, after all, is an historically bound social fabrication rather than an eternal and invariable phenomenon located in some uncomplicated repository—in the material object or in the subject or in the social realm. This brings us back to the matter of the dialectic.

Understanding this dialectical notion of knowledge is the most difficult feature of social-epistemic rhetoric. Psychological-epistemic rhetoric grants that rhetoric arrives at knowledge, but this meaning-generating activity is always located in a transcendent self, a subject who directs the discovery and arrives through it finally only at a better understanding of the self and its operation—this self-comprehension being the end of all knowledge. For social-epistemic rhetoric, the subject is itself a social construct that emerges through the linguistically circumscribed interaction of the individual, the community, and the material world. There is no universal, eternal, and authentic self that beneath all appearances is at one with all other selves. The self is always a creation of a particular historical and cultural moment. This is not to say that individuals do not ever act as individuals. It is to assert, however, that they never act with complete freedom. As Marx indicated, we make our own histories, but we do not make them just as we wish. Our consciousness is in large part a product of our material conditions. But our material conditions are also in part the products of our consciousness. Both consciousness and the material conditions influence each other, and they are both imbricated in social relations defined and worked out through language. In other words, the ways in which the subject understands and is affected by material conditions is circumscribed by socially devised definitions, by the community in which the subject lives. The community in turn is influenced by the subject and the material conditions of the moment. Thus, the perceiving subject, the discourse communities of which the subject is a part, and the material world itself are all the constructions of an historical discourse, of the ideological formulations inscribed in the language-mediated practical activity of a particular time and place. We are lodged within a hermeneutic circle, although not one that is impervious to change.

This scheme does not lead to an anarchistic relativism. It does, however, indicate that arguments based on the permanent rational structures of the universe or on the evidence of the deepest and most profound personal intuition should not be accepted without question. The material, the social, and the subjective are at once the producers and the products of ideology, and ideology must continually be challenged so as to reveal its economic and political consequences for individuals. In other words, what are the effects of our knowledge? Who benefits from a given version of truth? How are the material benefits of society distributed? What is the relation of this distribution to social relations? Do these relations encourage conflict? To whom does our knowledge designate power? In short, social-epistemic rhetoric views knowledge as an arena of ideological conflict: there are no arguments from transcendent truth since all arguments arise in ideology. It thus inevitably supports economic, social, political, and cultural democracy. Because there are no "natural laws" or "universal truths" that indicate what exists, what is good, what is possible, and how power is to be distributed, no class or group or individual has privileged access to decisions on these matters. They must be continually decided by all and for all in a way appropriate to our own historical moment. Finally, because of this historicist orientation, social-epistemic rhetoric contains within it the means for self-criticism and self-revision. Human responses to the material conditions of existence, the social relations they encourage, and the interpellations of subjects within them are always already ideological, are always already interpretations that must be constantly revised in the interests of the greater participation of all, for the greater good of all. And this of course implies an awareness of the ways in which rhetorics can privilege some at the expense of others, according the chosen few an unequal share of power, perquisites, and material benefits.

Social-epistemic rhetoric thus offers an explicit critique of economic, political, and social arrangements, the counterpart of the implicit critique found in expressionistic rhetoric. However, here the source and the solution of these arrangements are described quite differently. As Ira Shor explains, students must be taught to identify the ways in which control over their own lives has been denied them, and denied in such a way that they have blamed themselves for their powerlessness. Shor thus situates the individual within social processes, examining in detail the interferences to critical thought that would enable "students to be their own agents for social change, their own creators of democratic culture" (48). Among the most important forces preventing work toward a social order supporting the student's "full humanity" are forms of false consciousness — reification, pre-scientific thought, acceleration, mystification — and the absence of democratic practices in all areas of experience. Although Shor discusses these forms of false consciousness in their relation to working-class students, their application to all students is not hard to see, and I have selected for emphasis those features which clearly so apply.

In falling victim to reification, students begin to see the economic and social system that renders them powerless as an innate and unchangeable feature of the natural order. They become convinced that change is impossible, and they support the very practices that victimize them — complying in their alienation from their work, their peers, and their very selves. The most common form of reification has to do with the preoccupation with consumerism, playing the game of material acquisition and using it as a substitute for more self-fulfilling behavior. In pre-scientific thinking, the student is led to believe in a fixed human nature, always and everywhere the same. Behavior that is socially and self-destructive is then seen as inevitable, in the nature of things, or can be resisted only at the individual level, apart from communal activity. Another form of pre-scientific thinking is the belief in luck, in pure chance, as the source of social arrangements, such as the inequitable distribution of wealth. The loyalty to brand names, the faith in a "common sense" that supports the existing order, and the worship of heroes, such as actors and athletes, are other forms of this kind of thought, all of which prevent "the search for rational explanations to authentic problems" (66). Acceleration refers to the pace of everyday experience — the sensory bombardment of urban life and of popular forms of entertainment — which prevents critical reflection. Mystifications are responses to the problems of a capitalist society which obscure their real sources and solutions, responses based on racism, sexism, nationalism, and other forms of bigotry. Finally, students are constantly told they live in the most free, most democratic society in the world, yet they are at the same time systematically denied opportunities for "self-discipline, self-organization, collective work styles, or group deliberation" (70), instead being subjected at every turn to arbitrary authority in conducting everyday affairs.

Shor's recommendations for the classroom grow out of an awareness of these forces and are intended to counter them. The object of this pedagogy is to enable students to "*extraordinarily reexperience the ordinary*" (93), as they critically examine their quotidian experience in order to externalize false consciousness. (Shor's use of the term "critical" is meant to recall Freire as well as the practice of the Hegelian Marxists of the Frankfurt School.) The point is to "address self-in-society and social-relations-in-self" (95). The self then is regarded as the product of a dialectical relationship between the individual and the social, each given significance by the other. Self-autonomy and self-fulfillment are thus possible not through becoming detached from the social, but through resisting those social influences that alienate and disempower, doing so, moreover, in and through social activity. The liberatory classroom begins this resistance process with a dialogue that inspires "a democratic model of social relations, used to problematize the undemocratic quality of social life" (95). This dialogue — a model inspired by Paulo Freire — makes teacher and learner equals engaged in a joint practice that is "[l]oving, humble, hopeful, trusting, critical" (95). This is contrasted with the unequal power relations in the authoritarian classroom, a place where the teacher holds all power and knowledge and the student is the receptacle into which information is poured, a classroom that is "[l]oveless, arrogant, hopeless, mistrustful, acritical" (95). Teacher and student work together to shape the content of the liberatory classroom, and this includes creating the materials of study in the class — such as textbooks and media. Most important, the students are to undergo a conversion from "manipulated objects into active, critical subjects" (97), thereby empowering them to become agents of social change rather than victims. Shor sums up these elements: "social practice is studied in the name of freedom for critical consciousness; democracy and awareness develop through the form of dialogue; dialogue externalizes false consciousness, changing students from re-active objects into society-making subjects: the object-subject switch is a social psychology for empowerment; power through study creates the conditions for reconstructing social practice" (98).

This approach in the classroom requires interdisciplinary methods, and Shor gives an example from the study of the fast-food hamburger: "Concretely my class's study of hamburgers not only involved English and philosophy in our use of writing, reading, and conceptual analysis, but it also included economics in the study of the commodity relations which bring hamburgers to market, history and sociology in an assessment of what the everyday diet was like prior to the rise of the hamburger, and health science in terms of the nutritional value of the ruling burger" (114). This interdisciplinary approach to the study of the reproduction of social life can also lead to "the unveiling of hidden social history" (115), the discovery of past attempts to resist self-destructive experience. This in turn can lead to an examination of the roots of sexism and racism in our culture. Finally, Shor calls upon comedy to reunite pleasure and work, thought and feeling, and upon a resourceful use of the space of the classroom to encourage dialogue that provides students with information withheld elsewhere on campus — "informational, conceptual, personal, academic, financial" (120) — ranging from the location of free or inexpensive services to the location of political rallies.

This survey of the theory and practice of Ira Shor's classroom is necessarily brief and reductive. Still, it suggests the complexity of the behavior recommended in the classroom, behavior that is always open-ended, receptive to the unexpected, and subversive of the planned. Most important, success in this classroom can never be guaranteed. This is a place based on dialectical collaboration — the interaction of student, teacher, and shared experience within a social, interdisciplinary framework — and the outcome is always unpredictable. Yet, as Shor makes clear, the point of this classroom is that the liberated consciousness of students is the only educational objective worth considering, the only objective worth the risk of failure. To succeed at anything else is no success at all.

It should now be apparent that a way of teaching is never innocent. Every pedagogy is imbricated in ideology, in a set of tacit assumptions about what is real, what is good, what is possible, and how power ought to be distributed. The method of cognitive psychology is the most likely to ignore this contention, claiming that the rhetoric it recommends is based on an objective understanding of the unchanging structures of mind, matter, and language. Still, despite its commitment to the empirical and scientific, as we have seen, this rhetoric can easily be made to serve specific kinds of economic, social, and political behavior that works to the advantage of the members of one social class while disempowering others — doing so, moreover, in the name of objective truth. Expressionistic rhetoric is intended to serve as a critique of the ideology of corporate capitalism, proposing in its place an ideology based on a radical individualism. In the name of empowering the individual, however, its naivete about economic, social, and political arrangements can lead to the marginalizing of the individuals who would resist a dehumanizing society, rendering them ineffective through their isolation. This rhetoric also is easily co-opted by the agencies of corporate capitalism, appropriated and distorted in the service of the mystifications of bourgeois individualism. Social-epistemic rhetoric attempts to place the question of ideology at the center of the teaching of writing. It offers both a detailed analysis of dehumanizing social experience and a self-critical and overtly historicized alternative based on democratic practices in the economic, social, political, and cultural spheres. It is obvious that I find this alternative the most worthy of emulation in the classroom, all the while admitting that it is the least formulaic and the most difficult to carry out. I would also add that even those who are skeptical of the Marxian influence found in my description of this rhetoric have much to learn from it. As Kenneth Burke has shown, one does not have to accept the Marxian premise in order to realize the value of the Marxian diagnosis (109). It is likewise not necessary to accept the conclusions of Ira Shor about writing pedagogy in order to learn from his analysis of the ideological practices at work in the lives of our students and ourselves. A rhetoric cannot escape the ideological question, and to ignore this is to fail our responsibilities as teachers and as citizens.

Works Cited

Bartholomae, David. "Inventing the University." *When a Writer Can't Write: Research on Writer's Block and Other Writing Problems*. Ed. Mike Rose. New York: Guilford, 1986.

Berlin, James A. "Contemporary Composition: The Major Pedagogical Theories." *College English* 44 (1982): 765–77.

———. *Rhetoric and Reality: Writing Instruction in American Colleges, 1900–1985*. Carbondale: Southern Illinois UP, 1987.

———. *Writing Instruction in Nineteenth-Century American Colleges*. Carbondale: Southern Illinois UP, 1984.

Bizzell, Patricia. "Cognition, Convention, and Certainty: What We Need to Know about Writing." *PRETEXT* 3 (1982): 213–43.

Bowles, Samuel, and Herbert Gintis. *Schooling in Capitalist America*. New York: Basic, 1976.

Braverman, Harry. *Labor and Monopoly Capital: The Degradation of Work in the Twentieth Century*. New York: Monthly Review P, 1974.

Brodkey, Linda. "Modernism and the Scene of Writing." *College English* 49 (1987): 396–418.

Bruner, Jerome S. *The Process of Education*. Cambridge: Harvard UP, 1960.

Burke, Kenneth. *A Rhetoric of Motives*. Berkeley: U of California P, 1969.

Clifford, John, and John Schilb. "A Perspective on Eagleton's Revival of Rhetoric." *Rhetoric Review* 6 (1987): 22–31.

Clines, Ray. "Composition and Capitalism." *Progressive Composition* 14 (Mar. 1987): 4–5.

Dowst, Kenneth. "The Epistemic Approach: Writing, Knowing, and Learning." *Eight Approaches to Teaching Composition*. Ed. Timothy Donovan and Ben W. McClelland. Urbana: NCTE, 1980.

———. "An Epistemic View of Sentence Combining: A Rhetorical Perspective." *Sentence Combining: A Rhetorical Perspective*. Eds. Donald A. Daiker, Andrew Kerek, and Max Morenberg. Carbondale: Southern Illinois UP, 1986. 321–33.

Elbow, Peter. *Embracing Contraries: Explorations in Learning and Teaching*. New York: Oxford, 1981.

———. *Writing without Teachers*. New York: Oxford UP, 1973.

———. *Writing with Power: Techniques for Mastering the Writing Process*. New York: Oxford UP, 1981.

Emig, Janet. *The Composing Process of Twelfth Graders*. Research Report No. 13. Urbana: NCTE, 1971.

Flower, Linda. *Problem-Solving Strategies for Writing*. 2nd ed. San Diego: Harcourt, 1985.

Flower, Linda, and John R. Hayes. "A Cognitive Process Theory of Writing." *College Composition and Communication* 32 (1981): 365–87.

Knoblauch, C. H. "Rhetorical Constructions: Dialogue and Commitment." *College English* 50 (1988): 125–40.

Knoblauch, C. H., and Lil Brannon. *Rhetorical Traditions and the Teaching of Writing*. Upper Montclair: Boynton, 1984.

Larrain, Jorge. *The Concept of Ideology*. Athens: U of Georgia P, 1979.

Larson, Richard. "Discovery through Questioning: A Plan for Teaching Rhetorical Invention." *College English* 30 (1968): 126–34.

———. "Invention Once More: A Role for Rhetorical Analysis." *College English* 32 (1971): 665–72.

———. "Problem-Solving, Composing, and Liberal Education." *College Composition and Communication* 23 (1972): 208–10.

Lutz, William D. "Making Freshman English a Happening." *College Composition and Communication* 22 (1971): 35–38.

Murray, Donald. "Finding Your Own Voice: Teaching Composition in an Age of Dissent." *College Composition and Communication* 20 (1969): 118–23.

———. *A Writer Teaches Writing*. Boston: Houghton, 1968.

Myers, Greg. "Reality, Consensus, and Reform in the Rhetoric of Composition Teaching." *College English* 48 (1986): 154–74.

Ohmann, Richard. "Literacy, Technology, and Monopoly Capital." *College English* 47 (1985): 675–89.

Paull, Michael, and Jack Kligerman. "Invention, Composition, and the Urban College." *College English* 33 (1972): 651–59.

Shor, Ira. *Critical Teaching and Everyday Life*. 1980. Chicago: U of Chicago P, 1987.

Therborn, Göran. *The Ideology of Power and the Power of Ideology*. London: Verso, 1980.

Vitanza, Victor. "'Notes' towards Historiographies of Rhetorics; or, Rhetorics of the Histories of Rhetorics: Traditional, Revisionary, and Sub/Versive." *PRETEXT* 8 (1987): 63–125.

Williams, Raymond. *Keywords: A Vocabulary of Culture and Society*. Rev. ed. New York: Oxford UP, 1977.

———. *Marxism and Literature*. New York: Oxford UP, 1977.

Berlin's Insights as a Resource for Your Reflections

1. Make some notes on the ideology that dominates your own teaching. Which moments in your classroom practice most clearly illustrate your commitment to this ideology? What moments suggest that your classroom practice incorporates more than one ideology? While Berlin's tripartite model is a powerful tool for organizing our sense of what goes on in our classroom, actual practice is far too "messy" to be contained and fully delineated by such a simplistic model. Explore ways in which certain aspects of your teaching advance more than one ideology. Are some of your assignments driven by all three modes?

2. Which of Berlin's approaches to writing instruction do your students seem most inclined to accept? Do you have some budding expressionists in your classroom? Do you have any cognitivists on board? Consider ways of using ideological differences among your students as the basis for class discussion, even for writing.

Berlin's Insights as a Resource for Your Writing Classroom

1. Classroom reality is always more complex than any clear-cut taxonomy or model. Monitor your teaching for a few weeks to see how the more successful moments in class discussion are grounded in ideology. If you find that you get the best results when you are an expressivist, then examine what within this approach causes the success. Can it be combined with the more appealing elements of other ideologies?
2. Have students write brief, informal accounts of how they see themselves as writers. Read through these accounts with Berlin's taxonomy in mind. Which ideologies rule your students' self-conceptions? Do ideological patterns emerge in the accounts of strong students as opposed to weak students? How might you use Berlin's thinking to address weaker students?

CHAPTER

2

Thinking about the Writing Process

Many in composition studies agree that the founding insight of our field, the idea around which our work as we recognize it today first began, is that writing should be taught as a process, a recursive series of linked activities. This idea is now so entrenched that the pedagogic approaches it supplanted are rather difficult to imagine, but presumably the contrary emphasis on writing as a "product" involved simply trying to mirror, somehow, certain idealized models. When the idea of teaching composition as a process took hold and became pervasive in the 1970s, it not only transformed the classroom but also the community of those who taught, for now a meaningful object of study and an endless stream of research questions could bring us together and professionalize us as academics with an identity distinct from our colleagues who focused only on literature.

The first selections in this chapter address the complex, intertwined processes by which individuals generate a draft, consider their audience, revise their manuscripts, and craft their sentences. Of course, no particular act of composing fits perfectly into these neat, discrete categories, but these readings offer a general map of the potential activities that often mark successful academic writing and that can inform day-to-day classroom teaching. The age-old question of rhetorical invention — where do writers get their ideas? — has recently entered a remarkable new phase of its history as the Internet has changed the way we do research and, in turn, opened up difficult discussions of plagiarism. But invention isn't the only dimension of rhetoric that computers have changed—the question of delivery, of how we present our texts, of the role of graphic design or visual rhetoric in the writing class has also recently come to the fore of much discussion of composition pedagogy. And therefore, in this section, you'll find articles that address these concerns as well as those focused on issues that have been central to our field since it first emerged around the insight that writing is a process.

Generating a Draft

Understanding Composing

Sondra Perl

How, in general, do we characterize the writing process? Most writing teachers and theorists share Sondra Perl's belief that writing is a recursive process and that writers engage in "retrospective structuring" as they generate drafts. In this 1990 article from College Composition and Communication, *Perl uses her own observations of the composing processes of a variety of writers to analyze the significance of those processes. She defines a "felt sense" that may be a very rich and necessary resource for the writer even as it may be one that the writer (and his or her audience) has difficulty describing and consciously triggering.*

Perl believes that "skilled writers" rely on a felt sense even when they don't know it, and she implies that "unskilled writers" might come to use this felt sense and to engage in "retrospective structuring" more productively. She theorizes that writers who have internalized a model of writing as a recursive process rather than a linear process may have an easier time attending to their inner reflections.

You may well find "new thoughts" about composing as you read Perl's conjectures about "felt sense." In particular, you may be interested in the link of "felt sense" with "projective structuring," Perl's name for the process in which writers make what they intend to say intelligible to others.

> Any psychological process, whether the development of thought or voluntary behavior, is a process undergoing changes right before one's eyes. . . . Under certain conditions it becomes possible to trace this development.[1]
>
> —L. S. Vygotsky

It's hard to begin this case study of myself as a writer because even as I'm searching for a beginning, a pattern of organization, I'm watching myself, trying to understand my behavior. As I sit here in silence, I can see lots of things happening that never made it onto my tapes. My mind leaps from the task at hand to what I need at the vegetable stand for tonight's soup to the threatening rain outside to ideas voiced in my writing group this morning, but in between "distractions" I hear myself trying out words I might use. It's as if the extraneous thoughts are a counterpoint to the more steady attention I'm giving to composing. This is all to point out that the process is more complex than I'm aware of, but I think my tapes reveal certain basic patterns that I tend to follow.

—Anne, New York City teacher

Anne is a teacher of writing. In 1979, she was among a group of twenty teachers who were taking a course in research and basic writing at New York University.[2] One of the assignments in the course was for the teachers to tape their thoughts while composing aloud on the topic "My Most Anxious Moment as a Writer." Everyone in the group was given the topic in the morning during class and told to compose later on that day in a place where they would be comfortable and relatively free from distractions. The result was a tape of composing aloud and a written product that formed the basis for class discussion over the next few days.

One of the purposes of this assignment was to provide teachers with an opportunity to see their own composing processes at work. From the start of the course, we recognized that we were controlling the situation by assigning a topic and that we might be altering the process by asking writers to compose aloud. Nonetheless we viewed the task as a way of capturing some of the flow of composing and, as Anne later observed in her analysis of her tape, she was able to detect certain basic patterns. This observation, made not only by Anne, then leads me to ask "What basic patterns seem to occur during composing?" and "What does this type of research have to tell us about the nature of the composing process?"

Perhaps the most challenging part of the answer is the recognition of recursiveness in writing. In recent years, many researchers including myself have questioned the traditional notion that writing is a linear process with a strict plan-write-revise sequence.[3] In its stead, we have advocated the idea that writing is a recursive process, that throughout the process of writing, writers return to substrands of the overall process, or subroutines (short successions of steps that yield results on which the writer draws in taking the next set of steps); writers use these to keep the process moving forward. In other words, recursiveness in writing implies that there is a forward-moving action that exists by virtue of a backward-moving action. The questions that then need to be answered are "To what do writers move back?" "What exactly is being repeated?" "What recurs?"

To answer these questions, it is important to look at what writers do while writing and what an analysis of their processes reveals. The descriptions that follow are based on my own observations of the composing processes of many types of writers including college students, graduate students, and English teachers like Anne.

Writing does appear to be recursive, yet the parts that recur seem to vary from writer to writer and from topic to topic. Furthermore, some recursive elements are easy to spot while others are not.

1. The most visible recurring feature or backward movement involves rereading little bits of discourse. Few writers I have seen write for long periods of time without returning briefly to what is already down on the page.

For some, like Anne, rereading occurs after every few phrases; for others, it occurs after every sentence; more frequently, it occurs after a "chunk" of information has been written. Thus, the unit that is reread is not necessarily a syntactic one, but rather a semantic one as defined by the writer.

2. The second recurring feature is some key word or item called up by the topic. Writers consistently return to their notion of the topic throughout the process of writing. Particularly when they are stuck, writers seem to use the topic or a key word in it as a way to get going again. Thus many times it is possible to see writers "going back," rereading the topic they were given, changing it to suit what they have been writing or changing what they have written to suit their notion of the topic.

3. There is also a third backward movement in writing, one that is not so easy to document. It is not easy because the move, itself, cannot immediately be identified with words. In fact, the move is not to any words on the page nor to the topic but to feelings or nonverbalized perceptions that *surround* the words, or to what the words already present evoke in the writer. The move draws on sense experience, and it can be observed if one pays close attention to what happens when writers pause and seem to listen or otherwise react to what is inside of them. The move occurs inside the writer, to what is physically felt. The term used to describe this focus of writers' attention is *felt sense*. The term "felt sense" has been coined and described by Eugene Gendlin, a philosopher at the University of Chicago. In his words, felt sense is

> the soft underbelly of thought . . . a kind of bodily awareness that . . . can be used as a tool . . . a bodily awareness that . . . encompasses everything you feel and know about a given subject at a given time. . . . It is felt in the body, yet it has meanings. It is body *and* mind before they are split apart.[4]

This felt sense is always there, within us. It is unifying, and yet, when we bring words to it, it can break apart, shift, unravel, and become something else. Gendlin has spent many years showing people how to work with their felt sense. Here I am making connections between what he has done and what I have seen happen as people write.

When writers are given a topic, the topic itself evokes a felt sense in them. This topic calls forth images, words, ideas, and vague fuzzy feelings that are anchored in the writer's body. What is elicited, then, is not solely the product of a mind but of a mind alive in a living, sensing body.

When writers pause, when they go back and repeat key words, what they seem to be doing is waiting, paying attention to what is still vague and unclear. They are looking to their felt experience, and waiting for an image, a word, or a phrase to emerge that captures the sense they embody.

Usually, when they make the decision to write, it is after they have a dawning awareness that something has clicked, that they have enough of a sense that if they begin with a few words heading in a certain direction, words will continue to come which will allow them to flesh out the sense they have.

The process of using what is sensed directly about a topic is a natural one. Many writers do it without any conscious awareness that that is what they are doing. For example, Anne repeats the words "anxious moments," using these key words as a way of allowing her sense of the topic to deepen. She asks herself, "Why are exams so anxiety provoking?" and waits until she has enough of a sense within her that she can go in a certain direction. She does not yet have the words, only the sense that she is able to begin. Once she writes, she stops to see what is there. She maintains a highly recursive composing style throughout and she seems unable to go forward without first going back to see and to listen to what she has already created. In her own words, she says:

> My disjointed style of composing is very striking to me. I almost never move from the writing of one sentence directly to the next. After each sentence I pause to read what I've written, assess, sometimes edit and think about what will come next. I often have to read the several preceding sentences a few times as if to gain momentum to carry me to the next sentence. I seem to depend a lot on the sound of my words and . . . while I'm hanging in the middle of this uncompleted thought, I may also start editing a previous sentence or get an inspiration for something which I want to include later in the paper.

What tells Anne that she is ready to write? What is the feeling of "momentum" like for her? What is she hearing as she listens to the "sound" of her words? When she experiences "inspiration," how does she recognize it?

In the approach I am presenting, the ability to recognize what one needs to do or where one needs to go is informed by calling on felt sense. This is the internal criterion writers seem to use to guide them when they are planning, drafting, and revising.

The recursive move, then, that is hardest to document but is probably the most important to be aware of is the move to felt sense, to what is not yet *in words* but out of which images, words, and concepts emerge.

The continuing presence of this felt sense, waiting for us to discover it and see where it leads, raises a number of questions.

Is "felt sense" another term for what professional writers call their "inner voice" or their feeling of "inspiration"?

Do skilled writers call on their capacity to sense more readily than unskilled writers?

Rather than merely reducing the complex act of writing to a neat formulation, can the term "felt sense" point us to an area of our experience from which we can evolve even richer and more accurate descriptions of composing?

Can learning how to work with felt sense teach us about creativity and release us from stultifyingly repetitive patterns?

My observations lead me to answer "yes" to all four questions. There seems to be a basic step in the process of composing that skilled writers rely on even when they are unaware of it and that less skilled writers can be taught. This process seems to rely on very careful attention to one's inner reflections and is often accompanied with bodily sensations.

When it's working, this process allows us to say or write what we've never said before, to create something new and fresh, and occasionally it provides us with the experience of "newness" or "freshness," even when "old words" or images are used.

The basic process begins with paying attention. If we are given a topic, it begins with taking the topic in and attending to what it evokes in us. There is less "figuring out" an answer and more "waiting" to see what forms. Even without a predetermined topic, the process remains the same. We can ask ourselves, "What's on my mind?" or "Of all the things I know about, what would I most like to write about now?" and wait to see what comes. What we pay attention to is the part of our bodies where we experience ourselves directly. For many people, it's the area of their stomachs; for others, there is a more generalized response and they maintain a hovering attention to what they experience throughout their bodies.

Once a felt sense forms, we match words to it. As we begin to describe it, we get to see what is there for us. We get to see what we think, what we know. If we are writing about something that truly interests us, the felt sense deepens. We know that we are writing out of a "centered" place.

If the process is working, we begin to move along, sometimes quickly. Other times, we need to return to the beginning, to reread, to see if we captured what we meant to say. Sometimes after rereading we move on again, picking up speed. Other times by rereading we realize we've gone off the track, that what we've written doesn't quite "say it," and we need to reassess. Sometimes the words are wrong and we need to change them. Other times we need to go back to the topic, to call up the sense it initially evoked to see where and how our words led us astray. Sometimes in rereading we discover that the topic is "wrong," that the direction we discovered in writing is where we really want to go. It is important here to clarify that the terms "right" and "wrong" are not necessarily meant to refer to grammatical structures or to correctness.

What is "right" or "wrong" corresponds to our sense of our intention. We intend to write something, words come, and now we assess if those words adequately capture our intended meaning. Thus, the first question we ask ourselves is "Are these words right for me?" "Do they capture what I'm trying to say?" "If not, what's missing?"

Once we ask "what's missing?" we need once again to wait, to let a felt sense of what is missing form, and then to write out of that sense.

I have labeled this process of attending, of calling up a felt sense, and of writing out of that place, the process of *retrospective structuring*. It is retrospective in that it begins with what is already there, inchoately, and brings whatever is there forward by using language in structured form.

It seems as though a felt sense has within it many possible structures or forms. As we shape what we intend to say, we are further structuring our sense while correspondingly shaping our piece of writing.

It is also important to note that what is there implicitly, without words, is not equivalent to what finally emerges. In the process of writing, we begin with what is inchoate and end with something that is tangible. In order to do so, we both discover and construct what we mean. Yet the term "discovery" ought not lead us to think that meaning exists fully formed inside of us and that all we need do is dig deep enough to release it. In writing, meaning cannot be discovered the way we discover an object on an archeological dig. In writing, meaning is crafted and constructed. It involves us in a process of coming-into-being. Once we have worked at shaping, through language, what is there inchoately, we can look at what we have written to see if it adequately captures what we intended. Often at this moment discovery occurs. We see something new in our writing that comes upon us as a surprise. We see in our words a further structuring of the sense we began with and we recognize that in those words we have discovered something new about ourselves and our topic. Thus when we are successful at this process, we end up with a product that teaches us something, that clarifies what we know (or what we knew at one point only implicitly), and that lifts out or explicates or enlarges our experience. In this way, writing leads to discovery.

All the writers I have observed, skilled and unskilled alike, use the process of retrospective structuring while writing. Yet the degree to which they do so varies and seems, in fact, to depend upon the model of the writing process that they have internalized. Those who realize that writing can be a recursive process have an easier time with waiting, looking, and discovering. Those who subscribe to the linear model find themselves easily frustrated when what they write does not immediately correspond to what they planned or when what they produce leaves them with little sense of accomplishment. Since they have relied on a formulaic approach, they often produce writing that is formulaic as well, thereby cutting themselves off from the possibility of discovering something new.

Such a result seems linked to another feature of the composing process, to what I call *projective structuring*, or the ability to craft what one intends to say so that it is intelligible to others.

A number of concerns arise in regard to projective structuring; I will mention only a few that have been raised for me as I have watched different writers at work.

1. Although projective structuring is only one important part of the composing process, many writers act as if it is the whole process. These writers focus on what they think others want them to write rather than looking to see what it is they want to write. As a result, they often ignore their felt sense and they do not establish a living connection between themselves and their topic.

2. Many writers reduce projective structuring to a series of rules or criteria for evaluating finished discourse. These writers ask, "Is what I'm writing correct?" and "Does it conform to the rules I've been taught?" While these concerns are important, they often overshadow all others and lock the writer in the position of writing solely or primarily for the approval of readers.

Projective structuring, as I see it, involves much more than imagining a strict audience and maintaining a strict focus on correctness. It is true that to handle this part of the process well, writers need to know certain grammatical rules and evaluative criteria, but they also need to know how to call up a sense of their reader's needs and expectations.

For projective structuring to function fully, writers need to draw on their capacity to move away from their own words, to decenter from the page, and to project themselves into the role of the reader. In other words, projective structuring asks writers to attempt to become readers and to imagine what someone other than themselves will need before the writer's particular piece of writing can become intelligible and compelling. To do so, writers must have the experience of being readers. They cannot call up a felt sense of a reader unless they themselves have experienced what it means to be lost in a piece of writing or to be excited by it. When writers do not have such experiences, it is easy for them to accept that readers merely require correctness.

In closing, I would like to suggest that retrospective and projective structuring are two parts of the same basic process. Together they form the alternating mental postures writers assume as they move through the act of composing. The former relies on the ability to go inside, to attend to what is there, from that attending to place words upon a page, and then to assess if those words adequately capture one's meaning. The latter relies on the ability to assess how the words on that page will affect someone other than the writer, the reader. We rarely do one without the other entering in; in fact, again in these postures we can see the shuttling back-and-forth movements of the composing process, the move from sense to words and from words to sense, from inner experience to outer judgment and from judgment back to experience. As we move through this cycle, we are continually composing and recomposing our meanings and what we mean. And in doing so, we display some of the basic recursive patterns that writers who observe themselves closely seem to see in their own work. After observing the process for a long time we may, like Anne, conclude that at any given moment the process is more complex than anything we are aware of; yet such insights, I believe, are important. They show us the fallacy of reducing the composing process to a simple linear scheme and they leave us with the potential for creating even more powerful ways of understanding composing.

Notes

1. L. S. Vygotsky, *Mind in Society*, trans. M. Cole, V. John-Steiner, S. Scribner, and E. Souberman (Cambridge: Harvard UP, 1978) 61.
2. [I team-taught this course with] Gordon Pradl, Associate Professor of English Education at New York University.
3. See Janet Emig, *The Composing Processes of Twelfth-Graders*, NCTE Research Report No. 13 (Urbana: NCTE, 1971); Linda Flower and J. R. Hayes, "The Cognition of Discovery," *CCC* 31 (Feb. 1980): 21–32; Nancy Sommers, "The Need for Theory in Composition Research," *CCC* 30 (Feb. 1979): 46–49.
4. Eugene Gendlin, *Focusing* (New York: Everest, 1978) 35, 165.

Perl's Insights as a Resource for Your Reflections

1. Perl models a "holistic perspective" on the composing process and pays careful attention to the composing processes of the students she teaches. As you read this article and reflect on it, jot down your own memories of this experience of a "felt sense" as well as statements your students have made about such experiences. How might you generalize further about what the felt sense is, how it works, and how teachers can engage it?

2. Explore your own writing process in your reflective teaching journal. Which steps recur most frequently in your own writing? Try to articulate your own processes of restrospective and projective structuring. As you grow more aware of how your own processes work, how might you wish to tinker with or adjust these processes to improve your writing?

Perl's Insights as a Resource for Your Writing Classroom

1. Many generating strategies — those used by individual writers as well as the more formally described heuristics like freewriting, brainstorming, and the reporter's questions — help students start to pay attention to inner reflections and accompanying physical sensations. After they have practiced with several formal heuristics, ask your students to describe, either in journal entries or in fifteen-minute writing sessions, what they notice about their "getting started" and their "beginning again." Use this freewriting as the basis for students to discuss their own notions of felt sense.

Rigid Rules, Inflexible Plans, and the Stifling of Language: A Cognitivist Analysis of Writer's Block

Mike Rose

What's really going on when a student writer can't write, even when an assignment's deadline looms closer and closer? In this study, Mike Rose finds ten students at UCLA who struggle with writer's block and compares their composing processes with those of students who do not have writer's block. Students are often blocked by very specific cognitive objects: they are stifled by rigid "dos and don'ts" that they have internalized from past teachers and textbooks, and what they finally, painstakingly produce inevitably never matches their inflexible plans. Writers who do not struggle with writer's block, on the other hand, are unimpeded by any such hypersensitivity to rules and plans: They just write, knowing that they can revise or retract later. In the next section of this chapter, Considering Audience, Peter Elbow focuses on how writers' concerns about audience — particularly in the generating and drafting stages — can inhibit or "block" writing (see pp. 172–194, "Closing My Eyes as I Speak"), in that students may feel bound by their preconceived ideas of audience expectation and thus conform their writing to "fit" these. It is when we try to fit our writing into predetermined molds that we become stymied by self-consciousness, making it nearly impossible to tap the resources of our imagination.

Ruth will labor over the first paragraph of an essay for hours. She'll write a sentence, then erase it. Try another, then scratch part of it out. Finally, as the evening winds on toward ten o'clock and Ruth, anxious about tomorrow's deadline, begins to wind into herself, she'll compose that first paragraph only to sit back and level her favorite exasperated interdiction at herself and her page: "No. You can't say that. You'll bore them to death."

Ruth is one of ten UCLA undergraduates with whom I discussed writer's block, that frustrating, self-defeating inability to generate the next line, the right phrase, the sentence that will release the flow of words once again. These ten people represented a fair cross-section of the UCLA student community: lower-middle-class to upper-middle-class backgrounds and high schools, third-world and Caucasian origins, biology to fine arts majors, C+ to A− grade point averages, enthusiastic to blasé attitudes toward school. They were set off from the community by the twin facts that all ten could write competently, and all were currently enrolled in at least one course that required a significant amount of writing. They were set off among themselves by the fact that five of them wrote with relative to enviable ease while the other five experienced moderate to nearly immobilizing writer's block. This blocking usually resulted in rushed, often late papers and resultant grades that did not truly reflect these students' writing ability. And then, of course, there were other less measurable but probably more serious results: a growing distrust of their abilities and an aversion toward the composing process itself.

What separated the five students who blocked from those who didn't? It wasn't skill; that was held fairly constant. The answer could have rested in the emotional realm — anxiety, fear of evaluation, insecurity, etc. Or perhaps blocking in some way resulted from variation in cognitive style. Perhaps, too, blocking originated in and typified a melding of emotion and cognition not unlike the relationship posited by Shapiro between neurotic feeling and neurotic thinking.[1] Each of these was possible. Extended clinical interviews and testing could have teased out the answer. But there was one answer that surfaced readily in brief explorations of these students' writing processes. It was not profoundly emotional, nor was it embedded in that still unclear construct of cognitive style. It was constant, surprising, almost amusing if its results weren't so troublesome, and, in the final analysis, obvious: the five students who experienced blocking were all operating either with writing rules or with planning strategies that impeded rather than enhanced the composing process. The five students who were not hampered by writer's block also utilized rules, but they were less rigid ones, and thus more appropriate to a complex process like writing. Also, the plans these non-blockers brought to the writing process were more functional, more flexible, more open to information from the outside.

These observations are the result of one to three interviews with each student. I used recent notes, drafts, and finished compositions to direct and hone my questions. This procedure is admittedly non-experimental, certainly more clinical than scientific; still, it did lead to several inferences that lay the foundation for future, more rigorous investigation: (a) composing is a highly complex problem-solving process[2] and (b) certain disruptions of that process can be explained with cognitive psychology's problem-solving framework. Such investigation might include a study using "stimulated recall" techniques to validate or disconfirm these hunches. In such a study, blockers and non-blockers would write essays. Their activity would be videotaped and, immediately after writing, they would be shown their respective tapes and questioned about the rules, plans, and beliefs operating in their writing behavior. This procedure would bring us close to the composing process (the writers' recall is stimulated by their viewing the tape), yet would not interfere with actual composing.

In the next section I will introduce several key concepts in the problem-solving literature. In section three I will let the students speak for themselves. Fourth, I will offer a cognitivist analysis of blockers' and non-blockers' grace or torpor. I will close with a brief note on treatment.

Selected Concepts in Problem Solving: Rules and Plans

As diverse as theories of problem solving are, they share certain basic assumptions and characteristics. Each posits an *introductory period* during which a problem is presented, and all theorists, from Behaviorist to Gestalt to Information Processing, admit that certain aspects, stimuli, or "functions" of the problem must become or be made salient and attended to in certain ways if successful problem-solving processes are to be engaged. Theorists also believe that some conflict, some stress, some gap in information in these perceived "aspects" seems to trigger problem-solving behavior. Next comes a *processing period*, and for all the variance of opinion about this critical stage, theorists recognize the necessity of its existence — recognize that man, at the least, somehow "weighs" possible solutions as they are stumbled upon and, at the most, goes through an elaborate and sophisticated information-processing routine to achieve problem solution. Furthermore, theorists believe — to varying degrees — that past learning and the particular "set," direction, or orientation that the problem solver takes in dealing with past experience and present stimuli have critical bearing on the efficacy of solution. Finally, all theorists admit to a *solution period*, an end-state of the process where "stress" and "search" terminate, an answer is attained, and a sense of completion or "closure" is experienced.

These are the gross similarities, and the framework they offer will be useful in understanding the problem-solving behavior of the students discussed in this paper. But since this paper is primarily concerned with the second stage of problem-solving operations, it would be most useful to focus this introduction on two critical constructs in the processing period: rules and plans.

Rules

Robert M. Gagné defines "rule" as "an inferred capability that enables the individual to respond to a class of stimulus situations with a class of performances."[3] Rules can be learned directly[4] or by inference through experience.[5] But, in either case, most problem-solving theorists would affirm Gagné's dictum that "rules are probably the major organizing factor, and quite possibly the primary one, in intellectual functioning."[6] As Gagné implies, we wouldn't be able to function without rules; they guide response to the myriad stimuli that confront us daily, and might even be the central element in complex problem-solving behavior.

Dunker, Polya, and Miller, Galanter, and Pribram offer a very useful distinction between two general kinds of rules: algorithms and heuristics.[7] Algorithms are precise rules that will always result in a specific answer if applied to an appropriate problem. Most mathematical rules, for example, are algorithms. Functions are constant (e.g., pi), procedures are routine (squaring the radius), and outcomes are completely predictable. However, few day-to-day situations are mathematically circumscribed enough to warrant the application of algorithms. Most often we function with the aid of fairly general heuristics or "rules of thumb," guidelines that allow varying degrees of flexibility when approaching problems. Rather than operating with algorithmic precision and certainty, we search, critically, through alternatives, using our heuristic as a divining rod—"if a math problem stumps you, try working backwards to solution"; "if the car won't start, check X, Y, or Z," and so forth. Heuristics won't allow the precision or the certitude afforded by algorithmic operations; heuristics can even be so "loose" as to be vague. But in a world where tasks and problems are rarely mathematically precise, heuristic rules become the most appropriate, the most functional rules available to us: "a heuristic does not guarantee the optimal solution or, indeed, any solution at all; rather, heuristics offer solutions that are good enough most of the time."[8]

Plans

People don't proceed through problem situations, in or out of a laboratory, without some set of internalized instructions to the self, some program, some course of action that, even roughly, takes goals and possible paths to that goal into consideration. Miller, Galanter, and Pribram have referred to this course of action as a plan: "A plan is any hierarchical process in the organism that can control the order in which a sequence of operations is to be performed" (16). They name the fundamental plan in human problem-solving behavior the TOTE, with the initial T representing a *test* that matches a possible solution against the perceived end-goal of problem completion. O represents the clearance to *operate* if the comparison between solution and goal indicates that the solution is a sensible one. The second T represents a further, post-operation, *test* or comparison of solution with goal, and if the two mesh and problem solution is at hand the person *exits* (E) from problem-solving behavior. If the second test presents further discordance between solution and goal, a further solution is attempted in TOTE-fashion. Such plans can be both long-term and global and, as problem solving is underway, short-term and immediate.[9] Though the mechanicality of this information-processing model renders it simplistic and, possibly, unreal, the central notion of a plan and an operating procedure is an important one in problem-solving theory; it at least attempts to metaphorically explain what earlier cognitive psychologists could not — the mental procedures . . . underlying problem-solving behavior.

Before concluding this section, a distinction between heuristic rules and plans should be attempted; it is a distinction often blurred in the literature, blurred because, after all, we are very much in the area of gestating theory and preliminary models. Heuristic rules seem to function with the flexibility of plans. Is, for example, "If the car won't start, try X, Y, or Z" a heuristic or a plan? It could be either, though two qualifications will mark it as heuristic rather than plan. (A) Plans subsume and sequence heuristic and algorithmic rules. Rules are usually "smaller," more discrete cognitive capabilities; plans can become quite large and complex, composed of a series of ordered algorithms, heuristics, and further planning "sub-routines." (B) Plans, as was mentioned earlier, include criteria to determine successful goal-attainment and, as well, include "feedback" processes — ways to incorporate and use information gained from "tests" of potential solutions against desired goals.

One other distinction should be made: that is, between "set" and plan. Set, also called "determining tendency" or "readiness,"[10] refers to the fact that people often approach problems with habitual ways of reacting, a predisposition, a tendency to perceive or function in one way rather than another. Set, which can be established through instructions or, consciously or unconsciously, through experience, can assist performance if it is appropriate to a specific problem,[11] but much of the literature on set has shown its rigidifying, dysfunctional effects.[12] Set differs from plan in that set represents a limiting and narrowing of response alternatives with no inherent process to shift alternatives. It is a kind of cognitive habit that can limit perception, not a course of action with multiple paths that directs and sequences response possibilities.

The constructs of rules and plans advance the understanding of problem solving beyond that possible with earlier, less developed formulations. Still, critical problems remain. Though mathematical and computer models move one toward more complex (and thus more real) problems than the earlier research, they are still too neat, too rigidly sequenced to approximate the stunning complexity of day-to-day (not to mention highly creative) problem-solving behavior. Also, information-processing models of problem solving are built on logic theorems, chess strategies, and simple planning tasks. Even Gagné seems to feel more comfortable with illustrations from mathematics and science rather than with social science and humanities problems. So although these complex models and constructs tell us a good deal about problem-solving behavior, they are still laboratory simulations, still invoked from the outside rather than self-generated, and still founded on the mathematico-logical.

Two Carnegie-Mellon researchers, however, have recently extended the above into a truly real, amorphous, unmathematical problem-solving process — writing. Relying on protocol analysis (thinking aloud while solving problems), Linda Flower and John Hayes have attempted to tease out the role of heuristic rules and plans in writing behavior.[13] Their research pushes problem-solving investigations to the real and complex and pushes, from the other end, the often mysterious process of writing toward the explainable. The latter is important, for at least since Plotinus many have viewed the composing process as unexplainable, inspired, infused with the transcendent. But Flower and Hayes are beginning, anyway, to show how writing generates from a problem-solving process with rich heuristic rules and plans of its own. They show, as well, how many writing problems arise from a paucity of heuristics and suggest an intervention that provides such rules.

This paper, too, treats writing as a problem-solving process, focusing, however, on what happens when the process dead-ends in writer's block. It will further suggest that, as opposed to Flower and Hayes's students who need more rules and plans, blockers may well be stymied by possessing rigid or inappropriate rules, or inflexible or confused plans. Ironically enough, these are occasionally instilled by the composition teacher or gleaned from the writing textbook.

"Always Grab Your Audience" — The Blockers

In high school, *Ruth* was told and told again that a good essay always grabs a reader's attention immediately. Until you can make your essay do that, her teachers and textbooks putatively declaimed, there is no need to go on. For Ruth, this means that beginning bland and seeing what emerges as one generates prose is unacceptable. The beginning is everything. And what exactly is the audience seeking that reads this beginning? The rule, or Ruth's use of it, doesn't provide for such investigation. She has an edict with no determiners. Ruth operates with another rule that restricts her productions as well: if sentences aren't grammatically "correct," they aren't useful. This keeps Ruth from toying with ideas on paper, from the kind of linguistic play that often frees up the flow of prose. These two rules converge in a way that pretty effectively restricts Ruth's composing process.

The first two papers I received from *Laurel* were weeks overdue. Sections of them were well written; there were even moments of stylistic flair. But the papers were late and, overall, the prose seemed rushed. Furthermore, one paper included a paragraph on an issue that was never mentioned in the topic paragraph. This was the kind of mistake that someone with Laurel's apparent ability doesn't make. I asked her about this irrelevant passage. She knew very well that it didn't fit, but believed she had to include it to round out the paper. "You must always make three or more points in an essay. If the essay has less, then it's not strong." Laurel had been taught this rule both in high school and in her first college English class; no wonder, then, that she accepted its validity.

As opposed to Laurel, *Martha* possesses a whole arsenal of plans and rules with which to approach a humanities writing assignment, and, considering her background in biology, I wonder how many of them were formed out of the assumptions and procedures endemic to the physical sciences.[14] Martha will not put pen to first draft until she has spent up to two days generating an outline of remarkable complexity. I saw one of these outlines and it looked more like a diagram of protein synthesis or DNA structure than the time-worn pattern offered in composition textbooks. I must admit I was intrigued by the aura of process (vs. the static appearance of essay outlines) such diagrams offer, but for Martha these "outlines" only led to self-defeat: the outline would become so complex that all of its elements could never be included in a short essay. In other words, her plan locked her into the first stage of the composing process. Martha would struggle with the conversion of her outline into prose only to scrap the whole venture when deadlines passed and a paper had to be rushed together.

Martha's "rage for order" extends beyond the outlining process. She also believes that elements of a story or poem must evince a fairly linear structure and thematic clarity, or — perhaps bringing us closer to the issue — that analysis of a story or poem must provide the linearity or clarity that seems to be absent in the text. Martha, therefore, will bend the logic of her analysis to reason ambiguity out of existence. When I asked her about a strained paragraph in her paper on Camus' "The Guest," she said, "I didn't want to admit that it [the story's conclusion] was just hanging. I tried to force it into meaning."

Martha uses another rule, one that is not only problematical in itself, but one that often clashes directly with the elaborate plan and obsessive rule above. She believes that humanities papers must scintillate with insight, must present an array of images, ideas, ironies gleaned from the literature under examination. A problem arises, of course, when Martha tries to incorporate her myriad "neat little things," often inherently unrelated, into a tightly structured, carefully sequenced essay. Plans and rules that govern the construction of impressionistic, associational prose would be appropriate to Martha's desire, but her composing process is heavily constrained by the nonimpressionistic and nonassociational. Put another way, the plans and rules that govern her exploration of text are not at all synchronous with the plans and rules she uses to discuss her exploration. It is interesting to note here, however, that as recently as three years ago Martha was absorbed in creative writing and was publishing poetry in high school magazines. Given what we know about the complex associational, often non-neatly-sequential nature of the poet's creative process, we can infer that Martha was either free of the plans and rules discussed earlier or they were not as intense. One wonders, as well, if the exposure to three years of university physical science either established or intensified Martha's concern with structure. Whatever the case, she now is hamstrung by conflicting rules when composing papers for the humanities.

Mike's difficulties, too, are rooted in a distortion of the problem-solving process. When the time of the week for the assignment of writing topics draws near, Mike begins to prepare material, strategies, and plans that he believes will be appropriate. If the assignment matches his expectations, he has done a good job of analyzing the professor's intentions. If the assignment *doesn't* match his expectations, however, he cannot easily shift approaches. He feels trapped inside his original plans, cannot generate alternatives, and blocks. As the deadline draws near, he will write something, forcing the assignment to fit his conceptual procrustean bed. Since Mike is a smart man, he will offer a good deal of information, but only some of it ends up being appropriate to the assignment. This entire situation is made all the worse when the time between assignment of topic and generation of product is attenuated further, as in an essay examination. Mike believes (correctly) that one must have a plan, a strategy of some sort in order to solve a problem. He further believes, however, that such a plan, once formulated, becomes an exact structural and substantive blueprint that cannot be violated. The plan offers no alternatives, no "sub-routines." So, whereas Ruth's, Laurel's, and some of Martha's difficulties seem to be rule-specific ("always catch your audience," "write grammatically"), Mike's troubles are more global. He may have strategies that are appropriate for various writing situations (e.g., "for this kind of political science assignment write a compare/contrast essay"), but his entire approach to formulating plans and carrying them through to problem solution is too mechanical. It is probable that Mike's behavior is governed by an explicitly learned or inferred rule: "Always try to 'psych out' a professor." But in this case this rule initiates a problem-solving procedure that is clearly dysfunctional.

While Ruth and Laurel use rules that impede their writing process and Mike utilizes a problem-solving procedure that hamstrings him, *Sylvia* has trouble deciding which of the many rules she possesses to use. Her problem can be characterized as cognitive perplexity: some of her rules are inappropriate, others are functional; some mesh nicely with her own definitions of good writing, others don't. She has multiple rules to invoke, multiple paths to follow, and that very complexity of choice virtually paralyzes her. More so than with the previous four students, there is probably a strong emotional dimension to Sylvia's blocking, but the cognitive difficulties are clear and perhaps modifiable.

Sylvia, somewhat like Ruth and Laurel, puts tremendous weight on the crafting of her first paragraph. If it is good, she believes the rest of the essay will be good. Therefore, she will spend up to five hours on the initial paragraph: "I won't go on until I get that first paragraph down." Clearly, this rule — or the strength of it — blocks Sylvia's production. This is one problem. Another is that Sylvia has other equally potent rules that she sees as separate, uncomplementary injunctions: one achieves "flow" in one's writing through the use of adequate transitions; one achieves substance to one's writing through the use of evidence. Sylvia perceives both rules to be "true," but several times followed one to the exclusion of the other. Furthermore, as I talked to Sylvia, many other rules, guidelines, definitions were offered, but none with conviction. While she *is* committed to one rule about initial paragraphs, and that rule is dysfunctional, she seems very uncertain about the weight and hierarchy of the remaining rules in her cognitive repertoire.

"If It Won't Fit My Work, I'll Change It" — The Non-blockers

Dale, Ellen, Debbie, Susan, and Miles all write with the aid of rules. But their rules differ from blockers' rules in significant ways. If similar in content, they are expressed less absolutely — e.g., "*Try* to keep audience in mind." If dissimilar, they are still expressed less absolutely, more heuristically — e.g., "I can use as many ideas in my thesis paragraph as I need and then develop paragraphs for each idea." Our non-blockers do express some rules with firm assurance, but these tend to be simple injunctions that free up rather than restrict the composing process, e.g., "When stuck, write!" or "I'll write what I can." And finally, at least three of the students openly shun the very textbook rules that some blockers adhere to: e.g., "Rules like 'write only what you know about' just aren't true. I ignore those." These three, in effect, have formulated a further rule that expresses something like: "If a rule conflicts with what is sensible or with experience, reject it."

On the broader level of plans and strategies, these five students also differ from at least three of the five blockers in that they all possess problem-solving plans that are quite functional. Interestingly, on first exploration these plans seem to be too broad or fluid to be useful and, in some cases, can barely be expressed with any precision. Ellen, for example, admits that she has a general "outline in [her] head about how a topic paragraph should look" but could not describe much about its structure. Susan also has a general plan to follow, but, if stymied, will quickly attempt to conceptualize the assignment in different ways: "If my original idea won't work, then I need to proceed differently." Whether or not these plans operate in TOTE-fashion, I can't say. But they do operate with the operate-test fluidity of TOTEs.

True, our non-blockers have their religiously adhered-to rules: e.g., "When stuck, write," and plans, "I couldn't imagine writing without this pattern," but as noted above, these are few and functional. Otherwise, these non-blockers operate with fluid, easily modified, even easily discarded rules and plans (Ellen: "I can throw things out") that are sometimes expressed with a vagueness that could almost be interpreted as ignorance. There lies the irony. Students that offer the least precise rules and plans have the least trouble composing. Perhaps this very lack of precision characterizes the functional composing plan. But perhaps this lack of precision simply masks habitually enacted alternatives and sub-routines. This is clearly an area that needs the illumination of further research.

And then there is feedback. At least three of the five non-blockers are an Information-Processor's dream. They get to know their audience, ask professors and T.A.s specific questions about assignments, bring half-finished products in for evaluation, etc. Like Ruth, they realize the importance of audience, but unlike her, they have specific strategies for obtaining and utilizing feedback. And this penchant for testing writing plans against the needs of the audience can lead to modification of rules and plans. Listen to Debbie:

> In high school I was given a formula that stated that you must write a thesis paragraph with *only* three points in it, and then develop each of those points. When I hit college I was given longer assignments. That stuck me for a bit, but then realized that I could use as many ideas in my thesis paragraph as I needed and then develop paragraphs for each one. I asked someone about this and then tried it. I didn't get any negative feedback, so I figured it was o.k.

Debbie's statement brings one last difference between our blockers and non-blockers into focus; it has been implied above, but needs specific formulation: the goals these people have, and the plans they generate to attain these goals, are quite mutable. Part of the mutability comes from the fluid way the goals and plans are conceived, and part of it arises from the effective impact of feedback on these goals and plans.

Analyzing Writer's Block

Algorithms Rather Than Heuristics

In most cases, the rules our blockers use are not "wrong" or "incorrect" — it is good practice, for example, to "grab your audience with a catchy opening" or "craft a solid first paragraph before going on." The problem is that these rules seem to be followed as though they were algorithms, absolute dicta, rather than the loose heuristics that they were intended to be. Either through instruction, or the power of the textbook, or the predilections of some of our blockers for absolutes, or all three, these useful rules of thumb have been transformed into near-algorithmic urgencies. The result, to paraphrase Karl Dunker, is that these rules do not allow a flexible penetration into the nature of the problem. It is this transformation of heuristic into algorithm that contributes to the writer's block of Ruth and Laurel.

Questionable Heuristics Made Algorithmic

Whereas "grab your audience" could be a useful heuristic, "always make three or more points in an essay" is a pretty questionable one. Any such rule, though probably taught to aid the writer who needs structure, ultimately transforms a highly fluid process like writing into a mechanical lockstep. As heuristics, such rules can be troublesome. As algorithms, they are simply incorrect.

Set

As with any problem-solving task, students approach writing assignments with a variety of orientations or sets. Some are functional, others are not. Martha and Jane (see note 14), coming out of the life sciences and social sciences respectively, bring certain methodological orientations with them — certain sets or "directions" that make composing for the humanities a difficult, sometimes confusing, task. In fact, this orientation may cause them to misperceive the task. Martha has formulated a planning strategy from her predisposition to see processes in terms of linear, interrelated steps in a system. Jane doesn't realize that she can revise the statement that "committed" her to the direction her essay has taken. Both of these students are stymied because of formative experiences associated with their majors — experiences, perhaps, that nicely reinforce our very strong tendency to organize experiences temporally.

The Plan That Is Not a Plan

If fluidity and multi-directionality are central to the nature of plans, then the plans that Mike formulates are not true plans at all but, rather, inflexible and static cognitive blueprints.[15] Put another way, Mike's "plans" represent a restricted "closed system" (vs. "open system") kind of thinking, where closed system thinking is defined as focusing on "a limited number of units or items, or members, and those properties of the members which are to be used are known to begin with and do not change as the thinking proceeds," and open system thinking is characterized by an "adventurous exploration of multiple alternatives with strategies that allow redirection once 'dead ends' are encountered."[16] Composing calls for open, even adventurous thinking, not for constrained, no-exit cognition.

Feedback

The above difficulties are made all the more problematic by the fact that they seem resistant to or isolated from corrective feedback. One of the most striking things about Dale, Debbie, and Miles is the ease with which they seek out, interpret, and apply feedback on their rules, plans, and productions. They "operate" and then they "test," and the testing is not only against some internalized goal, but against the requirements of external audience as well.

Too Many Rules — "Conceptual Conflict"

According to D. E. Berlyne, one of the primary forces that motivate problem-solving behavior is a curiosity that arises from conceptual conflict — the convergence of incompatible beliefs or ideas. In *Structure and Direction in Thinking*,[17] Berlyne presents six major types of conceptual conflict, the second of which he terms "perplexity":

> This kind of conflict occurs when there are factors inclining the subject toward each of a set of mutually exclusive beliefs. (257)

If one substitutes "rules" for "beliefs" in the above definition, perplexity becomes a useful notion here. Because perplexity is unpleasant, people are motivated to reduce it by problem-solving behavior that can result in "disequalization":

> Degree of conflict will be reduced if either the number of competing . . . [rules] or their nearness to equality of strength is reduced. (259)

But "disequalization" is not automatic. As I have suggested, Martha and Sylvia hold to rules that conflict, but their perplexity does *not* lead to curiosity and resultant problem-solving behavior. Their perplexity, contra Berlyne, leads to immobilization. Thus "disequalization" will have to be effected from without. The importance of each of, particularly, Sylvia's rules needs an evaluation that will aid her in rejecting some rules and balancing and sequencing others.

A Note on Treatment

Rather than get embroiled in a blocker's misery, the teacher or tutor might interview the student in order to build a writing history and profile: How much and what kind of writing was done in high school? What is the student's major? What kind of writing does it require? How does the student compose? Are there rough drafts or outlines available? By what rules does the student operate? How would he or she define "good" writing? etc. This sort of interview reveals an incredible amount of information about individual composing processes. Furthermore, it often reveals the rigid rule or the inflexible plan that may lie at the base of the student's writing problem. That was precisely what happened with the five blockers. And with Ruth, Laurel, and Martha (and Jane) what was revealed made virtually immediate remedy possible. Dysfunctional rules are easily replaced with or counter-balanced by functional ones if there is no emotional reason to hold onto that which simply doesn't work. Furthermore, students can be trained to select, to "know which rules are appropriate for which problems."[18] Mike's difficulties, perhaps because plans are more complex and pervasive than rules, took longer to correct. But inflexible plans, too, can be remedied by pointing out their dysfunctional qualities and by assisting the student in developing appropriate and flexible alternatives. Operating this way, I was successful with Mike. Sylvia's story, however, did not end as smoothly. Though I had three forty-five minute contacts with her, I was not able to appreciably alter her behavior. Berlyne's theory bore results with Martha but not with Sylvia. Her rules were in conflict, and perhaps that conflict was not exclusively cognitive. Her case keeps analyses like these honest; it reminds us that the cognitive often melds with, and can be overpowered by, the affective. So while Ruth, Laurel, Martha, and Mike could profit from tutorials that explore the rules and plans in their writing behavior, students like Sylvia may need more extended, more affectively oriented counseling sessions that blend the instructional with the psychodynamic.

Notes

1. David Shapiro, *Neurotic Styles* (New York: Basic, 1965).
2. Barbara Hayes-Ruth, a Rand cognitive psychologist, and I are currently developing an information-processing model of the composing process. A good deal of work has already been done by Linda Flower and John Hayes (see

note 13 and surrounding text). I have just received—and recommend—their "Writing as Problem Solving" (paper presented at American Educational Research Association, April 1979).

3. Robert M. Gagné, *The Conditions of Learning* (New York: Holt, 1970) 193.
4. E. James Archer, "The Psychological Nature of Concepts," *Analysis of Concept Learning*, ed. H. J. Klausmeirer and C. W. Harris (New York: Academic P, 1966) 37–44; David P. Ausubel, *The Psychology of Meaningful Verbal Behavior* (New York: Grune, 1963); Robert M. Gagné, "Problem Solving," *Categories of Human Learning*, ed. Arthur W. Melton (New York: Academic P, 1964) 293–317; George A. Miller, *Language and Communication* (New York: McGraw, 1951).
5. George Katona, *Organizing and Memorizing* (New York: Columbia UP, 1940); Roger N. Shepard, Carl I. Hovland, and Herbert M. Jenkins, "Learning and Memorization of Classifications," *Psychological Monographs*, 75.13 (1961) (entire no. 517); Robert S. Woodworth, *Dynamics of Behavior* (New York: Holt, 1958) chs. 10–12.
6. Gagné, *The Conditions of Learning*, 190–91.
7. Karl Dunker, "On Problem Solving," *Psychological Monographs*, 58.5 (1945) (entire no. 270); George A. Polya, *How to Solve It* (Princeton: Princeton UP, 1945); George A. Miller, Eugene Galanter, and Karl H. Pribram, *Plans and the Structure of Behavior* (New York: Holt, 1960).
8. Lyle E. Bourne, Jr., Bruce R. Ekstrand, and Roger L. Dominowski, *The Psychology of Thinking* (Englewood Cliffs: Prentice, 1971).
9. John R. Hayes, "Problem Topology and the Solution Process," *Thinking: Current Experimental Studies*, ed. Carl P. Duncan (Philadelphia: Lippincott, 1967) 167–81.
10. Hulda J. Rees and Harold E. Israel, "An Investigation of the Establishment and Operation of Mental Sets," *Psychological Monographs*, 46 (1925) (entire no. 210).
11. Ibid.; Melvin H. Marx, Wilton W. Murphy, and Aaron J. Brownstein, "Recognition of Complex Visual Stimuli as a Function of Training with Abstracted Patterns," *Journal of Experimental Psychology* 62 (1961): 456–60.
12. James L. Adams, *Conceptual Blockbusting* (San Francisco: Freeman, 1974); Edward DeBono, *New Think* (New York: Basic, 1958); Ronald H. Forgus, *Perception* (New York: McGraw, 1966) ch. 13; Abraham Luchins and Edith Hirsch Luchins, *Rigidity of Behavior* (Eugene: U of Oregon Books, 1959); N. R. F. Maier, "Reasoning in Humans. I. On Direction," *Journal of Comparative Psychology* 10 (1920): 115–43.
13. Linda Flower and John Hayes, "Plans and the Cognitive Process of Writing," paper presented at the National Institute of Education Writing Conference, June 1977; "Problem-Solving Strategies and the Writing Process," *College English* 39 (1977): 449–61. See also note 2.
14. Jane, a student not discussed in this paper, was surprised to find out that a topic paragraph can be rewritten after a paper's conclusion to make that paragraph reflect what the essay truly contains. She had gotten so indoctrinated with Psychology's (her major) insistence that a hypothesis be formulated and then left untouched before an experiment begins that she thought revision of one's "major premise" was somehow illegal. She had formed a rule out of her exposure to social science methodology, and the rule was totally inappropriate for most writing situations.

15. Cf. "A plan is flexible if the order of execution of its parts can be easily interchanged without affecting the feasibility of the plan . . . the flexible planner might tend to think of lists of things he had to do; the inflexible planner would have his time planned like a sequence of cause-effect relations. The former could rearrange his lists to suit his opportunities, but the latter would be unable to strike while the iron was hot and would generally require considerable 'lead-time' before he could incorporate any alternative sub-plans" (Miller, Galanter, and Pribram, 120).
16. Frederic Bartlett, *Thinking* (New York: Basic, 1958) 74–76.
17. *Structure and Direction in Thinking* (New York: Wiley, 1965) 255.
18. Flower and Hayes, "Plans and the Cognitive Process of Writing," 26.

Rose's Insights as a Resource for Your Reflections

1. Consider the risks in teaching students how to write: Invariably, a few students will be cowed by your authority and will internalize even the most idle and perfunctory observations that you make. Worse yet, they will treat those observations not simply as useful tips but as some sort of holy edict. When they do, their ability to compose will be curtailed. In a journal, reflect on ways to prevent your overly earnest students from damaging themselves this way. What are some strategies you might devise to teach in a way that minimizes this risk?

2. How do you help students who have come into your classroom blocked by mishandled writing advice? What can you say to them? Can you use some of Rose's theory when giving advice to students who have already mishandled the advice given them in the past?

Rose's Insights as a Resource for Your Writing Classroom

1. Consider how you respond to grammar errors in student writing. Could thorough marking of "incorrect" spots in a paper contribute to what Rose identifies as an overly zealous conscientiousness about following the rules? Hold a class discussion about students' reactions to your written comments on their papers. Based on the discussion and on Rose's insights, how might you modify the ways you comment on student writing?

2. Ask students to meet in small groups, and make a list of the five most important dos and don'ts of writing. Then have them write

their lists on the board. As you discuss these rules, emphasize their tentative nature, and encourage students to take all of them with a grain of salt. Explain to them that to be overly concerned with such matters can undermine the process of getting thoughts down on paper.

Considering Audience

The Rhetorical Stance

Wayne C. Booth

Although this essay was written over forty years ago, it continues to enjoy frequent reprinting and much discussion among those who teach writing. Wayne C. Booth mixes casual anecdotes about his classroom practice with a sophisticated study of traditional rhetoric. Booth's central insight is that the success or failure of a piece of writing hinges on how the writer stages the author-subject-audience relationships within the text. He defines the ideal balance, or "rhetorical stance," by contrasting it with several "corruptions"—unbalanced stances that result in dry, obscure, or vacuous writing. Booth includes practical strategies to help students achieve the rhetorical stance, the proper balance that underlies all effective, persuasive writing. Like all powerful pieces, Booth's essay raises many questions: what is the ideally balanced stance, for example, and how do we coach students in how different contexts will require us to make different moves in sustaining it?

Last fall I had an advanced graduate student, bright, energetic, well-informed, whose papers were almost unreadable. He managed to be pretentious, dull, and disorganized in his paper on *Emma*, and pretentious, dull, and disorganized on *Madame Bovary*. On *The Golden Bowl* he was all these and obscure as well. Then one day, toward the end of term, he cornered me after class and said, "You know, I think you were all wrong about Robbe-Grillet's *Jealousy* today." We didn't have time to discuss it, so I suggested that he write me a note about it. Five hours later I found in my faculty box a four-page polemic, unpretentious, stimulating, organized, convincing. Here was a man who had taught freshman composition for several years and who was incapable of committing any of the more obvious errors that we think of as characteristic of bad writing. Yet he could not write a decent sentence, paragraph, or paper until his rhetorical problem was solved—until, that is, he had found a definition of his audience, his argument, and his own proper tone of voice.

The word *rhetoric* is one of those catch-all terms that can easily raise trouble when our backs are turned. As it regains a popularity that it once seemed permanently to have lost, its meanings seem to range all the way from something like "the whole art of writing on any subject," as in Kenneth Burke's *The Rhetoric of Religion*, through "the special arts of persuasion," on down to fairly narrow notions about rhetorical figures and devices. And of course we still have with us the meaning of "empty bombast," as in the phrase "merely rhetorical."

I suppose that the question of the role of rhetoric in the English course is meaningless if we think of rhetoric in either its broadest or its narrowest meanings. No English course could avoid dealing with rhetoric in Burke's sense, under whatever name, and on the other hand nobody would ever advocate anything so questionable as teaching "mere rhetoric." But if we settle on the following, traditional, definition, some real questions are raised: "Rhetoric is the art of finding and employing the most effective means of persuasion on any subject, considered independently of intellectual mastery of that subject." As the students say, "Prof. X knows his stuff but he doesn't know how to put it across." If rhetoric is thought of as the art of "putting it across," considered as quite distinct from mastering an "it" in the first place, we are immediately landed in a bramble bush of controversy. Is there such an art? If so, what does it consist of? Does it have a content of its own? Can it be taught? Should it be taught? If it should, how do we go about it, head on or obliquely?

Obviously it would be foolish to try to deal with many of these issues in twenty minutes. But I wish that there were more signs of our taking all of them seriously. I wish that along with our new passion for structural linguistics, for example, we could point to the development of a rhetorical theory that would show just how knowledge of structural linguistics can be useful to anyone interested in the art of persuasion. I wish there were more freshman texts that related every principle and every rule to functional principles of rhetoric, or, where this proves impossible, I wish one found more systematic discussion of why it is impossible. But for today, I must content myself with a brief look at the charge that there is nothing distinctive and teachable about the art of rhetoric.

The case against the isolability and teachability of rhetoric may look at first like a good one. Nobody writes rhetoric, just as nobody ever writes writing. What we write and speak is always *this* discussion of the decline of railroading and *that* discussion of Pope's couplets and the other argument for abolishing the poll-tax or for getting rhetoric back into English studies.

We can also admit that like all the arts, the art of rhetoric is at best very chancy, only partly amenable to systematic teaching; as we are all painfully aware when our 1:00 section goes miserably and our 2:00 section of the same course is a delight, our own rhetoric is not entirely under control. Successful rhetoricians are to some extent like poets, born, not made. They are also dependent on years of practice and experience. And we can finally admit that even the firmest of principles about writing cannot be taught in the same sense that elementary logic or arithmetic or French can be taught. In my first year of teaching, I had a student who started his first two essays with a swear word. When I suggested that perhaps the third paper ought to start with something else, he protested that his high school teacher had taught him always to catch the reader's attention. Now the teacher was right, but the application of even such a firm principle requires reserves of tact that were somewhat beyond my freshman.

But with all of the reservations made, surely the charge that the art of persuasion cannot in any sense be taught is baseless. I cannot think that anyone who has ever read Aristotle's *Rhetoric* or, say, Whateley's *Elements of Rhetoric* could seriously make the charge. There is more than enough in these and the other traditional rhetorics to provide structure and content for a year-long course. I believe that such a course, when planned and carried through with intelligence and flexibility, can be one of the most important of all educational experiences. But it seems obvious that the arts of persuasion cannot be learned in one year, that a good teacher will continue to teach them regardless of his subject matter, and that we as English teachers have a special responsibility at all levels to get certain basic rhetorical principles into all of our writing assignments. When I think back over the experiences which have had any actual effect on my writing, I find the great good fortune of a splendid freshman course, taught by a man who believed in what he was doing, but I also find a collection of other experiences quite unconnected with a specific writing course. I remember the instructor in psychology who pencilled one word after a peculiarly pretentious paper of mine: *bull*. I remember the day when P. A. Christensen talked with me about my Chaucer paper, and made me understand that my failure to use effective transitions was not simply a technical fault but a fundamental block in my effort to get him to see my meaning. His off-the-cuff pronouncement that I should never let myself write a sentence that was not in some way explicitly attached to preceding and following sentences meant far more to me at that moment, when I had something I wanted to say, than it could have meant as part of a pattern of such rules offered in a writing course. Similarly, I can remember the devastating lessons about my bad writing that Ronald Crane could teach with a simple question mark on a graduate seminar paper, or a pencilled "Evidence for this?" or "Why this section here?" or "Everybody says so. Is it true?"

Such experiences are not, I like to think, simply the result of my being a late bloomer. At least I find my colleagues saying such things as "I didn't learn to write until I became a newspaper reporter," or "The most important training in writing I had was doing a dissertation under old *Blank*." Sometimes they go on to say that the freshman course was useless; sometimes they say that it was an indispensable preparation for the later experience. The diversity of such replies is so great as to suggest that before we try to reorganize the freshman course, with or without explicit confrontations with rhetorical categories, we ought to look for whatever there is in common among our experiences, both of good writing and of good writing instruction. Whatever we discover in such an enterprise ought to be useful to us at any level of our teaching. It will not, presumably, decide once and for all what should be the content of the freshman course, if there should be such a course. But it might serve as a guideline for the development of widely different programs in the widely differing institutional circumstances in which we must work.

The common ingredient that I find in all of the writing I admire—excluding for now novels, plays, and poems—is something that I shall reluctantly call the rhetorical stance, a stance which depends on discovering and maintaining in any writing situation a proper balance among the three elements that are at work in any communicative effort: the available arguments about the subject itself, the interests and peculiarities of the audience, and the voice, the implied character, of the speaker. I should like to suggest that it is this balance, this rhetorical stance, difficult as it is to describe, that is our main goal as teachers of rhetoric. Our ideal graduate will strike this balance automatically in any writing that he considers finished. Though he may never come to the point of finding the balance easily, he will know that it is what makes the difference between effective communication and mere wasted effort.

What I mean by the true rhetorician's stance can perhaps best be seen by contrasting it with two or three corruptions, unbalanced stances often assumed by people who think they are practicing the arts of persuasion.

The first I'll call the pedant's stance; it consists of ignoring or underplaying the personal relationship of speaker and audience and depending entirely on statements about a subject—that is, the notion of a job to be done for a particular audience is left out. It is a virtue, of course, to respect the bare truth of one's subject, and there may even be some subjects which in their very nature define an audience and a rhetorical purpose so that adequacy to the subject can be the whole art of presentation. For example, an article on "The relation of the ontological and teleological proofs," in a recent *Journal of Religion*, requires a minimum of adaptation of argument to audience. But most subjects do not in themselves imply in any necessary way a purpose and an audience and hence a speaker's tone. The writer who assumes that it is enough merely to write an exposition of what he happens to know on the subject will produce the kind of essay that soils our scholarly journals, written not for readers but for bibliographies.

In my first year of teaching I taught a whole unit on "exposition" without ever suggesting, so far as I can remember, that the students ask themselves what their expositions were *for*. So they wrote expositions like this one—I've saved it, to teach me toleration of my colleagues: the title is "Family Relations in More's *Utopia*." "In this theme I would like to discuss some of the relationships with the family which Thomas More elaborates and sets forth in his book, *Utopia*. The first thing that I would like to discuss about family relations is that overpopulation, according to More, is a just cause of war." And so on. Can you hear that student sneering at me, in this opening? What he is saying is something like "you ask for a meaningless paper, I give you a meaningless paper." He knows that he has no audience except me. He knows that I don't want to read his summary of family relations in *Utopia*, and he knows that I know that he therefore has no rhetorical purpose. Because he has not been led to see a question which he considers worth answering, or an audience that could possibly care one way or the other, the paper is worse than no paper at all, even though it has no grammatical or spelling errors and is organized right down the line, one, two, three.

An extreme case, you may say. Most of us would never allow ourselves that kind of empty fencing? Perhaps. But if some carefree foundation is willing to finance a statistical study, I'm willing to wager a month's salary that we'd find at least half of the suggested topics in our freshman texts as pointless as mine was. And we'd find a good deal more than half of the discussions of grammar, punctuation, spelling, and style totally divorced from any notion that rhetorical purpose to some degree controls all such matters. We can offer objective descriptions of levels of usage from now until graduation, but unless the student discovers a desire to say something to somebody and learns to control his diction for a purpose, we've gained very little. I once gave an assignment asking students to describe the same classroom in three different statements, one for each level of usage. They were obedient, but the only ones who got anything from the assignment were those who intuitively imported the rhetorical instructions I had overlooked — such purposes as "Make fun of your scholarly surroundings by describing this classroom in extremely elevated style," or "Imagine a kid from the slums accidentally trapped in these surroundings and forced to write a description of this room." A little thought might have shown me how to give the whole assignment some human point, and therefore some educative value.

Just how confused we can allow ourselves to be about such matters is shown in a recent publication of the Educational Testing Service, called "Factors in Judgments of Writing Ability." In order to isolate those factors which affect differences in grading standards, ETS set six groups of readers — businessmen, writers and editors, lawyers, and teachers of English, social science, and natural science — to reading the same batch of papers. Then ETS did a hundred-page "factor analysis" of the amount of agreement and disagreement, and of the elements which different kinds of graders emphasized. The authors of the report express a certain amount of shock at the discovery that the median correlation was only .31 and that 94 percent of the papers received either seven, eight, or nine of the nine possible grades.

But what *could* they have expected? In the first place, the students were given no purpose and no audience when the essays were assigned. And then all these editors and businessmen and academics were asked to judge the papers in a complete vacuum, using only whatever intuitive standards they cared to use. I'm surprised that there was any correlation at all. Lacking instructions, some of the students undoubtedly wrote polemical essays, suitable for the popular press; others no doubt imagined an audience, say, of *Reader's Digest* readers, and others wrote with the English teachers as implied audience; an occasional student with real philosophical bent would no doubt do a careful analysis of the pros and cons of the case. This would be graded low, of course, by the magazine editors, even though they would have graded it high if asked to judge it as a speculative contribution to the analysis of the problem. Similarly, a creative student who has been getting A's for his personal essays will write an amusing colorful piece, failed by all the social scientists present, though they would have graded it high if asked to judge it for what it was. I find it shocking that tens of thousands of dollars and endless hours should have been spent by students, graders, and professional testers analyzing essays and grading results totally abstracted from any notion of purposeful human communication. Did nobody protest? One might as well assemble a group of citizens to judge students' capacity to throw balls, say, without telling the students or the graders whether altitude, speed, accuracy or form was to be judged. The judges would be drawn from football coaches, jai-lai experts, lawyers, and English teachers, and asked to apply whatever standards they intuitively apply to ball throwing. Then we could express astonishment that the judgments did not correlate very well, and we could do a factor analysis to discover, lo and behold, that some readers concentrated on altitude, some on speed, some on accuracy, some on form—and the English teachers were simply confused.

One effective way to combat the pedantic stance is to arrange for weekly confrontations of groups of students over their own papers. We have done far too little experimenting with arrangements for providing a genuine audience in this way. Short of such developments, it remains true that a good teacher can convince his students that he is a true audience, if his comments on the papers show that some sort of dialogue is taking place. As Jacques Barzun says in *Teacher in America*, students should be made to feel that unless they have said something to someone, they have failed; to bore the teacher is a worse form of failure than to anger him. From this point of view we can see that the charts of grading symbols that mar even the best freshman texts are not the innocent time savers that we pretend. Plausible as it may seem to arrange for more corrections with less time, they inevitably reduce the student's sense of purpose in writing. When he sees innumerable W13s and P19s in the margin, he cannot possibly feel that the art of persuasion is as important to his instructor as when he reads personal comments, however few.

This first perversion, then, springs from ignoring the audience or overreliance on the pure subject. The second, which might be called the advertiser's stance, comes from *under*valuing the subject and overvaluing pure effect: how to win friends and influence people.

Some of our best freshman texts — Sheridan Baker's *The Practical Stylist*, for example — allow themselves on occasion to suggest that to be controversial or argumentative, to stir up an audience is an end in itself. Sharpen the controversial edge, one of them says, and the clear implication is that one should do so even if the truth of the subject is honed off in the process. This perversion is probably in the long run a more serious threat in our society than the danger of ignoring the audience. In the time of audience-reaction meters and pre-tested plays and novels, it is not easy to convince students of the old Platonic truth that good persuasion is honest persuasion, or even of the old Aristotelian truth that the good rhetorician must be master of his subject, no matter how dishonest he may decide ultimately to be. Having told them that good writers always to some degree accommodate their arguments to the audience, it is hard to explain the difference between justified accommodation — say changing *point one* to the final position — and the kind of accommodation that fills our popular magazines, in which the very substance of what is said is accommodated to some preconception of what will sell. "The publication of *Eros* [magazine] represents a major breakthrough in the battle for the liberation of the human spirit."

At a dinner about a month ago I sat between the wife of a famous civil rights lawyer and an advertising consultant. "I saw the article on your book yesterday in the *Daily News*," she said, "but I didn't even finish it. The title of your book scared me off. Why did you ever choose such a terrible title? Nobody would buy a book with a title like that." The man on my right, whom I'll call Mr. Kinches, overhearing my feeble reply, plunged into a conversation with her, over my torn and bleeding corpse. "Now with my *last* book," he said, "I listed twenty possible titles and then tested them out on four hundred businessmen. The one I chose was voted for by 90 percent of the businessmen." "That's what I was just saying to Mr. Booth," she said. "A book title ought to grab you, and *rhetoric* is not going to grab anybody." "Right," he said. "My *last* book sold fifty thousand copies already; I don't know how this one will do, but I polled two hundred businessmen on the table of contents, and . . ."

At one point I did manage to ask him whether the title he chose really fit the book. "Not quite as well as one or two of the others," he admitted, "but that doesn't matter, you know. If the book is designed right, so that the first chapter pulls them in, and you *keep* 'em in, who's going to gripe about a little inaccuracy in the title?"

Well, rhetoric is the art of persuading, not the art seeming to persuade by giving everything away at the start. It presupposes that one has a purpose concerning a subject which itself cannot be fundamentally modified by the desire to persuade. If Edmund Burke had decided that he could win more votes in Parliament by choosing the other side—as he most certainly could have done—we would hardly hail this party-switch as a master stroke of rhetoric. If Churchill had offered the British "peace in our time," with some laughs thrown in, because opinion polls had shown that more Britishers were "grabbed" by these than by blood, sweat, and tears, we could hardly call his decision a sign of rhetorical skill.

One could easily discover other perversions of the rhetorician's balance—most obviously what might be called the entertainer's stance—the willingness to sacrifice substance to personality and charm. I admire Walker Gibson's efforts to startle us out of dry pedantry, but I know from experience that his exhortations to find and develop the speaker's voice can lead to empty colorfulness. A student once said to me, complaining about a colleague, "I soon learned that all I had to do to get an A was imitate Thurber."

But perhaps this is more than enough about the perversions of the rhetorical stance. Balance itself is always harder to describe than the clumsy poses that result when it is destroyed. But we all experience the balance whenever we find an author who succeeds in changing our minds. He can do so only if he knows more about the subject than we do, and if he then engages us in the process of thinking—and feeling—it through. What makes the rhetoric of Milton and Burke and Churchill great is that each presents us with the spectacle of a man passionately involved in thinking an important question through, in the company of an audience. Though each of them did everything in his power to make his point persuasive, including a pervasive use of the many emotional appeals that have been falsely scorned by many a freshman composition text, none would have allowed himself the advertiser's stance; none would have polled the audience in advance to discover which position would get the votes. Nor is the highly individual personality that springs out at us from their speeches and essays present for the sake of selling itself. The rhetorical balance among speakers, audience, and argument is with all three men habitual, as we see if we look at their nonpolitical writings. Burke's work on the Sublime and Beautiful is a relatively unimpassioned philosophical treatise, but one finds there again a delicate balance: though the implied author of this work is a far different person, far less obtrusive, far more objective, than the man who later cried *sursum corda* to the British Parliament, he permeates with his philosophical personality his philosophical work. And though the signs of his awareness of his audience are far more subdued, they are still here: every effort is made to involve the *proper* audience, the audience of philosophical minds, in a fundamentally interesting inquiry, and to lead them through to the end. In short, because he was a man engaged with men in the effort to solve a human problem, one could never call what he wrote dull, however difficult or abstruse.

Now obviously the habit of seeking this balance is not the only thing we have to teach under the heading of rhetoric. But I think that everything worth teaching under that heading finds its justification finally in that balance. Much of what is now considered irrelevant or dull can, in fact, be brought to life when teachers and students know what they are seeking. Churchill reports that the most valuable training he ever received in rhetoric was in the diagramming of sentences. Think of it! Yet the diagramming of a sentence, regardless of the grammatical system, can be a live subject as soon as one asks not simply "How is this sentence put together," but rather "Why is it put together in this way?" or "Could the rhetorical balance and hence the desired persuasion be better achieved by writing it differently?"

As a nation we are reputed to write very badly. As a nation, I would say, we are more inclined to the perversions of rhetoric than to the rhetorical balance. Regardless of what we do about this or that course in the curriculum, our mandate would seem to be, then, to lead more of our students than we now do to care about and practice the true arts of persuasion.

Booth's Insights as a Resource for Your Reflections

1. Read any piece of writing by a student, and track the ways the author appeals to you as a reader. Where does the author adopt the pedant's stance? The advertiser's stance? How might these terms help you to comment on student work that needs improvement?

2. Consider the stance that you model for your students. Do you alternate between pedant and advertiser, or do you strike a rhetorical stance most of the time? How do the students respond to the various stances we model for them?

Booth's Insights as a Resource for Your Writing Classroom

1. Assign Booth's essay to your students. Once they've read it, have them explore it according to the terms Booth himself presents. Does Booth effectively balance the audience-subject-author relationships? If so, how and where does he manage to strike this balance? Are there any places where the stance seems imbalanced and starts to lean in one direction or another?

2. Ask students to examine their own work or each other's in light of Booth's essay. Have them focus on passages in their own writing that lean toward a pedant, advertiser, or entertainer stance. Can they use Booth's terms to diagnose and fix problems?

Closing My Eyes as I Speak: An Argument for Ignoring Audience

Peter Elbow

At one time or another, all writing teachers have probably fallen back on this familiar exhortation to students whose writing misses the mark: "Consider your audience!" But is that necessarily good advice? In the following selection, first published in College English *in 1987, Peter Elbow argues that writers often need simply to ignore audience. Even though he credits several arguments for audience awareness and agrees that a consideration of audience can invite and enable the writer to generate thought and feeling, he cautions that audience awareness can sometimes inhibit and even block writing. In particular, attention to audience in the earliest stages of writing may confuse and inhibit the writer, whereas during revision it may enlighten and liberate the writer.*

Elbow asserts that when a student's concern for audience inhibits his or her writing, the teacher should suggest that the student ignore audience and simply follow his or her own thoughts wherever they might lead. He disagrees that writers who shape "reader-based prose" are ipso facto more cognitively mature than those who produce "writer-based prose." Instead, he insists that the ability to turn off audience awareness when it is distracting or confusing is a higher skill. Writers who can switch off audience awareness and sustain quiet, thoughtful reflection — who can in private reflection make meaning for themselves and shape a discourse from such thinking alone — are independent and mature thinkers. Once these writers work out through drafts and "internal conversation" what they think, they can turn their attention back to audience. Elbow insists that "ignoring audience can lead to worse drafts but better revisions."

> Very often people don't listen to you when you speak to them. It's only when you talk to yourself that they prick up their ears.
>
> — John Ashbery

When I am talking to a person or a group and struggling to find words or thoughts, I often find myself involuntarily closing my eyes as I speak. I realize now that this behavior is an instinctive attempt to blot out awareness of audience when I need all my concentration for just trying to figure out or express what I want to say. Because the audience is so imperiously present in a speaking situation, my instinct reacts with this active attempt to avoid audience awareness. This behavior — in a sense impolite or antisocial — is not so uncommon. Even when we write, alone in a room to an absent audience, there are occasions when we are struggling to figure something out and need to push aside awareness of those absent readers. As Donald Murray puts it, "My sense of audience is so strong that I have to suppress my conscious awareness of audience to hear what the text demands" (Berkenkotter and Murray 171). In recognition of how pervasive the role of audience is in writing, I write to celebrate the benefits of ignoring audience.[1]

It will be clear that my argument for writing without audience awareness is not meant to undermine the many good reasons for writing *with* audience awareness some of the time. (For example, that we are liable to neglect audience because we write in solitude; that young people often need more practice in taking into account points of view different from their own; and that students often have an impoverished sense of writing as communication because they have only written in a school setting to teachers.) Indeed I would claim some part in these arguments for audience awareness — which now seem to be getting out of hand.

I start with a limited claim: even though ignoring audience will usually lead to weak writing at first — to what Linda Flower calls "writer-based prose" — this weak writing can help us in the end to better writing than we would have written if we'd kept readers in mind from the start. Then I will make a more ambitious claim: writer-based prose is sometimes better than reader-based prose. Finally I will explore some of the theory underlying these issues of audience.

A Limited Claim

It's not that writers should never think about their audience. It's a question of when. An audience is a field of force. The closer we come — the more we think about these readers — the stronger the pull they exert on the contents of our minds. The practical question, then, is always whether a particular audience functions as a helpful field of force or one that confuses or inhibits us.

Some audiences, for example, are *inviting* or *enabling*. When we think about them as we write, we think of more and better things to say — and what we think somehow arrives more coherently structured than usual. It's like talking to the perfect listener: we feel smart and come up with ideas we didn't know we had. Such audiences are helpful to keep in mind right from the start.

Other audiences, however, are powerfully *inhibiting* — so much so, in certain cases, that awareness of them as we write blocks writing altogether. There are certain people who always make us feel dumb when we try to speak to them: we can't find words or thoughts. As soon as we get out of their presence, all the things we want to say pop back into our minds. Here is a student telling what happens when she tries to follow the traditional advice about audience:

> You know ____ [author of a text] tells us to pay attention to the audience that will be reading our papers, and I gave that a try. I ended up without putting a word on paper until I decided the hell with ____; I'm going to write to who I damn well want to; otherwise I can hardly write at all.

Admittedly, there are some occasions when we benefit from keeping a threatening audience in mind from the start. We've been putting off writing that letter to that person who intimidates us. When we finally sit down and write *to* them — walk right up to them, as it were, and look them in the eye — we may manage to stand up to the threat and grasp the nettle and thereby find just what we need to write.

Most commonly, however, the effect of audience awareness is somewhere between the two extremes: the awareness disturbs or disrupts our writing and thinking without completely blocking it. For example, when we have to write to someone we find intimidating (and of course students often perceive teachers as intimidating), we often start thinking wholly defensively. As we write down each thought or sentence, our mind fills with thoughts of how the intended reader will criticize or object to it. So we try to qualify or soften what we've just written — or write out some answer to a possible objection. Our writing becomes tangled. Sometimes we get so tied in knots that we cannot even figure out what we *think*. We may not realize how often audience awareness has this effect on our students when we don't see the writing process behind their papers: we just see texts that are either tangled or empty.

Another example. When we have to write to readers with whom we have an awkward relationship, we often start beating around the bush and feeling shy or scared, or start to write in a stilted, overly careful style or voice. (Think about the cute, too-clever style of many memos we get in our departmental mailboxes — the awkward self-consciousness academics experience when writing to other academics.) When students are asked to write to readers they have not met or cannot imagine, such as "the general reader" or "the educated public," they often find nothing to say except clichés they know *they* don't even quite believe.

When we realize that an audience is somehow confusing or inhibiting us, the solution is fairly obvious. We can ignore that audience altogether during the *early* stages of writing and direct our words only to ourselves or to no one in particular — or even to the "wrong" audience, that is, to an *inviting* audience of trusted friends or allies. This strategy often dissipates the confusion; the clenched, defensive discourse starts to run clear. Putting audience out of mind is of course a traditional practice: serious writers have long used private journals for early explorations of feeling, thinking, or language. But many writing teachers seem to think that students can get along without the private writing serious writers find so crucial — or even that students will *benefit* from keeping their audience in mind for the whole time. Things often don't work out that way.

After we have figured out our thinking in copious exploratory or draft writing — perhaps finding the right voice or stance as well — *then* we can follow the traditional rhetorical advice: Think about readers and revise carefully to adjust our words and thoughts to our intended audience. For a particular audience it may even turn out that we need to *disguise* our point of view. But it's hard to disguise something while engaged in trying to figure it out. As writers, then, we need to learn when to think about audience and when to put readers out of mind.

Many people are too quick to see Flower's "writer-based prose" as an analysis of what's wrong with this type of writing and miss the substantial degree to which she was celebrating a natural, and indeed developmentally enabling, response to cognitive overload. What she doesn't say, however, despite her emphasis on planning and conscious control in the writing process, is that we can *teach* students to notice when audience awareness is getting in their way — and when this happens, consciously to put aside the needs of readers for a while. She seems to assume that when an overload occurs, the writer-based gear will, as it were, automatically kick into action to relieve it. In truth, of course, writers often persist in using a malfunctioning *reader*-based gear despite the overload — thereby mangling their language or thinking. Though Flower likes to rap the knuckles of people who suggest a "correct" or "natural" order for steps in the writing process, she implies such an order here: When attention to audience causes an overload, start out by ignoring them while you attend to your thinking; after you work out your thinking, turn your attention to audience.

Thus if we ignore audience while writing on a topic about which we are not expert or about which our thinking is still evolving, we are likely to produce exploratory writing that is unclear to anyone else — perhaps even inconsistent or a complete mess. Yet by doing this exploratory "swamp work" in conditions of safety, we can often coax our thinking through a process of new discovery and development. In this way we can end up with something better than we could have produced if we'd tried to write to our audience all along. In short, ignoring audience can lead to worse drafts but better revisions. (Because we are professionals and adults, we often write in the role of expert: we may know what we think without new exploratory writing; we may even be able to speak confidently to critical readers. But students seldom experience this confident professional stance in their writing. And think how much richer *our* writing would be if we defined ourselves as *in*expert and allowed ourselves private writing for new explorations of those views we are allegedly sure of.)

Notice then that two pieties of composition theory are often in conflict:

1. Think about audience as you write (this stemming from the classical rhetorical tradition).
2. Use writing for *making new meaning*, not just transmitting old meanings already worked out (this stemming from the newer epistemic tradition I associate with Ann Berthoff's classic explorations).

It's often difficult to work out new meaning while thinking about readers.

A More Ambitious Claim

I go further now and argue that ignoring audience can lead to better writing—immediately. In effect, writer-based prose can be *better* than reader-based prose. This might seem a more controversial claim, but is there a teacher who has not had the experience of struggling and struggling to no avail to help a student untangle his writing, only to discover that the student's casual journal writing or freewriting is untangled and strong? Sometimes freewriting is stronger than the essays we get only because it is expressive, narrative, or descriptive writing and the student was not constrained by a topic. But teachers who collect drafts with completed assignments often see passages of freewriting that are strikingly stronger *even* when they are expository and constrained by the assigned topic. In some of these passages we can sense that the strength derives from the student's unawareness of readers.

It's not just unskilled, tangled writers, though, who sometimes write better by forgetting about readers. Many competent and even professional writers produce mediocre pieces *because* they are thinking too much about how their readers will receive their words. They are acting too much like a salesman trained to look the customer in the eye and to think at all times about the characteristics of the "target audience." There is something too staged or planned or self-aware about such writing. We see this quality in much second-rate newspaper or magazine or business writing: "good-student writing" in the awful sense of the term. Writing produced this way reminds us of the ineffective actor whose consciousness of self distracts us: he makes us too aware of his own awareness of us. When we read such prose, we wish the writer would stop thinking about us—would stop trying to "adjust" or "fit" what he is saying to our frame of reference. "Damn it, put all your attention on what you are saying," we want to say, "and forget about us and how we are reacting."

When we examine really good student or professional writing, we can often see that its goodness comes from the writer's having gotten sufficiently wrapped up in her meaning and her language as to forget all about audience needs: the writer manages to "break through." The Earl of Shaftesbury talked about writers needing to escape their audience in order to find their own ideas (Cooper 1:109; see also Griffin). It is characteristic of much truly good writing to be, as it were, on fire with its meaning. Consciousness of readers is burned away; involvement in subject determines all. Such writing is analogous to the performance of the actor who has managed to stop attracting attention to her awareness of the audience watching her.

The arresting power in some writing by small children comes from their obliviousness to audience. As readers, we are somehow sucked into a more-than-usual connection with the meaning itself because of the child's gift for more-than-usual concentration on what she is saying. In short, we can feel some pieces of children's writing as being very writer-based. Yet it's precisely that quality which makes it powerful for us as readers. After all, why should we settle for a writer's entering our point of view, if we can have the more powerful experience of being sucked out of our point of view and into her world? This is just the experience that children are peculiarly capable of giving because they are so expert at total absorption in their world as they are writing. It's not just a matter of whether the writer "decenters," but of whether the writer has a sufficiently strong focus of attention to make the *reader* decenter. This quality of concentration is what D. H. Lawrence so admires in Melville:

> [Melville] was a real American in that he always felt his audience in front of him. But when he ceases to be American, when he forgets all audience, and gives us his sheer apprehension of the world, then he is wonderful, his book [*Moby Dick*] commands a stillness in the soul, an awe. (158)

What most readers value in really excellent writing is not prose that is right for readers but prose that is right for thinking, right for language, or right for the subject being written about. If, in addition, it is clear and well suited to readers, we appreciate that. Indeed we feel insulted if the writer did not somehow try to make the writing *available* to us before delivering it. But if it succeeds at being really true to language and thinking and "things," we are willing to put up with much difficulty as readers:

> Good writing is not always or necessarily an adaptation to communal norms (in the Fish/Bruffee sense) but may be an attempt to construct (and instruct) a reader capable of reading the text in question. The literary history of the "difficult" work — from Mallarmé to Pound, Zukofsky, Olson, etc. — seems to say that much of what we value in writing we've had to learn to value by learning how to read it. (Trimbur)

The effect of audience awareness on voice is particularly striking — if paradoxical. Even though we often develop our voice by finally "speaking up" to an audience or "speaking out" to others, and even though much dead student writing comes from students not really treating their writing as a communication with real readers, nevertheless, the opposite effect is also common: we often do not really develop a strong, authentic voice in our writing till we find important occasions for *ignoring* audience — saying, in effect, "To hell with whether they like it or not. I've got to say this the way I want to say it." Admittedly, the voice that emerges when we ignore audience is sometimes odd or idiosyncratic in some way, but usually it is stronger. Indeed, teachers sometimes complain that student writing is "writer-based" when the problem is simply the idiosyncrasy — and sometimes in fact the *power* — of the voice. They would value this odd but resonant voice if they found it in a published writer (see Elbow, "Real Voice," *Writing with Power*). Usually we cannot *trust* a voice unless it is unaware of us and our needs and speaks out in its own terms (see the Ashbery epigraph). To celebrate writer-based prose is to risk the charge of *romanticism*: just warbling one's woodnotes wild. But my position also contains the austere *classic* view that we must nevertheless *revise* with conscious awareness of audience in order to figure out which pieces of writer-based prose are good as they are — and how to discard or revise the rest.

To point out that writer-based prose can be *better* for readers than reader-based prose is to reveal problems in these two terms. Does *writer-based* mean:

1. That the text doesn't work for readers because it is too much oriented to the writer's point of view?
2. Or that the writer was not thinking about readers as she wrote, although the text *may* work for readers?

Does *reader-based* mean:

3. That the text works for readers — meets their needs?
4. Or that the writer was attending to readers as she wrote although her text *may* not work for readers?

In order to do justice to the reality and complexity of what actually happens in both writers and readers, I was going to suggest four terms for the four conditions listed above, but I gradually realized that things are even too complex for that. We really need to ask about what's going on in three dimensions — in the *writer*, in the *reader*, and in the *text* — and realize that the answers can occur in virtually any combination:

> Was the writer thinking about readers or oblivious to them?
>
> Is the *text* oriented toward the writer's frame of reference or point of view, or oriented toward that of readers? (A writer may be thinking about readers and still write a text that is largely oriented toward her own frame of reference.)
>
> Are the readers' needs being met? (The text may meet the needs of readers whether the writer was thinking about them or not, and whether the text is oriented toward them or not.)

Two Models of Cognitive Development

Some of the current emphasis on audience awareness probably derives from a model of cognitive development that needs to be questioned. According to this model, if you keep your readers in mind as you write, you are operating at a higher level of psychological development than if you ignore readers. Directing words to readers is "more mature" than directing them to no one in particular or to yourself. Flower relates writer-based prose to the inability to "decenter," which is characteristic of Piaget's early stages of development, and she relates reader-based prose to later more mature stages of development.

On the one hand, of course this view must be right. Children do decenter as they develop. As they mature they get better at suiting their discourse to the needs of listeners, particularly to listeners very different from themselves. Especially, they get better at doing so *consciously* — thinking *awarely* about how things appear to people with different viewpoints. Thus much unskilled writing is unclear or awkward *because* the writer was doing what it is so easy to do — unthinkingly taking her own frame of reference for granted and not attending to the needs of readers who might have a different frame of reference. And of course this failure is more common in younger, immature, "egocentric" students (and also more common in writing than in speaking since we have no audience present when we write).

But on the other hand, we need the contrary model that affirms what is also obvious once we reflect on it, namely that the ability to *turn off* audience awareness — especially when it confuses thinking or blocks discourse — is also a "higher" skill. I am talking about an ability to use language in "the desert island mode," an ability that tends to require learning, growth, and psychological development. Children, and even adults who have not learned the art of quiet, thoughtful, inner reflection, are often unable to get much cognitive action going in their heads unless there are other people present to have action *with*. They are dependent on live audience and the social dimension to get their discourse rolling or to get their thinking off the ground.

For in contrast to a roughly Piagetian model of cognitive development that says we start out as private, egocentric little monads and grow up to be public and social, it is important to invoke the opposite model that derives variously from Vygotsky, Bakhtin, and Meade. According to this model, we *start out* social and plugged into others and only gradually, through learning and development, come to "unplug" to any significant degree so as to function in a more private, individual and differentiated fashion: "Development in thinking is not from the individual to the socialized, but from the social to the individual" (Vygotsky 20). The important general principle in this model is that we tend to *develop* our important cognitive capacities by means of social interaction with others, and having done so we gradually learn to perform them alone. We fold the "simple" back-and-forth of dialogue into the "complexity" (literally, "foldedness") of individual, private reflection.

Where the Piagetian (individual psychology) model calls our attention to the obvious need to learn to enter into viewpoints other than our own, the Vygotskian (social psychology) model calls our attention to the equally important need to learn to produce good thinking and discourse *while alone*. A rich and enfolded mental life is something that people achieve only gradually through growth, learning, and practice. We tend to associate this achievement with the fruits of higher education.

Thus we see plenty of students who lack this skill, who have nothing to say when asked to freewrite or to write in a journal. They can dutifully "reply" to a question or a topic, but they cannot seem to *initiate* or *sustain* a train of thought on their own. Because so many adolescent students have this difficulty, many teachers chime in: "Adolescents have nothing to write about. They are too young. They haven't had significant experience." In truth, adolescents don't lack experience or material, no matter how "sheltered" their lives. What they lack is practice and help. Desert island discourse is a learned cognitive process. It's a mistake to think of private writing (journal writing and freewriting) as merely "easy"—merely a relief from trying to write right. It's also hard. Some exercises and strategies that help are Ira Progoff's "Intensive Journal" process, Sondra Perl's "Composing Guidelines," or Elbow's "Loop Writing" and "Open Ended Writing" processes (*Writing with Power* 50–77).

The Piagetian and Vygotskian developmental models (language-begins-as-private vs. language-begins-as-social) give us two different lenses through which to look at a common weakness in student writing, a certain kind of "thin" writing where the thought is insufficiently developed or where the language doesn't really explain what the writing implies or gestures toward. Using the Piagetian model, as Flower does, one can specify the problem as a weakness in audience orientation. Perhaps the writer has immaturely taken too much for granted and unthinkingly assumed that her limited explanations carry as much meaning for readers as they do for herself. The cure or treatment is for the writer to think more about readers.

Through the Vygotskian lens, however, the problem and the "immaturity" look altogether different. Yes, the writing isn't particularly clear or satisfying for readers, but this alternative diagnosis suggests a failure of the private desert island dimension: the writer's explanation is too thin because she didn't work out her train of thought fully enough *for herself*. The suggested cure or treatment is *not* to think more about readers but to think more for herself, to practice exploratory writing in order to learn to engage in that reflective discourse so central to mastery of the writing process. How can she engage readers more till she has engaged herself more?

The current emphasis on audience awareness may be particularly strong now for being fueled by *both* psychological models. From one side, the Piagetians say, in effect, "The egocentric little critters, we've got to *socialize* 'em! Ergo, make them think about audience when they write!" From the other side, the Vygotskians say, in effect, "No wonder they're having trouble writing. They've been bamboozled by the Piagetian heresy. They think they're solitary individuals with private selves when really they're just congeries of voices that derive from their discourse community. Ergo, let's intensify the social context — use peer groups and publication: make them think about audience when they write! (And while we're at it, let's hook them up with a better class of discourse community.)" To advocate ignoring audience is to risk getting caught in the crossfire from two opposed camps.

Two Models of Discourse: Discourse as Communication and Discourse as Poesis or Play

We cannot talk about writing without at least implying a psychological or developmental model. But we'd better make sure it's a complex, paradoxical, or spiral model. Better yet, we should be deft enough to use two contrary models or lenses. (Bruner pictures the developmental process as a complex movement in an upward reiterative spiral — not a simple movement in one direction.)

According to one model, it is characteristic of the youngest children to direct their discourse to an audience. They learn discourse *because* they have an audience; without an audience they remain mute, like "the wild child." Language is social from the start. But we need the other model to show us what is also true, namely that it is characteristic of the youngest children to use language in a *nonsocial* way. They use language not only because people talk to them but also because they have such a strong propensity to play and to build — often in a *nonsocial* or non-audience-oriented fashion. Thus although one paradigm for discourse is social communication, another is private exploration or solitary play. Babies and toddlers tend to babble in an exploratory and reflective way — to themselves and not to an audience — often even with no one else near. This archetypally private use of discourse is strikingly illustrated when we see a pair of toddlers in "parallel play" alongside each other — each busily talking but not at all trying to communicate with the other.

Therefore, when we choose paradigms for discourse, we should think not only about children using language to communicate, but also about children building sandcastles or drawing pictures. Though children characteristically show their castles or pictures to others, they just as characteristically trample or crumple them before anyone else can see them. Of course sculptures and pictures are different from words. Yet discourse implies more media than words; and even if you restrict discourse to words, one of our most mature uses of language is for building verbal pictures and structures for their own sake — not just for communicating with others.

Consider this same kind of behavior at the other end of the life cycle: Brahms staggering from his deathbed to his study to rip up a dozen or more completed but unpublished and unheard string quartets that dissatisfied him. How was he relating to audience here — worrying too much about audience or not giving a damn? It's not easy to say. Consider Glenn Gould deciding to renounce performances before an audience. He used his private studio to produce recorded performances for an audience, but to produce ones that satisfied *himself* he clearly needed to suppress audience awareness. Consider the more extreme example of Kerouac typing page after page — burning each as soon as he completed it. The language behavior of humans is slippery. Surely we are well advised to avoid positions that say it is "always X" or "essentially Y."

James Britton makes a powerful argument that the "making" or poesis function of language grows out of the expressive function. Expressive language is often for the sake of communication with an audience, but just as often it is only for the sake of the speaker — working something out for herself (66–67, 74ff). Note also that "writing to learn," which writing-across-the-curriculum programs are discovering to be so important, tends to be writing for the self or even for no one at all rather than for an outside reader. You throw away the writing, often unread, and keep the mental changes it has engendered.

I hope this emphasis on the complexity of the developmental process — the limits of our models and of our understanding of it — will serve as a rebuke to the tendency to label students as being at a lower stage of cognitive development just because they don't yet write well. (Occasionally they *do* write well — in a way — but not in the way that the labeler finds appropriate.) Obviously the psychologistic labeling impulse started out charitably. Shaughnessy was fighting those who called basic writers *stupid* by saying they weren't dumb, just at an earlier developmental stage. Flower was arguing that writer-based prose is a natural response to a cognitive overload and indeed developmentally enabling. But this kind of talk can be dangerous since it labels students as literally "retarded" and makes teachers and administrators start to think of them as such. Instead of calling poor writers *either* dumb or slow (two forms of blaming the victim), why not simply call them poor writers? If years of schooling haven't yet made them good writers, perhaps they haven't gotten the kind of teaching and support they need. Poor students are often deprived of the very thing they need most to write well (which is given to good students): lots of extended and adventuresome writing for self and for audience. Poor students are often asked to write only answers to fill-in exercises.

As children get older, the developmental story remains complex or spiral. Though the first model makes us notice that babies start out with a natural gift for using language in a social and communicative fashion, the second model makes us notice that children and adolescents must continually learn to relate their discourse better to an audience — must struggle to decenter better. And though the second model makes us notice that babies also start out with a natural gift for using language in a *private*, exploratory, and playful way, the first model makes us notice that children and adolescents must continually learn to master this solitary, desert island, poesis mode better. Thus we mustn't think of language only as communication—nor allow communication to claim dominance either as the earliest or as the most "mature" form of discourse. It's true that language is inherently communicative (and without communication we don't develop language), yet language is just as inherently the stringing together of exploratory discourse for the self—or for the creation of objects (play, poesis, making) for their own sake.

In considering this important poesis function of language, we need not discount (as Berkenkotter does) the striking testimony of so many witnesses who think and care most about language: professional poets, writers, and philosophers. Many of them maintain that their most serious work is *making*, not *communicating*, and that their commitment is to language, reality, logic, experience, not to readers. Only in their willingness to cut loose from the demands or needs of readers, they insist, can they do their best work. Here is William Stafford on this matter:

> I don't want to overstate this . . . but . . . my impulse is to say I don't think of an audience at all. When I'm writing, the satisfactions in the process of writing are my satisfactions in dealing with the language, in being surprised by phrasings that occur to me, in finding that this miraculous kind of convergent focus begins to happen. That's my satisfaction, and to think about an audience would be a distraction. I try to keep from thinking about an audience. (Cicotello 176)

And Chomsky:

> I can be using language in the strictest sense with no intention of communicating. . . . As a graduate student, I spent two years writing a lengthy manuscript, assuming throughout that it would never be published or read by anyone. I meant everything I wrote, intending nothing as to what anyone would [understand], in fact taking it for granted that there would be no audience. . . . Communication is only one function of language, and by no means an essential one. (Qtd. in Feldman 5–6)

It's interesting to see how poets come together with philosophers on this point—and even with mathematicians. All are emphasizing the "poetic" function of language in its literal sense—"poesis" as "making." They describe their writing process as more like "getting something right" or even "solving a problem" for its own sake than as communicating with readers or addressing an audience. The task is not to satisfy readers but to satisfy the rules of the system: "[T]he writer is not thinking of a reader at all; he makes it 'clear' as a contract with *language*" (Goodman 164).

Shall we conclude, then, that solving an equation or working out a piece of symbolic logic is at the opposite end of the spectrum from communicating with readers or addressing an audience? No. To draw that conclusion would be a fall again into a one-sided position. Sometimes people write mathematics *for* an audience, sometimes not. The central point in this essay is that we cannot answer audience questions in an *a priori* fashion based on the "nature" of discourse or of language or of cognition — only in terms of the different *uses* or *purposes* to which humans put discourse, language, or cognition on different occasions. If most people have a restricted repertoire of uses for writing — if most people use writing only to send messages to readers, that's no argument for constricting the *definition* of writing. It's an argument for helping people expand their repertoire of uses.

The value of learning to ignore audience while writing, then, is the value of learning to cultivate the private dimension: the value of writing in order to make meaning to oneself, not just to others. This involves learning to free oneself (to some extent, anyway) from the enormous power exerted by society and others, to unhook oneself from external prompts and social stimuli. We've grown accustomed to theorists and writing teachers puritanically stressing the *problem* of writing: the tendency to neglect the needs of readers because we usually write in solitude. But let's also celebrate this same feature of writing as one of its glories: writing *invites* disengagement too, the inward turn of mind, and the dialogue with self. Though writing is deeply social and though we usually help things by enhancing its social dimension, writing is also the mode of discourse best suited to helping us develop the reflective and private dimension of our mental lives.

"But Wait a Minute, ALL Discourse Is Social"

Some readers who see *all* discourse as social will object to my opposition between public and private writing (the "trap of oppositional thinking") and insist that *there is no such thing as private discourse*. What looks like private, solitary mental work, they would say, is really social. Even on the desert island I am in a crowd.

> By ignoring audience in the conventional sense, we return to it in another sense. What I get from Vygotsky and Bakhtin is the notion that audience is not really out there at all but is in fact "always already" (to use that poststructuralist mannerism . . .) inside, interiorized in the conflicting languages of others — parents, former teachers, peers, prospective readers, whomever — that writers have to negotiate to write, and that we do negotiate when we write whether we're aware of it or not. The audience we've got to satisfy in order to feel good about our writing is as much in the past as in the present or future. But we experience it (it's so internalized) as *ourselves*. (Trimbur, "Beyond Cognition")

(Ken Bruffee likes to quote from Frost: "'Men work together, . . . / Whether they work together or apart'" ["The Tuft of Flowers"]). Or —

putting it slightly differently — when I engage in what seems like private non-audience-directed writing, I am really engaged in communication with the "audience of self." For the self is multiple, not single, and discourse to self is communication from one entity to another. As Feldman argues, "The self functions as audience in much the same way that others do" (290).

Suppose I accept this theory that all discourse is really social — including what I've been calling "private writing" or writing I don't intend to show to any reader. Suppose I agree that all language is essentially communication directed toward an audience — whether some past internalized voice or (what may be the same thing) some aspect of the self. What would this theory say to my interest in "private writing"?

The theory would seem to destroy my main argument. It would tell me that there's no such thing as "private writing"; it's impossible *not* to address audience; there are no vacations from audience. But the theory might try to console me by saying not to worry, because we don't *need* vacations from audience. Addressing audience is as easy, natural, and unaware as breathing — and we've been at it since the cradle. Even young, unskilled writers are already expert at addressing audiences.

But if we look closely we can see that in fact this theory doesn't touch my central practical argument. For even if all discourse is naturally addressed to *some* audience, it's not naturally addressed to the *right* audience — the living readers we are actually trying to reach. Indeed the pervasiveness of past audiences in our heads is one more reason for the difficulty of reaching present audiences with our texts. Thus even if I concede the theoretical point, there still remains an enormous practical and phenomenological difference between writing "public" words for others to read and writing "private" words for no one to read.

Even if "private writing" is "deep down" social, the fact remains that, as we engage in it, we don't have to worry about whether it works on readers or even makes sense. We can refrain from doing all the things that audience-awareness advocates advise us to do ("keeping our audience in mind as we write" and trying to "decenter"). Therefore this social-discourse theory doesn't undermine the benefits of "private writing" and thus provides no support at all for the traditional rhetorical advice that we should "always try to think about (intended) audience as we write."

In fact this social-discourse theory reinforces two subsidiary arguments I have been making. First, even if there is no getting away from *some* audience, we can get relief from an inhibiting audience by writing to a more inviting one. Second, audience problems don't come only from *actual* audiences but also from phantom "audiences in the head" (Elbow, *Writing with Power* 186ff). Once we learn how to be more aware of the effects of both external and internal readers and how to direct our words elsewhere, we can get out of the shadow even of a troublesome phantom reader.

And even if all our discourse is *directed to* or *shaped by* past audiences or voices, it doesn't follow that our discourse is *well directed to* or *successfully shaped for* those audiences or voices. Small children direct much talk to others, but that doesn't mean they always *suit* their talk to others. They often fail. When adults discover that a piece of their writing has been "heavily shaped" by some audience, this is bad news as much as good: often the writing is crippled by defensive moves that try to fend off criticism from this reader.

As teachers, particularly, we need to distinguish and emphasize "private writing" in order to teach it, to teach that crucial cognitive capacity to engage in extended and productive thinking that doesn't depend on audience prompts or social stimuli. It's sad to see so many students who can reply to live voices but cannot engage in productive dialogue with voices in their heads. Such students often lose interest in an issue that had intrigued them—just because they don't find other people who are interested in talking about it and haven't learned to talk reflectively to *themselves* about it.

For these reasons, then, I believe my main argument holds force even if I accept the theory that all discourse is social. But, perhaps more tentatively, I resist this theory. I don't know all the data from developmental linguistics, but I cannot help suspecting that babies engage in *some* private poesis—or "play-language"—some private babbling in addition to social babbling. Of course Vygotsky must be right when he points to so much social language in children, but can we really trust him when he denies *all* private or nonsocial language (which Piaget and Chomsky see)? I am always suspicious when someone argues for the total nonexistence of a certain kind of behavior or event. Such an argument is almost invariably an act of definitional aggrandizement, not empirical searching. To say that *all* language is social is to flop over into the opposite one-sidedness that we need Vygotsky's model to save us from.

And even if all language is *originally* social, Vygotsky himself emphasizes how "inner speech" becomes more individuated and private as the child matures. "Egocentric speech is relatively accessible in three-year-olds but quite inscrutable in seven-year-olds: the older the child, the more thoroughly has his thought become inner speech" (Emerson 254; see also Vygotsky 134). "The inner speech of the adult represents his 'thinking for himself' rather than social adaptation. . . . Out of context, it would be incomprehensible to others because it omits to mention what is obvious to the 'speaker'" (Vygotsky 18).

I also resist the theory that all private writing is really communication with the "*audience of self*." ("When we represent the objects of our thought in language, we intend to make use of these representations at a later time. . . . [T]he speaker-self must have audience directed intentions toward a listener-self" [Feldman 289].) Of course private language often is a communication with the audience of self:

- When we make a shopping list. (It's obvious when we can't decipher that third item that we're confronting *failed* communication with the self.)
- When we make a rough draft for ourselves but not for others' eyes. Here we are seeking to clarify our thinking with the leverage that comes from standing outside and reading our own utterance as audience — experiencing our discourse as receiver instead of as sender.
- When we experience ourselves as slightly split. Sometimes we experience ourselves as witness to ourselves and hear our own words from the outside — sometimes with great detachment, as on some occasions of pressure or stress.

But there are other times when private language is not communication with audience of self:

- Freewriting to no one: for the *sake* of self but not *to* the self. The goal is not to communicate but to follow a train of thinking or feeling to see where it leads. In doing this kind of freewriting (and many people have not learned it), you don't particularly plan to come back and read what you've written. You just write along and the written product falls away to be ignored, while only the "real product" — any new perceptions, thoughts, or feelings produced in the mind by the freewriting — is saved and looked at again. (It's not that you don't experience your words *at all* but you experience them only as speaker, sender, or emitter — not as receiver or audience. To say that's the same as being audience is denying the very distinction between "speaker" and "audience.")

As this kind of freewriting actually works, it often *leads* to writing we look at. That is, we freewrite along to no one, following discourse in hopes of getting somewhere, and then at a certain point we often sense that we have *gotten* somewhere: we can tell (but not because we stop and read) that what we are now writing seems new or intriguing or important. At this point we may stop writing; or we may keep on writing, but in a new audience-relationship, realizing that we *will* come back to this passage and read it as audience. Or we may take a new sheet (symbolizing the new audience-relationship) and try to write out for ourselves what's interesting.

- Writing as exorcism is a more extreme example of private writing *not* for the audience of self. Some people have learned to write in order to get rid of thoughts or feelings. By freewriting what's obsessively going round and round in our head we can finally let it go and move on.

I am suggesting that some people (and especially poets and freewriters) engage in a kind of discourse that Feldman, defending what she calls a "communication-intention" view, has never learned and thus has a hard time imagining and understanding. Instead of always using language in an audience-directed fashion for the sake of communication, these writers unleash language for its own sake and let it function a bit on its own, without much *intention* and without much need for *communication*, to see where it leads — and thereby end up with some intentions and potential communications they didn't have before.

It's hard to turn off the audience-of-self in writing — and thus hard to imagine writing to no one (just as it's hard to turn off the audience of *outside* readers when writing an audience-directed piece). Consider "invisible writing" as an intriguing technique that helps you become less of an audience-of-self for your writing. Invisible writing prevents you from seeing what you have written: you write on a computer with the screen turned down, or you write with a spent ballpoint pen on paper with carbon paper and another sheet underneath. Invisible writing tends to get people not only to write faster than they normally do, but often better (see Blau). I mean to be tentative about this slippery issue of whether we can really stop being audience to our own discourse, but I cannot help drawing the following conclusion: just as in freewriting, suppressing the *other* as audience tends to enhance quantity and sometimes even quality of writing; so in invisible writing, suppressing the *self* as audience tends to enhance quantity and sometimes even quality.

Contraries in Teaching

So what does all this mean for teaching? It means that we are stuck with two contrary tasks. On the one hand, we need to help our students enhance the social dimension of writing: to learn to be *more* aware of audience, to decenter better and learn to fit their discourse better to the needs of readers. Yet it is every bit as important to help them learn the private dimension of writing: to learn to be *less* aware of audience, to put audience needs aside, to use discourse in the desert island mode. And if we are trying to advance contraries, we must be prepared for paradoxes.

For instance if we emphasize the social dimension in our teaching (for example, by getting students to write to each other, to read and comment on each other's writing in pairs and groups, and by staging public discussions and even debates on the topics they are to write about), we will obviously help the social, public, communicative dimension of writing — help students experience writing not just as jumping through hoops for a grade but rather as taking part in the life of a community of discourse. But "social discourse" can also help private writing by getting students sufficiently involved or invested in an issue so that they finally want to carry on producing discourse alone and in private — and for themselves.

Correlatively, if we emphasize the private dimension in our teaching (for example, by using lots of private exploratory writing, freewriting, and journal writing and by helping students realize that of course they may need practice with this "easy" mode of discourse before they can use it fruitfully), we will obviously help students learn to write better reflectively for themselves without the need for others to interact with. Yet this private discourse can also help public, social writing — help students finally feel full enough of their *own* thoughts to have some genuine desire to *tell* them to others. Students often feel they "don't have anything to say" until they finally succeed in engaging themselves in private desert island writing for themselves alone.

Another paradox: Whether we want to teach greater audience awareness or the ability to ignore audience, we must help students learn not only to "try harder" but also to "just relax." That is, sometimes students fail to produce reader-based prose because they don't *try* hard enough to think about audience needs. But sometimes the problem is cured if they just relax and write *to* people — as though in a letter or in talking to a trusted adult. By unclenching, they effortlessly call on social discourse skills of immense sophistication. Sometimes, indeed, the problem is cured if the student simply writes in a more social *setting* — in a classroom where it is habitual to share lots of writing. Similarly, sometimes students can't produce sustained private discourse because they don't try hard enough to keep the pen moving and forget about readers. They must persist and doggedly push aside those feelings of, "My head is empty, I have run out of anything to say." But sometimes what they need to learn through all that persistence is how to relax and let go — to unclench.

As teachers, we need to think about what it means to *be an audience* rather than just be a teacher, critic, assessor, or editor. If our only response is to tell students what's strong, what's weak, and how to improve it (diagnosis, assessment, and advice), we actually *undermine* their sense of writing as a social act. We reinforce their sense that writing means doing school exercises, producing for authorities what they already know — *not* actually trying to say things to readers. To help students experience us as *audience* rather than as assessment machines, it helps to respond by "replying" (as in a letter) rather than always "giving feedback."

Paradoxically enough, one of the best ways teachers can help students learn to turn off audience awareness and write in the desert island mode — to turn off the babble of outside voices in the head and listen better to quiet inner voices — is to be a special kind of private audience to them, to be a reader who nurtures by trusting and believing in the writer. Britton has drawn attention to the importance of teacher as "trusted adult" for school children (67–68). No one can be good at private, reflective writing without some *confidence and trust in self*. A nurturing reader can give a writer a kind of permission to forget about other readers or to be one's own reader. I have benefited from this special kind of audience and have seen it prove useful to others. When I had a teacher who believed in me, who was interested in me and interested in what I had to say, I wrote well. When I had a teacher who thought I was naive, dumb, silly, and in need of being "straightened out," I wrote badly and sometimes couldn't write at all. Here is an interestingly paradoxical instance of the social-to-private principle from Vygotsky and Meade: We learn to listen better and more trustingly to *ourselves* through interaction with trusting *others*.

Look for a moment at lyric poets as paradigm writers (instead of seeing them as aberrant), and see how they heighten *both* the public and private dimensions of writing. Bakhtin says that lyric poetry implies "the absolute certainty of the listener's sympathy" (113). I think it's more helpful to say that lyric poets learn to create more than usual privacy in which to write *for themselves* — and then they turn around and let *others overhear*. Notice how poets tend to argue for the importance of no-audience writing, yet they are especially gifted at being public about what they produce in private. Poets are revealers — sometimes even grandstanders or showoffs. Poets illustrate the need for opposite or paradoxical or double audience skills: on the one hand, the ability to be private and solitary and tune out others — to write only for oneself and not give a damn about readers, yet on the other hand, the ability to be more than usually interested in audience and even to be a ham.

If writers really need these two audience skills, notice how bad most conventional schooling is on both counts. Schools offer virtually no privacy for writing: everything students write is collected and read by a teacher, a situation so ingrained students will tend to complain if you don't collect and read every word they write. Yet on the other hand, schools characteristically offer little or no social dimension for writing. It is *only* the teacher who reads, and students seldom feel that in giving their writing to a teacher they are actually communicating something they really want to say to a real person. Notice how often they are happy to turn in to teachers something perfunctory and fake that they would be embarrassed to show to classmates. Often they feel shocked and insulted if we want to distribute to classmates the assigned writing they hand in to us. (I think of Richard Wright's realization that the naked white prostitutes didn't bother to cover themselves when he brought them coffee as a black bellboy because they didn't really think of him as a man or even a person.) Thus the conventional school setting for writing tends to be the least private and the least public — when what students need, like all of us, is practice in writing that is the most private and also the most public.

Practical Guidelines about Audience

The theoretical relationships between discourse and audience are complex and paradoxical, but the practical morals are simple:

1. Seek ways to heighten both the *public* and *private* dimensions of writing. (For activities, see the previous section.)
2. When working on important audience-directed writing, we must try to emphasize audience awareness *sometimes*. A useful rule of thumb is to start by putting the readers in mind and carry on as long as things go well. If difficulties arise, try putting readers out of mind and write either to no audience, to self, or to an inviting audience. Finally, always *revise* with readers in mind. (Here's another occasion when orthodox advice about writing is wrong — but turns out right if applied to revising.)
3. Seek ways to heighten awareness of one's writing process (through process writing and discussion) to get better at taking control and deciding when to keep readers in mind and when to ignore them. Learn to discriminate factors like these:
   a. The writing task. Is this piece of writing *really* for an audience? More often than we realize, it is not. It is a draft that only we will see, though the final version will be for an audience; or exploratory writing for figuring something out; or some kind of personal private writing meant only for ourselves.
   b. Actual readers. When we put them in mind, are we helped or hindered?
   c. One's own temperament. Am I the sort of person who tends to think of what to say and how to say it when I keep readers in mind? Or someone (as I am) who needs long stretches of forgetting all about readers?
   d. Has some powerful "audience-in-the-head" tricked me into talking to it when I'm really trying to talk to someone else — distorting new business into old business? (I may be an inviting teacher-audience to my students, but they may not be able to pick up a pen without falling under the spell of a former, intimidating teacher.)
   e. Is *double audience* getting in my way? When I write a memo or report, I probably have to suit it not only to my "target audience" but also to some colleagues or supervisor. When I write something for publication, it must be right for readers, but it won't be published unless it is also right for the editors — and if it's a book it won't be much read unless it's right for reviewers.

Children's stories won't be bought unless they are right for editors and reviewers *and* parents. We often tell students to write to a particular "real-life" audience — or to peers in the class — but of course they are also writing for us as graders. (This problem is more common as more teachers get interested in audience and suggest "second" audiences.)

f. Is *teacher-audience* getting in the way of my students' writing? As teachers we must often read in an odd fashion: in stacks of twenty-five or fifty pieces all on the same topic; on topics we know better than the writer; not for pleasure or learning but to grade or find problems (see Elbow, *Writing with Power* 216–36).

To list all these audience pitfalls is to show again the need for thinking about audience needs — yet also the need for vacations from readers to think in peace.

Acknowledgments

I benefited from much help from audiences in writing various drafts of this piece. I am grateful to Jennifer Clarke, with whom I wrote a collaborative piece containing a case study on this subject. I am also grateful for extensive feedback from Pat Belanoff, Paul Connolly, Sheryl Fontaine, John Trimbur, and members of the Martha's Vineyard Summer Writing Seminar.

Note

1. There are many different entities called audience: (a) The actual readers to whom the text will be given; (b) the writer's conception of those readers — which may be mistaken (see Ong; Park; Ede and Lunsford); (c) the audience that the text implies — which may be different still (see Booth); (d) the discourse community or even genre addressed or implied by the text (see Walzer); (e) ghost or phantom "readers in the head" that the writer may unconsciously address or try to please (see Elbow, *Writing with Power* 186ff. Classically, this is a powerful former teacher. Often such an audience is so ghostly as not to show up as actually "implied" by the text). For the essay I am writing here, these differences don't much matter: I'm celebrating the ability to put aside the needs or demands of *any* or all of these audiences. I recognize, however, that we sometimes cannot fight our way free of unconscious or tacit audiences (as in b or e above) unless we bring them to greater conscious awareness.

Works Cited

Bakhtin, Mikhail. "Discourse in Life and Discourse in Poetry." Appendix. *Freudianism: A Marxist Critique*. By F. N. Volosinov. Trans. I. R. Titunik. Ed. Neal H. Bruss. New York: Academic, 1976. (Holquist's attribution of this work to Bakhtin is generally accepted.)

Berkenkotter, Carol, and Donald Murray. "Decisions and Revisions: The Planning Strategies of a Publishing Writer and the Response of Being a Rat—or Being Protocoled." *College Composition and Communication* 34 (1983): 156–72.

Blau, Sheridan. "Invisible Writing." *College Composition and Communication* 34 (1983): 297–312.

Booth, Wayne. *The Rhetoric of Fiction*. Chicago: U Chicago P, 1961.

Britton, James. *The Development of Writing Abilities*, 11–18. Urbana: NCTE, 1977.

Bruffee, Kenneth A. "Liberal Education and the Social Justification of Belief." *Liberal Education* 68 (1982): 95–114.

Bruner, Jerome. *Beyond the Information Given: Studies in the Psychology of Knowing*. Ed. Jeremy Anglin. New York: Norton, 1973.

———. *On Knowing: Essays for the Left Hand*. Expanded ed. Cambridge: Harvard UP, 1979.

Chomsky, Noam. *Reflections on Language*. New York: Random, 1975.

Cicotello, David M. "The Art of Writing: An Interview with William Stafford." *College Composition and Communication* 34 (1983): 173–77.

Clarke, Jennifer, and Peter Elbow. "Desert Island Discourse: On the Benefits of Ignoring Audience." *The Journal Book*. Ed. Toby Fulwiler. Montclair: Boynton, 1987.

Cooper, Anthony Ashley, 3rd Earl of Shaftesbury. *Characteristics of Men, Manners, Opinions, Times, Etc*. Ed. John M. Robertson. 2 vols. Gloucester, MA: Smith, 1963.

Ede, Lisa, and Andrea Lunsford. "Audience Addressed/Audience Invoked: The Role of Audience in Composition Theory and Pedagogy." *College Composition and Communication* 35 (1984): 140–54.

Elbow, Peter. *Writing with Power*. New York: Oxford UP, 1981.

———. *Writing without Teachers*. New York: Oxford UP, 1973.

Emerson, Caryl. "The Outer Word and Inner Speech: Bakhtin, Vygotsky, and the Internalization of Language." *Critical Inquiry* 10 (1983): 245–64.

Feldman, Carol Fleisher. "Two Functions of Language." *Harvard Education Review* 47 (1977): 282–93.

Flower, Linda. "Writer-Based Prose: A Cognitive Basis for Problems in Writing." *College English* 41 (1979): 19–37.

Goodman, Paul. *Speaking and Language: Defense of Poetry*. New York: Random, 1972.

Griffin, Susan. "The Internal Voices of Invention: Shaftesbury's Soliloquy." Unpublished. 1986.

Lawrence, D. H. *Studies in Classic American Literature*. Garden City: Doubleday, 1951.

Ong, Walter. "The Writer's Audience Is Always a Fiction." *PMLA* 90 (1975): 9–21.

Park, Douglas B. "The Meanings of 'Audience.'" *College English* 44 (1982): 247–57.

Perl, Sondra. "Guidelines for Composing." Appendix A. *Through Teachers' Eyes: Portraits of Writing Teachers at Work*. By Sondra Perl and Nancy Wilson. Portsmouth: Heinemann, 1986.

Progoff, Ira. *At a Journal Workshop*. New York: Dialogue, 1975.

Shaughnessy, Mina. *Errors and Expectations: A Guide for the Teacher of Basic Writing*. New York: Oxford UP, 1977.

Trimbur, John. "Beyond Cognition: Voices in Inner Speech." *Rhetoric Review* 5 (1987): 211–21.

———. Letter to the author. September 1985.

Vygotsky, L. S. *Thought and Language*. Trans. and ed. E. Hanfmann and G. Vakar. 1934. Cambridge: MIT P, 1962.

Walzer, Arthur E. "Articles from the 'California Divorce Project': A Case Study of the Concept of Audience." *College Composition and Communication* 36 (1985): 150–59.

Wright, Richard. *Black Boy*. New York: Harper, 1945.

Elbow's Insights as a Resource for Your Reflections

1. Respond to Elbow's claim that writer-based prose is sometimes better than reader-based prose. Have you ever found students' journal writing or freewriting to be stronger than their formal writing? How might you implement Elbow's ideas to help such students write more effective final drafts? Does Elbow's argument impact the way that you will address the subject of audience awareness with your students in the future?

2. Elbow's recommendation is to turn off the screen while writing with a computer. Try this and then reflect on the results. Were you better able to ignore audience? Did this exercise have an effect on your writing?

Elbow's Insights as a Resource for Your Writing Classroom

1. Elbow's "ghost reader" — a student's sense of an inflexible teacher-as-evaluator — surfaces frequently in early essays from first-year writers and most often in diagnostic essays written the first week. Photocopy a few samples of writing where the ghost reader clearly frightened the writer into dense or unclear or stuffy or inauthentic prose. Ask the class to decide where the "ghost teacher as reader" intruded and to suggest ways to exorcise the ghost reader.

2. Ask students to describe, either in journal entries or a brainstorming session, strategies that they use or habits that they have when writing or preparing to write (which they may have dismissed as personal idiosyncrasies unrelated to writing), and how these strategies and habits are related to their personal approach to the writing process. Do these habits hinder or encourage the flow of ideas? How might students consciously adjust these habits to promote uninhibited writing?

Revising a Draft

Revision Strategies of Student Writers and Experienced Adult Writers

Nancy Sommers

First published in College Composition and Communication *in 1980, Nancy Sommers's landmark study of the revision strategies used by students and by experienced, adult writers arrives at a bold conclusion: a major distinction between the immature and the mature writer is how the two groups conceive revision. The former see it as little more than editing; the latter understand it as a global, recursive, generative process by which the whole text changes and improves in fundamental ways.*

Sommers cites or implies several reasons that students see revision only as a linear process attending to surface features of a manuscript: previous writing experiences, infrequent practice, traditional dicta about the nature of revising, and cognitive readiness. She asserts that writing teachers can assist student writers to mature and to acquire a perspective on writing as discovery and development. Furthermore, writing teachers can help student writers to realize, as experienced adult writers do, that "Good writing disturbs: it creates dissonance." How might Sommers complicate or extend some of the ideas on the writing process encountered earlier in this chapter?

Although various aspects of the writing process have been studied extensively of late, research on revision has been notably absent. The reason for this, I suspect, is that current models of the writing process have directed attention away from revision. With few exceptions, these models are linear; they separate the writing process into discrete stages. Two representative models are Gordon Rohman's suggestion that the composing process moves from prewriting to writing to rewriting and James Britton's model of the writing process as a series of stages described in metaphors of linear growth, conception—incubation—production.[1] What is striking about these theories of writing is that they model themselves on speech: Rohman defines the writer in a way that cannot distinguish him from a speaker ("A writer is a man who . . . puts [his] experience into words in his own mind" [15]); and Britton backs his theory of writing on what he calls (following Jakobson) the "expressiveness" of speech.[2] Moreover, Britton's study itself follows the "linear model" of the relation of thought and language in speech proposed by Vygotsky, a relationship embodied in the linear movement "from the motive which engenders a thought to the shaping of the thought, *first* in inner speech, *then* in meanings of words, and *finally* in words" (qtd. in Britton 40). What this movement fails to take into account in its linear structure—"first . . . then . . . finally"—is the recursive shaping of thought by language; what it fails to take into account is *revision*. In these linear conceptions of the writing process revision is understood as a separate stage at the end of the process—a stage that comes after the completion of a first or second draft and one that is temporally distinct from the prewriting and writing stages of the process.[3]

The linear model bases itself on speech in two specific ways. First of all, it is based on traditional rhetorical models, models that were created to serve the spoken art of oratory. In whatever ways the parts of classical rhetoric are described, they offer "stages" of composition that are repeated in contemporary models of the writing process. Edward Corbett, for instance, describes the "five parts of a discourse"—*inventio, dispositio, elocutio, memoria, pronuntiatio*—and, disregarding the last two parts since "after rhetoric came to be concerned mainly with written discourse, there was no further need to deal with them,"[4] he produces a model very close to Britton's conception [*inventio*], incubation [*dispositio*], production [*elocutio*]. Other rhetorics also follow this procedure, and they do so not simply because of historical accident. Rather, the process represented in the linear model is based on the irreversibility of speech. Speech, Roland Barthes says, "is irreversible":

> A word cannot be retracted, except precisely by saying that one retracts it. To cross out here is to add: if I want to erase what I have just said, I cannot do it without showing the eraser itself (I must say: "*or rather . . .*" "*I expressed myself badly . . .*"); paradoxically, it is ephemeral speech which is indelible, not monumental writing. All that one can do in the case of a spoken utterance is to tack on another utterance.[5]

What is impossible in speech is *revision*: like the example Barthes gives, revision in speech is an afterthought. In the same way, each stage of the linear model must be exclusive (distinct from the other stages) or else it becomes trivial and counterproductive to refer to these junctures as "stages."

By staging revision after enunciation, the linear models reduce revision in writing, as in speech, to no more than an afterthought. In this way such models make the study of revision impossible. Revision, in Rohman's model, is simply the repetition of writing; or to pursue Britton's organic metaphor, revision is simply the further growth of what is already there, the "preconceived" product. The absence of research on revision, then, is a function of a theory of writing which makes revision both superfluous and redundant, a theory which does not distinguish between writing and speech.

What the linear models do produce is a parody of writing. Isolating revision and then disregarding it plays havoc with the experiences composition teachers have of the actual writing and rewriting of experienced writers. Why should the linear model be preferred? Why should revision be forgotten, superfluous? Why do teachers offer the linear model and students accept it? One reason, Barthes suggests, is that "there is a fundamental tie between teaching and speech," while "writing begins at the point where speech becomes *impossible*."[6] The spoken word cannot be revised. The possibility of revision distinguishes the written text from speech. In fact, according to Barthes, this is the essential difference between writing and speaking. When we must revise, when the very idea is subject to recursive shaping by language, then speech becomes inadequate. This is a matter to which I will return, but first we should examine, theoretically, a detailed exploration of what student writers as distinguished from experienced adult writers *do* when they write and rewrite their work. Dissatisfied with both the linear model of writing and the lack of attention to the process of revision, I conducted a series of studies over the past three years which examined the revision processes of student writers and experienced writers to see what role revision played in their writing processes. In the course of my work the revision process was redefined as *a sequence of changes in a composition—changes which are initiated by cues and occur continually throughout the writing of a work.*

Methodology

I used a case study approach. The student writers were twenty freshmen at Boston University and the University of Oklahoma with SAT verbal scores ranging from 450–600 in their first semester of composition. The twenty experienced adult writers from Boston and Oklahoma City included journalists, editors, and academics. To refer to the two groups, I use the terms *student writers* and *experienced writers* because the principal difference between these two groups is the amount of experience they have had in writing.

Each writer wrote three essays, expressive, explanatory, and persuasive, and rewrote each essay twice, producing nine written products in draft and final form. Each writer was interviewed three times after the final revision of each essay. And each writer suggested revisions for a composition written by an anonymous author. Thus extensive written and spoken documents were obtained from each writer.

The essays were analyzed by counting and categorizing the changes made. Four revision operations were identified: deletion, substitution, addition, and reordering. And four levels of changes were identified: word, phrase, sentence, theme (the extended statement of one idea). A coding system was developed for identifying the frequency of revision by level and operation. In addition, transcripts of the interviews in which the writers interpreted their revisions were used to develop what was called a *scale of concerns* for each writer. This scale enabled me to codify what were the writer's primary concerns, secondary concerns, tertiary concerns, and whether the writers used the same scale of concerns when revising the second or third drafts as they used in revising the first draft.

Revision Strategies of Student Writers

Most of the students I studied did not use the terms *revision* or *rewriting*. In fact, they did not seem comfortable using the word *revision* and explained that revision was not a word they used, but the word their teachers used. Instead, most of the students had developed various functional terms to describe the type of changes they made. The following are samples of these definitions:

> *Scratch Out and Do Over Again*: "I say scratch out and do over, and that means what it says. Scratching out and cutting out. I read what I have written and I cross out a word and put another word in; a more decent word or a better word. Then if there is somewhere to use a sentence that I have crossed out, I will put it there."
>
> *Reviewing*: "Reviewing means just using better words and eliminating words that are not needed. I go over and change words around."
>
> *Reviewing*: "I just review every word and make sure that everything is worded right. I see if I am rambling; I see if I can put a better word in or leave one out. Usually when I read what I have written, I say to myself, 'that word is so bland or so trite,' and then I go and get my thesaurus."
>
> *Redoing*: "Redoing means cleaning up the paper and crossing out. It is looking at something and saying, no that has to go, or no, that is not right."
>
> *Marking Out*: "I don't use the word rewriting because I only write one draft and the changes that I make are made on top of the draft. The changes that I make are usually just marking out words and putting different ones in."
>
> *Slashing and Throwing Out*: "I throw things out and say they are not good. I like to write like Fitzgerald did by inspiration, and if I feel inspired then I don't need to slash and throw much out."

The predominant concern in these definitions is vocabulary. The students understand the revision process as a rewording activity. They do so because they perceive words as the unit of written discourse. That is, they concentrate on particular words apart from their role in the text. Thus one student quoted above thinks in terms of dictionaries, and, following the eighteenth-century theory of words parodied in *Gulliver's Travels*, he imagines a load of things carried about to be exchanged. Lexical changes are the major revision activities of the students because economy is their goal. They are governed, like the linear model itself, by the Law of Occam's razor that prohibits logically needless repetition: redundancy and superfluity. Nothing governs speech more than such superfluities; speech constantly repeats itself precisely because spoken words, as Barthes writes, are expendable in the cause of communication. The aim of revision according to the students' own description is therefore to clean up speech; the redundancy of speech is unnecessary in writing, their logic suggests, because writing, unlike speech, can be reread. Thus one student said, "Redoing means cleaning up the paper and crossing out." The remarkable contradiction of cleaning by marking might, indeed, stand for student revision as I have encountered it.

The students place a symbolic importance on their selection and rejection of words as the determiners of success or failure for their compositions. When revising, they primarily ask themselves: can I find a better word or phrase? A more impressive, not so clichéd, or less humdrum word? Am I repeating the same word or phrase too often? They approach the revision process with what could be labeled as a "thesaurus philosophy of writing"; the students consider the thesaurus a harvest of lexical substitutions and believe that most problems in their essays can be solved by rewording. What is revealed in the students' use of the thesaurus is a governing attitude toward their writing: that the meaning to be communicated is already there, already finished, already produced, ready to be communicated, and all that is necessary is a better word "rightly worded." One student defined *revision* as "redoing"; *redoing* meant "just using better words and eliminating words that are not needed." For the students, writing is translating: the thought to the page, the language of speech to the more formal language of prose, the word to its synonym. Whatever is translated, an original text already exists for students, one which need not be discovered or acted upon, but simply communicated.[7]

The students list repetition as one of the elements they most worry about. This cue signals to them that they need to eliminate the repetition either by substituting or deleting words or phrases. Repetition occurs, in large part, because student writing imitates — transcribes — speech: attention to repetitious words is a manner of cleaning speech. Without a sense of the developmental possibilities of revision (and writing in general) students seek, on the authority of many textbooks, simply to clean up their language and prepare to type. What is curious, however, is that students are aware of lexical repetition, but not conceptual repetition. They only notice the repetition if they can "hear" it; they do not diagnose lexical repetition as symptomatic of problems on a deeper level. By rewording their sentences to avoid the lexical repetition, the students solve the immediate problem, but blind themselves to problems on a textual level; although they are using different words, they are sometimes merely restating the same idea with different words. Such blindness, as I discovered with student writers, is the inability to "see" revision as a process: the inability to "re-view" their work again, as it were, with different eyes, and to start over.

The revision strategies described above are consistent with the students' understanding of the revision process as requiring lexical changes but not semantic changes. For the students, the extent to which they revise is a function of their level of inspiration. In fact, they use the word *inspiration* to describe the ease or difficulty with which their essay is written, and the extent to which the essay needs to be revised. If students feel inspired, if the writing comes easily, and if they don't get stuck on individual words or phrases, then they say that they cannot see any reason to revise. Because students do not see revision as an activity in which they modify and develop perspectives and ideas, they feel that if they know what they want to say, then there is little reason for making revisions.

The only modification of ideas in the students' essays occurred when they tried out two or three introductory paragraphs. This results, in part, because the students have been taught in another version of the linear model of composing to use a thesis statement as a controlling device in their introductory paragraphs. Since they write their introductions and their thesis statements even before they have really discovered what they want to say, their early close attention to the thesis statement, and more generally the linear model, function to restrict and circumscribe not only the development of their ideas, but also their ability to change the direction of these ideas.

Too often as composition teachers we conclude that students do not willingly revise. The evidence from my research suggests that it is not that students are unwilling to revise, but rather that they do what they have been taught to do in a consistently narrow and predictable way. On every occasion when I asked students why they hadn't made any more changes, they essentially replied, "I knew something larger was wrong, but I didn't think it would help to move words around." The students have strategies for handling words and phrases and their strategies helped them on a word or sentence level. What they lack, however, is a set of strategies to help them identify the "something larger" that they sensed was wrong and work from there. The students do not have strategies for handling the whole essay. They lack procedures or heuristics to help them reorder lines of reasoning or ask questions about their purposes and readers. The students view their compositions in a linear way as a series of parts. Even such potentially useful concepts as "unity" or "form" are reduced to the rule that a composition, if it is to have form, must have an introduction, a body, and a conclusion, or the sum total of the necessary parts.

The students decide to stop revising when they decide that they have not violated any of the rules for revising. These rules, such as "Never begin a sentence with a conjunction" or "Never end a sentence with a preposition," are lexically cued and rigidly applied. In general, students will subordinate the demands of the specific problems of their text to the demands of the rules. Changes are made in compliance with abstract rules about the product, rules that quite often do not apply to the specific problems in the text. These revision strategies are teacher-based, directed towards a teacher-reader who expects compliance with rules — with pre-existing "conceptions" — and who will only examine parts of the composition (writing comments about those parts in the margins of their essays) and will cite any violations of rules in those parts. At best the students see their writing altogether passively through the eyes of former teachers or their surrogates, the textbooks, and are bound to the rules which they have been taught.

Revision Strategies of Experienced Writers

One aim of my research has been to contrast how student writers define revision with how a group of experienced writers define their revision processes. Here is a sampling of the definitions from the experienced writers:

> *Rewriting*: "It is a matter of looking at the kernel of what I have written, the content, and then thinking about it, responding to it, making decisions, and actually restructuring it."
>
> *Rewriting*: "I rewrite as I write. It is hard to tell what is a first draft because it is not determined by time. In one draft, I might cross out three pages, write two, cross out a fourth, rewrite it, and call it a draft. I am constantly writing and rewriting. I can only conceptualize so much in my first draft — only so much information can be held in my head at one time; my rewriting efforts are a reflection of how much information I can encompass at one time. There are levels and agenda which I have to attend to in each draft."
>
> *Rewriting*: "Rewriting means on one level, finding the argument, and on another level, language changes to make the argument more effective. Most of the time I feel as if I can go on rewriting forever. There is always one part of a piece that I could keep working on. It is always difficult to know at what point to abandon a piece of writing. I like this idea that a piece of writing is never finished, just abandoned."
>
> *Rewriting*: "My first draft is usually very scattered. In rewriting, I find the line of argument. After the argument is resolved, I am much more interested in word choice and phrasing."
>
> *Revising*: "My cardinal rule in revising is never to fall in love with what I have written in a first or second draft. An idea, sentence, or even a phrase that looks catchy, I don't trust. Part of this idea is to wait a while. I am much more in love with something after I have written it than I am a day or two later. It is much easier to change anything with time."
>
> *Revising*: "It means taking apart what I have written and putting it back together again. I ask major theoretical questions of my ideas, respond to those questions, and think of proportion and structure, and try to find a controlling metaphor. I find out which ideas can be developed and which should be dropped. I am constantly chiseling and changing as I revise."

The experienced writers describe their primary objective when revising as finding the form or shape of their argument. Although the metaphors vary, the experienced writers often use structural expressions such as "finding a framework," "a pattern," or "a design" for their argument. When questioned about this emphasis, the experienced writers responded that since their first drafts are usually scattered attempts to define their territory, their objective in the second draft is to begin observing general patterns of development and deciding what should be included and what excluded. One writer explained, "I have learned from experience that I need to keep writing a first draft until I figure out what I want to say. Then in a second draft, I begin to see the structure of an argument and how all the various sub-arguments which are buried beneath the surface of all those sentences are related." What is described here is a process in which the writer is both agent and vehicle. "Writing," says Barthes, unlike speech, "develops like a seed, not a line,"[8] and like a seed it confuses beginning and end, conception and production. Thus, the experienced writers say their drafts are "not determined by time," that rewriting is a "constant process," that they feel as if they "can go on forever." Revising confuses the beginning and end, the agent and vehicle; it confuses, *in order to find*, the line of argument.

After a concern for form, the experienced writers have a second objective: a concern for their readership. In this way, "production" precedes "conception." The experienced writers imagine a reader (reading their product) whose existence and whose expectations influence their revision process. They have abstracted the standards of a reader and this reader seems to be partially a reflection of themselves and functions as a critical and productive collaborator—a collaborator who has yet to love their work. The anticipation of a reader's judgment causes a feeling of dissonance when the writer recognizes incongruities between intention and execution, and requires these writers to make revisions on all levels. Such a reader gives them just what the students lacked: new eyes to "re-view" their work. The experienced writers believe that they have learned the causes and conditions, the product, which will influence their reader, and their revision strategies are geared towards creating these causes and conditions. They demonstrate a complex understanding of which examples, sentences, or phrases should be included or excluded. For example, one experienced writer decided to delete public examples and add private examples when writing about the energy crisis because "private examples would be less controversial and thus more persuasive." Another writer revised his transitional sentences because "some kinds of transitions are more easily recognized as transitions than others." These examples represent the type of strategic attempts these experienced writers use to manipulate the conventions of discourse in order to communicate to their reader.

But these revision strategies are a process of more than communication; they are part of the process of *discovering meaning* altogether. Here we can see the importance of dissonance; at the heart of revision is the process by which writers recognize and resolve the dissonance they sense in their writing. Ferdinand de Saussure has argued that meaning is differential or "diacritical," based on differences between terms rather than "essential" or inherent qualities of terms. "Phonemes," he said, "are characterized not, as one might think, by their own positive quality but simply by the fact that they are distinct."[9] In fact, Saussure bases his entire *Course in General Linguistics* on these differences, and such differences are dissonant; like musical dissonances which gain their significance from their relationship to the "key" of the composition which itself is determined by the whole language, specific language (parole) gains its meaning from the system of language (langue) of which it is a manifestation and part. The musical composition — a "composition" of parts — creates its "key" as in an overall structure which determines the value (meaning) of its parts. The analogy with music is readily seen in the compositions of experienced writers: both sorts of composition are based precisely on those structures experienced writers seek in their writing. It is this complicated relationship between the parts and the whole in the work of experienced writers which destroys the linear model; writing cannot develop "like a line" because each addition or deletion is a reordering of the whole. Explicating Saussure, Jonathan Culler asserts that "meaning depends on difference of meaning."[10] But student writers constantly struggle to bring their essays into congruence with a predefined meaning. The experienced writers do the opposite: they seek to discover (to create) meaning in the engagement with their writing, in revision. They seek to emphasize and exploit the lack of clarity, the differences of meaning, the dissonance, that writing as opposed to speech allows in the possibility of revision. Writing has spatial and temporal features not apparent in speech — words are recorded in space and fixed in time — which is why writing is susceptible to reordering and later addition. Such features make possible the dissonance that both provokes revision and promises, from itself, new meaning.

For the experienced writers the heaviest concentration of changes is on the sentence level, and the changes are predominantly by addition and deletion. But, unlike the students, experienced writers make changes on all levels and use all revision operations. Moreover, the operations the students fail to use — reordering and addition — seem to require a theory of the revision process as a totality — a theory which, in fact, encompasses the *whole* of the composition. Unlike the students, the experienced writers possess a nonlinear theory in which a sense of the whole writing both precedes and grows out of an examination of the parts. As we saw, one writer said he needed "a first draft to figure out what to say," and "a second draft to see the structure of an argument buried beneath the surface." Such a "theory" is both theoretical and strategical; once again, strategy and theory are conflated in ways that are literally impossible for the linear model. Writing appears to be more like a seed than a line.

Two elements of the experienced writers' theory of the revision process are the adoption of a holistic perspective and the perception that revision is a recursive process. The writers ask: What does my essay as a *whole* need for form, balance, rhythm, or communication? Details are added, dropped, substituted, or reordered according to their sense of what the essay needs for emphasis and proportion. This sense, however, is constantly in flux as ideas are developed and modified; it is constantly "re-viewed" in relation to the parts. As their ideas change, revision becomes an attempt to make their writing consonant with that changing vision.

The experienced writers see their revision process as a recursive process — a process with significant recurring activities — with different levels of attention and different agenda for each cycle. During the first revision cycle their attention is primarily directed towards narrowing the topic and delimiting their ideas. At this point, they are not as concerned as they are later about vocabulary and style. The experienced writers explained that they get closer to their meaning by not limiting themselves too early to lexical concerns. As one writer commented to explain her revision process, a comment inspired by the summer 1977 New York power failure: "I feel like Con Edison cutting off certain states to keep the generators going. In first and second drafts, I try to cut off as much as I can of my editing generator, and in a third draft, I try to cut off some of my idea generators, so I can make sure that I will actually finish the essay." Although the experienced writers describe their revision process as a series of different levels or cycles, it is inaccurate to assume that they have only one objective. The same objectives and sub-processes are present in each cycle, but in different proportions. Even though these experienced writers place the predominant weight upon finding the form of their argument during the first cycle, other concerns exist as well. Conversely, during the later cycles, when the experienced writers' primary attention is focused upon stylistic concerns, they are still attuned, although in a reduced way, to the form of the argument. Since writers are limited in what they can attend to during each cycle (understandings are temporal), revision strategies help balance competing demands on attention. Thus, writers can concentrate on more than one objective at a time by developing strategies to sort out and organize their different concerns in successive cycles of revision.

It is a sense of writing as discovery — a repeated process of beginning over again, starting out new — that the students failed to have. I have used the notion of dissonance because such dissonance, the incongruities between intention and execution, governs both writing and meaning. Students do not see the incongruities. They need to rely on their own internalized sense of good writing and to see their writing with their "own" eyes. Seeing in revision — seeing beyond hearing — is at the root of the word *revision* and the process itself; current dicta on revising blind our students to what is actually involved in revision. In fact, they blind them to what constitutes good writing altogether. Good writing disturbs: it creates dissonance. Students need to seek the dissonance of discovery, utilizing in their writing, as the experienced writers do, the very difference between writing and speech — the possibility of revision.

Acknowledgments

The author wishes to express her gratitude to Professor William Smith, University of Pittsburgh, for his vital assistance with the research reported in this article and to Patrick Hays, her husband, for extensive discussions and critical help.

Notes

1. D. Gordon Rohman and Albert O. Wlecke, "Pre-writing: The Construction and Application of Models for Concept Formation in Writing," Cooperative Research Project No. 2174, U.S. Office of Education, Department of Health, Education, and Welfare; James Britton, Anthony Burgess, Nancy Martin, Alex McLeod, Harold Rosen, *The Development of Writing Abilities* (11–18) (London: Macmillan, 1975).
2. Britton is following Roman Jakobson, "Linguistics and Poetics," *Style in Language*, ed. T. A. Sebeok (Cambridge: MIT P, 1960).
3. For an extended discussion of this issue see Nancy Sommers, "The Need for Theory in Composition Research," *College Composition and Communication* 30 (Feb. 1979): 46–49.
4. *Classical Rhetoric for the Modern Student* (New York: Oxford UP, 1965) 27.
5. Roland Barthes, "Writers, Intellectuals, Teachers," *Image-Music-Text*, trans. Stephen Heath (New York: Hill, 1977) 190–91.
6. Barthes 190.
7. Nancy Sommers and Ronald Schleifer, "Means and Ends: Some Assumptions of Student Writers," *Composition and Teaching* 2 (1980): 69–76.
8. *Writing Degree Zero*, in *Writing Degree Zero and Elements of Semiology*, trans. Annette Lavers and Colin Smith (New York: Hill, 1968) 20.
9. *Course in General Linguistics*, trans. Wade Baskin (New York, 1966) 119.
10. Jonathan Culler, *Saussure*, Penguin Modern Masters Series (London: Penguin, 1976) 70.

Sommers's Insights as a Resource for Your Reflections

1. Sommers's article is, in a sense, about more than the revision and the writing process — it's about the process by which writers grow and develop intellectually. How might you help student writers

make the transition to relative maturity, and how might other selections in this chapter help you conceptualize that growth and how to promote it?

2. When you work with a writer who engages in "deep revision," ask whether that writer will give you permission to use excerpts from his or her multiple drafts. With these drafts, you can demonstrate to future students what can happen when a writer moves beyond surface revision. (Any time you want to use student writing—for teaching or research or published writing—you must receive permission.)

Sommers's Insights as a Resource for Your Writing Classroom

1. Use the categories Sommers sets up to prompt small-group discussion about revision. Ask the groups to list what they view as characteristics of good revising. Then introduce the concept of "student" and "mature or experienced student" and ask them to classify the characteristics they described as representative of one or the other. Often students will volunteer descriptions that echo those that Sommers lists. If they don't, summarize Sommers's list and ask students to consider their own revising strategies in light of Sommers's categories. If you establish with your students that a mature college writer views revision as a recursive process, you give them one criterion by which to assess their growth as writers.

2. Prepare a sampler of revision suggestions from completed peer editing checklists or from transcripts of workshop sessions. (Borrow such materials from a teaching colleague if you are teaching for the first time or find your students apprehensive about seeing their comments used anonymously.) Organize small groups to evaluate peer criticism. Students should be instructed to consider which comments encourage revisions to improve the form and substance of the writer's argument, which comments focus the writer's attention on the needs of multiple readers, and which comments address lexical concerns. Ask each group to list the comments they would welcome on working drafts and to define or describe specifically what makes those comments useful. Have them also explain, in as much detail as possible, what makes the other comments less useful or less accessible. Don't be surprised if some class members find the exercise challenging: Many have never been asked to reflect on their critical thinking or encouraged to regard peer criticism as a significant writing experience.

Toward an Excess-ive Theory of Revision

Nancy Welch

What values set the agenda when we ask students to revise? With its mix of immediately recognizable, real-life writing situations and powerful philosophical underpinnings, this excerpt, from Getting Restless: Rethinking Writing and Revision *(1997), disrupts our "continued insistence on words like* clarity, consistency, *and* completeness" *in describing what we want our students to achieve in their writing. More specifically, Nancy Welch questions the "dominant beliefs about revision as a one-way movement . . . from unruly, unsocialized first draft to socially adapted, socially meaningful final product." She describes a different idea of revision, one "in which individual identities exceed and transgress" these neat-and-tidy containers, for it is in this excess that she wants us to locate emergent identities, voices, and truly important acts of re-visioning, crafting, and shaping meaning.*

> I think there is more that I want in here. Here is where I start to feel that my ideas scatter. I feel like I need something else or that it's just missing something.
>
> —Brandie, a first-year composition student writing in the margins of a draft

While it's generally thought that students view revision as a mechanical activity of correcting errors or as punishment for not getting a piece of writing right the first time, my classroom and writing center experiences tell me that many of our students *do* understand revision as a rich, complex, and often dramatic life-changing process. They understand—and have experienced—the kind of revision Adrienne Rich (1979) describes: as a moment of awakening consciousness, as entering old texts and cherished beliefs from new critical directions, as seeing with fresh and troubled eyes how they've been led to name themselves and each other (pp. 34–35).

The problem: The students I've worked with don't always know how to take the next step of intervening in a draft's meanings and representations. Or, in the context of a composition classroom, they understand that "revision" means the very opposite of such work, the systematic suppression of all complexity and contradiction. Another problem: Composition teachers by and large haven't been asking questions like "Something missing, something else?" that promote revision as getting restless with familiar and constrictive ways of writing and being, as creating alternatives. We respond instead (so a look through recent classroom texts suggests) in ways that restrict revision to a "narrowing" of focus, the correction of an "inappropriate tone" or "awkward repetition," the changing of any passage that might "confuse, mislead, or irritate" readers.[1]

Historians and critics of rhetoric, composition, and literacy education like James Berlin (1984), Susan Miller (1994), and Frank Smith (1986) have traced numerous reasons for this emphasis on writing as the management of meaning. They've linked such emphasis to the rise and codification of English as a discipline, to the opening of universities to working-class and minority students judged "deficient" and in need of linguistic and social correction, and to the faith educators have placed in the tenets of behaviorism.[2] Teachers and researchers in composition, rhetoric, and women's studies have also been resisting and recasting this history: through the arguments of Ann Berthoff against behaviorist conceptions of composing, through the productive dissonance that collaborative writing can generate (Lunsford 1991, Trimbur 1989, the *JAC* Winter 1994 issue on collaboration), through experiments in blending or contrasting autobiographical and academic voices (Bloom 1992, Bridwell-Bowles 1995, Brodkey 1994, Fulwiler 1990, Tompkins 1987), and through critiques of static conceptions of genre and the privileging of argument over autobiography (Bleich 1989, Bridwell-Bowles 1992, Frey 1990, Lamb 1991, Tompkins 1992). Most recently compositionists have also engaged Mary Louise Pratt's (1991) metaphor of the *contact zone* and Gloria Anzaldúa's (1987) of *borderlands* in refiguring academic scenes of writing as dynamic sites for multiple, conflicting, and creative language practices that push against and redraw the bounds of particular communities and genres (Horner 1994, Lu 1994, Severino 1994). The work of these researchers and many others destabilizes set notions about what constitutes academic discourse, genre, and authority, and they open up a field of speculation about what forms, voices, audiences, and concerns might be available and valued as academic work in the future. "At stake," Gesa Kirsch (1993) writes, "is nothing less than a new vision of what constitutes reading and writing — our scholarly work — in the academy" (p. 134).

What we still need to examine, however, are how these critiques, experiments, and speculations might be brought to bear on our ideas about revision and, more specifically, ways of talking in classrooms about revision that, despite the displacements of postmodernity, continue to posit the ideal of a stable, clear, and complete text. We need to consider, too, what practices of revision — of seeing with fresh eyes, of entering old texts from new critical directions — we must figure into our speculations and in our pedagogies if we are to move beyond calls for change into enactments of change in our writing and in our classrooms both.

In this chapter I want to revisit composition's articulated theories of revision and consider another layer to their history that can help us understand this continued insistence on words like *clarity, consistency*, and *completeness* at a time when other cherished and problematic ideals have given way — a history that's underwritten first by readings of Sigmund Freud, later by readings of Jacques Lacan, and their narratives of the encounter between an individual and society.[3] In particular

I'll examine how one offshoot of Freud, "ego psychology," along with Lacanian rereadings, shape composition's dominant beliefs about revision as a one-way movement from writer-based to reader-based prose; from unruly, unsocialized first draft to socially adapted, socially meaningful final product.[4] Then, turning to feminist rereadings of Freud and Lacan, I'll consider a different story of revision that highlights the ways in which individual identities always exceed and transgress the discursive formations available to them — always confuse, mislead, and irritate not only a text's readers, but oftentimes its writer as well. More, contemporary feminist theorists stress that it's in the pursuit of what exceeds, what transgresses, what is restless and irritated, that we can locate the beginnings of identity, voice, and revision — revision as getting restless with a first draft's boundaries, revision as asking, "Something missing, something else?" of our texts and of our lives.

My short story "The Cheating Kind" (1994) started with a memory from my teenage years: riding the backroads in an old, beat-up Cadillac that my best friend's father and his girlfriend loaned us along with a six-pack of Black Label beer because, even though we were only fifteen, without licenses, our presence wasn't wanted in the house. When I started the story, those memories seemed charged with rebellion, possibility, heady high-speed freedom; as the drafting continued, though, I grew more and more uneasy with the narrator's point of view. She seemed capable of just about anything for a taste of adventure. Her desires seemed to eclipse completely whatever Marla, her friend, might be feeling as they drove around in that Cadillac, banished from her house, banished from the narrator's house, too, since the narrator's mother didn't regard Marla as a "nice" girl. Though a cherished myth of the fiction workshop, as Mary Cain (1995) writes, is that a writer is in control of the text and meanings she creates, seeking the advice of workshop members only to make her text and meanings clear and unambiguous to others, I didn't feel at all in control of this story and the questions it raised: Where was this narrator taking my memories? How much did she have to do with me? And what did social class, power, and status — the narrator from an exceedingly quiet, exceedingly polite middle-class family; Marla from a working-class household and the part of town where "things happen" — have to do with this story, with the memory from which it came?

Then came the story's end — a minor car wreck, the old Cadillac skidding off the road and into a corn field — I thought I was "dreaming up" since I couldn't quite remember how my friendship with the real Marla ended:

> *It was only slender stalks of corn, ripe and ready for picking, that we hit. They gave way easily, and Marla, of course, didn't die.*
>
> *It would be an easier story to tell if she had — the stuff of high drama like Gatsby face down and bleeding in a pool, the romance of a steak knife*

> *shivering between two ribs. I couldn't simply walk away then, pretend it had all never happened, brush off my acquaintance with Marla like a fine layer of dirt . . .*
>
> *"We'll have to get a tow truck," Marla said, looking down at the Cadillac's front end shoved through rows of broken stalks, the tires dug into soft, rutted earth. She stepped carefully around the undamaged plants, shook her head, and said, "We'll need help."*
>
> *A drop of blood clung to her lip, and she touched a finger to it. Probably I should have asked her, "Are you hurt?" But I was already thinking ahead to the tow truck, the sheriff, the call to my mother. I saw Bob Crofton shaking his head and saying no, of course he didn't give two fourteen-year-olds his Cadillac to drive.*
>
> *"I'll go," I said. I took one step back. Crisp leaves and stalks crackled beneath my feet. I kicked into the road a crushed, empty can of Black Label. "You stay here. I'll get help."*
>
> *I took another step back, then paused for the jagged bolt of lightning to strike me dead or for Marla to read my aura and explode, "Oh, like hell I'm going to let you leave me here to take the blame." But the sky stayed the same bruised rainless gray, and Marla remained by the car and nodded as if she believed me, as if she trusted me to do this one small, honest thing.*
>
> *"You stay here," I said again, turning now to run.* (p. 45)

In the end, the narrator leaves Marla with the wreck, Marla to take the blame, back to the quiet, polite, "nothing-ever-happens-here" part of town. Though this ending isn't autobiographical, didn't actually happen, it also strikes me as true.

Let me put it this way: As I drafted and revised "The Cheating Kind," and especially its last scene, I wasn't concerned with the questions, "How can I better adapt each scene to the story's central theme?" and "How can I get my message across to readers?"—questions of craft, questions of a writer detached from and in complete control of his or her meanings. I was too caught up in the questions instead, "How much of this narrator's point of view was mine, is mine?" and "What does this story say about how I am already adapted—and to what?"

The Ethics of Excess: Three Stories

Psychoanalysis, French feminism, excess: These are words, I know, that conjure up images of uncritical celebrations of "writing the body" and lead to the protest, "But it's not responsible to invite students to write to excess, given what they're asked to do in their other classes" and "This is unethical since we're not licensed in psychology and psychiatry and aren't trained to handle what might result from encouraging the excessive."[5] Following a 1994 MLA presentation in which Wendy Bishop and Hans Ostrom (1994) argued for "convention making" and "convention breaking" taught together in the classroom, one teacher remarked to another, "I don't think students need to be confused any more than they already are." These are concerns I will address directly at this chapter's end, as well as indirectly in revision narratives placed throughout this chapter. Here, to suggest why we need to address these issues of restlessness, confusion, and excess along the borders of convention and genre, I'll introduce three brief stories that will be on my mind throughout this chapter:

1. Brandie, a student in a first-year composition class is, like many students at this large Midwestern land-grant institution, viewing the university as a place of transition between her rural upbringing and an adulthood defined primarily by what she cannot do and where she cannot go. She knows that after graduation she can neither return to the farm her family no longer owns nor to the small town where her parents met and married; its shrinking economy can't support her and the numbers of other children raised and schooled there. Her mission at the university, as she vaguely understands and writes it, is "to get a teaching certificate so I can get a decent job somewhere or maybe to meet someone and get married which is weird since my parents always knew each other growing up and that won't be true for me and whoever 'he' may be." At the start of the semester she writes essays in a consistently upbeat tone about moving to the city and adjusting to a large university, stating, "I feel that in a huge place like the university you can very easily be just a number, but just as easily be somebody," and concluding, "I am making all I can of being a college student." As she reads this last paragraph aloud to her small group, another student, her background similar to Brandie's, begins to sing, "Be all that you can be. Get an edge on life . . ." Everyone laughs, Brandie too. "But, hey," Brandie says, "this is reality, right? We got to do it." Another student asks, "But don't you miss your old friends?" Brandie nods. "Aren't you ever homesick?" Brandie nods again and says, "But I don't want to put any of that into the story. It would take away from the positive idea I'm trying to get across. I don't want people to think I'm a mess."

2. To the writing center, Moira, a sophomore taking an intermediate writing class, brings a draft about her experience of going through a pregnancy, then placing the child up for adoption. The draft begins in the doctor's office where Moira learned she was pregnant, then proceeds through the adoption and her decision to return to school. Though the draft is seven pages long, Moira doesn't get past reading aloud in the writing center the first two paragraphs, stopping frequently to explain to me about her boyfriend, her parents, the plans she'd been making to move with her sister to another state, the uncertainty she shared with her boyfriend about whether they were really in love, her worries too that this uncertainty was created by her father who insisted she was too young for a serious relationship, how she sat on the examination table

waiting for the doctor, thinking of all of this, and telling herself, "There's nothing wrong, there's nothing wrong." When I ask her if all she's telling me and jotting down in the margins has a place in the draft, Moira says, "That's the problem. I feel like it does, but then I worry about boring readers with all this background. It's all set up for the doctor to come in and tell me the news, and I don't feel like I can just leave readers hanging."

3. Lisa, a composition instructor, stops me in the hallway between classes and asks me to talk to her sometime about revision. She continues:

> I don't feel comfortable asking my students to revise because I don't really know how to revise either. I've got all these journals and papers that I don't do anything with because even though I know they're not perfect, I don't want to take the life out of them, "do this" or "do that" like people tell me I need to. So they just sit there, and it's the same with my students. Maybe what they write isn't perfect, but it's got life and maybe cleaning it up would kill that life.

As Lisa talks, I wonder how many teachers moving down the hall around us might voice the same ambivalence, how many also have stacks of journals and papers they've written and are afraid to touch. Strangely, I think too of Tillie Olsen's (1976) short story "I Stand Here Ironing" and especially its closing phrase, "helpless before the iron" (p. 21).

These stories are on my mind now because each suggests to me the start of revisionary consciousness — as Brandie and her group members recognize a troubling cultural narrative that may be writing their lives, as Moira considers aloud the relationships that shape her experiences and that don't fit into the shape of her draft, as Lisa notes the tension between her classroom's generative theories of composing and dominant ideas of revision as cleaning up, closing down, even killing off. These stories also suggest to me the kind of helplessness that Olsen's narrator voices as she stands at the ironing board. Brandie, Moira, and Lisa aren't sure how they can intervene in these texts, they're not sure *that* they can intervene. They stand, in other words, at the intersection between full, excessive lives and the seemingly strict limits of texts that must be ironed out, made unwrinkled and smooth.

These stories also suggest that, difficult and discomforting as it is to linger at this intersection, real irresponsibility lies in denying its existence, in trying to push past this place as quickly and neatly as possible. It's here, at this intersection, that we need, first, to question the legacy of twentieth-century psychologies with their emphasis on the clear, the consistent, and the complete, and, second, to expand our understanding of the psychoanalytic frame to include what were, at least at times, Freud and Lacan's very much *plural* aims: the movement of individual desires toward social goals; the exploration too of ideas, feelings, experiences, and identities that exceed the rules of a given language, the margins of a given genre, the boundaries of the communities in which we live and write.

Sometimes it's surprisingly easy. In the writing center I ask Moira if she were to imagine writing out some of this "background," if she were to imagine that these details won't "bore" readers — including herself as reader — where would she want to begin? She takes her pencil and draws a line between one sentence about sitting on the exam table and the next in which the doctor arrives. We talk, then, about the idea of "space breaks" — a visual interruption of four spaces on the page, opening up room for writing about the relationships, questions, and hopes her first draft left out, then another space break signaling the return to the original narrative. When Moira returns to the writing center the next week, she's tried the space break and says she was surprised to realize that what she wrote within it wasn't "background" but the "heart of it all." She still feels restless, though, about one sentence, explaining, "I say here about my father being overbearing, and that's how it felt at the time but that's not always true or completely true." She pauses, then asks, "Can I take just that one sentence and write another essay from it?"

Yes. Yes, of course.

The Ego, the Id, and Revising with Freud

As Robert Con Davis (1987) observes in his introduction to *College English*'s second of two special issues on composition and psychoanalysis, we can find in the *Collected Works* not one Freud but (at least) two: the early Freud of the instinctual "drive" theory, and the later Freud of "ego" psychoanalysis from which springs mainstream American psychoanalytic and pop psychological practice. It's that later Freud who carved the mind into three not-at-all-distinct realms — the ego, the id, and the superego — giving us a three-part topography of a self at war with its selves. According to this model, the *id* is that part of agency, part of the self, that develops from the needs and impulses of the body and is inseparably bound to sensations of pain, pleasure, deprivation, and fulfillment. Out of the id develops the *ego*, that part of the self that seeks to regulate and control chaotic id impulses, and the *superego*, that part that represents parental, social, and institutional controls — the genesis of prohibition, censorship, and guilt, but also of social awareness and responsibility.

From this later Freud grew two popular versions of psychoanalytic practice. Id psychology focuses on and privileges the instinctual drives and an individual's "private" and "personal" fantasies that escape or speak in muted form through the ego's monitor. From id psychology comes the practice of dream analysis, classical Freudian readings of literature as revelations of an author's psyche, and the idea of automatic writing. Ego psychology, on the other hand, stresses the containment of id fantasy and the construction and maintenance of a social identity.[6] Defining psychoanalysis as an "instrument to enable the ego to achieve a progressive conquest of the id" (Freud 1962b, XIX, p. 56), ego psychology underwrites behaviorism (which places the superego outside the individual in external punishments and rewards that shape the ego's functioning), literature's reader-response theories (which follow an individual among others as he or she develops personal reactions into culturally shared interpretations), and, I'd like to argue, composition's dominant ideas about writing and revision.[7] Consider:

> Revision is by nature a strategic, adaptive process. . . . One revises only when the text needs to be better. (Flower, and colleagues 1986, p. 18)
>
> Perhaps the best definition of revising is this: revising is whatever a writer does to change a piece of writing for a particular reader or readers — whoever they may be. . . . (Elbow and Belanoff 1989, p. 166)
>
> [H]e must become like us. . . . He must become someone he is not. . . . The struggle of the student writer is not the struggle to bring out that which is within; it is the struggle to carry out those ritual activities that grant one entrance into a closed society. (Bartholomae 1983, p. 300)

These compositionists, usually divided into the separate realms of *cognitivist, expressivist*, and *social constructionist*, share *in common* an understanding of revision as movement from the individual (or writer-based) to the social (or reader-based), the increasingly strategized, adapted, socially integrated and socially meaningful finished product. Though Flower and colleagues have been criticized for ignoring the social dimensions of writing in their seemingly interior cognitivist model, they actually highlight the social in their definition of revision — the need for writers to reread and adapt their texts according to very much social ideas of what they should say, how a piece of writing should appear, what would make it "better." Similarly, though the pedagogy of Elbow and Belanoff has been labeled "expressivist" and might be read as a pedagogy of the id, they too construct revision (albeit with some discomfort) as changes made toward a social text and social functioning; they too (within *Community of Writers*, that is) share in common with ego psychology the belief that movement from individual to social, private fantasy to public meaning, is desirable or, at least, unavoidable.

But it's David Bartholomae especially who makes visible for me the intersections between our understandings of composing and the ideas of ego psychology, showing how Freud's tripartite model of the mind has been further codified into separate, distinct realms: the student as "id" who must not bring out that which is within — or rather, that which is formed by social languages and communities deemed unintelligible within academe, deemed "other" than academic discourse; the draft as developing, regulatory "ego"; the teacher as "superego," the embodiment of the closed society and its rituals for meaning. Bartholomae doesn't tone down this process as entirely natural and as always positive and progressive. Rather, noting that stories of learning to write in academic settings are often "chronicles of loss, violence, and compromise" (1985, p. 142), his construction of the writing scene suggests that revision has much more to do with politics than with brain biology or liberal humanism. In this construction, intentions are shaped by the community the writer wants to make his or her way into, and the revision process is not a simple matter of making a text "better" or "clearer." Revision is instead the very complicated matter of struggle between a full, excessive life and the seemingly strict limits of what can be written and understood within a particular discourse community. Here, Bartholomae and other social constructionists like Patricia Bizzell and Thomas Recchio share much in common with Jacques Lacan, his rereading of Freud, and his view that the making of identity and meaning are social acts from the very start.

At a midterm conference, Rachel, a student in my first-year composition course, tells me, "I'm learning a lot from your class." I cock my head, puzzled. Rachel is always in class, never late, always has a draft, neatly typed, never handwritten, for workshops. A model student. Disturbingly so. (I can't remember now, looking back, what Rachel wrote about, only that her drafts were always clear and concise, a thesis stated in the first paragraph and stuck to through the very end.) "Is there anything missing for you in class?" I ask. "Anything we're not doing that you wish we would or something we could be doing more of?" I'm fumbling about, trying to get at my sense that there's something that could be and isn't in Rachel's writing for class or that could be and isn't in the class for Rachel. But Rachel shakes her head. "No, everything's great. It really makes a lot of sense, you know: free write, think about what's at the center, free write some more, get some feedback, go with a new question. It's great." Maybe, I think, my sense of something missing is wrong; she's identifying what she's learning after all. Maybe I'm only imagining an underground, unarticulated frustration she feels with this class, and maybe I just can't see something that really is happening in her writing.

Then at the semester's end Rachel writes her evaluation for the course in a voice I hadn't heard from her before — one of anger, of frustration, and of intense involvement with this writing task: "Supposedly this was a course in composition, but I'll tell you I didn't learn one thing about composition from it."

Mirror-Mirror *or* Revising with Lacan

With Lacan's rereading of Freud and, particularly, his reading of Freud's early thinking on the development of ego in "Narcissism" (Freud 1962b, XIV), that sense of the inevitability of the movement from self to other, individual sensation to social codification, is both reinforced and rendered as troubling. Beginning with the infant in an amorphous and boundaryless state, just a "l'hommelette" or "omelette" (little man, mass of egg), Lacan explores the advent of the largely metaphoric "mirror stage" in which individuals confront and seek to connect with a smooth and consistent reflection of themselves (1977b, p. 197). The mirror images they find can be gratifying—giving a sense of shape and wholeness to what was before a chaotic jumble of needs and sensations—but such images are also a source of discord and anxiety. The outer image of containment and completion is at odds with the inner sensations of fragmentation and incoherence; it leads to conflict between the "Ideal-I" reflected in the mirror and the "turbulent movements that the subject feels are animating him [or her]," and it asks an individual to combat and contain those sensations increasingly in order to assume an identity that's outside, other, and alienating (1977a, p. 2). "It is this moment," Lacan writes, "that decisively tips the whole of human knowledge into mediatization through the desire of the other" (1977a, p. 5). It is at this moment, in other words, when American ego psychology's clear distinctions between individual and society break down, revealing how an individual sense of self, meaning, and reality is thoroughly mediated by social mirrors and the images of wholeness and coherence they reflect.

The story of Lacan's mirror stage helps me to understand why professional writers are so often reluctant to talk about revision and show to others early drafts of their work. Fiction writer Tobias Wolff, for instance, destroys all early versions of his stories, explaining, "They embarrass me, to tell you the truth. . . . I only want people to see my work at its very best" (quoted in Woodruff 1993, p. 23). "When I finish a piece of writing," says Joyce Carol Oates, notorious for her reticence about the subject of her own writing, "I try my best to forget the preliminary stages, which involve a good deal of indecision, groping, tension" (quoted in Woodruff 1993, p. 167). Those early drafts may not match up at all to social mirrors that tell us what a short story ought to look like or what a good writer's sentences ought to sound like. They may even pose a threat to the writer's sense of himself or herself as a good writer at all, a threat to the belief that this draft can ever be finished and published. (This is something against which students in my fiction-writing classes particularly struggle, saying that they want or need to put their story drafts aside "to cool," when, in fact, I suspect that they fear the unsettling images these drafts reflect, images they see not in terms of possibility, but of failure to match up and fit in.) Lacan's analysis of the mirror stage tells me, too, why students often respond in conferences and in peer groups (as Richard Beach observed in a 1986 essay) with "Oh, I feel pretty good [about this draft]" or "I don't feel good about it at all but I don't want to revise it." It makes sense, I think, especially in an environment of evaluation, of grades, to respond to dissonance and disjuncture by insisting, "No, this is clear enough, good enough" or to worry that any intervention might make a sense of misfit and distortion even worse.

In my view, the story of Lacan's mirror stage is the story that underwrites social constructionist understandings of writing and revision. "[I]t is evident," Thomas Recchio (1991) writes, "that we all have to find ways to function in a language [or languages] . . . that have already been configured" (p. 446). "[H]e must become like us," Bartholomae (1983) writes. ". . . He must become someone he is not" (p. 300). Like Lacan, both Recchio and Bartholomae stress how from the very first word, the very first draft, a student in the composition classroom encounters, grapples with, and tries to accommodate an alien, even alienating, way of writing. Both stress that a notion of revision as a clean movement from writer-based to reader-based prose is also fiction, since languages and contexts for writing are already social, already reader based. A writer doesn't create language in isolation and out of thin air, then work toward involving others; one's words are already deeply involved in the work and words of others, come from without rather than from within, and can seem, as Lacan writes, like "the assumption of the armour of an alienating identity . . ." (1977a, p. 4).

This isn't to say that Recchio, Bartholomae, and other social constructionists postulate a writer who has no agency within this armor. Through "orchestrating and subordinating" the multiple social discourses of a text, Recchio (1991) states, a student may "begin to find her own voice" (pp. 452–453). "The person writing," Bartholomae (1990) says, "can be found in the work, the labor, the deployment and deflection . . ." (p. 130). Still, here, as in the usual reading of Lacan, there is that overriding sense of inevitability: We can resist this narrative of being subsumed and written by the assumptions and rituals of a single community — through deployment and deflection, subordination and control — but we cannot fundamentally alter it.[8]

In "Fighting Words: Unlearning to Write the Critical Essay," Jane Tompkins (1988) examines the narratives — of movie westerns, of the biblical David and Goliath — that underwrite traditional forms of academic writing: critics gunning each other's readings down; a graduate student standing up at her first conference with her slingshot-of-a-paper, hoping to smite the big voices in her field so she has the right to speak. That's also the narrative of my first academic publication: Set up this authority, set up that, then tear them down, get on with what you want to say. I was shaken when, one year later, I met one of those authorities face to face. It occurred to me then, and should have occurred to me before, that she was more than the few words on the page I chose to quote: a living breathing person leading a complex life, asking complex questions — who she is and what her work is far exceeding the boundaries I'd drawn.

In this chapter, too, I'm doing it again, choosing quotations from writers whose work exceeds the space I'm giving them and the narrow focus of revision I've selected. This is a problem — one to which I have to keep returning, not skipping over with the gesture of a "However" or "Yet it's easy to see . . . ," creating a text that's problematically concise, simply clear.

The Trouble with Mirrors

Freud and Lacan are not figures I want to dismiss, and I don't think, either, that compositionists can or should shrug off the influence of twentieth-century psychologies. Freud remains appealing to me if for no other reason than because he located his research in narrative. Though he wasn't always a critical reader of his narratives with their traces of sentimental romance, Victorian melodrama, and the mechanistic metaphors of industrial capitalism, he illustrates why forms of narrative research — case studies, ethnographies, autobiographical literacy narratives — are crucial to the making of knowledge in composition: They make visible what is "uncanny" in our thinking and in our practices; they reveal the slips and contradictions that disrupt our broad generalizations (or we might say "wishes") about what's happening in our classrooms and in our discipline. Stories, as Mary Ann Cain (1995) observes, don't merely "mirror" our assumptions and expectations; they "talk back."

Similarly, all the slips and contradictions of a classroom text like Elbow and Belanoff's (1989) *Community of Writers* — with its conflicting id-based and ego-based assertions, "You write for yourself; you write for others" — make visible and talk back to my own slips, my own contradictions when I try to talk with students about revision. As for Lacan, though his theories may appear grim and deterministic, he does tell me why my students and I are sometimes so unsettled when we look back on our early drafts, those drafts distorting what we wished to see, declining to mirror back ideas smooth-surfaced and well-mannered, the gratifying images of a graceful writer, a good teacher. Composition's social constructionists have also worked to disturb the discipline's harmonious image of the writing process as natural, asocial, and apolitical; they stress that no classroom and no piece of writing can ever be free from the problematic encounter between an individual and society, the pressures and desires to see one's text neatly reflect a preplanned intention, a pleasing image, the certainty of one's membership in a closed society.

But no social mirror — and this is what usual readings of Lacan leave out — can ever reflect back to us, whole and complete, an image of ourselves and the true nature of things. There is always something missing, something else, or, as feminist critic Sheila Rowbotham (1973) writes, misfit and distortion as we lumber around "ungainly-like" in "borrowed concepts" that do not "fit the shapes we [feel] ourselves to be" (p. 30). This has to be the case as well for the mirrors that our readings of Freud and Lacan provide. Those mirrors offer some ideas about writing and revision, individual identity and social meaning, that we want and need. Those mirrors ought to make us restless with what they distort, what they miss, what else they imply.

My restlessness begins when I consider how both our Freudian and Lacanian constructions of revision position the teacher as superego, the representative of the "us" students must learn to write like or as the regulatory voice in the margins telling students where and how their texts need to adapt and change. As philosopher Michele Le Dœuff (1989) considers, the position of superego sets teachers up for a "tic"-like approach to responding to students' texts: "systematically correcting [any] infidelities" and "castigating the language of the student . . . by writing in red in the margin . . ." (p. 57). That castigation may be overt with insistent commands like "Be specific!" or "Focus!"; it can also take the seemingly benign forms of "Does this paragraph really belong here?" or "Some readers might be offended by this." Either way, this relationship between teacher and student, teacher and text, doesn't set us up for questioning the textual ideals we and our students are writing/responding to match. It doesn't set us up for understanding the encounter between teacher and text as a potentially rich "contact zone" or "borderland" for questioning, speculating, and, possibly, revising the teacher's response. It constructs instead (Le Dœuff's point as she examines the grading of doctoral exams in philosophy) a position of complete submission for the student, of utter mastery for the teacher. Meanwhile, the question doesn't even come up: *Just who or what has mastered the teacher?*

My restlessness increases when I recall that Lacan's thinking about the mirror stage, so influential to social constructionism, began with his reading of Freud's essay on narcissism — suggesting some disturbing answers to that question: Just who or what has mastered the teacher? In Lacan, the experience of the mirror stage sends an individual in a "fictional direction," toward an imaginary idea of an "us," of a community and its practices into which an individual wants to fit. As compositionist Kurt Spellmeyer observed in his 1994 MLA presentation, "Lost in the Funhouse: The Teaching of Writing and the Problem of Professional Narcissism," this fictional direction is also a *narcissistic* one. It can lead us to seek — in our own writing and in others', in academic journal articles, dissertations, and students' compositions — gratifying images of ourselves, and it can lead us to feel frustrated and annoyed when a piece of writing doesn't reflect such an image. These imaginary identifications don't always lead us to question what's being gratified when we write an article that others call graceful, witty, or astute or when we write in the margins of a student's essay "Nice work" or "Very smoothly written." These imaginary identifications don't always lead us to question, either, the longing among compositionists within their departments and institutions to project certain images of themselves to the exclusion and debasement of others — as in "I teach a cultural studies classroom [rather than a mere writing class]" or "I'm in rhetoric [not composition]" or "I'm a post-process theorist [disassociated, that is, from composition's research of the past twenty years]."

Stressing at the start and end of his presentation that our academic lives are carried out under powerful institutional gazes, very often within English departments that value literature over composition, the high and sweeping theoretical over the narrative, detailed, and everyday, Spellmeyer suggests that compositionists do have some means for resistance. We can shift our attention from texts by a Beckett or a Joyce to texts by students; we can, as Spellmeyer demonstrated in his presentation, deploy French terms in ironic tones and with raised eyebrows, calling for light laughter and an edge of skepticism. These forms of resistance aside, however, we cannot fundamentally revise the forms, voices, and subjects of the texts we write — not according to this story of the formation of academic identity.

Here my restlessness is most extreme as social constructionism (slipping into social determinism), which began with a radical intervention in too-smooth notions of "the writing process," ends with a denial of possibilities for further intervention, as it replaces questions with absolute statements of what must be, and so repeats the move of ego psychology, asserting the need to adapt to a prefigured principle of (institutional) reality: *He must learn to write like us; narratives of academic socialization will always be narratives of loss, violence, compromise, and alienation; academic production is the production of anxiety, narcissism, and neurosis — this is just the way things are.*

I thought about Tompkins's (1988) essay "Fighting Words" and my own David-and-Goliath article this past week while reading poems in Prairie Schooner. I read poems by T. Alan Broughton that meditate on letters written by Vincent Van Gogh to his brother Theo, one by Cornelius Eady written from a photograph of Dexter Gordon, another by Adrienne Su that takes its occasion from a sentence in Alice's Adventures in Wonderland*: "Everything is queer today." Funny that poets are often charged with sequestering themselves in silent garrets or with suffering the most from the anxiety of influence. These three poets model for me ways of beginning to write, of working with the words of others, and of finding a voice — ways that don't involve setting up and knocking down. They suggest we might revise our usual forms of academic production by remaining at, rather than trying to get past, that border between one's text* *and others. Maxine Hong Kingston also offers me an example of this border work between one's voice and another's. In* The Woman Warrior *Kingston (1976) creates, continually returns to, and enriches a portrait of her mother, making places in her text for the both of them, even where — or especially where — their voices, their views, aren't at all one and the same.*

"Too Much": Revising to Death

In "Professional Narcissism," Kurt Spellmeyer focuses on the anxious, even neurotic relationships that form between writer and text, text and reader, when we write to adapt to institutional mirrors. Two fictional stories about revision as adaptation — Margaret Atwood's "The Bog Man" (1991) and Paule Marshall's *Praisesong for the Widow* (1984) — also focus on those powers of social mirrors and suggest more chilling consequences still. In "The Bog Man," there is Julie who revises again and again the tale of her long-ago affair with Connor, a married archeology professor who brought her as his "assistant" on an excavation in Scotland. Throughout the story Julie revises Connor, revises herself, even revises the setting where they broke up because "Julie broke up with Connor in the middle of a swamp" sounds "mistier, more haunted" than "Julie broke up with Connor in the middle of a bog" or, the truth, in a pub (p. 77). In her revisions of the story, told "late at night, after the kids were in bed and after a few drinks, always to women," Julie works to shut out any details that might be less than amusing, too hard to figure out (p. 94). She "skims over the grief," "leaves out entirely any damage she may have caused," thinks that this or that fact "does not really fit into the story" (pp. 94–95). Connor, like the bog man they go to Scotland to excavate, "loses in substance every time she forms him in words" (p. 95). In the end, Julie has an ironic, consistent, and lifeless tale of an episode from her life. In the end, Connor is "almost an anecdote" and Julie is "almost old" (p. 95).

Avey, the main character in Paule Marshall's novel *Praisesong for the Widow*, is also "almost old" when she begins, with great restlessness and resistance, to look back on the narrative of middle-class socialization she and her now-dead husband, Jerome, followed as they moved "out" and "up" from a fifth-floor walk-up in Harlem to a suburban house in White Plains, New York. She remembers the "small rituals" they left behind: a coffee ring on Sunday morning, gospel choirs on the Philco, Jerome (who then called himself "Jay," even his name changing with their move) reciting the poetry of Langston Hughes (pp. 124–126). She remembers their "private lives," their lovemaking, that had seemed "inviolable" but that also "fell victim to the strains. . . . Love like a burden [Jerome] wanted to get rid of" (p. 129). And she remembers the dances Jerome led her in across their small living room, "declaring it to be the Rockland Palace or the Renny," in the days before his voice began to change to one that said, "If it was left to me I'd close down every dance-hall in Harlem and burn every drum! That's the only way these Negroes out here'll begin making any progress!" (pp. 95, 132). "*Too much!*" That's what Avey cries out as she finally lets herself remember and mourn the changes in her husband, in herself, the cost of their "progress." She doesn't romanticize the years on Halsey Street in Harlem and doesn't erase the grim hardship; she does ask herself, "Hadn't there perhaps been another way?" She thinks, "They had behaved, she and Jay, as if there had been nothing about themselves worth honoring" (p. 139).

Julie, Jerome, and Avey are cast within narratives of accommodation and change that point toward the not-always-acknowledged implications of composition's dominant theories and practices of revision. Julie, for instance, strategizes and adapts, alters and omits, so that her story's "effect" matches her "intention." She revises with the aim of better functioning within an already configured language — here, the already configured and even clichéd language of college girls who get into affairs with married professors, of a middle-aged, middle-class woman who makes light of younger, wilder days. While Recchio considers that an individual voice may be formed through the work of orchestration and subordination, coherence and control, Atwood's story dramatizes the opposite case as Julie's orchestrations and subordination lead, in the end, to no voice at all. The same is true and much more disturbing in Marshall's story of Jerome. His work to adapt his life and his words to a single course of action, one proper tone, ends with his lying in a coffin while everyone congratulates his widow "on how well she had held up in the face of her great loss" (pp. 132–133).

In feminist readings of psychoanalysis the revision process involves both *dream-work* (the exploration of identifications and meanings along the border of consciousness) and *death-work* (the critique and dismantling of beliefs and identifications we experience as our selves, making their loss a kind of death). Joining the work of discovering and questioning, dis-orienting and re-orienting, revision becomes that process Winnicott (1971) calls "creative living" and that Kristeva (1986a) calls "dissidence": a process through which one recognizes how he or she has been situated, the process through which one negotiates with reality "out there" to change that situation. In Marshall's depiction of Jerome's brief life, however, there is no room for dream-work, dissidence, and negotiation with reality "out there." While Lacan (1977a) defines death-work as working one's way toward a "new truth" that is "always disturbing" (p. 169), in Marshall's representation of Jerome there is no work, no activity, no confrontation with and reflection on what in these life changes are disturbing; there is only the literal and complete killing off of a whole history, a whole host of attachments, every one of his daily rituals for meaning, as he works to adapt his life to one principle of reality. It's a story not of *re-vision* but of assimilation.

With Julie, Jerome, and Avey's narratives in mind, we might reconsider resistance to revision and that fear Lisa expressed of revision taking the "life" from a piece of writing just as Jerome's process of change literally took the life from him. Lisa, unlike Jerome, is not marginalized by race; however, as an untenured instructor in the university, a Jewish woman in the predominantly Christian and Protestant Nebraskan culture, a woman who came to feminism in her forties and after an impoverishing divorce, Lisa is aware each time she sits down to write of working against the grain of the dominant culture, a working-against she's only recently found the confidence to try. Viewing revision as the work of toning down and fitting in, the work of moving away from, not into, disturbing new positions and truths, she fears the silencing of a voice she's only just begun to use. In some instances at least, Lisa persuades me, a refusal to revise may arise from an intuitive understanding of the intimate link between language and identity, an intuitive understanding that we really can revise a story, revise ourselves, to death.

That is, unless we return to that intersection between a full and excess-ive life and the limits of a particular society, asking, with Marshall's Avey, if there isn't another way.

Sometimes relationships in the classroom — to reading, to other students — can recast, rather than reinforce, the usual social mirrors teachers and students write and respond within. In an intermediate composition class, Scott, a senior in his midtwenties, reads aloud in class a narrative of a ski trip in which he and his friends abandon another friend, new to skiing, on the beginner's slope. In his draft, Scott represents this friend as "whining" and "annoying," comedically clumsy and inept, deserving, so the story implies, to be left behind. The students in class laugh as Scott reads. Except Amanda, Scott's journal partner, who writes to him in her next journal, "What about you? Weren't you a beginner on that trip too? Did you worry about being left?"

Meanwhile, Scott is also reading Tim O'Brien's (1990) semiautobiographical novel The Things They Carried *in which the narrator, Tim, recreates his decision to go to Vietnam, feeling as though there were "an audience" to his life, an audience shouting "Traitor!" and "Pussy!" as he tries to imagine swimming for Canada (p. 60). Later O'Brien's narrator considers what happened when he sent one of his published stories to Norman, a foot soldier who was with him in Vietnam on the night when Kiowa, another foot soldier, was killed in a "shit field." About the story, Norman writes back, "It's not terrible . . . but you left out Vietnam. Where's Kiowa? Where's the shit?" (p. 181). With O'Brien's words in mind, Scott considers the audiences to his own life who expect him to be amusing, to keep it light, to skip the shit. He considers that in his latest draft, about canoeing on the Niobrara River, he's repeated the move that Amanda noticed in his ski trip draft — displacing his confusion and fear onto others, setting them up as comedic and inept, almost writing himself out of the story altogether. During an in-class glossing activity, Scott lists in the margins of his draft, as O'Brien does in his short story "The Things They Carried," some of the events, problems, and questions that he carried on this trip. He writes, "We were all having problems, and I want to bring those out" and "What's really going on here? Where's my trip?"*

With his glosses, Scott begins to revise, adding a scene in which he and his friend Chuck, riding down the Niobrara one afternoon in a slowly meandering canoe, talk seriously about their lives, relationships, and futures — the kind of serious and meandering talk between two men that isn't usually represented in social (and classroom) discourse. This and other revised passages don't present a version of Scott as whole and complete, who he really is, the way it really was. In the margins of the revision and his journal, he continues to write, "I may be using Chuck to say some of how I was feeling and perceived things" and "I'm looking for a voice I can feel comfortable with" and "I need to try this paragraph again." The revision does, though, lead him to a next step: giving the draft to Chuck to read, "fidgeting" while Chuck read "very slowly," and feeling "a great weight lifted" when Chuck responded by asking for a copy to keep. "He didn't ask 'Where's the Niobrara?'" Scott writes. "He didn't complain that I'd left out the shit."

Wrestling with Lacanian Bondage

Like Marshall's Avey, film theorist Joan Copjec (1989) also seeks another way, one out of what she calls the "realtight" bond in contemporary psychoanalytic theory between the "symbolic" and the "imaginary," between individual identity and the social gazes thought to determine, wholly, completely, who we can be and what we can say (p. 227). That real-tight bond seals us off from any consideration of the "real" or of, as Freud (1962b) puts it, that "inch of nature" that exceeds any one construction of our selves (Copjec 1989, pp. 228–229; Freud 1962b, XXI, p. 91). It leads, for instance, to film theorists positing a single (male) gaze that women are positioned within and must take pleasure from as they view a film, with no room for restlessness, resistance, another way of watching.

But this real-tight bond, Copjec writes, is also the result of a *misreading* of Lacan and, in particular, the familiar Lacanian aphorism, "Desire is the desire of the Other" (Copjec 1989, p. 238). In this misreading — one exemplified not only in film theory but also in composition's social-constructionist theories of writing — writers and their texts are viewed as entirely determined by the social mirrors that surround them, by actual and identifiable "Others" to which we can point and say, "Yes, there's the locus of my desire, the mirror I want to match." According to this (mis)reading, Copjec writes, individuals take on social representations as images of their own "ideal being" — that "Ideal I" from Lacan's mirror stage. As we take a "narcissistic pleasure" from such images (because they offer us shape and symmetry), we become "cemented" or "glued" to them, coming to call them (no longer an alienating armor) our selves — or, in the classroom, our definition of good writing, what we want our teaching and our students' texts to reflect (Copjec 1989, p. 229; this is likewise Spellmeyer's point in "Professional Narcissism" [1994]).

The problem with this construction of desire and the formation of identity is that it overlooks the capital "O" Lacan places here on "Other." In Lacan, there are "others" — small "o" — who are the people, communities, histories, social representations, and social discourses with whom and with which we interact, influence, and are influenced by — that "mediatization" the end of the mirror stage tips us toward, others with identifiable shapes, locations, and limits. There is also a persistent sense of *Otherness* (capital "O") beyond the limits of those people, communities, and discourses, a persistent sense we can't quite see and name that we might call the "real," the "inch of nature" that exceeds, overflows, cannot be contained and copied. "[W]e *have no image* of the Other's desire . . . ," Copjec writes, no single representation that can bring "reunion"; there is always "something more, something indeterminate, some question of meaning's reliability" (pp. 236–238, my emphasis).

In Copjec's reading of Lacan, identity is produced "not in conformity to social laws," but "in response to our inability to conform" to social laws and discursive limits (p. 242): with the recognition of limits there's restlessness, movement, a desire that can't be satisfied with determined gazing into the reflection of one social mirror.[9] Copjec's reading takes us back to that intersection between individual and society, between excess and limits, with the understanding that a sense of something missing, something else isn't a mistake to be corrected, isn't an unruly id to be suppressed, but is instead the start of revisionary activity by a self that is neither singular and static nor entirely composed by a fixed set of social determinants.

In an introductory fiction-writing class, the instructor says to me, "Technically, your story is very good. Clear. Logical, Complete. Good details." He pauses. "It's just that — " He smiles, starts again. "I think maybe you haven't found your material yet. You need to let yourself be a little messy." He adds, handing me back my story, handing me another story too, "Read this. Maybe it'll say what I mean." I nod, make my exit, frustrated, angry, ready to write on an end-of-semester evaluation, "Supposedly this was a course in fiction writing, but I'll tell you . . ." My material? What is that? And why were none of the routines I'd followed to write news stories (I was then working for a daily paper) working for me now? How did Mona Simpson, the writer of the story this instructor handed me, manage to make her stuff sound so, well, real? Home now, I head straight to my computer, turn it on, then do something else: turn off the lighted screen. This semester I'm also taking a seminar for writing tutors. We're reading Mikhail Bakhtin (1981), who claims that words hold within them whole lives and histories, the suggestions of relationships, of conflicts, of resolutions that can't last for long. We're also reading Peter Elbow (1987), who advocates shutting off the computer screen, writing in the dark. Do I believe it? Try it? Let the words run along, then reread to see what story is being written there, one I hadn't planned and controlled? I begin to write, thinking that whatever happens will prove to my instructor that a mess is exactly what will come of this, thinking too about the last time I felt this mute, pent-up, and confused — when I was sixteen years old and running away from home. I write, "In Cincinnati the snow turned to rain . . ." Half an hour later I stop, print it out, and without looking at the pages, mail them to the instructor with an irritable note, "So. Is this my material?"

"Yes," he said.

This is not the story "How I Came to Discover My Own True Voice." (The fiction that came from writing in the dark, "The Road from Prosperity" [1996], ended up being seven years in the making — seven years of trusting, doubting, then trying to trust again Elbow and Bakhtin, seven years of discovering how to read and work with the Otherness of my own words, the unruliness of my writing.) It's a story instead about coming up against the limits of my writing, traveling over the curricular boundaries into another class (a so-called theory class), coming back, learning to write — maybe for the first time.

Writing in the "Chinks and Cracks"

One way of starting the kind of revision, Copjec's essay suggests, is through exploring practices of "prodigality" that can both highlight and take us beyond a particular community or genre's discursive limits. In an essay that begins with the either/or choice feminists face between "silence and cooptation," Jerry Aline Flieger (1990) considers that beyond the position of "dutiful daughter" to institutional forms of living and writing or that of "illegitimate mother's daughter" who rejects institutions (and voice, power, authority), there is the possibility of another position: that of the "Prodigal Daughter" (pp. 57–59). The prodigal daughter "is a daughter still" who "acknowledges her heritage," but who also "goes beyond the fold of restrictive paternal law" and returns not castigated and repentant, ready to settle down and fit in, but "enriched" (pp. 59–60). The prodigal daughter "is lush, exceptional, extravagant, and affirmative"; her participation in one community (like feminism) creates for her an identity that exceeds the limits of another (like psychoanalysis). That excess-iveness allows her to take exception to a community's limits and laws; it enables her to introduce new questions and rituals, to "enlarge its parameters" and "recast its meanings," changing the bounds of "what is permissible" (p. 60), changing, indeed, what constitutes that community and the practices of those within it.

Enlarging the parameters and reenvisioning limits also concerns Michele Le Dœuff as she reworks static notions of rationality in philosophy into practices of "migration" — writing with and through other social discourses and needs rather than positioning philosophy apart from and above others. "I am seeking the greatest possibility of movement," Le Dœuff writes, a practice of writing that migrates into and creates authority from "different fields of knowledge, 'disciplines' or discursive formations, between different periods of thought and between supposedly different 'levels' of thought, from everyday opinions to the original metaphysical system" (1991, p. 51). For Le Dœuff this means bringing her experiences with the Women's Movement in France into her work as a philosopher, rather than choosing a focus on one or the other. In this way Le Dœuff recasts her role from a "precious admirer" of and careful commentator on the texts of male philosophers (1989, p. 120). Migration shows her the limits of those texts, creates new questions and possibilities of projects beyond philosophy's usual bounds: critiques of philosophy's strategy for authority through displacing "theoretical incapacity" onto others in order to create its meanings (1989, p. 126); examination of the "erotico-theoretical transference" that has historically defined women's relationships to philosophy; exploration, too (since the prodigal daughter is also "affirmative"), of "plural work" with other writers and other disciplines that reconnects philosophy to daily social concerns.[10]

Flieger and Le Dœuff's practices of migration and prodigality aren't pendulum swings away from the social and back to the purely private and personal: an uncritical celebration of an untamed id, the mirage of an essentialized female language. Quite the opposite, the experience of migration, Le Dœuff writes, works to "exile" a writer from the conventions of a discipline and the assumptions of doctrinal bases, and by doing so denaturalizes those conventions and assumptions, preventing them from becoming commonplace, essential, the way it must be (1991, p. 222). Similarly, plural work, instead of promising escape and freedom, offers Le Dœuff a "continuing sense" of "limits," "the recognition that 'I do not do everything on my own,'" and that this incompleteness is not a "tragedy," but the opportunity to continue revising along that border of "the unknown and the unthought" (1989, pp. 126, 128). As Julia Kristeva writes, also working with these notions of migration and exile, the experience of traveling beyond disciplinary limits and comfortable ways of knowing and writing can take us out of "the mire of common sense" and enable us to become a "stranger" to the daily communities, discursive formations, and rituals for meaning we would otherwise take for granted, their limits and implications invisible to us (1986a, p. 298). Neither advocating a search for a singular self nor attachment to one social identity, these theorists seek instead the formation and recognition of multiple attachments, bringing *all* of one's identities to the scene of writing, working for a voice of lushness that's a powerful means of critique and creation both.

The writings of Teresa de Lauretis, Trinh T. Minh-ha, and Minnie Bruce Pratt also demonstrate the creative, critical, and socially responsive uses of migration and prodigality. In *Technologies of Gender*, de Lauretis (1987) argues for migration away from a focus on the "positions made available by hegemonic discourses" and toward "social spaces carved in the interstices of institutions," in the "chinks and cracks" where one can find—already in existence, not needing to be longed for, a utopian future not yet come—"new forms of community" and "micropolitical practices of daily life and daily resistances that afford both agency and sources of power . . ." (pp. 25–26). Writing away from the prevailing discourses and the positions they allow is what Trinh (1989) does in *Woman, Native, Other* as she moves away from the word *author* with its implications of a solitary genius and toward the word *storyteller* with its connection to dailiness, community, and collectivity. The essays of poet and lesbian activist Minnie Bruce Pratt (1991) also stress that the work of crossing limits isn't the trivial and apolitical pursuit of an ivory-towered class of writers, without consequence for the better or worse. In claiming her identity as a lesbian, "step[ping] over a boundary into the forbidden," Pratt lost her children to her husband's custody, the court ruling that she had committed a "crime against nature" (p. 24). In claiming that identity, she writes, she also gained the ability to keep crossing boundaries, connect her struggles as a lesbian to those of others subordinated by race, gender, or class, and take her poetry "beyond the bounds of law and propriety into life" (pp. 23–24, 241).

In the here and now, these writers offer examples of writing that seeks to name, understand, and transgress the limits of prefigured texts, understandings, and ways of living. They demonstrate revision not as that one-way movement from writer-based to reader-based prose, but instead as that moment of looking back on a text, asking how it's already reader based, already socialized and reproducing the limits of a given society, and whether there's something missing, something else. Doing so, they radically question Lacanian (and social constructionist) notions that coming into language always and only means compromise and alienation. In these writings there's a refusal to leave the intersection with a quick and uneasy compromise; there's the work of revision as seeking other options and attachments, as expanding one's focus, and as learning to write to excess.

That's true too for Paule Marshall's Avey in *Praisesong for the Widow* (1984) who does not remain within White Plains' bounds of middle-class propriety and within the narrative of loss, violence, and compromise that marked her husband's death. Moving instead into another story of revision, Avey abandons the security and strict itinerary of a middle-class cruise ship. She travels—disoriented, ill, weary from mourning her husband Jay and their early life together—to the island of Carriacou. There, in the company of others making their yearly excursion to this island of their birth and of their ancestors, Avey begins to dance, "[a]ll of her moving suddenly with a vigor and passion she hadn't felt in years," her feet picking up the rhythm of the Carriacou Tramp, "the shuffle designed to stay the course of history" (1984, pp. 249–250). At the novel's end Avey, like Flieger's prodigal daughter, is on her way back to New York—exceptional, extravagant, and prepared now to alter the former limits of her life.

In class, Brandie reads her draft and writes back to her words in the margins. She writes "Spark!" and "I was amazed when I wrote this" next to the first paragraph that ends, "I can't believe that it took me nineteen years, one month, and six days to realize that I, Brandie Marie Anderson, have no idea whatsoever what I want to do with the rest of my life." She writes, "Here is where I start to feel that my ideas scatter . . ." next to the final paragraph that concludes "I have learned that I can do anything I want in this world, or I can do nothing." In between these paragraphs she's told the story of bringing a college friend, who grew up in a large city, home to visit her family. She's described feeling proud ("I felt like I was the man who invented the whole farming system itself") and defensive ("I wanted to destroy her feelings that my house was like that on Little House on the Prairie*") and confused ("I don't know why I thought my life was the only kind there was. I don't know why I never questioned my future"). In the margins she writes, "But is that really so bad?"*

Then Brandie turns to her journal partner, Meg, and says, "Do you want to trade?" Brandie reads and writes back to Meg's draft, which is about growing up with two families—her mother, stepfather, and their children together; her father, stepmother, and their children together. Meg reads and writes back to Brandie's draft, responding primarily to Brandie's marginal glosses: "I think this paragraph is perfect!" and "Brandie, what exactly was different about your background, and what made you think June's was so exciting? There's the obvious—bigger town, more to do, but tell me in your own words!" and "You ask yourself if that [not questioning the future] is so bad. Can you try to answer the question?" Reading this, Brandie nods and starts to make a list called "Differences" at the bottom of the page. By the end of class when she gives the draft to me, its margins—top, bottom, right, and left—are filled with conversation, arrows, directions, questions. Next to the glosses I write, "Yes," "Yes," and "I'd like to hear about this too," then respond to one sentence near the end that says, "I can really see myself teaching . . . except to teach you have to know everything, and I know I don't." I write: "I'd like to hear more about what you see when you see yourself teaching. What creates the view that a teacher must know everything? . . . Let's talk about this—maybe in a journal?"

Brandie does choose this draft to revise, responding to Meg's questions and her own. There are other kinds of revision taking place, too, of which this particular essay, by itself, is only a part: revision as Brandie strays from writing essays in a consistently upbeat tone with one "positive idea" she wants to "get across"; revision as Brandie and Meg carry their conversation from the margins of each others' drafts into their journals, writing about the differences in their lives and families; revision as Brandie and I write in journals back and forth about the images of teachers we've grown up with and what it can mean to see one's self as a teacher. There's revision too as I no longer reserve the space in the margins for my pen. Have I eliminated teacher as "superego," as regulatory voice? No. But just as Freud didn't posit the id, the ego, and the superego as absolute, distinct realms, I'm trying to blur the boundaries and populate this space with multiple voices, relationships, and tones.

Toward an Excess-ive Theory of Revision

"[A]t every point of *opposition*," writes Gayle Elliott (1994) in an essay about the tensions between feminist theory and creative writing, "is a point—an *opportunity*—of *intersection*" (p. 107, Elliott's emphases). "Limits," Ann Berthoff (1981) writes, "make choice possible and thus free the imagination" (p. 77). These words also apply to that opposition between the fullness of a life and the limits of genre and community. Yes, writers do confront languages already configured for them. Yes, we do write within powerful institutional gazes that can seem as impervious and punishing as the barbed wire that lines this country's southern border, and yes, identities do exceed the bounds of what's called permissible and appropriate in a given genre, discipline, or classroom, creating narratives of loss and of compromise. But Copjec, Fleiger, Pratt, Le Dœuff, Trinh, Marshall, and a great many writers more demonstrate that opposition *can* become intersection, a contact zone populated with activity, meaning, and the kind of revision that comes from working at the borders of community, writing to exceed the limits of a given language and form.

These writers also demonstrate that the first-person narrative, accompanied by practices of re-vision, doesn't necessarily produce "the ideology of sentimental realism" and reification of "a single authoring point of view"—the troubling limits of an "expressivist" conception of composing that David Bartholomae (1995) argues convincingly against (p. 69). When we understand with Joan Copjec that the "real" can't be inhabited, that even the most seemingly "complete" and "authentic" narrative has its limits and inexpressible excesses, we can begin to read at the limits. We can value not so much the "genuine voice" of a personal narrative, or its "candor" or "unique sensibility," but rather the activity of this writer at the border between text and context, between the fullness of experience and the limits of language that can be worked, transgressed, and radically revised.

When I return to composition studies from this migration into psychoanalysis, feminism, philosophy, and fiction, I find plenty of examples of working at the borders and transforming opposition into intersection. Histories of rhetoric, for example, show the historical specificity, the historical *limits*, of conventional forms for teaching writing like the five-paragraph essay and the rhetorical modes. In making visible the boundaries those forms describe, these histories open up the possibility of—and need for—migration.[11] Teachers of creative writing like Gayle Elliott show how the borders separating composition, creative writing, and critical theory can be redrawn, urging the greatest possibility of movement across "creative" and "critical" genres and identities. Alice Gillam (1991) redefines writing centers from a "battleground" (where students must choose between either focusing, cutting, and controlling or leaving a first draft as is) to a site where writers "*flesh out* the contradictions" and "*puzzle over* the off-key shifts in voice," as a way of discovering rather than imposing focus (p. 7, my emphases). In "Dialogic Learning across Disciplines," Marilyn Cooper (1994b), like Gillam, migrates toward the theories of Mikhail Bakhtin to consider that disciplinary conventions aren't fixed entities to be acquired by students, but are subject to "the forces of unification and the forces of diversification," making it possible for students to participate in the work of diversification as well (p. 532). Min-Zhan Lu (1994) dramatizes how that participation takes place when members of her first-year composition class examine an apparent "error" in a student's text as a richly nuanced and meaningful stylistic choice. Through this revision, they create a contact zone between the official codes of school and other languages students bring to this setting; they reconsider academic production as involving "approximating, negotiating, and revising" among contending codes—*including* those traditionally excluded from academic discourse (p. 447).

Lu especially helps me respond to teachers who fear that encouraging an excess-ive understanding of revision will confuse and even harm students both struggling with alien academic discourses and writing for professors who value neatly managed and monovocal meanings. Forces of unification, as well as of diversification, are always present in a classroom as students and teachers bring with them a range of histories, experiences, and assumptions about the limits and possibilities of writing in classrooms.[12] Rather than taking academic conventions as natural or as unquestionably superior to other language practices, rather than ignore these varied histories and varied understandings of just what the limits are, Lu writes that "the process of negotiation encourages students to struggle with such unifying forces" (p. 457)—to resist for a moment the work of subordination, coherence, and control; to pause, reflect, and consider the complexities of their choices; to realize that there *are* choices. Instead of confusing or misleading students, this renaming of error as style to be *puzzled over, thought through* (the same way teachers and students would puzzle over and think through the stylistic choices of a Gertrude Stein) offers those who want to resist a single official style, the community-based practices of revision, reflection, and argumentation they need to do so; it also offers those familiar with the discourses of school a view of that style's limits, as well as a view of the chinks and the cracks through which they might stray.

In composition's process legacy we can also find, I believe, practices of revision and reflection that can guide students and teachers as they consider revision as getting restless with a draft's initial meanings and representations, as seeking alternatives. Ann Berthoff's philosophy and practices, for instance, have always sought to engage the "form-finding and form-creating powers of the mind" in the "possibility of changing" a reality (1981, pp. 85, 92). Her practice of glossing invites students to reflect and revise along the borders of their texts — to "think about their thinking" and "interpret their interpretations," to see the limits and the choices there — while her practice of interpretive paraphrase offers a writer the means to write toward what exceeds. The double-entry notebook creates a visible space of critical exile where one can look back on, name, and rename initial meanings and representations; the question, "What's the opposite case?" encourages migrating from and complicating a first draft's focus.

I could continue — migrating from Berthoff's revisionary pedagogy to considering Elbow and Belanoff's loop writing as prodigality, Sondra Perl's open-ended composing process as creating a contact zone between forces of unification and diversification. But my point is this: These theorists tell me we need to remain at the intersection between "process" and "post-process" conceptions of composing, not quickly push past that intersection, not call one side the "past" and the other the "present." We need more border talk between the classroom practices and detailed case studies of the 1970s and 1980s, and current calls for institution-wide revisions of community, genre, academic discourse, and academic authority. (It's Flower and Hayes, I realize, who first showed me what I could learn about my classrooms through writing and reflecting on case studies; Elbow continues to invite me to turn off the computer screen as I draft.) Investigating the borders, we can refuse the gesture of projecting theoretical incapacity onto others; we resist *that* mirror for establishing authority. At the intersection, process pedagogies can be revitalized through examining how race, class, gender, ethnicity, sexual orientation — students' and teachers' many and varied cultural and personal histories — inform their writing, reading, and revising. And at the intersection teachers can both question and reclaim practices of revision we and our students need if we are to enact our many visions of change, if we are to be able, on a day-to-day basis, to question, intervene, and create; if we are to be able, on a day-to-day basis, to confront confusion, turn opposition into intersection, and create from the experience of limits the experience of choice.

Taking the sentence about her father from her adoption draft, Moira revises, creating another essay that considers her father's beliefs about what her decisions should be. With that draft comes another source of restlessness, though, as Moira considers that her responses, her beliefs, aren't in this writing. In the writing center she places another sheet of paper beside the draft and, asking of each paragraph, "Where am I in this?" she begins to write back to her draft on the new page—a kind of excess-ive version of glossing. "I think," she says after twenty minutes of this writing, "that the thing is this: My father always taught me that the decisions we make should bring us peace. But what we both have to learn is that we may have different ideas about what peace is, what decisions are right for me." It's close to the end of our meeting in the writing center and Moira checks her syllabus to see when her draft is due. She talks about leaving the draft as is or cutting up the paragraphs of both writings seeing what would happen if she tried to put them together. She talks about rewriting the first paragraph with a new emphasis on what she and her father need to learn, and she talks too about taking both pieces of writing to her composition class' next draft workshop, asking her small-group members what they think.

Moira talks too, as she's packing up, about her father's uneasy childhood, how he dropped out of school, why it's so important to him that her life be perfect. "Is that history a part of what you're talking about in your draft?" I ask, and Moira nods. "It should be," she says. "It says why. It tells me why."

Something Missing, Something Else

When Moira, like Brandie, whose words began this chapter, dares to consider that there's something missing in her text, something more, she recognizes the limits of that text and there, at the limit, she imagines what might happen next. What happens next is talking and writing on the borders of a neat and tidy draft, recognizing that its incompleteness isn't a tragedy at all, but a site of choice including the choice to stop for now, including the choice to continue. What happens is Moira and I both know that in a few weeks some of this writing will be graded, that she will decide which. Meanwhile there's time, here and there, in the chinks and cracks of her work and school schedule, for Moira to migrate toward questions other than: *What will get me an A?*

But this kind of work can only happen —*really happen* — within settings like Moira's writing class that promote and support an excessive understanding of revision: one that questions the ideal of the complete, contained, and disciplined body, the complete, contained, and disciplined text; one that takes the double perspective that revision involves both movement toward social goals *and* questioning what's being perpetuated or omitted in the process. Those questions can return a writer to invention as marginal glosses carry into other writings, as an interpretive paraphrase grows into something too big, too complicated to be easily integrated into the paper from which it came. So that students don't feel overwhelmed by the reflections these texts-in-progress mirror back, we also need to situate these practices in relationships that offer challenge and support like Brandie's with her journal partner and Scott with his reading of Tim O'Brien. Because investigating limits and straying from what may have been comfortable boundaries can be disorienting, dismaying, a threat to one's sense of self and to the life of a draft, students need the greatest possibility of choices about when to ask: *Something missing, something else?* In my classes this has meant that some students revise a particular draft by taking the same general topic, migrating into another genre, seeing how an autobiographical narrative, for instance, might look as a poem, a collage, a research project, a letter, or a fictional story. Meanwhile, others revise not by returning to a particular draft but to a journal entry (a kind of revision advocated by Ken Macrorie), seeing its limits and how this writing might be carried on. In one case a student struggling with the idea of revision reread a favorite book from his adolescence; his revision took the form of writing about that experience of rereading. In institutional settings, including my classrooms, revision *does* become another limit, another constraint, a social ideal to which students feel they must adapt. Around that word *revision*, though, there are borders students and teachers can name, question, negotiate, and rename, creating excess-ive understandings of what revisionary work can mean.

This kind of revision, however, depends on teachers supporting students' work at the intersection. It asks teachers to practice forms of response and evaluation that make sense of such work instead of operating out of a double standard that allows many of us to feel confident reading the excess-ive writings of a Joyce, Dickinson, or Foucault, but dismayed before a student who is writing at the line between what's comfortable and familiar and what's challenging, strange, and new.[13] This kind of revision depends on a teacher's ability to revise as well, to turn that question — Something missing, something else? — back on his or her reading of a student's draft, on what the limits of that reading are, what other ways of reading there might be.

Here, though, I come to the limits of this chapter and of this book, with a recognition that there's a great deal missing, a great deal more. Or I come to an intersection between this project I'm trying to finish and future projects I imagine, including:

- Where and when do teachers begin to feel restless with their ways of responding to students' texts, suggesting an intersection between a full, excess-ive experience of reading and the limits of prefigured forms for response? Where and when do teachers begin to ask, "Something missing, something else?" of their responses?
- What happens when teachers bring their reading of students' texts into dialogue with their reading of other writers whose work pushes against any single "Ideal Text" (to borrow Knoblauch and Brannon's apt and Lacanian phrase)?[14] Or, given that many teachers have argued precisely for such an intersection, what works against this happening or against this happening more?

- What would it mean to bring an excess-ive understanding of revision into dialogue with current research in the use of portfolios and of contract grading? To what extent do these practices of assessment in particular institutional contexts continue to perpetuate the ideal of complete, contained, disciplined texts? To what extent do these practices, again in particular institutional contexts, work to subvert such an ideal, pointing toward the excess-ive instead?
- What would it mean to alter the question, "How is this piece of writing finished?" into "What work does this writing suggest that might be carried on?" and "What are the future projects that might arise from it?"
- What would it mean to consider the literature classroom as a place that's also very much concerned with the investigation of "Something missing, something else?" Can we locate the work of interpretation in a literature class, as in the composition class, at the intersection between full, excess-ive experiences of reading and the limits of prefigured forms for response?
- What would happen in a fiction workshop if students and their teacher investigated, examined, and revised the limits of cultural notions of who a fiction writer or poet is and how he or she works? What would it mean to create such a workshop that actively seeks to address, as fiction writer Eve Shelnutt puts it, "the myth that works of the imagination and full consciousness are anti-thetical" (1989, p. 5)? What difference would this make to students' writing and to their reading of each others' work?[15]
- And since some ideas about just what "full consciousness" means in contemporary critical and literary theory make me restless, what intersections can I discover between my own excess-ive experiences as a writer of fiction and the limits of the theories through which I make sense of those experiences? How can Le Dœuff's project of working between philosophy and feminism become my own as I migrate between fiction and feminism, teacher and writer?

But all of these questions are, really, various versions of, departures from, and returns to this: What will happen when we begin to read, write, and teach at that tense, problematic, and fascinating boundary between *individual* and *society*—reading, writing, and teaching with an excess-ive and pluralized understanding of these terms and of the intricate braids that make it impossible for us to distinguish between the two? What if we read to see boundaries our texts and our students are getting restless within? What if we learned to watch for places where a text begins to resist, get unruly, and maybe even stray? What will happen when we read with the belief that our students do have, as Ross Winterowd wrote in 1965, "*restless minds*" that we can glimpse and encourage in their writing—if we get restless with static ways of reading, conventional forms of response (p. 93)?

Which suggests yet another question: What will happen when we begin to read to discover not *whether* a student needs to revise (suggesting the responses of no or yes, finished or not, still within that frame that values the complete and the contained), but to discover instead where and how, in or around this writing, he or she *has already started* to revise? That's work we can notice, work we can value, work that might continue within or beyond this not-so-single text. What would this mean for our students' writing? For how teachers and students talk about writing? For how students and teachers understand what revision can be?

As an undergraduate in an advanced composition class (before I migrated over into the fiction workshop, before I'd come up hard against the limits of my writing), I turned in an essay every Friday, got it back every Monday with an A. Especially since I then worked for a daily paper, I was a practiced writer—maybe too practiced and I knew it too. "Wonderfully wrought throughout" the professor wrote beside those A's. "Graceful." "Lovely." I felt gratified by those comments and A's. Restless too. Not so sure these essays really were so perfect and complete. Not sure what to do about it either, what questions to ask and where. At the semester's end the professor told us to return to the essay that received the lowest grade, revise it for a higher one.

"Mine were all A's," I told him after class. "What should I do?"

"You don't have to do anything," he said. "Your work is fine as is."

It wasn't, it isn't, not at all—but that's another story. Or the story of why I'm writing now, still restless, not satisfied.

Notes

1. I've taken these constructions of revision from three current composition textbooks but want to avoid attaching authors' names to them, since I found a dozen other textbooks that offered similar understandings of revision, telling me that none of these constructions can be attributed to a single author.
2. Michele Le Dœuff's (1989) *The Philosophical Imaginary*, which ties philosophy's systematic suppression of its own contradictions to its desire to gain and maintain academic status, also offers a way to read composition's history and particularly its history of teaching revision as the containment, rather than exploration, of dissonance. Likewise Mikhail Bakhtin's (1968) *Rabelais and His World* traces the ideological history of an emphasis on the text as a "classical body" that is "entirely finished, completed, strictly limited"—and, so, seemingly divorced from "living practice and class struggle" (pp. 320, 471).

3. In this chapter, I'll be looking at the most prominent and frequently cited constructions of revision from composition's *expressivist, cognitivist*, and *social constructionist* orientations. There are crucial differences, though, among composition teachers within these orientations and individual voices that have argued for or suggested different constructions of revision. Susan Osborn (1991), for instance, seeks to "provide a context in which re-vision and revision are explicated as both integral to the writing process and a way of knowing ourselves as readers and writers" (p. 270). Min-Zhan Lu (1994) also stresses "writing as a process of re-seeing"—including re-seeing, negotiating, and revising the conventions of academic discourse (p. 449). Recent articles in the *Writing Center Journal*—by, for instance, Alice Gillam (1991) and Cynthia Haynes-Burton (1994)—likewise work against the grain of revision as a one-way movement from writer-based to reader-based prose. In this chapter, then, I have the double aims of (1) explicating the construction of revision against which these teachers write and (2) writing toward the construction of revision their work suggests.
4. The terms *writer-based* and *reader-based* prose come from Linda Flower's (1979) essay "Writer-Based Prose: A Cognitive Basis for Problems in Writing," and her terms have given compositionists ways of thinking about the kind of audience for whom a piece of writing might be intended. This book, for instance, is decidedly intended for others to read and so it might be called *reader-based*, while the journal in which I considered the questions, problems, and breakthroughs of this book's writing is decidedly intended for me alone and so might be called *writer-based*. The problem I'm working with in this essay, though, is how these terms have been lifted from their original context, *writer-based* becoming increasingly used as synonymous with *solipsistic*, while *reader-based* is increasingly reduced to meaning *clear, concise, and instantly, easily understandable* and reduced to the single, unquestioned goal of revision.
5. The most thoughtful and searching critique I've found of the psychoanalytic frame, particularly the Lacanian psychoanalytic frame, in the classroom is Ann Murphy's (1989) "Transference and Resistance in the Basic Writing Classroom: Problematics and Praxis." Though I read that essay as underwritten by the assumptions of ego psychology—the need for students and teachers to adapt to and function within a social reality, a belief in stable and socially rewarding roles students can write toward, along with a promise to students that mastery of writing conventions can be "congruent with her or his own needs" (p. 185)—this statement from Murphy remains central to my thinking about revision in this book and in my teaching: "[A] process which seeks further to decenter [students] can be dangerous" (p. 180). Like Murphy's students in basic writing classrooms, the students I meet are already (often in ways that aren't readily apparent) decentered, divided, disoriented. They don't need or want a teacher, from her position of relative security and power, to create decentering experiences for them. What needs to be decentered instead, I think, is the view that learning and writing can ever be safe, neat, and tidy, leading us to be surprised, dismayed, and totally unprepared when we find again and again that no, learning and writing are not safe and neat at all. What needs to be decentered, too, I think, is the view that essays, unlike our lives, should contain nothing of disorientation, uncertainty, and division.

6. In *Dora* (Freud 1962a), for example, Freud contrasts the hysterical patient's "inability to give an ordered history" of her life with that of a patient whose "story came out perfectly clearly and connectedly" and whose case, Freud thus concluded, could not be one of hysteria (p. 31). In other words, Freud equates the unruly, disorderly, and discontinuous with emotional illness, and the clear, calm, and perfectly connected with emotional health. Ironically, Freud's own text might be called hysterical, then, with its many and sometimes acknowledged incompletenesses, contradictions, and omissions.
7. Elizabeth Wright (1989) takes a closer look at the forms of psychoanalysis that have influenced literary studies and theories and (by implication) composition, too.
8. Recently, however, Recchio (1994) suggests a much more dialogic and recursive process of revision in which society shapes individuals' texts, but in which many individuals in turn speak back to and shape society. "Realizing [this] potential of the essay in the Freshman English classroom, however," he writes, "is a thorny problem, for writing pedagogy has been dominated by formalized self-contained systematic thought where play, discovery, and recursiveness are squeezed out of discourse, and subordinated to a misleading formalist consistency and clarity" (p. 224).
9. Copjec's figuring of an unsatisfiable and restless desire runs against the grain of consumer culture that depends on our believing that if we can acquire the right sweater/car/hand cream/theoretical frame/language/publication/degree we will be satisfied, reunited with our complete being. There is no "Other" that can complete us, no matter what advertisements, textbooks, how-to guides, and academic programs may promise. She suggests to me that a classroom that seeks to understand this and at least question the ideal of the whole, complete, unified, and nothing-left-to-say text is also a classroom that prepares students and teachers to see themselves as critics and creators, rather than frustrated consumers, of culture.
10. For further exploration see Le Dœuff's essay "Long Hair, Short Ideas" in *The Philosophical Imaginary* (1989) and the "Second Notebook" in *Hipparchia's Choice* (1991).
11. See, for example, Sharon Crowley (1991) and James Berlin (1984).
12. Carrie Leverenz (1994) offers a careful and disturbing examination of such forces of unification at work in students' responses to each others' writing in a composition classroom.
13. I'm indebted to Wendy Bishop and Hans Ostrom (1994) who made this point in their 1994 MLA presentation, "Letting the Boundaries Draw Themselves."
14. Freud's *Dora* (1962a) or *Interpretation of Dreams* (1962b, IV), with all of their assertions, examples, clarifications, contradictions, caveats, and footnotes that continue for a page or more, strike me as excellent choices for disrupting stable notions of what can constitute "academic" writing. Try reading one of these, then telling someone, "Writing in academia must be clear, consistent, and concise." I don't think such an assertion is possible after Freud.
15. I think of these questions especially because recently a teacher remarked to me that students in her class who name themselves as "Writers"—capital "W"—also produce the most "writer-based" and "egocentric" work she's ever seen. I suspect, though, that the writing of such a student isn't

at all writer based, individualistic, divorced from readers and the social realm. Instead, that writing and that writer are probably very much caught up in and overdetermined by those social myths of the solitary, misunderstood, at-odds-with-society poetic genius — "a breath-mist," poet and fiction writer Fred Chappell (1992) writes, that one needs to clear away in order to begin to write (p. 21).

Works Cited

Ahlschwede, Margrethe. 1992. "No Breaks, No Time-Outs, No Place to Hide: A Writing Lab Journal." *Writing on the Edge* 3: 21–40.

Alton, Cheryl. 1993. Comment on "Crossing Lines," *College English* 6: 666–69.

Anzaldúa, Gloria. 1987. *Borderlands / La Frontera: The New Mestiza*. San Francisco, CA: Spinsters/Aunt Lute.

Atwell, Nancie. 1987. *In the Middle*. Portsmouth, NH: Boynton/Cook.

Atwood, Margaret. 1991. "The Bog Man." In *Wilderness Tips*. New York: Doubleday.

Bakhtin, Mikhail. 1968. *Rabelais and His World*. Translated by Helene Iswolsky. Cambridge, MA: MIT Press.

———. 1981. *The Dialogic Imagination*. Translated by Caryl Emerson and Michael Holquist. Edited by Michael Holquist. Austin, TX: University of Texas Press.

Bartholomae, David. 1983. "Writing Assignments: Where Writing Begins." In *Forum*. Edited by Patricia L. Stock. Upper Montclair, NJ: Boynton/Cook. 300–12.

———. 1985. "Inventing the University." In *When a Writer Can't Write*. Edited by Mike Rose. New York: Guilford Press. 134–65.

———. 1990. Response to "Personal Writing, Professional Ethos, and the Voice of 'Common Sense.'" *Pre / Text* 11.1–2: 122–30.

———. 1995. "Writing with Teachers: A Conversation with Peter Elbow." *College Composition and Communication* 46: 62–71.

Beach, Richard. 1986. "Demonstrating Techniques for Assessing Writing in the Writing Conference." *College Composition and Communication* 37: 56–65.

Berlin, James. 1984. *Writing Instruction in Nineteenth-Century American Colleges*. Carbondale, IL: Southern Illinois University Press.

Berthoff, Ann E. 1981. *The Making of Meaning*. Portsmouth, NH: Boynton/Cook.

Bigras, Julien. 1978. "French and American Psychoanalysis." In *Psychoanalysis, Creativity, and Literature*. Edited by Alan Roland. New York: Columbia University Press. 11–21.

Bishop, Wendy. 1990. *Something Old, Something New: College Writing Teachers and Classroom Change*. Carbondale, IL: Southern Illinois University Press.

———. 1993. "Writing Is/And Therapy?: Raising Questions about Writing Classrooms and Writing Program Administration." *Journal of Advanced Composition* 13: 503–516.

———. and Hans Ostrom. 1994. "Letting the Boundaries Draw Themselves: What Theory and Practice Have Been Trying to Tell Us." MLA Convention. San Diego, CA. 29 December.

Bizzell, Patricia. 1984. "William Perry and Liberal Education." *College English* 46: 447–454.

Bleich, David. 1988. *The Double Perspective: Language, Literacy, and Social Relations*. New York: Oxford University Press.

———. 1989. "Genders of Writing." *Journal of Advanced Composition* 9: 10–25.

Bloom, Lynn Z. 1992. "Teaching College English as a Woman." *College English* 54: 818–825.

Brand, Alice. 1991. "Social Cognition, Emotions, and the Psychology of Writing." *Journal of Advanced Composition* 11: 395–407.

Brannon, Lil, and C. H. Knoblauch. 1982. "On Students' Rights to Their Own Texts: A Model of Teacher Response." *College Composition and Communication* 33: 157–166.

Brannon, Lil. 1993. "M[other]: Lives on the Outside." *Written Communication* 10: 457–465.

———. 1994. "Rewriting the Story: Expressivism and the Problem of Experience." Conference on College Composition and Communication, Washington, DC. 23 March.

Bridwell-Bowles, Lillian. 1992. "Discourse and Diversity: Experimental Writing within the Academy." *College Composition and Communication* 43: 349–368.

———. 1995. "Freedom, Form, Function: Varieties of Academic Discourse." *College Composition and Communication* 46: 46–61.

Brodkey, Linda. 1994. "Writing on the Bias." *College English* 56: 527–547.

Brooke, Robert. 1987. "Lacan, Transference, and Writing Instruction." *College English* 49: 679–691.

———. 1988. "Modeling a Writer's Identity: Reading and Imitation in the Writing Classroom." *College Composition and Communication* 39: 23–41.

———. Judith Levin, and Joy Ritchie. 1994. "Teaching Composition and Reading Lacan: An Exploration in Wild Analysis." *Writing Theory and Critical Theory*. Edited by John Clifford and John Schilb. New York: MLA. 159–175.

Broughton, T. Alan. 1993. "Preparing the Way," "On This Side of the Canvas," "Death as a Cloudless Day," and "Refuge." *Prairie Schooner* 67 (Fall): 51–55.

Bruffee, Kenneth A. 1984. "Peer Tutoring and the 'Conversation of Mankind.'" In *Writing Centers: Theory and Administration*. Edited by Gary A. Olson. Urbana, IL: NCTE. 3–15.

Cain, Mary Ann. 1995. *Revisioning Writers' Talk: Gender and Culture in Acts of Composing*. Albany, NY: State University of New York Press.

Chappell, Fred. 1992. "First Attempts." In *My Poor Elephant: 27 Male Writers at Work*. Edited by Eve Shelnutt. Atlanta, GA: Longstreet. 17–29.

Clark, Beverly Lyon, and Sonja Weidenhaupt. 1992. "On Blocking and Unblocking Sonja: A Case Study in Two Voices." *College Composition and Communication* 43: 55–74.

Clark, Irene L. 1993. "Portfolio Grading and the Writing Center." *The Writing Center Journal* 13: 48–62.

Clark, Suzanne. 1994. "Rhetoric, Social Construction, and Gender: Is It Bad to Be Sentimental?" In *Writing Theory and Critical Theory*. Edited by John Clifford and John Schilb. New York: MLA. 96–108.

Con Davis, Robert. 1987. "Pedagogy, Lacan, and the Freudian Subject." *College English* 49: 749–755.

Cooper, Marilyn. 1994a. "Really Useful Knowledge: A Cultural Studies Agenda for Writing Centers." *The Writing Center Journal* 14: 97–111.

———. 1994b. "Dialogic Learning across Disciplines." *Journal of Advanced Composition* 14: 531–546.

Copjec, Joan. 1989. "Cutting Up." In *Between Feminism and Psychoanalysis*. Edited by Teresa Brennan. London: Routledge. 227–246.

Crowley, Sharon. 1991. "A Personal Essay on Freshman English." *Pre/Text* 12.3–4: 156–176.

Daniell, Beth. 1994. "Composing (as) Power." *College Composition and Communication* 45: 238–246.

de Beauvoir, Simone. 1959. *Memoirs of a Dutiful Daughter*. Translated by James Kirkup. Cleveland, OH: World Publishing.

———. 1962. *The Prime of Life*. Translated by Peter Green. Cleveland, OH: World Publishing.

de Lauretis, Teresa. 1987. *Technologies of Gender*. Bloomington, IN: Indiana University Press.

Deletiner, Carole. 1992. "Crossing Lines." *College English* 54: 809–817.

Eady, Cornelius. 1993. "Photo of Dexter Gordon, About to Solo, 1965." *Prairie Schooner* 67 (Fall): 11.

Ebert, Teresa L. 1991. "The 'Difference' of Postmodern Feminism," *College English* 53: 886–904.

Ede, Lisa. 1994. "Reading the Writing Process." In *Taking Stock: The Writing Process Movement in the 90s*. Edited by Lad Tobin and Thomas Newkirk. Portsmouth, NH: Boynton/Cook. 31–43.

Elbow, Peter. 1973. *Writing without Teachers*. New York: Oxford University Press.

———. 1981. *Writing with Power*. New York: Oxford University Press.

———. 1987. "Closing My Eyes as I Speak: An Argument for Ignoring Audience." *College English* 49: 50–69.

———. and Pat Belanoff. 1989. *Community of Writers*. New York: McGraw-Hill.

———. 1990. *What Is English?* New York: MLA.

Elliott, Gayle. 1994. "Pedagogy in Penumbra: Teaching, Writing, and Feminism in the Fiction Workshop." In *Colors of a Different Horse: Rethinking Creative Writing Theory and Pedagogy*. Edited by Wendy Bishop and Hans Ostrom. Urbana, IL: NCTE. 100–126.

Ellsworth, Elizabeth. 1989. "Why Doesn't This Feel Empowering? Working through the Repressive Myths of Critical Pedagogy." *Harvard Educational Review* 59: 297–324.

Faigley, Lester. 1992. *Fragments of Rationality: Postmodernity and the Subject of Composition*. Pittsburgh, PA: University of Pittsburgh Press.

———. and Stephen Witte. 1981. "Analyzing Revision." *College Composition and Communication* 32: 400–414.

Felman, Shoshana. 1987. *Jacques Lacan and the Adventure of Insight: Psychoanalysis in Contemporary Culture*. Cambridge, MA: Harvard University Press.

———. 1993. *What Does a Woman Want?: Reading and Sexual Difference*. Baltimore, MD: Johns Hopkins University Press.

Flax, Jane. 1990. *Thinking Fragments: Psychoanalysis, Feminism, and Postmodernism in the Contemporary West*. Berkeley, CA: University of California Press.

Flieger, Jerry Aline. 1990. "The Female Subject: (What) Does Woman Want?" In *Psychoanalysis and . . .* Edited by Richard Feldstein and Henry Sussman. New York: Routledge. 54–63.

Flower, Linda. 1979. "Writer-Based Prose: A Cognitive Basis for Problems in Writing." *College English* 41: 19–37.

———. John Hayes, Linda Carey, et al. 1986. "Detection, Diagnosis, and the Strategies of Revision." *College Composition and Communication* 37: 16–55.

Freire, Paulo. 1992 (1970). *Pedagogy of the Oppressed*. New York: Continuum.

Freud, Sigmund. 1962a. *Dora: An Analysis of a Case of Hysteria*. New York: Collier/Macmillan.

———. 1962b (1958). *The Standard Edition of the Complete Psychological Works of Sigmund Freud*. Edited and translated by James Strachey. London: Hogarth.

Frey, Olivia. 1990. "Beyond Literary Darwinism: Women's Voices and Critical Discourse." *College English* 52: 507–526.

Fuller, Margaret. 1992. *The Essential Margaret Fuller*. Edited by Jeffrey Steele. New Brunswick, NJ: Rutgers University Press.

Fulwiler, Toby. 1990. "Looking and Listening for My Voice." *College Composition and Communication* 41: 214–220.

Gallop, Jane. 1982. *The Daughter's Seduction: Feminism and Psychoanalysis*. Ithaca, NY: Cornell University Press.

———. 1988. "The Seduction of an Analogy." In *Thinking through the Body*. New York: Columbia University Press.

Gere, Anne Ruggles. 1994. "Kitchen Tables and Rented Rooms: The Extracurriculum of Composition." *College Composition and Communication* 45: 75–92.

Gillam, Alice M. 1991. "Writing Center Ecology: A Bakhtinian Perspective." *The Writing Center Journal* 11: 3–11.

Glass, James M. 1993. *Shattered Selves: Multiple Personality in a Postmodern World*. Ithaca, NY: Cornell University Press.

Gore, Jennifer. 1993. *The Struggle for Pedagogies: Critical and Feminist Discourses as Regimes of Truth*. New York: Routledge.

Harris, Muriel. 1995. "Talking in the Middle: Why Writers Need Writing Tutors." *College English* 57: 27–42.

Haynes-Burton, Cynthia. 1994. "'Hanging Your Alias on Their Scene': Writing Centers, Graffiti, and Style." *Writing Center Journal* 14: 112–124.

Heath, Shirley Brice. 1982. *Ways with Words: Language, Life, and Work in Communities and Classrooms*. Cambridge, MA: Cambridge University Press.

———. 1994. "Finding in History the Right to Estimate." *College Composition and Communication* 45: 97–102.

Helmers, Marguerite H. 1994. *Writing Students: Composition Testimonials and Representations of Students*. Albany, NY: State University of New York Press.

Herzberg, Bruce. 1994. "Community Service and Critical Teaching." *College Composition and Communication* 45: 307–319.

hooks, bell. 1989. *Talking Back*. Boston, MA: South End Press.

Horner, Bruce. 1994. "Mapping Errors and Expectations for Basic Writing: From the 'Frontier Field' to 'Border Country.'" *English Education* 26: 29–51.

Hunter, Ian. 1988. *Culture and Government: The Emergence of Literacy Education*. London: Macmillan.

Jardine, Alice. 1989. "Notes for an Analysis." In *Between Feminism and Psychoanalysis*. Edited by Teresa Brennan. London: Routledge. 73–85.

Jouve, Nicole Ward. 1991. *White Woman Speaks with Forked Tongue: Criticism as Autobiography*. London: Routledge.

Kalpakian, Laura. 1991. "My Life as a Boy." In *The Confidence Woman: 26 Women Writers at Work*. Edited by Eve Shelnutt. Atlanta, GA: Longstreet. 43–57.

Kingston, Maxine Hong. 1976. *The Woman Warrior: Memories of a Girlhood among Ghosts*. New York: Knopf.

Kirsch, Gesa B. 1993. *Women Writing the Academy: Audience, Authority, and Transformation*. Carbondale, IL: Southern Illinois University Press.

Knoblauch, C. H. 1990. "Literacy and the Politics of Education." In *The Right to Literacy*. Edited by Andrea A. Lunsford, Helene Moglen, and James Slevin. New York: MLA. 74–80.

———. 1991. "Critical Teaching and Dominant Culture." In *Composition and Resistance*. Edited by C. Mark Hurlbert and Michael Blitz. Portsmouth, NH: Heinemann. 12–21.

———. and Lil Brannon. 1993. *Critical Teaching and the Idea of Literacy*. Portsmouth, NH: Boynton/Cook.

Kristeva, Julia. 1986a. "A New Type of Intellectual: The Dissident." Translated by Sean Hand. In *The Kristeva Reader*. Edited by Toril Moi. New York: Columbia University Press.

———. 1986b. "Women's Time." Translated by Alice Jardine and Harry Blake. *The Kristeva Reader*. Edited by Toril Moi. New York: Columbia University Press.

———. 1987. *In the Beginning Was Love: Psychoanalysis and Faith*. Translated by Arthur Goldhammer. New York: Columbia University Press.

Lacan, Jacques. 1977a. *Ecrits: A Selection*. Translated by Alan Sheridan. New York: Norton.

———. 1977b. *The Four Fundamental Concepts of Psychoanalysis*. Translated by Alan Sheridan. London: Hogarth.

Lamb, Catherine. 1991. "Beyond Argument in Feminist Composition." *College Composition and Communication* 42: 11–24.

Le Dœuff, Michele. 1989. *The Philosophical Imaginary*. Translated by Colin Gordon. Stanford, CA: Stanford University Press.

———. 1990. "Women, Reason, Etc." *Differences: A Journal of Feminist Cultural Studies* 2: 1–13.

———. 1991. *Hipparchia's Choice: An Essay Concerning Women, Philosophy, etc.* Translated by Trista Selous. Oxford: Blackwell.

———. 1993. "Harsh Times." *New Left Review* 199 (May–June): 127–139.

Leverenz, Carrie Shively. 1994. "Peer Response in the Multicultural Composition Classroom: Dissensus—A Dream (Deferred)." *Journal of Advanced Composition* 14: 167–186.

Lorde, Audre. 1980. *The Cancer Journals*. Argyle, NY: Spinsters.

Lu, Min-Zhan. 1994. "Professing Multiculturalism: The Politics of Style in the Contact Zone." *College Composition and Communication* 45: 442–458.

Lunsford, Andrea. 1991. "Collaboration, Control, and the Idea of a Writing Center." *The Writing Center Journal* 12: 3–10.

———, Helene Moglen, and James Slevin, eds. 1990. *The Right to Literacy*. New York: MLA.

Macrorie, Ken. 1970. *Telling Writing*. Rochelle Park, NJ: Hayden.

Marshall, Paule. 1984. *Praisesong for the Widow*. New York: Dutton.

Miller, Susan. 1994. "Composition as Cultural Artifact: Rethinking History as Theory." In *Writing Theory and Critical Theory*. Edited by John Clifford and John Schilb. New York: MLA. 19–32.

Moi, Toril. 1989. "Patriarchal Thought and the Drive for Knowledge." In *Between Feminism and Psychoanalysis*. Edited by Teresa Brennan. London: Routledge. 189–205.

Morrison, Toni. 1970. *The Bluest Eye*. New York: Washington Square.
Morson, Gary Saul. 1994. *Narrative and Freedom: The Shadows of Time*. New Haven, CT: Yale University Press.
Mortensen, Peter, and Gesa E. Kirsch. 1993. "On Authority in the Study of Writing." *College Composition and Communication* 44: 556–572.
Murphy, Ann. 1989. "Transference and Resistance in the Basic Writing Classroom: Problematics and Praxis." *College Composition and Communication* 40: 175–187.
Murray, Donald M. 1982. "Teaching the Other Self: The Writer's First Reader." *College Composition and Communication* 33: 140–147.
———. 1995 (1991). *The Craft of Revision*. 2nd ed. Fort Worth, TX: Harcourt Brace.
North, Stephen. 1984. "The Idea of a Writing Center." *College English* 46: 433–446.
———. 1990. "Personal Writing, Professional Ethos, and the Voice of 'Common Sense.'" *Pre/Text* 11.1–2: 105–119.
O'Brien, Tim. 1990. *The Things They Carried*. New York: Penguin.
———. 1994. "The Vietnam in Me." *The New York Times Magazine* October 2: 48–57.
O'Connor, Frank. 1988. "Guests of the Nation." In *Fiction 100*, 5th ed. Edited by James H. Pickering. New York: Macmillan. 1227–1235.
Ohmann, Richard. 1976. *English in America: A Radical View of the Profession*. New York: Oxford University Press.
Olsen, Tillie. 1976 (1956). "I Stand Here Ironing." In *Tell Me a Riddle*. New York: Dell.
Osborn, Susan. 1991. "'Revision/Re-Vision': A Feminist Writing Class." *Rhetoric Review* 9: 258–273.
Pontalis, J. B. 1978. "On Death-Work in Freud, in the Self, in Culture." In *Psychoanalysis, Creativity, and Literature*. Edited by Alan Roland. New York: Columbia University Press. 85–95.
Pratt, Mary Louise. 1991. "Arts of the Contact Zone." In *Profession*. New York: MLA. 33–40.
Pratt, Minnie Bruce. 1991. *Rebellion: Essays 1980–1991*. Ithaca, NY: Firebrand.
Quandahl, Ellen. 1994. "The Anthropological Sleep of Composition." *Journal of Advanced Composition* 14: 413–429.
Ragland-Sullivan, Ellie. 1987. *Jacques Lacan and the Philosophy of Psychoanalysis*. Urbana and Chicago, IL: University of Illinois Press.
Recchio, Thomas. 1991. "A Bakhtinian Reading of Student Writing." *College Composition and Communication* 42: 446–454.
———. 1994. "On the Critical Necessity of 'Essaying.'" In *Taking Stock: The Writing Process Movement in the 90s*. Edited by Lad Tobin and Thomas Newkirk. Portsmouth, NH: Boynton/Cook. 219–235.
Rich, Adrienne. 1979. "When We Dead Awaken: Writing as Re-Vision." In *On Lies, Secrets, and Silence*. New York: Norton.
Ritchie, Joy. 1990. "Between the Trenches and the Ivory Towers: Divisions between University Professors and High School Teachers." In *Farther Along: Transforming Dichotomies in Rhetoric and Composition*. Edited by Kate Ronald and Hephzibah Roskelly. Portsmouth, NH: Boynton/Cook. 101–121.
Robinson, Marilynne. 1982. *Housekeeping*. New York: Bantam.
Rorty, Richard. 1991. "Feminism and Pragmatism." *Michigan Quarterly Review* 30 (Spring): 231–258.

Rose, Mike. 1989. *Lives on the Boundary: The Struggles and Achievements of America's Underprepared*. New York: Free Press; London: Collier Macmillan.

Rosenblatt, Louise. 1983 (1938). *Literature as Exploration*. 4th ed. New York: MLA.

———. 1993. "The Transactional Theory: Against Dualisms." *College English* 55: 377–386.

Rowbotham, Sheila. 1973. *Woman's Consciousness, Man's World*. London: Penguin.

Rushdie, Salman. 1990. *Haroun and the Sea of Stories*. New York: Viking.

Schuster, Charles I. 1985. "Mikhail Bakhtin as Rhetorical Theorist." *College English* 47: 594–607.

Severino, Carol. 1994. "Writing Centers as Linguistic Contact Zones and Borderlands." *The Writing Lab Newsletter* 19 (December): 1–5.

Shelnutt, Eve. 1989. *The Writing Room: Keys to the Craft of Fiction and Poetry*. Marietta, GA: Longstreet.

Silko, Leslie Marmon. 1977. *Ceremony*. New York: Viking Press.

Smith, Frank. 1986. *Insult to Intelligence: The Bureaucratic Invasion of Our Classrooms*. New York: Arbor House.

Sommers, Nancy. 1980. "Revision Strategies of Student Writers and Experienced Adult Writers." *College Composition and Communication* 31: 378–388.

Spellmeyer, Kurt. 1994. "Lost in the Funhouse: The Teaching of Writing and the Problem of Professional Narcissism." Division on the Teaching of Writing. MLA Convention. San Diego, CA. 29 December.

Sperling, Melanie, and Sarah Warshauer Freedman. 1987. "A Good Girl Writes Like a Good Girl." *Written Communication* 4: 343–369.

Spivak, Gayatri Chakravorty. 1989. "Feminism and Deconstruction Again: Negotiating with Unacknowledged Masculinism." In *Between Feminism and Psychoanalysis*. Edited by Teresa Brennan. London: Routledge. 206–223.

Stone, Leo. 1984. *Transference and Its Context: Selected Papers on Psychoanalysis*. New York: J. Aronson.

Su, Adrienne. 1993. "Alice Descending the Rabbit-Hole." *Prairie Schooner* 67 (Fall): 34–35.

Sunstein, Bonnie. 1994. *Composing a Culture: Inside a Summer Writing Program with High School Teachers*. Portsmouth, NH: Boynton/Cook.

Tobin, Lad. 1993. *Writing Relationships: What Really Happens in the Composition Class*. Portsmouth, NH: Boynton/Cook.

Tompkins, Jane. 1987. "Me and My Shadow." *New Literary History* 19: 169–178.

———. 1988. "Fighting Words: Unlearning to Write the Critical Essay." *Georgia Review* 42: 585–590.

———. 1992. "The Way We Live Now." *Change* 24 (November/December): 15–19.

Trimbur, John. 1989. "Consensus and Difference in Collaborative Learning." *College English* 51: 602–616.

———. 1994. "Taking the Social Turn: Teaching Writing Post-Process." *College Composition and Communication* 45: 108–118.

Trinh, T. Minh-ha. 1989. *Woman, Native, Other: Writing Postcoloniality and Feminism*. Bloomington, IN: Indiana University Press.

Warnock, Tilly, and John Warnock. 1984. "Liberatory Writing Centers: Restoring Authority to Writers." In *Writing Centers: Theory and Administration*. Edited by Gary A. Olson. Urbana, IL: NCTE. 16–23.

Weesner, Theodore. 1987 (1967). *The Car Thief*. New York: Vintage.
Welch, Nancy. 1993. "Resisting the Faith: Conversion, Resistance, and the Training of Teachers." *College English* 55: 387–401.
———. 1994. "The Cheating Kind." *Other Voices* 20 (Spring): 37–45.
———. 1996. "The Road from Prosperity." *Threepenny Review* 64 (Winter): 14–16.
Winnicott, D. W. 1971. *Playing and Reality*. London: Tavistock.
Winterowd, W. Ross. 1965. *Rhetoric and Writing*. Boston, MA: Allyn and Bacon.
Woodruff, Jay, ed. 1993. *A Piece of Work: Five Writers Discuss Their Revisions*. Iowa City, IA: University of Iowa Press.
Woolbright, Meg. 1992. "The Politics of Tutoring: Feminism with the Patriarchy." *The Writing Center Journal* 13: 16–30.
Wright, Elizabeth. 1989 (1984). *Psychoanalytic Criticism: Theory in Practice*. London: Routledge.

Welch's Insights as a Resource for Your Reflections

1. Welch values a vision of writing that runs counter to mainstream academic discourse. What practical difficulties might this vision present in your teaching, and how might you work around them?
2. What do you make of Welch's use of psychoanalytic concepts to understand revision? How might some of these tools be helpful in understanding other phases of composing and other aspects of teaching writing?

Welch's Insights as a Resource for Your Writing Classroom

1. Ask your students to reconsider a "finished" piece of writing. What would they add to it if they were to lengthen it a great deal? What digressions would they undertake? Help them to realize that they are not simply tacking on more prose but are free to explore digressions that may entirely change the focus and thrust of the paper.
2. Ask your students to reflect on some of the potential digressions they delineated in question 1 as potential topics for future essays. Would they want to pursue any of these further? If so, which ones, and why?

Crafting Sentences

The Erasure of the Sentence

Robert J. Connors

How might we focus student attention on developing good sentences? During the 1970s, the field of composition was briefly dominated by sentence-level pedagogies. In this article from the September 2000 issue of College Composition and Communication, *Robert J. Connors describes the emergence and reception of three teaching methods that focused on improving students' syntactical skills: Francis Christensen's generative rhetoric, exercises in imitation, and sentence combining. Connors goes on to account for several changes in teacher attitudes—including negative reactions to formalism, behaviorism, and empiricism—that contributed to the quick disappearance of sentence rhetorics. The discrediting of these methods owed little to a well-developed critique; in fact, the experimental results that supported sentence pedagogies were never disproved. Connors suggests that we re-evaluate the usefulness of sentence-level rhetorics and our reasons for neglecting them.*

In the 1980s, as composition studies matured, theoretical and critical interrogation of much of the field's received wisdom began in earnest. The field of composition studies, increasingly in the hands of the new generation of trained specialist Ph.D.'s, began to do more and more effectively what intellectual fields have always done: define, subdivide, and judge the efforts of members. Some elements of the older field of composition teaching became approved and burgeoned, while others were tacitly declared dead ends: lore-based and therefore uninteresting, scientistic and therefore suspect, mechanistic and therefore destructive. Little attention has been paid to these preterite elements in the older field of composition; they have been dropped like vestigial limbs, and most of those who once practiced or promoted those elements have retired or moved to more acceptable venues, maintaining a circumspect silence about their earlier flings with now-unpopular ideas such as paragraph theory, or structural linguistics, or stage-model developmental psychology. Of all of the inhabitants of this limbo of discarded approaches, there is no more dramatic and striking exemplar than what was called the school of syntactic methods. These sentence-based pedagogies rose from older syntax-oriented teaching methods to an extraordinary moment in the sun during the 1970s bidding fair to become methodologically hegemonic. But like the mayfly, their day was brief though intense, and these pedagogies are hardly mentioned now in mainstream composition studies except as of faint historical interest. The sentence itself as an element of composition pedagogy is hardly mentioned today outside of textbooks. But we can learn as much from watching the working out of Darwinian intellectual failures as from participating in the self-congratulatory normal science of the current winners, and so I offer this history of syntactic methods since 1960 in the spirit of the old New England gravestone: "As you are now, so once was I; as I am now, so you shall be."

From the earliest point in American composition-rhetoric, the sentence was a central component of what students were asked to study, practice, and become conversant with. From the 1890s onward, chapters on The Sentence in most textbooks were fairly predictable. Western rhetorical theories about the sentence date back to classical antiquity, with roots in Latin grammar and in the oral rhetorical theories of the classical period, and they came to their nineteenth-century form by a long process of accretion. Traditional sentence pedagogy assumed grammatical knowledge of the sort inculcated by Reed and Kellogg diagrams, but the prime elements in these textbook chapters were taxonomic, all this time focused on their place in sentence construction. Along with the breakdown of sentences by grammatical types — simple, compound, complex, and compound-complex — which was usually taken up in the grammar chapters of textbooks, the traditional classification of sentences is by function: declarative, imperative, interrogative, and exclamatory sentences. The traditional rhetorical classifications of sentences were also covered: long and short, loose and periodic, and balanced. In addition, sentence pedagogy nearly always included coverage of the old abstractions that informed modern composition-rhetoric from 1890 through the present: those of Adams Sherman Hill (clearness, energy, force), Barrett Wendell (unity, coherence, emphasis), or C. S. Baldwin (clearness and interest).[1]

All of these traditional sentence pedagogies included many exercises and much practice, and we fail to understand them if we think of them only as defined by their abstractions and classifications. Most sentence chapters in textbooks asked students to create many sentences, and indeed, sentence-level pedagogy was an important part of traditional writing courses. It became even more central during the 1950s, a period when composition teachers were looking to structural linguistics with expectation and sentence-writing was much discussed. But as I have discussed in more detail elsewhere (*Composition-Rhetoric* 162–70), it was just as structural linguistics was gaining a serious foothold in composition pedagogy that its theoretical bases came under sustained and successful attack from Noam Chomsky and the theory of transformational-generative grammar.

Here we enter a more familiar modern territory, the post-1960 era of composition and composition studies. And it is here that we find the beginnings of the three most important of the sentence-based rhetorics that were to seem so promising to writing teachers of the New Rhetoric era: the generative rhetoric of Francis Christensen, imitation exercises, and sentence-combining. I want to take up these three more modern syntactic methods in roughly chronological order, beginning with the ideas of Francis Christensen.

Christensen Rhetoric

Francis Christensen, a professor of English at the University of Southern California, began to publish essays in the early 1960s complaining that traditional theories of the sentence widely taught throughout the first sixty years of this century were primarily taxonomic rather than generative or productive. Except in providing examples, they were not of much real help to teachers in showing students how to write good sentences. In 1963, Christensen published what is arguably his most important article, "A Generative Rhetoric of the Sentence." In this article and in other works published up to his death in 1970, Christensen described a new way of viewing sentences and a pedagogical method that could be used to teach students how to write longer, more mature, more varied and interesting sentences.

In the opening sentence of "A Generative Rhetoric of the Sentence," he announced his intentions: "If a new grammar is to be brought to bear on composition, it must be brought to bear on the rhetoric of the sentence" (155). Christensen was certain that the sentence is the most important element in rhetoric because it is "a natural and isolable unit" ("Course" 168). Complaining that the traditional conceptions of the sentence were merely descriptive, Christensen argued that traditional sentence pedagogy simply did not help students learn to write. "We do not really teach our captive charges to write better — we merely expect them to" ("Generative" 155). Christensen indicated that both the grammatical and rhetorical classifications of sentences are equally barren in the amount of real assistance they give to students. "We need a rhetoric of the sentence that will do more than combine the ideas of primer sentences. We need one that will generate ideas" ("Generative" 155).

Christensen rhetoric did not follow the traditional canons of rhetoric, which begin with conceptualization or invention; instead it opted for a view that all other skills in language follow syntactic skills naturally. According to Christensen, you could be a good writer if you could learn to write a good sentence. His pedagogy consisted of short base-level sentences to which students were asked to attach increasingly sophisticated systems of initial and final modifying clauses and phrases — what he called "free modifiers." Effective use of free modifiers would result in effective "cumulative sentences," and Christensen's most famous observation about teaching the cumulative sentence was that he wanted to push his students "to level after level, not just two or three, but four, five, or six, even more, as far as the students' powers of observation will take them. I want them to become sentence acrobats, to dazzle by their syntactic dexterity" ("Generative" 160).

For some years after 1963, Christensen's syntactic rhetoric was widely discussed, praised, and damned. His few short articles—and all of them were contained in *Notes toward a New Rhetoric*, a book of 110 pages—created an intense interest in syntactic experimentation and innovation. Several experiments confirmed the effectiveness of using generative rhetoric with students. During the early 1970s, two published reports appeared on the use of the *Christensen Rhetoric Program* (an expensive boxed set of overhead transparencies and workbooks that had appeared in 1968). Charles A. Bond, after a rather loosely controlled experiment, reported that there was a "statistically significant difference" between the grades of a group of students taught using Christensen methods and those of a control group taught by conventional methods; he also mentioned that his students were enthusiastic about cumulative sentences. R. D. Walshe, teaching a group of adult night-class students in Australia (it is hard to imagine two groups of native-speaking English students as far removed from one another as Bond's American first-year students and Walshe's Australian working people), found that although some of Christensen's claims for his system were inflated, the *Christensen Rhetoric Program* generally worked well and was liked by his students.

These tests of Christensen's program were unscientific and anecdotal, and it was not until 1978 that a full-scale empirical research test was done on the Christensen system. The experiment's creator, Lester Faigley, began with two hypotheses: First, that the Christensen sentence method would increase syntactic maturity in those who used it (for a fuller discussion of the concept of syntactic maturity, see the next section of this paper), and second, that the Christensen rhetoric program as a whole would produce a measurable qualitative increase in writing skill. Faigley tested four experimental sections and four control sections in his experiment. The experimental sections used Christensen's *A New Rhetoric*, and the control sections used a well-known content-oriented rhetoric textbook, McCrimmon's *Writing with a Purpose*. Faigley proved both of his hypotheses; he found that the writing produced by the Christensen program not only was measurably more mature but also received better average ratings (.63 on a six-point scale; statistically significant) from blind holistic readings ("Generative" 179). Faigley's experiment showed that the Christensen method does produce measurable classroom results.

Imitation

The argument about Christensen rhetoric was in full swing during the middle 1960s when another syntactic method was first popularized: imitation exercises. Unlike Christensen rhetoric, imitation was part of the rediscovered trove of classical rhetorical theory that was coming to light in English departments. From the time of Isocrates and Aristotle, exercises in direct imitation and in the copying of structures had been recommended by theorists and teachers of rhetoric, and after Edward P. J. Corbett published his essay "The Uses of Classical Rhetoric" in 1963 and his *Classical Rhetoric for the Modern Student* in 1965, the use of imitation exercises in composition classes enjoyed a renaissance of popularity. There are, of course, different meanings for the term *imitation*, but in rhetoric it has always meant one thing: the emulation of the syntax of good prose models by students wishing to improve their writing or speaking styles. The recurring word used by the ancients concerning imitation, according to Corbett, was *similis*; the objective of imitation exercises was to make the student's writing similar to that of a superior writer ("Theory" 244). This similarity does not imply that the student's writing will be identical to the writing she imitates; the similarity that imitation promotes is not of content, but of form. Corbett recommends several different sorts of exercises, the first and simplest of which involved "copying passages, word for word from admired authors" ("Theory" 247). For students who have spent some time copying passages, Corbett recommends a second kind of imitation exercise: pattern practice. In this exercise, the student chooses or is given single sentences to use as patterns after which he or she is to design sentences of his or her own. "The aim of this exercise," says Corbett, "is not to achieve a word-for-word correspondence with the model but rather to achieve an awareness of the variety of sentence structure of which the English language is capable" ("Theory" 249). The model sentences need not be followed slavishly, but Corbett suggests that the student observe at least the same kind, number, and order of phrases and clauses.

After Corbett's initial arguments for imitation, other scholars took the method up as an important technique. As Winston Weathers and Otis Winchester put it in their 1969 textbook on imitation, *Copy and Compose*, writing "is a civilized art that is rooted in tradition" (2). The assumption that imitation makes about contemporary student writing is that it is often stylistically barren because of lack of familiarity with good models of prose style and that this barrenness can be remedied by an intensive course in good prose models. Weathers and Winchester—whose *Copy and Compose* and *The New Strategy of Style*, as well as Weathers's *An Alternate Style: Options in Composition*, recommended imitation as a primary exercise—became the most notable proponents of imitation. Weathers and Winchester used a slightly more complex model of imitation that did Corbett: They asked their students first to copy a passage, then to read a provided analysis of the model's structure, and finally to compose an imitation. During the 1970s, Frank D'Angelo, William Gruber, Penelope Starkey, S. Michael Halloran, and other writers all supported classically based imitation exercises as effective methods for attaining improved student sentence skills. A second set of imitation exercises proposed during the late 1960s and early 1970s were called "controlled composition exercises," and were actually a hybrid, melding some aspects of imitation and some aspects of sentence-combining. Controlled composition, according to Edmund Miller, is "the technique of having students copy a passage as they introduce some systematic change" (ii).

From the middle 1960s onward, a small but significant number of voices kept reproposing the value of imitation. Frank D'Angelo noted that imitation connoted counterfeiting and stereotyping in most people's minds, when it should connote originality and creativity. A student who practices imitation, he suggests, "may be spared at least some of the fumblings of the novice writer" for forms in which to express his thoughts (283). A "student will become more original as he engages in creative imitation," claimed D'Angelo (283). Weathers and Winchester took the argument further: "Originality and individuality are outgrowths of a familiarity with originality in the work of others, and they emerge from a knowledge of words, patterns, constructions and procedures that all writers use" (*Copy and Compose* 2).

Like Christensen rhetoric, imitation was put to the test, in this case by Rosemary Hake and Joseph Williams, who performed an experiment in 1977 that compared sentence-combining pedagogy with an imitation pedagogy that they evolved under the term "sentence expansion." Hake and Williams found that the students in their imitation group learned to write better expository prose with fewer flaws and errors than students using sentence-combining pedagogies ("Sentence" 143). Since sentence-combining was known by the late seventies to produce better syntactic results than non-sentence methods, this finding was important. Imitation, proponents claimed, provided students with practice in the "ability to design" that is the basis of a mature prose style. The different imitation techniques, whether they consist of direct copying of passages, composition of passages using models, or controlled mutation of sentence structures, all have this in common: They cause students to internalize the structures of the piece being imitated; as Corbett points out, internalization is the key term in imitation. With those structures internalized, a student is free to engage in the informed processes of choice, which are the wellspring of real creativity. William Gruber, writing in 1977, argued that imitation assists in design: "Standing behind imitation as a teaching method is the simple assumption that an inability to write is an inability to design — an inability to shape effectively the thought of a sentence, a paragraph, or an essay" (493–94). Gruber argued that imitation liberates students' personalities by freeing them of enervating design decisions, at least temporarily. Without knowledge of what has been done by others, claimed proponents of imitation exercises, there can be no profound originality.

The Sentence-Combining Juggernaut

Sentence-combining in its simplest form is the process of joining two or more short, simple sentences to make one longer sentence, using embedding, deletion, subordination, and coordination. In all probability sentence-combining was taught by the grammaticus of classical Rome, but such exercises have tended to be ephemera, and none has come down to us. Shirley Rose's article of 1983, "One Hundred Years of Sentence-Combining," traced the use of similar techniques back to the nineteenth century and argued that teachers asking students to combine short sentences into long ones was a pedagogy growing out of schoolbook grammar and structural grammar as well as more modern grammatical ideas (483).

While combining exercises can be found in the 1890s, it was not until 1957, when Noam Chomsky revolutionized grammatical theory with his book *Syntactic Structures*, that the theoretical base was established upon which modern sentence-combining pedagogies would be founded. This base was, of course, Chomskian transformational-generative (TG) grammar, which for a while caused tremendous excitement in the field of composition. TG grammar, which quickly swept both traditional and structural grammar aside in linguistics between 1957 and 1965, seemed at that time to present to composition the possibility of a new writing pedagogy based on the study of linguistic transformations. In 1963, Donald Bateman and Frank J. Zidonis of the Ohio State University conducted an experiment to determine whether teaching high-school students TG grammar would reduce the incidence of errors in their writing. They found that students taught TG grammar both reduced errors and developed the ability to write more complex sentence structures. Despite some questionable features in the Bateman and Zidonis study, it did suggest that learning TG grammar had an effect on student writing.

The Bateman and Zidonis study was published in 1964, and in that same year a study was published that was to have far more importance for sentence-combining: Kellogg Hunt's *Grammatical Structures Written at Three Grade Levels*. Francis Christensen had been using the term "syntactic fluency" since 1963, but Christensen's use of it was essentially qualitative and impressionistic. Hunt's work would become the basis for most measurements of "syntactic maturity," a quantitative term that came to be an important goal of sentence-combining. To recap Hunt's study quickly: He wished to find out what elements of writing changed as people matured and which linguistic structures seemed to be representative of mature writing. To this end he studied the writings of average students in the fourth, eighth, and twelfth grades and expository articles in *Harper's* and *The Atlantic*. At first Hunt studied sentence length, but he quickly became aware that the tendency of younger writers to string together many short clauses with "and" meant that sentence length was not a good indicator of maturity in writing. He studied clause length, and as he says, he "became more and more interested in what I will describe as one main clause plus whatever subordinate clauses happen to be attached to or embedded within it"

Table 1. Words per T-unit, Clauses per T-unit, Words per Clause

	Grade Level						
	3	4	5	7	8	12	Superior Adults
Words/T-unit	7.67	8.51	9.34	9.99	11.34	14.4	20.3
Clauses/T-unit	1.18	1.29	1.27	1.30	1.42	1.68	1.74
Words/Clause	6.5	6.6	7.4	7.7	8.1	8.6	11.5

O'Hare (22).

("Synopsis" 111). This is Hunt's most famous concept, the "minimal terminable unit" or "T-unit." "Each T-unit," says Hunt, is "minimal in length and each could be terminated grammatically between a capital and a period" (112).

The T-unit, Hunt found, was a much more reliable index of stylistic maturity than sentence length. Eventually he determined the three best indices of stylistic maturity: the average number of words per T-unit, the average number of clauses per T-unit, and the average number of words per clause. When applied to writing at different grade levels, he found that these numbers increased at a steady increment. [In Table 1] is a chart that Frank O'Hare adapted from Hunt's work and from similar work by Roy O'Donnell, William Griffin, and Raymond Norris. As you can see, the rise in these three indices over time is obvious. Although these preliminary studies of Bateman and Zidonis and of Hunt used no sentence-combining at all, they did represent the bases from which high-modern sentence-combining sprang: the methodological linguistic base of TG grammar and the empirical quantitative base of Hunt's studies of syntactic maturity.

These two bases were brought together in the first important experiment involving sentence-combining exercises, that of John Mellon in 1965. Mellon called the 1969 report of his experiment *Transformational Sentence-Combining: A Method for Enhancing the Development of Syntactic Fluency in English Composition*, and his was the first study actually asking students to practice combining kernel sentences rather than merely to learn grammar. "Research," wrote Mellon, ". . . clearly shows that memorized principles of grammar, whether conventional or modern, clearly play a negligible role in helping students achieve 'correctness' in their written expression" (15). What *could* help students do this, reasoned Mellon, was instruction in TG grammar plus practice exercises in combining short "kernel sentences" into longer, more complex sentences.

With Mellon's initial publication of his work in 1967 and then with the national publication by NCTE in 1969, sentence-combining was established as an important tool in helping students write more mature sentences. But the grammar question still remained open. Since Mellon had to spend so much time teaching the principles of TG grammar in order to allow his students to work on his complex exercises, there was doubt as to which activity — learning the grammar or doing the exercises — had gotten the results. After all, Bateman and Zidonis had gotten error reduction — though admittedly not scientifically measured growth — from mere TG grammar instruction alone. How much importance did the sentence-combining exercises really have?

These questions were put to rest once again and for all in 1973 with the publication of Frank O'Hare's research monograph *Sentence-Combining: Improving Student Writing without Formal Grammar Instruction*. This study, which was the spark that ignited the sentence-combining boom of the late 1970s, showed beyond a doubt that sentence-combining exercises, without any grammar instruction at all, could achieve important gains in syntactic maturity for students who used them. Testing seventh graders, O'Hare used sentence-combining exercises with his experimental group over a period of eight months without ever mentioning any of the formal rules of TG grammar. The control group was not exposed to sentence-combining at all.

O'Hare's test measured six factors of syntactic maturity and found that "highly significant growth had taken place on all six factors" (55). His experimental group of seventh graders, after eight months of sentence-combining, now wrote an average of 15.75 words per T-unit, which was 9 percent higher than the 14.4 words per T-unit Hunt had reported as the average of twelfth graders. The other factors were similarly impressive. Just as important as the maturity factors, though, were the results of a second hypothesis O'Hare was testing: whether the sentence-combining group would write compositions that would be judged better in overall quality than those of the control group. Eight experienced English teachers rated 240 experimental and control essays written after the eight-month test period, and when asked to choose between matched pairs of essays, chose an experimental-group essay 70 percent of the time. The results suggested that sentence-combining exercises not only improved syntactic maturity but also affected perceived quality of writing in general.

The O'Hare study focused interest in sentence-combining, which had been associated with Mellon's complex directions, as a pedagogic tool. A follow-up study by Warren E. Combs found that the gains in writing quality that were produced by O'Hare's methods persisted over time and were still notable as long as two months after the sentence-combining practice had been discontinued. Textbooks began to appear using sentence-combining exercises, notably William Strong's *Sentence-Combining: A Composing Book* in 1973, which used "open" exercises, and O'Hare's own *Sentencecraft* of 1975. There remained now only one important question about sentence-combining: Was it useful for first-year students in college, or were they too old to be helped by the practice it gave? There was no doubt that it worked at the secondary-school level, but an article by James Ney in 1975 describing his attempts to use sentence-combining in a first-year class cast doubt of the technique's usefulness for eighteen year olds. Some teachers who had tried small doses of sentence-combining in first-year classes anecdotally reported no noticeable change in student writing.

Were college students too old for syntactic methods? This last question was answered in 1978 by the publication of the first results of a large and impressively rigorous study conducted under an Exxon grant at Miami University of Ohio by Donald A. Daiker, Andrew Kerek, and Max Morenberg. This college-level study used ninety of William Strong's "open" exercises and others created by the Miami researchers. These "open" exercises, some of which were lengthy and gave considerable stylistic and creative leeway to students, gave no directions on how best to complete them, and thus there was no "correct" answer or combination. Daiker, Kerek, and Morenberg's experimental and control groups each consisted of six sections of first-year college students, and their experiment was conducted over a fifteen-week semester (245–48). The Miami researchers found that their experimental group, like O'Hare's, evidenced both statistically meaningful gains in syntactic maturity and a gain in overall quality of the writing they produced. Daiker, Kerek, and Morenberg's sentence-combining group moved during the experiment from a high-twelfth-grade-level of syntactic maturity to a level approximating high-sophomore- or junior-level college writing skills. In addition, their experimental group showed statistically significant gains in three qualitative measures of general essay quality: holistic, forced-choice, and analytic (Morenberg, Daiker, and Kerek 250–52).

The late 1970s, just after the Miami experiment, were the high-water mark for sentence-combining. The literature grew so fast it was difficult to keep up with it; Daiker and his colleagues hosted an entire large conference devoted to sentence-combining at Miami in 1978 and another in 1983; scores of normal-science experiments were conducted using it in classrooms across the nation during the early 1980s. The lesson of sentence-combining was simple but compelling; as O'Hare said, "writing behavior can be changed fairly rapidly and with relative ease" (68). The result: Sentence-combining was a land-rush for a time. Between 1976 and 1983, there were no fewer than 49 articles in major journals about sentence-combining and hundreds of papers and conference presentations.[2] The success of the method provoked nasty quarrels about who "owned" it or had a moral right to profit from it. Revisionist narratives about development of the technique were published. Everyone, it seemed, wanted a piece of the pie now that it had been proven so tasty.

With the potency during the early 1980s of the movement toward empirical research — a movement that had been materially strengthened by the popularity of some of the sentence-combining research — we might expect that sentence-combining would have continued as a potent force in the developing field of composition studies. The research was there; the pedagogy was usable by almost any teacher and provided results that could be seen impressionistically as well as measured; the method had powerful champions. It had been long assumed that sentence-combining could be a useful part of a complete rhetoric program, but by the late 1970s, the venerable Kellogg Hunt was suggesting that sentence-combining was so useful that it should take up all class time in a first-year course, that "in every sense, sentence-combining can be [a] comprehensive writing program in and of itself, for at least one semester" ("Anybody" 156).

Look upon my works, ye mighty, and despair.

The Counterforces

In an astonishing reversal of fortune for sentence rhetorics, the triumphalism, the quarrels, and the debates of the early 1980s — now mostly forgotten — died away after 1983 or so. The articles on sentence issues fell away radically, and those that were written were more and more about applications to learning disabilities, or English as a second language, or special education. Erstwhile syntactic rhetoricians turned to other issues. The devaluation of sentence-based rhetorics is a complex phenomenon, and we need to approach it with circumspection. Let me first try to establish the reality of what I'm calling the "erasure of the sentence" in clearly numerical terms. Table 2 lists raw numbers of books and articles appearing in general-composition journals about the three sentence rhetorics discussed in this essay.

While I can't claim that this chart, which I derived from a combination of ERIC searching and my own research, is exhaustive or even directly replicable, the numbers themselves are less important than the trends they show. And these numerical trends strongly match our intuitive sense

Table 2. Books and Composition Journal Articles about Sentence Rhetorics, 1960–1998

	Christensen	Imitation	Sentence-combining
1960–1965	4	1	1
1966–1970	13	2	2
1971–1975	12	5	3
1976–1980	6	4	31
1981–1985	2	3	23
1986–1990	2	5	3
1991–1998	1	2	2

of what has been going on. We see, starting with Christensen's first articles in the early 1960s, a strong interest in sentence-writing that was mostly taken up with generative rhetoric and imitation during the early period of the New Rhetoric, say, 1963–1975. After 1976, the interest in Christensen begins to peter out as sentence-combining gathers momentum; a truly extraordinary burst of activity occurred in the late 1970s and early 1980s. But after 1984, general articles on sentence-combining died out, and more and more of the essays published had to do with use of sentence-combining in classes in English as a second language or with behaviorally disordered or autistic students; an ERIC search shows only three essays published on general-composition sentence-combining after 1986. The few general articles that were published after 1986 came more and more to be critical, but even the criticisms died away. After the mid-1980s, the sentence rhetorics of the 1960s and 1970s were gone, at least from books and journals.[3] Shirley Rose's 1983 article on the history of sentence-combining, which probably felt when she wrote it like a historical background to a vital part of the field, now looks more like the *ave atque vale* of the field to sentence-combining.

What iceberg did this *Titanic* meet? It was not a sudden ending, certainly; there had been criticism of sentence rhetorics going back to the 1960s. There had been some sentence-combining studies reporting equivocal results. There had been arguments over the differences between Christensen's "syntactic fluency" and Hunt's "syntactic maturity." And there had been ongoing questions about the meaning and validity of T-units and the relationship between syntactic maturity and holistically rated writing quality. But all of these had been essentially in-house issues, methodological or pragmatic, mostly waged in the pages of *Research in the Teaching of English*. By the early 1980s, sentence rhetorics had been criticized by some theorists for over fifteen years — but finally the criticisms were coming to bite.

That this devaluation of sentence rhetorics took place slowly meant that it was not noticeable as such by most people in the field. But once noted, it stands out as quite an extraordinary phenomenon. The story of sentence rhetorics is analogous, perhaps, to that of the U.S. space exploration effort of the 1960s. John F. Kennedy determined in 1961 that we would beat the Russians to the moon, and as a result of amazing effort, technological breakthrough, heart-rending sacrifice, and incalculable spondulix, *Apollo 11* landed on the Mare Tranquilitatis in 1969. We went back a few more times, put up flags, drove about in dune-buggies, collected dusty gray rocks, and came home. We had seen what it had to offer. And after a while, we did not go back anymore.

Similarly, in the early 1960s, a few scholars in composition determined to update the ages-old notion that students needed to be able to write good sentences before they could write good essays. Through new discovery, imaginative application of literary ideas, grammatical theory, and empirical research breakthroughs, methods and measurements were evolved that could determine whether student writers were writing better sentences. Teaching methods relating to the measurements were tested, and they succeeded, repeatedly and incontrovertibly, in producing better sentence writers. In addition, researchers determined that there was indeed a correlation between sentence skill and general perceived writing skill, discovering repeatedly that experimental sentence-writing groups were also holistically rated better writers. The techniques were honed and refined for different levels, and they finally appear in easily usable textbooks available to all. We had said we wanted newer and better teaching techniques, and the sentence rhetorics of the 1960s and 1970s provided them. And, as a discipline, we then peered quizzically at what we had wrought, frowned, and declared that no, this was not what we had really wanted. We had seen what it had to offer. And after a while, we did not go back any more.

To understand the reasons for the erasure of sentence rhetorics, we need to look at the kinds of criticism that were leveled at them almost as soon as they demonstrated any success. It will become apparent, doing this, that sentence rhetorics were not dragged under by any sudden radical uprising in the early 1980s, but rather finally succumbed to an entire line of criticism that had been ongoing for at least fifteen years. The reasons for the erasure of the sentence are multiple and complex, but as we look back over the varied critiques of syntactic rhetorics that were leveled beginning with Johnson, I think we can induce some general themes — themes that I would argue represent an important, if sometimes tacit, set of underlife definitions for composition studies in the past two decades.

The first and most obvious of the lines of criticism that would engulf sentence rhetorics was what we might call anti-formalism — the idea that any pedagogy based in form rather than in content was automatically suspect. Some part of this anti-formalist position is a result of distrust of traditional textbook pedagogies, what we might call the reaction against rhetorical atomism. For much of rhetorical history, and certainly for all of the history of composition, the pedagogical method of taking discourse apart into its constituent components and working on those components separately had been accepted almost absolutely. In American composition-rhetoric, this meant the familiar textbook breakdown of the "levels" of discourse — the word, the sentence, the paragraph, the essay. The great difference between the early New Rhetoric of the 1960s and 1970s and the work that came after it is largely found in the New-Rhetoric acceptance of atomistic formal levels up until the late 1970s and the later rejection of them. The first exposition of this point was by James Moffett in his classic 1968 book *Teaching the Universe of Discourse*, in which Moffett surveyed sentence rhetorics (including Christensen and early [Mellon] sentence-combining) and concluded that teachers must "leave the sentence within its broader discursive context" (186). Teachers can help students relate to syntactic options only in the context of a whole discourse, Moffett believed, and thus a teacher can only help a student "if the units of learning are units larger than the hindsight sentence." He criticized traditional writing pedagogy for moving from "little particle to big particle" toward the whole composition. "For the learner," Moffett wrote, "basics are not the small-focus technical things but broad things like meaning and motivation, purpose and point, which are precisely what are missing from exercises" (205). This was a line of attack that came to be heard more and more often.

We first see it in responses to Francis Christensen's work, which began to draw criticism almost as soon as it was formulated. The ink was hardly dry on the large and ambitious *Christensen Rhetoric Program*, Christensen's expensive boxed set of workbooks and projector overlays, when the first serious critique of his theory was published in 1969. Sabina Thorne Johnson, in an article called "Some Tentative Strictures on Generative Rhetoric," admitted that Christensen offered "a revolution in our assessment of style and in our approach to the teaching of composition" (159), but she also had some important reservations about the *generative* nature of the cumulative sentence. Johnson's critique was essential: "Christensen seems to believe that form can generate content (*Program*, p. vi). I don't believe it can, especially if the content is of an analytical or critical nature" (159). Johnson went on to criticize Christensen's reliance upon narrative and descriptive writing for his examples and as the basis for his theory, complaining that narrative and descriptive skills seldom carry over to exposition. She initiated a line of argument against syntactic methods that later came to seem conclusive: that students need training in higher-level skills such as invention and organization more than they need to know how to be "sentence acrobats."

Christensen himself died (of natural causes) shortly after Johnson's article appeared, and the attack on his theory led to a colorful exchange between Johnson and Christensen's widow Bonniejean that can be surveyed in back issues of *College English*. This debate was joined by A. M. Tibbetts, who made several telling points. Although Christensen is useful in the classroom, said Tibbetts, the claims he made for his system are simply "not empirically true as stated" (142). It is true that pattern practice with cumulative sentences can help students learn to use free modifiers, Tibbetts continued, but that is only one of the skills writers need. While he admitted that Christensen's method produced clever sentences from students, Tibbetts complained that that was part of the problem. "What we are generally after in expository writing," Tibbetts warned, "is accuracy rather than cleverness" (144). He rearticulated Johnson's reservations about the formal generativity of the Christensen rhetoric program. Christensen's theory, argued Tibbetts, is not designed to teach young people how to do the most valuable things any grammar-rhetoric should be designed to teach—how to think; how to separate and define issues; how to isolate fallacies; how to make generalizations and value judgments—in brief, how to express the truths and realities of our time and how to argue for improvements. He criticizes, as did Johnson, Christensen's "fiction fallacy," as he calls it: the idea that students should learn to write like Welty and Faulkner. Narrative and descriptive writing, Tibbetts claims, require no logical analysis and lead to "arty, false descriptions of adolescent mental states" (143). If you want nothing but "sentence acrobats," Tibbetts warned, "you are likely to get what you deserve — dexterous rhetorical acrobats who dexterously tell untruths" (143).

W. Ross Winterowd, no enemy to linguistic issues in composition, also questioned Christensen's work in 1975, when he pointed out that Christensen rhetoric exercises "take sentences out of the living content of the rhetorical situation and make them into largely meaningless dry runs" (338). Although he was himself trained in linguistics, Winterowd had deep reservations about large claims made for formalist "technologies":

> I can envision no "technology" of composition, no effective programming of students for efficiency in learning to write — nor would most composition teachers want such efficiency. From my point of view, "efficient" exercises in sentence-building, for instance, are downright morbid because they miss the point concerning the creative act of producing meaningful language in a rhetorical situation. (90)

And when James Moffett reacted to the formalist orientation of early sentence-combining, his Parthian shot — "It's about time the sentence was put in its place" (187) — could have been the watchword on syntactic rhetorics for a whole group of theorists whose work was gaining power.

The two *loci classici* of this anti-formalist position were the papers given at the second Miami sentence-combining conference in 1983 by Donald Murray and by Peter Elbow (their invitation by the Miami group seems in retrospect not unlike Brutus's decision to allow Antony to speak at Caesar's funeral).[4] Murray's essay is one of the wildest and most subtle he ever wrote, an almost unreadable melange of brainstorming lists, poem drafts, and endless badly combined sentences that commit formal mayhem on sentence-combining while never mentioning the technique, inviting students to write as badly as he does here in order to learn to write well. Elbow was much more open in his challenges to the formalist assumptions of sentence-combining, and he deserves to be quoted at length:

> I think sentence-combining is vulnerable to attack for being so a-rhetorical — so distant from the essential process of writing. In sentence-combining the student is not engaged in figuring out what she wants to say or saying what is on her mind. And because it provides prepackaged words and ready-made thoughts, sentence-combining reinforces the push-button, fast-food expectations in our culture. As a result the student is not saying anything to anyone: The results of her work are more often "answers" given to a teacher for correction — not "writing" given to readers for reactions. (233)

Though Elbow followed up this frontal barrage with a quick statement that these were his misgivings in their most extreme form, the remainder of his essay is a careful assessment of the dangers of making sentence-based work any very important part of writing instruction. Believing that "every one of our students at every moment is *capable* of generating a perfectly intelligible, lively sentence," Elbow says that the way to bring student skills out most usefully is "by leaving syntax more alone — that is, by learning to do a better job of writing down words in the order in which they come to mind" (241). Indeed, the whole thesis of Elbow's essay is that students do better and are truer to their own language when they leave their syntax alone. Elbow's final word on form-based work is that it is not, cannot be, genuinely generative. "[Sentence-combining] gives the wrong model for generating by implying that when we produce a sentence we are making a package for an already completed mental act" (245).[5]

The second strand of criticism leveled against syntactic rhetorics is related to anti-formalism; we might call it anti-automatism or anti-behaviorism. This set of critiques was based in the idea that pedagogies that meant to tap into non-conscious behavioral structures and to manipulate them for a specific end were inherently demeaning to students. The debate on behaviorism had been raging since the 1950s, of course, but it was given new impetus in composition in 1969 with the notorious publication of Robert Zoellner's "Talk-Write: A Behavioral Pedagogy for Composition" in *College English*. Zoellner's open plea for consideration of behavioral aspects to writing pedagogy struck a powerful nerve; *College English* printed no fewer than eight passionate rejoinders to Zoellner in 1969 and 1970. Behaviorism in psychology was the subject of deep distrust on the part of most humanists, and any proposal for pedagogical uses of it was bound to be regarded with suspicion. It was here that syntactic pedagogies were problematical, because they all used exercises to build "skills" in a way that was not meant to be completely conscious. These skills would then be on tap for all conscious student-writing purposes. What most syntactic theorists wanted from their pedagogies was a systematic and intense exposure of student writers to models and activities that would not only teach them "correct structure," but would rather, as W. Ross Winterowd suggests, "activate their competence" in language so that it "spills over into the area of performance" (253). Effective generation, imitation, or combination would be praised, and incorrect syntactic manipulation could be corrected and criticized. But for many critics, the behaviorist, exercise-based formats of these pedagogies were deeply troubling. They were perceived as a-rhetorical, uncreative, and in some senses destructive of individuality.

Imitation exercises in particular were perceived as actively insulting to the creativity of student writers. Probably the most controversial of the syntactic methods in the 1970s, imitation exercises seemed to ask their team to play defense from the beginning. Objections to imitation were made on several grounds, and most theorists who discussed imitation even in the 1970s felt compelled to defend their interest in it. Frank D'Angelo claimed in 1973 that popular feeling against imitation existed because it was perceived as drudgery, "dull, heavy, and stultifying" (283), and spent his essay explicating how imitation was actually close to invention. But the complaint about drudgework was only a part of the reason that imitation was a pedagogy besieged from its inception. The main reason for the unpopularity of imitation was that it was perceived as "mere servile copying," destructive of student individuality and contributory to a mechanized, dehumanizing, Skinnerian view of writing. The romanticism of the age, seen clearly in much of the anti-Zoellner criticism, would grow more and more potent as the 1970s segued into the 1980s. Teachers and theorists reacted against any form of practice that seemed to compromise originality and the expression of personal feelings, and imitation exercises were among the most obvious indoctrinations to "tradition" and "the system." As a result of this fear of loss of individuality and originality in student writing, those who recommended imitation were fighting a battle that they were the first to join and, ultimately, the first to lose.

Although imitation's defenders sought to clear it of the charges of automatism leveled against it by the age, arguments against imitation never disappeared, even during its heyday, since it was the most overtly anti-romantic of the sentence-based writing pedagogies. D'Angelo noted in 1973 that imitation connotes counterfeiting and stereotyping in most people's minds, when it should connote originality and creativity. William Gruber, whose essay is titled "'Servile Copying' and the Teaching of English Composition," knew that imitation was distrusted by many teachers when he argued that imitation does not affect creativity. Gruber argued that imitation exercises liberate students' personalities by freeing them of enervating design decisions, at least temporarily. Without knowledge of what has been done by others, he claimed, there can be no profound originality: "Self-expression is possible only when the self has a defined area to work in" (497). But Gruber admitted that imitation "seems, I suppose, an 'inorganic' way of teaching writing" (495) and that his students initially seemed suspicious of it. "The greater part of students' mistrust of imitation . . . seems to derive more from emotional factors than from intellectual ones: for they grew up during the sixties, and they seem either to balk at any extreme formalization of the process of education, or to want one instant set of rules for all writing" (496). Gruber was indeed up against the powerful psychological backwash of the 1960s, as were, eventually, all proponents of sentence rhetorics.

The problem was in the exercises. Critics pointed out that sentence-combining exercises were quintessentially *exercises*, context-stripped from what students really wanted to say themselves. James Britton and his colleagues called such exercises "dummy runs," a term Britton's group evolved to describe tasks unrelated to the larger issues of creative composing in which a student is "called upon to perform a writing task in order (a) to exercise his capacity to perform that kind of task, and/or (b) to demonstrate to the teacher his proficiency in performing it" (104–05). And, as early as 1968, James Moffett was defining exercises as the central definition of old and discredited pedagogy:

> An exercise, by my definition, is any piece of writing practiced only in schools — that is, an assignment that stipulates arbitrary limits that leave the writer with no real relationships between him and a subject and an audience. I would not ask a student to write anything other than an authentic discourse, because the learning process proceeds from intent and content down to the contemplation of technical points, not the other way. (205)

Moffett was primarily attacking the old workbook "drill and kill" exercises that had stultified students since the 1920s, but he reports here on a keen resentment that had been building against all pedagogies based in the older ideas of exercises as "mental discipline." The wholesale (and heartfelt) assault on the teaching of grammar in composition that had been set off by Richard Braddock, Richard Lloyd-Jones, and Lowell Schoer's *Research in Written Composition* in 1963 was a related phenomenon. Many teachers had simply come to disbelieve in the efficacy of any exercise-based teaching. By 1980, this attack on the "from parts to the whole" tradition associated with exercises and textbooks had become much more general. Despite the flashy research claims to the contrary, many people felt that syntactic rhetorics were really not that much different from the old-time "grammar workbook" exercises whose usefulness had been aggressively challenged.

The final line in the congeries of criticism that brought down syntactic rhetorics was anti-empiricism. Now we are in complex territory, and I must be careful to limit my claims. The empirical-research strand in English studies had existed since the 1920s, when educational psychometricians first began to try testing classroom pedagogies against one another. Modern empirical research in composition, however, was much newer, dating back primarily to the potent critiques of Braddock, Lloyd-Jones, and Schoer in *Research in Written Composition*, which had pointed to serious methodological problems in most extant English research and laid the ground for defensible studies. In 1966, Braddock had founded the journal *Research in the Teaching of English* to publish the newer and better work he envisioned, and most compositionists cheered. For the next two decades the empirical strand in composition waxed powerful, with syntactic methods as its first great success and with the cognitive psychology-based research associated mainly with Carnegie-Mellon as its second. In the Big Tent atmosphere of the New Rhetoric era of the 1960s and early 1970s, there was a general air of good feeling produced by the vision, widely shared, that all—rhetoricians, process-based teachers, linguists, stylisticians, experimenters, psychologists—could work together to reform and improve the teaching of writing; workers in different vineyards need not be enemies. Once sentence rhetorics began to get serious ink in the late 1970s, however, a number of teachers looked at them more closely and began to feel some discomfort, especially with their pre- and post-test scientism, their quantifications, their whole atmosphere of horse race experimentalism. This discomfort was not eased by the huge success of sentence-combining, with its Huntian movement toward a possible pedagogical hegemony. So in the late 1970s, we see the first serious signals of an open anti-empiricism movement within the coalescing field of composition studies.

Anti-scientism and anti-empiricism were not completely novel in the field, of course. We saw a sort of prequel to the movement in the point-counterpoint debate about psychology and invention heuristics in 1971 and 1972 between Janice Lauer and Ann Berthoff.[6] In its modern form, however, the movement probably begins with Susan Wells's and Patricia Bizzell's work in the late 1970s. Wells looked carefully at Christensen's work, arguing that it was empiricist in both method and epistemology, with an asocial contemplation of static phenomena at its center. The natural attitude for a student doing Christensen exercises, said Wells, is

> minute and unquestioning attention to his or her own perceptions, passive receptivity to the messages of sensation, and the desire to work in isolation. . . . These characteristics amount to a sort of contemplation. . . . Contemplation is not distinguished by its objects, but by the relation of thinker to thought, and Christensen's rhetoric enforces a contemplative relation. (472)

And, in an important essay in 1979, Pat Bizzell made the point, which she and others would sharpen over the next decade, that cultural and community traditions would be "as important—if not more important—in shaping the outcome of our debate, as any empirical evidence adduced and interpreted by the competing schools of thought" (768).

This humanist- and theory-based criticism found its first voice in the late 1970s and early 1980s in attacks on the most obvious and successful empirical research going: syntactic pedagogical research.[7] We can see echoes of the anti-empirical position in some of the arguments I've mentioned against generative rhetoric and imitation, but the real edge of this criticism was directed at sentence-combining, whose basis in quantitative methods was almost total. One criticism resulting from this reliance on empiricism was that sentence-combining was a practice without a theory, a method without a principle, an *ars* without an *exercitatio*. As Winterowd complained in 1975, "in our self-made ghetto, compositionists have neglected theory, opting to concern ourselves with the pragmatics of everyday teaching" (90–91). James Kinneavy brought this complaint down to specifics in 1978, noting that ". . . few efforts have been made to place sentence-combining into a larger curricular framework," and that it still awaited a philosophic rationale (60, 76). This lack of a general theory was not seen at first as a particular problem, since the new research strand of sentence-combining was so novel and powerful that it submerged other questions.[8] But by 1983, when Miami held its second sentence-combining conference, the problem of theory had become obvious to many participants. The book that emerged from that conference, *Sentence-Combining: A Rhetorical Perspective*, is a fascinating collection, the last major statement made by the discipline about sentence rhetorics, and as a collection it shows clear awareness of the changing weather around sentence rhetorics.

By 1983, it was no longer enough to report that sentence-combining "worked" if no one could specify *why* it worked. Stars of the 1978 Miami conference Rosemary Hake and Joseph Williams were back, this time with more questions than answers. "Sentence-combining is at this moment operating at a very crude level of sophistication," they claimed, ". . . interesting theoretical speculation about sentence-combining has been very infrequent" ("Some" 100–01). Kenneth Dowst, in his essay "An Epistemic View of Sentence-Combining: Practice and Theories," takes on directly the popular perception that sentence-combining was "a practice devoid of a theory" (333). After examining the relation of sentence-combining to epistemic rhetoric, Dowst comes to the conclusion that sentence-combining *has* a theory, but that it is "a theory that many teachers are finding problematic and many students inadequately relevant. To wit: formalism" (333). The connection with formalism is not the only one possible, says Dowst, but other connections, to rhetoric or epistemic theory, "remain only to be enacted" (333). Despite the hopes expressed at the 1983 conference, they never were. And in the increasingly theoretical world of composition studies post-1985, practice without theory was increasingly associated with the lore-world of earlier composition and condemned.

Another criticism was that sentence-combining represented methodological hegemony of a kind destructive to a truly humanistic epistemology. Michael Holzman, in his "Scientism and Sentence Combining" in 1983, dry-gulches sentence-combining with such energy that he almost appears paranoid about its possibilities. After slashing and burning all the research findings down to the affirmation that "sentence-combining exercises do appear to help students learn how to combine sentences (although this skill deteriorates rapidly)" (77), Holzman makes his central claim for an end to "scientistic" research. "The humanities are the sciences of man," he writes, ". . . It would be a serious mistake to allow the fascination of methodologies for social scientific research to bring us to doubt that literacy is primarily a humanistic attainment" (78–79). Holzman's fear—that the clear-cut successes of the sentence-combining research might slant the whole evolving discipline of composition studies away from traditional humanistic/rhetorical lines and into the camp of social sciences and psychology—was beginning to be widely shared in the early 1980s and came to its real fruition four years later, with the wholesale reaction against cognitive approaches and empiricism in general that marked the beginning of the Social-Construction Era.[9] The best-known example of this methodological critique was Stephen North's famous chapter on the experimentalists in his *Making of Knowledge in Composition* in 1987, which calls out the Miami researchers in particular for criticism (although not as harshly as it does some other experimentalists).

The result of all of these lines of criticism of syntactic methods was that they were stopped almost dead in their tracks as a research program and ceased being a popular teaching project just a little later. The degree to which the attacks succeeded can be seen in the curious growth of the truly lore-oriented conception that "research has shown that sentence-combining doesn't work." When preparing to write this essay, I asked a number of friends and colleagues in composition studies what had ever happened to sentence-combining. At least half of them replied that it had lost currency because it had been shown not to work, not to help students write better. So far as I can determine, this is simply not true. Outside of a few essays, including Marzano's and Holzman's, that really did take a slash-and-burn attitude toward reporting balanced opinions of the research, I can find no work that genuinely "disproved" the gains created for students through sentence practice. It is true that Lester Faigley showed, in two essays in 1979 and 1980, that Hunt's concept of syntactic maturity did not correlate with generally perceived writing quality ("Problems"; "Names"). But Faigley himself did not question the holistic quality gains of the sentence-combining students, stating that the answer must be that sentence-combining and generative rhetoric "affect some part of the writing process more fundamental than the enhancement of syntactic maturity" ("Problems" 99).[10]

Warren Combs and Richard Smith published an essay in 1980 that reported that students would write demonstrably longer sentences if simply told to do so by the teacher ("Overt and Covert Cues"), but their experiment was short-term, and they specifically stated that their "findings in no way call the efficacy of SC [sentence-combining] instruction into question" (35).[11] It is true that the Miami group's last report, which appeared in the non-mainstream *Perceptual and Motor Skills*, found that absent other writing work, the gains made by the sentence-combiners were self-sustaining, but that the advantage that the experimental group had shown over the control group disappeared after two years. The control group, in other words, caught up to the sentence-combiners after twenty-eight months. This shows, as the Miami researchers comment, that the sentence-combining practice "simply accelerated the positive changes that would have occurred after a longer period of normal maturation and experience" (Kerek, Daiker, and Morenberg 1151). In other words, syntactic gains, if not practiced, only persisted for two years. But by this criterion, if our methods in any given first-year composition course don't measurably put our students ahead of other students *forever*, they don't work and are not worth doing. That's a high hurdle for any pedagogy to clear. There were, finally, a few articles published with "Questions" in their titles: Mary Rosner's "Putting 'This and That Together' to Question Sentence-Combining Research" in 1984 and Aviva Freedman's "Sentence Combining: Some Questions" in 1985, but these essays were concerned with specific queries about technical style and abstracting ability. Neither questioned the general writing success of students using the technique.

It really does seem that the current perception that somehow sentence rhetorics "don't work" exists as a massive piece of wish-fulfillment. Leaving aside the question of syntactic fluency or maturity entirely, the data from holistic and analytic general essay readings are unequivocal. George Hillocks, reviewing the research in 1986, looked closely into all the major sentence-combining research and found many lines of inquiry that needed to be followed up. But after his careful dissection, he still concluded his section on sentence rhetorics with a quote that recognized the value of the technique: "Even with so many questions left unanswered, one is tempted to agree with Charles Cooper (1975c) that 'no other single teaching approach has ever consistently been shown to have a beneficial effect on syntactic maturity and writing quality' (p. 72)" (151). In other words, if people believe that research has shown that sentence rhetorics don't work, their belief exists not because the record bears it out but because it is what people want to believe.

Why we want to believe it is the interesting part.

So what was it that erased the sentence, wiped what had been the "forefront in composition research today . . . at the cutting edge of research design" in 1980[12] off the radar screen of composition studies? What reduced it from a vital, if unfinished, inquiry into why a popular stylistic method worked so well to a half-hidden and seldom-discussed classroom practice on the level of, say, vocabulary quizzes? It was not, as we have seen, that sentence rhetorics were proved useless. Neither was this erasure the simple playing out of a vein of material before the onslaughts of the normal scientists who followed the major researchers of sentence rhetorics. If the last important work in sentence-combining, Daiker, Kerek, and Morenberg's *Rhetorical Perspective*, shows anything, it is that many of the most interesting questions about sentence rhetorics were still being raised and not answered.[13]

I think that we have, to a large extent, already seen what it was. The sentence was erased by the gradual but inevitable hardening into disciplinary form of the field of composition studies as a subfield of English studies. The anti-formalism, anti-behaviorism, and anti-empiricism that marked the criticism of sentence rhetorics can be found in some earlier writers and thinkers in the older field of composition, but not with the hegemony they gradually achieved as disciplinary structures were formed after 1975. These three attitudinal strands are hallmarks of English studies and not of works in the other fields — speech, psychology, education — from which composition grew after 1950. Departmental structures are lasting and durable, and as it became apparent that composition studies as a field would almost universally find its departmental home in the same place its primary course identity — first-year composition — resided, cross-disciplinary elements in the older composition-rhetoric world were likely to fade. The graduate students after 1975 who would make up the core of composition studies were, for better or worse, English graduate students, and they would go on to become English professors.

On a sheer demographic basis, it is not strange to see many default attitudes based around English departments — textuality, holism, stratification by status, theory-desire, distrust of scientism — gradually come to define composition studies. However complex the feelings composition people had and have about English departments, such departments are usually our native lands. Even if we reject much of the culture, we still speak the language. And one result of the increasing English-identification of composition studies has been a gradual movement away from connections that had helped define an earlier, looser version of composition that arose in the 1950s. We have dropped much of our relationship with non-English elements — with education and with high school teachers, with speech and communications and with oral rhetoric, with psychology and with quantitative research.

This is not the place for a complete discussion of the changing demographics of composition studies as it became a clear subfield of English. In this article I wanted to show, in a very delimited instance, evidence of the movement's power and potency by examining one part of its effects. When a phenomenon is hard to see or define, looking at what it has done may point to important realities about it. In this case, as in a tornado documentary, the effects exist as a trail of destruction. There was indeed much destruction in the wake of the disciplinary formation of composition studies, but since most of it was destruction of things few people after 1980 had ever believed in or fought for, the destruction was not noticed by many. Who remembers a vital NCTE College Section? Who mourns for the Four Communications Skills or the modes of discourse? But we should remember that swept away with the modes and the five types of paragraphs were other, newer, and potentially more valuable things. The loss of all defense of formalism has left some curious vacuums in the middle of our teaching. Rejection of all behaviorist ideas has left us with uncertainties about any methodology not completely rationalistic or any system of pedagogical rewards. Distrust of scientistic empiricism has left us with few proofs or certainties not ideologically based. More has been lost than sentence-combining here, but it seems somehow part of human nature to forget about the preterite. Many people still professionally active today have deep background as generative rhetoricians or imitation adepts or sentence-combining pioneers, but they have lost most of their interest; they do not do that much anymore. They have cut their losses and gone on. We all must.

Notes

1. C. S. Baldwin's terms, clearness and interest, were not used in his earlier textbook, *A College Manual of Rhetoric*, in 1902, which adopted Hill's version of Whately's terms. They are found in his later text, *Composition: Oral and Written*, from 1909.
2. These numbers do *not* include conference papers at the two Miami sentence-combining conferences, which became 45 separate essays in the two proceeding books.
3. Notice I'm not claiming that sentence rhetorics were gone from teaching. Anecdotal evidence seems to suggest that some teachers have continued to use sentence-combining and Christensen rhetoric even absent any mention of them in books or journals. They have thus become part of what Stephen North calls teacher lore. But isn't it ironic that such techniques, which made strong moves toward grammatical analyses and empirical proofs, have ended up as lore, which North defines (23) as being driven by pragmatic logic and experiential structure?
4. William Strong attempted to respond to Murray and Elbow in a heartbreaking piece with which the 1983 Miami conference (and collection) closes. Strong has read their papers, and his essay is an attempt to explain to them, and to the world at large, that sentence-combining is both more and less than they think and fear. Called "How Sentence Combining Works," Strong's essay admits that sentence-combining is not, cannot be, "real writing," and that it cannot and should never take the place of naturalistic experience. Still, though, Strong will not admit that sentence-combining is a-rhetorical or non-naturalistic, and he believes that "the language in sentence combining often triggers metalinguistic thinking beyond its own discursive content" and "helps students transfer power from oral language performance to writing" (350). Strong's is an extraordinary rhetorical performance, struggling at the end of the Era of Good Feelings for tolerance from a group that was moving inevitably away from him. But finally, his plea for compromise and understanding fell on stony ground. Composition studies after 1980 did not like or trust exercises. Any kind of exercises.
5. Today, more than fifteen years after the first carronades were fired at the various movements associated with the term "process," we are used to thinking of our world as "post-process" and of "expressivism" as a devil term and a dead letter. As an intellectual field, we have managed with considerable success to marginalize that movement, at least insofar as it existed as ongoing intellectual or non-pedagogical discourse. Its greatest champions—Moffett, Britton, Garrison, Emig, Murray, Macrorie, Stewart, Rohmann—have died or retired, leaving Peter Elbow nearly alone to carry the banner.

Many people see expressivism today—not unlike sentence-combining, ironically—as a hoary pedagogical survival, *exercitatio* with *ars*, old-time staffroom lore and instructor prejudice, the body still moving after the head has been cut off. It is difficult, on first consideration, to imagine the writing-process movement as a potent destructive force, or to think that we, in our shining theoretical plumage, are still living in the backwash of its great primary act of pedagogical creation/destruction: the wreck of formalism in all its versions.

But the powerful revolutionary doctrine of the process movement was, finally, terribly simple. It wished to do away with whatever was not authentic in writing and teaching writing. Its great enemy was modern composition-rhetoric, that huge carpetbag of textbook nostrums about modes and forms and methods and sentences and rules and paragraphs and vocabulary and punctuation and exercises and unity and coherence and emphasis. If rhetoric was a fox that knew many small things, process was a hedgehog that knew one great thing: you learn to write by writing and rewriting things important to you with the help of a sympathetic reader/teacher. Everything else is, finally, flummery. Formalism and atomism were huge and inescapable parts of modern composition-rhetoric, and the writing process movement laid down a constant challenge to them from 1960 onward. If, as was the case, formalism or atomism were charges that could be applied even to New Rhetoric ideas such as syntactic rhetorics, then applied they must be. Sadly, regretfully applied, yes, since many sentence-combiners had been friends. But when you build a set of positions based completely on authenticity and anti-formalism, you cannot easily choose some formalism you will be friends with.

Max Morenberg of the Miami sentence-combining group certainly had no doubt who had burnt his topless tower. In two conference presentations, in 1990 and 1992, he surveyed the wreckage and protested against the attitudes that had wrought it. His somewhat bitter titles tell the story: In 1990 he delivered "Process/Schmocess: Why Not Combine a Sentence or Two?" and in 1992 he delivered "'Come Back to the Text Ag'in, Huck Honey!'" Both blamed dichotomizing process/product thinking for the demise of sentence rhetorics. Unfortunately, Morenberg never published either talk outside of ERIC.

6. This whole argument can be seen most easily in Winterowd's *Contemporary Rhetoric* (99–103), along with Winterowd's thoughtful commentary on it.
7. Only a few people saw then that this movement would a few years later in 1987 enlarge the criticism to include the equally powerful cognitive-psychology strand of research; in retrospect it seems clear that the real relation between sentence research and cognitive research lay in their common nemesis. The enlarging reaction against quantitative research would eventually come to include all but the most narrative and humanistic qualitative research as well, and the results would, in the end, be the same: the effective ending of whole lines of research within mainstream composition studies. Of course, much research is still carried on, but it tends to be reported at NCTE and American Educational Research Association, rather than at CCCC. See Charney for the reaction of many researchers to this movement within composition studies.

8. As late as 1981, even such a noted practitioner of theory as the late James Berlin was co-authoring purely practical essays on sentence-combining containing such statements as, "In sum, the 'sentence skills' unit should not be relegated to a few hours devoted to 'style,' but should be seen as central to some of a writer's major concerns" (Broadhead and Berlin 306).
9. In my "Composition Studies and Science," published just a month before Holzman's essay, I made almost the exact plea for the primacy of humanities-based (which I called rhetorical) inquiry over social-science inquiry. Although I made my own howlers in that piece (lumping Pat Bizzell in with all other Kuhn-quoters as an advocate of empirical science!), I was not, I hope, slanting evidence as obviously as Holzman seems to do in his condemnation of sentence-combining, whose whole train of successes he dismisses with a sneer.
10. Faigley's and Holzman's work led to Forrest Houlette's 1984 article on reliability and validity in external criteria and holistic scoring, a piece that seems to suggest that neither criterion can be considered empirically dependable under all conditions without the context of the other. This was the level of epistemological humility syntactic research had reached by 1984: There was no longer any dependable way to determine what writing was actually good.
11. Richard Haswell and his co-authors recently mentioned the study of Combs and Smith as a rare example of replication of research in composition studies (5), and in terms of careful numerical enumeration of syntactic growth, this is true. But Combs and Smith studied their students over a much shorter period (six days) than did O'Hare or the Miami researchers and made no attempt to cover holistic writing-quality issues. (There is also some evidence that the overtly cued students [those told that their teacher would grade long sentences more favorably] simply began to string long sentences together in a few simple ways, since their T-unit numbers went up but their clause numbers did not [see pp. 33–35].)
12. This rather embarrassing quote is from my dissertation, written in 1979 and 1980. It's humbling to watch your own doxa turn into historical grist.
13. Janice Neuleib suggested, after hearing an earlier version of this paper, that another possible reason for the decline of sentence-combining was not that all of the research had been done, but that all of the impressive and groundbreaking research had been done. No one is much interested in the quotidian mopping-up work of normal science, especially in social science-based fields. The specialized and smaller scale studies that were called for (but not done) after 1983 were not career-makers. Although I thought at first that this idea might be too cynical, I have been gradually forced to admit its possibility.

Works Cited

Bateman, Donald R., and Frank J. Zidonis. *The Effect of a Study of Transformational Grammar on the Writing of Ninth and Tenth Graders*. Urbana: NCTE, 1966.

Bizzell, Patricia. "Thomas Kuhn, Scientism, and English Studies." *College English* 40 (1979): 764–71.

Bond, Charles A. "A New Approach to Freshman Composition: A Trial of the Christensen Method." *College English* 33 (1972): 623–27.

Braddock, Richard, Richard Lloyd-Jones, and Lowell Schoer. *Research in Written Composition*. Urbana: NCTE, 1963.

Britton, James, Tony Burgess, Nancy Martin, Alex McLeod, and Harold Rosen. *The Development of Writing Abilities* (11–18). Basingstoke: Macmillan, 1975.

Broadhead, Glenn J., and James A. Berlin. "Twelve Steps to Using Generative Sentences and Sentence Combining in the Composition Classroom." *College Composition and Communication* 32 (1981): 295–307.

Charney, Davida. "Empiricism Is Not a Four-Letter Word." *College Composition and Communication* 47 (1996): 567–93.

Christensen, Francis. "A Generative Rhetoric of the Sentence." *College Composition and Communication* 14 (1963): 155–61.

———. *Notes toward a New Rhetoric: Six Essays for Teachers*. New York: Harper, 1967.

———. "The Course in Advanced Composition for Teachers." *College Composition and Communication* 24 (1973): 163–70.

Christensen, Francis, and Bonniejean Christensen. *A New Rhetoric*. New York: Harper, 1975.

Combs, Warren E. "Sentence-Combining Practice: Do Gains in Judgments of Writing 'Quality' Persist?" *Journal of Educational Research* 70 (1977): 318–21.

Combs, Warren E., and William L. Smith. "The Effects of Overt and Covert Cues on Written Syntax." *Research in the Teaching of English* 14 (1980): 19–38.

Connors, Robert J. "Composition Studies and Science." *College English* 45 (1983): 1–20.

———. *Composition-Rhetoric: Backgrounds, Theory, and Pedagogy*. Pittsburgh: U of Pittsburgh P, 1997.

Cooper, Charles R. "Research Roundup: Oral and Written Composition." *English Journal* 64 (1975): 72–74.

Corbett, Edward P. J. *Classical Rhetoric for the Modern Student*. New York: Oxford UP, 1965.

———. "The Theory and Practice of Imitation in Classical Rhetoric." *College Composition and Communication* 22 (1971): 243–50.

Daiker, Donald A., Andrew Kerek, and Max Morenberg. "Sentence-Combining and Syntactic Maturity in Freshman English." *College Composition and Communication* 29 (1978): 36–41.

———, eds. *Sentence-Combining: A Rhetorical Perspective*. Carbondale: Southern Illinois UP, 1985.

———, eds. *Sentence-Combining and the Teaching of Writing*. Conway, AR: L&S Books, 1979.

———. *The Writer's Options: College Sentence-Combining*. New York: Harper and Row, 1979.

D'Angelo, Frank. "Imitation and Style." *College Composition and Communication* 24 (1973): 283–90.

Dowst, Kenneth. "An Epistemic View of Sentence-Combining: Practice and Theories." Daiker et al. *Sentence-Combining: A Rhetorical Perspective*. 321–33.

Elbow, Peter. "The Challenge for Sentence Combining." Daiker et al. *Sentence-Combining: A Rhetorical Perspective*. 232–45.

Faigley, Lester L. "Generative Rhetoric as a Way of Increasing Syntactic Fluency." *College Composition and Communication* 30 (1979): 176–81.

———. "Problems in Analyzing Maturity in College and Adult Writing." Daiker et al. *Sentence-Combining and the Teaching of Writing*. 94–100.

———. "Names in Search of a Concept: Maturity, Fluency, Complexity, and Growth in Written Syntax." *College Composition and Communication* 31 (1980): 291–300.

Freedman, Aviva. "Sentence Combining: Some Questions." *Carleton Papers in Applied Language Studies* 2 (1985): 17–32.

Graves, Richard L., ed. *Rhetoric and Composition: A Sourcebook for Teachers*. Rochelle Park, NJ: Hayden, 1976.

Gruber, William E. "'Servile Copying' and the Teaching of English Composition." *College English* 39 (1977): 491–97.

Hake, Rosemary, and Joseph M. Williams. "Sentence Expanding: Not Can, or How, but When." Daiker et al. *Sentence-Combining and the Teaching of Writing*. 134–46.

———. "Some Cognitive Issues in Sentence Combining: On the Theory that Smaller Is Better." Daiker et al. *Sentence-Combining: A Rhetorical Perspective*. 86–106.

Halloran, S. Michael. "Cicero and English Composition." Conference on College Composition and Communication. Minneapolis. 1978.

Haswell, Richard H., Terri L. Briggs, Jennifer A. Fay, Norman K. Gillen, Rob Harrill, Andrew M. Shupala, and Sylvia S. Trevino. "Context and Rhetorical Reading Strategies." *Written Communication* 16 (1999): 3–27.

Hillocks, George, Jr. *Research on Written Composition: New Directions for Teaching*. Urbana: NCTE, 1986.

Holzman, Michael. "Scientism and Sentence Combining." *College Composition and Communication* 34 (1983): 73–79.

Houlette, Forrest. "Linguistics, Empirical Research, and Evaluating Composition." *Journal of Advanced Composition* 5 (1984): 107–14.

Hunt, Kellogg W. *Grammatical Structures Written at Three Grade Levels*. Urbana: NCTE, 1965.

———. "A Synopsis of Clause-to-Sentence Length Factors." Graves 110–17.

———. "Anybody Can Teach English." Daiker et al. *Sentence-Combining and the Teaching of Writing*. 149–56.

Johnson, Sabina Thorne. "Some Tentative Strictures on Generative Rhetoric." *College English* 31 (1969): 155–65.

Kerek, Andrew, Donald A. Daiker, and Max Morenberg. "Sentence Combining and College Composition." *Perceptual and Motor Skills* 51 (1980): 1059–1157.

Kinneavy, James L. "Sentence Combining in a Comprehensive Language Framework." Daiker et al. *Sentence-Combining and the Teaching of Writing*. 60–76.

Marzano, Robert J. "The Sentence-Combining Myth." *English Journal* 65 (1976): 57–59.

Mellon, John. *Transformational Sentence-Combining: A Method for Enhancing the Development of Syntactic Fluency in English Composition*. Urbana: NCTE, 1969.

———. "Issues in the Theory and Practice of Sentence-Combining: A Twenty-Year Perspective." Daiker et al. *Sentence-Combining and the Teaching of Writing*. 1–38.

Miller, Edmund. *Exercises in Style*. Normal, IL: Illinois SUP, 1980.

Moffett, James. *Teaching the Universe of Discourse*. Boston: Houghton Mifflin, 1968.

Morenberg, Max. "Process/Schmocess: Why Not Combine a Few Sentences?" Conference on *College Composition and Communication*. Chicago. March 1990. ERIC ED 319040.

———. "'Come Back to the Text Ag'in, Huck Honey!'" NCTE Convention. Louisville. November 1992. ERIC ED 355557.

Morenberg, Max, Donald Daiker, and Andrew Kerek. "Sentence-Combining at the College Level: An Experimental Study." *Research in the Teaching of English* 12 (1978): 245–56.

Murray, Donald. "Writing Badly to Write Well: Searching for the Instructive Line." Daiker et al. *Sentence-Combining: A Rhetorical Perspective*. 187–201.

Ney, James. "The Hazards of the Course: Sentence-Combining in Freshman English." *The English Record* 27 (1976): 70–77.

North, Stephen M. *The Making of Knowledge in Composition*. Upper Montclair, NJ: Heinneman-Boynton/Cook, 1987.

O'Donnell, Roy C., William J. Griffin, and Raymond C. Norris. *Syntax of Kindergarten and Elementary School Children: A Transformational Analysis*. Urbana: NCTE, 1967.

O'Hare, Frank. *Sentence-Combining: Improving Student Writing without Formal Grammar Instruction*. Urbana: NCTE, 1973.

———. *Sentencecraft*. Lexington: Ginn, 1975.

Rose, Shirley K. "Down from the Haymow: One Hundred Years of Sentence-Combining." *College English* 45 (1983): 483–91.

Rosner, Mary. "Putting 'This and That Together' to Question Sentence-Combining Research." *Technical Writing Teacher* 11 (1984): 221–28.

Starkey, Penelope. "Imitatio Redux." *College Composition and Communication* 25 (1974): 435–37.

Strong, William. "How Sentence Combining Works." Daiker et al. *Sentence-Combining: A Rhetorical Perspective*. 334–50.

———. *Sentence-Combining: A Composing Book*. New York: Random House, 1973.

Tibbetts, A. M. "On the Practical Uses of a Grammatical System: A Note on Christensen and Johnson." *Rhetoric and Composition: A Sourcebook for Teachers*. E. Richard Graves. Rochelle Park, NJ: Hayden Books, 1976. 139–49.

Walshe, R. D. "Report on a Pilot Course on the Christensen Rhetoric Program." *College English* 32 (1971): 783–89.

Weathers, Winston. *An Alternate Style: Options in Composition*. Rochelle Park, NJ: Hayden Books, 1980.

Weathers, Winston, and Otis Winchester. *Copy and Compose*. Englewood Cliffs, NJ: Prentice-Hall, 1969.

———. *The New Strategy of Style*. New York: McGraw-Hill, 1978.

Wells, Susan. "Classroom Heuristics and Empiricism." *College English* 39 (1977): 467–76.

Winterowd, W. Ross. *Contemporary Rhetoric: A Conceptual Background with Readings*. New York: Harcourt Brace, 1975.

Zoellner, Robert. "Talk-Write: A Behavioral Pedagogy for Composition." *College English* 30 (1969): 267–320.

Connors's Insights as a Resource for Your Reflections

1. Beyond a purely grammatical perspective, what lessons about the construction of sentences have figured in your own development as a writer? Do you hold any general rules of thumb about crafting sentences that you share with your students? How might careful attention to the sentence — again, beyond a strict interest in grammatical correctness — benefit students?
2. In your view, which aspects of the sentence-based pedagogies that Connors describes seem most worth retaining? Which seem less valuable? Of the three pedagogies he sketches, which would you be most likely to adopt with your students, and why?

Connors's Insights as a Resource for Your Writing Classroom

1. In a recent batch of student drafts, identify sentences that you think could benefit from revision. Put students in small groups and assign each group a problem sentence; then have each group explain why their sentence is weak and how it could be improved.
2. Develop some sentence-combining or imitation exercises. You could have students work on these as a class, or you could require them as homework assignments, perhaps for extra credit. Talk with your students about their experiences with the exercises. Did students find them worthwhile? Why or why not?

A Generative Rhetoric of the Sentence

Francis Christensen

What might a carefully worked out "sentence level pedagogy," as Robert Connors calls it in the preceding article, actually look like in real detail? In the following chapter from his essay collection Notes Toward a New Rhetoric *(1963), Francis Christensen proposes that we train students to write the dynamic "cumulative sentence," a structure that invigorates writing by challenging students to reflect their minds at work. Teaching them to "grow" sentences by adding multiple levels of modifiers before, after, or within a base clause not only results in a mature, lively style, but it also gives students the sophistication and confidence to mimic the ebb-and-flow movement of thought. To cultivate "syntactical ingenuity," Christensen suggests breaking example sentences into their various layers of structure and discussing the relationships between the modifiers. This in turn opens the way for discussions of style in terms of four key principles: addition, direction, rhythm, and texture. Although critics may argue that cumulative sentences are too long for most first-year college students to handle, Christensen disagrees: "I try in narrative sentences to push to level after level, not just two or three, but four, five, or six, even more, as far as the students' powers of observation will take them. I want them to become sentence acrobats, to dazzle by their syntactic dexterity. I'd rather have to deal with hyperemia than anemia."*

We do not have time in our classes to teach everything about the rhetoric of the sentence. I believe in "island hopping," concentrating on topics where we can produce results and leaving the rest, including the "comma splice" and the "run-on sentence," to die on the vine. The balanced sentence deserves some attention in discursive writing, and the enormous range of coordinate structures deserves a bit more. The rhythm of good modern prose comes about equally from the multiple-tracking of coordinate constructions and the downshifting and backtracking of free modifiers. But the first comes naturally; the other needs coaxing along.

This coaxing is the clue to the meaning of *generative* in my title. (It is not derived from generative grammar; I used it before I ever heard of Chomsky.) The teacher can use the idea of levels of structure to urge the student to add further levels to what he has already produced, so that the structure itself becomes an aid to discovery.

This system of analysis by levels is essentially an application of immediate constituent analysis. IC analysis reveals what goes with what. The order in which initial, medial, and final elements are cut off is immaterial, but one might as well start at the beginning. Thus, in sentence 2 on page 281, the first cut would take off the whole set of initial modifiers. Then the members of a coordinate set are separated and, if the dissection is to be carried out to the ultimate constituents, analyzed one by one in order. In sentence 1 [p. 281], the first cut would come at the end of the base clause, taking off levels 2, 3, and 4 together since they are dependent on one another. Another cut would come at the end of level 2, taking off levels 3 and 4 together since 4 is a modifier of 3. Medial modifiers have to be cut *out* rather than *off*.

If the new grammar is to be brought to bear on composition, it must be brought to bear on the rhetoric of the sentence. We have a workable and teachable, if not a definitive, modern grammar; but we do not have, despite several titles, a modern rhetoric.

In composition courses we do not really teach our captive charges to write better—we merely *expect* them to. And we do not teach them how to write better because we do not know how to teach them to write better. And so we merely go through the motions. Our courses with their tear-out workbooks and four-pound anthologies are elaborate evasions of the real problem. They permit us to put in our time and do almost anything else we'd rather be doing instead of buckling down to the hard work of making a difference in the student's understanding and manipulation of language.

With hundreds of handbooks and rhetorics to draw from, I have never been able to work out a program for teaching the sentence as I find it in the work of contemporary writers. The chapters on the sentence all adduce the traditional rhetorical classification of sentences as loose, balanced, and periodic. But the term *loose* seems to be taken as a pejorative (it sounds immoral); our students, no Bacons or Johnsons, have little occasion for balanced sentences; and some of our worst perversions of style come from the attempt to teach them to write periodic sentences. The traditional grammatical classification of sentences is equally barren. Its use in teaching composition rests on a semantic confusion, equating complexity of structure with complexity of thought and vice versa. But very simple thoughts may call for very complex grammatical constructions. Any moron can say "I don't know who done it." And some of us might be puzzled to work out the grammar of "All I want is all there is," although any chit can think it and say it and act on it.

The chapters on the sentence all appear to assume that we think naturally in primer sentences, progress naturally to compound sentences, and must be taught to combine the primer sentences into complex sentences—and that complex sentences are the mark of maturity. We need a rhetoric of the sentence that will do more than combine the ideas of primer sentences. We need one that will *generate* ideas.

For the foundation of such a generative or productive rhetoric I take the statement from John Erskine, the originator of the Great Books courses, himself a novelist. In the essay "The Craft of Writing" (*Twentieth Century English*, Philosophical Library, 1946) he discusses a principle of the writer's craft which, though known he says to all practitioners, he has never seen discussed in print. The principle is this: "When you write, you make a point, not by subtracting as though you sharpened a pencil, but by adding." We have all been told that the formula for good writing is the concrete noun and the active verb. Yet Erskine says, "What you say is found not in the noun but in what you add to qualify the noun. . . . The noun, the verb, and the main clause serve merely as the base on which meaning will rise. . . . The modifier is the essential part of any sentence." The foundation, then, for a generative or productive rhetoric of the sentence is that composition is essentially a process of *addition*.

But speech is linear, moving in time, and writing moves in linear space, which is analogous to time. When you add a modifier, whether to the noun, the verb, or the main clause, you must add it either before the head or after it. If you add it before the head, the direction of modification can be indicated by an arrow pointing forward; if you add it after, by an arrow pointing backward. Thus we have the second principle of a generative rhetoric — the principle of *direction of modification* or *direction of movement*.

Within the clause there is not much scope for operating with this principle. The positions of the various sorts of close, or restrictive, modifiers are generally fixed and the modifiers are often obligatory — "The man who came to dinner remained till midnight." Often the only choice is whether to add modifiers. What I have seen of attempts to bring structural grammar to bear on composition usually boils down to the injunction to "load the patterns." Thus "pattern practice" sets students to accreting sentences like this: "The small boy on the red bicycle who lives with his happy parents on our shady street often coasts down the steep street until he comes to the city park." This will never do. It has no rhythm and hence no life; it is tone-deaf. It is the seed that will burgeon into gobbledegook. One of the hardest things in writing is to keep the noun clusters and verb clusters short.

It is with modifiers added to the clause — that is, with sentence modifiers — that the principle comes into full play. The typical sentence of modern English, the kind we can best spend our efforts trying to teach, is what we may call the *cumulative sentence*. The main clause, which may or may not have a sentence modifier before it, advances the discussion; but the additions move backward, as in this clause, to modify the statement of the main clause or more often to explicate or exemplify it, so that the sentence has a flowing and ebbing movement, advancing to a new position and then pausing to consolidate it, leaping and lingering as the popular ballad does. The first part of the preceding compound sentence has one addition, placed within it; the second part has 4 words in the main clause and 49 in the five additions placed after it.

The cumulative sentence is the opposite of the periodic sentence. It does not represent the idea as conceived, pondered over, reshaped, packaged, and delivered cold. It is dynamic rather than static, representing the mind thinking. The main clause ("the additions move backward" above) exhausts the mere fact of the idea; logically, there is nothing more to say. The additions stay with the same idea, probing its bearings and implications, exemplifying it or seeking an analogy or metaphor for it, or reducing it to details. Thus the mere form of the sentence generates ideas. It serves the needs of both the writer and the reader, the writer by compelling him to examine his thought, the reader by letting him into the writer's thought.

Addition and direction of movement are structural principles. They involve the grammatical character of the sentence. Before going on to other principles, I must say a word about the best grammar as the foundation for rhetoric. I cannot conceive any useful transactions between teacher and students unless they have in common a language for talking about sentences. The best grammar for the present purpose is the grammar that best displays the layers of structure of the English sentence. The best I have found in a textbook is the combination of immediate constituent and transformation grammar in Paul Roberts's *English Sentences*. Traditional grammar, whether oversimple as in the school tradition or overcomplex as in the scholarly tradition, does not reveal the language as it operates; it leaves everything, to borrow a phrase from Wordsworth, "in disconnection dead and spiritless." *English Sentences* is oversimplified and it has gaps, but it displays admirably the structures that rhetoric must work with—primarily sentence modifiers, including nonrestrictive relative and subordinate clauses, but, far more important, the array of noun, verb, and adjective clusters. It is paradoxical that Professor Roberts, who has done so much to make the teaching of composition possible, should himself be one of those who think that it cannot be taught. Unlike Ulysses, he does not see any work for Telemachus to work.

Layers of structure, as I have said, is a grammatical concept. To bring in the dimension of meaning, we need a third principle—that of *levels of generality* or *levels of abstraction*. The main or base clause is likely to be stated in general or abstract or plural terms. With the main clause stated, the forward movement of the sentence stops, the writer shifts down to a lower level of generality or abstraction or to singular terms, and goes back over the same ground at this lower level.[1] There is no theoretical limit to the number of structural layers or levels, each[2] at a lower level of generality, any or all of them compounded, that a speaker or writer may use. For a speaker, listen to Lowell Thomas; for a writer, study William Faulkner. To a single independent clause he may append a page of additions, but usually all clear, all grammatical, once we have learned how to read him. Or, if you prefer, study Hemingway, the master of the simple sentence: "George was coming down in the telemark position, kneeling, one leg forward and bent, the other trailing, his sticks hanging like some insect's thin legs, kicking up puffs of snow, and finally the whole kneeling, trailing figure coming around in a beautiful right curve, crouching, the legs shot forward and back, the body leaning out against the swing, the stick accenting the curve like points of light, all in a wild cloud of snow." Only from the standpoint of school grammar is this a simple sentence.

This brings me to the fourth, and last, principle, that of texture. *Texture* provides a descriptive or evaluative term. If a writer adds to few of his nouns or verbs or main clauses and adds little, the texture may be said to be thin. The style will be plain or bare. The writing of most of our students is thin—even threadbare. But if he adds frequently or much or both, then the texture may be said to be dense or rich. One of the marks of an effective style, especially in narrative, is variety in the texture, the texture varying with the change in pace, the variation in texture producing the change in pace. It is not true, as I have seen it asserted, that fast action calls for short sentences; the action is fast in the sentence by Hemingway above. In our classes, we have to work for greater density and variety in texture and greater concreteness and particularity in what is added.

I have been operating at a fairly high level of generality. Now I must downshift and go over the same points with examples. The most graphic way to exhibit the layers of structure is to indent the word groups of a sentence and to number the levels. The first three sentences illustrate the various positions of the added sentence modifiers—initial, medial, and final. The symbols mark the grammatical character of the additions: SC, subordinate clause; RC, relative clause; NC, noun cluster; VC, verb cluster; AC, adjective cluster; A + A, adjective series; Abs, absolute (i.e., a VC with a subject of its own); PP, prepositional phrase. The elements set off as on a lower level are marked as sentence modifiers by junctures or punctuation. The examples have been chosen to illustrate the range of constructions used in the lower levels; after the first few they are arranged by the number of levels. The examples could have been drawn from poetry as well as from prose. Those not attributed are by students.

1

1 He dipped his hands in the bichloride solution and shook them,
  2 a quick shake, (NC)
    3 fingers down, (Abs)
      4 like the fingers of a pianist above the keys. (PP)

Sinclair Lewis

2

  2 Calico-coated, (AC)
  2 small-bodied, (AC)
    3 with delicate legs and pink faces in which their mismatched eyes rolled wild and subdued, (PP)
1 they huddled,
  2 gaudy motionless and alert, (A + A)
  2 wild as deer, (AC)
  2 deadly as rattlesnakes, (AC)
  2 quiet as doves. (AC)

William Faulkner

3

1 The bird's eye, / , remained fixed upon him;

2 / bright and silly as a sequin (AC)

1 its little bones, / , seemed swooning in his hand.

2 / wrapped . . . in a warm padding of feathers (VC)

Stella Benson

4

1 The jockeys sat bowed and relaxed,

2 moving a little at the waist with the movement of their horses. (VC)

Katherine Anne Porter

5

1 The flame sidled up the match,

2 driving a film of moisture and a thin strip of darker grey before it. (VC)

6

1 She came among them behind the man,

2 gaunt in the gray shapeless garment and the sunbonnet, (AC)

2 wearing stained canvas gymnasium shoes. (VC)

Faulkner

7

1 The Texan turned to the nearest gatepost and climbed to the top of it,

2 his alternate thighs thick and bulging in the tight trousers, (Abs)

2 the butt of the pistol catching and losing the sun in pearly gleams. (Abs)

Faulkner

8

1 He could sail for hours,

2 searching the blanched grasses below him with his telescopic eyes, (VC)

2 gaining height against the wind, (VC)

2 descending in mile-long, gently declining swoops when he curved and rode back, (VC)

2 never beating a wing. (VC)

Walter Van Tilburg Clark

9

1 They regarded me silently,
2 Brother Jack with a smile that went no deeper than his lips, (Abs)
3 his head cocked to one side, (Abs)
3 studying me with his penetrating eyes; (VC)
2 the other blank-faced, (Abs)
3 looking out of eyes that were meant to reveal nothing and to stir profound uncertainty. (VC)

Ralph Ellison

10

1 He stood at the top of the stairs and watched me,
2 I waiting for him to call me up, (Abs)
2 he hesitating to come down, (Abs)
3 his lips nervous with the suggestion of a smile, (Abs)
3 mine asking whether the smile meant come, or go away. (Abs)

11

1 Joad's lips stretched tight over his long teeth for a moment, and
1 he licked his lips,
2 like a dog, (P)
3 two licks, (NC)
4 one in each direction from the middle. (NC)

Steinbeck

12

1 We all live in two realities:
2 one of seeming fixity, (NC)
3 with institutions, dogmas, rules of punctuation, and routines, (PP)
4 the calendared and clockwise world of all but futile round on round; (NC) and
2 one of whirling and flying electrons, dreams, and possibilities, (NC)
3 behind the clock. (PP)

Sidney Cox

13

1 It was as though someone, somewhere, had touched a lever and shifted gears, and
1 the hospital was set for night running,
2 smooth and silent, (A + A)
2 its normal clatter and hum muffled, (Abs)

2 the only sounds heard in the whitewalled room distant and unreal: (Abs)
3 a low hum of voices from the nurses' desk, (NC)
4 quickly stifled, (VC)
3 the soft squish of rubber-soled shoes on the tiled corridor; (NC)
3 starched white cloth rustling against itself, (NC) and, outside,
3 the lonesome whine of wind in the country night (NC) and
3 the Kansas dust beating against the windows. (NC)

14

1 The beach sounds are jazzy,
2 percussion fixing the mode—(Abs)
3 the surf cracking and booming in the distance, (Abs)
3 a little nearer dropped bar-bells clanking, (Abs)
3 steel gym rings, / , ringing, (Abs)
/ 4 flung together, (VC)
3 palm fronds rustling above me, (Abs)
4 like steel brushes washing over a snare drum, (PP)
3 troupes of sandals splatting and shuffling on the sandy cement, (Abs)
4 their beat varying, (Abs)
5 syncopation emerging and disappearing with changing paces. (Abs)

15

1 A small Negro girl develops from the sheet of glare-frosted walk,
2 walking barefooted, (VC)
3 her bare legs striking and coiling from the hot cement, (Abs)
4 her feet curling in, (Abs)
5 only the outer edges touching. (Abs)

16

1 The swells moved rhythmically toward us,
2 irregularly faceted, (VC)
2 sparkling, (VC)
2 growing taller and more powerful until the shining crest bursts, (VC)
3 a transparent sheet of pale green water spilling over the top, (Abs)
4 breaking into blue-white foam as it cascades down the front of the wave, (VC)
4 piling up in a frothy mound that the diminishing wave pushes up against the pilings, (VC)

5 with a swishsmash, (PP)
4 the foam drifting back, (Abs)
5 like a lace fan opened over the shimmering water as the spent wave returns whispering to the sea. (PP)

The best starting point for a composition unit based on these four principles is with two-level narrative sentences, first with one second-level addition (sentences 4, 5), then with two or more parallel ones (6, 7, 8). Anyone sitting in his room with his eyes closed could write the main clause of most of the examples; the discipline comes with the additions, provided they are based at first on immediate observation, requiring the student to phrase an exact observation in exact language. This can hardly fail to be exciting to a class: it is life, with the variety and complexity of life; the workbook exercise is death. The situation is ideal also for teaching diction — abstract-concrete, general-specific, literal-metaphorical, denotative-connotative. When the sentences begin to come out right, it is time to examine the additions for their grammatical character. From then on the grammar comes to the aid of the writing and the writing reinforces the grammar. One can soon go on to multilevel narrative sentences (1, 9–11, 15, 16) and then to brief narratives of three to six or seven sentences on actions with a beginning, a middle, and an end that can be observed over and over again — beating eggs, making a cut with a power saw, or following a record changer's cycle or a wave's flow and ebb. (Bring the record changer to class.) Description, by contrast, is static, picturing appearance rather than behavior. The constructions to master are the noun and adjective clusters and the absolute (13, 14). Then the descriptive noun cluster must be taught to ride piggyback on the narrative sentence, so that description and narration are interleaved: "In the morning we went out into a new world, a glistening crystal and white world, each skeleton tree, each leafless bush, even the heavy, drooping power lines sheathed in icy crystal." The next step is to develop the sense for variety in texture and change in pace that all good narrative demands.

In the next unit, the same four principles can be applied to the expository paragraph. But this is a subject for another paper.

I want to anticipate two possible objections. One is that the sentences are long. By freshman English standards they are long, but I could have produced far longer ones from works freshmen are expected to read. Of the sentences by students, most were written as finger exercises in the first few weeks of the course. I try in narrative sentences to push to level after level, not just two or three, but four, five, or six, even more, as far as the students' powers of observation will take them. I want them to become sentence acrobats, to dazzle by their syntactic dexterity. I'd rather have to deal with hyperemia than anemia. I want to add my voice to that of James Coleman (*CCC*, December 1962) deploring our concentration on the plain style.

The other objection is that my examples are mainly descriptive and narrative — and today in freshman English we teach only exposition. I deplore this limitation as much as I deplore our limitation to the plain style. Both are a sign that we have sold our proper heritage for a pot of message. In permitting them, the English department undercuts its own discipline. Even if our goal is only utilitarian prose, we can teach diction and sentence structure far more effectively through a few controlled exercises in description and narration than we can by starting right off with exposition (Theme One, 500 words, precipitates *all* the problems of writing). There is no problem of invention; the student has something to communicate — his immediate sense impressions, which can stand a bit of exercising. The material is not already verbalized — he has to match language to sense impressions. His acuteness in observation and in choice of words can be judged by fairly objective standards — is the sound of a bottle of milk being set down on a concrete step suggested better by *clink* or *clank* or *clunk?* In the examples, study the diction for its accuracy, rising at times to the truly imaginative. Study the use of metaphor, of comparison. This verbal virtuosity and syntactical ingenuity can be made to carry over into expository writing.

But this is still utilitarian. What I am proposing carries over of itself into the study of literature. It makes the student a better reader of literature. It helps him thread the syntactical mazes of much mature writing, and it gives him insight into that elusive thing we call style. Last year a student told of rereading a book by her favorite author, Willa Cather, and of realizing for the first time *why* she liked reading her: she could understand and appreciate the style. For some students, moreover, such writing makes life more interesting as well as giving them a way to share their interest with others. When they learn how to put concrete details into a sentence, they begin to look at life with more alertness. If it is liberal education we are concerned with, it is just possible that these things are more important than anything we can achieve when we set our sights on the plain style in expository prose.

I want to conclude with a historical note. My thesis in this paragraph is that modern prose like modern poetry has more in common with the seventeenth than with the eighteenth century and that we fail largely because we are operating from an eighteenth century base. The shift from the complex to the cumulative sentence is more profound than it seems. It goes deep in grammar, requiring a shift from the subordinate clause (the staple of our trade) to the cluster and the absolute (so little understood as to go almost unnoticed in our textbooks). And I have only lately come to see that this shift has historical implications. The cumulative sentence is the modern form of the loose sentence that characterized the anti-Ciceronian movement in the seventeenth century. This movement, according to Morris W. Croll,[3] began with Montaigne and Bacon and continued with such men as Donne, Browne, Taylor, Pascal. To Montaigne, its art was the art of being natural; to Pascal, its eloquence was the eloquence that mocks formal eloquence; to Bacon, it presented knowledge so that it could be examined, not so that it must be accepted.

But the Senecan amble was banished from England when "the direct sensuous apprehension of thought" (T. S. Eliot's words) gave way to Cartesian reason or intellect. The consequences of this shift in sensibility are well summarized by Croll:

> To this mode of thought we are to trace almost all the features of modern literary education and criticism, or at least of what we should have called modern a generation ago: the study of the precise meaning of words; the reference to dictionaries as literary authorities; the study of the sentence as a logical unit alone; the careful circumscription of its limits and the gradual reduction of its length; . . .[4] the attempt to reduce grammar to an exact science; the idea that forms of speech are always either correct or incorrect; the complete subjection of the laws of motion and expression in style to the laws of logic and standardization — in short, the triumph, during two centuries, of grammatical over rhetorical ideas. (*Style, Rhetoric and Rhythm*, p. 232)

Here is a seven-point scale any teacher of composition can use to take stock. He can find whether he is based in the eighteenth century or in the twentieth and whether he is consistent — completely either an ancient or a modern — or is just a crazy mixed-up kid.

Postscript

I have asserted that "syntactical ingenuity" can best be developed in narrative-descriptive writing and that it can be made to carry over into discursive writing. The count made for the article on sentence openers included all sentence modifiers — or free modifiers, as I prefer to call them. In the total number of free modifiers, the 2000 word samples were almost identical — 1545 in the fiction and 1519 in the nonfiction, roughly one in three sentences out of four. But they differ in position:

Nonfiction	initial 575	medial 492	final 452
Fiction	initial 404	medial 329	final 812

And they differ in some of the grammatical kinds used in the final position:

Nonfiction	NC 123	VC 63	Abs 9
Fiction	NC 131	VC 218	Abs 108

Thus the differences are not in the structures used, only in the position and in the frequency of the various kinds of structures. It will be well to look at a few more sentences of discursive prose.

17

1 His [Hemingway's] characters, / , wander through the ruins of Babel,
    2/ expatriates for the most part, (NC)
    2 smattering many tongues (VC) and
    2 speaking a demotic version of their own. (VC)

Harry Levin

18

1 From literal to figurative is one range that a word may take:
    2 from *foot* of a person to *foot* of a mountain, (PP)
        3 a substituted or metaphoric use. (NC)

1 From concrete to abstract is another range:
    2 from *foot* to *extremity*, (PP)
        3 stressing one of the abstract characteristics of foot, (VC)
            4 a contrast for which the terms *image* and *symbol* as distinguished from *concept* are also used. (NC)

Josephine Miles

19

    2 Going back to his [Hemingway's] work in 1944, (VC)
1 you perceive his kinship with a wholly different group of novelists,
    2 let us say with Poe and Hawthorne and Melville: (PP)
        3 the haunted and nocturnal writers, (NC)
        3 the men who dealt in images that were symbols of an inner world. (NC)

Malcolm Cowley

20

1 Even her style in it is transitional and momentous,
    2 a matter of echoing and reminiscing effects, and of little clarion notes of surprise and prophecy here and there; (NC)
        3 befitting that time of life which has been called the old age of youth and the youth of old age, (AC or VC)
            4 a time fraught with heartache and youthful tension. (NC)

Glenway Wescott, of Colette's *Break of Day*

21

    2 Aglow with splendor and consequence, (AC)
1 he [Sterne] rejoined his wife and daughter,

2 whom he presently transferred to his new parsonage at Coxwold, (RC)
3 an old and rambling house, (NC)
4 full of irregular, comfortable rooms, (AC)
4 situated on the edge of the moors, (VC)
5 in a neighborhood much healthier than the marshy lands of Sutton. (PP)

Peter Quennell

22

1 It is with the coming of man that a vast hole seems to open in nature,
2 a vast black whirlpool spinning faster and faster, (NC)
3 consuming flesh, stones, soil, minerals, (VC)
3 sucking down the lightning, (VC)
3 wrenching power from the atom, (VC)
4 until the ancient sounds of nature are drowned out in the cacophony of something which is no longer nature, (SC)
5 something instead which is loose and knocking at the world's heart, (NC)
5 something demonic and no longer planned — (NC)
6 escaped, it may be — (VC)
6 spewed out of nature, (VC)
6 contending in a final giant's game against its master. (VC)

Loren Eiseley

The structures used in prose are necessarily the structures used in poetry, necessarily because prose and poetry use the same language. Poets may take more liberties with the grammar than prose writers are likely to do; but their departures from the norm must all be understood by reference to the norm. Since poets, like the writers of narrative, work more by association than by logical connection, their sentences are likely to have similar structures. They seem to know the values of the cumulative sentence.

The first example here consists of the first two stanzas of "The Meadow Mouse"; the slashes mark the line ends. The other example constitutes the last four of the five stanzas of "The Motive for Metaphor." It shows well how structural analysis of the sentence reveals the tactics of a difficult poem.

23

1 In a shoebox stuffed in an old nylon stocking / Sleeps the baby mouse I found in the meadow, /

2 Where he trembled and shook beneath a stick / Till I caught him up by the tail and brought him in, / (RC)
3 Cradled in my hand, / (VC)
3 a little quaker, (NC)
4 the whole body of him trembling, / (Abs)
3 His absurd whiskers sticking out like a cartoon mouse, / (Abs)
3 His feet like small leaves, / (Abs)
4 Little lizard-feet, / (NC)
4 Whitish and spread wide when he tried to struggle away, / (AC)
5 Wriggling like a minuscule puppy. (VC)
1 Now he's eaten his three kinds of cheese and drunk from his bottle-cap watering trough — /
2 So much he just lies in one corner, / (AC)
3 His tail curled under him, (Abs)
3 his belly big / As his head, (Abs)
3 His bat-like ears / Twitching, (Abs)
4 tilting toward the least sound. (VC)

Theodore Roethke

24

2 In the same way, (PP)
1 you were happy in spring,
2 with the half colors of quarter-things, (PP)
3 The slightly brighter sky, (NC)
3 the melting clouds, (NC)
3 the single bird, (NC)
3 the obscure moon — (NC)
4 The obscure moon lighting an obscure world of things that would never be quite expressed, (NC)
5 where you yourself were never quite yourself and did not want nor have to be, (RC)
6 desiring the exhilarations of changes: (VC)
7 the motive for metaphor, (NC)
6 shrinking from the weight of primary noon, (VC)
7 the ABC of being, (NC)
7 the ruddy temper, (NC)
7 the hammer of red and blue, (NC)
7 the hard sound — (NC)
8 steel against intimation — (NC)
7 the sharp flash, (NC)
7 the vital, arrogant, fatal, dominant X. (NC)

Wallace Stevens

Notes

1. Cf. Leo Rockas, "Abstract and Concrete Sentences," *CCC*, May 1963. Rockas describes sentences as abstract or concrete, the abstract implying the concrete and vice versa. Readers and writers, he says, must have the knack of apprehending the concrete in the abstract and the abstract in the concrete. This is true and valuable. I am saying that within a single sentence the writer may present more than one level of generality, translating the abstract into the more concrete in added levels.
2. This statement is not quite tenable. Each helps to make the idea of the base clause more concrete or specific, but each is not more concrete or specific than the one immediately above it.
3. "The Baroque Style in Prose," *Studies in English Philology: A Miscellany in Honor of Frederick Klaeber* (1929), reprinted in *Style, Rhetoric, and Rhythm: Essays by Morris W. Croll* (1966) and A. M. Witherspoon and F. J. Warnke, *Seventeenth-Century Prose and Poetry*, 2nd ed. (1963). I have borrowed from Croll in my description of the cumulative sentence.
4. The omitted item concerns punctuation and is not relevant here. In using this scale, note the phrase "what we should have called modern a generation ago" and remember that Croll was writing in 1929.

Christensen's Insights as a Resource for Your Reflections

1. Consider Christensen's essay alongside the excerpts from Ann E. Berthoff's *The Making of Meaning* (pp. 292–304). How might Berthoff's conceptual framework aid you in implementing Christensen's pedagogy? Have you ever worked with language in this way or taught this sort of sentence analysis to your students? What were the results?

2. With Robert J. Connors's critique in mind ("The Erasure of the Sentence," pp. 247–275), consider what we might lose by ignoring Christensen's ideas and other sentence-level pedagogies. How might you guide your students in practicing Christensen's "generative rhetoric" as part of the composing process?

Christensen's Insights as a Resource for Your Writing Classroom

1. Ask your students to bring to class their most recent drafts of essay writing. Instruct students to isolate one of the shortest sentences in a draft and then work with them to "build upon" the

sentence by adding modifiers to its various parts. Discuss how these changes to one small, isolated moment in the essay might necessitate adjustments to other parts of the drafted essay.

2. Share with your students the point that Christensen makes about the "tone-deaf" sentence that can burgeon into "gobbledegook" (p. 279), and then share with them the formula that Christensen describes next, the formula for the cumulative sentence. Have students work in small groups to identify and reshape some of the longer, "tone-deaf" sentences in their drafts into cumulative sentences — that is, sentences that are, after revision, perhaps just as long as the original but much more elegant, readable, and meaningful.

From The Making of Meaning

Ann E. Berthoff

How, in the broadest sense, does the authorial imagination work? What do our minds do when we're creating a piece of writing? What, in short, does the writer, writing, do? In The Making of Meaning: Metaphors, Models, and Maxims for Writing Teachers *(1981), Ann E. Berthoff suggests that teachers can begin to improve writing by alerting students to how their minds work with language, imposing order on fundamentally ambiguous signs and abstracting from experience to establish categories and relationships. When students recognize the cognitive steps that underlie standard draft stages, they will be better equipped to make free and productive revisions of their work.*

Learning the Uses of Chaos

It is, perhaps, a measure of our sophistication that we English teachers can boldly set about discussing the topic *learning to write*, identifying an issue in nonpretentious terms while realizing that it isn't as simple a matter as it sounds. Holding a conference on the topic suggests an awareness that learning to write is a matter for theoretical consideration, not just recipe swapping; that the difficulties we must confront in teaching students how to write deserve something other than high-minded expressions of dismay. We need theory in order to find out what can be done about teaching composition and to define what it is we think we are doing. No theoretical premise is of greater importance to all the new rhetorics, from "free writing" to tagmemics, than that composing is a process; however, this idea, which is already on the way to becoming conventional wisdom, is not helping us as it should. That is to say, the idea that there is not just *composition* but *composing* is becoming dogma, an idea being handed on to teachers and students alike before the implications it might have for pedagogy and course design have been explored or understood.

What does it mean to say that composing is a process? Why is it important that, at all levels of development and in all grades, students of writing should understand that composing is a process? How do we design courses — sequences of assignments — which can make that understanding something other than received dogma? For unless composing as a process is what we actually teach, not just what we proclaim, the idea cannot be fruitful. In many instances, the language of the new rhetoric is used when there is no correspondingly new attitude towards what we are teaching, to say nothing of how we are teaching it. There may be talk of "pre-writing," but the term is misleading if it is taken to mean getting a thesis statement. (I have seen a writing lab manual for tutors that defines pre-writing as a matter of learning to outline.) A textbook that exhorts students in the first chapter to carry through discovery procedures and in the second discusses the rhetorical modes as they were defined in the eighteenth century has not encouraged students to understand the relationship of earlier and later phases of composing.

It is not instructive to talk about "the composing process" unless we have a conception of the kind of process writing is — or, at least, the kind of process it is not. Thus writing is *not* like cooking a particular dish; writing may resemble, at one stage or another, some phase of, say, making a cream sauce, but it is not sequential or "linear"; it is not measurement, followed by amalgamation and transformation. An analogy for writing that is based on culinary experience would have to include ways of calculating the guests' preferences, as well as ways of determining what's on the shelf — the cook's and the grocer's — and what's in the purse. Nor is the composing process like playing games or developing various motor skills. Such analogies leave out of account language, or they conceive of it in mechanistic or merely behavioral terms. But language is not merely a tool; it is not a set of counters to be moved about nor a set of conventions to be manipulated in order to express one or another idea. We don't have ideas that we put into words; we don't think of what we want to say and then write. In composing, we make meanings. We find the forms of thought by means of language, and we find the forms of language by taking thought. If we English teachers are to understand composing as the kind of process it is, we will need a philosophy of language that can account for this dialectic of forming. A hopeful sign that this is beginning to happen is that English teachers are beginning to study Vygotsky, a developmental psychologist who knew that language and thought do not bear one another a sequential relationship, but that they are simultaneous and correlative.

I believe we can best teach the composing process by conceiving of it as a continuum of making meaning, by seeing writing as analogous to all those processes by which we make sense of the world. It is generally a surprise to students to learn that writing has anything in common with anything else they have ever done — and for the very good reason that, as it has generally been taught them, it has indeed nothing much to do with anything they have ever done. But writing, taught as a process of making meanings, can be seen to be like taking in a happening, forming an opinion, deciding what's to be done, construing a text, or reading the significance of a landscape. Thinking, perceiving, writing are all acts of composing: any composition course should insure that students learn the truth of this principle, that making meanings is the work of the active mind and is thus within their natural capacity.

Meanings don't just happen: we make them; we find and form them. In that sense, all writing courses are creative writing courses. Learning to write is learning to do deliberately and methodically with words on the page what we do all the time with language. Meanings don't come out of the air; we make them out of a chaos of images, half-truths, remembrances, syntactic fragments, from the mysterious and unformed. The most useful slogan for the composition course — along with "how do I know what I mean 'till I hear what I say?" — is *ex nihilo nihil fit*: out of nothing, nothing can be made. When we teach pre-writing as a phase of the composing process, what we are teaching is not how to get a thesis statement but the generation and uses of chaos; when we teach revision as a phase of the composing process, we are teaching just that — reseeing the ways out of chaos.

Our students, because they are language animals, because they have the power of naming, can generate chaos; they can find ways out of chaos because language creates them. Language itself is the great heuristic. Any name implies generalization; any cluster of names implies classification; any classification implies statement. As Kenneth Burke says, to name something *A* is to declare simultaneously that it is not *not-A*.[Δ] All rhetorical functions can be derived from that most profound of linguistic facts, that words, in Vygotsky's formulation, come into being as verbal generalizations. It is the *discursive* character of language, its tendency to "run along," to be syntactical, which brings thought along with it. It is the discursive, generalizing, forming power of language that makes meanings from chaos.

Students can learn to write by learning the uses of chaos, which is to say, rediscovering the power of language to generate the sources of

Δ: As noted on p. 303, throughout *The Making of Meaning*, Berthoff uses this symbol to indicate source materials that she draws on repeatedly. The cited passages follow the article in the section titled "More Maxims."

meaning. Our job is to design sequences of assignments that let our students discover what language can do, what they can do with language. Kenneth Koch got poetry out of his youngsters because he gave them syntactic structures to play with; Sylvia Ashton-Warner's "key vocabulary" became what she called "the captions of the dynamic life itself"; Paulo Freire's "generative words" provided the means by which the peasants in his literacy classes — "culture circles" — could name the world. Our students can learn to write only if we give them back their language, and that means playing with it, working with it, using it instrumentally, making many starts. We want them to learn the truth of Gaston Bachelard's observation that "in the realm of mind, to begin is to know you have the right to begin again." Our students cannot learn the uses of chaos if we continue to make assignments appropriate not to these beginnings but to the final phases of the composing process. Beginnings, for instance, should never be graded: identifying mistakes is irrelevant when we are teaching making a start at the process of making meanings.

Now, chaos is scary: the meanings that can emerge from it, which can be discerned taking shape within it, can be discovered only if students who are learning to write can learn to tolerate ambiguity. It is to our teacherly advantage that the mind doesn't like chaos; on the other hand, we have to be alert to the fact that meanings can be arrived at too quickly, the possibility of other meanings being too abruptly foreclosed. What we must realize ourselves and make dramatically evident to our students is what I. A. Richards means when he calls ambiguities "the hinges of thought."

Learning to write is a matter of learning to tolerate ambiguity, of learning that the making of meaning is a dialectical process determined by perspective and context. Meanings change as we think about them; statements and events, significances and interpretations can mean different things to different people at different times. Meanings are not prebaked or set for all time; they are created, found, formed, and reformed. Even dictionary definitions change: that is a brand new discovery for most students, that language has a history. How we see something — a relationship between word and idea or object, or between two words or statements — depends on our experience, and on our purposes, our perspective, "where we're coming from." We know reality not directly but by means of the meanings we make. (The role of critical thinking is, of course, to review and revise those meanings.) What we know, we know in some form — perceptual or conceptual. We see relationships not in isolation but in a field of other relationships: as a text has a context, so events and ideas and objects have a "context of situation," in Malinowski's formulation. It is the nature of signifiers to be unclear, multivalent, polysemous, ambiguous, until perspective and context are determined. I consider it the most important advance of the semester if a student moves from "Webster tell us . . ." to "what this situation means depends on how you look at it." *It depends* is a slogan I would add to *ex nihilo nihil fit*.

For students to discover that ambiguities are "the hinges of thought," we surely will have to move from the inert, passive questions that we inscribe in the margins of papers and which we direct to student readers: "What do you mean here?" "What is the author trying to say?" Those are not critically useful questions; they elicit insubstantial responses or "I-thought-that-was-what-you-wanted" or, on occasion, students simply cast their eyes heavenward. We should focus on the shifting character of meaning and the role of perspective and context, and we can do so by raising such questions as these: "How does it change your meaning if you put it this way?" "If the author is saying *X*, how does that go with the *Y* we heard him saying in the preceding chapter — or stanza?" "What do you make of passage *A* in the light of passage *B?*" Students learn to use ambiguities as "the hinges of thought" as they learn to formulate alternate readings; to say it again, watching how the "it" changes. In my view, from my perspective, *interpretive paraphrase* is another name for the composing process itself. It is the means by which meanings are hypothesized, identified, developed, modified, discarded, or stabilized. And, furthermore, it is the only way I know to teach students how to edit their compositions. Interpretive paraphrase enacts the dialogue that is at the heart of all composing: a writer is in dialogue with his various selves and with his audience. And here is where the classroom hour can actively help us. The composition classroom ought to be a place where the various selves are heard and an audience's response is heard — listened to and responded to. Language is an exchange: we know what we've said and what can be understood from it when we get a response; we come to know what we mean when we hear what we say. It is this critical, reflexive character of language that allows us to think about thinking. Learning to write involves us all in many such unvicious circles whereby we interpret our interpretations.

Interpretive paraphrase — continually asking, "How does it change the meaning if I put it this way?" — is, of course, the principal method of all critical inquiry, but its importance for us in the composition classroom is that it teaches students to see relationships and to discover that that is what they do with their minds. It does not seem so to them: isolation and absurdity, not connectedness and meaningfulness, are for our students the characterizing qualities of most experience. Perhaps it's time to stop when one reaches the point of huge sociological generalization, but I think that this one is true; it is, after all, only another way of speaking of the alienation that is recognizably the mark of our era. If we can make the composition classroom a forum, a culture circle, a theatre, a version of Tolstoy's armchair aswarm with children questioning, talking, and arguing — if the composition classroom is the place where dialogue is the mode of making meaning, then we will have a better chance to dramatize not only the fact that language itself changes with the meanings we make from it and that its powers are generative and developmental, but also that it is the indispensable and unsurpassable means of reaching others and forming communities with them. The ability to speak is innate, but language can only be realized in a social context. Dialogue, that is to say, is essential to the making of meaning and thus to learning to write. The chief use of chaos is that it creates the need for that dialogue.

Discovering Limits

Our panel topic is rather less compelling than the convention slogan. The idea of the human mind as the supreme resource is more inspiriting than the notion of one more innovative this or that, and certainly the concept of mind is no more problematic than the notion of "students with learning and language difficulties." Of course, some difficulties are more difficult than others: you can't expect to teach someone to read a paragraph if he can't read a sentence, or a sentence if he can't read words, or words if he can't construe letters or letter groups. And yet that is not to say that we teach reading by teaching the alphabet. I realize that it is casuistry of a sort to stretch the idea of difficulty, but I do want to claim that "students with language and learning difficulties" is a pretty fair description of students entering college. If our freshmen were not burdened with such difficulties, if they encountered no such difficulties, we would not have to labor to teach them to write coherently, to read critically, and to think cogently. I believe that what is good for the best and brightest is essential for students who have difficulties. Those we used to call slow learners need the freedom and the opportunities we trouble to offer our prize students. And, in turn, what is important and worthwhile for disadvantaged students will prove to be useful and valuable for the good readers and the practiced writers.

If we tap this supreme resource, the minds of our students, we will find powerful, profoundly rooted capacities that cannot be identified solely in quantifiable terms and quotients, but which we can learn to identify and train. Mind in this sense is not reducible to what has been called "intelligence" by psychologists looking for something to measure; intelligence is a culture-bound concept as mind is not. Socrates demonstrated his method not with the head of the class but with an illiterate slave boy. Montessori's first school in Rome was for children who had been certified by the state as cretini—morons. It was Brazilian peasants who gained the experience of freedom in attending Paulo Freire's literacy classes. The point from which these great teachers of the disadvantaged begin is the mind's operation, the human mind in action. Now our convention slogan—Let the Minds of Our Students Be the

Supreme Resource — is a sound point of departure for the composition teacher because composing *is* the mind in action! The composing process that involves writing down words requires the same acts of mind as the composing process by which we make sense of the world. Jargon like "nonverbal communication" masks the fact that all perception, all communication, takes place in a world built by language. Man is the language animal and the operation of his mind is a linguistic operation, whether words are spoken or not.

It's very refreshing to have the NCTE and its affiliates publicly declaring an interest in mind. It's a welcome change from the pseudoscientific concepts we've grown used to: verbal behavior, communication skills, input and feedback, encoding and decoding. But we should be on our guard against becoming ensnared in the problem of defining what "mind" is; and, be warned, this is the game that psychologists and philosophers who deplore what they call "mentalism" like to play and win. (They do not equally enjoy the game of deciding what is "behavior.") Laboring under the delusion that they are being "scientific," English teachers have all too often asked such questions as, "What *is* creativity?" What *is* communication?" You may remember that the theme song of the Dartmouth Conference was, "What *is* English?" That kind of questioning gets us nowhere; it is neither pragmatic nor scientific. J. Robert Oppenheimer explains in discussing this misconception of scientific inquiry that Einstein did not ask, "What is a clock?" Rather, he framed questions about how we would measure time over immense distances. We will have to learn to ask not "what *is* mind?" but "what happens when we use our minds in writing that is comparable to what happens when we make sense of the world?" and "what happens in the composing process?" Josephine Miles has entitled one discussion of composition, "What Do We Compose?" and another, "How What's What in the English Language?" Such questions as these will help us develop a working concept of mind. A good name for the mind in action is *imagination*: Coleridge called the imagination "the prime agent of all human perception."[Δ] That is an epistemological concept that English teachers should make their own. I suggest, then, that this panel topic could be restated as follows: *Teaching the composing process by liberating the imagination.*

I will try in this talk to suggest what that might mean when we set about developing "innovative composition courses for students with learning and language difficulties."

The one sure principle of composition, as of imagination, is that nothing comes of nothing; *ex nihilo nihil fit*: nothing can be made from nothing. Recent textbooks in composition have begun to show signs of an interest in the subject of invention, though the process seems still unclear, if not misconceived. The first use of language that a student of composition has to learn, I think, is in the generation of chaos. If we don't begin there, we falsify the composing process because composition requires choosing all along the way, and you can't choose if there are no perceived alternatives: chaos is the source of alternatives. If we are unwilling to risk chaos, we won't have provided our students with the opportunity to discover that ambiguities are, as I. A. Richards has said, "the hinges of thought."[Δ]

Once we encourage the generation of chaos, however, we are morally as well as pedagogically bound to present very carefully the ways of emerging from it. Happily, the process of generating chaos provides, itself, the means of emerging from chaos by making something of it. I like to demonstrate how this can be so by having everybody in class name what he sees, what comes to mind in response to, say, a photograph from Steichen's *Family of Man*, with everyone writing down everybody else's word. Twice around the room and there begin to be repetitions; names group themselves like so many birds flocking; three times around the room and the blackboard is full, the sheet of paper covered. (That can illustrate the psychological advantage of having a full page rather than an empty sheet, and it suggests that chaos might be better than nothing.) The chaos begins to take shape: classifying, which is organized comparing, proceeds without the stimulus of prefabricated, loaded "study questions." The primary compositional modes of amalgamation and elimination begin to operate. All this happens more or less without guidance, though if there is a roadblock it can be exploded by asking the only study question anyone ever needs: How does who do what?

The reason that this natural ordering process takes place in the very act of naming is that the mind naturally abstracts. The human mind—but that is a redundancy: the mind naturally orders by comparing and differentiating. (That process of selection apparently goes on in the retinal cells at an electrochemical level.) We see in terms of classes and types; everything we see is seen as an example of a kind of thing. Perception is contingent on the mind's capacity for analogizing.

My point is that we do not have to teach our students *how* to abstract but *that* they abstract. What we do teach is how to listen in on the dialogue in progress when they are looking and classifying in the act of perception. That dialogue is thinking; it is dialectical. *Dialogue* and *dialectic* are cognate: learning to see what you're looking at really means learning to question and questioning is the life of thought. The composing process, I think we can say, is empowered from beginning to end by the dialectic of question and answer. The way to bring this fact to life for our students is to encourage writing from the start—not topic sentences and thesis statements of course, but lists, class names, questions, and tentative answers and new questions. This "pre-writing" is writing; a cluster of names is a protoparagraph; a cluster of clusters is a nascent composition.

To suggest the formal nature of this emergence from chaos I used to employ rather elaborate schematic devices—bits and pieces of signs from symbolic logic, tagmemic grids, flowcharts, and so on, but the trouble is—and it's not a problem peculiar to students with learning and language difficulties—the relationship of the sign to its referent is easily misconceived and the signs themselves become the focus of interest. I've collected pre-writing sheets covered with diagrams and charts that bore no relationship to the words employed, with whatever concepts might have emerged totally obscured by a mass of lines and boxes. Students have submitted first drafts with the appearance of sketches for a painting of the Martyrdom of St. Sebastian, because they were under the impression that "she likes arrows." Just as we can't teach reading by simply teaching the alphabet, so we can't teach composition by laying out unintelligible floor plans.

The alternative, I've come to believe, is a line drawn down the middle of the page. Overschematizing is no more conducive to the definition of choices than the formal outline, but opposition as an organizing concept, one which has been borrowed from linguistics by structuralists in all disciplines, can be very helpful to us in teaching composition. Opposition is a highly generalized term covering juxtapositions, alignments, echoes as well as antitheses, opposites, and counterpoint. Figure and ground are in opposition; beginning and end are in opposition; character and plot are in opposition. The ends of a scale and the banks of a river represent two kinds of opposition. It is a concept to think with; it is quickly grasped by all students because it is a name for what they are already doing when they judge size and distance and degrees of all kinds. Opposition is the principle informing every phrase they utter, every step they take. I have seen many a student weighed down with learning and language difficulties come to life smiling at the brand new discovery that composing has anything whatsoever to do with anything else he has ever done. Exercises in forming and developing oppositions not only provide the steps out of chaos; they also become the means of discovering that composing is a dialectical process: it starts and stops and starts again; it can proceed in circles; it is tentative, hypothetical, and recapitulative. Our students can learn, when they use the concept of opposition to think with, that composing means naming, differentiating, comparing, classifying, selecting, and thus defining; that composing means getting it together. Isn't that what we want to teach them?

"A composition is a bundle of parts": that is Josephine Miles' very useful definition.[Δ] Composing means identifying the parts and bundling them; in the composing process we recreate wholes by establishing relationships between the parts. All our innovative powers in designing composition courses should go to assuring that writing is involved at all stages of this process. The textbooks that warn glibly or sternly, "Don't begin to write until you know what you want to say," ought to be returned to the publishers. The motto of every composition course should be, "How do I know what I mean until I hear what I say?" I'm very fond of that old chestnut; here is a more weighty formulation: I. A. Richards, recalling Plato as usual, declares that "dialectic is the continuing audit of meaning."[Δ]

Some experienced writers can keep track of what they are saying in that interior dialogue and thus can audit their meanings in their heads, but students with learning and language difficulties should write it down, continually. In that way they can learn to recognize the interior dialogue and keep the dialectic going. Writing at all stages of composition brings to full consciousness the experience of the mind at work, the imagination in action. Writing can counter the notion that ideas fall from heaven, that some people just "have" them and others just don't. Writing at all stages is a way of seeing ideas develop. We want to assure that the student continually discovers that it is his mind that is giving form to chaos; that his language is ordering chaos; that his imagination is just what Coleridge tells him it is, "a shaping spirit."

We encourage that experience of writing and thereby the auditing of meaning by providing linguistic forms, syntactical and rhetorical structures, not for imitation but for use as speculative instruments. Forms are not cookie cutters superimposed on some given, rolled-out reality dough; forms are not alien structures that are somehow made appropriate to "what you want to say." Forms are our means of abstracting; or, rather, forming *is* abstracting. Abstracting is what the mind does; abstracting, forming is the work of imagination. But this can rapidly become more interesting as metaphysics than as pedagogy. I suggest that we think of forms by considering what they do: they provide limits. "A poet," in Allen Tate's definition, "is a man willing to come under the bondage of limitations—if he can find them." Limits make choice possible and thus free the imagination.

Consider what Kenneth Koch calls the "poetry idea" in his experimental writing assignments: that's the conception of form we need. Koch gets poetry out of his third graders by making forms available to them. He doesn't say, "Tell me what it would feel like to be a geranium in a sunny window." He reads poetry with them and then offers a form that can answer to their experience, their perceptions. "I used to be a ______, but now I am a ______." Or he says, "Talk to something that isn't a person; ask it a question":

> Dog, where did you get that bark?
> Dragon, where do you get that flame?
> Kitten, where did you get that meow?
> Rose, where did you get that red?
> Bird, where did you get those wings?

At first, Koch was apologetic about his dependence on form, but he soon came to see that it was the limits the forms provided that allowed the kids to discover their feelings and to shape their insights.

This conception of form as limit-providing structure can help us see more clearly that throughout the composing process the writer is engaged in limiting: selecting and differentiating are ways of limiting; we limit when we compare, classify, amalgamate, and discard; defining is, by definition, a setting of limits. How we limit is how we form. It is an idea that can help us develop sequences in our innovative composition courses. I. A. Richards has said that all learning depends upon a sequence of "partially parallel tasks." Any composition course should be organized so that learning something about syntactical structure prepares for learning something about paragraph structure. As it is, the new rhetorics every year lay out what the old rhetorics have been explaining since the eighteenth century; that, for instance, there are three modes of writing, called "exposition," "description," and "narrative." Do we create the occasions for our students to discover that argument can take the form of narrative, as in fable? that there is a logic of metaphor, in Robert Frost's sonnets as well as in Donne's? that description and analysis are both essential to definition? How many advanced composition courses incorporate so-called creative writing? It's time our composition courses were themselves composed, that we ask of them unity, coherence, and emphasis.

I have quoted I. A. Richards throughout because he has thought more deeply than anyone I know about the pedagogical implications of a philosophy of mind that stresses the shaping power of imagination. If we let the minds of our students be the supreme resource, it means we will be recognizing that language is "the supreme organ of the mind's self-ordering growth."[Δ] It is language — not vocabulary or a sophisticated repertory of syntactical structures, though we can work on this; not the students' very own language and not the teacher's — it is language as a form-finder and form-creator that makes possible naming and opposition and definition; it is the power of language as a form that creates order from chaos; it is language that frames the dialectic, limits the field, forms the questions and answers, starts the dialectic and keeps it going; it is language that makes choice possible. That is why we can say that to learn to compose is to discover both the power of the mind and the meaning of human freedom.

More Maxims

I have depended on certain formulations in trying to make the case for reclaiming the imagination in order to teach the composing process as a matter of making meaning. Throughout the talks and articles that constitute Part II, I have cited a few statements repeatedly. They are indicated in the text by this sign:△ For convenience's sake, I've gathered them here with bibliographic data.

> Implied in the use of the negative, there is both the ability to generalize and the ability to specify. That is, you cannot use the negative properly without by the same token exemplifying the two basic dialectical resources of merger and division. For you can use "no" properly insofar as you can classify under one head many situations that are, in their positive details, quite distinct from one another. In effect, you group them under the head of "Situations all of which are classes in terms of the negative." And in the very act of so classifying, you distinguish them from another class of situations that are "not No-Situations."
>
> —Kenneth Burke, *Language as Symbolic Action* (Berkeley: University of California Press, 1968), p. 425.

> The primary IMAGINATION I hold to be the living Power and prime Agent of all human Perception, and as a repetition in the finite mind of the eternal act of creation in the infinite I AM.
>
> —Samuel Taylor Coleridge, *Biographia Literaria*, Chap. XIII.

> *Questioner*: Like a whole composition, then, a word is a bundle of parts?
>
> *Speaker*: A bundle, a life, with a life history. . . .
>
> —Josephine Miles, "English: A Colloquy; or, How What's What in the Language," *California English Journal*, 2 (1966), 3–14.

> Language . . . is an organ — the supreme organ of the mind's self-ordering growth.
>
> Corresponding to all these studies [Mathematics, Physics, Chemistry, Biology, Sociology, Anthropology, Poetics, Dialectic] are characteristic uses of language. Poetics, I suggest, is faced by the most complex of them. Above Poetics I would put only Dialectic as being concerned with the relations of Poetics with all other studies and with their relations to one another. Dialectics would thus be the supreme study, with Philosophy as its Diplomatic Agent. All of them are both subject matter and language studies. That is the chief point here; there is no study which is not a language study, concerned with the speculative instruments it employs.
>
> —I. A. Richards, *Speculative Instruments* (N.Y.: Harcourt, 1955), p. 9; pp. 115–16.

> In general we will find that the more important a word is, and the more central and necessary its meanings are in our pictures of ourselves and the world, the more ambiguous and possibly deceiving the word will be. Naturally these words are also those which have been most used in philosophy. But it is not the philosophers who have made them ambiguous; it is the position of their ideas, as the very hinges of all thought. Our archproblem . . . has been "What should guide the reader's mind?" Our answer was "Our awareness of interdependence, of how things hang together, which makes us able to give and audit an account of what may be

meant in a discussion — that highest activity of REASON which Plato named "Dialectic."

—I. A. Richards, *How to Read a Page* (1942; rpt. Boston: Beacon Press, 1959), p. 24; p. 240.

Berthoff's Insights as a Resource for Your Reflections

1. Some of Berthoff's key terms — for example, *chaos, dialogue, meaning, process*, and *ambiguity* — are fairly generalized and abstract, and therefore invite the reader to link them to his or her own sense of practical contexts. How might you paraphrase Berthoff's ideas to students, and what sorts of classroom activities might enable your students to benefit from an understanding of these terms?
2. What might Berthoff mean by the extraordinarily concise assertion, "forming is abstracting"? As you elaborate the variety of implications of this assertion, consider ways that you could help students to understand, practice, and cultivate the skill of making meaning.

Berthoff's Insights as a Resource for Your Writing Classroom

1. Berthoff explains that when she teaches writing, she "offers linguistic forms, syntactical and rhetorical structures, not for imitation but for use as speculative instruments." Develop some of these structures for your students to work with. How will you introduce these forms, how will you grade them, and what role would you expect them to play in your students' composing processes?
2. Berthoff suggests that we would do well to show students how writing is closely akin to other activities that they perform constantly. Develop ways to illustrate this point for your students, and then ask them to describe everyday activities that function as metaphors for key aspects of the composing process.

Teaching Writing with Computers

Calling Off the Hounds: Technology and the Visibility of Plagiarism

James P. Purdy

Plagiarism has long been a hot-button issue in writing classrooms, and the Internet has radically complicated the issue. What are the best ways to think about plagiarism and how do we most successfully educate students about it? Purdy's article surveys the discourse about plagiarism, explores the ways schools most often fight the problem, evaluates the plagiarism-detection mechanisms available online, and delineates the implications for our classrooms.

Harvard's much publicized decision in summer 2003 to deny admission to Blair Hornstine because of allegations of plagiarism (Green and Russell 2003; Kantrowitz and Scelfo 2003) reminds those of us in English studies not only of the negative social stigma accompanying accusations of plagiarism, but also of the drastic actions academic institutions will take to avoid being labeled as tolerating plagiarism—or any behavior closely akin to it. Hornstine, who had already been accepted to Harvard, was accused of having "information from sources that was not properly attributed" in five articles published in Cherry Hill, New Jersey's *Courier-Post*, including sections copied from President Bill Clinton and Supreme Court justices William Brennan and Potter Stewart (Osenenko 2003: n.p.). Harvard revoked admission because Hornstine's actions were viewed as "behavior that brings into question . . . honesty, maturity, or moral character" (Green and Russell 2003).[1] Without a doubt, plagiarism continues to be fraught with concerns ethical and moral.

Now we must add technological. New technologies, such as the Internet, heralded simultaneously as promoting (e.g., see Kitalong 1998; DeVoss and Rosati 2002; Laird 2003) and thwarting (e.g., see Culwin and Lancaster 2000; Braumoeller and Gaines 2001) plagiarism, continue to keep concerns surrounding plagiarism in the forefront of the collective academic psyche. While plagiarism has arguably always been a function of technology—that is, plagiarizers could plagiarize only in ways the available technologies permitted—these new technologies increase the visibility of plagiarism, allowing interested parties to quickly and easily trace documents to those using similar language. As a result, writing teachers are more aware of plagiarism. In other words, if plagiarism is easier to commit because of the Internet, it is also easier to catch because of the Internet. We in English studies must, therefore, now think about plagiarism in light of technology. Just as Lisa Gitelman (1999: 119) argues that the phonograph and associated recording technology troubled nineteenth-century "visual norms of intellectual property," so too do new media technologies trouble the existing standards of plagiarism and intellectual property that rely on visual evidence. Treatment of intellectual property and plagiarism, however, does not necessarily evolve with this changing technology. As Gitelman notes, typing and related nineteenth-century literacy practices facilitated by new technologies, such as the typewriter and phonograph, were characterized by "anxiety about visuality and textual evidence" (211). Typewriters were thought to make writing — and error, because typewriters did not initially allow for mistakes to be corrected — more visible. They substantiated the presence of error and their own status as writing machines through the text they produced, that is, what people could see (211). New-media technology is still surrounded by this anxiety — largely because our standards of evidence still depend on visual proof. Little seems to have changed.

Plagiarism detection services that rely on the Internet allow instructors to search for this visual proof, to test their students' papers to determine if they include language copied directly from other sources. As Rebecca Moore Howard (2007) explains, the "logic" of these services is "if unethical writers have access to text online and plagiarize from it, then gatekeeping teachers can also access the plagiarized text and catch the offenders." Undoubtedly, many different services exist for instructors to tailor to their individual needs. In his 2001 report for Britain's Joint Information Systems Committee (JISC), Gill Chester (2003) identifies three types of plagiarism tested by detection services: cut and paste, paper mills, and collusion. Plagiarism detection services, in other words, can test if students copied text from Web sites, purchased papers from online paper mills, or copied text from other students. These services test for the first two types of plagiarism by comparing submitted papers against texts available via the Internet and test for the latter by comparing submitted papers against a database of student papers established by the instructor. Examples of the former services include EduTie,[2] Essay Verification Engine (EVE2), and Turnitin. Examples of the latter services include CopyCatch, Glatt, and WordCHECK. Some services, such as EVE2 and CopyCatch, download onto the user's computer, while others, such as EduTie and Turnitin, operate from remote servers. This distinction becomes significant when considering the accessibility of student papers submitted to be tested.

These technologies arguably have increased the fervor to eradicate plagiarism — or at least to capture and punish those who plagiarize. A 29 April 2004 *Primetime Thursday* special ("Cheaters Amok") largely devoted to the use of plagiarism detection services, specifically TurnItIn, to stop plagiarism serves as a case in point. The ability to detect plagiarism remains a priority for academic institutions, and the advent of plagiarism detection software seemingly provides the solution that many are seeking.

Sleuthing and Hunting: "Caught" in the Discourse of Plagiarism

The lead article in the University of Illinois at Urbana-Champaign's College of Liberal Arts and Sciences newsletter (*LAS News*, Spring 2003) exemplifies this heightened desire to apprehend plagiarists. The article, by Andrea Lynn, advances the importance of combating plagiarism in the classroom and advocates the use of plagiarism detection software, specifically EVE2, as one of the new "weapons" to "parry" plagiarism (1). At the outset the article's discussion of plagiarism is couched in terms of violence and struggle, and the work of the instructor is framed as combative and aggressive.

Such discourse about plagiarism, considered along with that mobilized by plagiarism detection software, makes it unclear whether the classroom is a United Nations summit or a nineteenth-century crime novel. EVE2, for instance, has a settable search function named "Call off the hounds when. . . ." The word choice here conjures images of the classic fox hunt—mobs of hunters on horseback galloping after dogs hot on the trail of their next kill. The use of plagiarism detection software, in other words, becomes a hunt for prey. This phrasing also positions the student as a wily and cunning trickster (the mythological image of the fox) and the instructor as a hunter out for the kill. While the former sadly may be true, we hope the latter never is. Moreover, this word choice also suggests an elite class chasing after lower creatures for sport. The pursuit of plagiarism becomes a game in which instructors seek to entrap students with a triumphant "Aha! I've got you!" As in the classic presentation of the private investigator or police officer at work, the criminal is caught red-handed in the glare of a flashlight. Instructors using plagiarism detection technology likewise seek to make visible students' acts of transgression. The goal here is far from pedagogical. Instructors, of course, often do not use these services with malicious intent, but the services as marketed do not lend themselves to effective pedagogy.

The aforementioned *LAS News* article, which offers recommendations based on Bear Braumoeller and Brian Gaines's 2001 study comparing simply warning students not to plagiarize with telling them their papers will be run through a plagiarism detection service, prompted action by the College of Liberal Arts and Sciences (LAS) at the University of Illinois at Urbana-Champaign (UIUC). LAS administration asked the Center for Writing Studies (the center), a cross-disciplinary academic unit devoted to the research and teaching of composition and rhetoric, to recommend a plagiarism detection service for use by instructors in identifying plagiarized work. The results of the investigation to determine which service would be most suitable reveal that these fee-based services appear to cause more problems than they solve. They raise not only ethical concerns, but also questions about their effectiveness as compared to free and readily available online search engines. Furthermore, plagiarism detection services direct our attention to the larger concerns of the role of the instructor and the definition of plagiarism in an academic environment where available technology both changes the writing practices of students and makes some of these practices, particularly those associated with plagiarism, more visible. In what follows, I detail the study and its results within the context of plagiarism scholarship to explore how new technologies affect our understanding of plagiarism and writing instruction.

Testing the Testers: Evaluating the Performance of Plagiarism Detection Software

Charged by LAS with the task of studying plagiarism detection services, with primary concern centering on Internet plagiarism, the center first established minimum requirements for any service suggested: the service had to search Internet sites and paper mills and the service could not maintain submitted papers in an internal database. Keeping such papers is a violation of students' intellectual property rights because students neither agree that their course papers be accessible to anyone on the Internet nor, even more disturbing, consent that their papers be used for profit. (While the former problem might be resolved by having students sign a waiver granting permission that their papers be submitted to the Web, the second problem is more complicated and not so easily solved.) Moreover, in their study of plagiarism detection services, Braumoeller and Gaines (2001) indicate that UIUC would not allow them to test services that kept copies of papers precisely because "students' essays are their own property." In this way, the university itself has taken a stand against services that retain student papers.

Elsewhere Andrea L. Foster (2002) and Rebecca Moore Howard (1995, 2000) discuss at greater length these ethical and moral concerns, as they apply to the use of plagiarism detection services and to the definition of plagiarism itself, respectively. Foster (2002: A37) addressed how some college lawyers now advise institutions that plagiarism detection services that maintain copies of submitted student papers, specifically Turnitin, not only potentially violate students' copyrights on their written work, but also violate their privacy since students often do not grant consent that their work be copied. She cites Howard as arguing that students can also protest the submission of their papers to plagiarism detection services under the Family Educational Rights and Privacy Act because it prohibits institutions of higher education from disclosing personal information about students without students' prior consent.

Howard (1995: 793), carrying these concerns to definitions of plagiarism itself, explores how writing studies often construct plagiarism as immoral or criminal (see also Howard 2000). She contends, however, that "morality is not a necessary component of plagiarism" as students may plagiarize for positive reasons (796–97). She addresses how when students do what she calls patchwriting—"writing passages that are not copied exactly but that have nevertheless been borrowed from another source, with some changes," a behavior closely allied with plagiarism—they can come to understand what was previously unfamiliar material (799). In other words, students who patchwrite do not plagiarize to cheat; they plagiarize because they lack confidence that they understand the material with which they are working. She ultimately argues that student writing be treated with the same respect as professional writing (796). Howard asks us, above all, to regard and value students as writers.

A 2003 case at McGill University illustrates such concerns regarding student copyright and privacy as well as another perspective on this issue of respect. Jesse Rosenfeld, a student at McGill, successfully argued his right to decline to submit his assignments to Turnitin. Initially, after refusing to submit his papers to the service for testing, Rosenfeld received zeros for the assignments. After two months of appeals, however, the professor who originally failed the papers agreed to grade them without requiring that they be submitted. Rosenfeld's objections to submitting to Turnitin were precisely how such a process views students and student work. He asserted, "frankly I'm offended that the university is violating students' rights by using a device that presumes students are guilty of plagiarism until proven innocent" and is sponsoring a service that "uses students' work to boost the company's profits" (Brown 2004). Rosenfeld's case and his eventual success at having the original decision of the university reversed underscore the validity and weight of these objections. It is of note here that these ethical concerns continue to circulate and invalidated the use of several plagiarism detection services for the purposes of my study.

For the study, I researched eight plagiarism detection services following the requirements established by the center and compared them based on the following criteria: type of testing, method of testing, treatment of papers, cost, and timeliness of reports. Only two services from this list, EduTie[3] and EVE2, met the aforementioned requirements; thus, they were selected to be tested for how effectively they traced plagiarized documents to their original sources. (Identifying the tested documents as "plagiarized" simply indicates that these documents were copied from online sources to mimic the process of plagiarizing online. This designation does not necessarily indicate that the original documents themselves were plagiarized. In fact, only one document tested was known to have been plagiarized.) Also selected for the study was the search engine Google to test whether the fee-based services performed more effectively than a free online search engine. Though Google is not marketed as a plagiarism detection service, its comprehensive Web search capabilities allow it to function as one. Other search engines might serve the same function.

Table 1. Tested Documents

Test	*Document*	*Description*
1	Plagiarized document compilation	A document, created specifically for the purposes of this study, with four sections, each copied from an online document in a different subject area: • section 1, the social sciences: a paper from the Electronic References online paper mill about the relationship between media and violence • section 2, the biological sciences: a scientific report on the relationship between hypothyroidism and prolactin levels • section 3, engineering: an article published in the *International Journal of Applied Electromagnetics* • section 4, literature: an analysis of book 1 of Homer's *The Iliad* provided by GradeSaver
2	Sexual harassment paper from online paper mill	The first paragraph of a paper on sexual harassment turned in by a student in a first-year composition course. The student presumably bought the paper from the Electronic References online paper mill. The student version used for the test differs slightly from the Electronic References version (i.e., the student added and deleted a few words)
3	President letter	A letter from the president of the University of Illinois
4	Braumoeller and Gaines article	The introduction, background, and conclusions sections from Braumoeller and Gaines's article "Actions Do Speak Louder than Words: Deterring Plagiarism with the Use of Plagiarism-Detection Software"
5	UIUC plagiarism policy	UIUC's Academic Integrity Policy for All Students, the university's official policy on plagiarism (without endnotes)

In June 2003 I ran five documents through each plagiarism detection service, as well as segments of these documents through Google. These documents comprise a variety of subject areas and document types to represent the range of sources from which writers might plagiarize. To test the types of documents students might hand in as part of their academic course work, the first two documents include examples of texts representative of the various discourse communities in the university environment. Documents for tests 3, 4, and 5 are examples of texts published by professionals to test how the plagiarism detection services and Google respond to such documents. The tested documents are described in Table 1.

Table 2. Test Methodology

Service	***Procedure***	***Reason***
EduTie	Each document was run once.	Searches are not customizable.
EVE2	Each document was run twice: • For the first run, the default options were used: search type was set as medium and "Call off the hounds when . . ." was set at 80 percent.[4] • For the second run, documents for tests 1, 2, 3, and 5 were rerun (EVE2 traced the document for test 4 directly to its online source and designated it as 100 percent plagiarized on medium), upgrading the search type to full strength to check whether EVE2 would determine the documents to be 100 percent plagiarized on a stronger setting.	In EVE2 there are several user options. Users can set the search type to quick, medium, or full strength and can set the option "Call off the hounds when . . ." to any whole number from 0–100 percent. The former determines the rigor of the test; that is, how many Web sites are examined and in what depth, and the latter determines at what percentage of plagiarism the search stops; that is, when the selected percentage of a submitted document is determined to be plagiarized, the search ceases.
Google	The first ten words of a section of a plagiarized document were entered for a search. For tests 1, 4, and 5, the first ten words of the multiple sections of each of the documents were tested.	Google allows a user to type in only ten words for a search; thus, the entire documents were not searched.

The methodology used for testing each of these documents differed slightly with each service, based on the services' different technical capabilities. The procedures followed are summarized in Table 2.

The following discussion of results centers on whether the tested services traced the submitted documents to their online sources and, for EVE2 and EduTie, to what extent (i.e., what percentage of) these documents were considered plagiarized—noting that all, except the student paper in test 2 that had only slight variations from its online source, were exact copies of online sources. In what follows I also address what online sources the submitted documents were traced to and consider the time required for each test. The report submitted to LAS not only outlined the performance of each service and compared the results across services, but also included an annotated list of resources on plagiarism for instructors interested in learning more about plagiarism.

Free versus Fee: Google's Capabilities as a Plagiarism Detection Service

Based on the results of the tests, I suggested the center not recommend that LAS advocate the purchase of EduTie, EVE2, or any such plagiarism detection service. While EduTie performed the best of all services tested, neither it nor EVE2 performed appreciably better than Google. Because Google, a free service for end users, generally performed on par with these fee-based services, there is no obvious advantage in purchasing them. Moreover, these fee-based services appear to cause more problems than they solve. The results of the tests are summarized in Table 3.

When Google found source sites, it found them within its first ten results five out of seven times, challenging the notion that using an online search engine is necessarily a more time-consuming endeavor than using plagiarism detection software. For the other two, section 4 of the test 1 document and the test 4 document, Google found the sources on the thirtieth and fifteenth entries, respectively. Although these results indicate that users would have to read through many search results before finding the correct source, it is worth noting that results from the medium-strength test and full-strength test runs on EVE2 were available after approximately fifty minutes and two hours and fifteen minutes, respectively, and results for EduTie were available after ap-

Table 3. Comparison of Results Across Services[5]

Test	*EduTie*	*EVE2*	*Google*
1	Sources found for sections 1, 2, and 4, not for section 3; plagiarism score 100 percent	Sources found for sections 1, 2, and 4, not for section 3; plagiarism score 100 percent	Sources found for sections 1, 2, and 4, not for section 3
2	Source found; plagiarism score 84 percent	Paper found at paper mills other than the source suspected to be copied from; plagiarism score 18.85 percent	Source found
3	Source found; plagiarism score 100 percent	Source not found	Source found
4	Source found; plagiarism score 100 percent	Source found; plagiarism score 100 percent	Source found on search of conclusions section
5	Source found; plagiarism score 100 percent	Closely related sites found, but not the original source	Closely related sites found, but not the original source

proximately twenty-four hours. Searches on Google provide nearly instantaneous results; thus, using Google can ultimately yield faster results, as instructors can begin checking sites within seconds. For this study Google traced plagiarized documents to their online sources more quickly for the tests, even counting the time it took to read through the search result entries. In the end, all services require instructors to check the Web sites provided as results to ensure they match the paper submitted for the test.

Especially notable in considering the results of this study is that other studies of plagiarism detection services do not consider online search engines. Sources that argue for the value of plagiarism detection software (e.g., Culwin and Lancaster 2000; Braumoeller and Gaines 2001; Gillis and Rockwell-Kincanon 2002) typically do not consider the potential of free search engines to provide comparable benefits to plagiarism detection software. Based on this study, such search engines, namely Google, yield benefits similar to the fee-based services. Even Braumoeller and Gaines (2001) turned to an Internet search engine to track down "an article that was particularly difficult to find" in their study of EVE2, suggesting that the Internet search engine proved more effective than EVE2 in this instance. Why, then, has scholarship advocating the use of plagiarism detection services not addressed free search engines?

Serving the Hand that Feeds You: A Potential Link between Plagiarism Detection Services and Online Paper Mills

After completing the tests I discovered that EduTie maintains copies of submitted papers on their server, which — though they claim these papers are accessible only to the submitting institution — is an intellectual property concern. An even greater concern, however, is elaborated in Jeffrey Young's March 2002 *Chronicle of Higher Education* article, which raises questions about EduTie's relationship with online paper mills. Young alleges that EduTie and PlagiServe, at the time a less comprehensive version of EduTie with the same parent company, have a business relationship with some online paper mills, which he suggests indicates these services are "secretly selling the very papers that they claim to check" (2002). Young traced the name of Oleksiy Shevchenko, a prominent official with EduTie and PlagiServe, to Cyber Breeze Networks, a company that operates several online paper mills: www.mightystudents.com, www.essaymill.com, and www.essaysonfile.com. While EduTie vehemently denies the charge that it is connected to any online paper mills, the possibility of such a connection is still troubling. This allegation raises additional questions about the appropriateness of EduTie as a plagiarism detection service, reinforcing that an endorsement of such a service would potentially risk, even if indirectly, supporting the existence of such paper-selling services.

The Weakness of Full Strength: Concerns over Consistency and Functionality of Multiple Runs of EVE2

While EVE2 does not raise the same ethical concerns as EduTie, EVE2's performance raises other functional concerns. EVE2's performance across multiple runs, though consistent overall, still shows disconcerting inconsistencies in the Web sites identified as potential sources. Although the results of the medium- and full-strength runs of EVE2 were not markedly different, the program nevertheless computed differing percentages of plagiarism and referenced additional and/or different Web sites. For the first two tests, the percentages of the documents determined to be plagiarized on the full-strength test are lower than those from the medium test (92.18 percent and 15.78 percent versus 100 percent and 18.85 percent, respectively); thus, when run at full strength EVE2 found a lesser percentage of these documents to be plagiarized, even though all (except the test 2 document) were copied word for word from their online sources. In other words, they were 100 percent plagiarized. So on full strength, EVE2 became less accurate in its determination of the amount of the documents that was plagiarized. The 100-percent value returned on the medium test, however, is also problematic. EVE2 (like EduTie) labeled the document from test 1 as 100 percent plagiarized, though it did not trace the third section to any Web sites. The amount of the document labeled as plagiarized, therefore, does not reflect the actual results provided by EVE2. EVE2 did not find the third section to be plagiarized: it did not trace this section to its online source, so its designation of the document as 100 percent plagiarized does not coincide with EVE2's actual performance.

The Web sites EVE2 returned as results were also sometimes quite different on multiple runs, particularly for the test 5 document. On full strength EVE2 traced the UIUC plagiarism policy to seven Web sites, only one the same as on the medium test (see below for more details). Additionally, on full strength EVE2 traced the test 2 document to one of the same Web sites as on medium, but to only that source, while medium traced it to three potential sources. What remained consistent, however, was that EVE2 was still unable to trace to their online sources section 3 of the test 1 document (the section on electromagnetics) and the University of Illinois president letter for test 3. More surprising, on the full-strength test EVE2 actually performed worse than on the medium test. On full strength EVE2 did not trace section 1 of the test 1 document to any Web site, whereas it did trace this section to the Academic Library online paper mill on medium. For the purposes of this study, then, increasing EVE2's testing strength did not yield more accurate results.

Also of particular note, both in terms of differing performance on multiple tests and in terms of the content of the test 5 document, on the full-strength test EVE2 traced UIUC's plagiarism policy to the plagiarism or academic integrity policies of several other universities, including Elmhurst College; California State University at Northridge; and Rutgers University at New Brunswick, which acknowledges that some of its material is drawn from Northwestern University. On the medium test, EVE2 traced UIUC's plagiarism policy to Rogers State University in Oklahoma. Even more fascinating, EVE2 determined the amount of UIUC's plagiarism policy to be plagiarized as 100 percent, which means that, according to EVE2, this document on plagiarism is itself 100 percent plagiarized. In his May 2003 *Chronicle of Higher Education* article, Dan Carnevale addresses a similarly provocative discovery: an article from *Syllabus* magazine written about online plagiarism appears to have been plagiarized from an online journal article, even if inadvertently. I am not arguing that UIUC's plagiarism policy is plagiarized. Instead I wish to point out that EVE2 suggests this possibility, which both draws attention to the potential for unintentional and perhaps inevitable borrowing of language,[6] especially at the institutional level, and, even more important, calls into question the veracity of the results of plagiarism detection services.[7]

Before we advocate the use of plagiarism detection technology to check if our students' papers are plagiarized, we should consider how these services treat the very policies that compel some people to use them. Their results should not be considered ironclad proof for accusation. We must pay careful attention to what these services designate as plagiarized because the technology is fallible. As with any technology, plagiarism detection technology requires human application and interpretation. As Gail E. Hawisher and Cynthia L. Selfe (1991: 64) remind us, positive change in the classroom requires human effort, not new technology. Plagiarism detection technology is not the solution to eradicating plagiarism. Thoughtful pedagogy addressing plagiarism is.

Implications for Defining Plagiarism and the Role of the Instructor

While blatant and intentional cheating should certainly be prevented and punished, the above results illustrate a need to revise our notions of plagiarism. Concerns of plagiarism are often disproportionately focused on students, positing that they are the only group (or at least the group most) guilty of plagiarism. Brian Martin (1994: 38–40) challenges such a view, exploring how current conceptions of plagiarism ignore what he calls "institutionalized plagiarism," which includes ghostwriting, honorary authorship, and attribution of authorship to higher officials in bureaucracies rather than the more novice workers who actually do the writing. He addresses how discussions of plagiarism nearly always focus on what he calls "competitive plagiarism," which includes word-for-word plagiarism, paraphrasing plagiarism, plagiarism of secondary sources, plagiarism of the form of a source, and plagiarism of authorship (37–38)—that is, the types of plagiarism of which students are accused. For Martin such plagiarism is often inadvertent and ultimately less serious than institutionalized plagiarism, which he argues is "pervasive and accepted" (38), even though it is more objectionable since it reinforces existing problematic power structures and reduces the accountability of subordinates who actually do the work because their work goes unrecognized (40–42). Andrea Abernethy Lunsford (1999: 532) extends Martin's claim here to address the problems of "corporate entities now assume[ing] the mantle of the 'author.'" She expresses alarm that large corporations now claim the rights of single authors—not only for the reasons Martin addresses, but also because such corporations come to reap the financial rewards that are due individuals and this "trend has resulted in a kind of 'gold-rush' mentality to copyright and patent everything under the sun."

The coverage of Blair Hornstine's case illustrates Martin's point. Though Hornstine is accused of plagiarizing President Bill Clinton's 17 November 2000 Thanksgiving Proclamation, for example, nowhere in articles covering this allegation is it addressed that Clinton likely did not write his own Thanksgiving Proclamation; speechwriters prepared it. In Martin's terms, Hornstine's commission of competitive plagiarism is seen as more egregious than Clinton's commission of institutionalized plagiarism. For Martin plagiarism is seemingly above all a hierarchical issue: plagiarism is acceptable when it harms subordinates or benefits superiors but unacceptable when it benefits subordinates or hurts superiors. From this perspective there exists a double standard surrounding plagiarism, one imbricated in a hierarchical society that situates students as a subordinate lower class. Ultimately, Martin proposes less attention be paid to competitive plagiarism and more attention be paid to institutionalized plagiarism, thus reminding us that accusations of plagiarism leveled at students might sometimes reflect writing practices espoused by professionals and, therefore, should be cause for reflection.

Gitelman's (1999: 74) rhetorical analysis of what she calls Thomas Edison's "idea letters," letters sent to Edison to offer suggestions and/or ask for help in developing an idea into an invention, provides further insight into current conceptualizations of plagiarism around which students are punished. She focuses on how authors of these letters treat an idea as a possessable entity, something one has or owns: "Writers perceived ideas as property, private and personal, with little sense of collectivity" (81). The same might be said of higher education's treatment of ideas today. This denial of collectivity still exists within academia (especially the humanities), where written papers—particularly those with the most significance (e.g., tenure publications, dissertations, theses)—must have single authors, reflecting a belief that only one person can lay claim to and own the ideas in a paper.[8] Ideas are framed as necessarily "private and personal," the possession of a sole author. This perspective seems somewhat ironic, if not disjunctive, given that many of us in our composition and literature classes require students to complete peer reviews for their papers to help them further develop their ideas. Lisa Ede and Andrea Lunsford (1990) explore at length the role of collaborative authorship in academia (and elsewhere) in their *Singular Texts/Plural Authors*. They conclude their preface by declaring, "Our ability to author anything at all is anchored in our experiences with others" (xii). This conclusion is seemingly lost in prominent conceptions of plagiarism.

Such a view of the singular ownership of ideas is clearly illustrated in the response displayed by clicking on one of the Web sites EduTie returned as a result of the test 2 document, the plagiarized student paper. EduTie returned the address lugovkyys@lakeland.edu (though this looks like an e-mail address, it was returned as a Web link, perhaps another problematic quirk of the program) as the source for the third sentence of the test 2 document, but access to this source was denied. Clicking on this link brought a page displaying the message "You do NOT own this paper!" Belief in the individual ownership of ideas as recorded in written documents clearly continues to predominate.

Yet the documents advancing and enforcing this belief are themselves collaboratively authored. Gitelman (1999: 111) addresses the somewhat ironic fact that a patent document, a foundational document in establishing current conceptions of plagiarism, does not have just one author. Rather, the inventor, his or her attorney, and the patent office itself all author the patent document. The actual authorship of the patent document belies the very logic of singular authorship on which it is based. Plagiarism detection software operates in much the same way. While purportedly seeking to combat "collaborative" authorship, plagiarism detection software itself depends on such collaborative authorship. In fact, for those services that maintain submitted student papers on a remote server, the very textual foundation that allows these services to operate has multiple authors. Thus, in practice, these services engage in a version of the very behavior they claim to abhor and combat.

For Karla Saari Kitalong (1998: 255) the uncritical application of the "print-oriented construct of plagiarism" to online spaces is particularly problematic. Following Pierre Bourdieu, she conceptualizes plagiarism as "symbolic violence" because it involves the perpetrator falsely appropriating someone else's linguistic capital, which may in turn lead to social and/or cultural capital (256–57) (in the example she cites, a journalism student named Dave copies the home page of Craig to turn in for a course assignment—that is, to achieve a certain form of cultural capital: a grade). At the same time, she stresses that the standard academic notion of plagiarism "clashes" (253) with online writing spaces that must allow for "uncertainty" and change in conceptions of writing (262). Dànielle DeVoss and Annette C. Rosati (2002: 196) further develop this point that online writing spaces change the definition of text by emphasizing how online texts "include sound and integrate visuals in ways that allow for more complex and fragmented presentation of connections, topics, and representations within richly layered systems." So while new technologies are changing what constitutes text, some people are employing these new technologies to hold texts to intellectual property standards that rely on print-based definitions of text. This changing definition of textuality does not mean that attributing authorship no longer matters and that multimedia texts are plunderable at will, but it does mean that notions of plagiarism and intellectual property need to evolve along with this technology.

Kitalong (1998: 260) cautions against "responding to the violence of plagiarism with more violence." For her, the unquestioned application of print-based plagiarism "doxa" to online spaces (260) and use of the Internet "to quickly, invisibly, and oppressively identify and punish suspected plagiarizers" (259) enact such violence, as both "reinforce polarized student/teacher relationships that cast teachers as uncoverers and punishers of plagiarism and place students on the defensive" (260). The use of online plagiarism detection services would seem to be an instance of the latter case. Thus, we might carry Kitalong's application of symbolic violence not only to plagiarism, but also to the use of plagiarism detection software.

Such reflection on the use of plagiarism detection software to combat certain constructs of plagiarism should also address how the use of plagiarism detection software changes the role of the instructor. To return to the EVE2 function title "Call off the hounds," the instructor becomes a hunter or, in friendlier terms, a sleuth or private investigator. In their study, Braumoeller and Gaines (2001) even thank a colleague for her "impressive sleuthing skills" in tracking down an article on the Internet to determine that a student had copied from sources listed in his or her bibliography. In this way, the instructor's goal becomes to find the elusive smoking gun. While the role of sleuth might be appealing when applied to archival research, the position is not appealing when applied to grading. In this role, instructors devote their time to finding what is wrong with students' papers, or, if you will, to finding the scene of the crime, rather than providing substantive, constructive feedback. Focus shifts from the writing process to the investigation of the "crime." Howard (2001) cogently addresses this issue in greater detail. She advocates structuring classes and assignments to prevent plagiarism rather than spending time trying to catch it. For her the latter creates a "criminal-police relationship," where students are labeled as either criminals or not and the complex and multiple meanings of plagiarism are ignored. She insists the role of a teacher is to be a mentor, not a cop.

I agree and would add that neither is the role of a teacher aristocratic hunter or super sleuth — unless perhaps it is to hunt down the most effective pedagogical approach to issues of plagiarism.

Clearly, instructors sometimes consult plagiarism detection services with the best of intentions. They rightly want to make students responsible writers by discouraging them from improperly using the work of others. Those who market these fee-based services present them as easy solutions to a difficult problem, so it is understandable that teachers might be interested in using them. As illustrated above, however, these plagiarism detection services, when used uncritically and as often marketed, are ultimately damaging to teaching and learning. Technology, of course, need not be detrimental to writing instruction. Google and similar Internet search engines can be used for productive pedagogical purposes — for example, to provide students with rapid access to a large variety of sources on a particular topic. The number and type of results Google searches return can also help students work to narrow or broaden a research topic. Perhaps most germane to the discussion here, such technology can assist students in learning how to incorporate source material. For example, search services that provide brief abstracts of results can provide models of effective (or ineffective) summaries against which students can compare their own summaries.

Conclusion: The (In)Visibility of Technology in Issues of Plagiarism

Hornstine's response to the allegations against her is particularly instructive in emphasizing the now undeniable role of technology in plagiarism. In responding to the *Courier-Post* editor's note that she had not attributed others' language included in her articles, she explains: "When finalizing my thoughts, I, like most every teenager who has use of a computer, cut and pasted my ideas together. I erroneously thought the way I had submitted the articles was appropriate. I now realize that I was mistaken. I was incorrect in also thinking that news articles didn't require as strict citation scrutiny as most school assignments because there was no place for footnotes or end notes" (2003). While clearly primary here are issues of genre and appropriate citation conventions, equally prevalent, I would argue, is the role of technology. Hornstine connects her writing practices directly to her use of computer technology, which allowed her to cut and paste her ideas together. How she used the available technology played a crucial role in how she prepared her articles and how she came to use outside sources. In this way, she illuminates how plagiarism is a problem of technology. And she emphasizes that this practice is followed by "most every teenager who has use of a computer." Hornstine is not alone in cutting and pasting from source to text — precisely because word processing and Internet technologies facilitate or, as Hornstine intimates, encourage this practice.

Computer technology has clearly become an integral part of the writing process, shaping how students compose and integrate sources. Because of this foundational role, we must be careful, as Bertram C. Bruce and Maureen P. Hogan (1998: 272) urge, that such technologies do not "become so enmeshed in daily experience that they disappear." Bruce and Hogan further argue that "teachers of literacy must consider how new technologies help to reconstruct reading and writing processes for their students" (271)—including, I would add, how such technologies make visible the practices associated with plagiarism. So rather than panic that students are now rampantly plagiarizing at numbers never known before, we must take a step back to consider the role the writing technologies they use play in their writing processes and consider how we as teachers—rather than hunters, police officers, or super sleuths—can pedagogically address these technologies. After all, isn't our time better spent in the classroom discussing ways to integrate sources beyond simply cutting and pasting from them and investigating the reasons for academic citation conventions, rather than at the computer testing student papers for unattributed language? Directing our attentions this way, of course, is not a magic solution to end plagiarism, but doing so keeps us from responding to plagiarism as an out-of-control plague[9] and keeps us focused on its connection to technology—and on our role as teachers.

The Hornstine case once again exemplifies how responses to plagiarism rely on ways in which technology makes plagiaristic practices visible. Hornstine's reputed plagiarism was made visible by media coverage of her lawsuit to protect her status as sole valedictorian of her high school. Thus she, rather than the potentially many other teenagers who engage in the same cut-and-paste writing practices and were admitted to Harvard, was punished. A recent article in the *New York Times* indicates that 38 percent of undergraduate students from a survey of 18,000 students admitted to engaging in these same cut-and-paste practices, taking material directly from Internet sources (Rimer 2003). This statistic reminds us that Hornstine is likely not the only student admitted to Harvard who cuts and pastes from the Internet. This is not at all to say that intentional plagiarism should go unpunished or that students now plagiarize more than in the past; as I am suggesting, available technology, such as plagiarism detection services, now simply makes cases of plagiarism more easily traceable and detectable. The larger, more crucial issue is understanding what writing practices available technology enables and considering what this technology makes visible so that we in English studies can frame writing instruction around those practices—not simply engage in a quest to use existing technology to punish plagiarizers. We need to be mindful of why we are unleashing the hounds in the first place.

Notes

I am grateful to Debra Hawhee, Gail E. Hawisher, Peter Mortensen, and Paul Prior for their invaluable feedback on the study and drafts of this article. I also wish to thank Amy Wan and Jody Shipka for pointing me to sources that proved important for this article. Finally, I am thankful to two anonymous reviewers for their insightful comments and suggestions.

1. It is particularly telling that this issue of plagiarism comes up at all in articles that are really about a student suing to defend her position as sole valedictorian of her high school. As Rebecca Moore Howard (2000: 475–85) suggests in her discussion of how plagiarism is constructed as a distinctly female violation, the fact that Hornstine is a woman undoubtedly played a significant role in the media blitz surrounding Hornstine's reputed plagiarism and Harvard's reaction to it. Furthermore, the shift in coverage of Hornstine to accusations of plagiarism speaks to the tabloid appeal of plagiarism and illustrates how plagiarism is often more about publicity than pedagogy. Articles about the allegations of plagiarism against Hornstine even appeared in international newspapers, including London's *Guardian* (Sutherland 2003). Would the story have been this popular had it just been about the valedictorian lawsuit?
2. EduTie no longer exists under this name. The services previously offered by EduTie are now (as of summer 2004) offered by a service titled MyDropBox. Little appears to have changed other than the name. This change in name is particularly interesting given the allegations surrounding EduTie's connection with online paper mills.
3. At the time the tests were run, it was unclear from its promotional materials whether EduTie maintains students' papers in any internal database. Assuming that it did not, I tested this service. Correspondence received from EduTie dated 28 June 2003, however, indicates that papers submitted to the service are maintained, albeit with reputed limited accessibility: "Submitted papers are maintained on the server, but they are accessible only for the institution (or individual user) that submitted them. Also, documents submitted by an institution are checked against all prior submissions of this institution" (Lytvyn 2003, e-mail correspondence). Given this treatment of submitted documents, which makes student papers accessible not only to the submitting institution but also to computer systems administrators and company personnel, the appropriateness of using EduTie as a plagiarism detection service is questionable.
4. In practice, selecting this "Call off the hounds when . . ." value seemed to have no noticeable effect on the search process. Some documents were still determined to be 100 percent plagiarized.
5. The results provided in Table 3 are for the medium-strength test of EVE2 because they represent the service's best performance.
6. After all, Mikhail Bakhtin (1986: 89–94) stresses that all utterances—including texts—are influenced by all previous utterances that an author has encountered (and future utterances that the author anticipates). From

this perspective, repetition in future texts of language from texts previously read is, to a certain extent, inevitable.

7. With all of its results, EVE2 appropriately provides the notice, "You should always check EVE's results carefully to make sure they are accurate." For results where the amount of the document detected to be plagiarized is below 15 percent, the caveat is even more emphatic: "Because plagiarism on this paper is below 15 percent, please check these results carefully to make sure plagiarism has in fact occurred." Particularly interesting, though, is that the threshold for greater concern that a document has actually been plagiarized is only 15 percent.
8. Andrea Lunsford (Lunsford et al. 1996) eloquently summarizes this issue when she declares that in the academy, individual "ownership of intellectual property is the key to advancement."
9. See Howard's "Sexuality, Textuality: The Cultural Work of Plagiarism" (2000) for more on the connection between plagiarism and disease.

Works Cited

Bakhtin, Mikhail. 1986. "The Problem of Speech Genres." In *Speech Genres and Other Late Essays*, ed. Caryl Emerson and Michael Holquist, trans. Vern W. McGee, 60–103. Austin: University of Texas Press.

Braumoeller, Bear, and Brian Gaines. 2001. "Actions Do Speak Louder than Words: Deterring Plagiarism with the Use of Plagiarism-Detection Software." *Political Science Online*, APSANet, December. www.apsanet.org/PS/dec01/braumoeller.cfm (accessed 11 June 2003).

Brown, Louise. 2004. "McGill Teen Wins Battle over Online Cheat Check." *Toronto Star*, 13 February. www.thestar.com/NASApp/cs/ContentServer?pagename=thestar/Layout/Article_Typet&c=Article&cid=1074208210446&call_pageid=968332188492&col=96 (accessed 13 February 2004).

Bruce, Bertram C., and Maureen P. Hogan. 1998. "The Disappearance of Technology: Toward an Ecological Model of Literacy." In *Handbook of Literacy and Technology: Transformations in a Post-Typographic World*, ed. David Reinking, Michael C. McKenna, Linda D. Labbo, and Ronald D. Kiffer, 269–81. Mahwah, NJ: Lawrence Erlbaum.

Carnevale, Dan. 2003. "Magazine's Essay on Plagiarism Appears to Have Copied Parts of Another." *Chronicle of Higher Education*, 28 May. chronicle.com/daily/2003/05/2003052801t.htm (accessed 1 July 2003).

"Cheaters Amok: A Crisis in America's Schools—How It's Done and Why It's Happening." 2004. *Primetime Thursday*, 29 April. Narr. Charles Gibson, dir. George Paul, prod. Shelley Ross, writ. Charles Gibson and Chris Whipple. ABC, WAND. Champaign, IL.

Chester, Gill. 2003. "Detection Technology." Joint Information Systems Committee. online.northumbria.ac.uk/faculties/art/information_studies/Imri/JISCPAS/site/pubs_detect_pilot.asp (accessed 10 June 2003).

Culwin, Fintan, and Thomas Lancaster. 2000. "A Review of Electronic Services for Plagiarism Detection in Student Submissions." www.ics.ltsn.ac.uk/pub/conf2000/Papers/culwin.htm (accessed 11 June 2003).

DeVoss, Dànielle, and Annette C. Rosati. 2002. "'It Wasn't Me, Was It?' Plagiarism and the Web." *Computers and Composition* 19:191–203.

Ede, Lisa, and Andrea Lunsford. 1990. *Singular Texts / Plural Authors: Perspectives on Collaborative Writing*. Carbondale: Southern Illinois University Press.

Foster, Andrea L. 2002. "Plagiarism-Detection Tool Creates Legal Quandary: When Professors Send Students' Papers to a Database, Are Copyrights Violated?" *Chronicle of Higher Education*, 17 May, A37.

Gillis, Theresa, and Janeanne Rockwell-Kincanon. 2002. "From Download Your Workload to the Evil House of Cheat: Cybercheating, Plagiarism, and Intellectual Property Theft." Cybercheating: Online Northwest: Comparison of Detection Services, 29 August. www.wou.edu/provost/library/staff/kincanon/plagiarism/chart.htm (accessed 11 June 2003).

Gitelman, Lisa. 1999. *Scripts, Grooves, and Writing Machines: Representing Technology in the Edison Era*. Stanford, CA: Stanford University Press.

Green, Elizabeth W., and J. Hale Russell. 2003. "Harvard Takes Back Hornstine Admission Offer: Decision Follows Allegations of Plagiarism by Controversial Admit." *Harvard Crimson Online*, 11 July. www.thecrimson.com/article.aspx?ref=348498 (accessed 29 August 2003).

Hawisher, Gail E., and Cynthia L. Selfe. 1991. "The Rhetoric of Technology and the Electronic Writing Class." *College Composition and Communication* 42:55–65.

Hornstine, Blair. 2003. [Untitled.] *Courier-Post*, 3 June, www.courierpostonline.com/static/sto60303g.html (accessed 29 August 2003).

Howard, Rebecca Moore. 1995. "Plagiarisms, Authorships, and the Academic Death Penalty." *College English* 57:788–806.

———. 2000. "Sexuality, Textuality: The Cultural Work of Plagiarism." *College English* 62:473–91.

———. 2001. "Forget about Policing Plagiarism. Just Teach." *Chronicle of Higher Education*, 16 November. chronicle.com/weekly/v48/i12/12b02401.htm (accessed 1 July 2003).

———. 2007. "Understanding 'Internet Plagiarism.'" *Computers and Composition*.

Kantrowitz, Barbara, and Julie Scelfo. 2003. "Harvard to Hornstine: No Way." *Newsweek*, 21 July, 50.

Kitalong, Karla Saari. 1998. "A Web of Symbolic Violence." *Computers and Composition* 15:253–64.

Laird, Ellen. 2001. "Internet Plagiarism: We All Pay the Price." *Chronicle of Higher Education*, 13 July. chronicle.com/weekly/v47/i44/44b00501.htm (accessed 1 July 2003).

Lunsford, Andrea Abernethy. 1999. "Rhetoric, Feminism, and the Politics of Textual Ownership." *College English* 61:529–44.

Lunsford, Andrea, Rebecca Rickly, Michael J. Salvo, and Susan West. 1996. "What Matters Who Writes? What Matters Who Responds? Issues of Ownership in the Writing Classroom." *Kairos: A Journal for Teachers of Writing in Webbed Environments* 1.1.english.tta.edu/kairos/1.1/features/Lunsford.html (accessed 12 July 2004).

Lynn, Andrea. 2003. "Parrying Plagiarism: Professors Show How New 'Weapons' Can Curb Cheating." *LAS News* (Spring):1.

Lytvyn, Max. 2003. "RE: question." E-mail to the author, 28 June.

Martin, Brian. 1994. "Plagiarism: A Misplaced Emphasis." *Journal of Information Ethics* 3.2:36–47.

Osenenko, Derek. 2003. "Stories, Essays Lacked Attribution." *Courier-Post*, 3 June. www.courierpostonline.com/static/st060303g.html (accessed 29 August 2003).

Rimer, Sara. 2003. "A Campus Fad That's Being Copied: Internet Plagiarism." *New York Times*, 3 Sept. nytimes.com/2003/09/03/education/03CHEA.html (accessed 3 September 2003).

Sutherland, John. 2003. "Clever Girl Destroyed: Blair Hornstine Was the Pride of Moorestown High—But Her Brilliant Career Was Too Good to Be True." *Guardian*, 21 July. www.guardian.co.uk/g2/story/0,,1002231,00.html (accessed 29 August 2003).

Young, Jeffrey R. 2002. "Anti-Plagiarism Experts Raise Questions about Services with Links to Sites Selling Papers." *Chronicle of Higher Education*, 12 March. Chronicle.com/free/2002/03/2002031201t.htm (accessed 28 June 2003).

Purdy's Insights as a Resource for Your Reflections

1. Rather than simply stating a policy against plagiarism in your syllabus, consider teaching students about how to avoid it as part of a larger lesson on intertextuality, how texts often originate, at least in part, in other texts, and how becoming a good writer means becoming adept at using the writings of others in a way that is both fair and empowering. How might you develop a unit that engages these possibilities? How might it include practice in quoting, summarizing, paraphrasing, alluding, and other strategies for positioning one's own text among others?
2. How might you link Purdy's ideas to those earlier in this chapter from Rose or Berthoff or others?

Purdy's Insights as a Resource for Your Writing Classroom

1. Offer your students several examples of artists or writers making use of the work of their peers or colleagues, some of which are guilty of plagiarism, others of which aren't, and, most important, some of which constitute ambiguous cases. Then have the students lead a discussion about which ones are problems and which ones aren't and why, and what's at stake.

When Blogging Goes Bad: A Cautionary Tale about Blogs, Email Lists, Discussion, and Interaction[1]

Steven D. Krause

How might the latest development in our cyberculture — "blogging" — enhance your writing classroom? Krause offers a cautionary tale, a story of one way that it won't. In this essay, which originally developed as a blog and appeared electronically at <http://english.ttu.edu/kairos/9.1/praxis/krause/>, Krause tells the story of how blogging backfired in his course and how e-mail, a considerably older technology in our mercurially evolving technocracy, emerged as a useful corrective. Krause, however, concludes that blogs "aren't all bad" and offers a direction for further experimentation.

Introduction

Like email and the World Wide Web in their times, blogs have become the "killer app" of the moment. Three years ago, all but the most hard-core of followers of Internet phenomenons would not have thought much of the term "blog," other than perhaps it was a misspelling of "blob." Now you know you are most certainly not a mainstream Internet user if you are unaware that "blog" is an adaptation of the term "Web Log," and that blogs exist as personal journals, professional writing spaces, news sources, or some combination of all of the above.

In their short history (Rebecca Blood pegs the beginning of sites we recognize as blogs as about 1998), blogs have been labeled as a form of "new journalism," and they have been a part of the news coverage of the war in Iraq (see, for example, "Where Is Raed?" at http://dearraed.blogspot.com/, and the March 29, 2003 NPR "Weekend Edition" story "News by Web Log"). As reported on NPR's "All Things Considered" on July 28, 2003, blogs were instrumental in democratic candidate Howard Dean's fund raising efforts, though not as important in his fall from political grace. Even Dear Abby (actually, the daughter of the original Abby) has weighed in on proper blog conduct.

Writing Teachers Using Blogs

And, of course, composition and rhetoric specialists have started to use blogs for their classes. For example, the students in Derek Mueller's Winter 2004 section of "Writing Purposes and Research" at Park University are writing in this blog space. Mueller's syllabus makes clear that from the third week of the class on, students are expected to post four times a week. As is evident by her links to "Class blogs" on her own blog space, Samantha Blackmon is using blogs as part of the class discussion for her classes at Purdue University. And then there are the numerous examples of weblogs developed primarily for writing classes at Joe Moxley's Writing Blogs space. Quite literally, hundreds of different blogs are hosted via Moxley's site, most presumably having to do with various types of writing and composition courses.

Clearly, the role of blogs in different writing classes varies considerably. However, a quick glance through these examples (especially Mueller's and Blackmon's) would suggest that many writing teachers seem to be using blog spaces as places to facilitate dynamic and interactive writing experiences. This approach to the use of blogs is consistent with what at least some advocates of weblogs in educational settings have suggested for a while now. In their *T.H.E. Journal Online* essay "Content Delivery in the 'Blogosphere,'" Richard E. Ferdig and Kaye D. Trammell claim that the benefits of blogs in classrooms include giving students a "legitimate" space to participate in discussions and to share diverse perspectives with readers in and outside of the classroom. Ferdig and Trammell argue that, "While blogging, students quickly learn that posted content can be read by those other than the teacher and their classmates. Blogging opens up assignments beyond the teacher-student relationship, allowing the world to grade students and provide encouragement or feedback on their writings." In a December 2003 "Talk at Brown" University, well-known blog writer Jill Walker suggested that blogs are one important way to "teach our students . . . *network* literacy: writing in a distributed, collaborative environment."

I am as excited about the uses of blogs in my own writing and teaching as any of these other innovators. But after a failed experiment in teaching with blogs, I have begun to wonder if it is advisable or even possible to see blogs as a collaborative or especially "interactive" writing environment.[2] Or, more accurately, I've come to believe we shouldn't substitute blogs for other electronic writing tools that foster discussion and interactive writing, particularly email lists, commonly known as "listservs."

What This Is All About

This text, which has grown out of my own experiences and a presentation I gave at the 2003 Computers and Writing Conference, offers a reason and a way to **NOT** use blogs in the writing classroom. Blogs certainly have a place in writing classes, and I discuss one such example in my concluding entry for this essay/blog. But I still see the dynamic and conversational exchange made possible by a rather "old fashioned" electronic writing genre, email — specifically, an electronic mailing list discussion — as uniquely valuable in writing classes. In fact, as I think my example of blogging gone bad demonstrates, I think my students' return to email as a discussion forum resulted in a reborn sense of collaboration and interaction.

Beginnings of My "Bad Example"

The source of my bad blogging example was a graduate seminar called "Rhetoric and Culture of Cyberspace." While it was a course part of Eastern Michigan University's "Teaching of Writing" MA program, our readings and discussions approached the idea of "cyberspace" from a lot of different directions: computers and the Internet of course, but also contemporary media, technical innovation in everyday life, technology and security/counter-terrorism efforts, and so forth. Most of the course work and course grade focused on fairly traditional assignments — a seminar paper, a book review presentation and essay, and a final.

The collaboratively written blog space was a small part of the class and described from the beginning as an "experiment" for me as a teacher. I thought the collaborative writing experience would be best if the groups were relatively small and if the subjects of the student writing spaces were not merely a response to the assigned reading. So, toward the end of our first class meeting, we brainstormed on the general topics of the blog spaces and then formed three collaborative groups each made up of four or five students. Their loosely defined subjects/topics for their different blog spaces were "Cyber-Communication," "Cyber-Terrorism/War/Surveillance," and "Cyber-Media." On this first night of class, I also introduced students to blogger.com and blogspot, the popular ad-based blog software/server we used for this project.

When I described this project as "an experiment," I meant just that. This is what I wrote in the course description which is available on the class web site:

> You may be wondering "what will this project look like?" and "what is he expecting from us here?" Quite honestly, I'm not completely sure yet. This is the first time I've tried this assignment, so when I describe it as an "experimental" writing assignment, I mean it. We will have to see how it goes. All I ask is that you give this experiment a chance by staying involved with it, that you be willing to take some chances, and that you remain open-minded.

Hindsight

I need to acknowledge three issues that, in hindsight, helped to make this blogging exercise turn out badly. First, we used blogger because it is extremely easy and it does not require any sort of server access (if using the blogspot option). It does support collaborative writing to the extent that blog writers can "invite" other users permission to post on the blog, but this project may have been more effective had I used a different blog-type option that better facilitated collaborative writing.

Second, this assignment did not have any specific requirements in terms of the number of postings, the subject of the postings, or just about anything else. While we set up subject groups on the first day of class, this was a quick and somewhat haphazard exercise, and I tried to make it clear that students were more than welcome to drift away from this initial focus.

Now, it's clear in hindsight that I could have headed off both of these problems had I pointed students to an example of a successful collaborative blog like Kairos News or Crooked Timber. However, I didn't do that at the time, in part because it simply didn't occur to me then, and in part because I wanted this assignment to be as "open-ended" as possible. I was unsure what the results of the assignment were going to be and because of that, I wanted the students' blog spaces to evolve more "organically" than they would have had I established more strict requirements.

Third and most important for my purposes here, the blog spaces were the only element of the class that was a full-fledged "electronic discussion." While there was a class electronic mailing list, one that figures prominently into my discussion here in a moment, there wasn't a specific requirement or expectation that students would post messages on the mailing list. The list was **supposed** to serve as a class housekeeping device where I would post updates to the evolving class activities and where students could post links or announcements of their own. The discussion and interaction was **supposed** to take place on the blogs.

Failure, Part I: Bad Blog Writing

As of August 2004, the class blog spaces are still up and running and available if you follow the links on the class homepage, though some of the archives were no longer functioning. Perhaps my expectations were too high, but I thought the blogs turned out poorly. Some students posted repeatedly, while other students barely posted at all. The amount of text per posting varied considerably. While there were times in which some students wrote longer messages, more often than not, the posts were short, merely links to other documents, or text that was "cut and pasted" from another source. There was very little writing that could be described as reflective, dynamic, collaborative, or interactive. There was almost no exchange or conversation between posters, and no "themed" group writing project emerged from any of the blogs, which was one of the goals of the assignment. It wasn't even clear if the students were reading other posts. Individuals made their posts in an erratic and inconsistent manner, and then they moved on.

In other words, the experiment failed.

Failure, Part II: Defining a Desire/Need to Write/Blog

Certainly, much of the failure of this assignment can be traced to its open-ended nature. As I already said, I purposefully gave my students minimal directions with this project because I didn't know what we would come up with (after all, I hadn't attempted blogging in my teaching before), but also because they were grad students (i.e., "grown-ups") and I thought in less need of the forced motivation by assignment than some of my undergraduate classes. I also thought that the blog technology very much called for this sort of open-ended and unformed writing assignment. My goal was to create an opportunity/space where my students would simply *just want to write*.

But what I found is my "open-ended" non-assignment translated into "vagueness."

Maybe I should have known before I began that this wasn't going to work, but I was disappointed that my students didn't "just write," if given the opportunity. I still feel a bit disappointed, actually. Every once in a while, in conference presentations or in essays in journals like *Kairos*, someone idealistically suggests that writing teachers ought to focus on fostering and nurturing an atmosphere where students can "learn" instead of being "taught," where students can write not because they are being *required* to do so by some sort of "teacherly" assignment but because they want to write, where students aren't *required* to write old-fashioned essays, but where they can create and explore new forms. And so forth.

Well, in the nutshell, that's what I felt I tried, and, in the nutshell, it didn't work. And when I talked with my students about this, they more or less said that they needed the direction of a teacherly assignment to write, and they weren't going to "just want to write" in a blog space (or anywhere else, for that matter) just because they were given the opportunity. Perhaps this is common sense, but it is a piece of common sense I think is too often forgotten in ideas about fostering student writing in general, and fostering student writing with various computer tools like blogs.

Students (or anyone else) don't just want to write, and certainly not in a blog space. As Walker puts it in her "Talk at Brown" notes, "How empowering is it to be forced to blog?" And yet, that is ultimately the power and even charm of web logs: it is very easy to master technology and interface in which just about anyone who *wants* to *can* post their writings and thoughts about anything. However, like the paper diaries and journals to which web logs are so often compared, the writer has to have a reason — and generally, a personal reason — to write in the first place.

A "Non-dynamic" Failure

I thought this blog assignment failed most interestingly in its inability to generate a dynamic discussion, particularly in comparison to an emailing list. This is the first class I have taught in a long time in which there was quite a bit of reading and there wasn't some sort of required discussion taking place on an electronic mailing list. In my other advanced writing classes, the mailing list is the place where students talk about the reading before the class, giving the group a starting point for discussion and giving me an idea about where students are "coming from" on the readings. But that wasn't the use of the mailing list for this seminar. In fact, before the events surrounding the Herring essay, there were fewer than two dozen messages sent to the list in three months' worth of class.

Turning Point: Discussion and the Class Emailing List

One of the last assignments I had for the blog groups was to come up with some readings to share with the rest of the class—essentially, I was asking for students to come up with relevant and current readings. One of the groups suggested the Susan Herring essay "Gender Differences in Computer-Mediated Communication: Bringing Familiar Baggage to the New Frontier." Now, I wasn't very happy with this group's choice because while I think the basic premise of the essay is true, I think it's very dated (it was published in 1994) and I think that Herring's approach to issues of gender online is a bit simplistic. At the risk of being reductive myself, her reading is more or less an essentialist one, where men are aggressive and uncooperative and from Mars, and women are kind and cooperative and from Venus. Again, it's not that I completely disagree with her; it's just that I think it's more complicated than what she seems to be suggesting.

We didn't get to talk about the essay in class because we talked about other essays that students had suggested, and without thinking very carefully, I off-handedly and inappropriately referred to it as "that feminist essay" at the close of that night's class. The next morning, I checked my email and found a message posted to the class mailing list from one of the more vocal female students in the class,[3] a post that was made at about 1 o'clock in the morning. She begins by qualifying herself and noting that this wasn't a criticism of me as the teacher, and also by noting that while she considers herself to be a feminist, she didn't want to come across as a "feminazi," so to speak. Then she wrote:

> I just wanted to draw a parallel to the one big article that we did not talk about tonight, just about the only thing this semester that I actually cared to read (which is odd because I'm interested in the topic, hmmm). It's the article that Steve called "the feminist article," the one that Lisa suggested, about gender differences in communication on the internet. I found it quite fascinating and wanted to discuss it tonight. But did I even feel comfortable enough to bring it up? Nope. But I think that it applies as accurately to "The Rhetoric of Cyberspace" as anything else we've read.

She went on to do a reading of the blogs, noting that there was some subtle flaming by the men in the class in the blog spaces, and some of the patterns of communication in the blogs were very much in line with what Herring was talking about in her essay. Finally, she noted that the male dynamics on the blogs ended up appearing again and again in our face-to-face class meetings as well.

As you can imagine, this email opened up quite a discussion, one where just over half the students in the class offered their take on the discussion practices in class and on the blogs, the Herring article, and what this student originally said. The email discussion carried on to the face-to-face meeting the following week, and all of this was done in a more or less polite though pointed and intellectually rigorous way. I found it to be a real turning point for the better in the class because it was the first time during the semester where I thought students fully engaged in the subject matter, and also the first time in which there was a connection between what happened in our face-to-face class meeting discussions and our electronic discussions.

I don't want to dwell on the specifics of this discussion, though it is arguable that it is indeed the specifics of the discussion that motivated this student and thus put this exchange in motion. It's arguable that it was not the mechanism being used or not used, but rather my bad treatment of an article this student was very interested in discussing that got the ball rolling here. However, it is very interesting that the student put this message on the class emailing list and *not* in a blog space.

Email as Discussion Space; Blogs as Publishing Space

My students' email exchange — how it came about and how I think we should understand it — is very much in line with what we have understood the uses and dynamics of email discussions to be for quite a while. As I noted in my 1995 essay "'How Will This Improve Student Writing?' Reflections on an Exploratory Study of Online and Off-line Texts," there were numerous studies in the late 1980's and early 1990's that specifically argued that email discussions fostered dynamic, interactive, and "real" writing activities.

Michael Spitzer suggested in his 1990 essay "Local and global networking: implications for the future" that networked communications could encourage a greater sense of audience by fostering an "online discourse community" where writers and readers are genuinely communicating with each other and see a purpose behind their writing beyond the assignment itself. He argued that because computer networks change the dynamic of the classroom to an interactive and social one, they "have the potential to transform student writing from listless academic drudgery into writing that is purposeful and reader-based" (59).

Gail Hawisher noted in her 1992 essay "Electronic meetings of the minds: research, electronic conferences, and composition studies" that online environments provide "a real and expanded audience" that student writers can return to with minimal restrictions on time and place (86). And in their 1989 article "Computer conferencing and collaborative learning: a discourse community at work," Delores K. Schriner and William C. Rice note that when students posted messages to each other via a computer network, "they knew they had an audience beyond the teacher, and as a result their writing emerged as 'real,' 'volunteered,' even urgent" (475).

There have been refinements over the years in our understandings of the discursive dynamics of email exchanges of course, but the basic premise of these articles (articles that, in computers and writing terms, are "ancient history") is still valid. I would argue that the student posted her message to the class electronic mailing list instead of to a blog space — even though there were very few messages posted to the class emailing list previous to her post — because she intuitively knew that her message would actually reach the "real audience" of the class community. She felt her message was urgent, important, and beyond the realm of an assignment, and that her best option for getting her message to her specific audience was with the class emailing list.

Blogs, on the other hand, do not foster this sort of dynamic discussion as well. The jury is still out, of course — blogs are still quite new, and as I hope I've made clear, my classes' failure with blogs had as much to do with my poor structure of the assignment as it had to do with the technology itself.

Nonetheless, while blogs are interactive and dynamic texts in the sense that there is a dialog between bloggers and their texts, the dialog is not the *literal* sort that is fostered and promoted by email exchanges. Email posts to mailing lists are drafts or works in progress, they are conversational in their direction toward an audience, and more often than not, they demand a literal response. Blog posts are more finished, are more personal in that the audience is the writer as much as it is a potential reader, and while readers might "respond" in some sort of metaphoric way, they are not as likely to write a direct response to the writer. Certainly, blog writers can enable commenting features that allow readers to respond on the writer's post.[4] But even when readers are invited to comment on blogs, they are only allowed to comment on posts initiated by the writer, and the writer can ultimately control who is or isn't allowed to post comments.

Finally, to the extent that collaboration is fostered by the "interaction" and "discussion" characterized by the exchange of ideas and the give and take of a group of writers, I think that email offers a much better opportunity for collaborative writing. After all, blogs are in their most basic sense electronic journals; more often than not, they are spaces for publishing highly individualistic writing.

Deliver and Publish; Discuss and Interact

In the end, I think this student made use of the emailing list in this instance because she understood something about the difference between a blog and an emailing list long before I did. If you have a piece of writing that you want to "deliver" or "publish" as a more or less finished text, put it on a blog. If you have something to say to a particular audience in order to enter into a discussion with them, put it on a mailing list.

Blogs Are "Individualistic" Rather than "Collaborative"

Blogs do not work well as a facilitator of dynamic discussion and interaction between members of a specific discourse community (a writing class, for example), and my point here has been that, in terms of writing pedagogy, they do not have the truly interactive or "collaborative" writing potential of an electronic mailing list.

I suppose though that much of this depends on what one means by "collaboration." For example, in his essay "Blogs and wikis: environments for on-line collaboration," Bob Goodwin-Jones speaks of the collaborative potentials of a variety of different asynchronous and synchronous technologies. I don't disagree with his general descriptions of the uses and values of these technologies. However, as he describes blogs, I do question the extent to which the writing done in these spaces is highly "collaborative." Goodwin-Jones writes:

> Blogs are well suited to serve as on-line personal journals for students, particularly since they normally enable uploading and linking of files. Language learners could use a personal blog, linked to a course, as an electronic portfolio, showing development over time. By publishing the blog on the Internet, the student has the possibility of writing for readers beyond classmates, not usually possible in discussion forums. Readers in turn can comment on what they're read, although blogs can be placed in secured environments as well. Self-publishing encourages ownership and responsibility on the part of students, who may be more thoughtful (in content and structure) if they know they are writing for a real audience. This same degree of personal responsibility is lacking in discussion forums.

I certainly agree with all of the possible and valuable uses for blogs that Goodwin-Jones outlines here for blogs, and I think these are some of the ways my colleagues and I are using blogs in our teaching. Blogs, as Goodwin-Jones points out, foster an *ownership* of text, a *personal responsibility* for writing that is distinctly different from the give and take interactions of the discussion in forums like email.

But in my way of thinking of it, these are not writing activities that are "collaborative," "interactive," or "dynamic." Quite the opposite. Blogs have the distinct advantage of allowing individuals to easily publish texts that can be responded to by others to be sure, but those texts are no more "collaborative" than texts published in conventional print.

But Blogs Aren't All Bad: Two "Good" Ideas for Teaching with Them

I don't want to conclude by giving the impression that I think blogs have little use or value in teaching or that emailing lists are always far superior to them. Far from it.

I like blogs. I read blogs frequently and I keep a blog of my own. At the 2003 CCCCs in New York City, I gave a presentation about how blogs could be a very useful tool for scholars to further the discussion they began in other publications. In this scenario, blogs could be a space for the writer to publish updates, reply to reader commentaries, and point interested readers to other publications.

There are several ways to take advantage of the strengths of web logs in the writing classroom, and in some ways, I believe some of the colleagues I mention earlier in this essay are leading the way. I'd like to briefly outline two other "good ideas," one that I've been using in my own teaching *after* my blog failure, and one that I am planning on using this coming school year.

The first approach is one I've been using in my sections of the class "Writing, Style, and Technology," a 300-level writing class for English majors and minors at EMU. My students are using blogs as part of a project where they examine two well-known writing style manuals, William Strunk, Jr. and E. B. White's *The Elements of Style* and Joseph Williams' *Style: Lessons Toward Clarity and Grace*. My goal with this project is not to simply study the "how to" advice in terms of "good writing" and style in these books — though both do offer advice that my students find useful. Rather, the purpose of the project is to ask students to look *below* the surface of the advice and to critically reflect on the definitions of "style" these different books offer. For example, we discuss in class some of the cultural assumptions apparent in even the revised version of Strunk and White's book, and we discuss how the fact that Williams is writing for an advanced audience is reflected in the complexity of the examples and advice.

Blog writing enters into this project as we read and discuss the books. In conjunction with the reading assignments, I ask students to respond to several writing prompts in their blog space. In spirit, the writing assignment is not unlike traditional "pen and paper" writing journals. In practice, I think the blog spaces have two significant advantages over paper. First, each posting is date-stamped and immediately accessible to readers (including me, of course) as soon as the writer publishes it. Second, the "public" and accessible nature of the blogs means that it is extremely easy for students to read each others' writing. One of the last blog writing prompts I've used for this exercise asks students to visit, browse through, and write about their colleagues' blog spaces.

Even though I routinely ask students to look at each others' writing in peer review of rough drafts and on the class email discussion, the response students have to each others' blog spaces has so far seemed unique and, for lack of a better word, more "authentic" than in some other forums. And in principle, this is the purpose and indeed spirit of blogs: a space where individual writers can easily publish texts that are easily accessed by interested readers.

The second approach is one I am trying for the first time during the Fall 2004 semester in a graduate course I will be teaching, Computers and Writing, Theory and Practice. The course is a required one for students in our MA program in "The Teaching of Writing," and while the title doesn't imply it, there is a pedagogical emphasis in the course. As a part of the research/seminar project this semester, I will be asking students to keep a "research blog" where they will post information about their ongoing project. While there will be due dates for certain posts (for example, students will need to post an entry about the topic of their project by a certain date), I am also hoping that students will come to see their class blog space as a useful research and prewriting tool — which is how I see my own academic blog work.

Of course, I haven't experienced any of the results of this project yet. But given what I've learned from when blogs go "bad" and also when blogs can work, I am confident that this assignment will be successful.

Last Word

No question, blogs are an exciting writing tool, one of the most interesting and potentially most useful to come to the writing classroom since email. Blogs work well for writing projects like the two I just described, where individual students publish texts they own. But it's become clear to me that blogs are not as useful as the relatively old-fashioned technology of electronic mailing lists for writing that is interactive and dynamic. How does the saying go? If it ain't broke . . .

Notes

1. My thanks for the advice and feedback from friends, colleagues, and the assigned readers/reviewers for *Kairos*. I found all of their different pieces of advice to be extremely interesting and helpful, and in several places in the essay/blog, I comment on their insights.
2. In the original version of this essay/blog, I placed a great deal more emphasis on the word "collaboration" in the sense of comparing the "collaborative" writing experiences of emailing lists and blogs. Yet, when I went to revise with the intention of explaining what I meant by "collaboration," I found that

most of my essay focuses on blogs and emailing lists for the purposes of discussion and interaction. While the "bad example" of a blog assignment was a collaborative one, this essay is less about collaboration and more about comparing blogs and emailing lists as places where students can *interact* with their writing and audiences in different ways. True, this interaction is itself collaborative in a sense. But I think both the "turning point" in my cautionary tale and my subsequent assignments using blogs are more about discussion and interaction than they are about collaboration, especially as individual student writing finds an audience.

3. The student who wrote the example I discuss here gave me permission to quote her work in this essay. She read the conference presentation version of my essay and agreed with my basic premise as well.
4. It's worth noting that at the time of this incident, commenting was *not* a feature included with Blogger. I don't believe an active commenting feature would have changed the results of this "cautionary tale" because I think the student took advantage of the emailing lists' superior interactive and conversational features of the emailing list. Still, it is an interesting difference between blogs then and now.

Works Cited

Ferdig, Richard E., and Kaye D. Trammell. "Content Delivery in the 'Blogosphere,'" *T.H.E. Journal Online*. February 13, 2004 (February 13, 2004).

Goodwin-Jones, Bob. "Blogs and Wikis: Environments for On-line Collaboration," *Language Learning and Technology*. Vol. 7, No. 2 (May 2003), 12–16.

Hawisher, G. "Electronic Meetings of the Minds: Research, Electronic Conferences, and Composition Studies." In *Re-imagining Computers in Composition: Teaching and Research in the Virtual Age*. Eds. G. Hawisher and P. LeBlanc. Portsmouth: Boynton, Cook, Heinmann, 1992. 81–101.

Krause, Steven D. "'How Will This Improve Student Writing?' Reflections on an Exploratory Study of Online and Off-Line Texts." *Computer Mediated Communication* (an electronic journal), May 1995.

Schriner, D., & Rice, W. "Computer Conferencing and Collaborative Learning: A Discourse Community at Work." *College Composition and Communication* (40), (December 1989:) 472–478.

Spitzer, M. "Local and Global Networking: Implications for the Future. In *Computers and Writing: Theory, Research, Practice.* Eds. D. Holdstein and C. Selfe. New York: MLA, 1990. 58–70.

Walker, Jill. "Talk at Brown," entry from *jill / txt*. December 3, 2003 (February 15, 2004).

Krause's Insights as a Resource for Your Reflections

1. Consider what failed or backfired in Krause's classroom. What additional adjustments can you think of that would have made the experiment more successful?

2. In comparing electronically mediated collaboration from face-to-face collaboration, what are the strengths and weaknesses of each and how might you design assignments that rely on a hybrid form of collaboration?

Krause's Insights as a Resource for Your Writing Classroom

1. Follow Krause's lead and design a unit of your course around blogging with e-mail Listservs operating in the course the way he describes as a useful corrective to the potential for too much open-endedness.
2. Ask your students to work in pairs to produce formal dialogues rather traditional single-author papers — that is, give them a topic, ask them to start e-mailing back and forth about it, and then, eventually, polish and edit this conversation into a formal exchange that can be posted electronically so that all the class members can read one anothers' exchanges and, perhaps, continue their exchange into a "sequel" that involves commenting on those of their peers.

Teaching Visual Literacy

Understanding Visual Rhetoric in Digital Writing Environments

Mary E. Hocks

As profoundly as the Internet has complicated the issue of plagiarism, and blogs and e-mail have expanded the possibilities of self-publishing and collaborating, there are in fact yet other ways that advances in computer technology have changed the lives of writing teachers. In the following article, first published in College Composition and Communication *in 2003, Mary E. Hocks states, "As writing technologies change, they require changes in our understanding of writing and rhetoric and, ultimately, in our writing pedagogy." Because students are increasingly both reading and producing online texts, Hocks argues that "we must help our students pay attention to the rhetorical features of these highly visual digital environments." To show how we can incorporate lessons on visual rhetoric into our writing courses, Hocks analyzes two interactive digital documents, defining and illustrating three key features of visual rhetoric: audience stance, transparency, and hybridity. By focusing on these concepts in our classes, we can teach visual rhetoric as a process, one that both overlaps with and significantly departs from more traditional, purely verbal models of the composing process. The online student project referred to on pages 352–357 was still available when this article was first published. It has since then expired and can no longer be accessed.*

Scholarship in rhetoric and composition has begun to emphasize the central role of visual rhetoric for writers, especially those working in digital writing environments. Visual rhetoric, or visual strategies used for meaning and persuasion, is hardly new, but its importance has been amplified by the visual and interactive nature of native hypertext and multimedia writing. The early developers of hypertextual writing as well as the scholars who study the effect technologies have on readers and writers in various settings have all influenced our understanding of how multimedia technologies use visual rhetoric. Since the appearance of hypertext and other interactive new media, these digital writing environments make it difficult to separate words from visuals or privilege one over the other.[1] Interactive digital texts can blend words and visuals, talk and text, and authors and audiences in ways that are recognizably postmodern.[2] Hypertext theorists and software designers Jay Bolter and Michael Joyce emphasized this visual and experimental character of digital hypertextual writing when they created the hypertext writing program *Storyspace*. Richard Lanham emphasized the rhetorical nature of digital writing, defining a "digital rhetoric" that recaptures the rhetorical paideia by making explicit oral and visual rhetorical concerns that were buried in the last two centuries of print culture and conventions (30). More recent scholarly work outlines the rhetorical practices possible with hypertext and multimedia, from Gary Heba's delineation of how html authoring mirrors rhetorical processes for composition to Patricia Sullivan's arguments that expand our definitions of electronic writing to include graphics, screen design, and other media forms. While professional writers rarely complete an entire interface or graphic design, early work in professional and technical communication by James Porter and Patricia Sullivan, Edward Tufte, and Barbara Mirel all demonstrated how rhetorical decisions impact the visual design of an online document or system: this work helped alert composition scholars to the visual nature of digital writing practices.[3] And as Anne Wysocki demonstrates in "Impossibly Distinct," computer-based interactive media can now blend text and images so thoroughly that they are indistinguishable on the screen (210). By using careful rhetorical analysis that is sensitive to audience, situation, and cultural contexts, Wysocki demonstrates how new media requires a complex relationship between verbal and visual meanings. This important line of rhetorical criticism tells us that new technologies simply require new definitions of what we consider writing.

Persuaded by these arguments, many teachers of writing who were trained in print-based rhetorics now want to articulate principles of visual rhetoric for our students. We sometimes borrow elements of visual rhetoric from moving image studies and design fields as well as draw more upon the fully visual culture within which our students work, live, and learn.[4] Whenever students look at artifacts such as online games or Web sites, we can begin by teaching them to "read" critically assumptions about gender, age, nationality, or other identity categories. Visual communication theories, however, tend to draw too easy a parallel between visual grammar and verbal grammar or to posit visual literacy as easier or more holistic than verbal literacy.[5] We need to recognize that these new media and the literacies they require are hybrid forms. Historical studies of writing technologies have demonstrated how all writing is hybrid—it is at once verbal, spatial, and visual.[6] Acknowledging this hybridity means that the relationships among word and image, verbal texts and visual texts, "visual culture" and "print culture" are all dialogic relationships rather than binary opposites.[7] Recognizing the hybrid literacies our students now bring to our classrooms, we need a better understanding of the increasingly visual and interactive rhetorical features of digital documents. As writing technologies change, they require changes in our understanding of writing and rhetoric and, ultimately, in our writing pedagogy.

With access to digital technologies increasing (or simply assumed) in our college writing courses, interactive digital media have increasingly become part of what we analyze and teach when we teach writing. Writers now engage in what Porter calls "internetworked writing"—writing that involves the intertwining of production, interaction, and publication in the online classroom or professional workplace as well as advocating for one's online audiences (12). Those of us who teach writing online find that we must help our students pay attention to the rhetorical features of these highly visual digital environments. I want to highlight the visual nature of these rhetorical acts and, conversely, the rhetorical nature of these visual acts as hybrid forms of reading and authoring in the digital medium of the World Wide Web. To explain visual rhetoric online to our students, we can begin by carefully articulating the rhetorical features we see in various interactive digital media. In our classrooms, we can also begin to break down the processes for creating successful digital documents, first by simply looking at the computers around us and analyzing them as intensely visual artifacts. The screen itself is a tablet that combines words, interfaces, icons, and pictures that invoke other modalities like touch and sound. But because modern information technologies construct meaning as simultaneously verbal, visual, and interactive hybrids, digital rhetoric *simply assumes* the use of visual rhetoric as well as other modalities.

This essay defines and illustrates some key features of visual rhetoric as they operate in two interactive digital documents designed for the World Wide Web. I first analyze features from two examples of academic hypertextual essays to demonstrate how visual and verbal elements work together to serve the rhetorical purposes and occasions for these publications. I then turn to how writing teachers can teach visual rhetoric by discussing work created by students and the strategies they used to create a visually persuasive and rhetorically effective Web site for Shakespeare studies. These examples demonstrate how analyzing interactive digital media can help students develop rhetorical abilities and become more reflective authors. I believe that teaching digital rhetoric requires profound changes in how all of us think about both writing and pedagogy: Critiquing and producing writing in digital environments actually offers a welcome return to rhetorical principles and an important new pedagogy of writing as design.

A Visual Digital Rhetoric

Any rhetorical theory works as a dynamic system of strategies employed for creating, reacting to, and receiving meaning. An individual author typically operates within multiple social and cultural contexts and, hopefully, advocates ethically for his or her audiences. Thus, digital rhetoric describes a system of ongoing dialogue and negotiations among writers, audiences, and institutional contexts, but it focuses on the multiple modalities available for making meaning using new communication and information technologies. I want to introduce some key features of digital rhetoric by analyzing two scholarly hypertexts by Anne Wysocki and Christine Boese. The following terms help us describe how visual rhetoric operates in digital writing environments:

> **Audience Stance:** The ways in which the audience is invited to participate in online documents and the ways in which the author creates an *ethos* that requires, encourages, or even discourages different kinds of interactivity for that audience.
>
> **Transparency:** The ways in which online documents relate to established conventions like those of print, graphic design, film, and Web pages. The more the online document borrows from familiar conventions, the more transparent it is to the audience.
>
> **Hybridity:** The ways in which online documents combine and construct visual and verbal designs. Hybridity also encourages both authors and audiences to recognize and construct multifaceted identities as a kind of pleasure.

Wysocki's and Boese's texts were published on the World Wide Web in 1998. The last decade marked a time when academic institutions and forms of writing began to change dramatically in their relationships to technology. Bolter called this period the "late age of print" in 1992 to describe how hypertext and multimedia technologies had brought us into an era where both print and digital forms are important to readers (10). When these two texts appeared during 1998, academics had been increasingly exposed to hypertexts (especially on the Web) as the publication opportunities and other institutional support grew for online academic work. Wysocki and Boese each had an interested readership and online community for their work, but each also clearly used the opportunities to educate a wider audience of academics and fans about the strategies important for design on the Web. Readers encountering this work brought with them the similarly postmodern hybridity of their own reading experiences, including experiences with linear print texts, changing scholarly conventions, online communities, and a growing familiarity with online texts. The authors of these documents met these readers' needs by using rhetorical features appropriate to a digital reading and writing environment, while also making concessions to the needs of their readers in a time of transition.

Although my analysis focuses on Web sites in relation to our changing academic conventions during a particular time period, I believe that these terms can help us develop an understanding of most interactive digital media as they change or reproduce more familiar forms. The kinds of features and categories I offer here focus on native hypertextual writing and reading processes, but they are hardly exhaustive categories. In these two works, the authors also bring up the subjects of changing literacies and the medium of the Web explicitly. Perhaps because these two authors have some experience (though no formal training) with digital graphic design and have taught visual communication, they offer both an execution of visual strategies and a self-conscious commentary that is inherently instructive for a visual rhetoric—what *Tristram Shandy* as experimental narrative was for early narrative theory. Each example uses these visual and interactive strategies in ways that are appropriate to the rhetorical situation and the hypertextual medium, but they go beyond formal innovation to help audiences take more conscious responsibility for making meaning out of the text. Audiences can experience the pleasures of agency and an awareness of themselves as constructed identities in a heterogeneous medium. How that agency gets played out, however, depends on the purpose and situation for the text in relation to the audience's need for linearity and other familiar forms.

Published in the online journal *Kairos* <http://english.ttu.edu/kairos/> in fall 1998, Wysocki's "Monitoring Order" is intended for teachers of writing in online environments who are experienced with Web-based hypertexts but are not as familiar with histories of design, the subject of her essay. This essay provides an important overview of the continuities between book design and Web page design, persuading us to be sensitive to the historical and cultural specificity of our current conventions for all designs, both book pages and Web browsers. Wysocki discusses how the order of designs and the contexts for reading all come from culturally framed experiences with literacy. We all "encounter designs individually, based on our particular bodily histories and presents" ("Monitoring Order"). She explains that, because the Web inherits book page design, it embeds the cultural assumptions about order on a page that come from our history with print texts: "[V]isual designs can

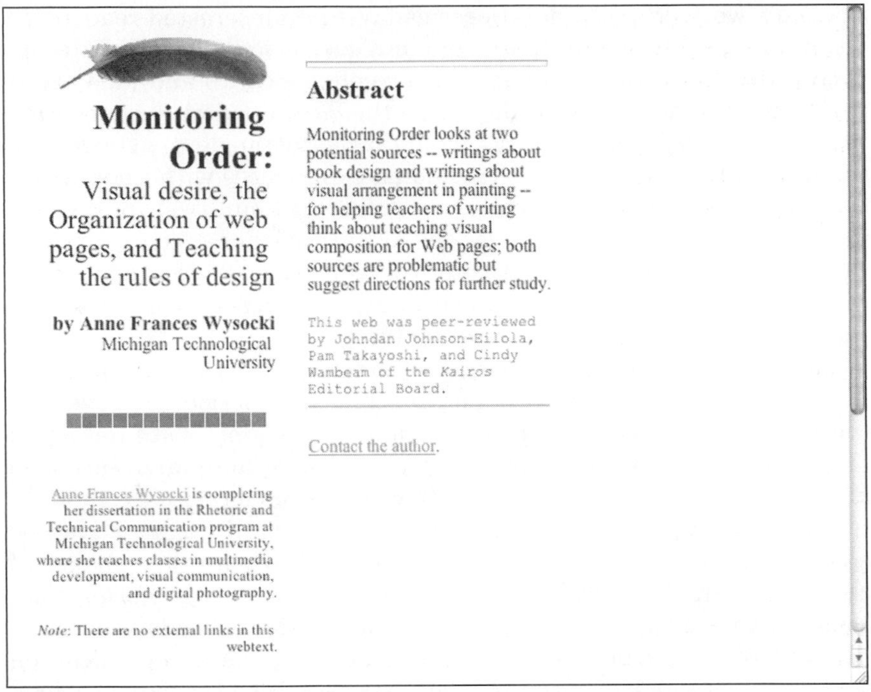

Monitoring Order: Visual desire, the Organization of web pages, and Teaching the rules of design

by Anne Frances Wysocki
Michigan Technological University

Anne Frances Wysocki is completing her dissertation in the Rhetoric and Technical Communication program at Michigan Technological University, where she teaches classes in multimedia development, visual communication, and digital photography.

Note: There are no external links in this webtext.

Abstract

Monitoring Order looks at two potential sources -- writings about book design and writings about visual arrangement in painting -- for helping teachers of writing think about teaching visual composition for Web pages; both sources are problematic but suggest directions for further study.

This web was peer-reviewed by Johndan Johnson-Eilola, Pam Takayoshi, and Cindy Wambeam of the *Kairos* Editorial Board.

Contact the author.

http://english.ttu.edu/kairos/3.2/features/wysocki/bridge.html

(as is most evident in what I've written about books) be expressions of and means for reproducing cultural and political structures, and . . . such visual orderings are likely to be those that are repeated. . . ." ("Monitoring Order"). The history of typography demonstrates that, because book design strives to be transparent, we don't necessarily think of it as designed or discuss the embedded assumptions about reading. Two-dimensional graphic design offers some guidance for designing Web pages but is also limited in its formalism. Ultimately, Wysocki wants readers to ask themselves "what the arrangement of images and words on a web page asks us to desire: what order is reinforced by a design, and what designs give us chances to re-order?" ("Monitoring Order"). The Web, while borrowing from both print and graphics design traditions, lends itself to looking again at the digital texts and pages whose structures and margins can change. Wysocki's argument and visual strategies work together to motivate readers and change their ways of seeing design.

Audience stance describes how the work visually gives readers a sense of agency and possibilities for interactive involvement. Wysocki's essay works visually by enacting in the interface the concepts about design and desire that it discusses while constructing the screen as page. The *ethos* created by Wysocki addresses the expected academic conventions for linear argument and also challenges those expectations.

Wysocki, an experienced designer of interactive media, originally delivered this piece at the Computers and Writing Conference, and she kept it within the linear format when designing this talk into an essay for *Kairos*.[8] When "Monitoring Order" appeared in September 1998, *Kairos* as a whole averaged 137,000 hits with 7,500 unique visitors per month, while today it averages 240,000 hits and 10,000 unique visitors per month.[9] Most direct involvement between this audience and the author in 1998 occurred in forms prescribed by the journal—the linear Web-text structure, the "Contact the author" e-mail link, and the discussion forum included in another section of the journal. But Wysocki uses the interface and the tone of her essay to create arguments using pages of texts and illustrations readers are familiar with, while subtly making readers construct a reading and a way of seeing the essay. She thus fulfills, and also plays with, the desire for ordered readings, using the essay itself to challenge the audience while also giving them the linearity they might want or even need.

The essay is divided into sections, or nodes, and the length of text in each node varies, but tiles in the upper frame allow readers to access the nodes, which are subsections of the argument, in any order. Each node can be read autonomously but also works to develop the overall argument of the essay. Some screens require scrolling to find all the examples; some screens are short, emphatic transitional and summary paragraphs. The final tile brings up the anticipated list of sources. The shape of each section thus develops and stresses points of the argument for readers familiar with academic arguments but also familiar with basic Web conventions like scrolling and clicking on buttons. If one clicks on a tile to navigate through the piece, subtle changes on the screen indicate movement through the document and reinforce the audience's sense of agency and interaction. The design of the essay invites readers to think beyond the familiar linear structure, to playfully reflect on the self-consciously linear structure. Readers are offered the pleasure of consciously "monitoring order" themselves by clicking on tiles and pursuing different orders as they read or re-read the essay. By creating this kind of interactive and reflective stance, Wysocki reminds readers of themselves as active readers and helps them be attentive to the features of design on the page. For readers with the ability to access its graphics and frames, the essay offers an interactive experience where color, shape, and text cannot be separated. The interface leaves these readers with a renewed sense of how design choices become contextualized in arguments, in this case about the changes in page and book designs throughout history.

Transparency refers to how the writer designs a document in ways familiar and clear to readers. Wysocki demonstrates how screen design of any new media document might use strategies borrowed from historically specific approaches to page design, graphic design, and the changing conventions (such as frames) for Web pages. "Monitoring Order" uses forms, color, and a familiar page layout to create a fairly transparent interface that quickly teaches a novice reader how to navigate it, relying primarily on repeated forms and colors as visual tools of organization.

Wysocki provides navigation through the text with the sequence of color tiles in the top frame. The tiles are different colors that correspond to the sections of the essay — blues for the sections on book design, reds for the sections on graphic design, and greens for the introduction and conclusion. These colors are repeated in the opening figure of the quill feather, an appropriately antiquated image of writing's material history represented on the computer screen. The quotations, subheadings, and reading instructions appear in slightly different colored text that stands out typographically. The feather and the graphic representing the subsection — here, a single green tile for the first node — appear at the top left of the main frame to orient the reader as if on a printed page. The bottom of this first page instructs us to click on the tiles to move through the paper. In this same location on subsequent pages, the tiles are repeated as a set of lines at the bottom of each screen so that we can visually identify the end of a section by its corresponding tiles. The tiles provide a navigational device and a kind of footprint of each screen. The forms on the screen are thus decorative and interactive, painterly, and significant representations for information. The screen is visually coherent primarily through the strategy of repetition — here, the use of repeated colors and forms. On the surface, this coherence provides a calm sense of modernist order that is simultaneously visual and navigational. Order reassures readers that they won't get lost and that the text has a structure that can be tracked visually as well as verbally.

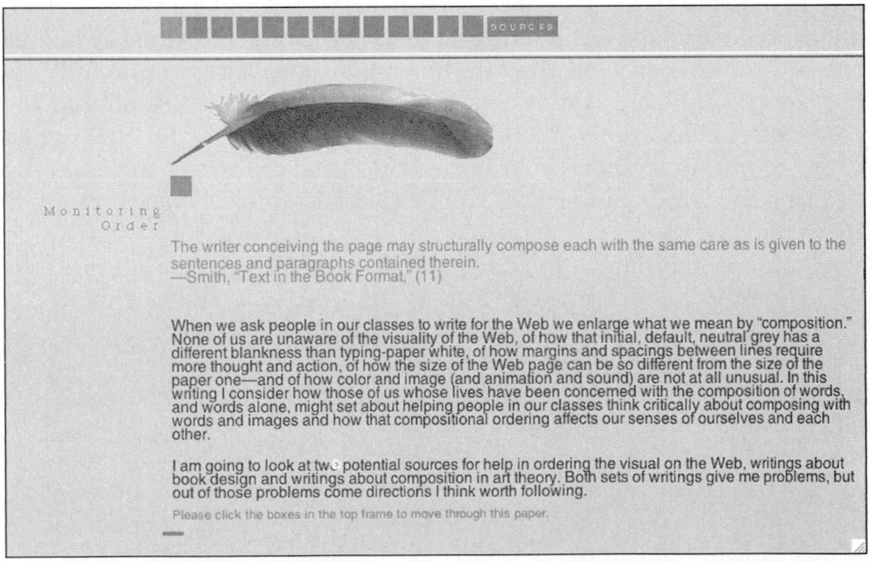

The **hybridity** of the Web medium refers to the interplay between the visual and the verbal in one constructed, heterogeneous semiotic space. Wysocki's site takes advantage of this hybridity to combine pictures and text in thoughtful and unconventional ways. The sections of text incorporate quotes and pictures and reproductions of texts as evidence for the arguments about visual design and its historical specificity. This strategy uses the juxtaposition of pictures, words, and unconventional margins to transform our understanding of the visual through the reading experience. For example, in the screen at the bottom of this page, Wysocki plays with the conventional relationships between texts and pictures on pages: the margins expand outward slightly on the left, reminding readers of how the digital page is not fixed but mutable. The illustration, a pictorial history book, is a startling example of how the production of such books served as an excuse for political oppression by conquerors who valued only verbal texts. Finally, the illustration is placed within the sentence without figure captions in the same way that verbal evidence supporting an argument might be.

Because of Wysocki's skillful use of examples like these to visually challenge the reader's sense of order and design, the readers of this journal leave this essay having actually experienced a new way of seeing what was previously invisible. An early example of what has become a hallmark of Wysocki's work, "Monitoring Order" uses colors, visual metaphors, and graphical repetitions to guide us through a meditation about our own perceptions, expectations, and attitudes regarding the visual in relation to text. In response, readers can imagine themselves as more thoughtful about designs or even as capable designers themselves.

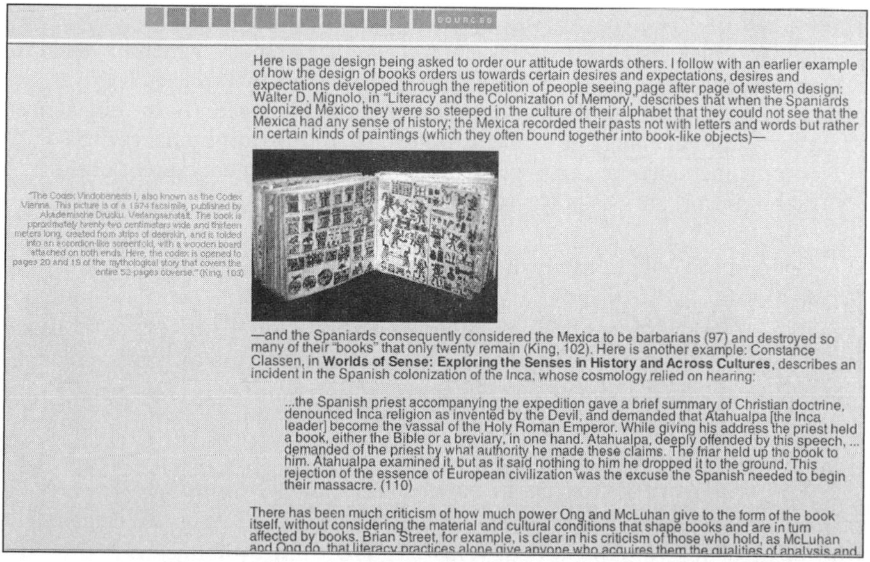
SOURCES

Here is page design being asked to order our attitude towards others. I follow with an earlier example of how the design of books orders us towards certain desires and expectations, desires and expectations developed through the repetition of people seeing page after page of western design: Walter D. Mignolo, in "Literacy and the Colonization of Memory," describes that when the Spaniards colonized Mexico they were so steeped in the culture of their alphabet that they could not see that the Mexica had any sense of history; the Mexica recorded their pasts not with letters and words but rather in certain kinds of paintings (which they often bound together into book-like objects)—

"The Codex Vindobonensis I, also known as the Codex Vienna. This picture is of a 1974 facsimile, published by Akademische Drucku. Verlangsanstalt. The book is pproximately twenty two centimeters wide and thirteen meters long, created from strips of deerskin, and is folded into an accordion-like screenfold, with a wooden board attached on both ends. Here, the codex is opened to pages 20 and 19 of the mythological story that covers the entire 52-pages obverse." (King, 103)

—and the Spaniards consequently considered the Mexica to be barbarians (97) and destroyed so many of their "books" that only twenty remain (King, 102). Here is another example: Constance Classen, in **Worlds of Sense: Exploring the Senses in History and Across Cultures**, describes an incident in the Spanish colonization of the Inca, whose cosmology relied on hearing:

> ...the Spanish priest accompanying the expedition gave a brief summary of Christian doctrine, denounced Inca religion as invented by the Devil, and demanded that Atahualpa [the Inca leader] become the vassal of the Holy Roman Emperor. While giving his address the priest held a book, either the Bible or a breviary, in one hand. Atahualpa, deeply offended by this speech, ... demanded of the priest by what authority he made these claims. The friar held up the book to him. Atahualpa examined it, but as it said nothing to him he dropped it to the ground. This rejection of the essence of European civilization was the excuse the Spanish needed to begin their massacre. (110)

There has been much criticism of how much power Ong and McLuhan give to the form of the book itself, without considering the material and cultural conditions that shape books and are in turn affected by books. Brian Street, for example, is clear in his criticism of those who hold, as McLuhan and Ong do, that literacy practices alone give anyone who acquires them the qualities of analysis and

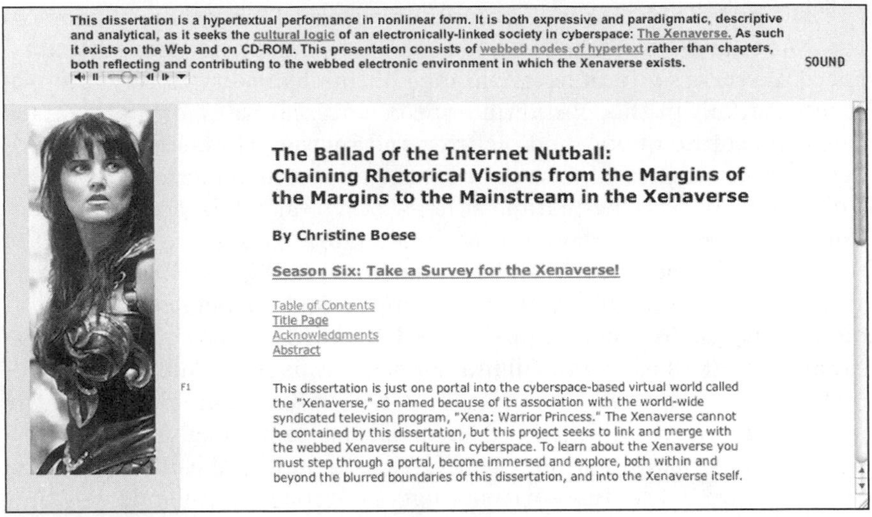
This dissertation is a hypertextual performance in nonlinear form. It is both expressive and paradigmatic, descriptive and analytical, as it seeks the cultural logic of an electronically-linked society in cyberspace: The Xenaverse. As such it exists on the Web and on CD-ROM. This presentation consists of webbed nodes of hypertext rather than chapters, both reflecting and contributing to the webbed electronic environment in which the Xenaverse exists.
SOUND
The Ballad of the Internet Nutball:
Chaining Rhetorical Visions from the Margins of the Margins to the Mainstream in the Xenaverse
By Christine Boese
Season Six: Take a Survey for the Xenaverse!
Table of Contents
Title Page
Acknowledgments
Abstract
F1
This dissertation is just one portal into the cyberspace-based virtual world called the "Xenaverse," so named because of its association with the world-wide syndicated television program, "Xena: Warrior Princess." The Xenaverse cannot be contained by this dissertation, but this project seeks to link and merge with the webbed Xenaverse culture in cyberspace. To learn about the Xenaverse you must step through a portal, become immersed and explore, both within and beyond the blurred boundaries of this dissertation, and into the Xenaverse itself.

http://www.nutball.com/dissertation/index.htm

Self-published and updated since 1998, Christine Boese's "The Ballad of the Internet Nutball" was the first hypertextual dissertation accepted by Rensselaer Polytechnic Institute. Boese's project is a participation/observer ethnography and analysis of the fans and online culture surrounding the popular fantasy television show, *Xena: Warrior Princess*. The original audiences for this site included the dissertation committee members and the *Xena* fans. Boese explains the goal in her dissertation is to

> explore the constellations of social forces in cyberspace, which have led to the success of a noncommercial, highly trafficked, dynamic culture or what is sometimes called a "community." . . . This research examines how the rhetorical visions of this culture are used to write the narratives of its ongoing existence, in a way that is increasingly independent of the dominant narratives of the television program itself.

Boese's ethnographic project analyzes show episodes, photographs, fan-authored fantasy narratives about the implicit lesbian subplot between Xena and her warrior-poet sidekick Gabrielle, surveys, and more than 1,100 Web sites devoted to the show and its fans online, and face-to-face interactions at fan conventions. This comprehensive study of a fan culture, or fandom, offers fresh definitions of both online community and hypertextual structure.

The **audience stance** is established on the opening screen as music, images, text, and hypertextual structure all set the stage for a highly interactive experience. With the freedom to design her own interface and the support of committee members to explore new techniques for hypertextual structure, Boese created a complex collage of visual and navigational strategies. Similarly, the kinds of agency presented to readers are complex and multifaceted, allowing many choices for interaction, including several ways to read the document. The *ethos* Boese creates is at once that of engaged insider, co-participant, and scholarly investigator, one that assumes an engaged online audience of fans. She emphasizes these multiple stances by providing equal amounts of narrative, analysis, personal reflection, and interaction. The familiar academic contexts for a dissertation, including title page and acknowledgments, are included as links from this first screen, as well as a traditional table of contents. But this document actively invites participation from those whom Boese calls in her acknowledgments “my co-authors” of the study, the fan audience for the site. These co-participants not only completed the expected surveys and interviews, but they have added online materials and interpretations to the site over time. Boese thus creates an experience of open-ended possibility with these proliferating texts and interpretations. When it first appeared on the Web, the site saw about 500 visits a month by these fans, but it continues to get a growing amount of traffic—up to 22,200 hits and 6,155 unique visitors a month at the time of this study. Its audience has apparently grown as academics and online journals have referenced Boese’s study as a cult fan site and a course resource.[10]

Like Wysocki’s visual strategies, Boese’s are integral to her argument, in this case to motivate and engage readers in the complex web of texts and interactions that make up the online culture called the Xenaverse. Boese’s interface design is not very **transparent**, offering instead an unfamiliar, multidimensional structure that includes complex linking and several forms of navigation:

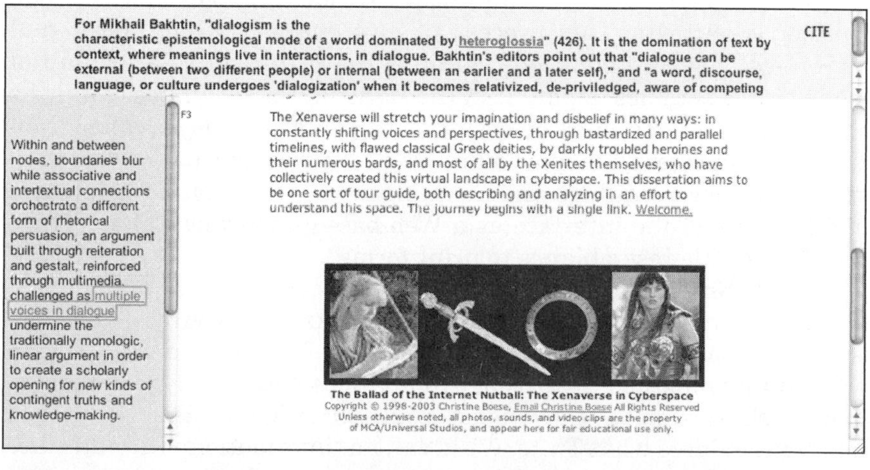
For Mikhail Bakhtin, "dialogism is the characteristic epistemological mode of a world dominated by heteroglossia" (426). It is the domination of text by context, where meanings live in interactions, in dialogue. Bakhtin's editors point out that "dialogue can be external (between two different people) or internal (between an earlier and a later self)," and "a word, discourse, language, or culture undergoes 'dialogization' when it becomes relativized, de-priviledged, aware of competing
CITE
F3
Within and between nodes, boundaries blur while associative and intertextual connections orchestrate a different form of rhetorical persuasion, an argument built through reiteration and gestalt, reinforced through multimedia, challenged as multiple voices in dialogue undermine the traditionally monologic, linear argument in order to create a scholarly opening for new kinds of contingent truths and knowledge-making.
The Xenaverse will stretch your imagination and disbelief in many ways: in constantly shifting voices and perspectives, through bastardized and parallel timelines, with flawed classical Greek deities, by darkly troubled heroines and their numerous bards, and most of all by the Xenites themselves, who have collectively created this virtual landscape in cyberspace. This dissertation aims to be one sort of tour guide, both describing and analyzing in an effort to understand this space. The journey begins with a single link. Welcome.
The Ballad of the Internet Nutball: The Xenaverse in Cyberspace
Copyright © 1998-2003 Christine Boese, Email Christine Boese All Rights Reserved
Unless otherwise noted, all photos, sounds, and video clips are the property of MCA/Universal Studios, and appear here for fair educational use only.

Boese's interface takes full advantage of nonlinear hypertextual form by using multiple frames, linking strategies, and multiple media in ways that draw attention to the constructed interface. Boese provides three frames, four navigational paths, and an image map to accommodate many kinds of readers. The use of three simultaneous frames in the screens gives an experience of nonhierarchical depth and multidimensionality to the screen space. Each frame is marked by a different color — blue at the top, pink at the side, and white in the middle — and the screen is assembled as a collage of contrasting colors, photographs, and links within the text and at the right margins of texts. Text appears organized by its graphical and spatial presentation in all frames. These texts also interact with one another to a great degree. Hypertextual links, when clicked, bring up explanations and citations in the other frames or in additional pop-up windows. Thus, one experiences many changes taking place through this cross-linking on what appears to be one level of information, creating what Janet Murray refers to as an experience of immersion that leads to increased agency (162).

To enhance that agency and also offer concessions to more linear readers, Boese uses several methods of navigation that provide multiple paths through the text. The picture of Gabrielle, the poet, leads to a narrative reading of the text. The sword, one of Xena's weapons, moves one to the argumentative theoretical portion of the text, while Xena's other weapon, the disc-shaped Shockrum, leads to a pop-up window that provides the image map — a clickable collage of photos offering a nonlinear path through the document. Finally, the picture of Xena leads to a discussion of interconnecting themes in the study. At every turn, then, readers are offered multiple choices, allowing them to construct very different readings of the text. At the same time, readers experience a dissonance between this text and other familiar forms (like linear fantasy narratives or academic arguments) that defamiliarizes their experiences with print narrative, argumentative forms, and even with other, simpler hypertexts. This process of awareness is what Bolter and Grusin call "hypermediation," because the historical relationship of media forms becomes apparent in the structure. In fact, Boese's aim, as she explains in her section on design, is to create what Joyce called "constructive hypertext," thereby encouraging audiences to actively construct their own readings and meanings (42–43). Boese's readers are highly aware of the interface as a Web-based, experimental structure that bears little resemblance to print forms.

The **hybridity** of the Web interface allows Boese to swap different kinds of media — texts, pictures, sounds, links, data sources, and citations — in and out of the various sections of the screen and pop up windows. She juxtaposes textual explanations with purely visual arguments. For example, this visual representation of the Xenaverse (on p. 349) — uses what Tufte would call an "information-rich" interface to present a large amount of data on a single level, with colors distin-

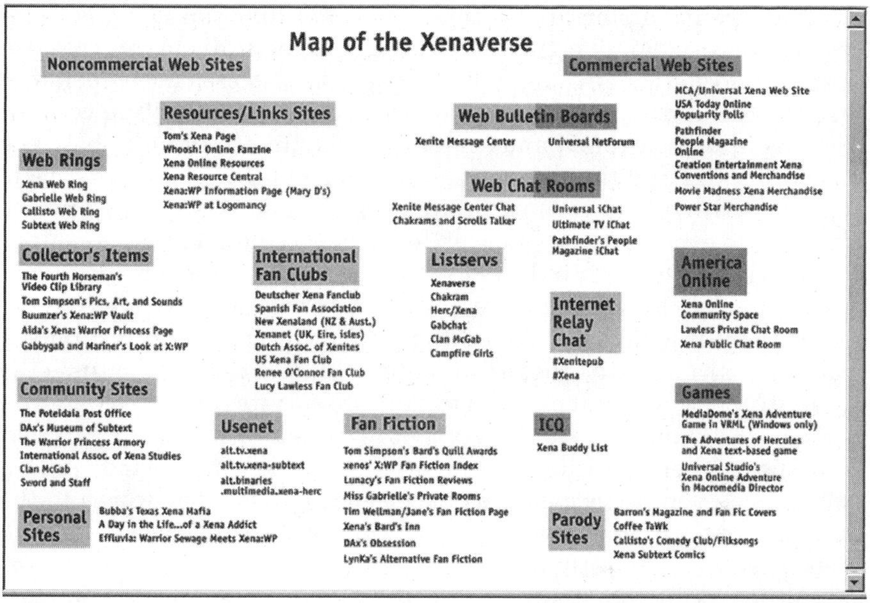

guishing the data (blue for noncommercial on the left, yellow for commercial on the right) and boxes and columns regularizing the data. While displaying many formal characteristics common to any two-dimensional design (alignment and clustering of similar data, highlighted headings, use of white space), the page asks readers to appreciate the depth and breadth of the online communities and to observe that noncommercial sites coded blue outnumbered commercial sites in yellow almost two to one. Readers, by grasping the scope of the Xenaverse and immersing themselves in the many sites and media included in the project, can help create the fan culture and construct themselves as fans, critics, or storytellers as they see fit.

Several important rhetorical features emerge from looking at both of these documents. First, each piece establishes an **audience stance** by offering readers different forms of interactivity and agency. This stance results largely from the author creating an *ethos* and a connection with readers that encourages different kinds of audience participation. Each author thus uses the interactive and performative potential of the hypertextual medium, encouraging the audience to explore the space created by the digital document and to reflectively participate in their own explorations and construction of the text. Secondly, each piece uses formal structures that mix old and new forms of reading and viewing conventions to create the audience's perception of **transparency**.

The document's historical relationship to familiar conventions helps create a sense of familiar structure and allows the audience to recognize desired information quickly. Transparency is also created by defamiliarizing the audience's experiences with reading and writing conventions by drawing explicit and sometimes playful attention to both the discontinuities and the continuities between older and newer forms of reading, writing, and viewing information. This process can allow the audience to experience the pleasure of constructing their own readings and playing with form. In the two examples, both documents make concession to and also disrupt the expectations of academic readers accustomed to traditional print and other media forms, but in quite different ways appropriate to the rhetorical context. Finally, each author uses the **hybridity** of the digital medium to capitalize on its constructed nature and also to encourage readers to be aware of their own hybrid identities. In a space where multifaceted identities can be constructed, experienced, and even performed, this experience of hybridity works to the audience's advantage by increasing the experience of pleasure through identification and multiplicity.

Although they obviously overlap, these categories provide a starting point for talking about the rhetorical and visual features of Web-based digital documents together, the contexts for designing these documents as visual arguments, and the potential impact of these designs on audiences, particularly through the use of interface designs and interactivity. Both essays use hypertextual form to underscore reflexively the arguments they make about conventions and about cultures. Both authors use the visual interactive medium to persuade their audiences to participate in and be changed by the reading experience. "Monitoring Order" uses academic readers' expectations about linearity and visual page design in a traditional "page" format and then subtly challenges those conventions using page designs and pictures as self-explanatory pieces of evidence to embody Wysocki's arguments about the historical specificity of all designs. Boese's dissertation immerses readers in a multidimensional structure that disrupts expectations about linearity up front but still provides many choices that lead to a linear path. The invitations to participate and be transformed by the online Xena cultures abound, driven by the agency offered to readers throughout the document. Analyzing professional models like this helps us demonstrate good techniques for how multimedia writing can then be taught as visual and verbal rhetorical practice.

Teaching Visual Digital Rhetoric

When we bring an understanding of digital rhetoric to our electronic classrooms, we need to expand our approach not only to rhetorical criticism but also to text production. Digital technologies can encourage what the New London School theorists call a multimodal approach to literacy, where using communication technologies engages students in a multisensory experience and active construction of knowledge. To use multimedia technologies effectively, writers have to use practices that are not just verbal but visual, spatial, aural, and gestural to meaning (Cope and Kalantzis 26; Kress, "Multimodality" 182). These theorists make a powerful case for redefining literacy practice and attending to the political and social impact made possible by technologies as complex artifacts that can help transform our lived experience. Their approach to pedagogy suggests that students can work from within their diverse cultures and multiple identities using their own languages as well as their everyday lived experiences to design new kinds of knowledge. This definition of literacy and its implications for teaching echo what Cynthia Selfe has called "critical technological literacy" in its recognition of the political implications of technological literacies and its commitment to diversity. This approach to literacy education reinforces the value of teaching students to think of themselves not just as critics but as designers of knowledge. Gunther Kress distinguishes how critique and design are two knowledge-making processes that manifest different social environments and epistemologies. Critique occurs when "existing forms, and the social relations of which they are manifestations, are subjected to a distanced, analytical scrutiny to reveal the rules of their constitution. . . . In periods of relative social stability critique has the function of introducing a dynamic into the system" ("'English' at" 87). Design becomes essential in times of intense social change: "While critique looks at the present through the means of past production, Design shapes the future through deliberate deployment of representational resources in the designer's interest" (77). In other words, design moves us from rhetorical criticism to invention and production. The "shaping" of resources gives students' work social and political impact and allows them to learn how to represent new forms of knowledge. To establish a balanced rhetorical approach, then, we must offer students experiences both in the analytic process of critique, which scrutinizes conventional expectations and power relations, and in the transformative process of design, which can change power relations by creating a new vision of knowledge.

In terms of visual rhetoric, students need to learn the "distanced" process of how to critique the saturated visual and technological landscape that surrounds them as something structured and written in a set of deliberate rhetorical moves. They then need to enact those visual moves on their own. Kress's notion of multimodal design helps to underscore how helpful design projects can be for learning visual rhetoric. If we can teach students to critique the rhetorical and visual features of professional hypertexts — the audience stance, presentations of *ethos*, transparency of the interface for readers, and the hybridity of forms and identities — we can also teach them to design their own technological artifacts that use these strategies but are more speculative or activist in nature. This approach to pedagogy asks teachers not only to incorporate new kinds of texts into our classrooms but new kinds of multimodal compositional processes that ask students to envision and create something that perhaps does not yet exist.

[Web address no longer available.]

To illustrate the transformative process of design, I want to turn to a student online project from a Shakespeare course at Spelman College, also self-published in 1998 when many students were designing their first Web-based documents.[11] The project focused on collecting professional and student opinions on colorblind casting in Shakespeare performances. The class Web site became an ongoing collaboration and a new experience for the English professor and the students. The professor explains that she hoped that students would "test their own ideas against those of a wide variety of people concerned with the study of Shakespeare" and "express their opinions to persons outside of their own school environment" (McDermott 2). She gave students the topic of colorblind casting, used by theaters to create more diversity in traditional theater, and cited the controversies regarding these casting practices. Students then identified key arguments about race and collected professional opinions online to create the first Web site that explicitly addresses race and casting practices in Shakespearean studies. They constructed an activist stance, using their identities as individual Black women and as a Spelman College community. Furthermore, publishing their work online highlighted the students' perceived impact on audiences and underscored the rhetorical ethics of internetworked writing emphasized by Porter. Students became designers of knowledge about Shakespeare by weaving together and visually representing their own perspectives and the perspectives of others on the Web. On the page, these voices become enacted as a visual mix of colored text, commercial and homemade visuals, seriousness and fun, as the students explain the occasion for their site and the controversies surrounding their topic, asking "Should Non-European Actors Be Cast in Major Roles?"

To construct the project, the students used **audience stance** to offer an engaging site with a layout and tone that would appeal to other students studying Shakespeare while also being responsible to the professionals with whom they had been communicating. The site includes interactive and inviting features that students designed specifically for other students. For example, the "guestbook" link visually marks a place where the students invite other students to respond to this controversial topic. Quotes in the guestbook compliment the students' work on the site, including a supporting quote by actor Raul Julia on his Shakespearean role. A student from another school wrote a deliberately informal note of recognition: "well i think that casting blacks and other colors into Shakespeare's work is very essential. as a student studying his arts i enjoyed acting out the parts that would of been issued to a white person. colorblindness is a great approach because then all can feel into the theme and not left out. thank you for your time and god bless." While few in number, these responses enhanced the class's sense of audience and purpose for designing the site.[12]

Another way students designed interactivity was to create a space where they could publish the ideas they collected from surveys. Students used the playful feature of a "thought bubble," an inherently visual/verbal semiotic space borrowed from comic book traditions, to represent their audience of professionals and their opinions culled from the surveys. Each thought bubble offers an opinion in its own unique color and a sense of incompleteness is suggested in the title's ellipsis:

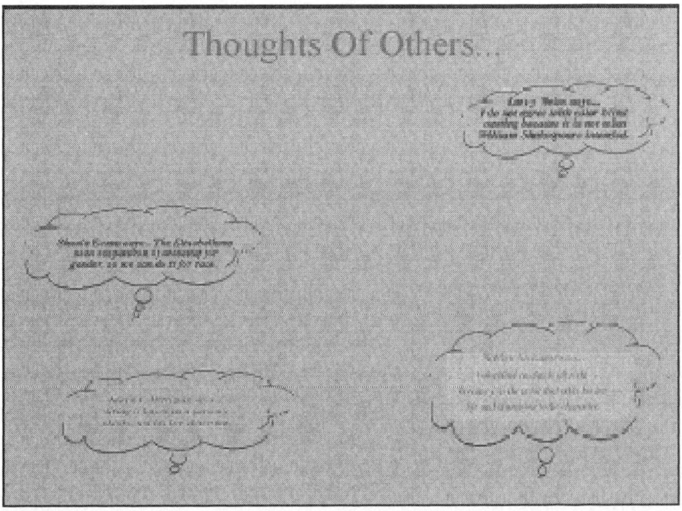

Students use these familiar forms to represent meaning for other students and professionals. The Spelman site works rhetorically to draw students into a dialogue about Shakespeare and race through its simple but engaging interface while also presenting research on the topic of Shakespeare to fulfill their responsibilities as researchers. By keeping these audience representations relatively separate, students hoped to persuade both audiences of the impact of colorblind casting. The students create an *ethos* of the collective voice of their class community that strikes a balance between professional academic discourse and authoritative self-identification, what Stephen Knadler, writing about online projects by students from the same college, calls a "*felt re-embodiment* online" (238). For example, on the next screen [at the top of p. 355], the students describe the "unanswered questions" they have and cite Errol Hill, a noted Caribbean scholar, as an authority, before they announce the purpose of their project. The clash between personal voice and professional discourse in this site exhibits the same kind of "double-consciousness" that Knadler saw in his students' portfolios and that teachers often find in students working to assimilate personal voices with distanced and objective academic discourse.

Students used a variety of familiar techniques to create a **transparent** interface appropriate for their rhetorical situation and for the audience. Keeping the site simple and straightforward for multiple audiences was a primary goal for the class as they were learning Web design. They use basic and familiar conventions for the Web at that time—linear arrangements and horizontal rules on pages, traditional book-style layout of pictures alongside text, and short nodes of explanatory text to help keep readers oriented. Students avoided using frames or other more complex hypertextual linking, opting instead for a few conventional in-text links. The pages use these familiar conventions but still take some advantage of the digital medium to go beyond traditional print-page format. Prompted by the idea of color, the students use multicolored text to provide a visual pun and argument to remind audiences that color is indeed visible. Students also playfully invite readers to explore the thoughts of others with the thought bubbles. The page is deceptively simple: It has a depth of resources offered through the few hypertextual links here, including the survey results linked to the "Thoughts of Others" box, a link to other Shakespeare sites, and a link to a class bulletin board with pictures, news, and reviews of ongoing productions.

While these pages appear "messy" in that they have less design continuity, onscreen spatial structure, and interface features than the professional examples, they illustrate the process of students learning to bring visual and verbal arguments together. The text on this page aims to balance opinions objectively, using black text for the opening summary and green text for their explicit purpose in making the site, thus establishing a firm sense of the class community as the occasion for this

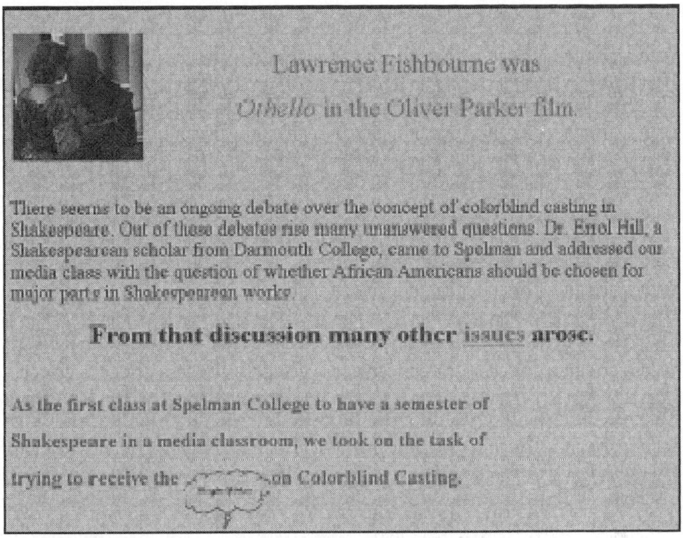

design. At the same time, commercial pictures with captions alongside them open the page and emphasize depictions of familiar Black actors cast in recent productions. Blue links lead to other issues from the class and opinions on the topic. The students thus build a visual argument about the track record of successful casting practices through the pictures as they introduce the controversy. They then work to balance perspectives and research about the topic. The **hybridity** of the medium thus lets students use texts, pictures, and other illustrations interchangeably to illustrate their learning and also to encourage engagement and responses from their dual audiences of students and theater professionals. Students can take on the role of offering professional perspectives and still be students.

If we understand this site as epistemic rhetoric (see James Berlin), it demonstrates how students can make their ongoing work and learning purposeful by directing it toward this particular situation and their audience of both professionals and students. By publishing it online as public discourse and new knowledge in the field, students have an immediate sense of their impact on audiences. The "Shakespeare in Color" Web site "makes an actual contribution to Shakespeare studies" while teaching students "investigative technique, analytical skills, and something about the process of publishing and taking responsibility for one's scholarly work" (McDermott 4). It thus becomes an authentic learning experience that has brought students in touch with a new experience of literature, of performance, and of theater culture through contact with their broader audience of professionals. Students themselves recognized the value of these activities and described their projects as "extremely creative," and including "alternate ways" of representing their understanding of the course material. Most importantly, students were extremely proud of their accomplishments, saw themselves as talented, and appreciated the "hands-on learning" and the opportunity to present their work in a public forum for an actual audience.[13] Design projects such as this not only bring the concept of multiliteracy squarely into the middle of the composition process but also help students design an activist academic project that represents new knowledge for a real audience.

How do we begin to help students enact their understanding of visual and digital rhetoric? Teachers must first develop assignments and projects that complement the goals of their courses. In this case, the professor wanted a multimodal experience of literary texts, interactions with professionals, and collaborative active learning experiences using multimedia technology. After these students looked critically at the visual elements of Web sites and other media, they then planned out their project together and designed the site for their two audiences. Students created a Web site and a PowerPoint project in this course and presented their preliminary designs in an oral presentation to other students and faculty from the department. When teaching design, I also begin by analyzing media and encouraging students to think broadly about visual elements and interactivity. I show them published new media titles and ask them to look for the rhetorical features like audience stance, *ethos*, transparency of the interface, and hybridity. They come to understand these features by analyzing the visual details: the use of elements like color, space, linearity; the use of conventions from film, print, advertisements, and typical Web sites; and the use of forms of agency for audiences. Students then draw conclusions about visual arguments and the purposes of interactivity. I have them sketch out or illustrate "borrowed" features they'd like to include in their projects. I do this so they will not limit their designs to their own production skills or to the technologies available at any one time in our classrooms. My students conduct research by starting with their own understandings of visual representations and their own perspectives as users of familiar and not-so-familiar technologies. This process of speculative design encourages students to think both creatively and rhetorically about everything from cell phones to online games, while paradoxically not limiting them to the time and place of particular software programs.

The next step is to teach students to map out or storyboard their projects. Storyboarding is a visual technique borrowed from documentary video production where every shot is planned out to correspond to a narrative script. In multimedia productions, storyboarding refers to planning and sketching out each screen of the digital production. To teach students the storyboarding process, I give them sheets of paper and ask them to draw every media element, each navigational link, and all text that appears on the screen. They also note the colors and any other graphics that will be used on each screen. This process makes them pay careful attention to visual arguments, to spatial placement on the screen, and to the consistency of the interface. It also forces them to narrow the scope of their projects in collaboration with one another and their audience. They think carefully about what the audience will see and how audience members will interact with the information in their projects. When students learn to storyboard a sequence of screens, they learn to think carefully about how visual information gets structured as part of the design. Their design and drawing skills can be minimal because storyboarding teaches students to *think through* the elements of design and navigation that meet the audience's needs. The speculative design process can be accomplished in a couple of weeks, and students don't need any specific technical skills to complete the assignments. I sometimes go on and teach students to use a scanner and an image software program that allows them to alter an already existing still image and change its meaning. If time permits, students can then create their own graphics and import them into a Web authoring program to be combined with links and other interactive features. This authoring of the project can take more weeks to accomplish, but it is well worth the time and effort if the ultimate goal is to have students publish a permanent Web site. Students in the Shakespeare class benefited from interacting with the target audience online and in oral presentations to other students as they decided how to design the content of the site. The oral critique of the site by other students is a very important part of the process — not only did students feel compelled to impress their audience of peers, but they also had the opportunity to revise their site before making it accessible online.

While this discussion offers only a starting point for teaching design, it shows how valuable all stages of design projects can be for students. Design projects require writers to look at successful models, to think deeply about audience, to design visual and verbal arguments together, and to actively construct new knowledge. Because the process of design is fundamentally visual and multimodal, it can be challenging, but it leads students to a new understanding of how designed spaces and artifacts impact audiences. Teaching design allowed these students to try to shape the social and cultural environment in which they found themselves by bringing together research and their own perspectives online to define a concept of English Studies. Nancy Kaplan ("Literacy and Technology"), Craig Stroupe ("Visualizing English"), and Randy Bass ("Story and Archive") have all demonstrated that the design of artifacts is an essential part of literacy and of enacting disciplinary knowledge in English Studies because those artifacts will ultimately determine how knowledge is received and perpetuated for our field. When designing digital documents and also seeing how people use and interpret them, our students can then see themselves as active producers of knowledge in their discipline.

Acknowledgments

I am grateful to Marilyn Cooper, Gary Bays, and the *CCC* reviewers for their helpful comments on this article. Special thanks to Jeff Grabill for his many readings and insights throughout the revision process. Thanks also to Chris Boese, Kristine McDermott, and Anne Wysocki for their contributions to this work, and to the Spelman students who allowed me to discuss their course work.

Notes

1. At the time that the hypertext theorists developed theories about electronic writing in the 1980s, they were primarily referring to elements of early hypertextual systems and the interactions in online communication before widespread use of graphical browsers on the World Wide Web. The early hypertext theorists focused immediately on both the visual and spatial character of electronic writing. For example, Jay Bolter defined the new writing technologies as "the visual writing space" (11) and outlined how they require a new visual literacy. Nancy Kaplan explained that "hypertextual writing systems [could] provide a graphic representation of textual structures, a dynamic map of the textual system in play" that "remain dynamic pictures of an evolving text" ("E-Literacies"). Michael Joyce highlighted Bolter's description of hypertext as "topographic writing" that implied its visual quality (47) and stated eloquently: "hypertext is, before anything else, a visual form" (19).
2. See, for example, Lester Faigley on the postmodern composing online self, George Landow on the connections between hypertext and postmodern literary theory, and Nancy Baym on the conversational features of online discourse. See Stuart Moulthrop and Peter Elbow on the postmodern forms of rhizome and collage for hypertext and for home pages. Hypertext seems to embody postmodern forms of writing, as Jane Yellowlees Douglass states: "The beauty of hypertext is . . . that it propels us from the straightened 'either/or' world that print has come to represent and into a universe where the 'and/and/and' is always possible" (146).
3. James Porter and Patricia Sullivan's early collaborative essay ends with a renewed emphasis on the visual challenges of electronic text (422). Barbara Mirel has demonstrated how database design has become an essential part of communication in the workplace and includes a "visual rhetoric" for effective data design (95). Similarly, Edward Tufte describes a successful computer interface as having a well-crafted parallelism and clustering of images that allows "visual reasoning" by the user. In two practical guides for authors, Domenic Stansberry points out in his guidelines for writers that designing content for new media focuses mostly on interactive design — the structure and flow of information pathways (17), while Karen Schriver includes chapters on interactive document design.
4. Not surprisingly, useful connections have been made between teaching writing and the visual arts as mutually reinforcing literacies in the classroom (e.g., Childers, Hobson, and Mullin). Theories for analyzing visual communication and visual culture have been highlighted in cross-disciplinary stud-

ies of culture and design, for example, the collections *The Visual Culture Reader* and *Design Discourse*. Industrial design discourse has been shown by Richard Buchanan as having a fully demonstrative rhetoric, drawing on the past and showing possibilities for the future in everyday objects (107). Hanno Ehses analyzes the visual rhetoric of performance posters, pointing out how the design medium of the poster collapses "visual and verbal" representation as the "structure itself becomes semiotic, since each of the two forms contains information over and above that pertaining to its own set" (193). The collection *Page to Screen* (Snyder) is a good example of cross-disciplinary scholarship that looks at the design processes involved in digital linguistic acts.

5. For examples of these parallels, see Michael Gibson and Donis Dondis. For critiques of these approaches to visual literacy and visual communication, see Mary Hocks, "Toward," and Anne Wysocki, "Seriously Visible."
6. See, for example, Jay Bolter, Richard Lanham, Christina Hass, and Michael Joyce.
7. See Mary Hocks and Michelle Kendrick for a complete discussion of hybridity in the history of visual and verbal language systems.
8. Personal communication with the author.
9. Personal communication with Doug Eyman, co-editor of *Kairos*. As Eyman explains it, the approximations of unique visitors, while more accurate than numbers of visits or hits, are probably underestimated due to technological constraints.
10. Personal communication with the author. As Christine Boese explains it, the increased traffic seems to correspond to moments when the site has been listed in articles or resources on cult fandoms. She adds that number of hits does indicate that some people might be reading fairly deep the thirty or so main screens and other pop up data windows in the site.
11. I did not teach this course, but as director of a faculty development program in communication across the curriculum I worked with a group of teachers from many disciplines who integrated multimedia design projects into their courses (see Mary Hocks and Daniele Bascelli). Faculty used an intensive summer workshop to develop online instructional resources like this site for their courses and to design writing-intensive assignments for their students that capitalized on the resources in the multimedia-equipped classroom.
12. I was unable to obtain data on visits to the Spelman College Writing Center site.
13. Results from an anonymous focus group of students, Spelman College, Atlanta, GA, May 2, 1992.

Works Cited

Bass, Randy. "Story and Archive in the Twenty-First Century." *College English* 61.6 (1999): 659–70.

Baym, Nancy. "From Practice to Culture on Usenet." In *The Cultures of Computing*. Ed. Susan Leigh Star. Oxford: Basil Blackwell, 1995. 29–52.

Berlin, James A. *Rhetorics, Poetics, and Cultures: Refiguring* College English *Studies*. Urbana, IL: NCTE, 1996.

Boese, Christine. "The Ballad of the Internet Nutball: Chaining Rhetorical Visions from the Margins to the Mainstream in the Xenaverse." Diss. online 1998 <http://www.nutball.com/dissertation/index.htm>.

Bolter, Jay David. *Writing Space: The Computer, Hypertext, and the History of Writing*. Hillsdale, NJ: Lawrence Erlbaum, 1991.

Bolter, Jay David, and Richard Grusin. *Remediation: Understanding New Media*. Cambridge: MIT P, 1999.

Buchanan, Richard. "Declaration by Design: Rhetoric, Argument, and Demonstration in Design Practice." In *Design Discourse: History, Theory, Criticism*. Ed. Victor Margolin. Chicago: U of Chicago P, 1989. 91–109.

Childers, Pamela B., Eric Hobson, and Joan A. Mullin. *ARTiculating: Teaching Writing in a Visual World*. Portsmouth, NH: Heinemann, 1998.

Cope, Bill, and Mary Kalantzis, eds. *Multiliteracies: Literacy Learning and the Design of Social Futures*. New York: Routledge, 2000.

Dondis, Donis A. *A Primer of Visual Literacy*. Cambridge: MIT P, 1973.

Douglass, Jane Yellowlees. "Will the Most Reflexive Relativist Please Stand Up: Hypertext, Argument, and Relativism." In *Page to Screen: Taking Literacy into the Electronic Era*. Ed. Ilana J. Snyder. London: Routledge, 1998. 144–62.

Ehses, Hanno H. J. "Representing MacBeth: A Case Study in Visual Rhetoric." In *Design Discourse: History, Theory, Criticism*. Ed. Victor Margolin. Chicago: U of Chicago P, 1989. 187–97.

Elbow, Peter. "Collage: Your Cheatin' Art." *Writing on the Edge* 9.1 (Fall/Winter 1997–98): 26–40.

Faigley, Lester. *Fragments of Rationality: Postmodernity and the Subject of Composition*. Pittsburgh, PA: U of Pittsburgh P, 1992.

Gibson, Michael. "Teaching Critical Analytical Methods in the Digital Typography Classroom." *Visible Language* 31.1 (1997): 300–25.

Hass, Christina. *Writing Technology: Studies on the Materiality of Literacy*. Mahwah, NJ: Lawrence Erlbaum, 1996.

Heba, Gary. "HyperRhetoric: Multimedia, Literacy, and the Future of Composition." *Computers and Composition* 14.1 (January 1997): 19–44.

Hocks, Mary E. "Toward a Visual Critical Electronic Literacy." *Works and Days* 17.1 & 2 (Spring/Fall 1999): 157–72.

Hocks, Mary E., and Daniele Bascelli. "Building a Multimedia Program across the Curriculum." In *Electronic Communication across the Curriculum*. Ed. Richard A. Selfe, Donna Reiss, and Art Young. Urbana, IL: NCTE. 40–56.

Hocks, Mary E., and Michelle Kendrick. "Introduction: Eloquent Images." In *Eloquent Images: Word and Image in the Age of New Media*. Cambridge: MIT P, 2003.

Joyce, Michael. *Of Two Minds: Hypertext Pedagogy and Poetics*. Ann Arbor: U of Michigan P, 1995.

Kaplan, Nancy. "E-Literacies: Politexts, Hypertexts, and Other Cultural Formations in the Late Age of Print." 1997 <http://iat.ubalt.edu/kaplan/lit/>.

———. "Literacy and Technology: Beyond the Book." <http://raven.ubalt.edu/staff/kaplan/parc/>.

Knadler, Stephen. "E-Racing Difference in E-Space: Black Female Subjectivity and the Web-Based Portfolio." *Computers and Composition* 18.3 (2001): 235–55.

Kress, Gunther. " 'English' at the Crossroads: Rethinking Curricula of Communication in the Context of the Turn to the Visual." *Passions, Pedagogies and 21st Century Technologies*. Ed. Gail E. Hawisher and Cynthia L. Selfe. Logan: Utah UP, 1999. 66–88.

———. "Multimodality." *Multiliteracies: Literacy Learning and the Design of Social Futures*. Ed. Bill Cope and Mary Kalantzis. New York: Routledge, 2000. 182–202.

Landow, George P. *Hypertext: The Convergence of Contemporary Critical Theory and Technology*. Baltimore: Johns Hopkins UP, 1992.

Lanham, Richard A. *The Electronic Word: Democracy, Technology, and the Arts*. Chicago: U of Chicago P, 1993.

McDermott, Kristine. "Report on Teaching and Technology Workshop for the Shakespeare Association of America." Unpublished manuscript. Atlanta, GA: Spelman College, 1998. 1–5.

Mirel, Barbara. "Writing and Database Technology: Extending the Definition of Writing in the Workplace." *Electronic Literacies in the Workplace: Technologies of Writing*. Ed. Patricia Sullivan and Jennie Dautermann. Urbana, IL: NCTE, 1996. 91–114.

Mirzoeff, Nicholas, ed. *The Visual Culture Reader*. New York: Routledge, 1998.

Mitchell, William J. *The Reconfigured Eye: Visual Truth in the Post-Photographic Era*. Cambridge: MIT P, 1992.

Moulthrop, Stuart. "Beyond the Electronic Book: A Critique of Hypertext Rhetoric." *Hypertext '91 Proceedings*. New York: The Association for Computing Machinery. 291–98.

Mullet, Kevin, and Darrell Sano. *Designing Visual Interfaces: Communication Oriented Techniques*. Mountain View, CA: Sun Microsystems, 1995.

Murray, Janet Horowitz. *Hamlet on the Holodeck: The Future of Narrative in Cyberspace*. Cambridge: MIT P, 1998.

Porter, James E. *Rhetorical Ethics and Internetworked Writing*. Greenwich, CT: Ablex, 1998.

Porter, James, and Patricia Sullivan. "Remapping Curricular Geography: Professional Writing in/and English Studies." *Journal of Business and Technical Communication* 7 (1993): 389–422.

Schriver, Karen A. *Dynamics in Document Design: Creating Text for Readers*. New York: John Wiley and Sons, 1997.

Selfe, Cynthia L. "Technology and Literacy: A Story about the Perils of Not Paying Attention." *College Composition and Communication* 50.3 (February 1999): 411–36.

Snyder, Ilana, ed. *Page to Screen: Taking Literacy into the Electronic Era*. London: Routledge, 1998.

Stansberry, Domenic. *Labyrinths: The Art of Interactive Writing and Design*. Belmont, CA: Wadsworth Publishing, 1998.

STORYSPACE™. Computer Software. Watertown, MA: Eastgate Systems, Inc. December 2, 2002 <http://www.eastgate.com/Storyspace.html>.

Stroupe, Craig. "Visualizing English: Recognizing the Hybrid Literacy of Visual and Verbal Authorship on the Web." *College English* 62.5 (May 2000): 607–32.

Tufte, Edward. *Visual Explanations: Images and Quantities, Evidence and Narrative*. Cheshire, CT: Graphics Press, 1997.

Wysocki, Anne Frances. "Impossibly Distinct: On Form/Content and Word/Image in Two Pieces of Computer-Based Interactive Multimedia." *Computers and Composition* 18 (2001): 209–34.

———. "Monitoring Order." Kairos 3.2 (Fall 1998). Online <http://english.ttu.edu/kairos/3.2/indx_f.html>.

———. "Seriously Visible." *Eloquent Images: Word and Image in the Age of New Media*. Ed. Mary E. Hocks and Michelle Kendrick. Cambridge: MIT P, 2003.

Hocks's Insights as a Resource for Your Reflections

1. Consider your students' level of preparedness for engaging the issues of visual rhetoric and new technology. What about your own level of comfort with the rhetoric that Hocks describes? Make a list of the aspects of visual rhetoric that feel familiar to you and those aspects that you would like to know more about. What resources are available at your school for teachers who want to learn more about technology?
2. How might certain features of your composition course, as currently configured, lend themselves particularly well to an online project? What about some of your own course materials? Would you consider asking your students to produce an online text? Why or why not?

Hocks's Insights as a Resource for Your Writing Classroom

1. Devise for your students a set of guidelines for analyzing the visual rhetoric of an online document. You might organize your guidelines around Hocks's concepts of audience stance, transparency, and hybridity.
2. Discuss with your students Hocks's concept of hybridity, and, in particular, how it can be used as a rhetorical strategy. Ask students to write a paper that explains the power of visual and verbal interplay in an online document of their choosing.

Delivering the Message: Typography and the Materiality of Writing

John Trimbur

Cartoons and photos, icons and emoticons, fonts, diagrams, charts, colors . . . the list of elements that can play a role in the printed page continues to grow, and if we consider multimodal composition of the sort involved in "writing" for Web sites, it grows exponentially. But what is the writing teacher to make of this? And how can we position this explosion of possibility within the more familiar context of our field's "process movement"? John Trimbur's essay engages these questions directly and shows how they open a great many others in this richly suggestive survey of the ideas that constitute typography (literally, the art of working with type as a material entity, just as painters work with paint or potters with clay), and he tracks the implications of these ideas for teachers of writing in today's whirlwind of technological change.

In recent years, those of us involved in the study and teaching of writing have been trying to adjust to life after the process movement. To be sure, the slogan "process not product" long ago lost any critical edge it might have possessed in the 1970s, and the once enabling notion that composing is the critical object of inquiry now seems, in Karl Marx's words, a "one-sided" view of the production of writing. One can no longer read, for example, Janet Emig's or Donald Graves's pioneer composing research without reading into it representations of their research subjects as gendered and racialized subjects of class society. And yet, the moment writing theorists are starting to call "post-process" must be seen not just as a repudiation of the process movement but also as an attempt to read into composition precisely the material conditions of the composer and the material pressures and limits of the composing process. As Robert J. Connors once remarked, the reason we feel we're living in a post-process era is that process has been so fully assimilated, so exhaustively read into and written over that we forget about the traces it has left in our theories and practices.

The dominant representations of writing typically offered by the process movement — voice, cognition, conversation — despite the crucial differences among them, all picture writing as an invisible process, an auditory or mental event that takes place at the point of composing, where meanings get made. In my contribution to this volume, I want to reread these dematerialized representations of writing in terms of the materiality of literacy, from the perspective that writing is a visible language produced and circulated in material forms. To put it another way, I want to suggest that the process movement's emphasis on the composer as the maker of meaning (whether that figure entails self-expression, mental activity, or participation in communal discourses) has obscured the composer's work in producing the resources of representation in order to signify at all, to make the special signs we call writing.

The Materiality of Writing

The line of thinking I propose holds that the figure of the composer we inherit from the process movement can still provide a generative topos in writing studies. The task, however, requires a thoroughgoing reconceptualization of the writer at work—one that locates the composer in the labor process, in relation to the available means of production. In certain respects, of course, such a project has already begun. No doubt the leading impetus to materialize literacy comes from the emergence of digital communication. Marshall McLuhan says that we can see human-made environments only once they have changed, and this is very much the case, I think, regarding the current shift from print to digital literacy. These changes in the technology of writing allow us to compare, say, mechanical means of production such as the typewriter or the Linotype machine and hot type of the late nineteenth-century print shop to the cool cybersurface and digital signals of the computer screen and digital signals. As Christina Haas points out, it is no longer quite so easy to treat the technologies of writing as transparent, to efface the material tools and embodied practices involved in the production of writing.

One of the main obstacles to *seeing* the materiality of writing has been the essayist tradition and its notion of a transparent text. (It is no accident that the process movement's favored genre has always been the essay, be it literary, journalistic, or academic.) I argued a few years ago that essayist literacy—from the scientific prose of the Royal Society to the essay of the coffeehouse and salon—emerged in the early modern period as a rhetoric of deproduction: a programmatic effort to reduce the figurative character of writing, minimize the need for interpretation, and thereby make the text more transparent ("Essayist"). What I was not aware of at the time, however, is how essayist literacy's compulsion to eliminate metaphor is linked to Old Testament warnings about graven images and to a Protestant desire to purge writing of all traces of visuality, a desire to replace, as Lester Faigley puts it, the "'mindless' auditory, visual, and olfactory credulity of Catholicism with the power of reason expressed in print" (174–75).

In Faigley's view, the notion of transparent text results from a great Alphabetic Literacy Narrative that runs through the work of Harold Innis, Jack Goody, Eric Havelock, and Walter Ong. This grand narrative identifies "'true' literacy" with the "abstract representation of sounds—a presupposition that subordinates syllabic and logographic writing systems and banishes pictographs and images to the status of illiteracy" (174). As the graphic design theorists J. Abbott Miller and Ellen Lupton say, "Westerners revere the alphabet as the most rational and transparent of all writing systems, the clearest of vessels for containing the words of speech" (21). By this account of literacy, the suppression of visuality in the alphabet's abstract coding system provides the groundwork for normative representations of both cultural and individual development as matters of overcoming a dependence on the visual that is taken to be immature, ephemeral, and manipulative. Accordingly, it should be no surprise that David Olson would want to make the essay into the culmination of alphabetic literacy precisely because it appears to transcend the visuality of writing by organizing the speech-sound abstractions of the alphabet into highly integrated grammatical and logical structures, forming self-sufficient, autonomous texts capable of speaking for themselves. The texts of essayist literacy, by Olson's account, appear to transmit meanings transparently, without reference to their mode and medium of production.

The fatal weakness of the Alphabetic Literacy Narrative and its commitment to textual transparency, however, is its scopophobia and how its fear of the visual causes it to align writing with speech. In this sense, the irony of the grand narrative is that it suppresses the full upshot of its own discovery — namely, that writing amounts to be less a recording of speech than a visual coding system that communicates by employing a range of nonphonetic elements such as spacing, punctuation, frames, and borders, not to mention the eccentricities in codes, such as in written English where different words can have the same sound (its/it's, meet/meat) and silent letters seem to defy phonetic strategies of pronunciation (might, paradigm). Haunted by suspicions of the visual (and hence of the visibility of writing), at just the moment when it elevates alphabetic literacy to a preeminent position in Western cultural history, the Alphabetic Literacy Narrative comes unglued, reminded by the very visuality of the alphabet, as Miller and Lupton say, that writing can only be a "faulty reflection of speech, an artificial byproduct of the otherwise natural workings of the mind" (24).

Now, you don't have to be much of a Derridean (I'm certainly not) to recognize a metaphysics of presence at work in such disappointment with writing, the overwhelming sense that what promised to be the vehicle for rational discourse is, in the end, a treacherous medium that continually betrays its own ostensible transparency by thickening into metaphor and material form. My view, perhaps uncharacteristically, is to follow Derrida out of the morass created by the Alphabetic Literacy Narrative and to picture writing not as a derivative of speech at all but instead as a typographical and rhetorical system of sign making. After all, as the turn-of-the-century Austrian architect and graphic designer Adolf Loos put it so concisely, "One cannot *speak* a capital letter" (qtd. in Helfand 50).

For post-process theorizing to rematerialize writing, we need to recast the figure of the composer and its essayist legacy — to see writers not just as making of meaning but as makers of the means of producing meaning out of the available resources of representation. To understand more fully the work of the composer in the labor process of writing, we must see, as Gunther Kress has argued, that individuals do not simply *acquire* literacy but actually *build* for themselves the tools to produce writing. As Kress shows in *Before Writing*, the multimodal activity of young children working with images, shapes, letterforms, the directionality of writing, the page, and an emergent understanding of genre amounts to an active incorporation of sign-making tools into their practices of signification. By the same token, instead of thinking of writers as "users" who confront computers as machines that they must learn to operate in order to write, we might think in terms of how individuals, through the labor process of writing, appropriate the means of digital literacy, in highly variable ways, into their own repertoire of sign-making tools. In either case, by locating the composer in a labor process that includes assembling the means of making meaning, we can begin to see, as Kress suggests, how writing transforms the signifying resources at hand by consuming them in the act of production and, in turn, how the material practice of writing transforms the composer's subjectivity and the world in which newly made signs appear.

Typography and Writing Studies

The line of thinking I want to advance starts with the recognition that the major images of writing from the process era (voice, cognition, conversation) neglect the materiality and visuality of writing. The next step is to devise a more adequate account. My claim is that studying and teaching typography as the culturally salient means of producing writing can help locate composers in the labor process and thereby contribute to the larger post-process work of rematerializing literacy. Typography, of course, has been a longtime topic in the writing curriculum. The problem is that, by and large, typography has been ghettoized in technical communication, where many compositionists think of it as a vocational skill. The concerns of typography — such as document design, page layout, fonts, infographics, and reading paths — are associated with at best commercial art and career training and at worst complicity with corporate culture. To put it bluntly, typography, for all practical purposes, has been assigned in the writing curriculum to the marketplace, at a far remove from the belletristic, critical, and academic work of the essay so cherished by the process movement.

There are good reasons to reconsider this marginalization and to bring typography into the mainstream of writing studies. For one thing, typography — quite literally "writing with type" — can help rematerialize literacy by calling attention to the visual design of writing, be it handwritten, print, or electronic. Typography enables us to *see* writing in material terms as letterforms, printed pages, posters, computer screens. It helps to name the available tools of representation that composers draw on to make their own means of production. For another, typography links writing to delivery—the fifth canon of rhetoric. Like typography, delivery has been neglected by the process movement, isolated from invention, arrangement, style, and memory, and, when mentioned at all, reduced to such afterthoughts as neat handwriting and manuscript preparation. From a typographical perspective, however, the visual design of writing figures prominently as the material form in which the message is delivered. That is, typography offers a way to think of writing not just in terms of the moment of composing but also in terms of its circulation, as messages take on cultural value and worldly force, moving through the Marxian dialectic of production, distribution, exchange, and consumption.[1] From the mass circulation of periodicals to the way junior high school girls write and fold the notes they pass in class (see Finders), the visual design of writing enters consequentially into the activity of composition.

Modern typography is associated with the rise of mass communication, consumer culture, and the society of the spectacle, with roots in both the popular culture of the metropolis and the agitations of the high modernist vanguard in art and politics. Typographical theory and practice developed largely within graphic design movements, from the art nouveau lithographs of Toulouse-Lautrec and Jules Cheret, William Morris, and the Viennese Secession at the turn of the previous century to the avant-garde of Futurism, Dada, and Soviet Constructivism, Jan Tschichold "new typography," Bauhaus, and the federal WPA posters of the 1920s and 1930s to the postwar ascendancy of Swiss Modern and its current postmodern challengers. Though now collected and displayed in art museums (see Friedman, *Graphic Design*; Rothschild, Lupton, and Goldstein; and Lupton for catalogues of major exhibits), typographical work has typically occurred outside the art world, in the realm of commerce and politics—or, in some instances, such as with Futurism and Dada, as an anti-art.

Only recently has there been an organized academic investigation of graphic design theory and history. During the 1980s, the professional journals *Print* and *AIGA Journal of Graphic Design* started to feature historical and critical articles. *Visible Language*, founded in 1967 as the quarterly *Journal of Typographical Research*, and journals started in the 1980s such as *Design Issues* and *Journal of Design History* have worked to make typography and graphic design, along with other types of design, into respectable objects of scholarly inquiry. Victor Margolin gives a sense of design history from 1977 to 1987 in an important review essay ("A Decade"). Two textbooks, Philip Meggs's *A History of Graphic Design* and Richard Hollis's *Graphic Design: A Concise History*, and Robin Kinross's *Modern Typography: An Essay in Critical History*, give overviews of graphic design movements and theories, and the three volumes of *Looking Closer* (edited by Michael Bierut et al.) collect both contemporary critical perspectives in the first two volumes and classic statements in the third. Book-length studies, such as Victor Margolin's *The Struggle for Utopia* (a study of the Soviet constructivists El Lissitzky and Alexander Rodchenko, as well as the associated figure Laslo Moholy-Nagi) and Johanna Drucker's *The Visible Word: Experimental Typography and Modern Art, 1909–1923*, have started to appear, providing both critical accounts and an alternative to the expensive, coffee-table productions that contain extensive illustrations but little analysis — publications that have tended to dominate publishing on typography and graphic design.

I offer this quick bibliographical tour as an outsider to the field of graphic design and with considerable misgivings. What I hope to suggest is the intellectual ferment that is currently taking place around what we might call in its most general sense "design studies." There are two points to be made. The first is that graphic designers and typographers have started to interrogate design theory and history in ways that are potentially of great interest to those of us who work in writing. I will look at a few of the specific questions they raise in the final section of this chapter. The second point is more general, for it has to do with the relevance of the very notion of "design" to writing theorists.[2] Design studies and design history are relatively new interdisciplinary fields that take not only typography and graphic design as their objects of inquiry but more broadly "the conception and planning of all the products made by human beings" (Buchanan and Margolin x). In other words, "design" has to do with the work of architects, urban planners, engineers, computer scientists, psychologists, sociologists, anthropologists, marketing and manufacturing experts, as well as industrial and graphic designers and communication specialists (see, for example, Buchanan and Margolin; and Margolin, *Design*). The various efforts to identify a discipline of design that can organize such a range of activities into intelligible patterns go far beyond the scope of this paper. For our purposes, what is worth noting is the persistent quest in modern design theory for "the essential unity of all forms of making in the circumstances of a new cultural environment strongly influenced by engineering, technology, and commerce" (Buchanan 36).

Importantly this search for what Richard Buchanan calls a "new architechtonic art of design" emerges in the modern era not so much out of the profit motive of the market as from a utopian vision of the designer's relationship to mass production, on the one hand, and to the fine arts, on the other. As Walter Gropius says of the Bauhaus:

> Our guiding principle was that design is neither an intellectual nor a material affair, but simply an integral part of the stuff of life, necessary for everyone in a civilized society. Our ambition was to arouse the creative

> artist from his other-worldiness and to reintegrate him into the workaday world of realities and, at the same time, to broaden and humanize the rigid, almost exclusively material mind of the businessman. Our conception of the basic unity of all design in relation to life was in diametric opposition to that of "art for art's sake" and the much more dangerous philosophy it sprang from, business as an end in itself. (20)

Gropius's desire to "humanize" the business classes may sound naïve, particularly after so much of modernist design has been assimilated by advertising, mass media, the "corporate identity" programs of the postwar period, and the current "branding" campaigns of global capital. Nonetheless, like the aspirations of Morris, Lissitzky, and others to design for social ends, the Bauhaus's utopian goal of dismantling the boundaries between fine and applied art and of designing for social usefulness and the enrichment of everyday life still retains its critical edge.[3]

The desire to design for life has particular relevance to the study and teaching of writing. Not only does it emphasize the rhetoricity of design as deliberation and argument about the possible worlds we might construct, it also calls attention to genres of writing that have traditionally fallen outside the mainstream of writing instruction. As Walter Benjamin says:

> Significant literary work can only come into being in a strict alternation between action and writing; it must nurture the inconspicuous forms that better fit its influence in active communities than does the pretentious, universal gesture of the book—in leaflets, brochures, articles, and posters. Only this prompt language shows itself actively equal to the moment. (qtd. in Kinross xv)

If we substitute here the "universal gesture" of *the essay* for that of *the book*, we can read Benjamin's remarks as a pertinent critique of contemporary writing instruction (and the residual hold of its essayist legacy). Benjamin's notion of "prompt language" amounts to the design of messages for mass circulation, timely responses to the twists and turns of class struggle "actively equal to the moment." Long considered ephemeral and beneath notice by writing teachers, Benjamin's "inconspicuous forms" break with the "universal gesture" of the essay to deliver messages in the history of the contemporary. And in this light, typography and the visual design of writing can no longer be marginalized in the writing curriculum as afterthoughts or preprofessional training; they appear instead as essential elements in an emergent civic rhetoric. If anything, the call to write for the social good found in public and community service writing can help to materialize Benjamin's figure of the author-as-producer as a post-process representation to replace the process movement's composer as the essayist maker of meaning.

Typography in Theory and Practice

Three issues in typographical theory and practice seem to me to be of particular interest to writing studies: the narrativity of letterforms, the page as a unit of discourse, and the division of labor that produces written text. The comments that follow are meant to be suggestive rather than programmatic, to indicate some of the paths typography opens to further investigation in our own intellectual work.

The Narrativity of Letterforms

The history of letterforms is a complex one involving changing philosophies, technologies, and social uses of writing. In Gutenburg's fifteenth-century print shop, handmade letterforms imitated the calligraphy of the older scribal tradition. During the Renaissance, humanist designers departed from the naturalistic pen strokes of handwriting to fix the ideal proportions of the alphabet by using the tools of geometry; and in 1693, Louis XIV commissioned a study of the Roman alphabet that imposed a rational grid on letterforms, resulting in the *romain du roi* that was meant to embody the authority of scientific method and bureaucratic power. Hopes for such an absolutist, idealized system of letterforms, however, disappeared within a century. According to Lupton and Miller, the Enlightenment typographers Giambattista Bodoni and Françoise Ambroise Didot broke the "ancestral bond between contemporary typefaces and a divine classical past" by reducing the alphabet to "a system of oppositions — thick and thin, vertical and horizontal, serif and stem," in effect paving the way to an understanding of letterforms "as a set of elements open to infinite manipulation" (55). From the nineteenth-century proliferation of display type to modernist experimentalism and now the vast repertoire of computer fonts (including inexact and degraded forms and bi-fontal crossbreedings), the alphabet has changed, as Miller and Lupton point out, from a "pedigreed line of fixed, self-contained symbols" to a "flexible system of difference." The emphasis in typography has shifted "from the individual letter to the overall series of characters," exchanging the "fixed identity of the letter for the relational system of the font" (23).

What this shift enables us to see is the figurative, narrative character of letterforms. We might read, for example, Josef Alber's 1925 stencil typeface, Herbert Bayer's 1925 "universal," and Tschichold's "new typography" not simply as failed modernist master codes to produce a rational font out of standardized, interchangeable parts but also as expressions of technological and humanistic optimism about to be shattered by the atavistic nationalism of black letter type under Hitler's Third Reich. By the same token, we can find the story in the use of vernacular forms by current typographical designers such as Jeffrey Keedy, whose 1990 Manuscript "combines an antiheroic amalgam of Modernist geometry and grade-school penmanship" to recall the "naïve yet normative scenario of learning to write"—an exercise that results "not only from external technologies but from the disciplinary socialization of the individual" (Lupton and Miller 24).[4] And finally, to bring things closer to home, we can read the manuscript conventions of the student essay as the story of the transparent text, where the neatness and clarity of standardized type on the printed page seek to efface the visuality of writing and bring the teacher-reader in direct and unmediated touch with the student's mind.

The Page as a Unit of Discourse

The standard units of discourse in writing instruction are the word, sentence, paragraph, and essay; and there is a sad—though now largely repudiated—history of arranging them as a developmental sequence. In the essayist tradition, the page itself is of little account, for as readers we are supposedly not looking at the visual design of writing but following the writer's thoughts. Typography, on the other hand, calls attention to how the look of the page communicates meaning by treating text as a visual element that can be combined with images and other nonverbal forms to produce a unit of discourse. Early printed books, for example, often sought to emulate the multimodal capacities of illuminated manuscripts by using borders, rules, columns, marginalia, textual inserts, and woodblock illustrations to design the page. Typography in the modern period has, in many respects, been eager to recover the visuality of the page from the monotony of standardized letterforms and dense monochromatic blocks of text by incorporating onto the printed page the available means of visual communication, from the engravings in such nineteenth-century periodicals as *Frank Leslie's Illustrated Newspaper* and *Harpers Weekly* to the mid-twentieth-century photo essays in *Life* and the computer infographics of *USA Today*. In addition, poets such as Stephane Mallarme, Guillaume Apollinaire, and Filippo Marinetti sought to free the word and the poetic line from the conventional horizontal and vertical structures of the printed page by mixing size, weight, and style of type and pasting letters and words in visual patterns to create nonlinear compositions. More recently, Dan Friedman's now famous design exercise, drawing on the mundane text of a weather report, raised questions about the emphasis on clarity, orderliness, and simplicity in the modernist use of the grid, rules, and information bands as the basis of page design to explore how "legibility (a quality of efficient, clear, and simple reading) is often in conflict with readability (a quality which promotes interest, pleasure, and challenge in reading)" ("Introductory" 139). And, with the advent of computers, designers such as Rudy VanderLans at *Emigre* magazine, April Greiman, and Katherine McCoy at Cranbrook Academy of Art have made use of the new digital technologies to give the page a formerly unimagined depth, layering and overlapping images and text in deep perspective in ways that confound the traditional opposition between seeing and reading and that call on reader/viewers to participate in making sense of the page.

The complicated relationship between reading and seeing text and image raises interesting questions for writing studies about how we might think about the page as a unit of discourse — about how, say, the juxtaposition of articles, photographs, and advertisements on a newspaper or magazine page creates larger messages than any single item can convey (see Kress, "Text," for an analysis of how the articles on a single newspaper page articulate complex and contradictory representations of poverty); about how "hyperactive" pages encourage browsing rather than reading (see Giovannini's warnings about the "capitulation of text to layout" [204]); and about how individuals find their own reading paths to negotiate the page. Finally, we might ask what is at stake in writing instruction by the common practice of taking articles and essays off the printed page on which they appear (along with other articles, images, and advertising) and reproducing them in handouts or anthologies.

Division of Labor

Typography was traditionally a craft, an artisan's labor that belongs to the print shop. In the early modern period, printing was often thought of as "black magic," and its secrets were guarded by guilds of craftsmen who passed their hermetic arts from master to apprentice. As printing spread, however, "a new occupational culture associated with the printing trades" began to appear, in which the print shop provided "a new setting for intellectual activity," and the master printer became a "hybrid figure" — by turns entrepreneur, lexicographer, editor, cultural impresario, sponsor of scientific research, and political activist — who "presided over the rise of a lay intelligentsia" (Eisenstein 24, 25). If printers like Benjamin Franklin played a central role in the scientific and democratic revolutions of the modern era, in the twentieth century, typography settled into the division of labor under corporate capital, becoming a career path for graphic artists in design studios, publishing, the media, advertising, and academia — another profession with its associations and publications.

I recount this brief historical overview to sketch a typical (if oversimplified) pattern of specialization in professional life and to suggest ways in which such specialization is now under pressure. With the rise of desktop publishing, the division of labor is beginning to flatten, and the distinctions between author, designer, and printer are starting to collapse. For example, the design, composition, production, and distribution of a memo or report may well be the continuous activity in virtual space of a single figure at a connected computer terminal. In the contemporary workplace, this is what new-age management gurus call "multitasking," where digital literacy overcomes the divisions of labor in the era of mechanical reproduction, eliminating secretarial pools and mimeograph machines and transforming managers into information designers.

But the pressure on specialization can do more than serve the ends of corporate restructuring. Benjamin's essay "The Author as Producer" anticipates the progressive possibilities inherent in a collapsing division of labor:

> What we require of the photographer is the ability to give his picture the caption that wrenches it from modish commerce and gives it revolutionary useful value. But we shall make this demand most emphatically when we — the writers — take up photography. Here, too, therefore, technical progress is for the author as producer of the foundation of political progress. (230)

Writing in 1934, Benjamin must have had in mind the work of revolutionary artists such as John Heartfield, whose photomontages used the airbrush, captions, and cut-and-paste techniques to turn the apparent transparency of the photograph into revolutionary messages ("prompt language") in the struggle against fascism (see Pachnicke and Honnef). At the same time, Benjamin raises questions for us today about how, with the rise of digital typography and online communication, we might imagine new possibilities for designers and authors to become producers, to take over the available tools of representation in order to transform the distribution and use of messages. Given the recent eruption of interest in visual culture within composition, Benjamin offers a way to think about how the study and teaching of writing might take up the visual (and the visibility of writing) as more than just new texts and topics for theorists and students to write about in interpretive and critical essays — though I certainly endorse the value of such work.[5] What remains to be seen, in theory and practice, is how typography — the productive art of writing with type — can be "actively equal to the moment."

Notes

1. For an extended argument on the importance of circulation to the study and teaching of writing, see Trimbur, "Composition."
2. The notion of "design" is already seeping into writing studies, as a possible replacement for "composing." See Kaufer and Butler; Petraglia; and Cope and Kalantzis. The view of "design" in this essay is aligned in important respects with the latter volume, but I think, at this point, it is important to keep the idea of "design" an open one — to see where it might lead us.
3. In this regard, see the three *Looking Closer* volumes (Bierut et al.) for the ongoing discussion of the social responsibilities of graphic designers. Also see Daniel Friedman, *Radical*, for an heroic attempt to join design and everyday life (as well as negotiate the demands of modernism and postmodernism

on the contemporary designer), and *Adbusters* magazine and Web site <www.adbusters.org>.

4. In this narrative vein, typographer Jonathan Barnbrook has designed a Nixon typeface "to tell lies" and Prozac to "simplify meanings."
5. *Reading Images: The Grammar of Visual Design* (Kress and van Leeuwen) provides, in my view, the preeminently useful social semiotic analysis of the "look of the page," but I can't resist pointing out the irony that it "explains" visual structures in terms of Hallydean linguistic ones.

Works Cited

Benjamin, Walter. "The Author as Producer." 1934. *Reflections: Essays, Aphorism, Autobiographical Writings*. Ed. Peter Demetz. New York: Schocken, 1978. 220–38.

Bierut, Michael, William Drenttel, Steven Heller, and D. K. Holland, eds. *Looking Closer: Critical Writings on Graphic Design*. Vols. 1–2. New York: Allworth, 1991, 1997.

Bierut, Michael, Jessica Helfand, Steven Heller, and Rich Poynor, eds. *Looking Closer: Classic Writings on Graphic Design*. Vol. 3. New York: Allworth, 1999.

Buchanan, Richard. "Rhetoric, Humanism, and Design." *Discovering Design: Explorations in Design Studies*. Ed. Richard Buchanan and Victor Margolin. Chicago: U of Chicago P, 1995. 23–66.

Buchanan, Richard, and Victor Margolin. Introduction. *Discovering Design: Explorations in Design Studies*. Ed. Richard Buchanan and Victor Margolin. Chicago: U of Chicago P, 1995. ix–xxvi.

Cope, Bill, and Mary Kalantzis, eds. *Multiliteracies: Literacy Learning and the Design of Social Futures*. London: Routledge, 2000.

Drucker, Johanna. *The Visible Word: Experimental Typography and Modern Art, 1909–1923*. Chicago: U of Chicago P, 1994.

Eisenstein, Elizabeth. "On the Printing Press as an Agent of Change." *Literacy, Language, and Learning: The Nature and Consequences of Reading and Writing*. Ed. David R. Olson, Nancy Torrance, and Angela Hildyard. Cambridge: Cambridge UP, 1985. 19–33.

Faigley, Lester. "Material Literacy and Visual Design." *Rhetorical Bodies*. Ed. Jack Selzer and Sharon Crowley. Madison: U of Wisconsin P, 1999. 171–201.

Finders, Margaret. *Just Girls: Hidden Literacies and Life in Junior High*. New York: Teachers College P, 1997.

Friedman, Daniel. "Introductory Education in Typography." *Visible Language* 7.2 (1973): 129–44.

———. *Radical Modernism*. New Haven: Yale UP, 1997.

Friedman, Mildred, ed. *Graphic Design in America: A Visual Language History*. Minneapolis: Walker Art Center, 1989.

Giovannini, Joseph. "A Zero Degree of Graphics." *Graphic Design in America: A Visual Language History*. Ed. Mildred Freidman. Minneapolis: Walker Art Center, 1989. 200–13.

Goody, Jack, and Ian P. Watt. "The Consequences of Literacy." *Comparative Studies in Society and History* 5 (1963): 304–45.

Gropius, Walter. "My Conception of the Bauhaus Idea." *Scope of Total Architecture*. Ed. Walter Gropius. New York: Colliers, 1962. 6–19.

Haas, Christina. *Writing Technology: Studies on the Materiality of Literacy*. Mahwah, NJ: Erlbaum, 1996.
Havelock, Eric. *The Literate Revolution in Greece and Its Cultural Consequences*. Princeton: Princeton UP, 1982.
Helfand, Jessica. "Electronic Typography: The New Visual Language." Bierut et al., vol. 2, 49–51.
Hollis, Richard. *Graphic Design: A Concise History*. London: Thames and Hudson, 1994.
Innis, Harold A. *The Bias of Communication*. Toronto: U of Toronto P, 1951.
Kaufer, David S., and Brian S. Butler. *Rhetoric and the Arts of Design*. Mahwah, NJ: Erlbaum, 1996.
Kinross, Robin. Introduction. *The New Typography: A Handbook for Modern Designers*. Jan Tschichold. Trans. Ruari McLean. Berkeley: U of California P, 1998. xv–xliv.
———. *Modern Typography: An Essay in Critical History*. London: Hyphen, 1992.
Kress, Gunther R. *Before Writing: Rethinking the Paths to Literacy*. London: Routledge, 1997.
———. "Text and Grammar as Explanation." *Text, Discourse, and Context: Representations of Poverty in Britain*. Ed. Ulrike H. Meinhof and Kay Richardson. London: Longman, 1994. 24–46.
Kress, Gunther R., and Theo van Leeuwen. *Reading Images: The Grammar of Visual Design*. New York: Routledge, 1996.
Lupton, Ellen. *Mixing Messages: Graphic Design in Contemporary Culture*. New York: Princeton Architectural P, 1996.
Lupton, Ellen, and J. Abbott Miller. "Laws of the Letter." *Design Writing Research: Writing on Graphic Design*. Ed. Ellen Lupton and J. Abbott Miller. London: Phaidon, 1996. 53–61.
Margolin, Victor. "A Decade of Design History in the United States, 1977–88." *Journal of Design History* 1.1 (1988): 51–72.
———, ed. *Design Discourse: History, Theory, Criticism*. Chicago: U of Chicago P, 1989.
———. *The Struggle for Utopia: Rodchenko, Lissitzky, Moholy-Nagy, 1917–1946*. Chicago: U of Chicago P, 1997.
Meggs, Philip B. *A History of Graphic Design*. 3rd ed. New York: Wiley, 1998.
Miller, J. Abbott, and Ellen Lupton. "A Natural History of Typography." Bierut et al., vol. 1, 19–25.
Olson, David R, "From Utterance to Text: The Bias of Language in Speaking and Writing." *Harvard Educational Review* 47 (1977): 257–81.
Ong, Walter J. *Orality and Literacy: The Technologizing of the Word*. New York: Methuen, 1982.
Pachnicke, Peter, and Klaus Honnef, eds. *John Heartfield*. New York: Abrams, 1992.
Petraglia, Joseph. *Reality by Design: The Rhetoric and Technology of Authenticity*. Mahwah, NJ: Erlbaum, 1998.
Rothschild, Deborah, Ellen Lupton, and Darra Goldstein. *Graphic Design in the Mechanical Age: Selections from the Merrill C. Berman Collection*. New Haven: Yale UP, 1998.
Trimbur, John. "Composition and the Circulation of Writing." *College Composition and Communication* 52 (2000): 188–219.
———. "Essayist Literacy and the Rhetoric of Deproduction." *Rhetoric Review* 9 (1990): 72–86.

Trimbur's Insights as a Resource for Your Reflections

1. Consider the three issues in typographical theory that Trimbur explores, and sketch ways that they might inform a set of remarks you might make to your students, and, in turn, a set of questions that you could offer them to stimulate a session of freewriting, more discussion, and perhaps a paper topic about what Trimbur calls the sheer "materiality of writing." After all, discovering this materiality is probably a powerful step in getting students to have more and more ambitious engagements with it and perhaps thereby become more and more effective writers. How might you facilitate this?
2. Consider Trimbur's ideas in the context of the essay by Hocks that immediately precedes it, and then make a list of the questions about the writing curriculum on your campus that you might want to discuss with colleagues. After all, writing today constitutes a fundamentally different set of possibilities than it did just fifteen years ago, and perhaps your school's curriculum is due for an upgrade. What challenges does such an upgrade need to overcome and how might it do so?

Trimbur's Insights as a Resource for Your Writing Classroom

1. In a short paper assignment, require your students to deviate in any three ways from the standard presentation of the printed page as conventionally, traditionally understood in the contemporary academy and then have students explain how those choices were appropriate to the message they intended to deliver.

CHAPTER

3

Responding to and Evaluating Student Writing

Teachers' responses to student texts are continuously cited as the most significant influence — positive or negative — on students' concepts of themselves as writers. And our commentary in the margins of student texts is potentially among our most powerful teaching tools. Although to many students "teacher response" signifies grades and summary comments, teachers may respond to student writing in several other ways: inside and outside the classroom, through structured feedback and spontaneously, and as both ally and gatekeeper.

Careful reflection on classroom practice prompted the articles in this chapter. Each essay is, of course, informed by philosophical perspectives, but all these readings focus very specifically on practical strategies for working with students at different skill levels in a variety of writing sites. You'll find many connections among the readings and a high degree of "intertextuality." Although you may be tempted to turn to just one of these readings only as a strong need arises, we recommend that you read them all and that you read them against the other pieces in this collection. These articles all resonate with a strong concern for student growth and empowerment, and from them you can carry away new ideas about ways of responding to student writing.

Responding to Student Writing

Nancy Sommers

Given the time and energy we devote to responding to student drafts, how should we go about it — how should we make the most of our efforts? In the conclusion of this landmark essay, first published in College Composition *and* Communication *in 1982, Nancy Sommers describes what continues to be a major responsibility for writing teachers: "The challenge we face as teachers is to develop comments which will provide an inherent reason for students to revise; it is a sense of revision as discovery, as a repeated process of beginning again, as starting out new, that our students have not learned. We need to show our students how to seek, in the possibility of revision, the dissonances of discovery—to show them through our comments why new choices would positively change their texts, and thus to show them the potential for development implicit in their own writing."*

Sommers's article reports the findings and the significance to teaching practice of collaborative research on the nature and effects of teachers' comments on first and second drafts. Lil Brannon, Cyril Knoblauch, and Sommers learned that instructor commentary can "appropriate" student texts—that is, distract writers from their own purposes in writing texts and focus them instead on responding to what they perceive the instructor wants in future drafts. They also found that instructor commentary was rarely text-based but rather exemplified the abstract, vague, and generic writing that we ask our students to avoid.

The article prompts writing teachers to analyze how they respond to student writing in all its stages, to adapt their comments on each draft to the needs and purpose of the writer, and to demonstrate through text-based comments the "thoughtful commentary" of attentive readers.

More than any other enterprise in the teaching of writing, responding to and commenting on student writing consumes the largest proportion of our time. Most teachers estimate that it takes them at least twenty to forty minutes to comment on an individual student paper, and those twenty to forty minutes times twenty students per class, times eight papers, more or less, during the course of a semester add up to an enormous amount of time. With so much time and energy directed to a single activity, it is important for us to understand the nature of the enterprise. For it seems, paradoxically enough, that although commenting on student writing is the most widely used method for responding to student writing, it is the least understood. We do not know in any definitive way what constitutes thoughtful commentary or what effect, if any, our comments have on helping our students become more effective writers.

Theoretically, at least, we know that we comment on our students' writing for the same reasons professional editors comment on the work of professional writers or for the same reasons we ask our colleagues to read and respond to our own writing. As writers we need and want thoughtful commentary to show us when we have communicated our ideas and when not, raising questions from a reader's point of view that may not have occurred to us as writers. We want to know if our writing has communicated our intended meaning and, if not, what questions or discrepancies our reader sees that we, as writers, are blind to.

In commenting on our students' writing, however, we have an additional pedagogical purpose. As teachers, we know that most students find it difficult to imagine a reader's response in advance, and to use such responses as a guide in composing. Thus, we comment on student writing to dramatize the presence of a reader, to help our students to become that questioning reader themselves, because, ultimately, we believe that becoming such a reader will help them to evaluate what they have written and develop control over their writing.[1]

Even more specifically, however, we comment on student writing because we believe that it is necessary for us to offer assistance to student writers when they are in the process of composing a text, rather than after the text has been completed. Comments create the motive for revising. Without comments from their teachers or from their peers, student writers will revise in a consistently narrow and predictable way. Without comments from readers, students assume that their writing has communicated their meaning and perceive no need for revising the substance of their text.[2]

Yet as much as we as informed professionals believe in the soundness of this approach to responding to student writing, we also realize that we don't know how our theory squares with teachers' actual practice—do teachers comment and students revise as the theory predicts they should? For the past year my colleagues, Lil Brannon, Cyril Knoblauch, and I have been researching this problem, attempting to discover not only what messages teachers give their students through their comments, but also what determines which of these comments the students choose to use or to ignore when revising. Our research has been entirely focused on comments teachers write to motivate revisions. We have studied the commenting styles of thirty-five teachers at New York University and the University of Oklahoma, studying the comments these teachers wrote on first and second drafts, and interviewing a representative number of these teachers and their students. All teachers also commented on the same set of three student essays. As an additional reference point, one of the student essays was typed into the computer that had been programmed with the "Writer's Workbench," a package of twenty-three programs developed by Bell Laboratories to help computers and writers work together to improve a text rapidly. Within a few minutes, the computer delivered editorial comments on the student's text, identifying all spelling and punctuation errors, isolating problems with wordy or misused phrases, and suggesting alternatives, offering a stylistic analysis of sentence types, sentence beginnings, and sentence lengths, and finally, giving our freshman essay a Kincaid readability score of eighth grade which, as the computer program informed us, "is a low score for this type of document." The sharp contrast between the teachers' comments and those of the computer highlighted how arbitrary and idiosyncratic most of our teachers' comments are. Besides, the calm, reasonable language of the computer provided quite a contrast to the hostility and mean-spiritedness of most of the teachers' comments.

The first finding from our research on styles of commenting is that *teachers' comments can take students' attention away from their own purposes in writing a particular text and focus that attention on the teachers' purpose in commenting*. The teacher appropriates the text from the student by confusing the student's purpose in writing the text with her own purpose in commenting. Students make the changes the teacher wants rather than those that the student perceives are necessary, since the teachers' concerns imposed on the text create the reasons for the subsequent changes. We have all heard our perplexed students say to us when confused by our comments: "I don't understand how you want me to change this" or "Tell me what *you* want me to do." In the beginning of the process there was the writer, her words, and her desire to communicate her ideas. But after the comments of the teacher are imposed on the first or second draft, the student's attention dramatically shifts from "This is what I want to say," to "This is what *you* the teacher are asking me to do."

This appropriation of the text by the teacher happens particularly when teachers identify errors in usage, diction, and style in a first draft and ask students to correct these errors when they revise; such comments give the student an impression of the importance of these errors that is all out of proportion to how they should view these errors at this point in the process. The comments create the concern that these "accidents of discourse" need to be attended to before the meaning of the text is attended to.

It would not be so bad if students were only commanded to correct errors, but, more often than not, students are given contradictory messages; they are commanded to edit a sentence to avoid an error or to condense a sentence to achieve greater brevity of style, and then told in the margins that the particular paragraph needs to be more specific or to be developed more. An example of this problem can be seen in the following student paragraph:

wordy; be precise — which Sunday? ↙ *comma needed*
Every year [on one Sunday in the middle of January] tens of
word choice
millions of people cancel all events, plans or work to watch the
wordy
Super Bowl. This audience includes [little boys and girls, old
be specific — what reason?
people, and housewives and men.] Many reasons have been
given to explain why the Super Bowl has become so popular
and why *(what spots?)* *awkward*
~~that~~ commercial spots cost up to $100,000.00. One explanation
another what?
is that people like to take sides and root for a team. Another is
spelling ↙
that some people like the pagentry and excitement of the event.
These reasons alone, however, do not explain
too colloquial
a happening as big as the Super Bowl.

You need to do more research.

This paragraph needs to be expanded in order to be more interesting to a reader.

In commenting on this draft, the teacher has shown the student how to edit the sentences, but then commands the student to expand the paragraph in order to make it more interesting to a reader. The interlinear comments and the marginal comments represent two separate tasks for this student; the interlinear comments encourage the student to see the text as a fixed piece, frozen in time, that just needs some editing. The marginal comments, however, suggest that the meaning of the text is not fixed, but rather that the student still needs to develop the meaning by doing some more research. Students are commanded to edit and develop at the same time; the remarkable contradiction of developing a paragraph after editing the sentences in it represents the confusion we encountered in our teachers' commenting styles. These different signals given to students, to edit and develop, to condense and elaborate, represent also the failure of teachers' comments to direct genuine revision of the text as a whole.

Moreover, the comments are worded in such a way that it is difficult for students to know what is the most important problem in the text and what problems are of lesser importance. No scale of concerns is offered to a student, with the result that a comment about spelling or a comment about an awkward sentence is given weight equal to a comment about organization or logic. The comment that seemed to represent this problem best was one teacher's command to his student: "Check your commas and semicolons and think more about what you are thinking about." The language of the comments makes it difficult for a student to sort out and decide what is most important and what is least important.

When the teacher appropriates the text for the student in this way, students are encouraged to see their writing as a series of parts — words, sentences, paragraphs — and not as a whole discourse. The comments encourage students to believe that their first drafts are finished drafts, not invention drafts, and that all they need to do is patch and polish their writing. That is, teachers' comments do not provide their students with an inherent reason for revising the structure and meaning of their texts, since the comments suggest to students that the meaning of their text is already there, finished, produced, and all that is necessary is a better word or phrase. The processes of revising, editing, and proofreading are collapsed and reduced to a single trivial activity, and the students' misunderstanding of the revision process as a rewording activity is reinforced by their teachers' comments.

It is possible, and it quite often happens, that students follow every comment and fix their texts appropriately as requested, but their texts are not improved substantially, or, even worse, their revised drafts are inferior to their previous drafts. Since the teachers' comments take the students' attention away from their own original purposes, students concentrate more, as I have noted, on what the teachers commanded them to do than on what they are trying to say. Sometimes students do not understand the purpose behind their teachers' comments and take these comments very literally. At other times students understand the comments, but the teacher has misread the text and the comments, unfortunately, are not applicable. For instance, we repeatedly saw comments in which teachers commanded students to reduce and condense what was written, when in fact what the text really needed at this stage was to be expanded in conception and scope.

The process of revising always involves a risk. But, too often revision becomes a balancing act for students in which they make the changes that are requested but do not take the risk of changing anything that was not commented on, even if the students sense that other changes are needed. A more effective text does not often evolve from such changes alone, yet the student does not want to take the chance of reducing a finished, albeit inadequate, paragraph to chaos—to fragments—in order to rebuild it, if such changes have not been requested by the teacher.

The second finding from our study is that *most teachers' comments are not text-specific and could be interchanged, rubber-stamped, from text to text.* The comments are not anchored in the particulars of the students' texts, but rather are a series of vague directives that are not text-specific. Students are commanded to "Think more about [their] audience, avoid colloquial language, avoid the passive, avoid prepositions at the end of sentences or conjunctions at the beginning of sentences, be clear, be specific, be precise, but above all, think more about what [they] are thinking about." The comments on the following student paragraph illustrate this problem:

Begin by telling your reader what you are going to write about.

In the sixties it was drugs, in the seventies it was rock and roll. Now in the eighties, one of the most controversial subjects is nuclear power. The United States is in great need of its own source of power. Because of environmentalists, coal is not an acceptable source of energy.[Solar and wind power have not yet received the technology necessary to use them.]It seems that nuclear power is the only feasible means right now for obtaining self-sufficient power. However, too large a percentage of the population are against nuclear power claiming it is unsafe. With as many problems as the United States is having concerning energy, it seems a shame that the public is so quick to "can" a very feasible means of power. Nuclear energy should not be given up on, but rather, more nuclear plants should be built.

avoid "one of the" · *elaborate* · *be specific* · *avoid "it seems"* · *be precise*

Think more about your reader.

Thesis sentence needed.

One could easily remove all the comments from this paragraph and rubber-stamp them on another student text, and they would make as much or as little sense on the second text as they do here.

We have observed an overwhelming similarity in the generalities and abstract commands given to students. There seems to be among teachers an accepted, albeit unwritten canon for commenting on student texts. This uniform code of commands, requests, and pleadings demonstrates that the teacher holds license for vagueness while the student is commanded to be specific. The students we interviewed admitted to having great difficulty with these vague directives. The students stated that when a teacher writes in the margins or as an end comment, "choose precise language," or "think more about your audience," revising becomes a guessing game. In effect, the teacher is saying to the student, "Somewhere in this paper is imprecise language or lack of awareness of an audience and you must find it." The problem presented by these vague commands is compounded for the students when they are not offered any strategies for carrying out these commands. Students are told that they have done something wrong and that there is something in their text that needs to be fixed before the text is acceptable. But to tell students that they have done something wrong is not to tell them what to do about it. In order to offer a useful revision strategy to a student, the teacher must anchor that strategy in the specifics of the student's text. For instance, to tell our student, the author of the above paragraph, "to be specific," or "to elaborate," does not show our student what questions the reader has about the meaning of the text, or what breaks in logic exist, that could be resolved if the writer supplied specific information; nor is the student shown how to achieve the desired specificity.

Instead of offering strategies, the teachers offer what is interpreted by students as rules for composing; the comments suggest to students that writing is just a matter of following the rules. Indeed, the teachers seem to impose a series of abstract rules about written products even when some of them are not appropriate for the specific text the student is creating.[3] For instance, the student author of our sample paragraph presented above is commanded to follow the conventional rules for writing a five-paragraph essay — to begin the introductory paragraph by telling his reader what he is going to say and to end the paragraph with a thesis sentence. Somehow these abstract rules about what five-paragraph products should look like do not seem applicable to the problems this student must confront when revising, nor are the rules specific strategies he could use when revising. There are many inchoate ideas ready to be exploited in this paragraph, but the rules do not help the student to take stock of his (or her) ideas and use the opportunity he has, during revision, to develop those ideas.

The problem here is a confusion of process and product; what one has to say about the process is different from what one has to say about the product. Teachers who use this method of commenting are formulating their comments as if these drafts were finished drafts and were not going to be revised. Their commenting vocabularies have not been adapted to revision and they comment on first drafts as if they were justifying a grade or as if the first draft were the final draft.

Our summary finding, therefore, from this research on styles of commenting is that the news from the classroom is not good. For the most part, teachers do not respond to student writing with the kind of thoughtful commentary which will help students to engage with the issues they are writing about or which will help them think about their purposes and goals in writing a specific text. In defense of our teachers, however, they told us that responding to student writing was rarely stressed in their teacher-training or in writing workshops; they had been trained in various prewriting techniques, in constructing assignments, and in evaluating papers for grades, but rarely in the process of reading a student text for meaning or in offering commentary to motivate revision. The problem is that most of us as teachers of writing have been trained to read and interpret literary texts for meaning, but, unfortunately, we have not been trained to act upon the same set of assumptions in reading student texts as we follow in reading literary texts.[4] Thus, we read student texts with biases about what the writer should have said or about what he or she should have written, and our biases determine how we will comprehend the text. We read with our preconceptions and preoccupations, expecting to find errors, and the result is that we find errors and misread our students' texts.[5] We find what we look for; instead of reading and responding to the meaning of a text, we correct our students' writing. We need to reverse this approach. Instead of finding errors or showing students how to patch up parts of their texts, we need to sabotage our students' conviction that the drafts they have written are complete and coherent. Our comments need to offer students revision tasks of a different order of complexity and sophistication from the ones that they themselves identify, by forcing students back into the chaos, back to the point where they are shaping and restructuring their meaning.[6]

For if the content of a student text is lacking in substance and meaning, if the order of the parts must be rearranged significantly in the next draft, if paragraphs must be restructured for logic and clarity, then many sentences are likely to be changed or deleted anyway. There seems to be no point in having students correct usage errors or condense sentences that are likely to disappear before the next draft is completed. In fact, to identify such problems in a text at this early first-draft stage, when such problems are likely to abound, can give a student a disproportionate sense of their importance at this stage in the writing process.[7] In responding to our students' writing, we should be guided by the recognition that it is not spelling or usage problems that we as writers first worry about when drafting and revising our texts.

We need to develop an appropriate level of response for commenting on a first draft, and to differentiate that from the level suitable to a second or third draft. Our comments need to be suited to the draft we are reading. In a first or second draft, we need to respond as any reader would, registering questions, reflecting befuddlement, and noting places where we are puzzled about the meaning of the text. Comments should point to breaks in logic, disruptions in meaning, or missing information. Our goal in commenting on early drafts should be to engage students with the issues they are considering and help them clarify their purposes and reasons in writing their specific text.

For instance, the major rhetorical problem of the essay written by the student who wrote the first paragraph (the paragraph on nuclear power) quoted above was that the student had two principal arguments running through his text, each of which brought the other into question. On the one hand, he argued that we must use nuclear power, unpleasant as it is, because we have nothing else to use; though nuclear energy is a problematic source of energy, it is the best of a bad lot. On the other hand, he also argued that nuclear energy is really quite safe and therefore should be our primary resource. Comments on this student's first draft need to point out this break in logic and show the student that if we accept his first argument, then his second argument sounds fishy. But if we accept his second argument, his first argument sounds contradictory. The teacher's comments need to engage this student writer with this basic rhetorical and conceptual problem in his first draft rather than impose a series of abstract commands and rules upon his text.

Written comments need to be viewed not as an end in themselves — a way for teachers to satisfy themselves that they have done their jobs — but rather as a means for helping students to become more effective writers. As a means for helping students, they have limitations; they are, in fact, disembodied remarks — one absent writer responding to another absent writer. The key to successful commenting is to have what is said in the comments and what is done in the classroom mutually reinforce and enrich each other. Commenting on papers assists the writing course in achieving its purpose; classroom activities and the comments we write to our students need to be connected. Written comments need to be an extension of the teacher's voice — an extension of the teacher as reader. Exercises in such activities as revising a whole text or individual paragraphs together in class, noting how the sense of the whole dictates the smaller changes, looking at options, evaluating actual choices, and then discussing the effect of these changes on revised drafts — such exercises need to be designed to take students through the cycles of revising and to help them overcome their anxiety about revising: that anxiety we all feel at reducing what looks like a finished draft into fragments and chaos.

The challenge we face as teachers is to develop comments which will provide an inherent reason for students to revise; it is a sense of revision as discovery, as a repeated process of beginning again, as starting out new, that our students have not learned. We need to show our students how to seek, in the possibility of revision, the dissonances of discovery — to show them through our comments why new choices would positively change their texts, and thus to show them the potential for development implicit in their own writing.

Notes

1. C. H. Knoblauch and Lil Brannon, "Teacher Commentary on Student Writing: The State of the Art," *Freshman English News* 10 (Fall 1981): 1–3.
2. For an extended discussion of revision strategies of student writers see Nancy Sommers, "Revision Strategies of Student Writers and Experienced Adult Writers," *College Composition and Communication* 31 (Dec. 1980): 378–88.
3. Nancy Sommers and Ronald Schleifer, "Means and Ends: Some Assumptions of Student Writers," *Composition and Teaching* 2 (Dec. 1980): 69–76.
4. Janet Emig and Robert P. Parker, Jr., "Responding to Student Writing: Building a Theory of the Evaluating Process," paper, Rutgers University.
5. For an extended discussion of this problem see Joseph Williams, "The Phenomenology of Error," *College Composition and Communication* 32 (May 1981): 152–68.
6. Ann Berthoff, *The Making of Meaning* (Upper Montclair: Boynton, 1981).
7. W. U. McDonald, "The Revising Process and the Marking of Student Papers," *College Composition and Communication* 24 (May 1978): 167–70.

Sommers's Insights as a Resource for Your Reflections

1. Examine your comments on several pieces of student writing. Analyze your commenting style on both early drafts and final papers. Do your comments clarify the papers' most important problems? Are your responses text-specific — that is, "anchored in the particulars of the students' texts" — or could they easily be "rubber-stamped" on any number of student essays? With Sommers's findings in mind, consider ways your comments might better help students engage in meaningful revision.

2. Ask a colleague teaching the same course to work with you on some early student drafts. Trade a set of drafts. Write your comments about revision on a separate sheet of paper; exchange and compare your comments, paying particular attention to the specificity of each comment and to precision of language. You'll both profit from the discussion and may find your reading of the text enhanced by this "external assessor."

   You might also use this technique when you evaluate final drafts. The ensuing conversation about your evaluative comments and criteria for evaluation will certainly give you both perspective on and confidence about your process of evaluating and grading.

Sommers's Insights as a Resource for Your Writing Classroom

1. Conduct an in-class session analyzing students' evaluative comments. After students have completed a shared writing task, ask them to respond using a peer editing checklist from the class text or one that you've constructed with the class. Ask students to write sentence-length, specific comments about issues of meaning and about attention to audience concerns. As a class, discuss specific comments, evaluating how well they do or do not promote substantive revision.
2. Ask class members to identify commentary that has assisted them in deep revision when they write a self-assessment to accompany a submitted draft. Ask questions like "What advice did your peer readers give?" and "What did you do with the advice?"

Ranking, Evaluating, and Liking: Sorting Out Three Forms of Judgment

Peter Elbow

What are the different kinds of things we do, most broadly, when we're engaging student texts? By distinguishing among the activities involved in grading student work, we cannot only do a better job of grading but can also keep grading from getting in the way of teaching and learning. In this article from a 1993 issue of College English, *Peter Elbow argues for the inadequacy of ranking, or "summing up one's judgment of a performance or person into a single, holistic number or score." In contrast, evaluating involves thoughtfully commenting on the strengths and weaknesses of different parts or dimensions of a work. He suggests shifting the emphasis from ranking to evaluating, making assessments of writing more informative and reliable. However, even evaluation, in large quantities, can hinder learning, so Elbow proposes that we consider how to create "evaluation free zones" in our classrooms, encouraging students to take risks and learn in ways that they otherwise might not. Finally, Elbow looks to redeem the undervalued reaction of "liking" student writing. By paying attention to what we like, we can connect with student work and discover its richest potential for growth.*

This essay is my attempt to sort out different acts we call assessment — some different ways in which we express or frame our judgments of value. I have been working on this tangle not just because it is interesting and important in itself but because assessment tends so much to drive and control *teaching*. Much of what we do in the classroom is determined by the assessment structures we work under.

Assessment is a large and technical area and I'm not a professional. But my main premise or subtext in this essay is that we nonprofessionals can and should work on it because professionals have not reached definitive conclusions about the problem of how to assess writing (or anything else, I'd say). Also, decisions about assessment are often made by people even less professional than we, namely legislators. Pat Belanoff and I realized that the field of assessment was open when we saw the harmful effects of a writing proficiency exam at Stony Brook and worked out a collaborative portfolio assessment system in its place (Belanoff and Elbow; Elbow and Belanoff). Professionals keep changing their minds about large-scale testing and assessment. And as for classroom grading, psychometricians provide little support or defense of it.

The Problems with Ranking and the Benefits of Evaluating

By ranking I mean the act of summing up one's judgment of a performance or person into a single, holistic number or score. We rank every time we give a grade or holistic score. Ranking implies a single scale or continuum or dimension along which all performances are hung.

By evaluating I mean the act of expressing one's judgment of a performance or person by pointing out the strengths and weaknesses of different features or dimensions. We evaluate every time we write a comment on a paper or have a conversation about its value. Evaluation implies the recognition of different criteria or dimensions — and by implication different contexts and audiences for the same performance. Evaluation requires going *beyond* a first response that may be nothing but a kind of ranking ("I like it" or "This is better than that"), and instead looking carefully enough at the performance or person to make distinctions between parts or features or criteria.

It's obvious, thus, that I am troubled by ranking. But I will resist any temptation to argue that we can get rid of all ranking — or even should. Instead I will try to show how we can have *less* ranking and *more* evaluation in its place.

I see three distinct problems with ranking; it is inaccurate or unreliable; it gives no substantive feedback; and it is harmful to the atmosphere for teaching and learning.

(1) First the unreliability. To rank reliably means to give a *fair* number, to find the single quantitative score that readers will agree on. But readers don't agree.

This is not news — this unavailability of agreement. We have long seen it on many fronts. For example, research in evaluation has shown many times that if we give a paper to a set of readers, those readers tend to give it the full range of grades (Diederich). I've recently come across new research to this effect — new to me because it was published in 1912. The investigators carefully showed how high school English teachers gave different grades to the same paper. In response to criticism that this was a local problem in English, they went on the next year to discover an even greater variation among grades given by high school geometry teachers and history teachers to papers in their subjects. (See the summary of Daniel Starch and Edward Elliott's 1913 *School Review* articles in Kirschenbaum, Simon, and Napier 258–59.)

We know the same thing from literary criticism and theory. If the best critics can't agree about what a text means, how can we be surprised that they disagree even more about the quality or value of texts? And we know that nothing in literary or philosophical theory gives us any agreed-upon rules for settling such disputes.

Students have shown us the same inconsistency with their own controlled experiments of handing the same paper to different teachers and getting different grades. This helps explain why we hate it so when students ask us their favorite question, "What do you want for an A?": it rubs our noses in the unreliability of our grades.

Of course champions of holistic scoring argue that they get *can* get agreement among readers — and they often do (White). But they get that agreement by "training" the readers before and during the scoring sessions. What "training" means is getting those scorers to stop reading the way they normally read — getting them to stop using the conflicting criteria and standards they normally use outside the scoring sessions. (In an impressive and powerful book, Barbara Herrnstein Smith argues that whenever we have widespread inter-reader reliability, we have reason to suspect that difference has been suppressed and homogeneity imposed — almost always at the expense of certain groups.) In short, the reliability in holistic scoring is not a measure of how texts are valued by real readers in natural settings, but only of how they are valued in artificial settings with imposed agreements.

Defenders of holistic scoring might reply (as one anonymous reviewer did), that holistic scores are not perfect or absolutely objective readings but just "judgments that most readers will agree are the appropriate ones given the purpose of the assessment and the system of communication." But I have been in and even conducted enough holistic scoring sessions to know that even that degree of agreement doesn't occur unless "purpose" and "appropriateness" are defined to mean acceptance of the single set of standards imposed on that session. We know too much about the differences among readers and the highly variable nature of the reading process. Supposing we get readings only from academics, or only from people in English, or only from respected critics, or only from respected writing programs, or only from feminists, or only from sound readers of my tribe (white, male, middle-class, full professors between the ages of fifty and sixty). We *still* don't get agreement. We can sometimes get agreement among readers from some subset, a particular community that has developed a strong set of common values, perhaps *one* English department or *one* writing program. But what is the value of such a rare agreement? It tells us nothing about how readers from other English departments or writing programs will judge — much less how readers from other domains will judge.

(From the opposite ideological direction, some skeptics might object to my skeptical train of thought: "So what else is new?" they might reply. "Of *course* my grades are biased, 'interested' or 'situated' — always partial to my interests or the values of my community or culture. There's no other possibility." But how can people consent to give grades if they feel that way? A single teacher's grade for a student is liable to have substantial consequences — for example on eligibility for a scholarship or a job or entrance into professional school. In grading, surely we must not take anything less than genuine fairness as our goal.)

It won't be long before we see these issues argued in a court of law, when a student who has been disqualified from playing on a team or rejected from a professional school sues, charging that the basis for his plight — teacher grades — is not reliable. I wonder if lawyers will be able to make our grades stick.

(2) Ranking or grading is woefully uncommunicative. Grades and holistic scores are nothing but points on a continuum from "yea" to "boo" — with no information or clues about the criteria behind these noises. They are 100 percent evaluation and 0 percent description or information. They quantify the degree of approval or disapproval in readers but tell nothing at all about what the readers actually approve or disapprove of. They say nothing that couldn't be said with gold stars or black marks or smiley-faces. Of course our first reactions are often nothing but global holistic feelings of approval or disapproval, but we need a system for communicating our judgments that nudges us to move beyond these holistic feelings and to articulate the basis of our feeling — a process that often leads us to change our feeling. (Holistic scoring sessions sometimes use rubrics that explain the criteria — though these are rarely passed along to students — and even in these situations, the rubrics fail to fit many papers.) As C. S. Lewis says, "People are obviously far more anxious to express their approval and disapproval of things than to describe them" (7).

(3) Ranking leads students to get so hung up on these oversimple quantitative verdicts that they care more about scores than about learning — more about the grade we put on the paper than about the comment we have written on it. Have you noticed how grading often forces us to write comments to justify our grades? — and how these are often *not* the comment we would make if we were just trying to help the student write better? ("Just try writing several favorable comments on a paper and then giving it a grade of D" [Diederich 21].)

Grades and holistic scores give too much encouragement to those students who score high — making them too apt to think they are already fine — and too little encouragement to those students who do badly. Unsuccessful students often come to doubt their intelligence. But oddly enough, many "A" students also end up doubting their true ability and feeling like frauds — because they have sold out on their own judgment and simply given teachers whatever yields an A. They have too often been rewarded for what they don't really believe in. (Notice that there's more cheating by students who get high grades than by those who get low ones. There would be less incentive to cheat if there were no ranking.)

We might be tempted to put up with the inaccuracy or unfairness of grades if they gave good diagnostic feedback or helped the learning climate; or we might put up with the damage they do to the learning climate if they gave a fair or reliable measure of how skilled or knowledgeable students are. But since they fail dismally on both counts, we are faced with the striking question of why grading has persisted so long.

There must be many reasons. It is obviously easier and quicker to express a global feeling with a single number than to figure out what the strengths and weaknesses are and what one's criteria are. (Though I'm heartened to discover, as I pursue this issue, how troubled teachers are by grading and how difficult they find it.) But perhaps more important, we see around us a deep *hunger to rank* — to create pecking orders: to see who we can look down on and who we must look up to, or in the military metaphor, who we can kick and who we must salute. Psychologists tell us that this taste for pecking orders or ranking is associated with the authoritarian personality. We see this hunger graphically in the case of IQ scores. It is plain that IQ scoring does not represent a commitment to looking carefully at people's intelligence; when we do that, we see different and frequently uncorrelated *kinds* or *dimensions* of intelligence (Gardner). The persistent use of IQ scores represents the hunger to have a number so that everyone can have a rank. ("Ten!" mutter the guys when they see a pretty woman.)

Because ranking or grading has caused so much discomfort to so many students and teachers, I think we see a lot of confusion about the process. It is hard to think clearly about something that has given so many of us such anxiety and distress. The most notable confusion I notice is the tendency to think that if we renounce ranking or grading, we are renouncing the very possibility of judgment and discrimination — that we are embracing the idea that there is no way to distinguish or talk about the difference between what works well and what works badly.

So the most important point, then, is that *I am not arguing against judgment or evaluation*. I'm just arguing against that crude, oversimple way of *representing* judgment — distorting it, really — into a single number, which means ranking people and performances along a single continuum.

In fact I am arguing *for evaluation*. Evaluation means looking hard and thoughtfully at a piece of writing in order to make distinctions as to the quality of different features or dimensions. For example, the process of evaluation permits us to make the following kinds of statements about a piece of writing:

- The thinking and ideas seem interesting and creative.
- The overall structure or sequence seems confusing.
- The writing is perfectly clear at the level of individual sentences and even paragraphs.
- There is an odd, angry tone of voice that seems unrelated or inappropriate to what the writer is saying.
- Yet this same voice is strong and memorable and makes one listen even if one is irritated.
- There are a fair number of mistakes in grammar or spelling: more than "a sprinkling" but less than "riddled with."

To rank, on the other hand, is to be forced to translate those discriminations into a single number. What grade or holistic score do these judgments add up to? It's likely, by the way, that more readers would agree with those separate, "analytic" statements than would agree on a holistic score.

I've conducted many assessment sessions where we were not trying to impose a set of standards but rather to find out how experienced teachers read and evaluate, and I've had many opportunities to see that good readers give grades or scores right down through the range of possibilities. Of course good readers sometimes agree—especially on papers that are strikingly good or bad or conventional, but I think I see difference more frequently than agreement when readers really speak up.

The process of evaluation, because it invites us to articulate our criteria and to make distinctions among parts or features or dimensions of a performance, thereby invites us further to acknowledge the main fact about evaluation: that different readers have different priorities, values, and standards.

The conclusion I am drawing, then, in this first train of thought is that we should do less ranking and more evaluation. Instead of using grades or holistic scores—single number verdicts that try to sum up complex performances along only one scale—we should give some kind of written or spoken evaluation that discriminates among criteria and dimensions of the writing—and if possible that takes account of the complex context for writing: who the writer is, what the writer's audience and goals are, who we are as readers and how we read, and how we might differ in our reading from other readers the writer might be addressing.

But how can we put this principle into practice? The pressure for ranking seems implacable. Evaluation takes more time, effort, and money. It seems as though we couldn't get along without scores on writing exams. Most teachers are obliged to give grades at the end of each course. And many students — given that they have become conditioned or even addicted to ranking over the years and must continue to inhabit a ranking culture in most of their courses — will object if we don't put grades on papers. Some students, in the absence of the crude gold star or black mark, may not try hard enough (though how hard is "enough" — and is it really our job to stimulate motivation artificially with grades — and is grading the best source of motivation?).

It is important to note that there are certain schools and colleges that do not use single-number grades or scores, and they function successfully. I taught for nine years at Evergreen State College, which uses only written evaluations. This system works fine, even down to getting students accepted into high quality graduate and professional schools.

Nevertheless we have an intractable dilemma: that grading is unfair and counterproductive but that students and institutions tend to want grades. In the face of this dilemma there is a need for creativity and pragmatism. Here are some ways in which I and others use *less ranking* and *more evaluation* in teaching — and they suggest some adjustments in how we score large-scale assessments. What follows is an assortment of experimental compromises — sometimes crude, seldom ideal or utopian — but they help.

(a) Portfolios. Just because conventional institutions oblige us to turn in a single quantitative course grade at the end of every marking period, it doesn't follow that we need to grade individual papers. Course grades are more trustworthy and less damaging because they are based on so many performances over so many weeks. By avoiding frequent ranking or grading, we make it *somewhat* less likely for students to become addicted to oversimple numerical rankings — to think that evaluation always translates into a simple number — in short, to mistake ranking for evaluation. (I'm not trying to defend conventional course grades since they are still uncommunicative and they still feed the hunger for ranking.) Portfolios permit me to refrain from grading individual papers and limit myself to writerly evaluative comments — and help students see this as a positive rather than a negative thing, a chance to be graded on a body of their best work that can be judged more fairly. Portfolios have many other advantages as well. They are particularly valuable as occasions for asking students to write extensive and thoughtful explorations of their own strengths and weaknesses.

A midsemester portfolio is usually an informal affair, but it is a good occasion for giving anxious students a ballpark estimate of how well they are doing in the course so far. I find it helpful to tell students that I'm perfectly willing to tell them my best estimate of their course grade—but only if they come to me in conference and only during the second half of the semester. This serves somewhat to quiet their anxiety while they go through seven weeks of drying out from grades. By midsemester, most of them have come to enjoy not getting those numbers and thus being able to think better about more writerly comments from me and their classmates.

Portfolios are now used extensively and productively in larger assessments, and there is constant experimentation with new applications (Belanoff and Dickson; *Portfolio Assessment Newsletter; Portfolio News*).

(b) Another useful option is to make a strategic retreat from a wholly negative position. That is, I sometimes do a *bit* of ranking even on individual papers, using two "bottom-line" grades: H and U for "Honors" and "Unsatisfactory." I tell students that these translate to about A or A− and D or F. This practice may seem theoretically inconsistent with all the arguments I've just made, but (at the moment, anyway) I justify it for the following reasons.

First, I sympathize with a *part* of the students' anxiety about not getting grades: their fear that they might be failing and not know about it—or doing an excellent job and not get any recognition. Second, I'm not giving *many* grades; only a small proportion of papers get these Hs or Us. The system creates a "non-bottom-line" or "non-quantified" atmosphere. Third, these holistic judgments about best and worst do not seem as arbitrary and questionable as most grades. There is usually a *bit* more agreement among readers about the best and worst papers. What seems most dubious is the process of trying to rank that whole middle range of papers—papers that have a mixture of better and worse qualities so that the numerical grade depends enormously on a reader's priorities or mood or temperament. My willingness to give these few grades goes a long way toward helping my students forgo most bottom-line grading.

I'm not trying to pretend that these minimal "grades" are truly reliable. But they represent a very small amount of ranking. Yes, someone could insist that I'm really ranking every single paper (and indeed if it seemed politically necessary, I could put an OK or S [for satisfactory] on all those middle range papers and brag, "Yes, I grade everything"). But the fact is that I am doing *much less sorting* since I don't have to sort them into five or even twelve piles. Thus there is a huge reduction in the total amount of unreliability I produce.

(It might seem that if I use only these few minimal grades I have no good way for figuring out a final grade for the course—since that requires a more fine-grained set of ranks. But I don't find that to be the case. For I also give these same minimal grades to the many other important parts of my course such as attendance, meeting deadlines, peer responding, and journal writing. If I want a mathematically computed grade on a scale of six or A through E, I can easily compute it when I have such a large number of grades to work from—even though they are only along a three-point scale.)

This same practice of crude or minimal ranking is a big help on larger assessments outside classrooms, and needs to be applied to the process of assessment in general. There are two important principles to emphasize. On the one hand we must be prudent or accommodating enough to admit that despite all the arguments against ranking, there *are* situations when we need that bottom-line verdict along one scale: which student has not done satisfactory work and should be denied credit for the course? which student gets the scholarship? which candidate to hire or fire? We often operate with scarce resources. But on the other hand we must be bold enough to insist that we do far more ranking than is really needed. We can get along not only with fewer occasions for assessment but also with fewer gradations in scoring. If we decide what the *real* bottom-line is on a given occasion—perhaps just "failing" or perhaps "honors" too—then the reading of papers or portfolios is enormously quick and cheap. It leaves time and money for evaluation—perhaps for analytic scoring or some comment.

At Stony Brook we worked out a portfolio system where multiple readers had only to make a binary decision: acceptable or not. Then individual teachers could decide the actual course grade and give comments for their own students—so long as those students passed in the eyes of an independent rater (Elbow and Belanoff; Belanoff and Elbow). The best way to begin to wean our society from its addiction to ranking may be to permit a tiny bit of it (which also means less unreliability)—rather than trying to go "cold turkey."

(c) Sometimes I use an analytic grid for evaluating and commenting on student papers. An example is given in Figure 1. I often vary the criteria in my grid (e.g. "connecting with readers" or "investment") depending on the assignment or the point in the semester.

Grids are a way I can satisfy the students' hunger for ranking but still not give in to conventional grades on individual papers. Sometimes I provide nothing but a grid (especially on final drafts), and this is a

Strong	OK	Weak	
			CONTENT, INSIGHTS, THINKING, GRAPPLING WITH TOPIC
			GENUINE REVISION, SUBSTANTIVE CHANGES, NOT JUST EDITING
			ORGANIZATION, STRUCTURE, GUIDING THE READER
			LANGUAGE: SYNTAX, SENTENCES, WORDING, VOICE
			MECHANICS: SPELLING, GRAMMAR, PUNCTUATION, PROOFREADING
			OVERALL [Note: this is not a sum of the other scores.]

Figure 1.

very quick way to provide a response. Or on midprocess drafts I sometimes use a grid in addition to a comment: a more readerly comment that often doesn't so much tell them what's wrong or right or how to improve things but rather tries to give them an account of what is *happening to me* as I read their words. I think this kind of comment is really the most useful thing of all for students, but it frustrates some students for a while. The grid can help these students feel less anxious and thus pay better attention to my comment.

I find grids extremely helpful at the end of the semester for telling students their strengths and weaknesses in the course — or what they've done well and not so well. Besides categories like the ones above, I use categories like these: "skill in giving feedback to others," "ability to meet deadlines," "effort," and "improvement." This practice makes my final grade much more communicative.

(d) I also help make up for the absence of ranking — gold stars and black marks — by having students share their writing with each other a great deal both orally and through frequent publication in class magazines. Also, where possible, I try to get students to give or send writing to audiences outside the class. At the University of Massachusetts at Amherst, freshmen pay a ten dollar lab fee for the writing course, and every teacher publishes four or five class magazines of final drafts a semester. The effects are striking. Sharing, peer feedback, and publication give the best reward and motivation for writing, namely, getting your words out to many readers.

(e) I sometimes use a kind of modified *contract grading*. That is, at the start of the course I pass out a long list of all the things that I most want students to do — the concrete activities that I think most lead to learning — and I promise students that if they do them *all* they are guaranteed a certain final grade. Currently, I say it's a B — it could be lower or higher. My list includes these items: not missing more than a week's worth of classes; not having more than one late major assignment; *substantive* revising on all major revisions; good copy editing on all final revisions; good effort on peer feedback work; keeping up the journal; and substantial effort and investment on each draft.

I like the way this system changes the "bottom-line" for a course: the intersection where my authority crosses their self-interest. I can tell them, "You have to work very hard in this course, but you can stop worrying about grades." The crux is no longer that commodity I've always hated and never trusted: a numerical ranking of the quality of their writing along a single continuum. Instead the crux becomes what I care about most: the *concrete behaviors* that I most want students to engage in because they produce more learning and help me teach better. Admittedly, effort and investment are not concrete observable behaviors, but they are no harder to judge than overall quality of writing. And since I care about effort and investment, I don't mind the few arguments I get into about them; they seem fruitful. ("Let's try and figure out why it looked to me as though you didn't put any effort in here.") In contrast, I hate discussions about grades on a paper and find such arguments fruitless. Besides, I'm not making fine distinctions about effort and investment—just letting a bell go off when they fall palpably low.

It's crucial to note that I am *not* fighting evaluation with this system. I am just fighting ranking or grading. I still write evaluative comments and often use an evaluative grid to tell my students what I see as strengths and weaknesses in their papers. My goal is not to get rid of evaluation but in fact to emphasize it, enhance it. I'm trying to get students to listen *better* to my evaluations—by uncoupling them from a grade. In effect, I'm doing this because I'm so fed up with students *following* or *obeying* my evaluations too blindly—making whatever changes my comments suggest but doing it for the sake of a grade; not really taking the time to make up their own minds about whether they think my judgments or suggestions really make sense to them. The worst part of grades is that they make students obey us without carefully thinking about the merits of what we say. I love the situation this system so often puts students in: I make a criticism or suggestion about their paper, but it doesn't matter to their grade whether they go along with me or not (so long as they genuinely revise in some fashion). They have to think; to decide.

Admittedly this system is crude and impure. Some of the really skilled students who are used to getting As and desperate to get one in this course remain unhelpfully hung up about getting those Hs on their papers. But a good number of these students discover that they can't get them, and they soon settle down to accepting a B and having less anxiety and more of a learning voyage.

The Limitations of Evaluation and the Benefits of Evaluation-Free Zones

Everything I've said so far has been in praise of evaluation as a substitute for ranking. But I need to turn a corner here and speak about the *limits* or *problems* of evaluation. Evaluating may be better than ranking, but it still carries some of the same problems. That is, even though I've praised evaluation for inviting us to acknowledge that readers and contexts are different, nevertheless the very word *evaluation* tends to imply fairness or reliability or getting beyond personal or subjective preferences. Also, of course, evaluation takes a lot more time and work. To rank you just have to put down a number; holistic scoring of exams is cheaper than analytic scoring.

Most important of all, evaluation harms the climate for learning and teaching—or rather *too much* evaluation has this effect. That is, if we evaluate *everything* students write, they tend to remain tangled up in the assumption that their whole job in school is to give teachers "what they want." Constant evaluation makes students worry more about psyching out the teacher than about what they are really learning. Students fall into a kind of defensive or on-guard stance toward the teacher: a desire to hide what they don't understand and try to impress. This stance gets in the way of learning. (Think of the patient trying to hide symptoms from the doctor.) Most of all, constant evaluation by someone in authority makes students reluctant to take the risks that are needed for good learning — to try out hunches and trust their own judgment. Face it: if our goal is to get students to exercise their own judgment, that means exercising an immature and undeveloped judgment and making choices that are obviously wrong to us.

We see around us a widespread hunger to be evaluated that is often just as strong as the hunger to rank. Countless conditions make many of us walk around in the world wanting to ask others (especially those in authority), "How am I doing, did I do OK?" I don't think the hunger to be evaluated is as harmful as the hunger to rank, but it can get in the way of learning. For I find that the greatest and most powerful breakthroughs in learning occur when I can get myself and others to *put aside* this nagging, self-doubting question ("How am I doing? How am I doing?") — and instead to take some chances, trust our instincts or hungers. When everything is evaluated, everything counts. Often the most powerful arena for deep learning is a kind of "time out" zone from the pressures of normal evaluated reality: make-believe, play, dreams — in effect, the Shakespearian forest.

In my attempts to get away from too much evaluation (not from all evaluation, just from too much of it), I have drifted into a set of teaching practices which now feel to me like the *best* part of my teaching. I realize now what I've been unconsciously doing for a number of years: creating "evaluation-free zones."

(a) The paradigm evaluation-free zone is the ten minute, nonstop freewrite. When I get students to freewrite, I am using my authority to create unusual conditions in order to contradict or interrupt our pervasive habit of always evaluating our writing. What is essential here are the two central features of freewriting: that it be private (thus I don't collect it or have students share it with anyone else); and that it be nonstop (thus there isn't time for planning, and control is usually diminished). Students quickly catch on and enter into the spirit. At the end of the course, they often tell me that freewriting is the most useful thing I've taught them (see Belanoff, Elbow, and Fontaine).

(b) A larger evaluation-free zone is the single unevaluated assignment — what people sometimes call the "quickwrite" or sketch. This is a piece of writing that I ask students to do — either in class or for homework — without any or much revising. It is meant to be low stakes writing. There is a bit of pressure, nevertheless, since I usually ask them to share it with others and I usually collect it and read it. But I don't write any comments at all — except perhaps to put straight lines along some passages I like or to write a phrase of appreciation at the end. And I ask students to refrain from giving evaluative feedback to each other—and instead just to say "thank you" or mention a couple of phrases or ideas that stick in mind. (However, this writing-without-feedback can be a good occasion for students to discuss the *topic* they have written about—and thus serve as an excellent kick-off for discussions of what I am teaching.)

(c) These experiments have led me to my next and largest evaluation-free zone—what I sometimes call a "jump start" for my whole course. For the last few semesters I've been devoting the first three weeks *entirely* to the two evaluation-free activities I've just described: freewriting (and also more leisurely private writing in a journal) and quickwrites or sketches. Since the stakes are low and I'm not asking for much revising, I ask for *much more* writing homework per week than usual. And every day we write in class: various exercises or games. The emphasis is on getting rolling, getting fluent, taking risks. And every day all students read out loud something they've written—sometimes a short passage even to the whole class. So despite the absence of feedback, it is a very audience-filled and sociable three weeks.

At first I only dared do this for two weeks, but when I discovered how fast the writing improves, how good it is for building community, and what a pleasure this period is for me, I went to three weeks. I'm curious to try an experiment with teaching a whole course this way. I wonder, that is, whether all that evaluation we work so hard to give really does any more good than the constant writing and sharing (Zak).

I need to pause here to address an obvious rejoinder: "But withholding evaluation is not normal!" Indeed, it is *not* normal—certainly not normal in school. We normally tend to emphasize evaluations—even bottom-line ranking kinds of evaluations. But I resist the argument that if it's not normal we shouldn't do it.

The best argument for evaluation-free zones is from experience. If you try them, I suspect you'll discover that they are satisfying and bring out good writing. Students have a better time writing these unevaluated pieces; they enjoy hearing and appreciating these pieces when they don't have to evaluate. And *I* have a much better time when I engage in this astonishing activity: reading student work when I don't have to evaluate and respond. And yet the writing improves. I see students investing and risking more, writing more fluently, and using livelier, more interesting voices. This writing gives me and them a higher standard of clarity and voice for when we move on to more careful and revised writing tasks that involve more intellectual pushing—tasks that sometimes make their writing go tangled or sodden.

The Benefits and Feasibility of Liking

Liking and disliking seem like unpromising topics in an exploration of assessment. They seem to represent the worst kind of subjectivity, the merest accident of personal taste. But I've recently come to think that the phenomenon of liking is perhaps the most important evaluative response for writers and teachers to think about. In effect, I'm turning another corner in my argument. In the first section I argued against ranking — with evaluating being the solution. Next I argued not *against* evaluating — but for no-evaluation zones in *addition* to evaluating. Now I will argue neither against evaluating nor against no-evaluation zones, but for something very different in addition, or perhaps underneath, as a foundation: liking.

Let me start with the germ story. I was in a workshop and we were going around the circle with everyone telling a piece of good news about their writing in the last six months. It got to Wendy Bishop, a good poet (who has also written two good books about the teaching of writing), and she said, "In the last six months, I've learned to *like* everything I write." Our jaws dropped; we were startled — in a way scandalized. But I've been chewing on her words ever since, and they have led me into a retelling of the story of how people learn to write better.

The old story goes like this: We write something. We read it over and we say, "This is terrible. I *hate* it. I've got to work on it and improve it." And we do, and it gets better, and this happens again and again, and before long we have become a wonderful writer. But that's not really what happens. Yes, we vow to work on it — but we don't. And next time we have the impulse to write, we're just a *bit* less likely to start.

What really happens when people learn to write better is more like this: We write something. We read it over and we say, "This is terrible. . . . But I *like* it. Damn it, I'm going to get it good enough so that others will like it too." And this time we don't just put it in a drawer, we actually work hard on it. And we try it out on other people too — not just to get feedback and advice but, perhaps more important, to find someone else who will like it.

Notice the two stories here — two hypotheses. (a) "First you improve the faults and then you like it." (b) "First you like it and then you improve faults." The second story may sound odd when stated so badly, but really it's common sense. Only if we like something will we get involved enough to work and struggle with it. Only if we like what we write will we write again and again by choice — which is the only way we get better.

This hypothesis sheds light on the process of how people get to be published writers. Conventional wisdom assumes a Darwinian model: poor writers are unread; then they get better; as a result, they get a wider audience; finally they turn into Norman Mailer. But now I'd say the process is more complicated. People who get better and get published really tend to be driven by how much *they* care about their writing. Yes, they have a small audience at first — after all, they're not very good. But they try reader after reader until finally they can find people who like and appreciate their writing. I certainly did this. If someone doesn't like her writing enough to be pushy and hungry about finding a few people who also like it, she probably won't get better.

It may sound so far as though all the effort and drive comes from the lonely driven writer — and sometimes it does (Norman Mailer is no joke). But, often enough, readers play the crucially active role in this story of how writers get better. That is, the way writers *learn* to like their writing is by the grace of having a reader or two who likes it — even though it's not good. Having at least a few appreciative readers is probably indispensable to getting better.

When I apply this story to our situation as teachers I come up with this interesting hypothesis: *good writing teachers like student writing* (and like students). I think I see this borne out — and it is really nothing but common sense. Teachers who hate student writing and hate students are grouchy all the time. How could we stand our work and do a decent job if we hated their writing? Good teachers see what is only *potentially* good, they get a kick out of mere possibility — and they encourage it. When I manage to do this, I teach well.

Thus, I've begun to notice a turning point in my courses — two or three weeks into the semester: "Am I going to like these folks or is this going to be a battle, a struggle?" When I like them everything seems to go better — and it seems to me they learn more by the end. When I don't and we stay tangled up in struggle, we all suffer — and they seem to learn less.

So what am I saying? That we should like bad writing? How can we see all the weaknesses and criticize student writing if we just like it? But here's the interesting point: if I *like* someone's writing it's *easier* to criticize it.

I first noticed this when I was trying to gather essays for the book on freewriting that Pat Belanoff and Sheryl Fontaine and I edited. I would read an essay someone had written, I would want it for the book, but I had some serious criticism. I'd get excited and write, "I really like this, and I hope we can use it in our book, but you've got to get rid of this and change that, and I got really mad at this other thing." I usually find it hard to criticize, but I began to notice that I was a much more critical and pushy reader when I liked something. It's even fun to criticize in those conditions.

It's the same with student writing. If I like a piece, I don't have to pussyfoot around with my criticism. It's when I don't like their writing that I find myself tiptoeing: trying to soften my criticism, trying to find something nice to say — and usually sounding fake, often unclear. I see the same thing with my own writing. If I like it, I can criticize it better. I have faith that there'll still be something good left, even if I train my full critical guns on it.

In short — and to highlight how this section relates to the other two sections of this essay — liking is not the same as ranking or evaluating. Naturally, people get them mixed up: when they like something, they assume it's good; when they hate it, they assume it's bad. But it's helpful to uncouple the two domains and realize that it makes perfectly good sense to say, "This is terrible, but I like it." Or, "This is good, but I hate it." In short, I am not arguing here *against* criticizing or evaluating. I'm merely arguing *for* liking.

Let me sum up my clump of hypotheses so far:

- It's not improvement that leads to liking, but rather liking that leads to improvement.
- It's the mark of good writers to like their writing.
- Liking is not the same as evaluating. We can often criticize something better when we like it.
- We learn to like our writing when we have a respected reader who likes it.
- Therefore, it's the mark of good teachers to like students and their writing.

If this set of hypotheses is true, what practical consequences follow from it? How can we be better at liking? It feels as though we have no choice — as though liking and not-liking just happen to us. I don't really understand this business. I'd love to hear discussion about the mystery of liking — the phenomenology of liking. I sense it's some kind of putting oneself out — or holding oneself open — but I can't see it clearly. I have a hunch, however, that we're not so helpless about liking as we tend to feel.

For in fact I can suggest some practical concrete activities that I have found fairly reliable at increasing the chances of liking student writing:

(a) I ask for lots of private writing and merely shared writing, that is, writing that I don't read at all, and writing that I read but don't comment on. This makes me more cheerful because it's so much easier. Students get *better* without me. Having to evaluate writing — especially bad writing — makes me more likely to hate it. This throws light on grading: it's hard to like something if we know we have to give it a D.

(b) I have students share lots of writing with each other — and after a while respond to each other. It's easier to like their writing when I don't feel myself as the only reader and judge. And so it helps to build community in general: it takes pressure off me. Thus I try to use peer groups not only for feedback, but for other activities too, such as collaborative writing, brainstorming, putting class magazines together, and working out other decisions.

(c) I increase the chances of my liking their writing when I get better at finding what *is* good — or *potentially* good — and learn to praise it. This is a skill. It requires a good eye, a good nose. We tend — especially in the academic world—to assume that a good eye or fine discrimination means *criticizing*. Academics are sometimes proud of their tendency to be bothered by what is bad. Thus I find I am sometimes looked down on as dumb and undiscriminating: "He likes bad writing. He must have no taste, no discrimination." But I've finally become angry rather than defensive. It's an act of discrimination to see what's good in bad writing. Maybe, in fact, this is the secret of the mystery of liking: to be able to see potential goodness underneath badness.

Put it this way. We tend to stereotype liking as a "soft" and sentimental activity. Mr. Rogers is our model. Fine. There's nothing wrong with softness and sentiment—and I love Mr. Rogers. But liking can also be hard-assed. Let me suggest an alternative to Mr. Rogers: B. F. Skinner. Skinner taught pigeons to play ping-pong. How did he do it? Not by moaning, "Pigeon standards are falling. The pigeons they send us these days are no good. When I was a pigeon . . ." He did it by a careful, disciplined method that involved close analytic observation. He put pigeons on a ping-pong table with a ball, and every time a pigeon turned his head 30 degrees toward the ball, he gave a reward (see my "Danger of Softness").

What would this approach require in the teaching of writing? It's very simple . . . but not easy. Imagine that we want to teach students an ability they badly lack, for example how to organize their writing or how to make their sentences clearer. Skinner's insight is that we get nowhere in this task by just telling them how much they lack this skill: "It's disorganized. Organize it!" "It's unclear. Make it clear!"

No, what we must learn to do is to read closely and carefully enough to show the student little bits of *proto*-organization or *sort of* clarity in what they've already written. We don't have to pretend the writing is wonderful. We could even say, "This is a terrible paper and the worst part about it is the lack of organization. But I will teach you how to organize it. Look here at this little organizational move you made in this sentence. Read it out loud and try to feel how it pulls together this stuff here and distinguishes it from that stuff there. Try to remember what it felt like writing that sentence—creating that piece of organization. Do it some more." Notice how much more helpful it is if we can say, "Do *more* of what you've done here," than if we say, "Do something *different* from anything you've done in the whole paper."

When academics criticize behaviorism as crude it often means that they aren't willing to do the close careful reading of student writing that is required. They'd rather give a cursory reading and turn up their nose and give a low grade and complain about falling standards. No one has undermined behaviorism's main principle of learning: that reward produces learning more effectively than punishment.

(d) I improve my chances of liking student writing when I take steps to get to know them a bit as people. I do this partly through the assignments I give. That is, I always ask them to write a letter or two to me and to each other (for example about their history with writing). I base at least a couple of assignments on their own experiences, memories, or histories. And I make sure some of the assignments are free choice pieces — which also helps me know them.

In addition, I make sure to have at least three conferences with each student each semester — the first one very early. I often call off some classes in order to keep conferences from being too onerous (insisting nevertheless that students meet with their partner or small group when class is called off). Some teachers have mini-conferences with students during class — while students are engaged in writing or peer group meetings. I've found that when I deal only with my classes as a whole — as a large group — I sometimes experience them as a herd or lump — as stereotyped "adolescents"; I fail to experience them as individuals. For me, personally, this is disastrous since it often leads me to experience them as that scary tribe that I felt rejected by when *I* was an eighteen-year-old — and thus, at times, as "the enemy." But when I sit down with them face to face, they are not so stereotyped or alien or threatening — they are just eighteen-year-olds.

Getting a glimpse of them as individual people is particularly helpful in cases where their writing is not just bad, but somehow offensive — perhaps violent or cruelly racist or homophobic or sexist — or frighteningly vacuous. When I know them just a bit I can often see behind their awful attitude to the person and the life situation that spawned it, and not hate their writing so much. When I know students I can see that they are smart behind that dumb behavior; they are doing the best they can behind that bad behavior. Conditions are keeping them from acting decently; something is holding them back.

(e) It's odd, but the more I let myself show, the easier it is to like them and their writing. I need to share some of my own writing — show some of my own feelings. I need to write the letter to them that they write to me — about my past experiences and what I want and don't want to happen.

(f) It helps to work on my own writing — and work on learning to *like* it. Teachers who are most critical and sour about student writing are often having trouble with their own writing. They are bitter or unforgiving or hurting toward their own work. (I think I've noticed that failed PhDs are often the most severe and difficult with students.) When we are stuck or sour in our own writing, what helps us most is to find spaces free from evaluation such as those provided by freewriting and journal writing. Also, activities like reading out loud and finding a supportive reader or two. I would insist, then, that if only for the sake of our teaching, we need to learn to be charitable and to like our own writing.

A final word. I fear that this sermon about liking might seem an invitation to guilt. There is enough pressure on us as teachers that we don't need someone coming along and calling us inadequate if we don't *like* our students and their writing. That is, even though I think I am right to make this foray into the realm of feeling, I also acknowledge that it is dangerous — and paradoxical. It strikes me that we also need to have permission to hate the dirty bastards and their stupid writing.

After all, the conditions under which they go to school bring out some awful behavior on their part, and the conditions under which we teach sometimes make it difficult for us to like them and their writing. Writing wasn't meant to be read in stacks of twenty-five, fifty, or seventy-five. And we are handicapped as teachers when students are in our classes against their will. (Thus high school teachers have the worst problem here, since their students tend to be the most sour and resentful about school.)

Indeed, one of the best aids to liking students and their writing is to be somewhat charitable toward ourselves about the opposite feelings that we inevitably have. I used to think it was terrible for teachers to tell those sarcastic stories and hostile jokes about their students: "teacher room talk." But now I've come to think that people who spend their lives teaching *need* an arena to let off this unhappy steam. And certainly it's better to vent this sarcasm and hostility with our buddies than on the students themselves. The question, then, becomes this: do we help this behavior function as a venting so that we can move past it and not be trapped in our inevitable resentment of students? Or do we tell these stories and jokes as a way of staying stuck in the hurt, hostile, or bitter feelings — year after year — as so many sad teachers do?

In short I'm not trying to invite guilt, I'm trying to invite hope. I'm trying to suggest that if we do a sophisticated analysis of the difference between liking and evaluating, we will see that it's possible (if not always easy) to like students and their writing — without having to give up our intelligence, sophistication, or judgment.

Let me sum up the points I'm trying to make about ranking, evaluating, and liking:

- Let's do as little ranking and grading as we can. They are never fair and they undermine learning and teaching.
- Let's use evaluation instead — a more careful, more discriminating, fairer mode of assessment.
- But because evaluating is harder than ranking, and because too much evaluating also undermines learning, let's establish small but important evaluation-free zones.
- And underneath it all — suffusing the whole evaluative enterprise — let's learn to be better likers: liking our own and our students' writing, and realizing that liking need not get in the way of clear-eyed evaluation.

Works Cited

Belanoff, Pat, and Marcia Dickson, eds. *Portfolios: Process and Product.* Portsmouth, NH: Boynton/Cook-Heinemann, 1991.

Belanoff, Pat, and Peter Elbow. "Using Portfolios to Increase Collaboration and Community in a Writing Program." *WPA: Journal of Writing Program Administration* 9.3 (Spring 1986): 27–40. (Also in *Portfolios: Process and Product.* Ed. Pat Belanoff and Marcia Dickson. Portsmouth, NH: Boynton/Cook-Heinemann, 1991.)

Belanoff, Pat, Peter Elbow, and Sheryl Fontaine, eds. *Nothing Begins with N: New Investigations of Freewriting.* Carbondale: Southern Illinois UP, 1991.

Bishop, Wendy. *Released into Language: Options for Teaching Creative Writing.* Urbana: NCTE, 1990.

———. *Something Old, Something New: College Writing Teachers and Classroom Change.* Carbondale: Southern Illinois UP, 1990.

Diederich, Paul. *Measuring Growth in English.* Urbana: NCTE, 1974.

Elbow, Peter. "The Danger of Softness." *What Is English?* New York: MLA, 1990. 197–210.

Elbow, Peter, and Pat Belanoff. "State University of New York: Portfolio-Based Evaluation Program." *New Methods in College Writing Programs: Theory into Practice.* Ed. Paul Connolly and Teresa Vilardi. New York: MLA, 1986. 95–105. (Also in *Portfolios: Process and Product.* Ed. Pat Belanoff and Marcia Dickson. Portsmouth, NH: Boynton/Cook-Heinemann, 1991.)

Gardner, Howard. *Frames of Mind: The Theory of Multiple Intelligences.* New York: Basic, 1983.

Kirschenbaum, Howard, Sidney Simon, and Rodney Napier. *Wad-Ja-Get? The Grading Game in American Education.* New York: Hart Publishing, 1971.

Lewis, C. S. *Studies in Words.* 2d ed. London: Cambridge UP, 1967.

Portfolio Assessment Newsletter. Five Centerpointe Drive, Suite 100, Lake Oswego, Oregon 97035.

Portfolio News. c/o San Dieguito Union High School District, 710 Encinitas Boulevard, Encinitas, CA 92024.

Smith, Barbara Herrnstein. *Contingencies of Value: Alternative Perspectives for Critical Theory.* Cambridge: Harvard UP, 1988.

White, Edward M. *Teaching and Assessing Writing.* San Francisco: Jossey-Bass, 1985.

Zak, Frances. "Exclusively Positive Responses to Student Writing." *Journal of Basic Writing* 9.2 (1990): 40–53.

Elbow's Insights as a Resource for Your Reflections

1. Reflect on your own grading procedures: Which of Elbow's three activities — ranking, evaluating, or liking — have influenced them the most? Why?

2. Consider what Elbow says about liking, and trace the ups and downs of your enjoyment of student writing. Can you imagine ways to like it more, and, more important, to articulate this liking more effectively?

Elbow's Insights as a Resource for Your Writing Classroom

1. How might your composition course make more room for what Elbow calls "evaluation-free zones"? Try to make such moments become a regular feature of your students' drafting and revising processes.
2. As you respond to your next batch of student drafts, strive to make at least one sincere, positive comment on each of them. When you receive the final drafts, try to determine whether the positive reinforcement appreciably altered the ways your students approached the task of final revision.

Portfolio Standards for English 101

Douglas D. Hesse

Douglas D. Hesse developed the following guidelines, reprinted in Strategies for Teaching First-Year Composition *(2002), for instructors at Illinois State University. Provided to English 101 students as well as to the teachers, this set of standards for assessing portfolios offers detailed discussion of exactly what distinguishes the best portfolios from the merely good ones, and the good ones from those that are flawed. A carefully stated rubric can be a useful dimension of any syllabus for any writing course, for it gives both students and teachers a clear and explicit set of guidelines for evaluating student work.*

Unlike individual paper grading, portfolio evaluation involves judging a collection of texts written by a writer. The grade reflects an overall assessment of the writer's ability to produce varied kinds of texts, not an average of grades on individual papers. Raters will choose the description that best fits the portfolio. In other words, not all of the criteria in a selected grade range may apply to a given set of papers, but that cluster of criteria more accurately describes the portfolio than any other. Feedback to student portfolios will usually consist of some indication to the students of how their work measures against these various criteria, plus a few sentences of written response to the portfolio as a whole. Individual papers are not marked.

The "A" Portfolio

"A" portfolios demonstrate the writer's skillful ability to perform in a variety of rhetorical situations. "A" portfolios suggest that the writer will be able to adroitly handle nearly any task an undergraduate student writer might encounter, in both academic and public forums. The papers, the drafting materials, and, most important, the reflective introduction demonstrate the writer's sense of his or her development through the semester, his or her ability to reflect analytically and critically on his or her writing, and the relations among works submitted in the portfolio.

Individual works in "A" portfolios tend consistently to be appropriate to their intended audiences, audiences who are characterized as well read or knowledgeable on the topics and ideas addressed. These readers would often be struck by the freshness of ideas, strategies, perspective, or expression in the work. Writers are usually able to bridge knowledge or opinion gaps between themselves and their readers and effectively create a context for the writing.

The quality of thought in "A" portfolios is generally ambitious and mature. Not only is the writer able to state claims or ideas clearly and effectively, but also he or she is generally able to provide support and discuss warrants for those claims in a manner that reflects the complexity of issues and yet still takes a plausible position. Not only is the writer able to describe phenomena or events clearly and effectively, but also he or she is able to analyze and interpret their possible meanings, going beyond the obvious. "A" writers usually have a keen eye for detail. Individual works are most often characterized by an effective texture of general and specific ideas or by such compelling specific ideas or accounts that generalizations are implicit.

Through allusions, interpretive strategies, and stylistic sophistication, "A" portfolios often suggest that their authors read or have read widely, not only materials assigned for courses but also a variety of public texts: newspapers, magazines, and books. These writers are able to incorporate ideas and insights gained from reading into their texts, sometimes critically, sometimes generatively, sometimes as support or illustration of ideas. This is not to suggest, however, that all works in portfolios must be documented. Indeed, reference to outside sources in many papers would be contrived, inappropriate, and undesirable.

"A" portfolios frequently show how their writers are able to draw on personal experience and direct observations of the world around them. They are able to connect these experiences and observations to readings or to new situations. Their writing often displays analogical or metaphorical thinking.

"A" portfolios may show frequent evidence of the writer's ability to make conceptual or global revisions — wide-ranging changes at the idea level — as well as local revisions — changes that affect meaning primarily in sentences and paragraphs. The writer is often able to use the entire range of revision operations: addition, subtraction, transposition. The writer is frequently able to use teacher and peer response generatively, moving beyond a single, narrow comment to revise other aspects of the paper — or to initiate revisions on her or his own.

"A" portfolios are generally marked by a range of sophisticated stylistic features appropriate to a given writing situation, perhaps including sentences of various types and lengths (especially cumulative and other subordinated structures), striking word choices that are appropriate to the situation of the paper, and the effective use of metaphor and analogy, often extended. Papers often reflect a distinctive voice. The opening strategies of "A" papers are generally creative and engaging, the conclusions more than simple restatements of preceding ideas.

"A" portfolios, although not necessarily perfect, are virtually free of the kinds of errors that compromise the effectiveness of the piece, and have virtually no stigmatized errors.

"A" portfolios are neatly printed and organized as described in "Guidelines for Turning in Portfolios."

Incomplete portfolios may not be graded "A."

The "B" Portfolio

"B" portfolios generally suggest the writer's skillful ability to perform in a variety of rhetorical situations, though a few areas may not be as strong as others. "B" portfolios suggest that the writer will be able successfully to handle nearly any task an undergraduate student writer might encounter, in both academic and public forums. The papers, the drafting materials, and, most important, the reflective introduction suggest progress toward the writer's becoming conversant with his or her development, toward an ability to reflect analytically and critically on his or her writing, and toward understanding the relations among works submitted in the portfolio.

Individual works in "B" portfolios are usually appropriate to their intended audiences, audiences who are characterized as well read or knowledgeable on the topics and ideas addressed. "B" portfolios may be less ambitious in their choice of intended topics or audience, or may be less sophisticated in the way they address their readers than "A" portfolios. "B" writers are often able to bridge knowledge or opinion gaps between themselves and their readers and to create a plausible context for the writing.

The quality of thought in "B" portfolios is often ambitious and mature. Not only is the writer able to state claims or ideas clearly and effectively, but also he or she is frequently able to provide support and discuss warrants for those claims in a manner that frequently reflects the complexity of issues. Not only is the writer able to describe phenomena or events clearly and effectively, but also he or she is generally able to analyze and interpret their meaning. Individual works are often characterized by an effective texture of general and specific ideas.

Through allusions, interpretive strategies, and stylistic sophistication, "B" portfolios suggest that their authors read widely, not only materials assigned for courses but also a variety of public texts: newspapers, magazines, and books. These writers are able to incorporate ideas and insights from reading into their texts, sometimes critically, sometimes generatively, sometimes as support or illustration of ideas, although this is often done less fluently or facilely than in "A" portfolios. This is not to suggest, however, that all works must be documented. Indeed, reference to outside sources in many papers would be contrived, inappropriate, and undesirable.

"B" portfolios occasionally show how their writers are able to draw on personal experience and observations of the world around them. They suggest that their writers are able to connect experience and direct observations to readings or to new situations. Occasionally, their writing may display analogical or metaphorical thinking.

"B" portfolios show occasional evidence of the writer's ability to make conceptual or global revision (or frequent evidence of such revisions that are not always fully successful). They show the writer's ability to make effective local revisions and to use a variety of revision strategies. The writer is sometimes able to use teacher and peer response generatively, moving beyond a single, narrow comment to revise other aspects of the paper.

"B" portfolios display a variety of sophisticated stylistic features, including sentences of various types and lengths (perhaps including cumulative and other subordinated structures), word choices that are appropriate to the rhetorical situation of the paper, and the occasional use of metaphor and analogy, though sometimes these features may not be fully controlled or appropriate. There is frequently a distinctive voice to the papers, although this may be uneven. The opening strategies of "B" papers are creative and engaging, the conclusions more than simple restatements of preceding ideas.

"B" portfolios, although not necessarily perfect, are virtually free of the kinds of errors that compromise the rhetorical effectiveness of the piece, and have virtually no stigmatized errors.

"B" portfolios are neatly printed and organized as described in "Guidelines for Turning in Portfolios."

Incomplete portfolios may not be graded "B."

The "C" Portfolio

"C" portfolios demonstrate the writer's ability to perform competently in a variety of rhetorical situations, perhaps even showing skills in some writings. The set of papers, the drafting materials, and, most important, the writer's reflective introduction suggest progress toward the writer's becoming conversant with his or her development, toward an ability to reflect analytically and critically on his or her writing, and toward understanding the relations among works submitted in the portfolio. "C" writers, however, may not be nearly as perceptive as "B" writers in making connections between projects, in discussing and illustrating general tendencies in their writing, or in critically analyzing their drafting processes. These portfolios may seem to be more compilations of isolated works than at least partially connected wholes. Again, the reflective introduction will be most useful in making this judgment.

Writing in "C" portfolios adequately addresses knowledge and attitudes of peers. While this writing may often successfully address a well-read and knowledgeable outside audience, the context and occasion for the writing tend to be confined more to the classroom situation itself.

The quality of thought in "C" portfolios is competent and sometimes compelling, though often standard or familiar. Not only is the writer able to state claims or ideas clearly and effectively, but also he or she is able to provide support and discuss warrants for those claims, although the complexities of the issues involved may be suggested rather than fully treated — or perhaps dealt with very little. Not only is the writer able to describe phenomena or events clearly and effectively, but also he or she is able to analyze and interpret their meaning, although the interpretations may be obvious or sometimes perfunctory. Individual works are often characterized by a texture of general and specific elements, but paraphrase and repetition may often take the place of development. Papers may be developed more by partition or addition, in the mode of the five-paragraph theme, rather than by logical or organic development of a central idea.

"C" portfolios demonstrate the writer's ability to read course materials critically and analytically and to incorporate ideas from reading into his or her texts. There may be some suggestions of the writer's facility with outside readings, but they may not be well integrated into papers, used rather in a more cut-and-paste fashion than a more organic one.

"C" writers may be able to draw on personal experience and observations of the world around them and connect these to readings or to new situations. The connections, however, may not be as fully integrated, explored, or subtle as in "B" portfolios.

"C" portfolios demonstrate the writer's ability to make local revisions, perhaps with one dominant strategy (addition, for example). While these portfolios may suggest the writer's ability to make global revisions, this ability is not clearly demonstrated. Revisions are frequently tied narrowly to specific comments made by the teacher or peers; the writer is less clearly a self-starter when it comes to revision than the "A" or "B" student.

"C" portfolios display a reasonable range of stylistic features, although sentences tend to be of a fairly uniform type (usually subject-verb-complement) and sentence length is mostly a function of coordination rather than subordination. There is infrequent use of metaphor and analogy. The voice of these papers is perhaps generic, competent but largely indistinct from other student prose. The opening strategies of writings in "C" portfolios may rely fairly directly on the assignment sheets or use some version of a funnel strategy. Conclusions tend to summarize the preceding ideas.

"C" portfolios are virtually free of the kinds of errors that compromise the rhetorical effectiveness of the piece, and they have few stigmatized errors and no consistent patterns of stigmatized errors.

"C" portfolios are neatly printed and organized as described in "Guidelines for Turning in Portfolios."

Incomplete portfolios may not be graded "C."

The "D" Portfolio

"D" portfolios suggest the writer's inability to write competently in several rhetorical situations. Writers of "D" portfolio work will likely have difficulty in other college or public writing situations. The set of papers, the drafting materials, and, most important, the writer's reflective introduction suggest that the writer is not fairly conversant with his or her development as a writer and is fairly unable to reflect analytically and critically on his or her writing. These portfolios generally seem to be more compilations of isolated works than partially connected wholes.

While the writing is sometimes appropriate to an audience that is knowledgeable on the topics and ideas addressed, frequently the writer assumes less — or more — of his or her readers than is appropriate. There are considerable knowledge or opinion gaps between the writer and his or her reader, and the context for the writing is usually limited to the classroom assignments themselves.

The quality of thought in "D" portfolios is frequently stock or perfunctory. The writer may be able to state claims or ideas clearly but is able to provide only minimal support and discuss virtually no warrants for that support. The writer may be able to describe phenomena or events clearly, but his or her interpretations may be obvious or perfunctory. While works may sometimes display a texture of general and specific elements, paraphrase and repetition may often take the place of development. "D" portfolios may contain papers that are consistently shorter than is needed to successfully engage the tasks.

"D" portfolios suggest their authors' difficulties in reading course materials critically and analytically. These writers may have some difficulty summarizing complex ideas. Or they may be able to summarize but unable to respond critically or interpretively. They incorporate ideas from reading into their texts in ways that are frequently not well integrated, in more of a cut-and-paste fashion than an organic one.

"D" portfolios suggest the writer's ability to make local revisions, but these are often infrequent or do not substantially improve the paper from draft to draft. Revisions may take the form primarily of proofreading or direct responses only to the teacher's or peers' comments.

"D" portfolios may display a narrow range of stylistic features, with most sentences of a fairly uniform type. The result may be an overly predictable text, at levels all the way from the sentence, to paragraphs, to openings and closings.

"D" portfolios may display some of the kinds of errors that compromise the rhetorical effectiveness of individual works and may have some stigmatized errors, even a pattern of one such error.

"D" portfolios may not be neatly printed, or they may not be neatly organized as described in "Guidelines for Turning in Portfolios."

"D" portfolios may be incomplete.

The "F" Portfolio

"F" portfolios demonstrate the writer's inability to write competently in various aims (persuasive, explanatory, and narrative), although the writer may be better in some than in others; writers of "F" portfolio work will have difficulty in most writing situations. The set of papers, the drafting materials, and, most important, the writer's reflective introduction generally indicate that the writer is not conversant with his or her development as a writer and that he or she is unable to reflect analytically and critically on his or her writing. These portfolios generally seem to be more compilations of isolated works than at least partially connected wholes.

The writing is almost never appropriate to an audience that is knowledgeable on the topics and ideas addressed; the writer assumes less — or more — of his or her readers than is appropriate, expecting readers to fill in all the gaps, to make all the connections, and automatically agree with the writer's perspective.

The quality of thought in "F" portfolios is perfunctory, obvious, or unclear. The writer may offer claims or ideas but be unable to provide much support. The writer may be able to describe phenomena or events but be unable to analyze or interpret them. Paraphrase and repetition often take the place of development. "F" portfolios may contain papers that are consistently shorter than is needed to successfully engage the tasks.

"F" portfolios demonstrate their authors' difficulties in reading course materials critically and analytically. These writers may have considerable difficulty summarizing complex ideas. They are unable to respond critically or interpretively. They incorporate ideas from reading into their texts in a cut-and-paste fashion rather than a more organic one.

"F" portfolios show relatively little evidence of revision, and what is there is frequently done at the sentence level or narrowly in response to a teacher's comment.

"F" portfolios may display the kinds of errors that compromise the rhetorical effectiveness of individual works; they may have patterns of stigmatized errors.

"F" portfolios may not be neatly printed, or they may not be neatly organized as described in "Guidelines for Turning in Portfolios."

"F" portfolios may be incomplete.

English 101 Final Portfolio Cover Sheet and Checklist, Spring 1999

Please provide the following information, which will help make sure you submit all the appropriate materials with your final portfolio. Turn this sheet in with your final portfolio. Thank you.

Name ____________________ Social Security Number ____________
Instructor and Section Number ______________________________
Local Address and Phone:
____
Permanent Address:
____

I. A check on the right numbers and kinds of works

_____ This portfolio contains a total of 20–30 pages.

_____ This portfolio contains a reflective introduction (Part I, Course Guide, p. 8).

_____ This portfolio contains at least 17 pages of revised writing from the course, appx. 5000–7500 words (Part II, p. 8).

_____ The writings in Part II consist of at least 4 but not more than 8 papers.

Note: It's acceptable to list a paper in more than one category below:
One persuasive paper in the portfolio is titled:
One paper that has analysis or critique as its primary aim is titled:
One paper that makes substantial use of readings is titled:

_____ This portfolio contains an analysis of writing done for another course and a copy of that paper (Part III, p. 8).

II. A check of format for the portfolio

_____ I have included drafts for each paper. These are arranged exactly as described in step 3 on page 11 of the English 101 Course Guide.

I understand that the Writing Program strongly urges me to keep a photocopy.

_____ I have provided an electronic second copy of the portfolio exactly as described in step 7 on page 11.

_____ I have turned in all materials in a two-pocket folder. On the outside of the folder is the information requested in step 9 on page 11 of the Course Guide. I understand that I can pick up my portfolio from my teacher at the beginning of next semester.

III. Permission: Choosing to give or withhold permission will not affect your grade in any way. Report any concerns or irregularities to the director of Writing Programs or the program ombudsperson.

I give my permission to the English Department to reproduce writings from this portfolio in future editions of Language and Composition I Course Guide: yes _____ no _____

I give permission to my instructor or to the English Department to reproduce or otherwise use my writings for teaching training or research purposes. This includes permission to quote from my work in published articles or books. I understand that I will not be identified in any way, that my participation is completely voluntary, and that I may withdraw my permission, in writing, at any time. yes _____ no _____

IV. Certification

The works submitted in this portfolio do not violate the plagiarism policy stated in the Course Guide. I understand that plagiarism will result in an F for the course.

____

(signed) (date)

Hesse's Insights as a Resource for Your Reflections

1. Look closely at the criteria Hesse sets forth for the "A" portfolio, the "B" portfolio, and so on. How would adopting Hesse's set of standards change your course? What challenges or obstacles might they create in your particular institution? How might you revise these standards to fit your own situation?
2. Consider the potential uses — beyond evaluation — of student portfolios. How might you use them when you yourself are evaluated by supervisors? How might they function, systematically, in your own ongoing "reflective practice" as a teacher? Try to devise some particular ways of tracking broad trends in student portfolios over a couple of semesters.

Hesse's Insights as a Resource for Your Writing Classroom

1. Hesse suggests that the reflective portfolio introduction that students must write at the end of the semester is quite important. What guidelines would you offer your students to assist them in this task? How long should the introduction be? What sorts of terms are they expected to use as conceptual tools for understanding their work over the semester? How directly must they refer to your own evaluative commentary on their work?
2. Early in the semester, distribute a set of criteria among your students for grading portfolios and discuss with them, in detail, what these criteria mean. Another possibility is to devote the first week of the semester to discussing standards with your students so that they have significant input into the terms by which their work will be evaluated. Take careful notes throughout the discussion, and at the next class meeting present a draft of the criteria for revision. As a class, work together to finalize the standards by way of ending the introduction to the course. Beginning the course in this way can enable broad discussion about the definition of good writing, what sorts of things first-year students should learn, and so on. It will also give students a crucial sense of responsibility for the class, since they will have had a hand in developing the grading criteria.

Error

Joseph Harris

What are the institutional traditions that have conspired to make such a hot-button issue out of grammatical error—and how should we handle this issue? In this chapter from his 1997 book A Teaching Subject: Composition Since 1966, *Joseph Harris situates the discussion of error historically, looking closely at the debate between John Rouse and Gerald Graff over the meaning of Mina Shaughnessy's widely known work,* Errors and Expectations, *and detailing the broader politics that make this such a heated debate. Harris argues that we are obligated to teach students to write correctly, not because of any naïve faith in the transcendent value of the "standard" but because these issues are inextricably linked to the need for authority and credibility that brings students to the university in the first place. Supporting a shift from issues of phrasing and correctness to matters of stance and argument, Harris's beliefs complement David Bartholomae's overall goal—to help students gain the authority in their discourse that will provide them access to academic and professional communities (see "Inventing the University," Chapter 1).*

How Rouse makes his living is none of my business, but I venture that if he manages a decent livelihood it is only because he has somewhere or other submitted to enough socialization to equip him to do something for which somebody is willing to pay him" (852). So thundered Gerald Graff in the pages of *College English* in 1980, as part of a response to an article John Rouse had published in the same journal a year before. Not only was Graff's tone here sententious and overbearing, his question was also rhetorical to the point of being disingenuous, since how Rouse made his living should have been clear to anyone who had read his article, which was on the teaching of college writing and included a standard biographical note on its title page identifying him as "a teacher of English and an administrator in public schools" as well as the author of previous pieces in *College English* and of a book called *The Completed Gesture: Myth, Character, and Education* ("Politics" 1). So Rouse was a teacher and writer, "managing his livelihood" in much the same way as Graff, and probably drawing on much the same sort of skills and "socialization" in order to do so. Except not quite. For what Graff—who was identified by a similar note on the first page of his response as the chair of the English department at Northwestern University, as well as the author of articles in several prestigious literary journals and of a book published by the University of Chicago Press (851)—was hinting rather broadly at was that he didn't know who this guy was, that Rouse (schoolteacher rather than professor; articles in *College English* rather than *Salmagundi*; book published by trade rather than university press) was not a player in the academic world that Graff moved about in. And perhaps why this seemed so important was that Rouse had presumed to criticize the work of someone who was such a player, someone who by then had in fact become a kind of revered figure in the literary establishment, its sanctioned representative of the good teacher—and that was Mina Shaughnessy.

Although in many ways, Rouse had seemed to ask for precisely the sort of response he got from Graff and others.[1] His article on "The Politics of Composition" offered what I still see as a trenchant critique of Shaughnessy's 1977 *Errors and Expectations*, a book on the teaching of "basic" or underprepared college writers that had almost immediately gained the status of a classic. Rouse argued that Shaughnessy's relentless focus on the teaching of grammar might in many cases actually hinder the attempts of anxious and inexperienced students to elaborate their thoughts effectively in writing. I agree. But his criticism was couched in language that sometimes seemed deliberately aimed to provoke: Rouse failed to acknowledge, for instance, the crucial political importance and difficulty of the role that Shaughnessy took on in the late 1960s when she set up the first Basic Writing Program at City College of New York, and thus found herself in charge of diagnosing and responding to the academic needs of thousands of newly admitted and severely underprepared open admissions students. He also failed to note the clear sympathy and respect for such students that runs throughout *Errors and Expectations* and which all of her many admirers argue was central to Shaughnessy's work as a teacher and intellectual. And he was either unaware of or did not see the need to mention her tragic and early death from cancer the year before in 1978. Instead, Rouse went ferociously on the attack, arguing that Shaughnessy's "overriding need to socialize these young people in a manner politically acceptable accounts, I think, for her misinterpretations of student work and her disregard of known facts of language learning" (1–2). This rabble-rousing tone led right into Graff's magisterial response, and a much needed argument over teaching aims and strategies became clouded with competing accusations of elitism and pseudoradicalism, as snide guesses about Mina Shaughnessy's psychopolitical needs or John Rouse's means of earning a living were followed by insinuations about who *really* had the best interests of students in mind. "Is this submission with a cheerful smile? 'Mrs. Shaughnessy, we do know our verbs and adverbs,'" sneered Rouse (8). "John Rouse's article . . . illustrates the predicament of the thoughtful composition teacher today," replied Graff, who then went on to explain that it was the very conscientiousness of such teachers that left them "open to attack from critics of Rouse's persuasion" (851).

I want to do two things in this chapter: First, to work through what might actually be at stake in this argument over error and socialization, to sort out what competing views of the aims and practices of teaching are being offered in it, and, second, to try to understand why this particular issue in teaching, more than any other that I know of, seems to spark such strong feeling. I begin by looking more closely at Mina Shaughnessy, who figures in this debate, I think, less as an advocate of a position which many people now find very compelling than as a kind of icon, a model of what it might mean to be, in Graff's words, a "thoughtful composition teacher."

Shaughnessy was an elegant but evidently also rather slow writer. Her entire body of work consists of a few essays and talks along with a single book, *Errors and Expectations*. This has been enough, though, to secure her place in the history of the field. *Errors and Expectations* showed how students who had often been presumed uneducable, hopelessly unprepared for college work, could in fact be helped to compose reasonably correct academic prose—that their problems with college writing stemmed not from a lack of intelligence but from inexperience. As Shaughnessy put it, "BW students write the way they do, not because they are slow or non-verbal, indifferent to or incapable of academic excellence, but because they are beginners and must, like all beginners, learn by making mistakes" (5). The students whom Shaughnessy worked with (she calls them "BWs" or "basic writers"), and whose writings fill the pages of her book, were for the most part blacks and Hispanics who had been given the chance to attend City through its (then) new and controversial program of open admissions for graduates of New York high schools.[2] Shaughnessy's work with these students was thus an intrinsic part of one of the most ambitious democratic reforms of American higher education — as the glowing reviews of her book in popular liberal magazines like *The Nation* and *Atlantic Monthly* attested.

But while politically liberal, the plan of work sketched out in *Errors and Expectations* is in many ways quite intellectually conservative. What people tend to remember and admire about *Errors and Expectations* is Shaughnessy's early defense of the aims of open admissions, her attentiveness throughout to the language of students, and her analysis late in the book of the difficulties students often have in taking on the critical and argumentative stance of much academic writing. What tends to be forgotten or glossed over is that the bulk of *Errors and Expectations* is a primer on teaching for correctness, pure and simple, as the titles of its Chapters 2 through 6 show: Handwriting and Punctuation, Syntax, Common Errors, Spelling, and Vocabulary. And even the much more celebrated seventh chapter on Beyond the Sentence offers what seems to me a distressingly formulaic view of academic writing and how to teach it. For instance, an extraordinarily detailed "sample lesson" on helping students write about reading (251–55) offers students an extended list of quotations culled from the book they are reading (*Black Boy*), followed by a set of procedures (Observation, Idea, and Analysis — the three of which are themselves broken into substeps) that they are to use in analyzing this list of details, and ends up by instructing them to

> Follow the steps given above. Make observations on parts, repetitions, omissions, and connections. Write down the main idea you get from your observations. Develop that main idea into an essay that makes a general statement, an explanation of the statement, an illustration of the statement, and a concluding statement. (255)

Follow the steps given above. I can't imagine a less compelling representation of the work of a critic or intellectual. Students are not asked in this assignment to say anything about what they thought or felt about their reading, or to connect what the author is writing about with their own experiences, or to take a stand on what he has to say; rather, they are simply told to generate and defend "a main idea" about a list of details that their teacher has given them from the book. What is the point of having students read books (like *Black Boy*) that might speak to their situations and concerns if they are not then encouraged to draw on their life experiences in speaking back to it? The tame parody of critical analysis sketched out in this assignment is "academic" in the worst sense: its form predetermined, its aim less to say something new or interesting than to demonstrate a competence in a certain kind of school writing.

Errors and Expectations thus argues for a new sort of student but not a new sort of intellectual practice. It says that basic writers can also do the kind of work that mainstream students have long been expected to do; it doesn't suggest this work be changed in any significant ways. This is a strong part of its appeal. Throughout her writings Shaughnessy offers a consistent image of herself as an *amateur* and a *reformer*. Even as she helped to set up the new field of "basic writing," Shaughnessy identified herself less with composition than with mainstream literary studies. Few of her admirers miss the chance to note how she was the product of a quite traditional education (B.A. in speech from Northwestern, M.A. in literature from Columbia) or to mark her love of Milton and drama.[3] Her method in *Errors and Expectations* is essentially that of the literary critic: a close and careful explication of difficult texts—except that in this case the difficulty springs from the inexperience of students rather than from the virtuosity of professionals. And her list of references and suggested readings at the end of her book has an undisciplined and eclectic quality: some literature, some criticism, some linguistics, some psychology, some work on second language learning and on the writing process—whatever, it seems, that could be found which might help with the task at hand.

This image of the autodidact or amateur was carefully constructed. Shaughnessy often depicts herself and her colleagues as "pioneers" working on a new "frontier," who need to "dive in" and explore previously uncharted waters (the metaphor varies a bit) so they can form a new kind of knowledge and expertise to use in teaching a new kind of college student. In "Mapping Errors and Expectations for Basic Writing," Bruce Horner points to the troubling (indeed, almost unconsciously racist) implications of describing teachers and students in terms of pioneers and natives. I would add that the "frontier" Shaughnessy claimed to stumble upon was already quite well developed, that even though the field of composition was not disciplined or professionalized in the same ways it is now, many teachers and writers had for some time been dealing with much the same sorts of issues.

There is no question that Shaughnessy brought a new sense of urgency to the problem of teaching underprepared writers. But it wasn't a new problem. In 1961, for instance, David Holbrook had written his moving book on *English for the Rejected* (still perhaps the bluntest and most accurate name for "basic" writers); in 1967, John Dixon was writing in *Growth through English* about students like Joan, the third grader with an IQ of 76 who wrote her poem about "the yellow bird." (It is this British and school-based tradition that John Rouse identifies himself with in his response to Shaughnessy.) And in America, in 1977, the same year that *Errors and Expectations* came out, Geneva Smitherman published *Talkin and Testifyin*, a book that urged teachers to spend less time correcting the language of black students and more time responding to what they had to say. And throughout the 1970s, the very time that Shaughnessy was most active in the profession, what remains perhaps the liveliest and most vehement debate in the history of CCCC was going on around the drafting and eventual approval of its 1974 statement on "The Students' Right to Their Own Language," a document which militantly asserted the need for teachers to move beyond a simple concern with having students write standard written English. None of these texts or authors can be placed in easy agreement with the approach taken by Shaughnessy in *Errors and Expectations*, which remains, again, after everything else is said about it, a book on teaching grammar. What Shaughnessy depicts as a sparse and unpopulated frontier of inquiry, then, looks from another perspective (to make use of a competing cliché) more like a marketplace of ideas as contending factions hawk their positions and argue against the views of others.

But this contrast also shows the appeal of the metaphor of the frontier, which allowed Shaughnessy to present herself less as criticizing than *extending* the reach of English studies. (Contrast this with critics, like Rouse, who positioned themselves as outsiders arguing *against* the status quo.) Even at her angriest moments (as in her article on "The English Professor's Malady," in which she complains of her colleagues' unwillingness to take on the hard work of teaching students not already familiar with their preferred ways of reading and writing), Shaughnessy's argument was for the profession to live up to its own stated values. Her message was consistently one of *inclusion*—that we can (and should) teach a kind of student, the "basic writer," who has too often slipped beneath the notice of the professoriate. And not only that, but she also showed how this sort of teaching could draw on precisely the sort of skills that people trained in English were likely to have, as well as to offer them much the sort of intellectual rewards which they most valued. The pleasures of *Errors and Expectations* are strikingly like that of good literary criticism: Passages of student writing that seem almost impossibly convoluted and obscure are patiently untangled and explicated. Shaughnessy thus offered the profession of English studies a useful image of one of its own best selves: The teacher who happily takes on the class of boneheads that the rest of us dread encountering and who patiently teaches them the very "basics" which we want to be able to assume they already know.

But *what* Shaughnessy argues can (and should) be taught to these new students is dismaying. Here, for instance, is the plan she offers for a basic writing course near the end of *Errors and Expectations*:

Weeks 1–5	Combined work on syntax and punctuation, following recommendations in Chapters 2 and 3.
Weeks 6–7	Spelling — principles of word formation, diagnostic techniques. (After this, spelling instruction should be individualized.)
Weeks 8–12	Common errors — verb inflections for number, noun inflections for number, verb tenses, agreement.
Weeks 13–15	Vocabulary — prefixes, suffixes, roots, abstract-concrete words, precision. (289)

Fifteen weeks and the focus never moves past correctness. Nowhere here (or anywhere else in her book) do we get a sense that the work of a basic writing course might be not only to train students in the mechanics of writing correct sentences but also to engage them in the life of the mind, to offer them some real experience in testing out and elaborating their views in writing. At no point in *Errors and Expectations* does Shaughnessy talk about how teachers might respond to the gist or argument of student writings, or about how to help students use writing to clarify or revise what they think. Indeed, as Rouse pointed out, Shaughnessy does not even seem to notice how many of the students whose work she cites change what they actually have to say in the process of trying to write more correct sentences.[4] Coupled with this is her nearly complete lack of interest in revision. Almost all of the student writings that Shaughnessy analyzes are timed first drafts; her goal in teaching was not to have students go back to edit and revise what they had written but to write new impromptu pieces with fewer mistakes in them. Her measures of good writing, that is to say, centered on fluency and correctness at the almost total expense of meaning. A footnote near the end of her book strikingly shows this mechanistic emphasis. Comparing some pieces written early in the term with those composed later on by the same students, Shaughnessy remarks,

> In all such before-and-after examples, the "after" samples bear many marks of revision (crossed-out words, corrected punctuation, etc.), suggesting that students have acquired the important habit of going back over their sentences with an eye to correctness. (277)

Revision here is pictured simply as a habit of proofreading. *Errors and Expectations* is thus the sort of book that tells you everything but why — as students and teachers labor together to perfect the form of prose whose actual or possible meanings they never seem to talk about.

Compare this to the sort of work that, at precisely the same time, Geneva Smitherman was arguing ought to go on in writing classes. A sociolinguist active in political and legal debates over the schooling of black children, Smitherman was also a strong influence in the framing of the 1974 CCCC statement on the "Students' Right to Their Own Language." (Shaughnessy was conspicuously absent from this debate.) Her 1977 *Talkin and Testifyin* is an impassioned and lucid defense of the richness and complexity of black English. In its final chapter, Smitherman turns to language education, which she argues should center (for both black and white students) on skills in reading and writing that are "intellectual competencies that can be taught in any dialect or language" (228). To teach such a "communicative competence," teachers need to move beyond a fetishizing of correctness and instead focus on the more substantive, difficult, and rhetorical

> aspects of communication such as content and message, style, choice of words, logical development, originality of thought and expression, and so forth. Such are the real components of language power, and they cannot be measured by narrow conceptions of "correct grammar." While teachers frequently correct student language on the basis of such misguided conceptions, saying something correctly, and saying it well, are two entirely different Thangs. (229)

This emphasis on forming something to say and working to say it well could hardly be more different than Shaughnessy's focus on error. Smitherman continues to drive this emphasis home by comparing her responses to two student pieces: one a vacuous (and stylistically bland) comment on Baraka's *Dutchman* by a white student teacher, and the other a poorly developed paragraph on the evils of war by a black ninth grader. What I find striking is how Smitherman uses much the same strategy in responding to both writers, challenging them to articulate their positions more fully before working to correct their phrasings. To the white student, Smitherman said,

> as kindly as I could, that his "essay" was weak in content and repetitious, and that it did not demonstrate command of the literary critical tools that teachers of literature are supposed to possess, *plus it didn't really say nothing!* (229)

While in responding to the black ninth grader writing on war, she asked things like:

> "Some say . . ." Who is "some"? . . .
>
> Exactly who are the two sides you're talking about here? What category of people? Name them and tell something about them. . . .
>
> Give me an example showing when and how such a disagreement leads to war. . . . (230)

While these two responses show some differences in tone (and perhaps appropriately so, given the varying situations of the writers), their aim is quite similar: to get students to think about what they want to say in their writing and about the effects their words have on readers. Smitherman is quick to say that she is not advocating an "off-the-deep-end permissiveness of letting their kids get away with anything," but rather that she is teaching toward a rhetorical and stylistic awareness that is "deeper and more expansive" than that encouraged by a focus on norms of correctness (233). Her position is much the same as that taken by Rouse in his response to Shaughnessy, and indeed something like it has become in recent years the consensus view of the profession, at least as represented in the pages of *CCC* and *College English* and at the annual meetings of CCCC: Students must learn not simply how to avoid mistakes but how to write in ways that engage the attention of educated readers. Teachers need then to respond to what students are trying to say, to the effectiveness of their writing as a whole, and not simply to the presence or absence of local errors in spelling, syntax, or usage. Correctness thus becomes not the single and defining issue in learning how to write but simply one aspect of developing a more general communicative competence.

This shift in focus was given articulate and moving expression by Mike Rose in his 1989 *Lives on the Boundary*, a book which, like *Errors and Expectations*, gained almost immediate acclaim both within and outside the profession. Like Shaughnessy, Rose argues for the intelligence and promise of students who are too often dismissed as unprepared or even unfit for college work, and like her too, his work and writing speaks to the linkings between education and politics, since the underprepared students he works with are so often also (and not coincidentally) people of color or from lower socioeconomic classes. And, certainly, even though the students Rose works with in Los Angeles in the 1980s often seem to live in an almost completely different world than those Shaughnessy worked with in New York in the 1970s, what both groups most need to learn is how to find their way into a system of education that seems at many points purposely designed to exclude them. But rather than assuming, like Shaughnessy, that what such students need is yet more training in the "basics," Rose argues that an unremitting focus on the more routine and dull aspects of intellectual work can instead act to dim their ambitions and limit their chances of success. One of the most telling bits of evidence Rose has to offer for this view comes from his own life, since as a boy he was placed in the vocational track of his local schools and so learned of the boredom and condescension of such classrooms firsthand. He was only retracked into college prep when a teacher noticed he was doing suspiciously well in biology. You don't know what you don't know, Rose suggests: "The telling thing is how chancy both my placement into and exit from Voc. Ed. was; neither I nor my parents had anything to do with it" (30). We can't expect students to grow proficient at kinds of intellectual work that they don't know about, that they've never really been given a chance to try their hands at.

What struggling students need, then, is not more of the basics but a sense of what others find most exciting and useful about books, writing, and ideas. Here's how Rose describes how he began to form his own aims for teaching while working with a group of Vietnam veterans studying to return to college:

> Given the nature of these men's needs and given the limited time I would have with them, could I perhaps orient them to some of the kinds of reading and writing and ways of thinking that seem essential to a liberal course of study, some of the habits of mind that Jack MacFarland and the many [of Rose's own teachers] that followed him helped me develop? . . . I was looking for a methodical way to get my students to think about thinking. Thinking. Not a fussbudget course, but a course about thought. I finally decided to build a writing curriculum on four of the intellectual strategies my education had helped me develop — some of which, I later learned were as old as Aristotle — strategies that kept emerging as I reflected on the life of the undergraduate: summarizing, classifying, comparing, and analyzing. (138)

The crucial words here are *habits of mind*, a phrasing even older than Aristotle, at least as it is often used to translate the Greek notion of *arete*, those "virtues" or "excellences" required by the citizens of a democracy.[5] There is an admirable hardheadedness in this teaching project that is reminiscent of Shaughnessy; like her, Rose wants to demystify the workings of the academy for his students. But a course on habits or strategies of thinking is in practice quite different from one focused on issues of correctness in language. As Rose outlines his course,

> Each quarter, I began by having the students summarize short simple readings, and then moved them slowly through classifying and comparing to analyzing. . . . I explained and modeled, used accessible readings, tried to incorporate what the veterans learned from one assignment to the next, slowly increased difficulty, and provided a lot of time for the men to talk and write. (143)

Malcolm Kiniry and Rose offer a more elaborate version of such a course in their 1990 *Critical Strategies for Academic Writing*, a text whose aim is to engage students in reading and writing, at a beginning and approximate level, about the kinds of issues and questions that academics in various fields take on. Similarly, in their 1986 *Facts, Artifacts, and Counterfacts*, David Bartholomae and Anthony Petrosky sketch out a plan for a basic writing course that is set up very much like a graduate seminar: Students read, write, and talk together about a particular intellectual issue over the course of a term, coming at the same topic from a number of different angles, reading one another's writings, seeing how the individual concerns they bring to their common subject influence what each of them has to say about it. The trick of such teaching is, of course, to find a set of readings that underprepared students will find accessible, and not only speak to their concerns but also push their ways of understanding and talking about them. (Some of the classes described in *Facts, Artifacts*, for instance, had students read and write on "Growth and Adolescence," or "Work," or "Creativity.") But what's more important is how this sort of teaching signals a shift in focus from *error* to *academic discourse*, from issues of phrasing and correctness to matters of stance and argument.

I support this shift myself, and, again, feel that Shaughnessy's failure to attend in any sustained way to issues beyond the sentence is what now makes her work, less than twenty years after its appearance, seem of merely historical interest rather than of practical use. (There is a dark irony here: The subtitle of *Errors and Expectations* is *A Guide for the Teacher of Basic Writing*, and Shaughnessy is often invoked as a model practitioner whose scholarship was deeply rooted in her day-to-day work with students. And yet I can't now imagine giving *Errors and Expectations* as a guide to a beginning teacher of basic writing, although I still often offer new teachers other writings from the 1960s and 1970s by people like Moffett, Britton, Elbow, and Coles.) Still one can see how this downplaying of error might seem to outsiders simply a way of slipping past the difficulty and drudgery of actually teaching writing. "Students and parents complain that they are being patronized, that the more relaxed, more personalist pedagogy fails to teach anybody how to write" (852), was how Graff (who is no cultural reactionary) put it in 1980. Given his distrust of Rouse and defense of Shaughnessy, it seems clear that for Graff learning "how to write" involves strong attention to issues of correctness, and his complaint about "relaxed" standards has been echoed in countless ways not only by students and parents but also by college faculty and administrators, as well as by writers in the popular press.[6] As one of my colleagues, a biologist, said to me recently after a curriculum meeting in which I argued for a new structuring of introductory writing courses at my college: "The thing is, most of us think that too many students can't write worth a damn, and we wish you'd just do something about it."

It's tempting to dismiss such complaints as misinformed, as in many ways they surely are. But that is also precisely the problem. Again, for some time now, most compositionists have held that a focus on error can often block the attempts of beginning writers to form their thoughts in prose, and indeed that the explicit teaching of grammatical forms usually has little effect on the abilities of students to write fluently or correctly.[7] But ask anyone *outside* the field (and this includes many writing teachers who are not active in CCCC) what they expect students to learn in a composition course, and you are likely to hear a good bit about issues of proper form and correctness. As even someone like the distinguished liberal philosopher Richard Rorty put it, when asked in an interview about what the aims of a writing course might be,

> I think the idea of freshman English, mostly, is just to get them to write complete sentences, get the commas in the right place, and stuff like that—the stuff we would like to think the high schools do and, in fact, they don't. But as long as there's a need for freshman English, it's going to be primarily a matter of the least common denominator of all the jargon. (Olson 6–7)

Although Rorty's interviewer, Gary Olson, expresses surprise at this response (since Rorty's views on language have influenced many progressive composition theorists), it seems to me both familiar and reasonable enough. What I find more distressing has been the ongoing inability of compositionists (myself among them) to explain ourselves to people like Graff and Rorty. Instead we have too often retreated behind the walls of our professional consensus, admonishing not only our students and university colleagues but the more general public as well when they fail to defer to our views on language learning—answering their concerns about correctness by telling them, in effect, that they should not want what they are asking us for.

This is an unfortunate stance for a field that defines itself through its interest in teaching and the practical workings of language. I am not advocating a return to Shaughnessy-like focus on error, but I do think we can learn from her responsiveness to the concerns of people outside our field. Rather than either meekly acceding to or simply dismissing what Smitherman called "the national mania for correctness" (229), we need to argue for a view of literacy that clearly recognizes and includes such concerns but is not wholly defined by them.

A first step might be to reinterpret worries about "grammar" or "correctness" in a more generous and expansive way. Rather than reading them as moves to trivialize the issues involved in learning to write, to turn everything into a simple matter of proofreading, we might see such remarks as somewhat clumsy attempts to voice concerns about how one gains or loses authority in writing. For even if mistakes do not interfere with what a writer has to say, they can still do serious harm to her credibility. Indeed, it is precisely because many mistakes (lapses in spelling or punctuation, for instance) seem so trivial that their appearance in a writer's text can seem to speak of a lack of care or ability. People don't want to be caught out in their writing or to have their students or children caught out. And so many struggling writers speak of their "problems with grammar" as a kind of shorthand for a whole set of difficulties they have with writing that are much harder to name, much as many readers will begin to complain about fairly trivial errors in a text they have grown impatient with for other less easily defined reasons. It is one thing to feel that in a particular classroom your language will not be held up for ridicule; it is another to feel confidence in your abilities to write to an indifferent or even hostile reader — to a different sort of teacher or examiner, perhaps, or to an applications committee or potential employer. Something like this is, I think, what lies behind many worries about "relaxed" or "permissive" forms of teaching. To gloss over such concerns is to dodge questions about the workings of power in language at their most naked.

Not that responding to them is all that easy either. As I've noted before, simply drilling students in proper forms has been shown to have little effect — and besides, the problem of gaining authority is not merely a matter of getting rid of error; students must also and at the same time acquire a rhetorical ease and power, an ability to write persuasively as well as correctly. And standards of correctness vary from one context to the other, along with the readiness of readers to look for mistakes, as Joseph Williams points out in his stunning 1981 article on "The Phenomenology of Error," in which he shows how the authors of writing handbooks often commit the same errors they decry, and sometimes in the very act of stating them — as when, for instance, while inveighing against the use of negative constructions, one text declares that "the following example . . . is not untypical"; or when in "Politics and the English Language" Orwell casts his famous polemic against the passive voice *in the passive voice*; or when yet another handbook advises that "Emphasis is often achieved . . . by the use of verbs in the active rather than in the passive voice" (158). The reason we don't tend to notice such problems, Williams argues, is that we're not looking for them. And, conversely, why we find so many mistakes in student papers is because we expect to, we're on the watch for them. (Williams clinches his case by revealing, at the end of his article, that he has deliberately inserted about a hundred "errors" in his own text. I have never met a reader who claimed to notice more than two or three on a first reading.)

Williams's point is not that we should downplay the significance of error but that we should focus our attention and energies on those mistakes which really count, on those that seriously impugn a writer's authority. (Maxine Hairston added to this line of thinking in a piece that appeared that same year in *College English*, "Not All Errors Are Created Equal: Nonacademic Readers in the Professions Respond to Lapses in Usage.") This makes good sense, but even more important is how Williams locates "error" as something that exists not simply as marks on a page but also as a part of the consciousness of writers, readers, and (in the form of handbooks and such) the culture at large. A mistake is not a mistake unless it's noticed as one, is how the argument goes, and it's a line of thought that sheds light both on why some writers have such difficulty proofreading their work and on the role that readers play in creating a mania of correctness. For what is involved in detecting errors seems to be not only an awareness of rules but a shift in attentiveness: One needs to learn how to read for mistakes as well as meaning.[8] This suggests the need for a kind of double approach to the issue of error, one that deals frankly with the practical politics of the situation: What writers need to learn is how to read their work for those lapses that will send many readers into a tailspin; what readers (and the culture) need to learn is to lighten up, to recognize the writing of reasonably correct prose as a fairly complex intellectual achievement and to be a little less quick to damn a writer for a few mistakes.

In practice one often sees this sort of double approach. In the *Facts, Artifacts* course, for instance, students are asked to revise and edit one of their writings for publication in a class book, a process which requires them to carefully proofread and correct their prose. And while his *Lives on the Boundary* is a plea to reform education in America, to make it more forgiving of error and more willing to work with difference, the picture Mike Rose offers of himself *as a teacher* throughout the book is of someone who wants to help students claim whatever power they can in the system as it stands. As one woman tells him,

> You know, Mike, people always hold this shit over you, make you . . . make you feel stupid with their fancy talk. But now *I've* read it, I've read Shakespeare, I can say I, *Olga*, have read it. I won't tell you I like it, 'cause I don't know if I do or I don't. But I like knowing what it's about. (223)

While in another context, I might want to quibble with the term *fancy talk*, what is crucial to realize here, I think, is that unless you already feel at home in the workings of critical or intellectual discourse, that's all it's likely to seem to you: fancy talk. And I don't see how you could possibly begin to feel at ease in any sort of fancy talk unless you also felt sure both that what you had to say would be listened to seriously and that you weren't likely to commit any egregious nails-on-the-chalkboard kinds of mistakes (*c'est je*, that sort of thing) in trying to speak or write it. So while we can't teach for correctness alone, we also can't *not* teach for it either. I think of the joke in Calvin Trillin's 1977 novel *Runestruck*, when a lawyer goes out "on a drive to relax from the pressures of a civil liberties case he was arguing in a nearby town — the case of an elementary school teacher of progressive views who claimed that she was fired by the local school board solely because she had refused to teach her students to spell" (23). "Better watch my grammar" versus "won't really teach kids how to write." Some choice. (And Trillin probably actually knew something about the debate over error in the 1970s, since he is married to Alice Trillin, who taught basic writing with Shaughnessy at City College.) We need to make sure that in distancing ourselves from poor practice (a focus on error alone) we don't seem to advocate an equally unconvincing stance (no concern with error at all).

In the mid-1980s, a number of teachers and theorists tried to break out of this rhetorical bind by arguing that the job of writing teachers was to initiate students into the workings of the academic discourse community, to learn the specific conventions of college writing. For now, I simply want to say that the power of this view has much to do with the elasticity of the term *convention* — which can describe almost anything from a critical habit of mind to a preferred form of citing sources to specific usages and phrasings. Using a term like *convention*, you can argue (and indeed I would) that in learning to write at college, students need to work on everything from spelling and punctuation to active verbs to self-reflexivity — and to do all this at once. Nothing can ruin the credibility of an academic piece more than poor proofreading (I know from hard experience as both a writer and journal editor), but errorless typing doesn't make up for a lack of critical insight either. To gain control over academic discourse, writers need to work on several levels at once — as do their teachers.

There is both a conceptual and rhetorical problem, though, I think, with a stress on specifically academic writing. In her 1991 rereading of *Errors and Expectations*, Min-Zhan Lu criticizes Shaughnessy's tendency to pit the ways with words that students bring with them to college against a seemingly neutral "language of public transactions" (*Errors* 125), a move which Lu argues allows Shaughnessy to gloss over the fact that academic writing is both characterized by the use of certain linguistic forms and often associated with a particular set of political values. We do not teach a contextless Standard Written English, Lu argues, but a specific kind of writing closely tied to the particular aims and needs of university work. We thus need to recognize there are other Englishes, tied to other contexts or communities, which are not simply underdeveloped or less public versions of academic discourse, but that work toward different ends and whose use may express a competing or oppositional politics — as when, for instance, Geneva Smitherman draws on the forms and phrasings of black English throughout *Talkin and Testifyin*. This view of academic discourse as a limited and specific *use* of language, whose characteristic forms and gestures can thus be defined and taught, has proven a powerful tool in sharpening our sense of what might go on in a college writing class. But it can also seem once more to cast its advocates in the role of simply teaching a professional jargon. For instance, when asked by Gary Olson if writing teachers should try to teach students the "normal discourse" of the academic fields they are studying, Richard Rorty replies,

> It strikes me as a terrible idea. . . . I think that America has made itself a bit ridiculous in the international academic world by developing distinctive disciplinary jargon. It's the last thing we want to inculcate in the freshmen. (Olson 6–7)

Rorty's tone here is sneering, but even still the issue he raises is an important one: Is the point of undergraduate study to prepare students to become professional intellectuals? Or to put it another way, even if our aim is to teach students a particular form of writing (and not some neutral "standard"), is that form best described as "academic"? For some time now in composition, *academic* has served as the opposing term to words like *personal* or *expressive*. That is, if one does not ask students to write directly from experience but instead sets them to writing about books and ideas, then, according to common usage, their work is "academic."[9] But I'm not so sure about the usefulness of the term, which at best tends to suggest a stylistic distance or formality and at worst to serve as a shorthand for pretension and bad writing. And I don't think that the sort of writing I usually imagine myself as teaching toward is in any strict sense *academic* (although it is not simply personal either). That is, while I almost always ask undergraduates to write on texts and ideas, I rarely ask them to do the sort of reading through the relevant academic literature that I would routinely require of graduate students (who *are* training to become professional intellectuals), and I don't spend much time on issues of citation, documentation, and the like.[10] (I rarely even teach anything like the "research paper.") I'm more interested in having students read the work of others closely and aggressively, and to use their reading in thinking and writing about issues that concern them. I would like my students to begin to think of themselves as critics and intellectuals. But that is not at all the same as preparing them to become academics.

I think this is more than a fussing over terms. In his 1994 "Travels to the Hearts of the Forest: Dilettantes, Professionals, and Knowledge," Kurt Spellmeyer shows how academics routinely lay claim to expertise by denigrating the knowledge of nonspecialists or amateurs (a kind of sinister version of the critical move defined by David Bartholomae in "Inventing the University"). By way of example, Spellmeyer shows how university ethnographers and art historians labored to assert the authority of their own systematized and restricted bodies of knowledge over the more idiosyncratic works of "mere" travel writers and connoisseurs. But he might just as easily have chosen to talk about how academic literary scholars have over the years differentiated themselves from mere reviewers or how a newly disciplined generation of composition scholars now seek to distinguish themselves from mere classroom practitioners. With Spellmeyer, I believe we need to be wary of an increasingly narrow professionalization of knowledge — and thus that we should resist equating the "critical" with the "academic."

In making this distinction I also think of books like Peter Medway's 1980 *Finding a Language*, in which he reports on his attempts to do something more than simply pass time as the teacher of a set of working-class British youths near the end of their formal schooling, none of whom were likely to go on to university and all of whom had resisted most other attempts to interest them in their course work. Medway had these students define an issue that mattered to them in their lives outside of school (jobs, politics, sports, and so on), and then had them spend the rest of the term reading and writing about it. There's little about the course, as thoughtful as it is, that would be likely to startle an informed American teacher of basic writing; in fact, it seems very much like the sort of course described in *Facts, Artifacts*. But that's precisely my point. Medway's aim was not to help his students enter the academy (there was little realistic hope of doing so for all but one or two of them); his goal was to have them reflect critically on the world they were part of right then. Freed from having to prepare his students to write according to the formal standards of an academy they would never enter, Medway was able instead to think about how to engage their intellectual curiosity and urge them toward a self-reflectiveness.

Of course Medway was only freed from such expectations by working in a culture that is more stratified by social class than ours. His students had little prospect of moving out of the circumstances that they were born into, whatever they did in school. But the promise of America is to be able to do just that — and education has long been advertised as one way of doing it. Underneath all the worries about correctness in writing, then, there is hope — that getting it right will mean getting ahead (or at least allow the chance of getting ahead). But there is fear, too: What is the point of having a standard that includes everyone, a marker that fails to separate? Language is not only a means of communicating but a form of identification, a badge that seems to define its wearer and yet, paradoxically, can be changed. It is the fear and hope of such change that so powerfully charges the debate on error.

Notes

1. *College English* published sharply critical responses to Rouse by Graff, Michael Allen, and William Lawlor, along with a counterstatement by Rouse, "Feeling Our Way Along." That none of Rouse's critics identified themselves with the field of composition studies points to the politically charged quality of the debate about error.
2. City College's experiment with open admissions sparked a remarkable number of accounts from its faculty, both advocates and opponents, radicals and conservatives. Sidney Hook (*Out of Step*) and Irving Howe (*A Margin of Hope*), for instance, have interesting things to say in their memoirs about the struggles of the 1970s at City. And there have also been a number of accounts by people involved in some way with the teaching of English or basic writing, although this did not always mitigate the sententiousness of their prose — as is shown in the titles of Geoffrey Wagner's *The End of Education* and Theodore Gross's *Academic Turmoil*. And for a quick overview of the events of the 1970s at City, see James Traub's *City on a Hill*.
3. Shaughnessy's career has perhaps been documented more thoroughly than any other recent figure in composition studies. Janet Emig briefly traced

her work in an obituary appearing in the February 1979 issue of *CCC*, and a series of writers—including E. D. Hirsch, Benjamin DeMott, John Lyons, Richard Hogart, and Sarah D'Eloia—commented on her work in a special issue, "Towards a Literate Democracy," of the *Journal of Basic Writing* in 1980, and then the same journal published still more reminiscences of Shaughnessy in 1994. John Lyons has a detailed and affectionate, although not uncritical, biographical essay on Shaughnessy in Brereton's *Traditions of Inquiry*. And, more recently, James Traub writes respectfully of Shaughnessy in a book, *City on a Hill*, that is more often quite critical of the open admissions experiment at City College.

4. In "Politics," Rouse points to how Shaughnessy's first example of a basic writer in action shows "his desperate effort to find *something* to say about the assigned topic" given him by his teacher, as he changes his position on the prompt no less than four times in an attempt to get his essay started (2). Similarly, in an article written some ten years later on "Redefining the Legacy of Mina Shaughnessy," Min-Zhan Lu analyzes the writings of a student whom Shaughnessy singles out for praise, pointing out that while the student does indeed seem to grow stylistically more fluent, the political positions she expresses in her successive writings also seem to shift significantly—although this attracts no comment from Shaughnessy.
5. There is a gendered subtext here as well that I can only begin to hint at: The Greek view of *arete* is closely connected with manliness, valor (the word is etymologically related to *Ares*, the god of war). It is thus peculiarly suggestive (even if also coincidental) that Rose should begin to form his notion of teaching toward "habits of mind" while working with a set of war veterans, and certainly the kind of teaching that he, David Bartholomae, and others have been associated with has strong masculinist overtones. ("Reading involves a fair measure of push and shove" is the first sentence of the introduction to Bartholomae and Petrosky's *Ways of Reading*.) On the other hand, the sort of "fussbudget" course that Rose wants to avoid, and that Shaughnessy provides with her emphasis on form and correctness, has a stereotypically feminine and nurturing (or perhaps schoolmarmish) quality. James Catano offers an interesting look into this issue in his 1990 article on "The Rhetoric of Masculinity."
6. A 1994 poll of parents of public school students, for instance, found them strongly suspicious of "new methods of teaching composition" and desirous for a return to "the basics" (Johnson and Immerwahr); more sustained outsider criticisms of progressive language teaching have also appeared in magazines like *The New Republic* (Traub) and *The Atlantic Monthly* (Levine).
7. The first and still most ringing statement of this professional consensus came from Braddock, Lloyd-Jones, and Schoer in their 1963 *Research on Written Composition*: "In view of the widespread agreement of research studies based upon many types of students and teachers, the conclusion can be stated in strong and unqualified terms: the teaching of grammar has a negligible or, because it usually displaces some instruction and practice in composition, even a harmful effect on improvement in writing" (37–38). In 1985, Patrick Hartwell revisited the research on the effectiveness of explicit teaching of rules of correctness and once again concluded (along with virtually everyone he cites) that such teaching has little usefulness

and thus that we ought to "move on to more interesting areas of inquiry" ("Grammar, Grammars, and the Teaching of Grammar" 127).

8. Some of the practical difficulties of teaching and learning proofreading are hinted at by the very number of people who have written on its complexities. The first issue of the *Journal of Basic Writing*, founded and edited by Mina Shaughnessy in 1975, was devoted entirely to the topic of error and included pieces by Sarah D'Eloia, Isabella Halstead, and Valerie Krishna. The 1980s saw more work on the subject from David Bartholomae ("Study of Error"), Mary Epes, Glynda Hull, and Elaine Lees; more recently, Bruce Horner ("Editing") and Min-Zhan Lu ("Professing") have written on the problematic relations between "error" and "style."
9. This standoff between the "academic" and the "personal" gets played out in a 1995 *CCC* interchange between David Bartholomae ("Writing with Teachers") and Peter Elbow ("Being a Writer vs. Being an Academic") — although, tellingly, when pushed, Bartholomae ends up defending not "academic" writing but something he calls *criticism*. Kurt Spellmeyer offers a powerful reading of this exchange, which began as a series of talks at CCCC, in the last chapter of *Common Ground*.
10. We do sometimes talk, though, about the rhetorical and stylistic uses of footnotes.

Works Cited

Bartholomae, David. "Inventing the University." *When a Writer Can't Write: Studies in Writer's Block and Other Composing-Process Problems*. Ed. Mike Rose. New York: Guilford, 1985. 134–65.

———. "A Reply to Stephen North." *Pre/Text* 11 (1990): 122–30.

———. "The Study of Error." *CCC* 31 (1980): 253–69.

———. "Writing with Teachers: A Conversation with Peter Elbow." *CCC* 46 (1995): 62–71, 84–87.

Bartholomae, David, and Anthony Petrosky. *Facts, Artifacts, and Counterfacts: Theory and Method for a Reading and Writing Course*. Upper Montclair, NJ: Boynton, 1986.

———. *Ways of Reading: An Anthology for Writers*. 2nd ed. Boston: Bedford, 1990.

"The Basic Issues in the Teaching of English." *PMLA* 74.4 (1959): 1–19.

Britton, James. "The Distinction between Participant and Spectator Role Language in Research and Practice." *Research in the Teaching of English* 18 (1984): 320–31.

———. *Language and Learning*. Harmondsworth: Penguin, 1970.

———. "Response to Working Party Paper No. 1. — What Is English?" *Working Papers of the Dartmouth Seminar*. ERIC, 1966. ED 082 201.

———. "The Spectator as Theorist: A Reply." *English Education* 21 (1989): 53–60.

Britton, James, Tony Burgess, Nancy Martin, Alex McLeod, and Harold Rosen. *The Development of Writing Abilities* (11–18). London: Macmillan, 1975.

Coles, William E., Jr. *Composing: Writing as a Self-Creating Process*. Rochelle Park, NJ: Hayden, 1974.

———. "Literacy for the Eighties: An Alternative to Losing." *Literacy for Life: The Demand for Reading and Writing*. Ed. Richard W. Bailey and Robin Melanie Fosheim. New York: MLA, 1983. 248–62.

———. *The Plural I*. New York: Holt, 1978.

———. *Seeing through Writing*. New York: Harper, 1988.

———. *Teaching Composing*. Rochelle Park, NJ: Hayden, 1974.

———. "An Unpetty Pace." *CCC* 23 (1972): 378–82.

Coles, William E., Jr., and James Vopat. *What Makes Writing Good? A Multiperspective*. Lexington, MA: Heath, 1985.

Dixon, John. "Conference Report: The Dartmouth Seminar." *Harvard Educational Review* 39 (1969): 366–72.

———. *Growth through English: A Record Based on the Dartmouth Seminar 1966*. Reading, England: NATE, 1967.

———. *Growth through English (Set in the Perspective of the Seventies)*. 3rd ed. London: NATE, 1974.

Elbow, Peter. "Being a Writer vs. Being an Academic: A Conflict in Goals." *CCC* 46 (1995): 72–83, 87–92.

———. "Forward: About Personal Expressive Academic Writing." *Pre/Text* 11 (1990): 7–20.

———. "The Pleasures of Voice in the Literary Essay: Explorations in the Prose of Gretel Ehrlich and Richard Selzer." *Literary Nonfiction: Theory, Criticism, Pedagogy*. Ed. Chris Anderson. Carbondale: Southern Illinois UP, 1989. 211–34.

———. "Reflections on Academic Discourse: How It Relates to Freshmen and Colleagues." *College English* 53 (February 1991): 135–55.

———. *Writing without Teachers*. New York: Oxford UP, 1973.

———. *Writing with Power: Techniques for Mastering the Writing Process*. New York: Oxford UP, 1981.

Graff, Gerald. "The Politics of Composition: A Reply to John Rouse." *College English* 41 (1980): 851–56.

———. *Professing Literature: An Institutional History*. Chicago: U of Chicago P, 1987.

Hairston, Maxine. "Breaking Our Bonds and Reaffirming Our Connections." *CCC* 36 (1985): 272–82.

———. "Not All Errors Are Created Equal: Nonacademic Readers in the Professions Respond to Lapses in Usage." *College English* 43 (1981): 794–806.

———. "The Winds of Change: Thomas Kuhn and the Revolution in the Teaching of Writing." *CCC* 33 (1982): 76–88.

Holbrook, David. *English for Meaning*. New York: Taylor, 1979.

———. *English for the Rejected*. London: Cambridge UP, 1964.

Horner, Bruce. "Mapping Errors and Expectations for Basic Writing: From 'Frontier Field' to 'Border Country.'" *English Education* 26 (1994): 29–51.

———. "Rethinking the 'Sociality' of Error: Teaching Editing as Negotiation." *Rhetoric Review* 11 (1992): 172–99.

Kiniry, Malcolm, and Mike Rose. *Critical Strategies for Academic Writing*. Boston: Bedford, 1990.

Lu, Min-Zhan. "Conflict and Struggle: The Enemies or Preconditions of Basic Writing?" *College English* 54 (1992): 887–913.

———. "Professing Multiculturalism: The Politics of Style in the Contact Zone." *CCC* 45 (1994): 305–21.

———. "Redefining the Legacy of Mina Shaughnessy: A Critique of the Politics of Linguistic Innocence." *Journal of Basic Writing* 10 (1991): 26–40.
Medway, Peter. *Finding a Language: Autonomy and Learning in School*. London: Writers and Readers, 1980.
Moffett, James. *Coming on Center: English Education in Evolution*. Montclair, NJ: Boynton/Cook, 1981.
———. "Liberating Inner Speech." *CCC* 36 (1985): 304–08.
———. *Storm in the Mountains: A Case Study of Censorship, Conflict, and Consciousness*. Carbondale: Southern Illinois UP, 1988.
———. *A Student-Centered Language Arts Curriculum*, K–12. Boston: Houghton, 1968.
———. *Teaching the Universe of Discourse*. Boston: Houghton, 1968.
———. "Writing, Inner Speech, and Meditation." *Coming on Center* 133–81.
Moffett, James, and Kenneth R. McElheny. *Points of View: An Anthology of Short Stories*. New York: Mentor, 1966.
Olson, Gary A. "Social Construction and Composition Theory: A Conversation with Richard Rorty." *Journal of Advanced Composition* 9 (1989): 1–9.
Rose, Mike. *Lives on the Boundary*. New York: Free Press, 1989.
Rosen, Jay. "Making Journalism More Public." *Communication* 12 (1991): 267–84.
Rouse, John. "Feeling Our Way Along." *College English* 41 (1980): 868–75.
———. "The Politics of Composition." *College English* 41 (1979): 1–12.
Shaughnessy, Mina. "The English Professor's Malady." *Journal of Basic Writing* 3.1 (1980): 91–97.
———. *Errors and Expectations: A Guide for the Teacher of Basic Writing*. New York: Oxford UP, 1977.
Smitherman, Geneva. *Talkin and Testifyin: The Language of Black America*. Detroit: Wayne State UP, 1977.
Spellmeyer, Kurt. *Common Ground: Dialogue, Understanding, and the Teaching of Composition*. New York: Prentice Hall, 1993.
———. "Foucault and the Freshman Writer: Considering the Self in Discourse." *College English* 51 (1989): 715–29.
———. "Travels to the Hearts of the Forest: Dilettantes, Professionals, and Knowledge." *College English* 56 (1994): 788–809.
Trillin, Calvin. *Runestruck*. Boston: Little, Brown, 1977.
Williams, Joseph. "The Phenomenology of Error." *CCC* 32 (1981): 152–68.

Harris's Insights as a Resource for Your Reflections

1. Think about conversations you've had about grammar with students, colleagues, and acquaintances. Did they address the sorts of polarities that Harris discusses? Did they reflect the larger politics that interest him? If not, what aspects of the issue has Harris neglected, and how might you use his thinking to address these hidden problems?

2. What do you think of Harris's suggestion that a principal goal of the classroom must be to honor the students' search for a certain kind of identity and sense of authority and credibility? Do you think that this goal might conflict with other agendas? With what specific issues might this goal be in conflict?

Harris's Insights as a Resource for Your Writing Classroom

1. Ask your students to record their initial ideas of, or associations with, grammar. Next, outline Harris's basic principles for students. Ask your students if they had ever thought of grammar not as a fixed standard, but in terms of having social and cultural ramifications, and have them read the powerful last two lines of the article, which identify grammar as a hot-button issue:

   > Language is not only a means of communicating but a form of identification, a badge that seems to define its wearer and yet, paradoxically, can be changed. It is the fear and hope of such change that so powerfully charges the debate on error.

   Have their perceptions of grammar changed after reflecting on these issues? How? How is this awareness important or relevant to their own lives and learning?

2. Outline the basic principles of the Graff-Rouse debate for your students and ask them which position they support, and why. List specific points of support on the board during the ensuing discussion. Consider having students use these points as a basis for developing a paper topic.

Grammar, Grammars, and the Teaching of Grammar

Patrick Hartwell

How do we navigate the bottomless complexity of the problems swirling around all questions of grammatical error? First published in College English *in 1985, this classic essay offers a powerful remedy to the widespread and high-stakes confusion. Patrick Hartwell begins by offering five different definitions of* grammar; *in doing so, he eliminates the confusion generated by competing senses of the term. These five different grammars range from the basic linguistic programming that is an intrinsic feature of human beings, like the opposable thumb, up through the sort of grammar that he calls "metalinguistic," a kind of context-sensitive sophistication about style that one develops after years of careful reflection. By setting forth these different definitions of grammar, Hartwell provides us with a clear way of dealing with this delicate subject.*

For me the grammar issue was settled at least twenty years ago with the conclusion offered by Richard Braddock, Richard Lloyd-Jones, and Lowell Schoer in 1963.

> In view of the widespread agreement of research studies based upon many types of students and teachers, the conclusion can be stated in strong and unqualified terms: the teaching of formal grammar has a negligible or, because it usually displaces some instruction and practice in composition, even a harmful effect on improvement in writing.[1]

Indeed, I would agree with Janet Emig that the grammar issue is a prime example of "magical thinking": the assumption that students will learn only what we teach and only because we teach.[2]

But the grammar issue, as we will see, is a complicated one. And, perhaps surprisingly, it remains controversial, with the regular appearance of papers defending the teaching of formal grammar or attacking it.[3] Thus Janice Neuleib, writing on "The Relation of Formal Grammar to Composition" in *College Composition and Communication* (23 [1977], 247–250), is tempted "to sputter on paper" at reading the quotation above (p. 248), and Martha Kolln, writing in the same journal three years later ("Closing the Books on Alchemy," *CCC*, 32 [1981], 139–151), labels people like me "alchemists" for our perverse beliefs. Neuleib reviews five experimental studies, most of them concluding that formal grammar instruction has no effect on the quality of students' writing nor on their ability to avoid error. Yet she renders in effect a Scots verdict of "Not proven" and calls for more research on the issue. Similarly, Kolln reviews six experimental studies that arrive at similar conclusions, only one of them overlapping with the studies cited by Neuleib. She calls for more careful definition of the word *grammar*—her definition being "the internalized system that native speakers of a language share" (p. 140)—and she concludes with a stirring call to place grammar instruction at the center of the composition curriculum: "our goal should be to help students understand the system they know unconsciously as native speakers, to teach them the necessary categories and labels that will enable them to think about and talk about their language" (p. 150). Certainly our textbooks and our pedagogies—though they vary widely in what they see as "necessary categories and labels"—continue to emphasize mastery of formal grammar, and popular discussions of a presumed literacy crisis are almost unanimous in their call for a renewed emphasis on the teaching of formal grammar, seen as basic for success in writing.[4]

An Instructive Example

It is worth noting at the outset that both sides in this dispute — the grammarians and the anti-grammarians — articulate the issue in the same positivistic terms: What does experimental research tell us about the value of teaching formal grammar? But seventy-five years of experimental research has for all practical purposes told us nothing. The two sides are unable to agree on how to interpret such research. Studies are interpreted in terms of one's prior assumptions about the value of teaching grammar: their results seem not to change those assumptions. Thus the basis of the discussion, a basis shared by Kolln and Neuleib and by Braddock and his colleagues — "what does educational research tell us?" — seems designed to perpetuate, not to resolve, the issue. A single example will be instructive. In 1976 and then at greater length in 1979, W. B. Elley, I. H. Barham, H. Lamb, and M. Wyllie reported on a three-year experiment in New Zealand, comparing the relative effectiveness at the high school level of instruction in transformational grammar, instruction in traditional grammar, and no grammar instruction.[5] They concluded that the formal study of grammar, whether transformational or traditional, improved neither writing quality nor control over surface correctness.

> After two years, no differences were detected in writing performance or language competence; after three years small differences appeared in some minor conventions favoring the TG [transformational grammar] group, but these were more than offset by the less positive attitudes they showed towards their English studies. (p. 18)

Anthony Petrosky, in a review of research ("Grammar Instruction: What We Know," *English Journal*, 66, No. 9 [1977], 86–88), agreed with this conclusion, finding the study to be carefully designed, "representative of the best kind of educational research" (p. 86), its validity "unquestionable" (p. 88). Yet Janice Neuleib in her essay found the same conclusions to be "startling" and questioned whether the findings could be generalized beyond the target population, New Zealand high school students. Martha Kolln, when her attention is drawn to the study ("Reply to Ron Shook," *CCC*, 32 [1981], 139–151), thinks the whole experiment "suspicious." And John Mellon has been willing to use the study to defend the teaching of grammar; the study of Elley and his colleagues, he has argued, shows that teaching grammar does no harm.[6]

It would seem unlikely, therefore, that further experimental research, in and of itself, will resolve the grammar issue. Any experimental design can be nitpicked, any experimental population can be criticized, and any experimental conclusion can be questioned or, more often, ignored. In fact, it may well be that the grammar question is not open to resolution by experimental research, that, as Noam Chomsky has argued in *Reflections on Language* (New York: Pantheon, 1975), criticizing the trivialization of human learning by behavioral psychologists, the issue is simply misdefined.

> There will be "good experiments" only in domains that lie outside the organism's cognitive capacity. For example, there will be no "good experiments" in the study of human learning.
>
> This discipline . . . will, of necessity, avoid those domains in which an organism is specially designed to acquire rich cognitive structures that enter into its life in an intimate fashion. The discipline will be of virtually no intellectual interest, it seems to me, since it is restricting itself in principle to those questions that are guaranteed to tell us little about the nature of organisms. (p. 36)

Asking the Right Questions

As a result, though I will look briefly at the tradition of experimental research, my primary goal in this essay is to articulate the grammar issue in different and, I would hope, more productive terms. Specifically, I want to ask four questions:

1. Why is the grammar issue so important? Why has it been the dominant focus of composition research for the last seventy-five years?
2. What definitions of the word *grammar* are needed to articulate the grammar issue intelligibly?
3. What do findings in cognate disciplines suggest about the value of formal grammar instruction?
4. What is our theory of language, and what does it predict about the value of formal grammar instruction? (This question — "what does our theory of language predict?" — seems a much more powerful question than "what does educational research tell us?")

In exploring these questions I will attempt to be fully explicit about issues, terms, and assumptions. I hope that both proponents and opponents of formal grammar instruction would agree that these are useful as shared points of reference: care in definition, full examination of the evidence, reference to relevant work in cognate disciplines, and explicit analysis of the theoretical bases of the issue.

But even with that gesture of harmony it will be difficult to articulate the issue in a balanced way, one that will be acceptable to both sides. After all, we are dealing with a professional dispute in which one side accuses the other of "magical thinking," and in turn that side responds by charging the other as "alchemists." Thus we might suspect that the grammar issue is itself embedded in larger models of the transmission of literacy, part of quite different assumptions about the teaching of composition.

Those of us who dismiss the teaching of formal grammar have a model of composition instruction that makes the grammar issue "uninteresting" in a scientific sense. Our model predicts a rich and complex interaction of learner and environment in mastering literacy, an interaction that has little to do with sequences of skills instruction as such. Those who defend the teaching of grammar tend to have a model of composition instruction that is rigidly skills-centered and rigidly sequential: The formal teaching of grammar, as the first step in that sequence, is the cornerstone or linchpin. Grammar teaching is thus supremely interesting, naturally a dominant focus for educational research. The controversy over the value of grammar instruction, then, is inseparable from two other issues: the issues of sequence in the teaching of composition and of the role of the composition teacher. Consider, for example, the force of these two issues in Janice Neuleib's conclusion: After calling for yet more experimental research on the value of teaching grammar, she ends with an absolute (and unsupported) claim about sequences and teacher roles in composition.

> We do know, however, that some things must be taught at different levels. Insistence on adherence to usage norms by composition teachers does improve usage. Students can learn to organize their papers if teachers do not accept papers that are disorganized. Perhaps composition teachers can teach those two abilities before they begin the more difficult tasks of developing syntactic sophistication and a winning style. ("The Relation of Formal Grammar to Composition," p. 250)

(One might want to ask, in passing, whether "usage norms" exist in the monolithic fashion the phrase suggests and whether refusing to accept disorganized papers is our best available pedagogy for teaching arrangement.)[7]

But I want to focus on the notion of sequence that makes the grammar issue so important: first grammar, then usage, then some absolute model of organization, all controlled by the teacher at the center of the learning process, with other matters, those of rhetorical weight—"syntactic sophistication and a winning style"—pushed off to the future. It is not surprising that we call each other names: Those of us who question the value of teaching grammar are in fact shaking the whole elaborate edifice of traditional composition instruction.

The Five Meanings of "Grammar"

Given its centrality to a well-established way of teaching composition, I need to go about the business of defining grammar rather carefully, particularly in view of Kolln's criticism of the lack of care in earlier discussions. Therefore I will build upon a seminal discussion of the word *grammar* offered a generation ago, in 1954, by W. Nelson Francis, often excerpted as "The Three Meanings of Grammar."[8] It is worth reprinting at length, if only to re-establish it as a reference point for future discussions.

> The first thing we mean by "grammar" is "the set of formal patterns in which the words of a language are arranged in order to convey larger meanings." It is not necessary that we be able to discuss these patterns self-consciously in order to be able to use them. In fact, all speakers of a language above the age of five or six know how to use its complex forms of organization with considerable skill; in this sense of the word—call it "Grammar 1"—they are thoroughly familiar with its grammar.
>
> The second meaning of "grammar"—call it "Grammar 2"—is "the branch of linguistic science which is concerned with the description, analysis, and formulization of formal language patterns." Just as gravity was in full operation before Newton's apple fell, so grammar in the first sense was in full operation before anyone formulated the first rule that began the history of grammar as a study.
>
> The third sense in which people use the word "grammar" is "linguistic etiquette." This we may call "Grammar 3." The word in this sense is often coupled with a derogatory adjective: we say that the expression "he ain't here" is "bad grammar." . . .
>
> As has already been suggested, much confusion arises from mixing these meanings. One hears a good deal of criticism of teachers of English couched in such terms as "they don't teach grammar any more." Criticism of this sort is based on the wholly unproven assumption that teaching Grammar 2 will improve the student's proficiency in Grammar 1 or improve his manners in Grammar 3. Actually, the form of Grammar 2 which is usually taught is a very inaccurate and misleading analysis of the facts of Grammar 1; and it therefore is of highly questionable value in improving a person's ability to handle the structural patterns of his language. (pp. 300–301)

Francis' Grammar 3 is, of course, not grammar at all, but usage. One would like to assume that Joseph Williams' recent discussion of usage ("The Phenomenology of Error," *CCC*, 32 [1981], 152–168), along with his references, has placed those shibboleths in a proper perspective. But I doubt it, and I suspect that popular discussions of the grammar issue will be as flawed by the intrusion of usage issues as past discussions have been. At any rate I will make only passing reference to Grammar 3—usage—naïvely assuming that this issue has been discussed elsewhere and that my readers are familiar with those discussions.

We need also to make further discriminations about Francis' Grammar 2, given that the purpose of his 1954 article was to substitute for one form of Grammar 2, that "inaccurate and misleading" form "which is usually taught," another form, that of American structuralist grammar. Here we can make use of a still earlier discussion, one going back to the days when *PMLA* was willing to publish articles on rhetoric and linguistics, to a 1927 article by Charles Carpenter Fries, "The Rules of the Common School Grammars" (42 [1927], 221–237). Fries there distinguished between the scientific tradition of language study (to which we will now delimit Francis' Grammar 2, scientific grammar) and the separate tradition of "the common school grammars," developed unscientifically, largely based on two inadequate principles — appeals to "logical principles," like "two negatives make a positive," and analogy to Latin grammar; thus, Charlton Laird's characterization, "the grammar of Latin, ingeniously warped to suggest English" (*Language in America* [New York: World, 1970], p. 294). There is, of course, a direct link between the "common school grammars" that Fries criticized in 1927 and the grammar-based texts of today, and thus it seems wise, as Karl W. Dykema suggests ("Where Our Grammar Came From," *CE*, 22 [1961], 455–465), to separate Grammar 2, "scientific grammar," from Grammar 4, "school grammar," the latter meaning, quite literally, "the grammars used in the schools."

Further, since Martha Kolln points to the adaptation of Christensen's sentence rhetoric in a recent sentence-combining text as an example of the proper emphasis on "grammar" ("Closing the Books on Alchemy," p. 140), it is worth separating out, as still another meaning of *grammar*, Grammar 5, "stylistic grammar," defined as "grammatical terms used in the interest of teaching prose style." And, since stylistic grammars abound, with widely variant terms and emphases, we might appropriately speak parenthetically of specific forms of Grammar 5 — Grammar 5 (Lanham); Grammar 5 (Strunk and White); Grammar 5 (Williams, *Style*); even Grammar 5 (Christensen, as adapted by Daiker, Kerek, and Morenberg).[9]

The Grammar in Our Heads

With these definitions in mind, let us return to Francis' Grammar 1, admirably defined by Kolln as "the internalized system of rules that speakers of a language share" ("Closing the Books on Alchemy," p. 140), or, to put it more simply, the grammar in our heads. Three features of Grammar 1 need to be stressed: first, its special status as an "internalized system of rules," as tacit and unconscious knowledge; second, the abstract, even counterintuitive, nature of these rules, insofar as we are able to approximate them indirectly as Grammar 2 statements; and third, the way in which the form of one's Grammar 1 seems profoundly affected by the acquisition of literacy. This sort of review is designed to firm up our theory of language, so that we can ask what it predicts about the value of teaching formal grammar.

A simple thought experiment will isolate the special status of Grammar 1 knowledge. I have asked members of a number of different groups — from sixth graders to college freshmen to high-school teachers — to give me the rule for ordering adjectives of nationality, age, and number in English. The response is always the same: "We don't know the rule." Yet when I ask these groups to perform an active language task, they show productive control over the rule they have denied knowing. I ask them to arrange the following words in a natural order:

French the young girls four

I have never seen a native speaker of English who did not immediately produce the natural order, "the four young French girls." The rule is that in English the order of adjectives is first, number, second, age, and third, nationality. Native speakers can create analogous phrases using the rule — "the seventy-three aged Scandinavian lechers"; and the drive for meaning is so great that they will create contexts to make sense out of violations of the rule, as in foregrounding for emphasis: "I want to talk to the French four young girls." (I immediately envision a large room, perhaps a banquet hall, filled with tables at which are seated groups of four young girls, each group of a different nationality.) So Grammar 1 is eminently usable knowledge — the way we make our life through language — but it is not accessible knowledge; in a profound sense, we do not know that we have it. Thus neurolinguist Z. N. Pylyshyn speaks of Grammar 1 as "autonomous," separate from common-sense reasoning, and as "cognitively impenetrable," not available for direct examination.[10] In philosophy and linguistics, the distinction is made between formal, conscious, "knowing about" knowledge (like Grammar 2 knowledge) and tacit, unconscious, "knowing how" knowledge (like Grammar 1 knowledge). The importance of this distinction for the teaching of composition — it provides a powerful theoretical justification for mistrusting the ability of Grammar 2 (or Grammar 4) knowledge to affect Grammar 1 performance — was pointed out in this journal by Martin Steinmann, Jr., in 1966 ("Rhetorical Research," *CE*, 27 [1966], 278–285).

Further, the more we learn about Grammar 1 — and most linguists would agree that we know surprisingly little about it — the more abstract and implicit it seems. This abstractness can be illustrated with an experiment, devised by Lise Menn and reported by Morris Halle,[11] about our rule for forming plurals in speech. It is obvious that we do indeed have a "rule" for forming plurals, for we do not memorize the plural of each noun separately. You will demonstrate productive control over that rule by forming the spoken plurals of the nonsense words below:

thole flitch plast

Halle offers two ways of formalizing a Grammar 2 equivalent of this Grammar 1 ability. One form of the rule is the following, stated in terms of speech sounds:

a. If the noun ends in /s ž š ž č j/, add /ɨ/
b. otherwise, if the noun ends in /p t k f Ø/, add /s/;
c. otherwise, add /z/.

This rule comes close to what we literate adults consider to be an adequate rule for plurals in writing, like the rules, for example, taken from a recent "common school grammar," Eric Gould's *Reading into Writing: A Rhetoric, Reader, and Handbook* (Boston: Houghton Mifflin, 1983):

> *Plurals* can be tricky. If you are unsure of a plural, then check it in the dictionary.
> The general rules are:
> Add *s* to the singular: *girls, tables*
> Add *es* to nouns ending in *ch, sh, x* or *s; churches, boxes, wishes*
> Add *es* to nouns ending in *y* and preceded by a vowel once you have changed *y* to *i: monies, companies*. (p. 666)

(But note the persistent inadequacy of such Grammar 4 rules: here, as I read it, the rule is inadequate to explain the plurals of *ray* and *tray*, even to explain the collective noun *monies*, not a plural at all, formed from the mass noun *money* and offered as an example.) A second form of the rule would make use of much more abstract entities, sound features:

a. If the noun ends with a sound that is [coronal, strident], add /ɨ/;
b. otherwise, if the noun ends with a sound that is [non-voiced], add /s/;
c. otherwise, add /z/.

(The notion of "sound features" is itself rather abstract, perhaps new to readers not trained in linguistics. But such readers should be able to recognize that the spoken plurals of *lip* and *duck*, the sound [s], differ from the spoken plurals of *sea* and *gnu*, the sound [z], only in that the sounds of the latter are "voiced"—one's vocal cords vibrate—while the sounds of the former are "non-voiced.")

To test the psychologically operative rule, the Grammar 1 rule, native speakers of English were asked to form the plural of the last name of the composer Johann Sebastian *Bach*, a sound [x], unique in American (though not in Scottish) English. If speakers follow the first rule above, using word endings, they would reject (a) and (b), then apply (c), producing the plural as */baxz/*, with word-final /z/. (If writers were to follow the rule of the common school grammar, they would produce the written plural *Baches*, apparently, given the form of the rule, on analogy with *churches*.) If speakers follow the second rule, they would have to analyze the sound [x] as [non-labial, non-coronal, dorsal, non-voiced, and non-strident], producing the plural as */baxs/*, with word-final /s/. Native speakers of American English overwhelmingly produce the plural as */baxs/*. They use knowledge that Halle characterizes as "unlearned and untaught" (p. 140).

Now such a conclusion is counterintuitive — certainly it departs maximally from Grammar 4 rules for forming plurals. It seems that native speakers of English behave as if they have productive control, as Grammar 1 knowledge, of abstract sound features (± coronal, ± strident, and so on) which are available as conscious, Grammar 2 knowledge only to trained linguists — and, indeed, formally available only within the last hundred years or so. ("Behave as if," in that last sentence, is a necessary hedge, to underscore the difficulty of "knowing about" Grammar 1.)

Moreover, as the example of plural rules suggests, the form of the Grammar 1 in the heads of literate adults seems profoundly affected by the acquisition of literacy. Obviously, literate adults have access to different morphological codes: the abstract print *-s* underlying the predictable /s/ and /z/ plurals, the abstract print *-ed* underlying the spoken past tense markers /t/, as in "walked," /əd/, as in "surrounded," /d/, as in "scored," and the symbol /Ø/ for no surface realization, as in the relaxed standard pronunciation of "I walked to the store." Literate adults also have access to distinctions preserved only in the code of print (for example, the distinction between "a good sailer" and "a good sailor" that Mark Aranoff points out in "An English Spelling Convention," *Linguistic Inquiry*, 9 [1978], 299–303). More significantly, Irene Moscowitz speculates that the ability of third graders to form abstract nouns on analogy with pairs like *divine: :divinity* and *serene: :serenity*, where the spoken vowel changes but the spelling preserves meaning, is a factor of knowing how to read. Carol Chomsky finds a three-stage developmental sequence in the grammatical performance of seven-year-olds, related to measures of kind and variety of reading; and Rita S. Brause finds a nine-stage developmental sequence in the ability to understand semantic ambiguity, extending from fourth graders to graduate students.[12] John Mills and Gordon Hemsley find that level of education, and presumably level of literacy, influence judgments of grammaticality, concluding that literacy changes the deep structure of one's internal grammar; Jean Whyte finds that oral language functions develop differently in readers and non-readers; José Morais, Jésus Alegria, and Paul Bertelson find that illiterate adults are unable to add or delete sounds at the beginning of nonsense words, suggesting that awareness of speech as a series of phonemes is provided by learning to read an alphabetic code. Two experiments — one conducted by Charles A. Ferguson, the other by Mary E. Hamilton and David Barton — find that adults' ability to recognize segmentation in speech is related to degree of literacy, not to amount of schooling or general ability.[13]

It is worth noting that none of these investigators would suggest that the developmental sequences they have uncovered be isolated and taught as discrete skills. They are natural concomitants of literacy, and they seem best characterized not as isolated rules but as developing schemata, broad strategies for approaching written language.

Grammar 2

We can, of course, attempt to approximate the rules or schemata of Grammar 1 by writing fully explicit descriptions that model the competence of a native speaker. Such rules, like the rules for pluralizing nouns or ordering adjectives discussed above, are the goal of the science of linguistics, that is, Grammar 2. There are a number of scientific grammars — an older structuralist model and several versions within a generative-transformational paradigm, not to mention isolated schools like tagmemic grammar, Montague grammar, and the like. In fact, we cannot think of Grammar 2 as a stable entity, for its form changes with each new issue of each linguistics journal, as new "rules of grammar" are proposed and debated. Thus Grammar 2, though of great theoretical interest to the composition teacher, is of little practical use in the classroom, as Constance Weaver has pointed out (Grammar for Teachers [Urbana, Ill.: NCTE, 1979], pp. 3–6). Indeed Grammar 2 is a scientific model of Grammar 1, not a description of it, so that questions of psychological reality, while important, are less important than other, more theoretical factors, such as the elegance of formulation or the global power of rules. We might, for example, wish to replace the rule for ordering adjectives of age, number, and nationality cited above with a more general rule — what linguists call a "fuzzy" rule — that adjectives in English are ordered by their abstract quality of "nouniness": adjectives that are very much like nouns, like French or Scandinavian, come physically closer to nouns than do adjectives that are less "nouny," like four or aged. But our motivation for accepting the broader rule would be its global power, not its psychological reality.[14]

I try to consider a hostile reader, one committed to the teaching of grammar, and I try to think of ways to hammer in the central point of this distinction, that the rules of Grammar 2 are simply unconnected to productive control over Grammar 1. I can argue from authority: Noam Chomsky has touched on this point whenever he has concerned himself with the implications of linguistics for language teaching, and years ago transformationalist Mark Lester stated unequivocally, "there simply appears to be no correlation between a writer's study of language and his ability to write."[15] I can cite analogies offered by others: Francis Christensen's analogy in an essay originally published in 1962 that formal grammar study would be "to invite a centipede to attend to the sequence of his legs in motion,"[16] or James Britton's analogy, offered informally after a conference presentation, that grammar study would be like forcing starving people to master the use of a knife and fork before allowing them to eat. I can offer analogies of my own, contemplating the wisdom of asking a pool player to master the physics of momentum before taking up a cue or of making a prospective driver get a degree in automotive engineering before engaging the clutch. I consider a hypothetical argument, that if Grammar 2 knowledge affected Grammar 1 performance, then linguists would be our best writers. (I can certify that they are, on the whole, not.) Such a position, after all, is only in accord with other domains of science: the formula for catching a fly ball in baseball ("Playing It by Ear," *Scientific American*, 248, No. 4 [1983], 76) is of such complexity that it is beyond my understanding — and, I would suspect, that of many workaday centerfielders. But perhaps I can best hammer in this claim — that Grammar 2 knowledge has no effect on Grammar 1 performance — by offering a demonstration.

The diagram [below] is an attempt by Thomas N. Huckin and Leslie A. Olsen (*English for Science and Technology* [New York: McGraw-Hill, 1983]) to offer, for students of English as a second language, a fully explicit formulation of what is, for native speakers, a trivial rule of the language — the choice of definite article, indefinite article, or no definite article. There are obvious limits to such a formulation, for article choice in English is less a matter of rule than of idiom ("I went to college" versus "I went to a university" versus British "I went to university"), real-world knowledge (using indefinite "I went into a house" instantiates definite "I looked at the ceiling," and indefinite "I visited a university" instantiates definite "I talked with the professors"), and stylistic choice (the last sentence above might alternatively end with "the choice of the definite article, the indefinite article, or no article"). Huckin and Olsen invite non-native speakers to use the rule consciously to justify article choice in technical prose, such as the passage below from

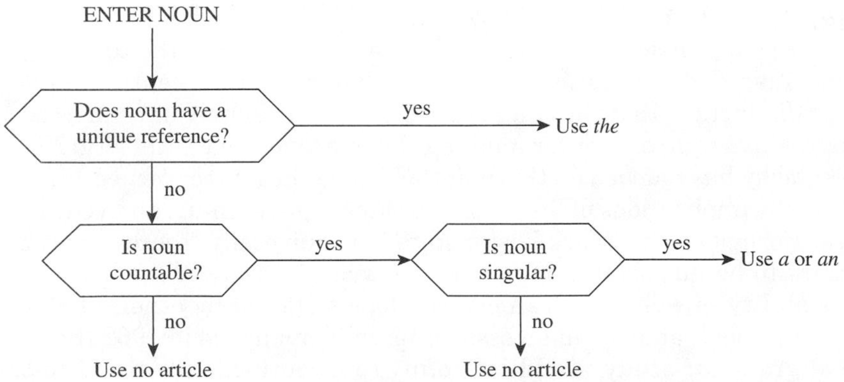

P. F. Brandwein (*Matter: An Earth Science* [New York: Harcourt Brace Jovanovich, 1975]). I invite you to spend a couple of minutes doing the same thing, with the understanding that this exercise is a test case: You are using a very explicit rule to justify a fairly straightforward issue of grammatical choice.

> Imagine a cannon on top of ______ highest mountain on earth. It is firing ______ cannonballs horizontally. ______ first cannonball fired follows its path. As ______ cannonball moves, ______ gravity pulls it down, and it soon hits ______ ground. Now ______ velocity with which each succeeding cannonball is fired is increased. Thus, ______ cannonball goes farther each time. Cannonball 2 goes farther than ______ cannonball 1 although each is being pulled by ______ gravity toward the earth all ______ time. ______ last cannonball is fired with such tremendous velocity that it goes completely around ______ earth. It returns to ______ mountaintop and continues around the earth again and again. ______ cannonball's inertia causes it to continue in motion indefinitely in ______ orbit around earth. In such a situation, we could consider ______ cannonball to be ______ artificial satellite, just like ______ weather satellites launched by ______ U.S. Weather Service. (p. 209)

Most native speakers of English who have attempted this exercise report a great deal of frustration, a curious sense of working against, rather than with, the rule. The rule, however valuable it may be for non-native speakers, is, for the most part, simply unusable for native speakers of the language.

Cognate Areas of Research

We can corroborate this demonstration by turning to research in two cognate areas, studies of the induction of rules of artificial languages and studies of the role of formal rules in second language acquisition. Psychologists have studied the ability of subjects to learn artificial languages, usually constructed of nonsense syllables or letter strings. Such languages can be described by phrase structure rules:

$$S \Rightarrow VX$$
$$X \Rightarrow MX$$

More clearly, they can be presented as flow diagrams, as below:

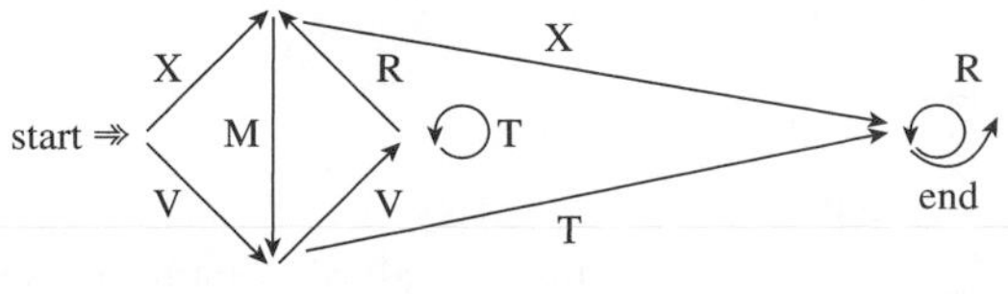

This diagram produces "sentences" like the following:

VVTRXRR.	XMVTTRX.	XXRR.
XMVRMT.	VVTTRMT.	XMTRRR.

The following "sentences" would be "ungrammatical" in this language:

*VMXTT.	*RTXVVT.	*TRVXXVVM.

Arthur S. Reber, in a classic 1967 experiment, demonstrated that mere exposure to grammatical sentences produced tacit learning: subjects who copied several grammatical sentences performed far above chance in judging the grammaticality of other letter strings. Further experiments have shown that providing subjects with formal rules—giving them the flow diagram above, for example—remarkably degrades performance: subjects given the "rules of the language" do much less well in acquiring the rules than do subjects not given the rules. Indeed, even telling subjects that they are to induce the rules of an artificial language degrades performance. Such laboratory experiments are admittedly contrived, but they confirm predictions that our theory of language would make about the value of formal rules in language learning.[17]

The thrust of recent research in second language learning similarly works to constrain the value of formal grammar rules. The most explicit statement of the value of formal rules is that of Stephen D. Krashen's monitor model.[18] Krashen divides second language mastery into *acquisition*—tacit, informal mastery, akin to first language acquisition—and formal learning—conscious application of Grammar 2 rules, which he calls "monitoring" output. In another essay Krashen uses his model to predict a highly individual use of the monitor and a highly constrained role for formal rules:

> Some adults (and very few children) are able to use conscious rules to increase the grammatical accuracy of their output, and even for these people, very strict conditions need to be met before the conscious grammar can be applied.[19]

In *Principles and Practice in Second Language Acquisition* (New York: Pergamon, 1982) Krashen outlines these conditions by means of a series of concentric circles, beginning with a large circle denoting the rules of English and a smaller circle denoting the subset of those rules described by formal linguists (adding that most linguists would protest that the size of this circle is much too large):

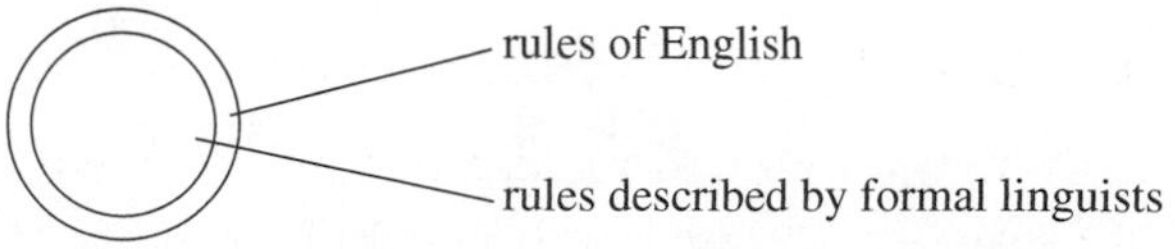

Krashen then adds smaller circles, as shown below—a subset of the rules described by formal linguists that would be known to applied linguists, a subset of those rules that would be available to the best teachers, and then a subset of those rules that teachers might choose to present to second language learners:

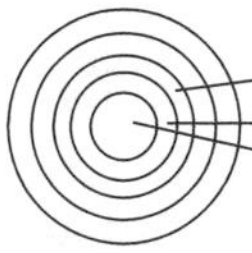

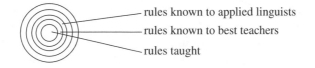

Of course, as Krashen notes, not all the rules taught will be learned, and not all those learned will be available, as what he calls "mental baggage" (p. 94), for conscious use.

An experiment by Ellen Bialystock, asking English speakers learning French to judge the grammaticality of taped sentences, complicates this issue, for reaction time data suggest that learners first make an intuitive judgment of grammaticality, using implicit or Grammar 1 knowledge, and only then search for formal explanations, using explicit or Grammar 2 knowledge.[20] This distinction would suggest that Grammar 2 knowledge is of use to second language learners only after the principle has already been mastered as tacit Grammar 1 knowledge. In the terms of Krashen's model, learning never becomes acquisition (*Principles*, p. 86).

An ingenious experiment by Herbert W. Seliger complicates the issue yet further ("On the Nature and Function of Language Rules in Language Learning," *TESOL Quarterly*, 13 [1979], 359–369). Seliger asked native and non-native speakers of English to orally identify pictures of objects (e.g., "an apple," "a pear," "a book," "an umbrella"), noting whether they used the correct form of the indefinite articles *a* and *an*. He then asked each speaker to state the rule for choosing between *a* and *an*. He found no correlation between the ability to state the rule and the ability to apply it correctly, either with native or non-native speakers. Indeed, three of four adult non-native speakers in his sample produced a correct form of the rule, but they did not apply it in speaking. A strong conclusion from this experiment would be that formal rules of grammar seem to have no value whatsoever. Seliger, however, suggests a more paradoxical interpretation. Rules are of no use, he agrees, but some people think they are, and for these people, assuming that they have internalized the rules, even inadequate rules are of heuristic value, for they allow them to access the internal rules they actually use.

The Incantations of the "Common School Grammars"

Such a paradox may explain the fascination we have as teachers with "rules of grammar" of the Grammar 4 variety, the "rules" of the "common school grammars." Again and again such rules are inadequate to the facts of written language; you will recall that we have known this since Francis' 1927 study. R. Scott Baldwin and James M. Coady, studying how readers respond to punctuation signals ("Psycholinguistic Approaches to a Theory of Punctuation," *Journal of Reading Behavior*, 10 [1978], 363–383), conclude that conventional rules of punctuation are "a complete sham" (p. 375). My own favorite is the Grammar 4 rule for showing possession, always expressed in terms of adding *-'s* or *-s'* to nouns, while our internal grammar, if you think about it, adds possession to noun phrases, albeit under severe stylistic constraints: "the horses of the Queen of England" are "the Queen of England's horses" and "the feathers of the duck over there" are "the duck over there's feathers." Suzette Haden Elgin refers to the "rules" of Grammar 4 as "incantations" (*Never Mind the Trees*, p. 9: see note 3).

It may simply be that as hyperliterate adults we are conscious of "using rules" when we are in fact doing something else, something far more complex, accessing tacit heuristics honed by print literacy itself. We can clarify this notion by reaching for an acronym coined by technical writers to explain the readability of complex prose — COIK: "clear only if known." The rules of Grammar 4 — no, we can at this point be more honest — the incantations of Grammar 4 are COIK. If you know how to signal possession in the code of print, then the advice to add *-'s* to nouns makes perfect sense, just as the collective noun *monies* is a fine example of changing *-y* to *-i* and adding *-es* to form the plural. But if you have not grasped, tacitly, the abstract representation of possession in print, such incantations can only be opaque.

Worse yet, the advice given in "the common school grammars" is unconnected with anything remotely resembling literate adult behavior. Consider, as an example, the rule for not writing a sentence fragment as the rule is described in the best-selling college grammar text, John C. Hodges and Mary S. Whitten's *Harbrace College Handbook*, 9th ed. (New York: Harcourt Brace Jovanovich, 1982). In order to get to the advice, "as a rule, do not write a sentence fragment" (p. 25), the student must master the following learning tasks:

Recognizing verbs.

Recognizing subjects and verbs.

Recognizing all parts of speech. (*Harbrace* lists eight.)

Recognizing phrases and subordinate clauses. (*Harbrace* lists six types of phrases, and it offers incomplete lists of eight relative pronouns and eighteen subordinating conjunctions.)

Recognizing main clauses and types of sentences.

These learning tasks completed, the student is given the rule above, offered a page of exceptions, and then given the following advice (or is it an incantation?):

> Before handing in a composition, . . . proofread each word group written as a sentence. Test each one for completeness. First, be sure that it has at least one subject and one predicate. Next, be sure that the word group is not a dependent clause beginning with a subordinating conjunction or a relative clause. (p. 27)

The school grammar approach defines a sentence fragment as a conceptual error — as not having conscious knowledge of the school grammar definition of *sentence*. It demands heavy emphasis on rote memory, and it asks students to behave in ways patently removed from the behaviors of mature writers. (I have never in my life tested a sentence for completeness, and I am a better writer — and probably a better person — as a consequence.) It may be, of course, that some developing writers, at some points in their development, may benefit from such advice — or, more to the point, may think that they benefit — but, as Thomas Friedman points out in "Teaching Error, Nurturing Confusion" (*CE*, 45 [1983], 390–399), our theory of language tells us that such advice is, at the best, COIK. As the Maine joke has it, about a tourist asking directions from a farmer, "you can't get there from here."

Redefining Error

In the specific case of sentence fragments, Mina P. Shaughnessy (*Errors and Expectations* [New York: Oxford University Press, 1977]) argues that such errors are not conceptual failures at all, but performance errors — mistakes in punctuation. Muriel Harris' error counts support this view ("Mending the Fragmented Free Modifier," *CCC*, 32 [1981], 175–182). Case studies show example after example of errors that occur *because* of instruction — one thinks, for example, of David Bartholomae's student explaining that he added an *-s* to *children* "because it's a plural" ("The Study of Error," *CCC*, 31 [1980], 262). Surveys, such as that by Muriel Harris ("Contradictory Perceptions of the Rules of Writing," *CCC*, 30 [1979], 218–220), and our own observations suggest that students consistently misunderstand such Grammar 4 explanations (COIK, you will recall). For example, from Patrick Hartwell and Robert H. Bentley and from Mike Rose, we have two separate anecdotal accounts of students, cited for punctuating a *because*-clause as a sentence, who have decided to avoid using *because*. More generally, Collette A. Daiute's analysis of errors made by college students shows that errors tend to appear at clause boundaries, suggesting short-term memory load and not conceptual deficiency as a cause of error.[21]

Thus, if we think seriously about error and its relationship to the worship of formal grammar study, we need to attempt some massive dislocation of our traditional thinking, to shuck off our hyperliterate perception of the value of formal rules, and to regain the confidence in the tacit power of unconscious knowledge that our theory of language gives us. Most students, reading their writing aloud, will correct in essence all errors of spelling, grammar, and, by intonation, punctuation, but usually without noticing that what they read departs from what they wrote.[22] And Richard H. Haswell ("Minimal Marking," *CE*, 45 [1983], 600–604) notes that his students correct 61.1 percent of their errors when they are identified with a simple mark in the margin rather than by error type. Such findings suggest that we need to redefine error, to see it not as a cognitive or linguistic problem, a problem of not knowing a "rule of grammar" (whatever that may mean), but rather, following the insight of Robert J. Bracewell ("Writing as a Cognitive Activity," *Visible Language*, 14 [1980], 400–422), as a problem of metacognition and metalinguistic awareness, a matter of accessing knowledges that, to be of any use, learners must have already internalized by means of exposure to the code. (Usage issues — Grammar 3 — probably represent a different order of problem. Both Joseph Emonds and Jeffrey Jochnowitz establish that the usage issues we worry most about are linguistically unnatural, departures from the grammar in our heads.)[23]

The notion of metalinguistic awareness seems crucial. The sentence below, created by Douglas R. Hofstadter ("Metamagical Themas," *Scientific American*, 235, No. 1 [1981], 22–32), is offered to clarify that notion; you are invited to examine it for a moment or two before continuing.

> Their is four errors in this sentance. Can you find them?

Three errors announce themselves plainly enough, the misspellings of *there* and *sentence* and the use of *is* instead of *are*. (And, just to illustrate the perils of hyperliteracy, let it be noted that, through three years of drafts, I referred to the choice of *is* and *are* as a matter of "subject-verb agreement.") The fourth error resists detection, until one assesses the truth value of the sentence itself — the fourth error is that there are not four errors, only three. Such a sentence (Hofstadter calls it a "self-referencing sentence") asks you to look at it in two ways, simultaneously as statement and as linguistic artifact — in other words, to exercise metalinguistic awareness.

A broad range of cross-cultural studies suggest that metalinguistic awareness is a defining feature of print literacy. Thus Sylvia Scribner and Michael Cole, working with the triliterate Vai of Liberia (variously literate in English, through schooling; in Arabic, for religious purposes; and in an indigenous Vai script, used for personal affairs), find that metalinguistic awareness, broadly conceived, is the only cognitive skill underlying each of the three literacies. The one statistically significant skill shared by literate Vai was the recognition of word boundaries. Moreover, literate Vai tended to answer "yes" when asked (in Vai), "Can you call the sun the moon and the moon the sun?" while illiterate Vai tended to have grave doubts about such metalinguistic play. And in the United States Henry and Lila R. Gleitman report quite different responses by clerical workers and Ph.D. candidates asked to interpret nonsense compounds like "house-bird glass": clerical workers focused on meaning and plausibility (for example, "a house-bird made of glass"), while Ph.D. candidates focused on syntax (for example, "a very small drinking cup for canaries" or "a glass that protects house-birds").[24] More general research findings suggest a clear relationship between measures of metalinguistic awareness and measures of literacy level.[25] William Labov, speculating on literacy acquisition in inner-city ghettoes, contrasts "stimulus-bound" and "language-bound" individuals, suggesting that the latter seem to master literacy more easily.[26] The analysis here suggests that the causal relationship works the other way, that it is the mastery of written language that increases one's awareness of language as language.

This analysis has two implications. First, it makes the question of socially nonstandard dialects, always implicit in discussions of teaching formal grammar, into a non-issue.[27] Native speakers of English, regardless of dialect, show tacit mastery of the conventions of Standard English, and that mastery seems to transfer into abstract orthographic knowledge through interaction with print.[28] Developing writers show the same patterning of errors, regardless of dialect.[29] Studies of reading and of writing suggest that surface features of spoken dialect are simply irrelevant to mastering print literacy.[30] Print is a complex cultural code — or better yet, a system of code — and my bet is that, regardless of instruction, one masters those codes from the top down, from pragmatic questions of voice, tone, audience, register, and rhetorical strategy, not from the bottom up, from grammar to usage to fixed forms of organization.

Second, this analysis forces us to posit multiple literacies, used for multiple purposes, rather than a single static literacy, engraved in "rules of grammar." These multiple literacies are evident in cross-cultural studies.[31] They are equally evident when we inquire into the uses of literacy in American communities.[32] Further, given that students, at all levels, show widely variant interactions with print literacy, there would seem to be little to do with grammar — with Grammar 2 or with Grammar 4 — that we could isolate as a basis for formal instruction.[33]

Grammar 5: Stylistic Grammar

Similarly, when we turn to Grammar 5, "grammatical terms used in the interest of teaching prose style," so central to Martha Kolln's argument for teaching formal grammar, we find that the grammar issue is simply beside the point. There are two fully articulated positions about "stylistic grammar," which I will label "romantic" and "classic," following Richard Lloyd-Jones and Richard E. Young.[34] The romantic position is that stylistic grammars, though perhaps useful for teachers, have little place in the teaching of composition, for students must struggle with and through language toward meaning. This position rests on a theory of language ultimately philosophical rather than linguistic (witness, for example, the contempt for linguists in Ann Berthoff's *The Making of Meaning: Metaphors, Models, and Maxims for Writing Teachers* [Montclair, N.J.: Boynton/Cook, 1981]); it is articulated as a theory of style by Donald A. Murray and, on somewhat different grounds (that stylistic grammars encourage overuse of the monitor), by Ian Pringle. The classic position, on the other hand, is that we can find ways to offer developing writers helpful suggestions about prose style, suggestions such as Francis Christensen's emphasis on the cumulative sentence, developed by observing the practice of skilled writers, and Joseph Williams' advice about predication, developed by psycholinguistic studies of comprehension.[35] James A. Berlin's recent survey of composition theory (*CE*, 45 [1982], 765–777) probably understates the gulf between these two positions and the radically different conceptions of language that underlie them, but it does establish that they share an overriding assumption in common: that one learns to control the language of print by manipulating language in meaningful contexts, not by learning about language in isolation, as by the study of formal grammar. Thus even classic theorists, who choose to present a vocabulary of style to students, do so only as a vehicle for encouraging productive control of communicative structures.

We might put the matter in the following terms. Writers need to develop skills at two levels. One, broadly rhetorical, involves communication in meaningful contexts (the strategies, registers, and procedures of discourse across a range of modes, audiences, contexts, and purposes). The other, broadly metalinguistic rather than linguistic, involves active manipulation of language with conscious attention to surface form. This second level may be developed tacitly, as a natural adjunct to developing rhetorical competencies — I take this to be the position of romantic theorists. It may be developed formally, by manipulating language for stylistic effect, and such manipulation may involve, for pedagogical continuity, a vocabulary of style. But it is primarily developed by any kind of language activity that enhances the awareness of language as language.[36] David T. Hakes, summarizing the research on metalinguistic awareness, notes how far we are from understanding this process:

> the optimal conditions for becoming metalinguistically competent involve growing up in a literate environment with adult models who are themselves metalinguistically competent and who foster the growth of that competence in a variety of ways as yet little understood. ("The Development of Metalinguistic Abilities," p. 205: see note 25)

Such a model places language, at all levels, at the center of the curriculum, but not as "necessary categories and labels" (Kolln, "Closing the Books on Alchemy," p. 150), but as literal stuff, verbal clay, to be molded and probed, shaped and reshaped, and, above all, enjoyed.

The Tradition of Experimental Research

Thus, when we turn back to experimental research on the value of formal grammar instruction, we do so with firm predictions given us by our theory of language. Our theory would predict that formal grammar instruction, whether instruction in scientific grammar or instruction in "the common school grammar," would have little to do with control over surface correctness nor with quality of writing. It would predict that any form of active involvement with language would be preferable to instruction in rules or definitions (or incantations). In essence, this is what the research tells us. In 1893, the Committee of Ten (*Report of the Committee of Ten on Secondary School Studies* [Washington, D.C.: U.S. Government Printing Office, 1893]) put grammar at the center of the English curriculum, and its report established the rigidly sequential mode of instruction common for the last century. But the committee explicitly noted that grammar instruction did not aid correctness, arguing instead that it improved the ability to think logically (an argument developed from the role of the "grammarian" in the classical rhetorical tradition, essentially a teacher of literature — see, for example, the etymology of *grammar* in the *Oxford English Dictionary*).

But Franklin S. Hoyt, in a 1906 experiment, found no relationship between the study of grammar and the ability to think logically; his research led him to conclude what I am constrained to argue more than seventy-five years later, that there is no "relationship between a knowledge of technical grammar and the ability to use English and to interpret language" ("The Place of Grammar in the Elementary Curriculum," *Teachers College Record*, 7 [1906], 483–484). Later studies, through the 1920s, focused on the relationship of knowledge of grammar and ability to recognize error; experiments reported by James Boraas in 1917 and by William Asker in 1923 are typical of those that reported no correlation. In the 1930s, with the development of the functional grammar movement, it was common to compare the study of formal grammar with one form or another of active manipulation of language; experiments by I. O. Ash in 1935 and Ellen Frogner in 1939 are typical of studies showing the superiority of active involvement with language.[37] In a 1959 article, "Grammar in Language Teaching" (*Elementary English*, 36 [1959], 412–421), John J. DeBoer noted the consistency of these findings.

> The impressive fact is . . . that in all these studies, carried out in places and at times far removed from each other, often by highly experienced and disinterested investigators, the results have been consistently negative so far as the value of grammar in the improvement of language expression is concerned. (p. 417)

In 1960 Ingrid M. Strom, reviewing more than fifty experimental studies, came to a similarly strong and unqualified conclusion:

> direct methods of instruction, focusing on writing activities and the structuring of ideas, are more efficient in teaching sentence structure, usage, punctuation, and other related factors than are such methods as nomenclature drill, diagramming, and rote memorization of grammatical rules.[38]

In 1963 two research reviews appeared, one by Braddock, Lloyd-Jones, and Schorer, cited at the beginning of this paper, and one by Henry C. Meckel, whose conclusions, though more guarded, are in essential agreement.[39] In 1969 J. Stephen Sherwin devoted one-fourth of his *Four Problems in Teaching English: A Critique of Research* (Scranton, Penn.: International Textbook, 1969) to the grammar issue, concluding that "instruction in formal grammar is an ineffective way to help students achieve proficiency in writing" (p. 135). Some early experiments in sentence combining, such as those by Donald R. Bateman and Frank J. Zidonnis and by John C. Mellon, showed improvement in measures of syntactic complexity with instruction in transformational grammar keyed to sentence combining practice. But a later study by Frank O'Hare achieved the same gains with no grammar instruction, suggesting to Sandra L. Stotsky and to Richard Van de Veghe that active manipulation of language, not the grammar unit, explained the earlier results.[40] More recent summaries of research—by Elizabeth I. Haynes, Hillary Taylor Holbrook, and Marcia Farr Whiteman—support similar conclusions. Indirect evidence for this position is provided by surveys reported by Betty Bamberg in 1978 and 1981, showing that time spent in grammar instruction in high school is the least important factor, of eight factors examined, in separating regular from remedial writers at the college level.[41]

More generally, Patrick Scott and Bruce Castner, in "Reference Sources for Composition Research: A Practical Survey" (*CE*, 45 [1983],

756–768), note that much current research is not informed by an awareness of the past. Put simply, we are constrained to reinvent the wheel. My concern here has been with a far more serious problem: that too often the wheel we reinvent is square.

It is, after all, a question of power. Janet Emig, developing a consensus from composition research, and Aaron S. Carton and Lawrence V. Castiglione, developing the implications of language theory for education, come to the same conclusion: that the thrust of current research and theory is to take power from the teacher and to give that power to the learner.[42] At no point in the English curriculum is the question of power more blatantly posed than in the issue of formal grammar instruction. It is time that we, as teachers, formulate theories of language and literacy and let those theories guide our teaching, and it is time that we, as researchers, move on to more interesting areas of inquiry.

Notes

1. *Research in Written Composition* (Urbana, Ill.: National Council of Teachers of English, 1963), pp. 37–38.
2. "Non-magical Thinking: Presenting Writing Developmentally in Schools," in *Writing Process, Development and Communication*, Vol. II of *Writing: The Nature, Development and Teaching of Written Communication*, ed. Charles H. Frederiksen and Joseph F. Dominic (Hillsdale, N.J.: Lawrence Erlbaum, 1980), pp. 21–30.
3. For arguments in favor of formal grammar teaching, see Patrick F. Basset, "Grammar — Can We Afford Not to Teach It?" *NASSP Bulletin*, 64, No. 10 (1980), 55–63; Mary Epes et al., "The COMP-LAB Project: Assessing the Effectiveness of a Laboratory-Centered Basic Writing Course on the College Level" (Jamaica, N.Y.: York College, CUNY, 1979) ERIC 194 908; June B. Evans, "The Analogous Ounce: The Analgesic for Relief," *English Journal*, 70, No. 2 (1981), 38–39; Sydney Greenbaum, "What Is Grammar and Why Teach It?" (a paper presented at the meeting of the National Council of Teachers of English, Boston, Nov. 1982) ERIC 222 917; Marjorie Smelstor, *A Guide to the Role of Grammar in Teaching Writing* (Madison: University of Wisconsin School of Education, 1978) ERIC 176 323; and A. M. Tibbetts, *Working Papers: A Teacher's Observations on Composition* (Glenview, Ill.: Scott, Foresman, 1982).

   For attacks on formal grammar teaching, see Harvey A. Daniels, *Famous Last Words: The American Language Crisis Reconsidered* (Carbondale: Southern Illinois University Press, 1983); Suzette Haden Elgin, *Never Mind the Trees: What the English Teacher Really Needs to Know about Linguistics* (Berkeley: University of California College of Education, Bay Area Writing Project Occasional Paper No. 2, 1980) ERIC 198 536; Mike Rose, "Remedial Writing Courses: A Critique and a Proposal," *College English*, 45 (1983), 109–128; and Ron Shook, Response to Martha Kolln, *College Composition and Communication*, 34 (1983), 491–495.
4. See, for example, Clifton Fadiman and James Howard, *Empty Pages: A Search for Writing Competence in School and Society* (Belmont, Calif.:

Fearon Pitman, 1979); Edwin Newman, *A Civil Tongue* (Indianapolis, Ind.: Bobbs-Merrill, 1976); and *Strictly Speaking* (New York: Warner Books, 1974); John Simons, *Paradigms Lost* (New York: Clarkson N. Potter, 1980); A. M. Tibbetts and Charlene Tibbetts, *What's Happening to American English?* (New York: Scribner's, 1978); and "Why Johnny Can't Write," *Newsweek*, 8 Dec. 1975, pp. 58–63.

5. "The Role of Grammar in a Secondary School English Curriculum," *Research in the Teaching of English*, 10 (1976), 5–21; *The Role of Grammar in a Secondary School Curriculum* (Wellington: New Zealand Council of Teachers of English, 1979).
6. "A Taxonomy of Compositional Competencies," in *Perspectives on Literacy*, ed. Richard Beach and P. David Pearson (Minneapolis: University of Minnesota College of Education, 1979), pp. 247–272.
7. On usage norms, see Edward Finegan, *Attitudes toward English Usage: The History of a War of Words* (New York: Teachers College Press, 1980), and Jim Quinn, *American Tongue in Cheek: A Populist Guide to Language* (New York: Pantheon, 1980); on arrangement, see Patrick Hartwell, "Teaching Arrangement: A Pedagogy," *CE*, 40 (1979), 548–554.
8. "Revolution in Grammar," *Quarterly Journal of Speech*, 40 (1954), 299–312.
9. Richard A. Lanham, *Revising Prose* (New York: Scribner's, 1979); William Strunk and E. B. White, *The Elements of Style*, 3rd ed. (New York: Macmillan, 1979); Joseph Williams, *Style: Ten Lessons in Clarity and Grace* (Glenview, Ill.: Scott, Foresman, 1981); Christensen, "A Generative Rhetoric of the Sentence," *CCC*, 14 (1963), 155–161; Donald A. Daiker, Andrew Kerek, and Max Morenberg, *The Writer's Options: Combining to Composing*, 2nd ed. (New York: Harper & Row, 1982).
10. "A Psychological Approach," in *Psychobiology of Language*, ed. M. Studdert-Kennedy (Cambridge, Mass.: MIT Press, 1983), pp. 16–19. See also Noam Chomsky, "Language and Unconscious Knowledge," in *Psychoanalysis and Language: Psychiatry and the Humanities*, Vol. III, ed. Joseph H. Smith (New Haven, Conn.: Yale University Press, 1978), pp. 3–44.
11. Morris Halle, "Knowledge Unlearned and Untaught: What Speakers Know about the Sounds of Their Language," in *Linguistic Theory and Psychological Reality*, ed. Halle, Joan Bresnan, and George A. Miller (Cambridge, Mass.: MIT Press, 1978), pp. 135–140.
12. Moscowitz, "On the Status of Vowel Shift in English," in *Cognitive Development and the Acquisition of Language*, ed. T. E. Moore (New York: Academic Press, 1973), pp. 223–260; Chomsky, "Stages in Language Development and Reading Exposure," *Harvard Educational Review*, 42 (1972), 1–33; and Brause, "Developmental Aspects of the Ability to Understand Semantic Ambiguity, with Implications for Teachers," *RTE*, 11 (1977), 39–48.
13. Mills and Hemsley, "The Effect of Levels of Education on Judgments of Grammatical Acceptability," *Language and Speech*, 19 (1976), 324–342; Whyte, "Levels of Language Competence and Reading Ability: An Exploratory Investigation," *Journal of Research in Reading*, 5 (1982), 123–132; Morais et al., "Does Awareness of Speech as a Series of Phones Arise Spontaneously?" *Cognition*, 7 (1979), 323–331; Ferguson, *Cognitive Effects of Literacy: Linguistic Awareness in Adult Non-readers* (Washington, D.C.: National Institute of Education Final Report, 1981) ERIC 222 857; Hamilton and Barton, "A Word Is a Word: Metalinguistic Skills in Adults of

Varying Literacy Levels" (Stanford, Calif.: Stanford University Department of Linguistics, 1980) ERIC 222 859.

14. On the question of the psychological reality of Grammar 2 descriptions, see Maria Black and Shulamith Chiat, "Psycholinguistics without 'Psychological Reality,'" *Linguistics*, 19 (1981), 37–61; Joan Bresnan, ed., *The Mental Representation of Grammatical Relations* (Cambridge, Mass.: MIT Press, 1982); and Michael H. Long, "Inside the 'Black Box': Methodological Issues in Classroom Research on Language Learning," *Language Learning*, 30 (1980), 1–42.
15. Chomsky, "The Current Scene in Linguistics," *College English*, 27 (1966), 587–595; and "Linguistic Theory," in *Language Teaching: Broader Contexts*, ed. Robert C. Meade, Jr. (New York: Modern Language Association, 1966), pp. 43–49; Mark Lester, "The Value of Transformational Grammar in Teaching Composition," *CCC*, 16 (1967), 228.
16. Christensen, "Between Two Worlds," in *Notes toward a New Rhetoric: Nine Essays for Teachers*, rev. ed., ed. Bonniejean Christensen (New York: Harper & Row, 1978), pp. 1–22.
17. Reber, "Implicit Learning of Artificial Grammars," *Journal of Verbal Learning and Verbal Behavior*, 6 (1967), 855–863; "Implicit Learning of Synthetic Languages: The Role of Instructional Set," *Journal of Experimental Psychology: Human Learning and Memory*, 2 (1976), 889–894, and Reber, Saul M. Kassin, Selma Lewis, and Gary Cantor, "On the Relationship Between Implicit and Explicit Modes in the Learning of a Complex Rule Structure," *Journal of Experimental Psychology: Human Learning and Memory*, 6 (1980), 492–502.
18. "Individual Variation in the Use of the Monitor," in *Principles of Second Language Learning*, ed. W. Richie (New York: Academic Press, 1978), pp. 175–185.
19. "Applications of Psycholinguistic Research to the Classroom," in *Practical Applications of Research in Foreign Language Teaching*, ed. D. J. James (Lincolnwood, Ill.: National Textbook, 1983), p. 61.
20. "Some Evidence for the Integrity and Interaction of Two Knowledge Sources," in *New Dimensions in Second Language Acquisition Research*, ed. Roger W. Andersen (Rowley, Mass.: Newbury House, 1981), pp. 62–74.
21. Hartwell and Bentley, *Some Suggestions for Using Open to Language: A New College Rhetoric* (New York: Oxford University Press, 1982), p. 73; Rose, *Writer's Block: The Cognitive Dimension* (Carbondale: Southern Illinois University Press, 1983), p. 99; Daiute, "Psycholinguistic Foundations of the Writing Process," *RTE*, 15 (1981), 5–22.
22. See Bartholomae, "The Study of Error"; Patrick Hartwell, "The Writing Center and the Paradoxes of Written-Down Speech," in *Writing Centers: Theory and Administration*, ed. Gary Olson (Urbana, Ill.: NCTE, 1984), pp. 48–61; and Sondra Perl, "A Look at Basic Writers in the Process of Composing," in *Basic Writing: A Collection of Essays for Teachers, Researchers, and Administrators* (Urbana, Ill.: NCTE, 1980), pp. 13–32.
23. Emonds, *Adjacency in Grammar: The Theory of Language-Particular Rules* (New York: Academic, 1983); and Jochnowitz, "Everybody Likes Pizza, Doesn't He or She?" *American Speech*, 57 (1982), 198–203.
24. Scribner and Cole, *Psychology of Literacy* (Cambridge, Mass.: Harvard University Press, 1981); Gleitman and Gleitman, "Language Use and Language

Judgment," in *Individual Differences in Language Ability and Language Behavior*, ed. Charles J. Fillmore, Daniel Kemper, and William S.-Y. Wang (New York: Academic Press, 1979), pp. 103–126.

25. There are several recent reviews of this developing body of research in psychology and child development: Irene Athey, "Language Development Factors Related to Reading Development," *Journal of Educational Research*, 76 (1983), 197–203; James Flood and Paula Menyuk, "Metalinguistic Development and Reading/Writing Achievement," *Claremont Reading Conference Yearbook*, 46 (1982), 122–132; and the following four essays: David T. Hakes, "The Development of Metalinguistic Abilities: What Develops?" pp. 162–210; Stan A. Kuczaj II and Brooke Harbaugh, "What Children Think about the Speaking Capabilities of Other Persons and Things," pp. 211–227; Karen Saywitz and Louise Cherry Wilkinson, "Age-Related Differences in Metalinguistic Awareness," pp. 229–250; and Harriet Salatas Waters and Virginia S. Tinsley, "The Development of Verbal Self-Regulation: Relationships between Language, Cognition, and Behavior," pp. 251–277; all in *Language, Thought, and Culture*, Vol. II of *Language Development*, ed. Stan Kuczaj, Jr. (Hillsdale, N.J.: Lawrence Erlbaum, 1982). See also Joanne R. Nurss, "Research in Review: Linguistic Awareness and Learning to Read," *Young Children*, 35, No. 3 (1980), 57–66.

26. "Competing Value Systems in Inner City Schools," in *Children In and Out of School: Ethnography and Education*, ed. Perry Gilmore and Allan A. Glatthorn (Washington, D.C.: Center for Applied Linguistics, 1982), pp. 148–171; and "Locating the Frontier between Social and Psychological Factors in Linguistic Structure," in *Individual Differences in Language Ability and Language Behavior*, ed. Fillmore, Kemper, and Wang, pp. 327–340.

27. See, for example, Thomas Farrell, "IQ and Standard English," *CCC*, 34 (1983), 470–484; and the responses by Karen L. Greenberg and Patrick Hartwell, *CCC*, 35 (1984): 455–478.

28. Jane W. Torrey, "Teaching Standard English to Speakers of Other Dialects," in *Applications of Linguistics: Selected Papers of the Second International Conference of Applied Linguistics*, ed. G. E. Perren and J. L. M. Trim (Cambridge, Mass.: Cambridge University Press, 1971), pp. 423–428; James W. Beers and Edmund H. Henderson, "A Study of the Developing Orthographic Concepts among First Graders," *RTE*, 11 (1977), 133–148.

29. See the error counts of Samuel A. Kirschner and G. Howard Poteet, "Non-Standard English Usage in the Writing of Black, White, and Hispanic Remedial English Students in an Urban Community College," *RTE*, 7 (1973), 351–355; and Marilyn Sternglass, "Close Similarities in Dialect Features of Black and White College Students in Remedial Composition Classes," *TESOL Quarterly*, 8 (1974), 271–283.

30. For reading, see the massive study by Kenneth S. Goodman and Yetta M. Goodman, *Reading of American Children Whose Language Is a Stable Rural Dialect of English or a Language Other than English* (Washington, D.C.: National Institute of Education Final Report, 1978) ERIC 175 754; and the overview by Rudine Sims, "Dialect and Reading: Toward Redefining the Issues," in *Reader Meets Author/Bridging the Gap: A Psycholinguistic and Sociolinguistic Approach*, ed. Judith A. Langer and M. Tricia Smith-Burke (Newark, Del.: International Reading Association, 1982),

pp. 222–232. For writing, see Patrick Hartwell, "Dialect Interference in Writing: A Critical View," *RTE*, 14 (1980), 101–118; and the anthology edited by Barry M. Kroll and Roberta J. Vann, *Exploring Speaking-Writing Relationships: Connections and Contrasts* (Urbana, Ill.: NCTE, 1981).

31. See, for example, Eric A. Havelock, *The Literary Revolution in Greece and Its Cultural Consequences* (Princeton, N.J.: Princeton University Press, 1982); Lesley Milroy on literacy in Dublin, *Language and Social Networks* (Oxford: Basil Blackwell, 1980); Ron Scollon and Suzanne B. K. Scollon on literacy in central Alaska, *Interethnic Communication: An Athabascan Case* (Austin, Tex.: Southwest Educational Development Laboratory Working Papers in Sociolinguistics, No. 59, 1979) ERIC 175 276; and Scribner and Cole on literacy in Liberia, *Psychology of Literacy* (see note 24).
32. See, for example, the anthology edited by Deborah Tannen, *Spoken and Written Language: Exploring Orality and Literacy* (Norwood, N.J.: Ablex, 1982); and Shirley Brice Heath's continuing work: "Protean Shapes in Literacy Events: Ever-Shifting Oral and Literate Traditions," in *Spoken and Written Language*, pp. 91–117; *Ways with Words: Language, Life and Work in Communities and Classrooms* (New York: Cambridge University Press, 1983); and "What No Bedtime Story Means," *Language in Society*, 11 (1982), 49–76.
33. For studies at the elementary level, see Dell H. Hymes et al., eds., *Ethnographic Monitoring of Children's Acquisition of Reading / Language Arts Skills In and Out of the Classroom* (Washington, D.C.: National Institute of Education Final Report, 1981) ERIC 208 096. For studies at the secondary level, see James L. Collins and Michael M. Williamson, "Spoken Language and Semantic Abbreviation in Writing," *RTE*, 15 (1981), 23–36. And for studies at the college level, see Patrick Hartwell and Gene LoPresti, "Sentence Combining as Kid-Watching," in *Sentence Combining: Toward a Rhetorical Perspective*, ed. Donald A. Daiker, Andrew Kerek, and Max Morenberg (Carbondale: Southern Illinois University Press, 1984).
34. Lloyd-Jones, "Romantic Revels — I Am Not You," *CCC*, 23 (1972), 251–271; and Young, "Concepts of Art and the Teaching of Writing," in *The Rhetorical Tradition and Modern Writing*, ed. James J. Murphy (New York: Modern Language Association, 1982), pp. 130–141.
35. For the romantic position, see Ann E. Berthoff, "Tolstoy, Vygotsky, and the Making of Meaning," *CCC*, 29 (1978), 249–255; Kenneth Dowst, "The Epistemic Approach," in *Eight Approaches to Teaching Composition*, ed. Timothy Donovan and Ben G. McClellan (Urbana, Ill.: NCTE, 1980), pp. 65–85; Peter Elbow, "The Challenge for Sentence Combining"; and Donald Murray, "Following Language toward Meaning," both in *Sentence Combining: Toward a Rhetorical Perspective* (Carbondale: Southern Illinois University Press, 1984); and Ian Pringle, "Why Teach Style? A Review-Essay," *CCC*, 34 (1983), 91–98.

    For the classic position, see Christensen's "A Generative Rhetoric of the Sentence"; and Joseph Williams' "Defining Complexity," *CE*, 41 (1979), 595–609; and his *Style: Ten Lessons in Clarity and Grace* (see note 9).
36. Courtney B. Cazden and David K. Dickinson, "Language and Education: Standardization versus Cultural Pluralism," in *Language in the USA*, ed. Charles A. Ferguson and Shirley Brice Heath (New York: Cambridge

University Press, 1981), pp. 446–468; and Carol Chomsky, "Developing Facility with Language Structure," in *Discovering Language with Children*, ed. Gay Su Pinnell (Urbana, Ill.: NCTE, 1980), pp. 56–59.

37. Boraas, "Formal English Grammar and the Practical Mastery of English." Diss. University of Illinois, 1917; Asker, "Does Knowledge of Grammar Function?" *School and Society*, 17 (27 January 1923), 109–111; Ash, "An Experimental Evaluation of the Stylistic Approach in Teaching Composition in the Junior High School," *Journal of Experimental Education*, 4 (1935), 54–62; and Frogner, "A Study of the Relative Efficacy of a Grammatical and a Thought Approach to the Improvement of Sentence Structure in Grades Nine and Eleven," *School Review*, 47 (1939), 663–675.
38. "Research on Grammar and Usage and Its Implications for Teaching Writing," *Bulletin of the School of Education*, Indiana University, 36 (1960), pp. 13–14.
39. Meckel, "Research on Teaching Composition and Literature," in *Handbook of Research on Teaching*, ed. N. L. Gage (Chicago: Rand McNally, 1963), pp. 966–1006.
40. Bateman and Zidonis, *The Effect of a Study of Transformational Grammar on the Writing of Ninth and Tenth Graders* (Urbana, Ill.: NCTE, 1966); Mellon, *Transformational Sentence Combining: A Method for Enhancing the Development of Fluency in English Composition* (Urbana, Ill.: NCTE, 1969); O'Hare, *Sentence-Combining: Improving Student Writing without Formal Grammar Instruction* (Urbana, Ill.: NCTE, 1971); Stotsky, "Sentence-Combining as a Curricular Activity: Its Effect on Written Language Development," *RTE*, 9 (1975), 30–72; and Van de Veghe, "Research in Written Composition: Fifteen Years of Investigation," ERIC 157 095.
41. Haynes, "Using Research in Preparing to Teach Writing," *English Journal*, 69, No. 1 (1978), 82–88; Holbrook, "ERIC/RCS Report: Whither (Wither) Grammar," *Language Arts*, 60 (1983), 259–263; Whiteman, "What We Can Learn from Writing Research," *Theory into Practice*, 19 (1980), 150–156; Bamberg, "Composition in the Secondary English Curriculum: Some Current Trends and Directions for the Eighties," *RTE*, 15 (1981), 257–266; and "Composition Instruction Does Make a Difference: A Comparison of the High School Preparation of College Freshmen in Regular and Remedial English Classes," *RTE*, 12 (1978), 47–59.
42. Emig, "Inquiry Paradigms and Writing," *CCC*, 33 (1982), 64–75; Carton and Castiglione, "Educational Linguistics: Defining the Domain," in *Psycholinguistic Research: Implications and Applications*, ed. Doris Aaronson and Robert W. Rieber (Hillsdale, N.J.: Lawrence Erlbaum, 1979), pp. 497–520.

Hartwell's Insights as a Resource for Your Reflections

1. Make a list of the different ways in which you might "teach grammar," and then try to identify the assumptions that underlie each one. Which methods are most appropriate, given Hartwell's argument? Which are the least appropriate?

2. Hartwell's "Grammar 5" is clearly the sort of grammar and usage that we want our students to master. What types of difficulties might you expect to encounter in striving to teach this approach? How would you prepare for these?

Hartwell's Insights as a Resource for Your Writing Classroom

1. Briefly outline for your students Hartwell's five different types of grammar. Ask them to describe what specific components they think might constitute the all-important "Grammar 5."
2. Ask your students to describe their chief concerns about grammar. Challenge them to address these concerns by following Hartwell's ideas about formal grammar instruction and considering specific methods to engage active language involvement.

CHAPTER

4

Issues in Writing Pedagogy: Institutional Politics and the Other

What is a university, and with whom, upon whom, for whom does it do its work? Of the many issues that challenge and encourage teachers of writing, one continues to dominate much of our focus: How might writing teachers acknowledge the diversity of our students' experience? Answers to this question can lead us down a variety of paths, and the readings in Chapter 4 are portals to the many subtopics within the larger discussion of diversity. Each reading provides both an entry to the discussion and reading paths to follow when you decide to broaden and deepen your engagement.

Paradigms of writing, language acquisition, and reading as recursive processes have led to recognition of and respect for the individual engaged in learning. This recognition and respect has in turn informed the discussion, research, and practice in many areas: admissions policies; the teaching of writing, English as a second language, and composition as cultural critique; collaborative learning; whole-language learning; the "feminization" of composition; and assessment. There is also greater awareness of multicultural perspectives on writing, reading, and the gaining of wisdom.

Nouns such as *literacy, diversity, feminism, multiculturalism, social construction, negotiation, discourse communities*, and *postmodernism* resonate in our professional conversations. We hear national, state, local, and institutional mandates for increasing and enhancing literacy, for acknowledging and respecting diversity, and for broadening our awareness of and inquiry into the multiple perspectives, issues, and cultures (ethnic, regional, social, political, gender-linked, religious, and so on) that make up the mosaic of "America" and of the world community. The selections in this chapter can help bring us to a more concrete understanding of how these often vaguely defined issues impact teaching and learning in our classrooms.

The community of writers with whom we work brings together individuals who have traditionally been welcomed to and included in knowledge communities and individuals who have been excluded. We teach these students in times of vigorous debate about how education could and should serve all these learners. The task is daunting and exciting. Look to the Annotated Bibliography for more readings to guide you in reflecting on your practices within this environment.

Can Teaching, of All Things, Prove to Be Our Salvation?

Kurt Spellmeyer

The power academic institutions wield is, paradoxically, also a weakness. Their extraordinary authority over the intellectual legacies and traditions we inherit can also articulate itself as a debilitating slowness in responding to cultural change and pressing international crises. How can we narrow the gap that separates the "ivory tower" from the lives of those struggling today in a world that—perhaps more desperately than ever—needs meaningful intellectual and cultural leadership?

In this chapter from Arts of Living: Reinventing the Humanities for the Twenty-First Century *(2003), Kurt Spellmeyer describes one university's attempt to create a curriculum that would provide students with essential knowledge and skills. The administration devised a plan that, rather than decide what young people needed to know—which is the aim of the great books courses—instead attempted to anticipate the problems they would have to solve. Spellmeyer reports that within the rigid structure and demands of the academy, this interdisciplinary initiative was almost doomed from the start. It succeeded, however, in finding an accommodating home in the writing program.*

Just before noon on September 11, 2001, while I was working at home on revisions to this book, my wife Barbara phoned to tell me that New York City was under siege. Of course I thought she was joking. Like millions of Americans that morning, I sat speechless as the World Trade Towers burned and fell, again and again in endless televised replays.

In the immediate aftermath, it become commonplace to say that nothing would ever be the same, and in a certain sense this was true. Candidate Bush had eschewed "nation building," but President Bush found himself preoccupied with the forging of multicontinental coalitions while sending many thousands of troops overseas — the exact figure still remains under wraps — to a semiarid plateau more than seven thousand miles away from his "ranch" in Crawford, Texas. But this was not the only change. Long regarded with suspicion by most Americans west of the Hudson, New Yorkers were suddenly transformed into global ambassadors of a nation that had shown it could "pull together in crisis," its police and fire squads hailed as heros, its abrasive and scandal-tainted mayor elevated to *Time*'s "Person of the Year," in the company of Gandhi and Winston Churchill. And if the memory of massacres at My Lai and Kent State had soured aging boomers on the use of armed forces, the popular press compared troops landing in Kabul to the liberating armies of D-Day. At this moment, no one can even begin to foresee the ramifications of such developments.

Yet at the same time, nothing has changed in at least one important sense. The education most Americans now receive is essentially the same as a century ago, in form if not in content. Yes, more Americans finish high school, more get to college and take degrees, but the organization of basic knowledge, the stock-in-trade of the humanities, assumed its current appearance well before the invention of airplanes and cars, before the two World Wars, before people understood the structure of the atom, before the United Nations, before the discovery of penicillin, and before the mapping of space beyond our solar system. For many people working in the humanities, however, the failure to address such developments is not a failure at all: as they see it, their purpose is to keep the past alive for its own sake and not because it might happen to have some utility now. They might agree that people need to know a bit about world politics, contemporary geography, advances in science, and so on, but they might say that all of this is evanescent and superficial. Anyone can keep track of current events simply by reading the papers, but the knowledge that really matters stays the same no matter what the future brings. We humanists value foundations, traditions, and canons, whether we wish to preserve them in amber or subversively explode them. This is why eleventh graders in the state where I live — who may someday bear arms in Africa or Indonesia — still read Hawthorne's "Young Goodman Brown" and memorize events from U.S. history that get forgotten the day after the exam. My guess is that the current innovation of national standardized testing will only make matters worse: students will get better at standardized tests, but nothing will have altered the enormous disparity between the world that young Americans actually inhabit and the image of the world preserved and purveyed by the knowledge apparatus.

After 9/11 at my university there were teach-ins and a special lecture series, but no one in the flurry of information seemed to recall a debate that flamed up and then died out less than a decade earlier, a debate that had consumed the time and energy of key faculty for several years on end. It had begun in response to the "Qualls Report," a document that called for fundamental change in undergraduate education here at Rutgers. Under the direction of Barry Qualls, chair of the English Department and later Dean of the Humanities, a committee had acknowledged openly what everyone knew but seldom vocalized: that college students across the United States graduate without an adequate understanding of their society, their world, and their times. But agreement about the problem did not produce agreement about potential remedies. If the committee had begun its discussions by attempting to define a core curriculum, it soon ran up against an immovable wall: no one could concur about whose knowledge counted as "essential." Very quickly every discipline and subdiscipline made the claim that its particular specialization could not be cut from the list. Students needed to know about Reconstruction, the nature-versus-nurture debate, Quattrocento painting, Aristotle on politics, Wordsworth and Keats, as well as recent achievements in psychology, philosophy, and the sciences. Not only did the members of the committee disagree about what constituted "cultural literacy," but they could not even reach consensus on the definition of culture itself, in spite of their evident respect for one another and the good intentions they all shared.

After many fruitless hours stuck at this impasse, the committee took a radically different tack: instead of beginning with the effort to define the kinds of knowledge educated people ought to have, it tried to identify the problems that college graduates might be expected to face in the next twenty years or so, not as doctors or lawyers or Indian chiefs, but as ordinary citizens. And here, it turned out, agreement came more readily. Of course, a list of this sort would look different now. No committee member ten years ago could have foreseen how quickly human cloning might become a reality, just as no one could have anticipated the machinations of al-Qaeda. The committee overlooked other matters as well. Since 1990, the ruination of the world's environment has continued to accelerate, and the growing convergence of opinion on global warming has failed to produce any meaningful response. In 1990, the Kyoto Agreement lay seven years ahead. Today, it has apparently died and gone to heaven reserved for noble but stillborn ideas. Who would have guessed ten years ago that the next world war might begin, not in the Middle East as so many have suspected, but on the border between India and Pakistan? And who then could have predicted bioterrorism? The list drawn up by the Qualls committee might look distinctly dated now. Yet to point out that the present moment's urgencies will become tomorrow's old news is not to deny the importance of events as they unfold in the here and now. I would say the committee had exactly the right idea.

What Qualls and his associates concretely proposed instead of a core curriculum were courses designed around "dialogues" on the issues of consequence to society as a whole. The idea was to give students the intellectual tools—the information and the interpretive paradigms—to explore both the problems of the coming century and their possible solutions. As originally imagined, the "dialogues courses" were supposed to instigate a rich cross mixing of the disciplines, as enticing to the faculty as they would be to students. According to the final plan, the Dean's office would release a list of dialogues courses for each coming year, and on the way to graduation all our students were supposed to complete several of these special courses. While the conventional divisions of knowledge would remain in place, supported by the iron scaffolding of departments and disciplines, the dialogues courses would eventually become the centerpiece of undergraduate intellectual life.

What actually happened? Initially, very little. As the report circulated downward from the deaconal level to individual faculty, they quickly grasped that nothing in the university's structure of promotion and reward would compensate them for the special efforts they would have to make if they got involved. They felt uncomfortable, as well, teaching out of their field: historians knew little about ecology, English professors might explore "economies of signs" but in fact they knew next to nothing about economies of dollars. To make matters worse, the teaching done in the dialogues courses would seldom translate easily into publication, and the willingness of some faculty to participate might keep them locked below decks with the undergraduates instead of mounting freely to the vistas of graduate study. Besides, they would have to work with strangers from other departments who might look at them askance, or at whom they might look in much the same manner. The faculty responded, in other words, with all the reservations inculcated by their long and arduous training, and by the culture of the University itself, which would, indeed, punish them through benign neglect when raises were handed out. No one at our Research 1 institution gets a raise for better teaching. Ultimately, the administration, which had called for the report and convened the committee, distanced itself from the whole debate, preferring not to squander its political capital on a contest so clearly destined to end with the innovators' defeat.

More was at stake, however, than the dreams of a few idealists and the intransigence of the professoriate. Consider 9/11. Consider, too, that right now, by most estimates, species are disappearing at a rate without precedent since mammals first appeared on earth. Should global warming become a reality, we are not likely to enjoy a future of springlike weather at Christmas. Years of record drought in Afghanistan, record cold in Mongolia, record floods in Bangladesh—these may offer us a foretaste of things to come, not outright cataclysm but a slow, steady, and irreparable deterioration of the natural order. On its own, this deterioration might pose mortal challenges to many societies around the globe, but it is just now intersecting with an orgy of first-world-style consumption and first-world-style pollution to match, combined with a projected fivefold increase in the world population since 1900. While the triumph of Western democracy, such as it is, may seem virtually assured, environmental degradation could easily undermine not only economic progress but political stability as well. If people are willing to fight wars over oil, they will surely spill blood over water when that resource becomes desperately scarce, as many observers now predict. We may assume that the extensiveness and redundancy of our social systems will safeguard us against disaster, but the world's economy in 1929 collapsed within a few weeks, while the Soviet Union fell apart just as fast and just as unexpectedly.

What have we done to prepare the next generation for these problems and possibilities? At my institution six or seven years ago, the great majority of the faculty apparently resolved that we couldn't do much, and probably shouldn't. For the soundest of institutional and historical reasons, we were quite willing to perpetuate an arrangement guaranteeing that *none* of the coming century's major problems will be studied formally at the university: for the most part, whatever students happened to learn about these matters they will have to learn on their own. As for their professors, we continue to believe — or at least to claim — that a knowledge of Plato, a reading of Shakespeare, a brush with current historiography, an immersion in possible world theory, or an acquaintance with the New York Fluxus artists circa 1960, will somehow enable young Americans to make better decisions than if they actually had more pertinent information at their ready command. As far as I'm concerned, this is the sheerest superstition.

But the story does not end with the shelving of the Qualls report. The one place at our university where the proposal could be instituted was our writing program. That it happened there, and only there, was no accident. Although housed in an English department, the program had a long record of interdisciplinary instruction. In fact, it drew its teachers, for the most part TAs or adjunct instructors, from across the spectrum of the humanities and social sciences. Its marginal status, without so much as a budget line of its own, and its position at the bottom of the ladder of prestige, made it an ideal place for innovation. With so few tenured faculty employed in the teaching of writing, and with such poor compensation for those engaged with that work, the stakes were too low to spark much of a fight. One day, with few dust-ups to speak of, English 101 became the foundation course for a program of interdisciplinary study that reached about eleven thousand undergraduates every year.

Most students in college composition classes nationwide do exactly what they did in high school, writing about short stories, novels, poetry, and plays — literary pseudo-scholarship masquerading as something else. Or the students read "short essays" that might have appeared originally as opinion pieces in the major daily papers, something by Shelby Steele on affirmative action, for instance, or by Katie Roiphe on the perfidy of various feminists, or a classic from the archives like E. B. White's "Once More to the Lake" or Nora Ephron's infamous "Breasts." Alternately, students learn to practice cultural critique, unmasking class anxieties in *ER* or celebrating gangsta rap as counterhegemonic. The thinking behind such absurdities, which only the force of long tradition can obscure, is that English 101 should somehow bridge the gap between the home world of the students themselves and the specialized concerns of the university. But what an image of that "home world" most courses conjure up! Can the students or their instructors really bring themselves to believe in it?

The teaching of E. B. White in 2002 is the product of an all-too-familiar compromise in English 101: the students pretend to learn, and will do so in good humor so long as little effort is required from them, while the faculty, often indifferent and underpaid, pretend to teach. The same might be said, however, of lower-level courses across the curriculum. Complaints about this predicament have become a permanent fixture of university life, much like statues of forgotten Confederate generals in empty, sun-baked Southern parks. But the champions of teaching have misunderstood why it might have value for us once again: not because teaching possesses some intrinsic merit, like hard manual labor or cold morning baths. Teaching has lost its value precisely because the humanities no longer see their fate as linked to the future lives of ordinary citizens. Instead of asking how we might enable those citizens to act in the world that is likely to emerge ten or fifteen years from now, we have imagined ourselves as our society's principle actors, while those citizens, our students, have become superfluous in our eyes. But what should really matter, and what might really save us, is our attention to the problems they will have to address, and the skills they will need in order to improve on our common life. Our job is not to lead, but to prepare and support.

After several years of trial and error, it became possible for beginning students at my institution to read Benjamin Barber on civil society, Martha Nussbaum on women and human rights, Malcolm Gladwell on the dynamics of change in commercial culture, and Michael Pollan on Monsanto's genetic engineering. Students had the opportunity to write papers on health care in the Third World, global trade and environmental decline, the Internet and rates of voter turnout, artificial intelligence and religious tradition. Certainly, the writing classes taught students how to write; but more important, these classes taught them how to use academic knowledge, fixed and formalized as it probably has to be, in order to make sense of a perpetually shifting real-world terrain. As texts for reading and writing, Benjamin Barber or Karen Armstrong demand a great deal more than a four-page theme on teenagers and abortion, and not simply because the prose is conceptually difficult and presupposes a wide range of background knowledge. Instead of urging students to take sides on an issue whose contours are already familiar and well-defined, thinkers like Barber and Armstrong expect those who engage with their ideas to move beyond the accustomed contours. Barber and Armstrong enact synthetic thinking, and they require it as well.

These demands we acknowledged openly in the preface to the reader we assembled for the writing program's flagship course, which still carries the antiquated title of "Expository Writing." Here's one part of what we told the students themselves:

> Although the articles and essays in this book deal with subjects as diverse as the anthropology of art and the ethics of science, the book is not really "about" art or science or any of the other subjects explored by the readings. Instead this book is about the need for new ways of thinking, and it does not pretend that those ways of thinking already exist. Never before have people faced uncertainty in so many different areas. How, for instance, will the information technologies affect our personal lives? As corporations spread across the continents, will our identity as Americans continue to be important, or will we need to see ourselves in other ways? Will genetic technology lead to a Brave New World of "designer babies" and made-to-order soldier-clones or will its breakthroughs revolutionize food production and eliminate genetic disease?
>
> Unlike most questions posed by textbooks, the right answers to these questions aren't waiting for us in the teacher's edition. Not even the best educated and the most experienced can foresee with certainty how the life of our times will turn out. Our problems today are not only much more sweeping than humankind has encountered before, they are also more complex. Globalization is not just an issue for economists, or political scientists, or historians, or anthropologists; it is an issue for all of them together. The degradation of the biosphere is not just an ecological matter, but a political, social, and cultural matter as well. The uniqueness of our time requires us to devise new understandings of ourselves and the world. One purpose of this course is to provide a place for these understandings to emerge.
>
> It may seem strange, perhaps, that we would have such lofty goals in a course for undergraduates. Surely the experts are better equipped than college students to respond to the issues our world now confronts. But this assumption may be unjustified. In a certain sense, the current generation of students needs to reinvent the university itself, not by replacing one department or methodology with another, but by building broad connections across areas of knowledge that still remain in relative isolation.

Clearly, this is a manifesto and not the innocuous course description it pretends to be. It tells students that the university's knowledge has reached its historical and institutional limits, and that their role as social actors after graduation will require them to think and act in ways beyond the imaginings of most of their professors.

Earlier, I claimed that English 101 had become "the foundation course for a program of interdisciplinary study that reached about eleven thousand undergraduates every year." While that figure is entirely accurate, and even a bit conservative, the foundation stands alone as of this writing, uncrowned by the soaring architecture of any new curriculum. Perhaps this is how change always has to come. In a certain sense, after all, the situation of the academic humanities is nothing short of hopeless: few of those ensconced within the institution's cocoon have any pressing reason to pursue systemic change. For this very reason, however, any future life the humanities might enjoy will depend on our students — those raw, unlettered citizen-dilettantes — and on our efforts to prepare them for their world, not ours, should we make such effort at all. And this too we said, more or less, in the preface to our book:

> The humanities will have succeeded in their work only when students take the knowledge of the university beyond the university itself. In a certain sense, this means that students have to become their own best teachers: they need to find in their own lives — their own goals, values, and commitments — an organizing principle for a learning experience which is bound to seem disorganized. The great, unspoken secret of the university now is that the curriculum has no center: specialization makes sure of that. Historians write primarily for historians; literary critics for other literary critics. As students shuttle back and forth between these specialized domains, the only coherence they can take away from their education is a coherence they have made for themselves.

Ironically the humanities may find themselves better off if they abandon all hope of recovering a centrality they have never really had, not in Plato's time nor Shakespeare's nor Lionel Trilling's. The very effort to protect something called "the past" from something called "the present" already testifies to the limitations of our temporal perspective. When we gaze a thousand years into the past, or a thousand years into the future, the worlds we envision there are only reflections of our world right now, and it is to this fragile, fearful world that we must turn with all our energy, intelligence, and care.

Spellmeyer's Insights as a Resource for Your Reflections

1. Consider Spellmeyer's critique of college composition classes. How closely does his indictment of the typical composition course apply to what goes on in your own class? Which elements of your course might Spellmeyer favor? How might you expand those elements?

2. Consider the quote from Spellmeyer's preface to the collection of readings that he and his colleagues prepared for a writing course. Although he admits that "such lofty goals" might seem strange, he holds that "building broad connections across areas of knowledge" is the paramount purpose of education in our times. What do you make of his goals? How are your teaching goals similar to or different from Spellmeyer's? What connections might you seek to build in your composition classroom, and how might you go about doing so?
3. With Spellmeyer's vision of teaching and the university foremost in mind, return to the selections in the first chapter of the book and consider how it magnifies or undermines the significance of certain elements in those readings. How does your reading of those pieces change when viewed "through the lens" of Spellmeyer's point?

Spellmeyer's Insights as a Resource for Your Writing Classroom

1. Sketch Spellmeyer's argument for your students and then ask them to freewrite about their reactions to Spellmeyer's ideas for ten minutes. Follow this freewriting session with a class discussion about their responses.
2. After outlining Spellmeyer's argument to students, ask them about their hopes for your course: What, ideally, will the course enable them to do outside the classroom for themselves and for their community?

Diversity, Ideology, and Teaching Writing

Maxine Hairston

What is the proper relation of politics to pedagogy? This essay has been highly controversial since it first appeared some fifteen years ago, and having remained so interesting for so long, it surely deserves to be called a classic. How might you synthesize the viewpoint here with the one in the preceding selection by Kurt Spellmeyer? Although our work is undoubtedly political (see Berlin's essay on ideology in Chapter 1), a great many questions remain that each teacher needs to answer personally, for him- or herself, and also that institutions need to sort out.

Where We Have Come From

In 1985, when I was chair of CCCC, as my chair's address I gave what might be called my own State of the Profession Report. On the whole it was a positive report. I rejoiced in the progress we had made in the previous fifteen years in establishing our work as a discipline and I pointed out that we were creating a new paradigm for the teaching of writing, one that focused on process and on writing as a way of learning. I asserted that we teach writing for its own sake, as a primary intellectual activity that is at the heart of a college education. I insisted that writing courses must not be viewed as service courses. Writing courses, especially required freshman courses, should not be *for* anything or *about* anything other than writing itself, and how one uses it to learn and think and communicate.

I also warned in my Chair's address that if we hoped to flourish as a profession, we would have to establish our psychological and intellectual independence from the literary critics who are at the center of power in most English departments; that we could not develop our potential and become fully autonomous scholars and teachers as long as we allowed our sense of self-worth to depend on the approval of those who define English departments as departments of literary criticism.

We've continued to make important strides since 1985. We have more graduate programs in rhetoric and composition, more tenure track positions in composition created each year, more and larger conferences, and so many new journals that one can scarcely keep up with them. In those years, I've stayed optimistic about the profession and gratified by the role I've played in its growth.

Where We Seem to Be Heading

Now, however, I see a new model emerging for freshman writing programs, a model that disturbs me greatly. It's a model that puts dogma before diversity, politics before craft, ideology before critical thinking, and the social goals of the teacher before the educational needs of the student. It's a regressive model that undermines the progress we've made in teaching writing, one that threatens to silence student voices and jeopardize the process-oriented, low-risk, student-centered classroom we've worked so hard to establish as the norm. It's a model that doesn't take freshman English seriously in its own right but conceives of it as a tool, something to be used. The new model envisions required writing courses as vehicles for social reform rather than as student-centered workshops designed to build students' confidence and competence as writers. It is a vision that echoes that old patronizing rationalization we've heard so many times before: students don't have anything to write about so we have to give them topics. Those topics used to be literary; now they're political.

I don't suggest that all or even most freshman writing courses are turning this way. I have to believe that most writing teachers have too much common sense and are too concerned with their students' growth as writers to buy into this new philosophy. Nevertheless, everywhere I turn I find composition faculty, both leaders in the profession and new voices, asserting that they have not only the right, but the duty, to put ideology and radical politics at the center of their teaching.

Here are four revealing quotations from recent publications. For instance, here is James Laditka in the *Journal of Advanced Composition*:

> All teaching supposes ideology; there simply is no value free pedagogy. For these reasons, my paradigm of composition is changing to one of critical literacy, a literacy of political consciousness and social action. (361)

Here is Charles Paine in a lead article in *College English*:

> Teachers need to recognize that methodology alone will not ensure radical visions of the world. An appropriate course content is necessary as well. . . . [E]quality and democracy are not transcendent values that inevitably emerge when one learns to seek the truth through critical thinking. Rather, if those are the desired values, the teacher must recognize that he or she must influence (perhaps manipulate is the more accurate word) students' values through charisma or power—he or she must accept the role as manipulator. Therefore it is of course reasonable to try to inculcate into our students the conviction that the dominant order is repressive. (563–64)

Here is Patricia Bizzell:

> We must help our students . . . to engage in a rhetorical process that can collectively generate . . . knowledge and beliefs to displace the repressive ideologies an unjust social order would prescribe. . . . I suggest that we must be forthright in avowing the ideologies that motivate our teaching and research. For instance, [in an experimental composition course he teaches at Purdue] James Berlin might stop trying to be value-neutral and anti-authoritarian in the classroom. Berlin tells his students he is a Marxist but disavows any intention of persuading them to his point of view. Instead, he might openly state that this course aims to promote values of sexual equality and left-oriented labor relations and that this course will challenge students' values insofar as they conflict with these aims. Berlin and his colleagues might openly exert their authority as teachers to try to persuade students to agree with their values instead of pretending that they are merely investigating the nature of sexism and capitalism and leaving students to draw their own conclusions. (670)

Here is C. H. Knoblauch:

> We are, ultimately, compelled to choose, to make, express, and act upon our commitments, to denounce the world, as Freire says, and above all oppression and whatever arguments have been called upon to validate it. Moreover our speech may well have to be boldly denunciative at times if it is to affect its hearers in the midst of their intellectual and political comfort. . . . We are obliged to announce ourselves so that, through the very process of self-assertion, we grow more conscious of our axioms. . . . The quality of our lives as teachers depends on our willingness to discover through struggle ever more fruitful means of doing our work. The quality of our students' lives depends on [it]. ("Rhetorical" 139)

These quotations do not represent just a few instances that I ferreted out to suit my thesis; you will find similar sentiments if you leaf through only a few of the recent issues of *College English, Rhetoric Review, College Composition and Communication, Journal of Advanced Composition, Focuses*, and others. Some names that you might look for in addition to the ones I've quoted are James Berlin, John Trimbur, Lester Faigley, Richard Ohmann, and Linda Brodkey. At least forty percent of the essays in *The Right to Literacy*, the proceedings of a 1988 conference sponsored by the Modern Language Association in Columbus, Ohio, echo such sentiments, and a glance at the program for the 1991 CCCC convention would confirm how popular such ideas were among the speakers. For that same convention, the publisher HarperCollins sponsored a contest to award grants to graduate students to attend; the topic they were asked to write on was "Describe the kind of freshman writing course you would design." Nearly all of the contestants described a politically-focused course. All ten essays in the 1991 MLA publication *Contending with Words* recommend turning writing courses in this direction.

Distressingly often, those who advocate such courses show open contempt for their students' values, preferences, or interests. For example, in an article in *College English*, Ronald Strickland says, "The teacher can best facilitate the production of knowledge by adapting a confrontational stance toward the student. . . . Above all, the teacher should avoid the pretense of detachment, objectivity, and autonomy." He admits that his position "conflicts with the expectations of some students [and] these students make it difficult for me to pursue my political/intellectual agenda" (293).

David Bleich dismisses his students' resistance with equal ease:

> There is reason to think that students want to write about what they say they don't want to write about. They want a chance to write about racism, classism, and homophobia even though it makes them uncomfortable. But what I think makes them most uncomfortable is to surrender the paradigm of individualism and to see that paradigm in its sexist dimensions.

He cites his students' religion as one of the chief obstacles to their enlightenment:

> Religious views collaborate with the ideology of individualism and with sexism to censor the full capability of what people can say and write. . . . By "religious values" I mean belief in the savability of the individual human soul. The ideal of the nuclear family, as opposed to the extended or communal family, permits the overvaluation of the individual child and the individual soul. (167)

And here is Dale Bauer in an article from *College English*:

> I would argue that political commitment — especially feminist commitment — is a legitimate classroom strategy and rhetorical imperative. The feminist agenda offers a goal toward our students' conversions to emancipatory critical action. . . . In teaching identification and teaching feminism, I overcome a vehement insistence on pluralistic relativism or on individualism.

Bauer acknowledges that her students resist her political agenda. She says,

> There is an often overwhelming insistence on individualism and isolation . . . [They] labor at developing a critical distance to avoid participating in "the dialectic of resistance and identification."

Bauer quotes one of her students as saying in an evaluation,

> "The teacher consistently channels class discussions around feminism and does not spend time discussing the comments that oppose her beliefs. In fact, she usually twists them around to support her beliefs."

Bauer dismisses such objections, however, claiming she has to accept her authority as rhetor because "anything less ends up being an expressivist model, one which reinforces . . . the dominant patriarchal culture" (389).

Often these advocates are contemptuous of other teachers' approaches to teaching or the goals those teachers set for their students. For example, Lester Faigley assails the advice given about writing a job application letter in a standard business writing text:

> In the terms of [the Marxist philosopher] Althusser, [the applicant who writes such a letter] has voluntarily assented his subjectivity within the dominant ideology and thus has reaffirmed relations of power. By presenting himself as a commodity rather than as a person, he has not only made an initial gesture of subservience like a dog presenting its neck, but he has also signaled his willingness to continue to be subservient. (251)

In discussing Linda Flower's cognitive, problem-solving approach to teaching writing, James Berlin calls it, "the rationalization of economic activity. The pursuit of self-evident and unquestioned goals in the composing process parallels the pursuit of self-evident and unquestioned profit-making goals in the corporate market place." (What a facile non-logical leap!) He continues in the same article to deride Donald Murray's and Peter Elbow's approaches to writing because of their focus on the individual, saying

> Expressionist rhetoric is inherently and debilitatingly divisive of political protest. . . . Beyond that, expressionist rhetoric is easily co-opted by the very capitalist forces it opposes. After all, this rhetoric can be used to reinforce the entrepreneurial virtues capitalism values most: individualism, private initiative, the confidence for risk taking, the right to be contentious with authority (especially the state). (491)

How We Got Here

But how did all this happen? Why has the cultural left suddenly claimed writing courses as their political territory?

There's no simple answer, of course. Major issues about social change and national priorities are involved, and I cannot digress into those concerns in this essay. But my first response is, "You see what happens when we allow writing programs to be run by English departments?" I'm convinced that the push to change freshman composition into a political platform for the teacher has come about primarily because the course is housed in English departments.

As the linguistics scholar John Searle pointed out in a detailed and informative article in *The New York Review of Books*, the recent surge of the cultural left on major American campuses has centered almost entirely in English departments. He says,

> The most congenial home left for Marxism, now that it has been largely discredited as a theory of economics and politics, is in departments of literary criticism. And [because] many professors of literature no longer care about literature in ways that seemed satisfactory to earlier generations . . . they teach it as a means of achieving left-wing political goals or as an occasion for exercises in deconstruction, etc. (38)

I theorize that the critical literary theories of deconstruction, post-structuralism (both declining by now), and Marxist critical theory have trickled down to the lower floors of English departments where freshman English dwells. Just as they have been losing their impact with faculty above stairs, they have taken fresh root with those dwelling below.

Deconstructionists claim that the privileged texts of the canon are only reflections of power relations and the dominant class structures of their eras. Thus the job of the literary critic is to dissect Shakespeare or Milton or Eliot or Joyce to show how language reflects and supports the "cultural hegemony" of the time. They also claim that all meaning is indeterminate and socially constructed; there is no objective reality nor truth that can be agreed on.

Marxist criticism echoes these sentiments. For example, Ronald Strickland writes in *College English*:

> Marxist critics have demonstrated that conventional literary studies have been more complicitous . . . than any other academic discipline in the reproduction of the dominant ideology. . . . Traditional English studies helps to maintain liberal humanism through its emphasis on authorial genius. . . . [Thus] there is a political imperative to resist the privileging of individualism in this practice, for, as Terry Eagleton has demonstrated, it amounts to a form of coercion in the interests of conservative, elitist politics. (293)

All these claims strike me as silly, simplistic, and quite undemonstrable. Nevertheless, if one endorses these intellectual positions—and sympathizes with the politics behind them—it's easy to go to the next step and equate conventional writing instruction with conventional literary studies. Then one can say that because standard English is the dialect of the dominant class, writing instruction that tries to help students master that dialect merely reinforces the status quo and serves the interest of the dominant class. An instructor who wants to teach students to write clearly becomes part of a capitalistic plot to control the workforce. What nonsense! It seems to me that one could argue with more force that the instructor who fails to help students master the standard dialect conspires against the working class.

How easy for theorists who, by the nature of the discipline they have chosen, already have a facile command of the prestige dialect to denigrate teaching that dialect to students. Have they asked those students what *they* want to learn? And how easy for these same theorists to set up straw men arguments that attack a mechanistic, structuralist, literature-based model of composition and call it "conservative, regressive, deterministic, and elitist" (Knoblauch, "Literacy" 76) when they know such models have long been discredited in the professional literature.

But I think this is what happens when composition theorists remain psychologically tied to the English departments that are their base. Partly out of genuine interest, I'm sure, but also out of a need to belong to and be approved by the power structure, they immerse themselves in currently fashionable critical theories, read the authors that are chic—Foucault, Bahktin, Giroux, Eagleton, and Cixous, for example—then look for ways those theories can be incorporated into their own specialty, teaching writing.

This, according to Searle's article, means that they subscribe to a view of the role of the humanities in universities that is

> . . . based on two primary assumptions. 1. They believe that Western civilization in general, and the United States in particular, are in large part oppressive, patriarchal, hegemonic, and in need of replacement or at least transformation. 2. The primary function of teaching the humanities is political; they [the cultural left] do not really believe the humanities are valuable in their own right except as a means of achieving social transformation. (38)

Searle goes on to point out that this debate about what is "hegemonic," "patriarchal," or "exclusionary" has been focused almost entirely in English departments.

I find it hard to believe that most English professors seriously hold these opinions or that they are ready to jettison their lifelong commitment to the humanities, but evidently significant numbers do. News releases and many professional articles suggest that these attitudes have permeated the Modern Language Association, and the associate chair of the English Department at the University of Texas recently said in a colloquium of the College of Liberal Arts that the "mission of English departments is always to oppose the dominant culture."

For those who agree, how natural to turn to the freshman writing courses. With a huge captive enrollment of largely unsophisticated students, what a fertile field to cultivate to bring about political and social change. Rhetoric scholars who go along will also get new respect now that they have joined the ideological fray and formed alliances with literature faculty who have been transforming their own courses.

Composition faculty who support such change can bring fresh respectability and attention to those often despised introductory English courses now that they can be used for "higher purposes." They may even find some regular faculty who will volunteer to teach freshman writing when they can use it for a political forum. Five years ago the regular faculty in our department at Texas tried to get rid of freshman English altogether by having it taught entirely in extension or at the local community college; this past year, many of those who had previously advocated abandoning the course were in the forefront of the battle to turn it into a course about racism and sexism. Now the course was suddenly worth their time.

The opportunity to make freshman English a vehicle for such social crusades is particularly rich: in many universities, graduate students in English teach virtually all of the sections, graduate students who are already steeped in post-structuralism and deconstruction theory, in the works of Foucault, Raymond Williams, Terry Eagleton, and Stanley Fish, and in feminist theory. Too often they haven't been well trained in how to teach writing and are at a loss about what they should be doing with their students. How easy then to focus the course on their own interests, which are often highly political. Unfortunately, when they try to teach an introductory composition course by concentrating on issues rather than on craft and critical thinking, large numbers of their students end up feeling confused, angry — and cheated.

I also believe that two major social forces outside the liberal arts are contributing to creating the environment that has given rise to this new model.

The first is the tremendous increase in diversity of our student population, especially in states like California and Texas and in all our major cities. With changing demographics, we face an ethnic and social mix of students in our classes that previews for us what our institutions are going to be like in the year 2000. These students bring with them a kaleidoscope of experiences, values, dialects, and cultural backgrounds that we want to respond to positively and productively, using every resource we can to help them adapt to the academic world and become active participants in it. The code words for our attempts to build the kind of inclusive curriculum that we need have become "multiculturalism" and "cultural diversity." They're good terms, of course. Any informed and concerned educator endorses them in the abstract. The crucial question, however, is how one finds concrete ways to put them into practice, and also how one guards against their becoming what Richard Weaver called "god terms" that can be twisted to mean anything an ideologue wants them to mean.

As writing teachers, I think all of us are looking for ways to promote genuine diversity in our classes and yet keep two elements that are essential for any state-of-the-art composition course.

First, students' own writing must be the center of the course. Students need to write to find out how much they know and to gain confidence in their ability to express themselves effectively. They do not need to be assigned essays to read so they will have something to write about — they bring their subjects with them. The writing of others, except for that of their fellow students, should be supplementary, used to illustrate or reinforce.

Second, as writing teachers we should stay within our area of professional expertise: helping students to learn to write in order to learn, to explore, to communicate, to gain control over their lives. That's a large responsibility, and all that most of us can manage. We have no business getting into areas where we may have passion and conviction but no scholarly base from which to operate. When classes focus on complex issues such as racial discrimination, economic injustices, and inequities of class and gender, they should be taught by qualified faculty who have the depth of information and historical competence that such critical social issues warrant. Our society's deep and tangled cultural conflicts can neither be explained nor resolved by simplistic ideological formulas.

But one can run a culturally diverse writing course without sacrificing any of its integrity as a writing course. Any writing course, required or not, can be wonderfully diverse, an exciting experience in which people of different cultures and experience learn about difference first-hand. More about that shortly.

Forces from Outside

The second major force I see at work is directly political. There's no question in my mind that this new radical stance of many composition faculty is in some ways a corollary of the angry response many intellectuals have to the excesses of right-wing, conservative forces that have dominated American politics for the past decade. Faculty in the liberal arts tend to be liberals who are concerned about social problems and dislike the trends we've seen in cutting funds for human services and for education. We're sick over the condition of our country: one child in five living in poverty; one person in eight hungry; 33 million people with no health insurance; a scandalous infant mortality rate; hundreds of thousands homeless. Yet we see our government spend billions on a dubious war. No need to go on — we all know the terrible inequities and contradictions of our society.

As educators of good will, we shouldn't even have to mention our anger about racism and sexism in our society — that's a given, as is our commitment to work to overcome it. I, for one, refuse to be put on the defensive on such matters of personal conscience or to be silenced by the fear that someone will pin a label on me if I don't share his or her vision of the world or agree on how to improve it. *Ad hominem* arguments don't impress me.

But it's entirely understandable that academics who are traditional liberals sympathize at first with those who preach reform, even when they sound more radical than we'd like. On the surface we share common ground: we'd all like to bring about a fairer, more compassionate society. But I fear that we are in real danger of being co-opted by the radical left, coerced into acquiescing to methods that we abhor because, in the abstract, we have some mutual goals. Some faculty may also fear being labeled "right-wing" if they oppose programs that are represented as being "liberating." But we shouldn't be duped. Authoritarian methods are still authoritarian methods, no matter in what cause they're invoked. And the current battle is *not* one between liberals and conservatives. Those who attempt to make it so — columnists like George Will — either do not understand the agenda of the cultural left, or they make the association in order to discredit liberal goals. Make no mistake — those on the cultural left are not in the least liberal; in fact, they despise liberals as compromising humanists. They're happy, however, to stir up traditional liberal guilt and use it for their purposes.

What's Wrong with Their Goals?

Why do I object so strongly to the agenda that these self-styled radical teachers want to establish for composition courses and freshman English in particular?

First, I vigorously object to the contention that they have a right—even a *duty*—to use their classrooms as platforms for their own political views. Such claims violate all academic traditions about the university being a forum for the free exchange of ideas, a place where students can examine different points of view in an atmosphere of honest and open discussion, and, in the process, learn to think critically. It is a teacher's obligation to encourage diversity and exploration, but diversity and ideology will not flourish together. By definition, they're incompatible.

By the logic of the cultural left, any teacher should be free to use his or her classroom to promote any ideology. Why not facism? Racial superiority? Religious fundamentalism? Anti-abortion beliefs? Can't any professor claim the right to indoctrinate students simply because he or she is right? The argument is no different from that of any true believers who are convinced that they own the truth and thus have the right to force it on others. My colleague John Ruszkiewicz compares them to Milton's "the new forcers of conscience." We don't have to look far to see how frightening such arguments really are. They represent precisely the kind of thinking that leads to "re-education camps" in totalitarian governments, to putting art in the service of propaganda, and to making education always the instrument of the state.

Those who want to bring their ideology into the classroom argue that since any classroom is necessarily political, the teacher might as well make it openly political and ideological. He or she should be direct and honest about his or her political beliefs; then the students will know where they stand and everyone can talk freely. Is any experienced teacher really so naïve as to believe that? Such claims are no more than self-serving rationalizations that allow a professor total freedom to indulge personal prejudices and avoid any responsibility to be fair. By the same reasoning, couldn't one claim that since we know it is impossible to find absolute, objective truths, we might just as well abandon the search for truth and settle for opinion, superstition, and conjecture? Would that advance our students' education? Couldn't one also say that since one can never be completely fair with one's children, one might as well quit trying and freely indulge one's biases and favoritism? It's astonishing that people who purport to be scholars can make such specious arguments.

The real political truth about classrooms is that the teacher has all the power; she sets the agenda, she controls the discussion, and she gives the grades. She also knows more and can argue more skillfully. Such a situation is ripe for intellectual intimidation, especially in required freshman composition classes, and although I think it is unprofessional for teachers to bring their ideology into any classroom, it is those freshman courses that I am especially concerned about.

The Threat to Freshman Courses

I believe that the movement to make freshman English into courses in which students must write about specific social issues threatens all the gains we have made in teaching writing in the last fifteen years. I also think that rather than promoting diversity and a genuine multicultural environment, such courses actually work against those goals. Here are my reasons.

First, we know that students develop best as writers when they can write about something they care about and want to know more about. Only then will they be motivated to invest real effort in their work; only then can we hope they will avoid the canned, clichéd prose that neither they nor we take seriously. Few students, however, will do their best when they are compelled to write on a topic they perceive as politically charged and about which they feel uninformed, no matter how thought-provoking and important the instructor assumes that topic to be. If freshmen choose to write about issues involving race, class, and gender, that's fine. They should have every encouragement. I believe all topics in a writing class should be serious ones that push students to think and to say something substantial. But the topic should be their choice, a careful and thoughtful choice, to be sure, but not what someone else thinks is good for them.

Second, we know that young writers develop best as writers when teachers are able to create a low-risk environment that encourages students to take chances. We also know that novice writers can virtually freeze in the writing classroom when they see it as an extremely high-risk situation. Apprehensive about their grades in this new college situation, they nervously test their teachers to see what is expected of them, and they venture opinions only timidly. It is always hard to get students to write seriously and honestly, but when they find themselves in a classroom where they suspect there is a correct way to think, they are likely to take refuge in generalities and responses that please the teacher. Such fake discourse is a kind of silence, the silence we have so often deplored when it is forced on the disadvantaged. But when we stifle creative impulse and make students opt for survival over honesty, we have done the same thing. In too many instances, the first lesson they will learn as college students is that hypocrisy pays — so don't try to think for yourself.

My third objection to injecting prescribed political content into a required freshman course is that such action severely limits freedom of expression for both students and instructors. In my view, the freshman course on racism and sexism proposed at the University of Texas at

Austin in the spring of 1990 would have enforced conformity in both directions. Students would have had no choice of what to write about, and the instructors who were graduate students would have had no choice about what to teach. Even if they felt unqualified to teach the material — and many did — or believed that the prescribed curriculum would work against their students' learning to write — and many did — they had to conform to a syllabus that contradicted their professional judgment, and, often, their personal feelings. That course has since been revised and the freshman course in place since the fall of 1991 offers choices to both students and teachers.

New Possibilities for Freshman Courses

I believe we can make freshman English — or any other writing course — a truly multicultural course that gives students the opportunity to develop their critical and creative abilities and do it in an intellectually and ethically responsible context that preserves the heart of what we have learned about teaching writing in the past two decades.

First, I resist the effort to put any specific multicultural content at the center of a writing course, particularly a freshman course, and particularly a required course. Multicultural issues are too complex and diverse to be dealt with fully and responsibility in an English course, much less a course in which the focus should be on writing, not reading. Too often attempts to focus on such issues encourage stereotyping and superficial thinking. For instance, what English teacher wouldn't feel presumptuous and foolish trying to introduce Asian culture into a course when he or she can quickly think of at least ten different Asian cultures, all of which differ from each other drastically in important ways? What about Hispanic culture? Can the teacher who knows something of Mexico generalize about traditions of other Hispanic cultures? Can anyone teach the "black experience"? Do black men and women whose forebears come from Haiti and Nigeria and Jamaica share the experiences and heritage of African-Americans? Is Southern culture a valid topic for study? Many people think so. What about Jewish culture? But I don't need to labor the point. I only want to highlight the concerns any of us should have when the push for so-called multicultural courses threatens the integrity of our discipline and the quality of our teaching.

I believe, however, that we can create a culturally inclusive curriculum in our writing classes by focusing on the experiences of our students. *They* are our greatest multicultural resource, one that is authentic, rich, and truly diverse. Every student brings to class a picture of the world in his or her mind that is constructed out of his or her cultural background and unique and complex experience. As writing teachers, we can help students articulate and understand that experience, but we also have the important job of helping every writer to understand that each of us sees the world through our own particular lens, one shaped by unique experiences. In order to communicate with others, we must learn to see through their lenses as well as try to explain to them what we see through ours. In an interactive classroom where students collaborate with other writers, this process of decentering so one can understand the "other" can foster genuine multicultural growth.

Imagine, for example, the breadth of experience and range of difference students would be exposed to in a class made up of students I have had in recent years.

One student would be from Malawi. The ivory bracelet he wears was put on his arm at birth and cannot be removed; he writes about his tribal legends. Another student is a young Vietnamese man who came to America when he was eight; he writes about the fear he felt his first day in an American school because there were no walls to keep out bullets. Another is a young Greek woman whose parents brought her to America to escape poverty; she writes about her first conscious brush with sexism in the Greek orthodox church. One student is the son of illegal aliens who followed the harvests in Texas; he writes with passion about the need for young Hispanics to get their education. A young black man writes about college basketball, a culture about which he is highly knowledgeable. A young man from the Texas panhandle writes about the traditions of cowboy boots and the ethical dimensions of barbed wire fences. Another young black man writes about the conflicts he feels between what he is learning in astronomy, a subject that fascinates him, and the teachings of his church.

It's worth noting here that religion plays an important role in the lives of many of our students — and many of us, I'm sure — but it's a dimension almost never mentioned by those who talk about cultural diversity and difference. In most classrooms in which there is an obvious political agenda, students — even graduate students — are very reluctant to reveal their religious beliefs, sensing they may get a hostile reception. And with reason — remember the quotation from David Bleich. But a teacher who believes in diversity must pay attention to and respect students with deep religious convictions, not force them too into silence.

Real diversity emerges from the students themselves and flourishes in a collaborative classroom in which they work together to develop their ideas and test them out on each other. They can discuss and examine their experiences, their assumptions, their values, and their questions. They can tell their stories to each other in a nurturant writing community. As they are increasingly exposed to the unique views and experiences of others, they will begin to appreciate differences and understand the rich tapestry of cultures that their individual stories make up. But they will also see unified motifs and common human concerns in that tapestry.

In this kind of classroom not all writing should be personal, expressive writing. Students need a broader range of discourse as their introduction to writing in college. The teacher can easily design the kinds of writing assignment that involve argument and exposition and suggest options that encourage cross-cultural awareness. For instance, some suggested themes for development might be these: family or community rituals; power relationships at all levels; the student's role in his or her family or group; their roles as men and women; the myths they live by; cultural tensions within groups. There are dozens more rich possibilities that could be worked out with the cooperation of colleagues in other departments and within the class itself.

The strength of all the themes I've mentioned is that they're both individual and communal, giving students the opportunity to write something unique to them as individuals yet something that will resonate with others in their writing community. The beauty of such an approach is that it's *organic*. It grows out of resources available in each classroom, and it allows students to make choices, then discover more about others and themselves through those choices. This approach makes the teacher a midwife, an agent for change rather than a transmitter of fixed knowledge. It promotes a student-centered classroom in which the teacher doesn't assume, as our would-be forcers of conscience do, that he or she owns the truth. Rather the students bring their own truths, and the teacher's role is to nurture change and growth as students encounter individual differences. Gradually their truths will change, but so will ours because in such a classroom one continually learns from one's students.

This is the kind of freshman English class from which students can emerge with confidence in their ability to think, to generate ideas, and to present themselves effectively to the university and the community. It is a class built on the scholarship, research, and experience that has enabled us to achieve so much growth in our profession in the last fifteen years. It is the kind of classroom we can be proud of as a discipline. I don't think we necessarily have to take freshman English out of English departments in order to establish this model, but we do have to assert our authority as writing professionals within our department and fiercely resist letting freshman English be used for anyone else's goals. We must hold on to the gains we have made and teach writing in the ways we know best. Above all, we must teach it for the *students'* benefit, not in the service of politics or anything else.

Freshman English is a course particularly vulnerable to takeover because English departments in so many universities and colleges refuse to take it seriously and thus don't pay much attention to what happens in it. They can wake up, however, to find that some political zealots take the course very seriously indeed and will gladly put it to their own uses. The scores of us who have been studying, writing, speaking, and publishing for two decades to make freshman English the solid intellectual enterprise that it now is must speak out to protect it from this kind of exploitation. It is time to resist, time to speak up, time to reclaim freshman composition from those who want to politicize it.

What is at stake is control of a vital element in our students' education by a radical few. We can't afford to let that control stand.

Works Cited

Bauer, Dale. "The Other 'F' Word: Feminist in the Classroom." *College English* 52 (Apr. 1990): 385–96.

Berlin, James A. "Rhetoric and Ideology in the Writing Class." *College English* 50 (Sep. 1988): 477–94.

Bizzell, Patricia. "Beyond Anti-Foundationalism to Rhetorical Authority: Problems in Defining 'Cultural Literacy.'" *College English* 52 (Oct. 1990): 661–75.

Bleich, David. "Literacy and Citizenship: Resisting Social Issues." Lunsford, Moglen, and Slevin 163–69.

Faigley, Lester. "The Study of Writing and the Study of Language." *Rhetoric Review* 7 (Spring 1989): 240–56.

Harkin, Patricia, and John Schilb. *Contending with Words: Composition and Rhetoric in a Postmodern Age*. New York: MLA, 1991.

Knoblauch, C. H. "Literacy and the Politics of Education." Lunsford, Moglen, and Slevin, 74–80.

———. "Rhetorical Constructions: Dialogue and Commitment." *College English* 50 (Feb. 1988): 125–40.

Laditka, James N. "Semiology, Ideology, Praxis: Responsible Authority in the Composition Classroom." *Journal of Advanced Composition* 10.2 (Fall 1990): 357–73.

Lunsford, Andrea A., Helen Moglen, and James Slevin, eds. *The Right to Literacy*. New York: MLA and NCTE, 1990.

Paine, Charles. "Relativism, Radical Pedagogy, and the Ideology of Paralysis." *College English* 51 (Oct. 1989): 557–70.

Searle, John. "The Storm Over the University." Rev. of *Tenured Radicals*, by Roger Kimball; *The Politics of Liberal Education*, ed. by Darryl L. Gless and Barbara Herrnstein Smith; and *The Voice of Liberal Learning: Michael Oakeshott on Education*, ed. by Timothy Fuller. *The New York Review of Books* 6 Dec. 1990: 34–42.

Strickland, Ronald. "Confrontational Pedagogy and Traditional Literary Studies." *College English* 52 (Mar. 1990): 291–300.

Weaver, Richard M. *The Ethics of Rhetoric*. Chicago: Henry Regnery, 1953.

Hairston's Insights as a Resource for Your Reflections

1. How have you handled the culture wars in your classroom? What have been some of your better moments in engaging these inevitable and quite profound differences in opinion on matters of public policy? And what have been some moments you wish you'd handled more successfully?

2. Can we ever wholly strip our classrooms of explicit political discussion? At what cost? What do we gain?

Hairston's Insights as a Resource for Your Writing Classroom

1. Early in the semester, have your students develop a set of guidelines for discussing social issues, as these occur in the readings and student drafts, that keeps issues of rhetoric (ethos, style, tone, discourse communities, and what Slevin, in Chapter 1, called "evidence") foregrounded.

The Politics of Teaching Literate Discourse

Lisa Delpit

Not all of our students grew up speaking Standard American English as their primary language, and thus the move into that language can be fraught with a variety of challenges. How should teachers respond? Do students have a right to their own language and must their teachers simply honor that right? Some thirty years ago, many in the field of composition studies would have said yes. But Lisa Delpit offers a careful reconsideration of this view, one that suggests, finally, that we have a very different obligation.

I have encountered a certain sense of powerlessness and paralysis among many sensitive and well-meaning literacy educators who appear to be caught in the throes of a dilemma. Although their job is to teach literate discourse styles to all of their students, they question whether that is a task they can actually accomplish for poor students and students of color. Furthermore, they question whether they are acting as agents of oppression by insisting that students who are not already a part of the "mainstream" learn that discourse. Does it not smack of racism or classism to demand that these students put aside the language of their homes and communities and adopt a discourse that is not only alien, but that has often been instrumental in furthering their oppression? I hope here to speak to and help dispel that sense of paralysis and powerlessness and suggest a path of commitment and action that not only frees teachers to teach what they know, but to do so in a way that can transform and subsequently liberate their students.

Discourse, Literacy, and Gee

This article got its start as I pondered the dilemmas expressed by educators. It continued to evolve when a colleague sent a set of papers to me for comment. The papers, authored by literacy specialist James Paul Gee ("Literacy, Discourse, and Linguistics: Introduction" and "What Is Literacy?"), are the lead articles of a special issue of the *Journal of Education*[1] devoted solely to Gee's work. The papers brought to mind many of the perspectives of the educators I describe. My colleague, an academic with an interest in literacy issues in communities of color, was disturbed by much of what she read in the articles and wanted a second opinion.

As I first read the far-reaching, politically sensitive articles, I found that I agreed with much that Gee wrote, as I have with much of his previous work. He argues that literacy is much more than reading and writing, but rather that it is part of a larger political entity. This larger entity he calls a discourse, construed as something of an "identity kit," that is, ways of "saying-writing-doing-being-valuing-believing," examples of which might be the discourse of lawyers, the discourse of academics, or the discourse of men. He adds that one never learns simply to read or write, but to read and write within some larger discourse, and therefore within some larger set of values and beliefs.

Gee maintains that there are primary discourses, those learned in the home, and secondary discourses, which are attached to institutions or groups one might later encounter. He also argues that all discourses are not equal in status, that some are socially dominant — carrying with them social power and access to economic success — and some nondominant. The status of individuals born into a particular discourse tends to be maintained because primary discourses are related to secondary discourses of similar status in our society (for example, the middle-class home discourse to school discourse, or the working-class African-American home discourses to the black church discourse). Status is also maintained because dominant groups in a society apply frequent "tests" of fluency in the dominant discourses, often focused on its most superficial aspects — grammar, style, mechanics — so as to exclude from full participation those who are not born to positions of power.

These arguments resonate in many ways with what I also believe to be true. However, as I reread and pondered the articles, I began to get a sense of my colleague's discomfort. I also began to understand how that discomfort related to some concerns I have about the perspectives of educators who sincerely hope to help educate poor children and children of color to become successful and literate, but who find themselves paralyzed by their own conception of the task.

There are two aspects of Gee's arguments which I find problematic. First is Gee's notion that people who have not been born into dominant discourses will find it exceedingly difficult, if not impossible, to acquire such a discourse. He argues strongly that discourses cannot be "overtly" taught, particularly in a classroom, but can only be acquired by enculturation in the home or by "apprenticeship" into social practices. Those who wish to gain access to the goods and status connected to a dominant discourse must have access to the social practices related to that discourse. That is, to learn the "rules" required for admission into a particular dominant discourse, individuals must already have access to the social institutions connected to that discourse—if you're not already in, don't expect to get in.

This argument is one of the issues that concerned my colleague. As she put it, Gee's argument suggests a dangerous kind of determinism as flagrant as that espoused by the geneticists: instead of being locked into "your place" by your genes, you are now locked hopelessly into a lower-class status by your discourse. Clearly, such a stance can leave a teacher feeling powerless to effect change, and a student feeling hopeless that change can occur.

The second aspect of Gee's work that I find troubling suggests that an individual who is born into one discourse with one set of values may experience major conflicts when attempting to acquire another discourse with another set of values. Gee defines this as especially pertinent to "women and minorities," who, when they seek to acquire status discourses, may be faced with adopting values that deny their primary identities. When teachers believe that this acceptance of self-deprecatory values is *inevitable* in order for people of color to acquire status discourses, then their sense of justice and fair play might hinder their teaching these discourses.

If teachers were to adopt both of these premises suggested by Gee's work, not only would they view the acquisition of a new discourse in a classroom impossible to achieve, but they might also view the goal of acquiring such a discourse questionable at best. The sensitive teacher might well conclude that even to try to teach a dominant discourse to students who are members of a nondominant oppressed group would be to oppress them further. And this potential conclusion concerns me. While I do agree that discourses may embody conflicting values, I also believe there are many individuals who have faced and overcome the problems that such a conflict might cause. I hope to provide another perspective on both of these premises.

Overcoming Obstacles to Acquisition

One remedy to the paralysis suffered by many teachers is to bring to the fore stories of the real people whose histories directly challenge unproductive beliefs. Mike Rose has done a poignantly convincing job of detailing the role of committed teachers in his own journey toward accessing literate discourse, and his own role as a teacher of disenfranchised veterans who desperately needed the kind of explicit and focused instruction Rose was able to provide in order to "make it" in an alien academic setting.[2] But there are many stories not yet documented which exemplify similar journeys, supported by similar teaching.

A friend and colleague who teaches in a college of education at a major Midwestern university told me of one of her graduate students whom we'll call Marge. Marge received a special fellowship funded by a private foundation designed to increase the numbers of faculty holding doctorates at black colleges. She applied to the doctoral program at my friend's university and traveled to the institution to take a few classes while awaiting the decision. Apparently, the admissions committee did not quite know what to do with her, for here was someone who was already on campus with a fellowship, but who, based on GRE scores and writing samples, they determined was not capable of doing doctoral-level work. Finally, the committee agreed to admit Marge into the master's program, even though she already held a master's degree. Marge accepted the offer. My friend—we'll call her Susan—got to know Marge when the department head asked her to "work with" the new student who was considered "at risk" of not successfully completing the degree.

Susan began a program to help Marge learn how to cope with the academic setting. Susan recognized early on that Marge was very talented but that she did not understand how to maneuver her way through academic writing, reading, and talking. In their first encounters, Susan and Marge discussed the comments instructors had written on Marge's papers, and how the next paper might incorporate the professor's concerns. The next summer Susan and Marge wrote weekly synopses of articles related to educational issues. When they met, Marge talked through her ideas while Susan took notes. Together they translated the ideas into the "discourse of teacher education." Marge then rewrote the papers referring to their conversations and Susan's extensive written comments.

Susan continued to work with Marge, both in and out of the classroom, during the following year. By the end of that year, Marge's instructors began telling Susan that Marge was a real star, that she had written the best papers in their classes. When faculty got funding for various projects, she became one of the most sought-after research assistants in the college. And when she applied for entry into the doctoral program the next fall, even though her GRE scores were still low, she was accepted with no hesitation. Her work now includes research and writing that challenge dominant attitudes about the potential of poor children to achieve.

The stories of two successful African-American men also challenge the belief that literate discourses cannot be acquired in classroom settings, and highlight the significance of teachers in transforming students' futures. Clarence Cunningham, now a vice chancellor at the largest historically black institution in the United States, grew up in a painfully poor community in rural Illinois. He attended an all-African-American elementary school in the 1930s in a community where the parents of most of the children never even considered attending high school. There is a school picture hanging in his den of a ragtag group of about thirty-five children. As he shows me that picture, he talks about the one boy who grew up to be a principal in Philadelphia, one who is now a vice president of a major computer company, one who was recently elected attorney general of Chicago, another who is a vice president of Harris Bank in Chicago, another who was the first black pilot hired by a major airline. He points to a little girl who is now an administrator, another who is a union leader. Almost all of the children in the photo eventually left their home community, and almost all achieved impressive goals in life.

Another colleague and friend, Bill Trent, a professor and researcher at a major research university, told me of growing up in the 1940s and 1950s in inner-city Richmond, Virginia, "the capital of the Confederacy." His father, a cook, earned an eighth-grade education by going to night school. His mother, a domestic, had a third-grade education. Neither he nor his classmates had aspirations beyond their immediate environment. Yet, many of these students completed college, and almost all were successful, many notable. Among them are teachers, ministers, an electronics wizard, state officials, career army officers, tennis ace Arthur Ashe, and the brothers Max and Randall Robinson, the national newscaster and the director of Trans-Africa, respectively.

How do these men explain the transformations that occurred in their own and their classmates' lives? Both attributed their ability to transcend the circumstances into which they were born directly to their teachers. First, their teachers successfully taught what Gee calls the "superficial features" of middle-class discourse — grammar, style, mechanics — features that Gee claims are particularly resistant to classroom instruction. And the students successfully learned them.

These teachers also successfully taught the more subtle aspects of dominant discourse. According to both Trent and Cunningham, their teachers insisted that students be able to speak and write eloquently, maintain neatness, think carefully, exude character, and conduct themselves with decorum. They even found way to mediate class differences by attending to the hygiene of students who needed such attention — washing faces, cutting fingernails, and handing out deodorant.

Perhaps more significant than what they taught is what they believed. As Trent says, "They held visions of us that we could not imagine for ourselves. And they held those visions even when they themselves were denied entry into the larger white world. They were determined that, despite all odds, we would achieve." In an era of overt racism when much was denied to African-Americans, the message drilled into students was "the one thing people can't take away from you is what's between your ears." The teachers of both men insisted that they must achieve because "you must do twice as well as white people to be considered half as good."

As Cunningham says, "Those teachers pushed us, they wouldn't let us fail. They'd say, 'The world is tough out there, and you have to be tougher.'" Trent recalls that growing up in the "inner-city," he had no conception of life beyond high school, but his high school teachers helped him to envision one. While he happily maintained a *C* average, putting all of his energy into playing football, he experienced a turning point one day when his coach called him inside in the middle of a practice. There, while he was still suited up for football, all of his teachers gathered to explain to him that if he thought he could continue making *C*s and stay on the team, he had another thing coming. They were there to tell him that if he did not get his act together and make the grades they knew he was capable of, then his football career would be over.

Like similar teachers chronicled elsewhere, these teachers put in overtime to ensure that the students were able to live up to their expectations. They set high standards and then carefully and explicitly instructed students in how to meet them. "You can and will do well," they insisted, as they taught at break times, after school, and on weekends to ensure that their students met their expectations. All of these teachers were able to teach in classrooms the rules for dominant discourses, allowing students to succeed in mainstream America who were not only born outside of the realms of power and status, but who had no access to status institutions. These teachers were not themselves a part of the power elite, not members of dominant discourses. Yet they were able to provide the keys for their students' entry into the larger world, never knowing if the doors would ever swing open to allow them in.

The renowned African-American sociologist E. Franklin Frazier also successfully acquired a discourse into which he was not born. Born in poverty to unschooled parents, Frazier learned to want to learn from his teachers and from his self-taught father. He learned his lessons so well that his achievements provided what must be the ultimate proof of the ability to acquire a secondary dominant discourse, no matter what one's beginnings. After Frazier completed his master's degree at Clark University, he went on to challenge many aspects of the white-dominated oppressive system of segregation. Ironically, at the time Frazier graduated from Clark, he received a reference from its president, G. Stanley Hall, who gave Frazier what he must have thought was the highest praise possible in a predominantly white university in 1920. "Mr. Frazier . . . seems to me to be quite gentlemanly and *mentally white*."[3] What better evidence of Frazier's having successfully acquired the dominant discourse of academe?

These stories are of commitment and transformation. They show how people, given the proper support, can "make it" in culturally alien environments. They make clear that standardized test scores have little to say about one's actual ability. And they demonstrate that supporting students' transformation demands an extraordinary amount of time and commitment, but the teachers *can* make a difference if they are willing to make that commitment.

Despite the difficulty entailed in the process, almost any African-American or other disenfranchised individual who has become "successful" has done so by acquiring a discourse other than the one into which he or she was born. And almost all can attribute that acquisition to what happened as a result of the work of one or more committed teachers.

Acquisition and Transformation

But the issue is not only whether students can learn a dominant secondary discourse in the classroom. Perhaps the more significant issue is, should they attempt to do so? Gee contends that for those who have been barred from the mainstream, "acquisition of many mainstream Discourses . . . involves active complicity with the values that conflict with one's home and community-based Discourses." There can be no doubt that in many classrooms students of color do reject literacy, for they feel that literate discourses reject them. Keith Gilyard, in his jolting autobiographical study of language competence, graphically details his attempt to achieve in schools that denied the very existence of this community reality:

> I was torn between institutions, between value systems. At times the tug of school was greater, therefore the 90.2 average. On the other occasions the streets were a more powerful lure, thus the heroin and the 40 in English and a brief visit to the Adolescent Remand Shelter. I . . . saw no middle ground or, more accurately, no total ground on which anomalies like me could gather. I tried to be a hip schoolboy, but it was impossible to achieve that persona. In the group I most loved, to be fully hip meant to repudiate a school system in which African-American consciousness was undervalued or ignored; in which, in spite of the many nightmares around us, I was urged to keep my mind on the Dream, to play the fortunate token, to keep my head straight down and "make it." And I pumped more and more dope into my arms. It was a nearly fatal response, but an almost inevitable one.[4]

Herb Kohl writes powerfully about individuals, young and old, who choose to "not-learn" what is expected of them rather than to learn that which denies them their sense of who they are:

> Not-learning tends to take place when someone has to deal with unavoidable challenges to her or his personal and family loyalties, integrity, and identity. In such situations there are forced choices and no apparent middle ground. To agree to learn from a stranger who does not respect your integrity causes a major loss of self. The only alternative is to not-learn and reject the stranger's world.[5]

I have met many radical or progressive teachers of literacy who attempt to resolve the problem of students who choose to "not-learn" by essentially deciding to "not-teach." They appear to believe that to remain true to their ideology, their role must be to empower and politicize their most disenfranchised students by refusing to teach what Gee calls the superficial features (grammar, form, style, and so forth) of dominant discourses.[6] Believing themselves to be contributing to their students' liberation by deemphasizing dominant discourses, they instead seek to develop literacy *solely* within the language and style of the students' home discourse.

Feminist writer bell hooks writes of one of the consequences of this teaching methodology. During much of her postsecondary school career she was the only black student in her writing courses. Whenever she would write a poem in black Southern dialect, the teachers and fellow students would praise her for using her "true authentic voice" and encourage her to write more in this voice.[7] hooks writes of her frustration with these teachers who, like the teachers I describe, did not recognize the need for African-American students to have access to many voices and who maintained their stance even when adult students or the parents of younger students demanded that they do otherwise.

I am reminded of one educator of adult African-American veterans who insisted that her students needed to develop their "own voices" by developing "fluency" in their home language. Her students vociferously objected, demanding that they be taught grammar, punctuation, and "Standard English." The teacher insisted that such a mode of study was "oppressive." The students continued venting their objections in loud and certain tones. When asked why she thought her students had not developed "voice" when they were using their voices to loudly express their displeasure, she responded that it was "because of who they are," that is, apparently because they were working-class, black, and disagreed with her. Another educator of adults told me that she based her teaching on liberating principles. She voiced her anger with her mostly poor, working-class students because they rejected her pedagogy and "refused to be liberated." There are many such stories to recount.[8]

There are several reasons why students and parents of color take a position that differs from the well-intentioned position of the teachers I have described. First, they know that members of society need access to dominant discourses to (legally) have access to economic power. Second, they know that such discourses can be and have been acquired in classrooms because they know individuals who have done so. And third, and most significant to the point I wish to make now, they know that individuals have the ability to transform dominant discourses for liberatory purposes — to engage in what Henry Louis Gates calls "changing the joke and slipping the yoke,"[9] that is, using European philosophical and critical standards to challenge the tenets of European belief systems.

bell hooks speaks of her black women teachers in the segregated South as being the model from which she acquired both access to dominant discourses and a sense of the validity of the primary discourse of working-class African-American people. From their instruction, she learned that black poets were capable of speaking in many voices, that the Dunbar who wrote in dialect was as valid as the Dunbar who wrote sonnets. She also learned from these women that she was capable of not only participating in the mainstream, but redirecting its currents: "Their work was truly education for critical consciousness. . . . They were the teachers who conceptualized oppositional world views, who taught us young black women to exult and glory in the power and beauty of our intellect. They offered to us a legacy of liberatory pedagogy that demanded active resistance and rebellion against sexism and racism."[10]

Carter G. Woodson called for similar pedagogy almost seventy years ago. He extolled teachers in his 1933 *Mis-Education of the Negro* to teach African-American students not only the language and canon of the European "mainstream," but to teach as well the life, history, language, philosophy, and literature of their own people. Only this kind of education, he argued, would prepare an educated class which would serve the needs of the African-American community.

Acquiring the ability to function in a dominant discourse need not mean that one must reject one's home identity and values, for discourses are not static, but are shaped, however reluctantly, by those who participate within them and by the form of their participation. Many who have played significant roles in fighting for the liberation of people of color have done so through the language of dominant discourses, from Frederick Douglass to Ida B. Wells, to Mary McCloud Bethune, to Martin Luther King, to Malcolm X. As did bell hooks' teachers, today's teachers can help economically disenfranchised students and students of color both to master the dominant discourses and to transform them. How is the teacher to accomplish this? I suggest several possibilities.

What can teachers do? First, teachers must acknowledge and validate students' home language without using it to limit students' potential. Students' home discourses are vital to their perception of self and sense of community connectedness. One Native American college student I know says he cannot write in Standard English when he writes about his village "because that's about me!" Then he must use his own "village English" or his voice rings hollow even to himself. June Jordan has written a powerful essay about teaching a course in Black English and the class's decision to write a letter of protest in that language when the brother of one of the students was killed by police.[11] The point must not be to eliminate students' home languages, but rather to add other voices and discourses to their repertoires. As bell hooks and Henry Gates have poignantly reminded us, racism and oppression must be fought on as many fronts and in as many voices as we can muster.[12]

Second, teachers must recognize the conflict Gee details between students' home discourses and the discourse of school. They must understand that students who appear to be unable to learn are in many instances choosing to "not-learn," as Kohl puts it, choosing to maintain their sense of identity in the face of what they perceive as a painful choice between allegiance to "them" or "us." The teacher, however, can reduce this sense of choice by transforming the new discourse so that it contains within it a place for the students' selves. To do so, they must saturate the dominant discourse with new meanings, must wrest from it a place for the glorification of their students and their forebears.

An interesting historical example is documented by James Anderson. Anderson writes of Richard Wright, an African-American educator in the post-Reconstruction era, who found a way through the study of the "classical" curriculum to claim a place of intellectual respect for himself and his people. When examined by the U.S. Senate Committee on Education and Labor, one senator questioned Wright about the comparative inferiority and superiority of the races. Wright replied:

> It is generally admitted that religion has been a great means of human development and progress, and I think that about all the great religions which have blessed this world have come from the colored races — all . . . I believe, too, that our methods of alphabetic writing all came from the colored race, and I think the majority of the sciences in their origin have come from the colored races. . . . Now I take the testimony of those people who know, and who, I feel are capable of instructing me on this point, and I find them saying that the Egyptians were actually wooly-haired Negroes. In Humboldt's *Cosmos* (Vol. 2, p. 531) you will find that testimony, and Humboldt, I presume, is a pretty good authority. The same thing is stated in Herodotus, and in a number of other authors with whom you gentlemen are doubtless familiar. Now if that is true, the idea that the negro race is inherently inferior, seems to me to be at least a little limping.[13]

Noted educator Jaime Escalante prepared poor Latino students to pass the tests for advanced calculus when everyone else thought they would do well to master fractions. To do so, he also transformed a discourse by placing his students and their ancestors firmly within its boundaries. In a line from the movie chronicling his success, *Stand and Deliver*, he entreated his students, "You *have* to learn math. The Mayans discovered zero. Math is in your blood!"

And this is also what those who create what has been called "Afrocentric" curricula do. They too seek to illuminate for students (and their teachers) a world in which people with brown and black skin have achieved greatness and have developed a large part of what is considered the great classical tradition. They also seek to teach students about those who have taken the language born in Europe and transformed it into an emancipatory tool for those facing oppression in the "new world."

In the mouths and pens of Bill Trent, Clarence Cunningham, bell hooks, Henry Louis Gates, Paul Lawrence Dunbar, and countless others, the "language of the master" has been used for liberatory ends. Students can learn of that rich legacy, and they can also learn that they are its inheritors and rightful heirs.

A final role that teachers can take is to acknowledge the unfair "discourse-stacking" that our society engages in. They can discuss openly the injustices of allowing certain people to succeed, based not upon merit but upon which family they were born into, upon which discourse they had access to as children. The students, of course, already know this, but the open acknowledgement of it in the very institution that facilitates the sorting process is liberating in itself. In short, teachers must allow discussions of oppression to become a part of language and literature instruction. Only after acknowledging the inequity of the system can the teacher's stance then be "Let me show you how to cheat!" And of course, to cheat is to learn the discourse which would otherwise be used to exclude them from participating in and transforming the mainstream. This is what many black teachers of the segregated South intended when they, like the teachers of Bill Trent and Clarence Cunningham, told their students that they *had* to "do better than those white kids." We can again let our students know that they can resist a system that seeks to limit them to the bottom rung of the social and economic ladder.

Gee may not agree with my analysis of his work, for, in truth, his writings are so multifaceted as not to be easily reduced to simplistic positions. But that is not the issue. The point is that some aspects of his work can be disturbing for the African-American reader, and reinforcing for those who choose — wrongly, but for "right" reasons — not to educate black and poor children.

Individuals *can* learn the "superficial features" of dominant discourses, as well as their more subtle aspects. Such acquisition can provide a way both to turn the sorting system on its head and to make available one more voice for resisting and reshaping an oppressive system. This is the alternative perspective I want to give to teachers of poor children and children of color, and this is the perspective I hope will end the paralysis and set teachers free to teach, and thereby to liberate. When teachers are committed to teaching all students, and when they understand that through their teaching change *can* occur, then the chance for transformation is great.

Notes

1. *Journal of Education*, special issue: *Literacy, Discourse, and Linguistics: Essays by James Paul Gee* 171.1 (1989).
2. Mike Rose, *Lives on the Boundary* (New York: Free Press, 1989).
3. Anthony M. Platt, *E. Franklin Frazier Reconsidered* (New Brunswick, N.J.: Rutgers University Press, 1991), p. 15.

4. Keith Gilyard, *Voice of the Self* (Detroit: Wayne State University Press, 1991), p. 160.
5. Herbert Kohl, *I Won't Learn from You! The Role of Assent in Education* (Minneapolis, Minn.: Milkweed Editions, 1991).
6. Gee's position here is somewhat different. He argues that grammar and form should be taught in classrooms, but that students will never acquire them with sufficient fluency to gain entry into dominant discourses. Rather, he states, such teaching is important because it allows students to gain "meta-knowledge" of how language works, which in turn "leads to the ability to manipulate, to analyze, to resist while advancing" (*Journal of Education*, special issue 171.1, p. 13).
7. bell hooks, *Talking Back* (Boston: South End Press, 1989), p. 11.
8. See, for example, Carlos Yorio, "The Other Side of the Looking Glass," *Journal of Basic Writing* 8.1 (1989).
9. Henry Louis Gates, Jr., quoted in Reginald Martin, "Black Writer as Black Critic: Recent Afro-American Writing," *College English* 52.2 (Feb. 1990), p. 204.
10. hooks, *Talking Back*, p. 50.
11. June Jordan, "Nobody Mean More to Me Than You and the Future Life of Willie Jordan," *Harvard Educational Review* 58.3 (1988).
12. hooks, *Talking Back*; and Henry Louis Gates, Jr., *Race, Writing, and Difference* (Chicago: University of Chicago Press, 1986).
13. James D. Anderson, *The Education of Blacks in the South, 1860–1935* (Chapel Hill, N.C.: University of North Carolina Press, 1988), p. 30.

Delpit's Insights as a Resource for Your Reflections

1. Consider the ideas about discourse and identity that Delpit has engaged. What, thus, is at stake in instances that we sometimes benignly flag as dialectic interference or nonstandard linguistic forms?

2. Return for a moment to Dawn Skorczewski's ideas in Chapter 1: How would she complicate Delpit's response to Gee?

Delpit's Insights as a Resource for Your Writing Classroom

1. Sketch these concepts of discourse for your students and ask them to identify how many they feel they've achieved a sort of fluency in and which ones they are struggling to master now.

2. Many people feel inclined to defend African American vernacular English for what they see as its poetic qualities, which raises an

interesting question: How do these ideas of discourse account for those moments when we're caught off guard by a refreshing, witty, even poetic utterance, one that surprises, entertains, captivates, and that we want to remember and use with others? In short, ask your students to use Delpit's terms to define poetry and wit.

Tutoring ESL Students: Issues and Options

Muriel Harris and Tony Silva

Anyone who has worked in a writing center knows that a great many of the students who come for help fall into a category that can also be the most vexing — the ESL student. For new tutors encountering ESL students for the first time, the questions quickly proliferate and overwhelm. Muriel Harris, a writing center administrator and theorist, and Tony Silva, an English as a Second Language specialist, wrote this piece for colleagues who train tutors to work with ESL writers. However, the essay, which appeared in College Composition and Communication *(1993), also provides composition teachers a clear overview of issues and practical teaching strategies for working with ESL writers. The questions that nag new peer tutors and their responses to texts written by ESL students differ only by degree of apprehension from the questions and reading responses of writing teachers. The "tutorial principles" cited are also standard teaching practices of writing instructors. The recommended readings are useful additions to the professional library of a writing instructor. Use this essay as a jumping-in point for thinking about, and planning to work with, students who compose in English as their second — or third or fourth — language.*

For students whose first language is not English, the writing classroom cannot provide all the instructional assistance that is needed to become proficient writers. For a variety of reasons, these students need the kind of individualized attention that tutors offer, instruction that casts no aspersions on the adequacy of the classroom or the ability of the student. We should recognize that along with different linguistic backgrounds, ESL students have a diversity of concerns that can only be dealt with in the one-to-one setting where the focus of attention is on that particular student and his or her questions, concerns, cultural presuppositions, writing processes, language learning experiences, and conceptions of what writing in English is all about. Typically, the tutorial assistance available for these students is provided by writing centers, and much of the personal help available there is precisely the same as for any native speaker of English: The goal of tutors who work in the center is to attend to the individual concerns of every writer who walks in the door — writing process questions, reader feedback, planning conversations, and so on. But also typically, tutors, who bring to their work a background of experience and knowledge in interacting effectively with native speakers of English, are not adequately equipped to deal with some additional concerns of non-native speakers of English — the unfamiliar grammatical errors, the sometimes bewilderingly different rhetorical patterns and conventions of other languages, and the expectations that accompany ESL writers when they come to the writing center. Tutors can be reduced to stunned silence when they try to explain why "I have many homeworks to completed" is wrong or why we say "on Monday" but "in June."

Tutors need some perspective on rhetorical approaches other than those they expect to find, such as a direct statement of the topic or discourse with a linear development. When tutors find, instead, an implicitly stated point or when they become lost in a long, seemingly meandering introduction or digressions that appear irrelevant, they flounder, not recognizing that implicitness and digressions may be acceptable rhetorical strategies in the writing of some other cultures. Because the need to learn more about how to work with ESL writers in tutorials is immediate and real, one of the authors of this essay, a writing center director, asked the other author, the coordinator of ESL writing courses at our university, for help. The conversations that ensued are summarized here in terms of the questions that guided our discussion of various issues and options, and our hope is that our exchanges will be of interest to others who train tutors to work with ESL students. We also hope that composition teachers looking for guidance when conferencing with ESL students will find useful suggestions for their own interactions with these students.

Plunging In: How Do We Prioritize among Errors?

In the peer tutor training course in our writing center, peer tutors are especially eager to meet and work with ESL students, but their initial contacts can be somewhat frightening because some unfamiliar concerns crop up. To the untrained tutor's eye what is most immediately noticeable is that a draft written by an ESL student looks so different. Vocabulary choices might be confusing, familiar elements of essays are missing, and sentences exhibit a variety of errors — some we can categorize, some we cannot. Tutors' first concern is often a matter of wanting some guidance about where to plunge in. Where should they start? New tutors who have not yet completely internalized the concept of the tutorial as focusing only on one or two concerns think initially it is their responsibility to help the writer fix everything in the draft in front of them. As tutors learn the pedagogy of the tutorial, they become more comfortable with selecting something to work on for that session, but they still need suggestions for a hierarchy and some sense of what is most important.

When tutors ask how to prioritize among errors, they should be encouraged to begin by looking for what has been done well in the paper, acknowledge that, and go from there. Such a suggestion fits in well with the tutorial principle of beginning all interaction with writers on a positive note and reminds us that ESL writers should not be separated out as different or unlike other students in this regard. And tutors should also be encouraged to let their students know that errors are a natural part of language learning and that most readers will be interested primarily in what writers have to say. So tutors need to distinguish between errors that will interfere with the intended reader's understanding of the text (global errors) and those that will not (local errors) and to give priority to the former. To illustrate for tutors this notion of global vs. local errors at the sentence level, the following example can help. Suppose an ESL student, attempting to describe some classmates as uninspired by a particular lecture, wrote: "Those students are boring" instead of "Those students are bored." This would constitute a global error. On the other hand, a construction such as "Those student are bored" would represent a local error.

Using Research: How Helpful Is It to Look for Patterns?

With our heightened awareness of multiculturalism, we are also more aware of cultural preferences that are reflected in writing, such as the often-cited Asian preference for indirection. The question in working one-to-one with ESL students is how helpful such generalizations really are. Work in contrastive rhetoric would seem to be particularly valuable because it describes patterns of rhetorical preferences in other cultures, patterns which may explain the seemingly inappropriate rhetorical strategies used by ESL students. But to what degree is such knowledge useful? To what extent should we help tutors become aware of such differences? On the one hand, there is a danger that they can begin to use general patterns as givens, expecting all speakers of other languages to fit the models they have learned. On the other hand, without any knowledge of cultural preferences tutors are likely to see differences as weaknesses and to assume that the ESL student needs basic writing help. For example, instead of introducing the American intolerance of digression as culturally appropriate for American discourse, a tutor might treat an ESL student purposefully using digression as an inadequate writer who has problems with organization. If the tutor assumes that student is deficient, the tutor's tendency might be to work on outlining and to leave aside any rationale for why digressions should be avoided. Tutors need to introduce preferences and conventions of American discourse for what they are — alternate conventions and preferences.

However, to consider the extent to which such knowledge is helpful, we have to begin with some background information. The study of first-language transfer at or below the sentence level, typically referred to as "contrastive analysis" (see Brown 153–63 for a concise summary of this work), and the study of differences in rhetorical preferences among various cultures, usually termed "contrastive rhetoric" (see, for example, Grabe and Kaplan; Leki), have given us useful insights into how the writing of ESL students may differ from accepted standards of American discourse. The question of the transfer of first-language (L1) linguistic and rhetorical patterns to second-language (L2) writing has been a central and contentious issue in ESL studies since the beginning of work in this area. In the early days it was believed that L1 transfer (then called interference) was the primary if not exclusive cause of L2 problems. Therefore, it was felt that if one could catalog the differences between a student's L1 and L2, one could anticipate — and thus be prepared to deal with — any problems that student might encounter in the L2. However, research showed that this was not the case. There were many problems that could not be accounted for by L1 interference. Other factors, such as cognitive development, prior language and/or writing instruction, and experience were also implicated. Today, it is generally believed that transfer can be positive or negative and that it is only one of the potential causes of L2 writing problems. Thus we have to approach the question of the use of such knowledge with some hedging. On one hand, being cognizant of typical problems associated with particular groups of ESL students can be helpful — especially if tutors work largely with one or two particular groups. At the very least, this would make tutors very familiar with these problems and perhaps enhance their ability to deal with them. However, tutors need to keep two things in mind: (1) not all members of a particular group may manifest all of the problems or cultural preferences associated with that group; and (2) not all problems will be a result of transfer of L1 patterns.

A related issue is that of culturally conditioned patterns of behavior, some articulated, some not. In the Writing Lab's tutor-training course, we dip into Edward Hall's work to help tutors-to-be become aware of the variety of human behaviors which are conditioned, consciously or unconsciously, by one's culture. Since some of these behaviors can impede communication in a tutorial, it's important to recognize that such differences occur. A few favorite topics among the tutors-in-training are their reactions to the preference for or avoidance of eye contact, the differences among cultures in regard to the amount of space that people expect to maintain between themselves and others, the acceptability of touching between strangers, and so on. The cautionary advice about not doing too much large-scale or whole-group predicting is worth recalling here, but we also have to be aware that we might make unconscious judgments about others based on our expectations about such behaviors. In addition, we have to deal with different cultural assumptions about time, keeping appointments vs. showing up (if at all) much later, and so on. Understanding and accommodating cultural differences is, to a great extent, what ESL instruction is all about. This is especially true when working with students who are very new to and not very cognizant of the workings of American culture.

Recognizing Differences: How Do We Distinguish Language Learning from Writing Process Needs?

There is a tendency to think about ESL students as if they're all alike when obviously they're not. And in writing centers our focus is on working with individual differences of all kinds. So when the tutor and student negotiate the agenda of what they'll work on, the tutor has to do some assessment about a variety of things, including some sense of what skills the student has or doesn't have — not an easy matter when it might be that the writer's low level of language proficiency, not weak writing skills, is causing the problem. For example, does the thin, undeveloped two-paragraph essay an ESL student brings in indicate the need to talk about how to develop topics or is the student's lack of language proficiency in English keeping her from expressing a rich internal sense of what she wants to write about? As tutors we know that our conversation would take on a somewhat different emphasis depending on our analysis of the situation. The question then becomes one of how to decide whether the student needs help with language or with writing processes.

While the distinction between language proficiency and writing ability is not clear cut, it is crucial to make such a distinction in order to understand and address a given ESL writer's problems (see Barbara Kroll's "The Rhetoric and Syntax Split" for an excellent discussion of this issue). In some cases, a very low level of English proficiency will prevent a student from producing any kind of coherent prose. For such a student some basic language instruction, preceding or accompanying writing instruction, would be indicated. Then there is the student with enough English proficiency to make it unclear whether problems result primarily from rhetorical or linguistic difficulties or from both. There are a number of ways tutors can proceed when trying to ascertain the cause of the problem — assuming they will see the student more than once. They can try to locate the student's results on general English proficiency tests or tests of English writing ability. They can consult with an ESL professional. They can analyze some samples of the student's writing and make a judgment of their own. They can ask the student's opinion about what the basic difficulty is.

Exploring Writing Process Differences: Do ESL Writers Compose Differently?

A rather small but growing body of research, reviewed and synthesized by Silva, compares the composing of ESL and native English-speaking

(NES) writers. The findings of this research suggest that while the composing processes of these two groups are similar in their broad outlines, that is, for both groups writing is a recursive activity involving planning, writing, and revising, there are some salient and important differences. The findings (and these should be seen as very tentative) suggest that adult ESL writers plan less, write with more difficulty (primarily due to a lack of lexical resources), reread what they have written less, and exhibit less facility in revising by ear, that is, in an intuitive manner — on the basis of what "sounds" right, than their NES peers. One implication that can be drawn from this research is that those who deal with ESL writers might find it helpful to stretch out the composing process: (1) to include more work on planning — to generate ideas, text structure, and language — so as to make the actual writing more manageable; (2) to have their ESL students write in stages, e.g., focusing on content and organization in one draft and focusing on linguistic concerns in another subsequent draft; and (3) to separate their treatments of revising (rhetorical) and editing (linguistic) and provide realistic strategies for each, strategies that do not rely on intuitions ESL writers may not have.

Confronting Error: Does It Help to Categorize Sentence-Level Concerns?

When working on grammar with native speakers, tutors categorize types of error so that they can address seemingly disparate problems by focusing on a larger language principle at work. While it's useful to know how to do this so that one can figure out what the problem is and explain it in an effective way to the student, such categorization in the writing of ESL students is often difficult. To do such categorizing well, tutors may need to take a course in the grammar of modern English. Or maybe a short in-service seminar or self-study would do the trick. In any case, a merely intuitive understanding of how English works would not be sufficient for helping ESL writers — who do not share the tutor's native speaker intuitions and who often need explicit explanations. We should also remember that the "rules" of English vary in terms of level of usefulness. Most don't work all the time; some have as many exceptions as cases covered by the rule. So knowing the rules can help tutors a lot; but they can't count on the rules solving their problems in every case. Such advice should make tutors feel more comfortable with their role as writing collaborators rather than as grammarians whose function it is to spout rules. Tutors are there to help with the whole spectrum of writing processes, not to be talking grammar handbooks.

Although tutors do not work primarily on grammar and mechanics, some ESL writers — especially those whose first acquaintance with English was as a foreign language taught in classrooms in other countries — have a tendency to want to know rules. For example, in a tutorial with a native speaker of English or a student born in the United States who spoke another language before entering school, the student might ask "Is this sentence OK?" or "How do I fix this sentence?" But an ESL student who comes to the United States after studying English as a foreign language in another country is more likely to ask "Why is this wrong?" Such students seem to have a strong inclination toward organizing their knowledge of English by rules. Though things are changing, many foreign language classes (and this includes foreign language classes in the United States) privilege the learning of grammatical rules, of learning about the language as an object, and neglect the learning of how to actually communicate, orally or in writing, in the foreign language. Certainly, this can make learners very rule-oriented in their outlook. However, there is something else that may also contribute to an ESL student's seeming preoccupation with rules. It's necessary to keep in mind that non-native speakers of a language (especially ones with lower levels of second language proficiency) simply don't have the intuitions about the language that native speakers do; that is, it is harder for them to recognize when something "sounds good." Therefore, in lieu of these intuitions, these students will have to rely on explicit rules to a certain extent.

Adjusting Expectations: How Do We Withstand the Pressure to Correct Every Error?

ESL writers often come to the writing center seeking an editor, someone who will mark and correct their errors and help them fix the paper. On one hand, as tutors we are collaborators who listen to the student's concerns when setting the tutorial agenda. On the other hand, as tutors we also want to begin with rhetorical concerns before looking at sentence-level matters. This causes delicate negotiating between tutor and student when these differing preferences for the agenda collide. But tutors should be firm about dealing with rhetorical matters before linguistic ones (recognizing that sometimes this distinction is hard to make), a sequence as beneficial for ESL writers as it is for native speakers. Tutors should remind ESL writers that their linguistic options may be determined to a large degree by the rhetorical requirements of their papers and that, correlatively, it doesn't make sense to focus initially on grammatical or mechanical problems which may disappear as a result of rhetorically based revisions.

A related problem is that when ESL students are particularly insistent on having tutors correct all grammatical errors in a paper, tutors are at a loss to explain in meaningful ways why this is not productive. Resisting such pressure is very difficult, especially when ESL students are writing papers for other courses where they think the paper should be "correct." One way to address this is for tutors to adjust expectations. Tutors need to tell ESL writers that it is unrealistic for them to expect to be able to write like native speakers of English—especially when it comes to the small but persistent problems like articles and prepositions. Tutors can explain that even non-native speakers of English who live in an English-speaking area for many years and write regularly in English maintain a written accent. It might help to compare this to a foreign accent in pronunciation and to remind ESL students that most native speakers (their professors included) will probably not penalize them much or at all for minor problems in their writing. It also helps to remind such students to focus on substance and not worry so much about style. But there are faculty who do have unrealistic demands about the level of correctness, who expect non-native speakers of English to write error-free prose—not to have a written accent, so to speak. If an ESL student's teacher has such unrealistic expectations, then the student is justified in seeking out editing help, and a native English-speaking colleague, friend, or tutor is justified in providing such help.

Another way that tutors can deal with students' insistence on having all errors corrected is to explain the role of a tutor. ESL students need to know that tutors are expected to help them with strategies that will make them effective, independent writers. We need to explicitly state that tutors are supposed to be educators, not personal editors. This problem is often a result of a mismatch between the assumptions and expectations of tutors and students, though tutors do tend to hang on to their kind-hearted desire to help the student turn in a good paper. Writing center specialists endlessly quote Steve North's now famous one-liner that the tutor's job "is to produce better writers, not better writing" (438). But we still suffer pangs when the student leaves with less than an "A" paper in hand. Offering editorial services is not a learning experience—except for the editor, of course—and tutors need to resist their impulse to help as much as ESL students need to resist their desire to have every grammatical error corrected.

Setting Goals: What Can We Accomplish?

Since second-language learning is typically a long, slow process, tutors have to confront the realities of the time constraints they face in tutorials. Sometimes tutors meet briefly with ESL writers who are about to hand in a paper, sometimes tutors may have a few more leisurely tutorials with the same student, and sometimes tutors are able to meet over a more extended period of time, including sessions when the student is not working on a particular paper. The question then becomes one of deciding what can reasonably be done in the varying situations tutors find themselves in. In terms of last-minute encounters, a tutor can't do much with a paper that is about to be handed in—except act as a proofreader or offer moral support. And neither of these has much instructional value in the long run. However, dealing with an early or intermediate draft of a paper at one or more short sessions can be very useful if tutors can resist trying to deal with all of a draft's problems at once. It is more realistic and more useful to focus on one or two salient difficulties, the things that strike the tutor as most problematic for the reader. To do more would probably overload and frustrate the student and wind up being counterproductive. Going this slowly will probably not result in great improvements in a particular paper, but is more likely to facilitate real learning and writing improvement over time.

When tutors are able to meet with ESL students over a period of time and meet when the student is not working on a particular paper, there are several kinds of tutorial activities that might be useful in helping the student build language proficiency. To begin this sequence, a tutor should first look at one or more samples of the student's writing to get a feel for what linguistic features need to be addressed and in what order (global first, local later). Then, always working with a text the student has written previously or writes in the tutorial, the tutor can help the student identify and remedy errors or help the student generate lexical and/or syntactic options that would improve the student's text. This sort of procedure would help with building language proficiency and might also help the student develop effective personalized strategies for generating language, revising, and editing. Such an approach also harmonizes with the writing center philosophy that what we do particularly well in the tutorial setting is to help writers develop strategies individually matched to their own preferences and differences. Because the tutorial is also especially well suited to working through writing processes, to engaging in various processes such as planning, organizing, revising, and editing with the writer, working through various texts the ESL writer is drafting and revising is easily accomplished in a one-to-one setting.

Resisting the Urge to "Tell": How Do We Stop Supplying All the Answers?

Since writing center pedagogy has given high priority to working collaboratively and interactively, a major goal of a tutor is to help students find their own solutions. Tutors thus don't see themselves as "instructors" who "tell" things. Yet the ESL student cannot easily come to some of the realizations that native speakers can as a result of tutorial questioning and collaboration. To confound the problem even more, while the tutor is uncomfortable straying from the role of collaborator, ESL writers are likely to find such a situation strange or uncomfortable when they come from cultures/educational systems where teachers are expected to be "tellers," where those who don't "tell" are seen as poor teachers, or where such casual interaction with relative strangers is seen as odd or inappropriate. This means that tutors cannot assume that a pattern of interaction that is common and accepted in their culture will be familiar or comfortable for their ESL students. Therefore, tutors might find it useful to make sure that they and their ESL students understand each other's goals and expectations vis-à-vis their tutoring sessions.

In terms of the tutor's role, there may have to be adjustments in their pedagogical orientation. Tutors who work with ESL students may have to be "tellers" to some extent because they will probably need to provide cultural, rhetorical, and/or linguistic information which native speakers intuitively possess and which ESL students do not have, but need to have to complete their writing assignments effectively. That is, regardless of their level of skill in collaboration or interpersonal interaction, tutors will not be able to elicit knowledge from ESL students if the students don't have that knowledge in the first place. This is not to suggest that "telling" should become a tutor's primary style of interacting with ESL writers; they should use it when they feel it would be necessary or appropriate, just as they assume the role of informant occasionally when working with native speakers of English. Tutors can also make minor accommodations in their tutoring style when working with ESL writers. For example, with non-native students who are used to hearing directive statements from teachers, Judith Kilborn has suggested that where it is appropriate, tutors modify the normal mode of asking questions so that instead of asking "Why . . ." or "How . . . ," tutors can, for example, say, "Please explain. . . ." An answer to a relatively open-ended request for explanation might be more useful and enlightening for both the ESL student and the tutor.

Making Hierarchies: What Aspects of Grammar Are Most Important?

Although tutorials should begin with discussions of larger rhetorical concerns, at some point ESL students will want help with grammatical correctness. When tutors do confront working with grammar, problems with verb endings and tenses, prepositions, and deleted articles often are the most noticeable. But are these the most useful things to start with? One way to define the most important areas is functionally; that is, the ones most important to address are those that most interfere with the reader's understanding of what the writer wants to say (global errors) regardless of their structural characteristics. Research suggests that ESL writers most commonly make the following errors:

Verbs

Inflectional morphology (agreement with nouns in person, number, etc.)

Verbal forms (participials, infinitives, gerunds)

Verb complementation (the types of clauses or constructions that must follow a particular verb)

Nouns

Inflection (especially in terms of singular/plural and count/mass distinctions)

Derivation (deriving nouns from other parts of speech, e.g., *quick — quickness*, which often seems quite arbitrary to non-native speakers)

Articles (related to problems in classifying nouns)

Use of wrong article

Missing article

Use of an article when none is necessary or appropriate

Prepositions (primarily a result of limited lexical resources)

Knowing which one goes with a particular noun, verb, adjective, or adverb

These four error types account for most of the errors made by ESL writers with a fairly high level of English proficiency; ESL writers with lower levels of proficiency may also exhibit more problems with basic sentence, clause, and phrase structure — which (when combined with vocabulary limitations) result in writing that is very difficult to decipher. Article problems can be important, too; that is, they can seriously obscure meaning in some contexts. But they generally do not cause readers any serious difficulties, and because they are so hard to eradicate, they should not be a high priority for tutors. It might help both tutors and ESL writers to think of article problems in writing as akin to a slight foreign accent in writing — something that doesn't pose serious difficulties and disappears only gradually — if at all.

When working with the complicated matter of articles and prepositions and non-rule-governed matters such as idioms, tutors need some new pedagogies as well as guidance for explaining topics not normally discussed in grammar handbooks. But, while we can develop an explanation of article use in English, such an explanation will not be simple by any means. It would involve making sequential decisions about the noun phrase that an article modifies — common or proper, count or non-count, singular or plural, definite or indefinite. Then, of course, there are the several classes of special cases and the many outright exceptions to the rules (Ann Raimes's *Grammar Troublespots* is helpful here; see 85–92). ESL writers could understand such explanations — but it's not clear that this understanding would translate into greatly improved performance in making correct article decisions while actually writing. Article use can improve gradually with increased exposure to English, but it's not realistic to expect that an ESL writer will ever use articles like a native speaker does. ESL students should be encouraged to do the best they can and then get a native speaker to proofread their work — if proofreading is absolutely necessary. As for preposition problems, they are lexical rather than grammatical problems. We either know the correct preposition in a given context or we don't — there are really no rules we can appeal to. Therefore, ESL writers need to learn prepositions the same way they learn other vocabulary items — through study or exposure to the language. Idioms are also a lexical rather than a grammatical matter. Second language learners usually have a keen interest in idiomatic expressions and are eager to learn and use them. Tutors can capitalize on this interest by providing students with idiomatic options for words and expressions they have used in their text. Both tutor and student might find this a useful and enjoyable activity. One proviso: When introducing an idiom, tutors need to also supply information about the appropriate context for the use of that idiom in order to avoid putting the student in a potentially embarrassing situation.

Encouraging Proofreading: What Strategies Work Well?

With native English speakers we are often successful in helping them learn to edit for correctness by reading aloud, something some ESL students can also learn how to do. Some are able to find their own mistakes, even add omitted articles, and it really works. But for other ESL students, this doesn't seem to be an effective strategy. ESL writers who can't successfully edit "by ear" aren't proficient enough in English to have a "feel" for what is correct and what isn't. It follows that those with higher levels of proficiency will have more success with reading aloud, but even the most proficient aren't likely to display native-speaker-like intuitions. Therefore, some recourse to more mechanical rule-based proofreading strategies or to outside help, such as a native speaker reader, will probably be necessary.

Adding Resources: What Are Useful Readings for Tutors?

Since many tutors and directors would like to better prepare themselves to work with ESL students but have limited time to spend, we will limit our suggestions for further reading to a small fraction of the abundant literature produced in recent years on ESL writing and ESL writers. The resources described in this section were chosen on the basis of their timeliness, breadth, and accessibility.

The first resources are book-length treatments of issues in ESL writing and writing instruction. One is Ilona Leki's, *Understanding ESL Writers: A Guide for Teachers*. This introductory book addresses the history of ESL writing instruction, relevant models of second language acquisition, differences between basic writers and ESL writers, personal characteristics of ESL writers, ESL writers' expectations, writing behaviors, and composing processes, contrastive rhetoric, common sentence-level errors, and responding to ESL writing. The second is Joy M. Reid's *Teaching ESL Writing*. This work deals with the special problems and concerns that distinguish first and second language writing instruction, addressing in particular the variables of language and cultural background, prior education, gender, age, and language proficiency. Reid also provides an overview of different ESL composition teaching methodologies and offers specific information on developing curricula, syllabi, and lesson plans for basic, intermediate, and advanced ESL writing classes. Also useful are two collections covering a broad range of issues in ESL writing. The first is Barbara Kroll's *Second Language Writing: Research Insights for the Classroom*, which contains thirteen papers in two major sections. The papers in the first section address theories of L2 writing and provide overviews of research in a number of basic areas of ESL composition. The second section is comprised of reports of empirical research on current issues in L2 writing instruction. The second collection, Donna M. Johnson and Duane H. Roen's *Richness in Writing: Empowering ESL Students*, includes eighteen papers in three sections which deal respectively with contexts for ESL writing, specific rhetorical concerns of L2 writers, and cultural issues in the writing of ESL students.

Two additional resources are the *Journal of Second Language Writing*, a scholarly journal which publishes reports of research and discussions of issues in second and foreign language writing and writing instruction, and *Resources for CCCC Members Who Want to Learn about Writing in English as a Second Language*, a fact sheet of information about professional organizations, conferences, publications, and educational and employment opportunities for those interested in working with ESL writers. (For a copy of the *Resources* fact sheet, write to Tony Silva, CCCC Committee on ESL, Department of English, Heavilon Hall, Purdue University, West Lafayette, Indiana 47907–1356.)

Conclusion

ESL instructors and writing center people need to keep interacting with and learning from each other. We each have insights, methods, research, and experiences to share. For those of us in writing centers, it's useful to know that writing center tutors can draw on both research and language teaching approaches used in ESL classrooms. Writing center directors can share with ESL teachers one-to-one pedagogies that work in the writing center as well as our perceptions of how individual differences interact with various classroom pedagogies on different students. We can also share our awareness of the kinds of questions students really ask, our first-hand observations of how students cope with writing assignments and teacher responses, and our encounters with nonnative differences that interfere with learning how to write in American classrooms. Such information can only serve to illuminate the work of ESL teachers. Similarly, insights from ESL writing theory, research, and practice can help writing centers, and mainstream composition in general, to deal effectively with their increasingly multilingual and multicultural student populations.

Works Cited

Brown, H. Douglas. *Principles of Language Learning and Teaching*. 2nd ed. Englewood Cliffs: Prentice, 1987.

CCCC Committee on ESL. *Resources for CCCC Members Who Want to Learn about Writing in English as a Second Language (ESL)*. Urbana: NCTE, 1992.

Grabe, William, and Robert B. Kaplan. "Writing in a Second Language: Contrastive Rhetoric." *Richness in Writing: Empowering ESL Students*. Ed. Donna Johnson and Duane Roen. New York: Longman, 1989. 263–83.

Hall, Edward. *The Silent Language*. New York: Doubleday, 1959.

Johnson, Donna M., and Duane H. Roen, eds. *Richness in Writing: Empowering ESL Students*. New York: Longman, 1989.

Kilborn, Judith. "Tutoring ESL Students: Addressing Differences in Cultural Schemata and Rhetorical Patterns in Reading and Writing." Minnesota, TESOL Conference. St. Paul, 2 May 1992.

Kroll, Barbara. "The Rhetoric and Syntax Split: Designing a Curriculum for ESL Students." *Journal of Basic Writing* 9 (Spring 1990): 40–45.

———, ed. *Second Language Writing: Research Insights for the Classroom*. New York: Cambridge UP, 1990.

Leki, Ilona. "Twenty-Five Years of Contrastive Rhetoric: Text Analysis and Writing Pedagogies." *TESOL Quarterly* 25 (Spring 1991): 123–43.

———. *Understanding ESL Writers: A Guide for Teachers*. Portsmouth: Boynton, 1992.

North, Stephen. "The Idea of a Writing Center." *College English* 46 (Sept. 1984): 433–46.

Raimes, Ann. *Grammar Troublespots: An Editing Guide for Students*. 2nd ed. New York: St. Martin's, 1992.

Reid, Joy M. *Teaching ESL Writing*. Englewood Cliffs: Regents, 1993.

Silva, Tony. "Differences in ESL and Native Speaker Writing." *Writing in Multicultural Settings*. Ed. Johnnella Butler, Juan Guerra, and Carol Severino. New York: MLA, 1997.

Harris and Silva's Insights as a Resource for Your Reflections

1. Harris and Silva's advice that ESL tutors distinguish global errors from local errors is also a rule of thumb for writing teachers.

Have you worked with ESL students who seem to have a product-centered introduction to writing in English and assume "correctness" will be your first criterion for evaluation? How might you emphasize in your comments on drafts or in your conferences with ESL writers that your first concern is with the message and that you will focus primarily on errors that impede you in understanding what the writer wants to say? You might remind students that, as they revise for ideas and structure, some of their global errors will disappear. Remind them to separate revising (rhetorical concerns) from editing (linguistic concerns).

2. In the conclusion of their article, Harris and Silva stress the need for interaction between ESL instructors and writing center tutors and administrators. If you work with ESL writers in your classroom, meet with some tutors or faculty from the writing center to share insights and experiences. What successful writing center strategies might work well in the classroom? In turn, what insights from your research or classroom practice might help the writing center more effectively work with non-native speakers?

3. How might Lisa Delpit add to this article and what might she take from it to apply to the particular students that interest her?

Harris and Silva's Insights as a Resource for Your Writing Classroom

1. Early in the semester, invite all your students to write you letters describing their histories as writers and scholars and detailing anything you need to know about them to work with them as writers. In conferences with individual writers, use your reading of and response to an early writing assignment, journal entries, and the letter to initiate a conversation about the ESL student's writing experiences and about his or her confidence and fluency in spoken and written English. Anticipate that some ESL students — perhaps because of their fluency level or lack of proficiency with basic communication skills in English or perhaps because of cultural communication patterns — will need to become comfortable with one-to-one conferences. They may not articulate their concerns and questions clearly in a first conference or may send verbal and nonverbal messages that they comprehend what you say when in fact they don't. Anticipate that some students will be silent in classroom discussions because they fear speaking incorrectly or they lack cognitive readiness.

2. Collaborative activities are high-risk experiences for some ESL students and familiar experiences for others. To introduce small-group discussions or projects and peer critique, ask class members to write a three-minute letter about their expectations for and fears about working collaboratively. Merge the letters and make a handout for large-group discussion. Ask the class to agree on some shared responsibilities for collaborative activities. On self-assessment protocols afterward, ask students to evaluate how well these responsibilities were met. (Return the letter and protocols and ask students to keep them to use in conferences when they assess their work in groups later in the semester.)

Becoming a Writerly Self: College Writers Engaging Black Feminist Essays

Juanita Rodgers Comfort

What's the difference between self-expression and self-indulgence, and, more important, how can matters of race not only complicate the issue but actually help lead us to a more refined sense of how to manage that difference in our classrooms and writing assignments? This article, from a 2000 issue of College Composition and Communication, *describes a method for enabling student writers to connect their personal and social identities in ways that will enhance their writing while avoiding the "self-indulgence" teachers typically fear when introducing the personal into writing. Juanita Rodgers Comfort argues, "Writing instruction should enable students to recognize the writerly self as a* persuasive instrument *that can be strategically deployed and to learn to make effective use of their own multiple locations to take personal stands on public issues* that transcend the confessional." *Black feminist writers, she feels, have mastered this effective juxtaposition with essays that go beyond the mere narrative while still invoking the self, and thus serve as excellent models of authoritative and contextualized writing.*

> My work requires me to think about how free I can be as an African-American woman writer in my genderized, sexualized, wholly racialized world. To think about (and wrestle with) the full implications of my situation leads me to consider what happens when other writers work in a highly and historically racialized society. For them, as for me, imagining is not merely looking or looking at; nor is it taking oneself intact into the other. It is for the purposes of the work, *becoming.*
>
> —Toni Morrison, *Playing in the Dark*

Whenever I tell people that I am studying the rhetoric of contemporary black feminist essayists, I'm inevitably asked why rhetoricians should pay attention to the writings of African American women. I'm asked to account for what makes their discursive situations "noteworthy"; after all, my questioners reason, isn't the struggle for personal power, for voice, for credibility, shared by *all* writers? Then why focus on *black women's writing*, specifically—what can *they* show *us?* This question always echoes in my ears for days after each encounter with it. Despite my sense that most of the time it is asked out of intellectual curiosity and in a spirit of goodwill, it has always felt like a trick question to me, designed to somehow betray me as an academic "outsider," to put me in my place and, perhaps, out of the business of locating black women's voices more centrally within the discipline. I've always managed to give what I hoped was an acceptably distanced, "scholarly" response (one that I always hope does not saddle me with the burden of defending my well-considered standpoint as a black feminist rhetorician or the contributions of African American women's writing to "mainstream" scholarly projects):

> I study these works *as I think any rhetorician would*, in order to gain more insight into the challenges faced by all speakers and writers in negotiating an influential ethos for themselves. I examine the writing of African American women, specifically, because *their* texts document the authoritative spaces *they* have created for *themselves* within and against particular configurations of social, cultural, political, and economic power. This work represents *one scholarly direction to take among many*, but it is of vital importance because it contributes to *a useful culturally grounded theory* of rhetorical power.

This answer, for the most part, has satisfied my interlocutors. But I am usually left wondering how my answer, in positioning my black female self as critically distant from the issues involved, removes me from my own work and somehow impoverishes the meaning of that work. As I reread this answer, I see that several strategies of disengagement are apparent (and in fact work to negate the "I" that I have used twice): I locate myself in a mainstream—"as any rhetorician would"—that historically has been populated by white men. I exclude myself from the world of African American writers, obscuring the fact that I happen to be one, eschewing the self-inclusive pronouns "our," "we," and "ourselves" in favor of their self-excluding counterparts "their," "they," and "themselves." I assign myself almost anonymous status among a cohort of scholars. I choose to reduce my conclusions to the neutral terms of "*a* (generic) theory" instead of the "*my* (personally located) theory." And I choose not to articulate at all what is perhaps the most important part of my answer: *I'm doing this work because what "I" (a black woman who is also, ostensibly, an academic "insider") have to say about the African American women's discursive practices contributes to making those practices matter.*

I invoke this brief self-analysis to frame my vision of how literary essays by black feminist writers can be used by college writers at both the first-year and advanced levels to gain valuable insight into writing as a self-defining activity. Displayed through features comprising specific texts as well as through a rhetor's general reputation (whether that rhetor is a professional or student writer), her image in the minds of her audiences can be one of the most powerful influences on their judgments of her work. The enfranchisement of African American women as makers of knowledge in situations where forces work toward muting or silencing us may very well hinge on the task of distinguishing ourselves to audiences (for whom white male perspectives are the norm) specifically as black and female in our grounding assumptions, strategies of argument, and writing style, while simultaneously eliciting from those audiences a favorable impression of our perceived characters. Like all rhetors (student writers included), black feminist essayists must invent effective ways to answer readers' fundamental question: Who is this person and why should I believe what she says?

Cornel West's description of the struggle of the black diaspora to obtain and maintain status and credibility within a Eurocentric (masculinist) cultural framework invokes for me a similar struggle engaged in by student writers within the cultural framework of the academy. West analyzes the problematic of *invisibility* and *namelessness*, enacted by cultural authorities, which "promoted Black inferiority and constituted the European background against which Black diaspora struggles for identity, dignity . . . and material resources took place" (102). Perhaps because of my own search for a writerly self that is at once influential in the academic arena, representative of the places I come from outside the academy, and comfortable as a self-image, questions about the writerly self condition everything I write. Over the ten years that I have been teaching composition and rhetoric courses, I've observed that my most insightful students have generally sought to use their writing assignments as tools to help themselves mature as thinking individuals and become more powerful as social beings. Through their writerly eyes, I've come to see that successful college writing demands, and ultimately achieves, something more personally enriching than merely "inventing the university," as David Bartholomae would say. The most successful student writers in my experience learn how to move beyond merely imitating the prose styles and interpretive schemes of disciplinary discourses. They animate those discourses by inventing complex and versatile writerly selves who are able to place their extra-academic worlds into a carefully constructed relationship with those discourse communities.

Universities are, of course, part of the genderized, racialized society that Morrison speaks of. A genderized, racialized society is one in which the statuses and roles of the people in its institutions (educational, military, economic, governmental . . .) and communities (neighborhood, social, religious . . .)—and even the very structures of those institutions and communities — are influenced, even dictated on some level, by gender and race. Racial and gender groups, of course, must be understood not merely in terms of differential physical attributes, but also in terms of discursive habits and social practices, along with perceptions of intelligence, morality, values, and so forth that are typically associated with those attributes, habits, and practices.

The discourses of the university are heavily invested with markers of white race, male gender, and middle and upper socioeconomic classes. As an African American woman who studies and teaches rhetoric and composition at a university, I am keenly aware of the ways in which language constructs the person who knows as much as it defines what one knows. And I am unwilling to pretend that disciplinary discourses are value-neutral enclaves where race, gender, class, spirituality, and other cultural issues don't matter. And so, echoing Morrison, I think it's important for rhetoricians and composition specialists to ask important questions about what happens when *student writers* of any gender or any race work in a genderized, racialized society. If imagining, through composing, is something more significant to students than exercises in critical detachment, and if we do not expect them to remain essentially unchanged by their encounters with the ideas they write about, then composing text must be for the purposes of these students' education, *becoming* insurgent intellectuals (to use a term coined by West and bell hooks) who are personally invested in the world of ideas.

The rhetorical implications of writing one's way toward becoming in a racialized society came into particular focus for me last year, after teaching a graduate seminar on contemporary African American women essayists. The course employed methods of rhetorical criticism to draw insights from literary essays by black feminist writers June Jordan, Alice Walker, bell hooks, Nikki Giovanni, and Pearl Cleage. As I led the class of nine students through the semester (seven black women and two white women, along with several others who sat in on occasional sessions), we all felt strongly attracted to — and sometimes troubled by — the range of essayistic voices that were speaking to us. We raised numerous questions and engaged in more than a few debates about merits of the essayists' personal approaches to public issues. Class discussions defined spaces where issues of identity, location, and meaning emerged from a wide range of experiences with work, family, community, spirituality, and often, the academy. Our encounters with the diversity of these essayists' world views certainly complicated the taken-for-granted, almost stereotypical notions of "black" and "female" identity that were initially prevalent in the class. Regardless of the direction of our critiques, however, none of us doubted the powerful *presence* of these women in their works. As we moved through our reading list, it became increasingly evident to us that who these writers portray themselves to be as African American women had great bearing on their ability to entice us to entertain their positions, share their social agenda, or accept their conclusions. And their self-portrayals as distinctively raced and gendered beings posed a challenge to my students, both black and white, to reconsider what they themselves were about.

An extended example underscores this point. One of my students, a middle-aged white woman, whom I'll call Eleanor, was deeply troubled by the way June Jordan's essay "Requiem for the Champ" (which we read from her collection, *Technical Difficulties*) seemed to defend the aberrant personal behavior of heavyweight boxer Mike Tyson. On the day students presented proposals for their semester projects, Eleanor told the class that because she had always felt connected to Jordan, a renowned poet and political activist, as a "feminist thinker," she could not comprehend why the essayist would stoop to dignify Tyson with what she called an apology, and so she was planning to write a paper arguing for her misgivings. I don't think she realized it at the time she developed her proposal, but Eleanor was beginning an important journey toward a racialized consciousness made possible by Jordan's writing self.

Let me give some background about the essay. In "Requiem," Jordan outlines the horrific conditions of poverty and oppression under which Mike Tyson learned the life rules that have governed his personal behavior as an adult. In keeping with the theme identified by the subtitle of *Technical Difficulties* — "African-American Notes on the State of the Union" — she asks of readers to consider the attitudes of politicians, military personnel, filmmakers, recording artists, and others who authorize, carry out, and applaud both acts of violence and the objectification of women (226). She indicts those who might share responsibility for maintaining the kind of social order that could dehumanize not only Tyson, but even someone as apparently different from him as Jordan herself. It is upon this point that she makes a crucial connection between herself and Tyson, designed to disrupt readers' easy categorizations of either one of them.

The message in Jordan's essay is especially powerful because of its "self-disclosures" — bits of information about herself that Jordan endows with salience, places in specific locations in the essay, packages with other images, flags as revelatory, and connects to the essay's central message. Rhetorically, self-disclosures foreground the embodied nature of the self, which, through selective, insightful sharing, can build connections between writers and readers that authorize the writer to make claims and ensure the acceptability of those claims.

Jordan opens the essay with an assertion of physical proximity to Tyson:

> Mike Tyson comes from Brooklyn. And so do I. Where he grew up was about a twenty-minute bus ride from my house. (221)

Then, she confesses that it took her most of her own life to learn the social lessons that Tyson apparently had not, emphasizing that she was, *for most of her life*, very much like Tyson is now:

> *Mike Tyson comes from Brooklyn. And so do I.* In the big picture of America, I never had much going for me. And he had less. *I only learned, last year*, that I can stop whatever violence starts with me. *I only learned, last year*, that love is infinitely more interesting, and more exciting, and more powerful, than really winning or really losing a fight. *I only learned, last year*, that all war leads to death and that all love leads you away from death. (223, italics mine)

It is difficult to overlook that in the middle of this passage, Jordan speaks words that could easily have come from Tyson (which I indicate here in boldface):

> *I am more than twice Mike Tyson's age. And I'm not stupid. Or slow.* ***But I'm Black. And I come from Brooklyn. And I grew up fighting. And I grew up and I got out of Brooklyn because I got pretty good at fighting. And winning***. Or else, intimidating my would-be adversaries with my fists, my feet, and my mouth. And I never wanted to fight. *I never wanted anybody to hit me. And I never wanted to hit anybody*. But the bell would ring at the end of another dumb day in school and I'd head out with dread and a nervous sweat because I knew some jackass more or less my age and more or less my height would be waiting for me because she or he had nothing better to do than to wait for me and hope to kick my butt or tear up my books or break my pencils or pull hair out of my head. (223, italics mine)

Then a little later in the essay, she identifies herself with Tyson again, and this time the connection moves beyond Tyson to identify Jordan with African Americans generally:

> *I'm Black. Mike Tyson is Black*. And neither one of us was ever supposed to win anything more than a fight between the two of us. And if you check out the mass-media material on "*us*," and if you check out the emergency-room reports on "*us*," you might well believe we're losing the fight to be more than our enemies have decreed. . . . (224, italics mine)

These passages illustrate two ways that self-disclosures function as a persuasive element. First, as a matter of strategy, Jordan provides specially chosen personal information in order to place herself directly—almost physically—between her readers and Mike Tyson. For the space of reading this essay, Jordan insists that readers perceive of her and Tyson not separately, but together, and as explicitly raced beings. The physical identification becomes a point of *stasis*: If Jordan is so much like Tyson, then we should either dislike Jordan as much as we dislike Tyson, or (the preferred reading) translate our respect for Jordan into a greater valuing of Tyson.

Second, the psychological power of Jordan's disclosures relies on her readers' sense that a defining relationship is taking place between the essayist and her subject. I'm drawn to Sharon Crowley's explanation for this phenomenon, that the writing subject is enmeshed in multiple relations, but when writing, the "writer becomes audience" as well (34). So, in the process of working through the problems posed by assuming a personal association with Tyson, Jordan constructs a self who speaks back to her from the pages of her work-in-progress. Having written part of Tyson's life into her own, and then reading reflexively what she has written from the subject position she created for herself, Jordan presumably has on some level become self-identified as "June Jordan, sister of Mike Tyson." So, in a sense, this is a "real" June Jordan who speaks to readers, not a mechanistically crafted persona. And as readers become familiar with the person in the essay who asserts a similar background to Tyson's but demonstrates a decidedly different outcome, Jordan can hope that readers will better understand her stance on the fallen Tyson and why a requiem for him might be justified.

These effects of self-disclosure can shed light on the challenge that Eleanor was faced with. Until she encountered "Requiem," she seems to have been comfortable in a relationship with the essayist that foregrounded gender solidarity over race division. As long as race can be ignored, the two of them can be kindred spirits. "Although I can't share her experience as a black person," Eleanor could reason, "I can certainly share her experiences as a woman, and I can feel good about that." The feminist values that she believed she already shared with Jordan should have precluded either of them from having sympathies for people like Tyson. But the Tyson/Jordan connection in "Requiem," in both its textual strategy and psychological implications, confounded her: How is it possible that Jordan and Tyson can co-exist on the same moral or intellectual plane?

As the essay unfolds, Tyson's rape conviction and its underpinnings of misogyny and violence, about which Eleanor expected Jordan to have an overriding outrage, seem far less of an issue for the essayist than the implications of their shared oppression as black people. Even though Jordan clearly states at one point that she *does not* condone Tyson's behavior, the essay's rhetoric of black identification seems to counter that disclaimer. Eleanor witnesses her woman-to-woman connection with Jordan disrupted by Jordan's identification as a *black* woman, something that Eleanor herself can never be. Therefore, Eleanor must decide how to establish a new relationship with the person that Jordan becomes in the essay, so that she can begin to understand Jordan's message.

As I read Eleanor's semester-project essay, "Down for the Count: The Selection of Metaphor in 'Requiem for the Champ,'" I saw that Jordan's self-disclosures had inspired Eleanor to measure herself against the emergent image of Jordan and to decide what it meant for her to identify with a feminist thinker who claimed the violent sensibility of a Mike Tyson. Her essay dealt with the challenge to her own self-identity by emulating Jordan's strategy of self-disclosure. Her struggle to accomplish this illustrates a theory of modern rhetoric that is, in the words of Michael Halloran, "distinguished by its emphasis on the responsibility of speakers to articulate their own worlds, and thereby their own selves" (342–43). "It is no longer valid," asserts Halloran, "to assume that speaker and audience live in the same world and to study the techniques by which the speaker moves his audience to act or think in a particular way. One must turn instead to the more fundamental problem of why the gap between the speaker's and audience's worlds is so broad and how one might bridge it smoothly" (336). Jordan forces Eleanor to take on the responsibility of first acknowledging and then attempting to bridge the racial gap between their feminist worlds.

Eleanor uses Jordan's self-representational strategies to help her interrogate Jordan's position, placing herself between her own readers (her classmates and me) and the June Jordan and Mike Tyson who are the joint subjects of her essay.

Eleanor opens her essay with a disclosure about her eyesight that becomes a metaphor for her struggle to gain insight into Jordan's message:

> The truth is that at age fifty-three, I see less clearly than I did at thirty-three. I now wear glasses most of the time so that my field of vision will not be so limited and the words on the page in front of me will be large enough for me to see without hyper-extending my arms. So you see, I have done my best to correct my vision. . . . so why am I having so much trouble "seeing" what June Jordan wants me to see? For the life of me, I just can't go along with her *apologia* for the troubled life of Mike Tyson, former heavyweight champion and lost soul. Or at least what I see as her defense of the fallen champ.

She answers her own question in a way that discloses her status as a white person:

> . . . but perhaps I am constitutionally incapable of seeing or hearing what you **are** saying. Perhaps it is, as my African American classmates suggest, the myopia that accompanies white skin. This is my limitation, my visual impairment.

And later, responding to, and echoing Jordan's disclosures about encountering the war-like devastation of the neighborhood where Tyson grew up, Eleanor offers her own growing-up story:

> I've never been to Brooklyn and I have not seen war up close and personal. I've never been in combat nor did I grow up in a war zone. I have only seen TV wars. I have not known the ugliness of racism and poverty, and I grew up in a neighborhood where you could buy tulips and ribbons for a girl.[1] . . . And mostly, *I have never been seen as "other"* the way Mike Tyson and June Jordan have. Maybe this is why I cannot see her point; but I can see that she has one. (my emphasis)

Jordan's assertion of a shared identity with Tyson became the catalyst for Eleanor to confront her feminist perspective *with her own whiteness*. I am defining "whiteness" here as a cultural construction of individual and group identity that is associated with the images of race that underpin the structure of our society. The cultural construction of whiteness may be one possible answer to bell hooks' question, "from what political perspective do we dream, look, create, and take action?" (4). In a culturally pluralistic society like America, whiteness does not exist in isolation from non-white cultural constructions such as "blackness"; it must exist in juxtaposition against those other constructions. Whiteness has been a locus of (often abusive) power and privilege for those in society who can claim it and a source of subjugation for those who cannot. Certainly, part of the advantage vested in whiteness lies in its ability to mask its own power and privilege — to render them normative, even invisible, in the minds of most whites, in order to maintain the framework of white supremacy. This dynamic is often painfully visible to those who cannot claim the power and privilege of whiteness.

What June Jordan's essay did for Eleanor, I think, was to force upon her a representation of whiteness that could only be conveyed from the vantage point of Jordan's blackness. The essay's intention and effect were to make uncomfortably visible the taken-for-granted privilege of whiteness, along with its potential to dominate the non-white. It disallowed Eleanor's attempt to claim a "sameness" of perspective with Jordan based on gender solidarity. She responded in her course paper with a set of personal disclosures that certainly cannot be dismissed as merely confessional or self-indulgent, but are in fact essential to the problem of race that Jordan has challenged her to resolve.

The kind of critical engagement exhibited by Eleanor and her classmates at the graduate level has led me to envision the *undergraduate* composition classroom as a place where students can learn strategies for expressing themselves meaningfully within the context of academic discourse. Because first-year and advanced composition courses are a large part of my teaching load, the essayist course enabled me to view authorship issues in student writing in a more focused way. I was particularly able to see that the experiences of my master's-level students, reflected in their class discussions and course papers, displayed important similarities to those of my undergraduate writers. They both seemed to share a strong desire to call upon the resources of their personal lives in order to make sense of their subject matter and to negotiate their stances relative to the conventional demands of academic discourse. While the writing of my master's students was somewhat more proficient, in a technical sense, than that of my undergraduates, the ability to effectively integrate personal stances into academically oriented discussions seemed about the same at both levels.

I further saw that the range of experiences that my undergraduate students—white and non-white, female and male—bring to their classrooms resonates strongly with experiences asserted in the black feminist essays from the seminar. Significant parallels exist between the lives of my students and those of the essayists, in their relationships with spouses/lovers, in their child-rearing responsibilities, in their religious and political affiliations, in their work situations, and in the depth of their community involvement. These students have taken on numerous sophisticated roles, such as parents of children with disabilities, litigants in major lawsuits, career military members, entrepreneurs and businesspeople, and caregivers for relatives with disabilities and catastrophic illnesses. Many of the social, political, and humanistic issues that they expressed a personal stake in resolving in their course papers were the same issues raised by the essayists that my graduate students studied. So whenever I was able to suggest the idea of infusing their school papers with personal stances (using excerpts from essayists to illustrate self-disclosure techniques), my writing students were as attentive as my seminar students. And anxious as well, since few of them felt that they had been given meaningful opportunities to express personal standpoints, and fewer still had been given explicit instruction in how to do so effectively.

What is most memorable about both the professional essayists and my students is what I believe most college writers can be convinced of—that, as Halloran asserts, "the rigor and passion with which they *disclose their world* to the audience, is their *ethos*" (343). Yet I am aware that many composition teachers have considerable difficulty in granting their student writers that *ethos*. Even while assigning compositions they call "essays," these teachers have largely denied to academic writing the essay's invitation to *explicit* personal engagement with its subject matter, viewing most attempts to assert such a personal relationship as incompatible with the critical detachment valued in much disciplinary discourse. I've heard teachers routinely insinuate, and sometimes even state outright, the criticism that Kurt Spellmeyer has described, that students are no more than incomplete knowers whose "right to speak must be learned—or perhaps more accurately, earned—through what is essentially the effacement of subjectivity" (265).

Anxiety over the disclosure of personal information has occasionally been expressed in our professional journals. In a *College English* article, for example, Gordon Harvey suggests that the overt "personal" gesture is often construed by academic readers as irrelevant, inconsequential, and counterproductive. He tries to resolve some of that anxiety by considering ways in which academic writing can be "*informed* by personal experience without injecting personal *information*" (649). Such a dance around the embodied self may well be based on an assumption that one's subjectivity is an element separate from the world being written about, and — especially when expressed through personal disclosures — somehow interferes with clear, logical, critical thinking. However, I am concerned that this attitude can hinder efforts of student writers to integrate disciplinary knowledge with other aspects of their lives, in order to define themselves as distinctive intellectual agents in academic and professional situations and thereby locate meaningful vantage points from which to interpret and apply the information they are learning. Such wholesale dismissal of college students' capability to assert credible knowledge created through placing one's knowledge about a subject within the framework of one's life experiences, which is reflected in the rather cynical teacherly question, "What do *students* know?" perverts the powerfully heuristic question, *Que sais je?* — what do *I* know? — that has driven the development of the essay genre from the time of Montaigne.

Harvey seems to reduce the territory of personal disclosure, advocated mainly by feminist theorists and scholars of the familiar essay, to narrative and autobiography motivated by a desire to make the public voice of academic discourse more connected with lived experience and empathetic to others, less abstract, and less competitive. In Harvey's view, the impulse toward personal disclosure, so defined, often produces bad writing by both college students and professional academic writers. He cites, in particular, the difficulty of contextualizing close analysis of primary texts with personal report; the analytical and the personal (which he admits is an arbitrary distinction), when treated as separate entities, are much like oil and water for most of his student writers.

> The students devote their energy to finding whatever personal connections they can, not to wrestling the issues out of the text or finding things to say besides summaries and platitudes. For students who can't yet manage an extended development of an idea in a "linear" fashion, the invitation to jump back and forth is added disincentive to extending thinking. The textual and the personal sections, sometimes jarringly different in style, are only very roughly stitched together — prompting one teacher I know to call these "Frankenstein" papers. But the assignment also provides an excuse to avoid even the more basic work of focusing closely and describing accurately. The picture given of the text in these essays is distorted, reductive, fudged to fit. (645)

Key for me in this statement is that students are often, at least implicitly, invited to invoke the personal, but not given any explicit rhetorical insight regarding its effective use. Jumping back and forth between personal and analytical is, as even Harvey later acknowledges, arbitrary. That the personal can be analytical, that the analytical can be usefully located from a personal vantage point, seems impossible not only for the student writer to manage but for the teacher to work from as well.

The idea that the essay might be faulted for being "personal" in the ways advanced by Harvey might be attributed, at least in part, to critics' reliance on the notion that identities are the private property of the individuals — as Celia Kitzinger asserts, "freely created products of introspection or the unproblematic reflections of the private sanctum of the 'inner self'" (82). The questionable relevance of the "personal" may stem from viewing the essay's subjectivity as an element separate from the world being written about that can cloud or detract from that world. From this perspective, the "personal" gesture is often construed as irrelevant, inconsequential, and counterproductive, as Harvey suggests. However, looking at the personal dimension from the perspective of black feminist writers, for example, can show how subjectivity is indeed inseparable from the world of ideas — from their interpretation and analysis — and thus essential for ideas to be properly developed by writers and understood by readers.

The problems that Harvey has encountered in many student compositions certainly should not be discounted. Engaging the overt personal gesture is indeed a strategy mishandled in much student writing. Many would agree, I think, that we would like students to go beyond writing that is personal, as Wendell Harris would say, "merely by virtue of narrating a personal experience" (941). Harvey does have an answer, in terms of his concept of "presence" that incorporates, among other things, a sense of motive or why a text needs writing; a development that allows the writer to explore and shape a topic as ideas dictate rather than as a thesis-plus-three ideas formula; use of details such as original metaphors, non-academic analogies; opening up larger questions and issues; and elaborating on reasons for judgments (651–53).

However, I disagree with Harvey's attempt to render *embodied* writers invisible — particularly student writers who, in his eyes, merely "drag in their personal experiences" or allow personal narrative to "infiltrate" traditional academic analysis. I am convinced that significant problems arise with student writing precisely when they have not defined and located themselves as effectively self-authorized knowers for their evaluative audiences. The problem I identify in much personal writing by students is a lack of skill in articulating a self that genuinely contributes to the rhetorical power of their compositions. But identifying a student's lack of skill in this area does not invalidate the *concept* of personal engagement of his or her subject matter as a potentially powerful strategy, which is what I believe happens too often. Dismissing the self-disclosure strategies themselves because students have not yet mastered those strategies seems senseless if the strategies are not being taught to them in the first place. The problematic *ethos* of student writers, which often seems to trigger their instructors' denial of their right to ask (heuristically) and then answer the question "what do I know" from all of their intellectual resources, strongly resonates with the struggle of many African American women writers to do the same. It is this connection between these two groups that allows me, as a composition instructor, to investigate how black feminist essayists attempt to solve the problematic, described by Cornel West, of "present[ing] themselves to themselves and others as complex human beings" (102), and to investigate what students might learn from studying their essays.

Pamela Klass Mittlefehldt's work provides considerable insight on issues involved in the construction of self-identity that black feminist writers typically bring to the essay form. For Mittlefehldt, the essay's focus on the author's voice, the visible process of contemplation, its grounding in particular experience, the reconsideration of and resistance to the orthodox, "make it a useful genre for Black feminists who are writing to change their worlds" (198). The essay's rhetorical edge, rather than the dispassionate contemplation that has characterized Western male essay traditions, is the attraction for black feminist writers. Essays by black feminist writers deal with the dynamic of social identity in provocative ways. Mittlefehldt explains that in the essay, "the author matters intensely. When that author is a black woman, the voice that comes through is one of radical import, for it is a voice that has been traditionally obliterated in Western thought and literature" (198). Having moved from the margins and established a space for their voices by virtue of their success as writers, black women find the essay to be an important space for continually re-forming, re-visioning, and renegotiating personal identity in light of the past and ongoing experiences that shape their lives.

In fact, it becomes even more important for these essayists to allow readers to enter their lives, after they have become more centrally located. Kevin Murray states: "Whereas social identity is a problem for marginal individuals . . . personal identity becomes difficult for people who have achieved a successful moral career to the point where it is hard to distinguish oneself from the official social order" (181). In ways not unlike black women in American society at large, college students constitute a social and cultural category within an institutional hierarchy that includes professors, administrators, support staff, and other members of the college/university community. In light of the diversity of our student populations (in terms of race, ethnicity, class, age, gender/sexual orientation, literacies, and so forth), it is all the more striking that college students, like members of other hierarchies in our society, are subject to the same kinds of invisibility and namelessness.

Black feminist essays teach many possibilities for negotiating self-identity and promoting *ethos* given *the multiple locations from which the authors speak as African American women* (gendered, cultural, economic, generational, spiritual). It is the skillful interweaving of those locations into the subject matter under discussion that allows African American women writers to claim authoritative voices. Two concepts related to this notion of *ethos* are of great import for writing instruction. The first, as expressed by Patricia Hill Collins, concerns the development of an "ethic of personal accountability," wherein individuals place themselves in positions of direct responsibility for their own knowledge claims. For Collins and other black feminist theorists,

> Assessments of an individual's knowledge claims simultaneously evaluate an individual's character, values, and ethics. African Americans reject the Eurocentric, masculinist belief that probing into an individual's personal viewpoint is outside the boundaries of discussion. Rather, all views expressed and actions taken are thought to derive from a central set of core beliefs that cannot be other than personal. . . . Knowledge claims made by individuals respected for their moral and ethical connections to their ideas will carry more weight than those offered by less respected figures. (218)

The second concept is a suggestion that black women's essays can in fact model for student writers those strategies that would enable them to create a distinctive place for themselves in a given discourse community. Mittlefehldt asserts that black women's essays

> . . . are a resistance, a refusal to be silenced, a refusal to be *said*. By telling the stories of their own and other Black women's lives, [the essays] counter the attempts to erase and deny the experiences of Black women in American culture. At the same time, they also challenge the seductive ease of connection by engaging in dialectic tensions of difference. (199)

These two concepts contribute to an understanding of the strategic nature of the essay as a means of knowledge-making grounded in the creation and manifestation of a writerly self. Writing instruction should enable students to recognize the writerly self as a *persuasive instrument* that can be strategically deployed and to learn to make effective use of their own multiple locations to take personal stands on public issues *that transcend the confessional*. A large part of what writing does for people is to help with their personal growth; as writers develop and then read their own work, they place themselves in subject positions relative to their texts and adapt to the role they have laid out for themselves in relation to the subject under discussion. Every text that is produced (in college or elsewhere) contributes to this re-visioning of the self that has been constructed for the writer and includes that self in the social dynamic that is writing. As Stuart Hall asserts:

> we . . . occupy our identities very retrospectively: having produced them, we then know who we are. We say, "Oh that's where I am in relation to this argument and for these reasons." So, it's exactly the reverse of what I think is the common sense way of understanding it, which is that we already know our "self" and then put it out there. Rather, having put it into play in language, we *then* discover what we are. I think that only then do we make an investment in it, saying, "Yes, I like that position, I am that sort of person, I'm willing to occupy that position." (qtd. in Drew 173)

This reciprocal movement between writer and text, I believe, must be as much a part of a writing student's rhetorical education as the movement between writer and reader. Since every text represents a cultural position, drawing texts by African American women into writing instruction may serve to make student writers more keenly aware of how their own (and other) texts are constructing them, so that they can exercise greater influence over the Eurocentric masculinist vantage point that has been promoted as objectivity, even though it reinscribes Eurocentric masculinist scientistic vision and values.

Judicious use of these essays may also avoid another significant danger, articulated in Gesa Kirsch and Joy Ritchie's critique of the essay's invitation to the personal. They charge that the essayistic writing that has become popular in feminist scholarship offers essentialist renderings of a confessional voice leading to more master narratives (8). A sophisticated understanding of self-disclosure as rhetorical strategy can, I believe, be a way out of such a trap. According to Mittlefehldt, "The self that is constructed in [black feminist] essays emerges from the complexity of each writer's personal experiences as a Black woman. It is strikingly apparent that for these women, that self is multi-voiced and in constant dialogue with others" (201). The multi-layered voice of the writing self that speaks in the essays offers new angles of vision, unique juxtapositions of understanding and accountability. There is a passionate sense of connection in these writings, a clear impression that these words are directed towards others and that they invite response. The self that emerges here is one "grounded in a community. . . . It includes a spectrum of relationships, including ancestors, family, Black women, Black people, women, all living beings" (201–02).

The way a writer uses language to describe, report, narrate, or argue actually shapes a particular self-image both for the writer and the readers. This "rhetorical identity"—the presence invested in the text, developed by the writer to accomplish particular persuasive effects in the minds of readers, not only contributes to the writer's authority/credibility but also helps build a mutual relationship to readers as fellow scholars. Effective rhetorical identity defines a textual voice that is at once distinctive and strongly resonant with readers. My essayist course afforded my students a measure of comfort and a greater sense of strategy in developing their own ideas, which I think can be transferred effectively to the undergraduate writing classroom. The results in my courses, in terms of the rhetorical impact of the writing produced, validated for me the claims of Kurt Spellmeyer, W. Ross Winterowd, William Zieger, and other composition scholars, summarized by Janis Forman, that critical reading of and writing essays in composition classes "open up for students ways of knowing that are too often underrepresented in the curriculum — a willingness to value ambiguity, to invent, to suspend closure, to situate the self in multiple and complex ways through discourse" (5).

What do writing teachers need to consider in helping student writers to develop a more sophisticated approach to personal disclosure, with help from black feminist essayists? One approach would be to consider how these essayists can increase our sensitivity to the situational factors that generate a writer's *ethos*, to compare the constraints of school writing with those traditionally imposed upon African American women writers, and ultimately to draw conclusions regarding the contribution of *ethos*, in turn, to the evolution of the essayist and the student writer alike as an intellectual, as a professional communicator, as an enlightened self.

Having seen personal power at work in the essays by black feminist writers that we studied, Eleanor and the other students in my essayist course managed to enhance the rhetorical force of their own writing. They were able to recognize more circumstances that invite writers to invoke personal statements, to use specific kinds of words, images, and signals that construct a personal perspective; to see how distinctions between spiritual and secular, or between blackness and whiteness, can be manipulated for various reasons; and to learn how these discursive actions taken by essayists make considerable difference in how readers think about a given topic. And sometimes, as happened with Eleanor, students followed up on their observations by taking the risk of asserting their writerly selves more explicitly in their papers. Reflecting on Eleanor's project and the rest of that semester's work, I have come to see that the questions and concerns — even complaints — raised in that class regarding self-portrayal and authorization to speak demand closer examination, not only in seminars on the essay, but also in first-year and advanced composition classes, as well as in writing-intensive courses across disciplines, where student writers are struggling for the kind of credibility born out of rhetorically meaningful self-representations, the kind of credibility that these essayists, at their best, were able to achieve.

One important goal of writing instruction, of course, is to help students become effective communicators in academic and professional situations, where the expectations of audiences constrain what and how something should be said. In a society that is so culturally diverse, technologically sophisticated, and hierarchically complex, finding a vantage point, a place to stand, and a locus of authority, respect, influence, and power cannot be ignored as a teachable subject in rhetoric and composition courses. What many student writers seem to long for, even without knowing exactly how to articulate it, is meaningful instruction in using writing to assess, define, and assert who they are becoming as knowing beings. I think these students would find black feminist essayists useful for their ability to reconcile social and personal identities and for directing those identities toward rhetorically useful ends.

Note

1. Here Eleanor is responding to the question posed by Jordan in describing Tyson's desolate environment: "In his neighborhood, where could you buy ribbons for a girl, or tulips?" (223).

Works Cited

Collins, Patricia Hill. *Black Feminist Thought: Knowledge, Consciousness, and the Politics of Empowerment*. New York: Routledge, 1990.

Crowley, Sharon. *A Teacher's Introduction to Deconstruction*. Urbana, IL: NCTE, 1989.

Drew, Julie. "Cultural Composition: Stuart Hall on Ethnicity and the Discursive Turn." *JAC* 18 (1998): 171–96.

Forman, Janis, ed. *What Do I Know: Reading, Writing, and Teaching the Essay*. Portsmouth, NH: Heinemann-Boynton/Cook, 1996.

Halloran, S. Michael. "On the End of Rhetoric, Classical and Modern." *Professing the New Rhetorics: A Sourcebook*. Eds. Theresa Enos and Stuart C. Brown. Englewood Cliffs, NJ: Blair/Prentice, 1994. 331–43.

Harris, Wendell. "Reflections on the Peculiar Status of the Personal Essay." *College English* 58 (1996): 934–53.

Harvey, Gordon. "Presence in the Essay." *College English* 56 (1994): 642–54.

hooks, bell. *Black Looks: Race and Representation*. Boston: South End, 1992.

Jordan, June. "Requiem for the Champ." *Technical Difficulties: African-American Notes on the State of the Union*. Ed. June Jordan. New York: Vintage/Random, 1994. 221–26.

Kirsch, Gesa E., and Joy S. Ritchie. "Beyond the Personal: Theorizing a Politics of Location in Composition Research." *College Composition and Communication* 46 (1995): 7–29.

Kitzinger, Celia. "Liberal Humanism as an Ideology of Social Control: The Regulation of Lesbian Identities." Shotter and Gergen 83–98.

Mittlefehldt, Pamela Klass. "A Weaponry of Choice: Black American Women Writers and the Essay." *Politics of the Essay: Feminist Perspectives*. Eds. Ruth-Ellen Boetcher Joeres and Elizabeth Mittman. Bloomington: Indiana UP, 1993. 196–208.

Morrison, Toni. *Playing in the Dark: Whiteness and the Literary Imagination.* Cambridge, MA: Harvard UP, 1992.
Murray, Kevin. "Construction of Identity in the Narratives of Romance and Comedy." Shotter and Gergen 177–205.
Shotter, John, and Kenneth J. Gergen. *Texts of Identity*. London: Sage, 1989.
Spellmeyer, Kurt. "A Common Ground: The Essay in the Academy." *College English* 51 (1989): 262–76.
West, Cornel. "The New Cultural Politics of Difference." *October* 53 (Summer 1990): 93–109.

Comfort's Insights as a Resource for Your Reflections

1. Comfort offers a pedagogy that tightly braids the personal and the political to improve student writing. How can you realistically ensure that in introducing the personal you do not invite the confessional? What other challenges do you anticipate this pedagogy presenting, and how would you meet them?
2. If you are to introduce this pedagogy or aspects of it, it is crucial to provide students with a variety of solid models to analyze. Discuss with your students how the writer juxtaposes the personal and the public. What other writers or essays would provide a solid model like June Jordan's?
3. How might Comfort respond to the ideas Lisa Delpit set forth earlier in this chapter? Can you delineate a set of points upon which they would agree or disagree? And which side would you take?

Comfort's Insights as a Resource for Your Writing Classroom

1. Comfort's essay offers a powerful tool for teaching students about the bottomless complexity of the idea of "ethos" (the persona or worldview evinced by an author in his or her writing). Try using some of Comfort's ideas in a lesson or series of lessons on ethos.
2. Using essays that explicitly question the dominant culture provides an especially powerful means to enhance students' skills as critical thinkers. Consider how Comfort's use of the Jordan essay in her class might provide a model for your own attempts to enhance students' capacity for critique.

Bi, Butch, and Bar Dyke: Pedagogical Performances of Class, Gender, and Sexuality

Michelle Gibson, Martha Marinara, and Deborah Meem

"We offer [these stories] not as models for teachers, but rather as possibilities for complicating the experience of Otherness in the academy." So concludes this powerful blend of radical theory and personal anecdote about the identities we bring to the academy and that, in various ways, we perform there, in and through and against and among the variety of historical and ideological forces that are also in play. But perhaps this article does, in the end, offer teachers a set of models: What might be illustrated here about the gendered self and the self-as-teacher within the larger context of the institution?

Current theories of radical pedagogy stress the constant undermining, on the part of both professors and students, of fixed essential identities. Trinh Minh-Ha, for example, describes an "Inappropriate/d Other who moves about with always at least two/four gestures: and that of reminding 'I am different' while unsettling every definition of otherness arrived at" (8). Elizabeth Ellsworth applies Minh-Ha's idea to "classroom practices that facilitate such moving about" and the nature of identity that obtains in such classrooms:

> Identity in this sense becomes a vehicle for multiplying and making more complex the subject positions possible, visible, and legitimate at any given historical moment, requiring disruptive changes in the way social technologies of gender, race, ability, and so on define Otherness and use it as a vehicle for subordination. (113)

In the stories that make up this article, we hope to show our own strategies, partial and varied though they are, for disrupting several assumptions that animate the dynamics of the academy: the assumption that the university represents a set of attributes that can be acquired by various Others that will enable them to realize a stereotyped dream of success, the assumption that the process of acquiring such attributes involves jettisoning undesirable traits and associations that the Other has brought with her, the assumption that power in the academy is consistently associated with a predictable and unchanging set of personal characteristics, and the assumption that professor self-presentation must reflect only those "power" characteristics and no other.

Presented as a set of theorized narratives in three voices, this article examines the way three feminist, queer teachers of writing experience and perform their gender, class, and sexual identities. We hope to critique both the academy's tendency to neutralize the political aspects of identity performance and the essentialist identity politics that still inform many academic discussions of gender, class, and sexuality. Through our "stories," we hope to complicate the notion that identities can be performed in clean, organized, distinct ways by examining and theorizing our own experiences of class, gender, and sexual identity performance. We want to acknowledge the conscious ways we perform our multiple subjectivities and to examine our political/economic/pedagogical uses of those performances. In short, we want to move beyond the essentialist act of situating ourselves as scholars authorized to speak about specific issues; we want instead to argue for a kind of universal authorization of discourse. We present these three "papers" as one multivoiced article because the narratives seem to us to be alive both with continuity and with conflict, and we believe that maintaining the integrity of each voice helps highlight its relationship to (and against) the others.

Bi: Playing with Fixed Identities

Late last Friday afternoon, as I do every Friday after work, I stopped at Kroger to pick up groceries for the weekend. I don't like the complication of grocery shopping when I'm hungry and tired and thinking about the paper I'm writing or the assignments I need to put together. On this particular Friday, the juice aisle was blocked by a young woman shopping with her daughter. The little girl, who couldn't have been much more than three, sat in the grocery cart while her mother asked her what kind of juice she wanted. Not an unusual scene, except that there were no limits placed on the child's choices. No "I have a coupon for Ocean Spray Cranapple 64 ounces, the Welch's White Grape Juice is on sale, and the 28-ounce Kroger Apple Juice is two for one, so you can have one of those." It's not that I don't believe in giving children choices, but there are always financial limits to the choices my children can make. And time limits as well. This little girl was reveling in the power of her choices and had already changed her mind three times, each time just as her mother reached for the juice she had asked for. Because I was in a hurry and becoming annoyed, I said, "After you change your mind three times, all the juice disappears." The little girl sat up in the grocery cart seat, looked straight at me for a few long seconds, flexed her little slippered feet, shook out her golden locks, touched her rosy cheek, and said, "Oh, you're one of those people that makes up stories." "Yes," I answered her, "but all my stories come true." I knew she meant the *magic dream princess secret identity riddle treasure* kind of story, not the kind of stories I tell in writing classes. But I had to wonder as I finished my shopping and drove home if the stories I tell don't at least try to serve the same purpose as the mismatched, mistaken identity fairy tale where all the characters figure out who they *really* are by the end, where knowing who they *really* are means they get to live happily ever after. Despite the inability of the storytellers of personal narratives to easily manipulate a happy ending or any ending at all, storytelling is the way we compose our lives; all identity, all social construction, begins with narratives. Although my stories and many fairy tales represent a struggle for identity, the difference between fairy tales and personal narratives comes from autobiography's necessary interplay of fiction and reality, the constant dialogue between an emerging identity and social institutions. My stories are different from fairly tales because they represent people and culture in process; there is no fixed identity, no happily ever after. I have to wonder why if I can feel that pea under my mattress, I'm still eating cold porridge.

The nexus created by the juxtaposition of that uncomfortable pea and the cold porridge illustrates an important connection between autobiography and social critique; the writing of individual lives actively constructs culture and politics by establishing the narrative codes, the parameters of subject and community. Both our cultural context (the cold porridge) and social identity (feeling that hard pea) depend on their reciprocal relationship for structure and definition. The narratives told about social institutions are embedded in or with the narratives of individuals whose lives, whose joys and pains, and whose struggles for survival have been involved with building, manipulating, and rebuilding the cultural context(s) in which they form their social identities. And these identities give us a critical apparatus, one that enables us to reflect on how and why we tell stories and how we use our stories to produce culture.

The stories told by both lesbians and working-class academics help form class consciousness and serve a strategic political purpose. In marking stories "lesbian" or "working class," the lives contained therein are less invisible and give the narrators — students and faculty — a political site from which to speak and act. Playing with the notion of an "essential voice" allows the storytellers to claim a recognizable, politically engaged identity from a narrative that is already academically codified; however "speakable," this politicized voice emerges from a self-empowerment that hinges on an appeal to universalities of class and sexuality, a self-empowerment that depends on binary oppositions. We think we tell stories to illustrate the particular, to demarcate culture as marked and shaped by difference. Claims of universalism have given way to the demands of the particular, but the particulars have their own universalisms. Most lesbian and working-class autobiographies, rather than defying the fixity of identity, merely redraw the boundaries and serve to categorize individual subjects as different from those defined as "straight" and "professional." These stories create a common experience, and the personal narratives suggest that there is something coherently the same about all lesbians, about all working-class persons, and, consequently, something coherently the same about the "straight" or "middle-class" experience that is being resisted. But there are stories that conform to neither category of identification.

Using lesbian and working-class experiences to strive for a political identity is both significant and necessary; I have no wish to deny those voices their political direction. But the communal voice that is created tends to erase the differences within those communities and ignore the complex, intertwined relationship between public and personal narratives. Consequently, writing students — working class or middle class, gay or straight — either embrace or resist the collective voice and often find themselves defending a "real me" that is a mix of essentialist beliefs about good and bad thinking, right and wrong behaviors, and inclusion and exclusion. "Their own" interpretations of social texts tend to be ahistorically driven and grounded in universals. Writing students define "real me" voices as safe, static, inherent, and inviolate; public voices, though, are required to listen to other public voices, and listening can cause uncomfortable changes. The tension, the uncertain space writing teachers and students find between the familiar, "real me" voice and an emerging public voice should not necessarily be resolved with already codified positions; rather, the tension should be a space to work from and with because the language of any personal narrative contests static identities. Defining the personal, the "real me" as the product of an individual (but universally human) psyche would construct rhetorical studies as insular and drained of political content, ideological analysis, and intellectual rigor (the tools necessary to understand and change social hierarchies and cultural institutions). In parallel fashion, recognizing identity as grounded or fixed in particular political locations negates the possibility for inter-reference between any two narrative landscapes. Because the formation of any story is not fixed within some individual identity or within an established public position — but rather is formed among competing public and private voices — identity, the writer's story and voice, includes the writer's shifting relationships with the peculiarities of our culture.

Despite the complexities of self-construction, the dependence of cultural identity on a dualistic system of thought makes it impossible for me to come out of the closet; when one can be "straight" and "lesbian" simultaneously, one doesn't get an already codified, easily recognizable closet narrative. In this case, difference is more than a presence; it is a pressure that acts constantly, if unevenly, along the boundaries constructed by "straight" and "lesbian" narratives. This pressure promises heterosexual protection with its already disclosed rules of social recognition while still shifting the contours of sexuality and desire. Bisexuality, defined as an incomplete dominance of either sexual trait, defies easy social categorization; it is an identity without visible rules, almost without referent.

Because a politically productive identity demands a culturally recognizable political self (or at least someone who can make up her mind), the closet story I live in is without a collective identity. Entangled in the dynamics of difference, my public identity as both lesbian and straight is as conflicted as my private identity. In a similar fashion, no one can be both professional and working class; so one's "new" identity is perceived as a positive step up, a successful crossing of class barriers. The resulting narrative reflects the American Dream, the "rags to riches" story, and *The Little Engine That Could*. In these narratives, "working class" has a transient quality, and a successful performance makes the previous identity go away. Those are the fairy tales; the reality is an identity that never quite fits, is never quite comfortable, authentic, or believable. The politics of the professional narrative promises the dream of the street, but cannot carry with it the drama of labor, cannot live back in the neighborhood.

Recently, back for a short visit to the neighborhood where I lived most of my adult life, I found myself sitting in my sister's kitchen at 6:30 on a Saturday morning wishing someone else — anyone else who could figure out her new coffeemaker — would wake up. I decided finally to walk the seven blocks up Putnam Avenue to the market where I worked for the eight years it took me to finish my undergraduate degree. I knew the Faricellis would have hot coffee. When I walked in the back door, Mace (the produce manager) looked at me and said, "So Marta, what are ya' dreamin'? Bring in the newspapers and the hard rolls." The hard rolls weren't on the back porch and that resulted in an argument I had listened to every morning as Patrice and Johnny the butcher yelled back and forth in a mixture of English and Italian. This particular argument started with the missing hard rolls and escalated to the conflicts between genders. I found the whole scene amusing and comfortable.

The comfortable feeling I recognized even before I finished making the coffee — I knew what to expect here, what I could safely say, and what would get me in trouble. (And I knew how to work the coffeemaker.) The amusement came from a different space. I could now observe them from a distance, an educated distance that kept me from being a part of or really caring about their argument, a distance that in fact made it possible for me to analyze the argument and realize why Patrice always won. Before I left the market for one final time, more final than the last time I left, I collected hugs and kisses, heard "we're so proud of you" and "don't be a stranger." I promised I wouldn't, but I knew I already was, because if I had made the kind of success the Faricellis could understand an autographed photo of me shaking Johnny's hand would be hung up on the wall behind the deli counter and I'd be able to order filet, large shrimp, casaba melons, and asparagus like their successful customers. So, there's that uncomfortable pea, planted under my mattress the minute I went back to college. I can talk or write about my working-class past, but I no longer live in it. I have no *real* identity there, and I have no *real* identity in the professional class; I only have the dream.

The dream state makes one unable to belong to a particular social identity because the lack of authenticity, however problematic the concept, makes one's class, as well as one's sexual orientation, invisible. I once had a student who, when angered by the text we were discussing, loudly proclaimed, "I don't believe in lesbians." There I stood, feeling like Tinker Bell as her life breath slipped away and her little twinkling light faded from sight, hoping that some child somewhere could proclaim, "I do. I do believe in fairies" and clap his or her hands so I could continue to live. I asked my students to clap for me, but most of them just appeared confused or thought I was joking and with good reason: I'm not lesbian by every definition and certainly not by the definitions of students who cling to the sexual stereotypes that construct their worlds. I don't look like a dyke and I have two children. Caught in the tension between individual desires and communal cohesion, the flux of my identity resists the established parameters of subjectivity and community. This rebellious identity really is a matter of both believing and resisting, but it can't be shaped by the clapping of hands.

What it can be shaped by is exploring the differences within difference and welcoming the friction that an animated identity represents. This difference undermines the very idea of identity and becomes a conflicted, but productive, space in which signifiers and codes of cultural representation are questioned. The space created by opening up identity allows for a more open-ended model of collective identity and poses hard questions about the nature and definitions of political subject positions as one is both enlarged and oppressed by constantly shifting alliances. In the classroom, this space lies in the often tense relationship between students' experiences and what they are learning in class. In the same class where I felt like Tinker Bell, the students who hadn't dropped the class were reading and discussing a poem by David Budbill, "Roy McInnes." At one point the narrator of the poem states, "When you shake his hand his grip is warm and gentle / and you can feel the calm he carries in his person / flow into your arm" (14–16). Questioning what Budbill might have meant by writing these lines resulted in a discussion about whether or not the narrator was "male" or "female." Most of the class finally decided the character was female because "men," real or fictive, "don't shake hands with each other like that." For most students who lack different cultural experiences, the question of physicality is always a question of sexuality, especially female sexuality. I thought at first that I would merely offer the definitions of the difference between *affection* and *sexual desire*, but the three pairs of eyes from the three lesbians in the class challenged me: "You're one of us, Dr. Marinara. Don't cop out on us." So, instead, knowing those differences are not as acute as social mores would like us to believe, I asked the students to blur the emotional differences between affection and sex, sexuality and physicality. We began the discussion by making a list on the board of those people in our lives whom we "touch warmly," for whom we feel a deep emotional, almost electric bond. We put the "same sex" experiences, the hugging of friends and relatives, in a separate column. I mentioned not being able to keep my hands off my children, how burying my face in my younger daughter's hair and smelling her sun-warmed scalp is a sensual experience, an affection that cannot be divorced from the physical experience of touching. Others shared their experiences of enjoying the touch of warm fingers, the smell of soft skin. Somewhere along the way, most of the class agreed that it is physically satisfying, not just emotionally satisfying, to hug our friends. The class left that day with no clear definitions, with a narrator whose gender and sexuality couldn't be determined, whose physical affection could not be wholly separated from sexuality or sensuality, a narrator who had to speak from difference.

The "About the Author" page inserted at the end of my dissertation reflects my difference from the academy, as does the epigraph I chose for the beginning. My dissertation opens with a few bars of Bruce Springsteen's "Thunder Road" and ends with my life up until that point. My story of singing with a rock band; hitching cross-country with my best friend Rachel; working for Dunkin' Donuts, Baskin-Robbins, and the Whitneyville Market; giving birth to one daughter and adopting another overwhelms the last line about receiving graduate degrees. I think I "got away" with this because I was expected to put those experiences in the past and behave like a professional from then on.

My students also feel the pressure to give up something about their lives in order to take on the new, professional roles or careers they are trying so hard to achieve. What makes this giving up so difficult is the fact that most of our cultural texts have been shaped by persistent binaries: working class/professional class, heterosexual/homosexual, college preparation/vocational. Choosing a subject position seems to entail resisting a previous position or identity. Like many writing faculty who want their classrooms to be a "contact zone" where students can reflect on and negotiate identities within different cultural perspectives, I find telling stories of living with an identity that moves in and out of centers of power and combines often conflicting identities to be a useful pedagogical tool.

I tell stories to explain my feminist position, a position that was shaped by my working-class life: When I was in my late twenties, I worked the graveyard shift at Dunkin' Donuts. One night a customer leaned over the counter and bit my cheek because, as he explained, my earrings looked like fishing lures. The other customers, all male including two police officers who were drinking their "free" coffee at the end of the counter, laughed as if this were the funniest thing they'd ever heard (and sadly enough, it probably was). There was nothing I could do at that point, no possible resistance except for serving him regular coffee instead of decaffeinated and the stalest donut I could find. I've told my students about the boss I had when I was a waitress (and I'm purposefully saying waitress rather than waitstaff because I think there is a difference) who every day offered me $100 not to wear a bra to work. I needed that job, so every day I said, "For $300, I might consider it." Some of my students will tell me that this was sexual harassment; they can't believe someone who changes every "mankind" in their papers to "humankind" would have put up with it. We talk about the sexual harassment lawsuits that make it to *Court TV*. They are all high-profile cases, and the women involved are most always professionals, women with some power, women who are not working class. For many working-class women, sexual harassment is just another unfortunate part of the workday.

Sexual harassment, under the guise of the inability to work with difference, is still a part of my everyday life. Last quarter I taught an advanced composition class in which most of the students were planning careers in education, most of the students were non-traditional, and all of the students were female. Toward the end of the quarter, the classroom had become a comfortable working environment, and the students had developed an open, tolerant way of speaking about and sharing their differences from one another as they worked out problems in their essays. I was unprepared for what happened the day we were to discuss Adrienne Rich's "When We Dead Awaken: Writing as Re-Vision." A large percentage of the students couldn't or wouldn't work with Rich's theories, life, or poetry because she is lesbian. I never thought that a class whose inside joke was "you don't need a penis to do that" would be so threatened by a woman who theoretically in language and materially in her life and politics resisted and then rejected penises altogether. Threatened by Rich's collective "we," the women in the class felt compelled to take a position that resisted Rich's inclusive definition of "lesbian." But the term "lesbian" for Rich referred to "nothing so simple and dismissible as the fact that two women might go to bed together." I had made the mistake of becoming too comfortable with this class; by enjoying what made us all the same, I had forgotten how different I am from many women. When one of the students said, "Maybe we shouldn't talk about this. There aren't any of *them* in here, are there?" fear almost kept me silent. But instead I did what I've always done when I've felt harassed or threatened. I used sarcasm: "Let's check and see who has 'lesbian' tattooed on their butt." I told them that I did and talked about how my life causes me to read Rich's essay in ways that were different from their readings, in ways that found her language intellectually stimulating rather than threatening. We moved into a discussion about how our lives shape our theoretical positions and how theoretical positions shape our lives and politics. But for the most part the class was silent. The journal entries I received, however, were plenty loud:

> Rich tried to justify her actions by blaming culture and men, rather than acknowledging her own problems with sex.
>
> Rich's unhappiness is innate and she shouldn't point a finger at outside forces or the cultural environment.
>
> Rich's "awakened" way of life was degrading in the 70s and is now as well.

And, of course, I had to read an awful lot of quasi-biblical, Christian with a capital *C* rhetoric as well. Most of the class completely missed out on Rich's insistence on feminine language, a language that begins with "the act of looking back, of seeing with fresh eyes, of entering an old text from a new critical direction" (467), and moves on to "renaming." No longer willing to share my life, I answered their journal entries with academic, theoretical arguments, something useful I had learned in graduate school.

The last piece we discussed in this class was Joyce Carol Oates's short story "Theft." The class was still, for the most part, and silent. But one student brought up the question of Marya's denial of her lesbian sexuality as contributing to the stresses that made her steal, an interpretation that had in previous classes remained invisible. A few students were even willing to discuss Marya's love for Imogene and found a place for this love within other cultural stories of attraction and betrayal. Several passages where Marya describes Imogene or watches Imogene walk across campus were used to highlight this interpretation. I brought up the question of difference between the heterosexual relationships in the story and Marya's and Imogene's relationship, and some of the class discussed how the best friendships can survive sometimes blurred sexual boundaries and changing roles. A very small triumph to be sure, but the stories of teaching writing are fed by such successes, by the little workings with difference.

Differences between identities that are comprehended as absolute stifle the multiplicity of difference. The controlled dramatic or dynamic quality of a teacher's flexible identity as a bisexual and working-class academic can accommodate both an understanding of the necessity for an essential, collective consciousness to engage political issues and the equally compelling need to continually question this political identity. Keeping identity from becoming "fixed" leaves room to construct other useful political positions, still more "Other" places from which to speak. Increasing our understanding of those who tell stories from the social margins means exploring contradictions — the changing shapes of difference — so we can locate ourselves within/as the process of negotiating class and sexuality.

Butch: Personal Pedagogy and the Butch Body

In the late 1980s, I participated in a seminar series designed to help faculty members trained in traditional disciplines "retool" (a decidedly non-feminist word choice) with a view toward teaching interdisciplinary women's studies courses. There for the first time I encountered a chart (which I now know to be commonly used in introductory women's studies classes and elsewhere) outlining two areas: (1) some of an individual's multiple identities and (2) the relative experience of privilege associated with each. Through positioning myself on this chart, I was able to articulate to myself for the first time some of the ways I partake of unearned privilege: through my whiteness, through my family's adequate middle-class income, through access to education and other entranceways into a lifetime of status and financial security. At the same time, I was able to see how two specific aspects of my identity operated to deny me privilege: my femaleness and my lesbianism. (For the moment I'll ignore the butch aspect of my lesbian identity.) I began to understand how I occupy both the center and the margins of American society.

I focus on the implications of my identity presentation for my personal pedagogy and my collegial experience in the academy. I argue that many issues of diversity are so fully embodied that they cannot be meaningfully discussed, but rather exist primarily in the realm of performance. I believe that in my writing classrooms, the kind of multicultural consciousness I hope to encourage can arise at least as much from my own performance of (multiple) personal identities as from *Life Studies, Living in America, Writing About Diversity* or any other anthology. And I believe that in my interactions with colleagues, strange and (sometimes) wonderful transformations frequently take place at a visceral, not an intellectual, level. Don't get me wrong: I don't preach, and I don't act. But I have observed, for instance, that my femaleness, complicated both by a butch self-presentation and by the fact that I have children my students' ages, leads students and colleagues to react to me in ways that indicate their (not fully conscious) awareness of multiple, incongruent identities.

I suppose I should begin by pinning down what I mean by the word "butch." In lesbian parlance, the terms butch and femme refer to "qualities that exert a mutual attraction" related to stereotypical notions of masculinity and femininity (Laporte 210); the butch is "a lesbian whose self-identity takes on aspects of the traditionally 'masculine'" (Tracey and Pokorny 12). In the early twentieth century, the butch was seen as a "mannish lesbian," an invert, containing the soul of a man in a woman's body. By mid-century, butch and femme "roles" organized working-class lesbian bar culture, even to the extent that, as Elizabeth Kennedy and Madeline Davis have written, "For many women, their identity was in fact butch or fem, rather than gay or lesbian" (5). The lesbian-feminists of the 1970s rejected the butch/femme binary because they felt that rigid same-sex gender roles replicated the oppressive sexism of the larger society. What they forgot was that the very rigidity of butch/femme roles had given lesbians much-needed visibility in the years after World War II. After a decade underground, butch/femme reemerged as a form of "lesbian erotic identity" (Nestle 14) during the "lesbian sex wars" of the 1980s. As Arlene Stein puts it, "Eighties butch-femme — if it can accurately be termed such — is a self-conscious aesthetic that plays with style and power, rather than an embracing of one's 'true' nature against the constraints of straight society" (434–35).

Today, in the era of lesbian chic, butch is a woman's performance of the stereotypically masculine.

In connecting my own butch gender performance with my experience as an academic, I want to tell three stories. The first took place in the late 1980s, when I coordinated an ongoing study of computers and basic writers. In gathering data, we ended up with some intriguing results that didn't fit anywhere in our stated purpose. Seven faculty took part in the study, three men and four women; over a period of four and a half years, the seven of us taught developmental writing to over 1,000 student participants. Every student completed a standard course evaluation at the end of the quarter. On a whim, we looked at the evaluation results by professor's sex and found that, taken together as a group, the three men averaged higher ratings in *instrumental* categories (knowledge, fairness) while the four women as a group averaged higher ratings in *affective* categories (helpfulness, availability). This result was, of course, the expected trend based on the research. But when we compared the four women with one another, we found another trend: Two of the women received much higher affective than instrumental scores while the other two (myself and another woman) had instrumental scores as high as the men's and affective scores just slightly lower than those of the other two women's. We theorized at the time that this result was obtained because the two of us women who scored high in instrumental categories are more butch than the other two women, who are more traditionally feminine. We considered having all seven faculty participants take the Bem Sex-Role Inventory test and actually measure the degree of (stereotypical) masculinity and femininity that each of us projects. We didn't do it, because we had enough on our hands just analyzing the data that pertained to the computer study, but now I wish we had. I suspect that the two butches would have scored high in masculine traits, which might very well have explained the difference in how our students reacted to us.

The second story is a coming-out story. In October 1994 I received a phone call from Jay Schatz, a TV reporter for Cincinnati's Channel 12 news, asking me to be a "sample dyke at work" for a feature timed to coincide with National Coming-Out Day. We arranged that he would film me in my writing class the next morning; I requested that he not arrive until half past the hour because I had not yet come out to the students in that class and needed some time to get past that sometimes thorny moment. When class began the next day, I launched into my coming-out speech: "Channel 12 is doing a feature on lesbians and gay men at work, and since I'm a lesbian and this is my work, they are coming to film us. If any of you prefer not to be shown on TV, let me know, because they'll be here any minute." There was a beat of silence, that moment of dysphoria every queer experiences every time we come out. Then a young man sitting near me pulled off his baseball cap, ran his fingers through his hair, and said, "How do I look?" Everyone laughed and the filming went off without incident. The point is that my coming out surprised no one, because, as Kristin Esterburg writes, in all areas "the coding of lesbians as not feminine *and therefore in some way masculine* predominate[s]" (276). As a butch or masculine woman, I project a "lesbian" persona without formally coming out.

The third story tells of my relationship to a (certain type of) male colleague. I should explain that I have been at the University of Cincinnati for sixteen years and am now a full professor. As such I have been involved in college and departmental policy planning, especially in the area of reappointment, promotion, and tenure (RPT). Since 1990 I have chaired two major college committees, one on the evaluation of teaching and the other on the revision of the college RPT guidelines. In the fall of 1997, I served for one quarter as acting academic dean of the college, a position I did not seek and agreed to fill only until a full-time person could be hired. That said, my story begins with the RPT guidelines committee during 1996–97. As chair, I was already struggling with a number of difficult personalities on the committee (you know them, I'm sure: the prima donna, the whiner, the obstructionist) and trying to keep the group on task and at least a little bit focused. On this committee was a man I'll call Professor Bluster, who at the time was recently tenured and also serving as chair of the committee that reviews promotion and tenure dossiers at the college level. In the few months that he had chaired that committee, he had done such a lousy job that faculty members throughout the college were calling for the elimination of the entire committee. Nevertheless, Professor Bluster thought he knew everything about how academic units should govern themselves, and he made it abundantly clear to the guidelines committee that he intended to tell us what we needed to know, while of course never volunteering for any of the real grunt work. My strategy for dealing with him was simply to allow him to say his piece, do a quick read of how the rest of the committee felt about it, then either bring his idea up for a quick decision or thank him for sharing and move on. He never protested openly, and the committee concluded its work in timely fashion. Later that year, however, I heard from another colleague that Professor Bluster had cornered her in her office and complained, "That Deb Meem — she's so bossy!" Here again I suspect it's my butchness that troubled Professor Bluster. Had I been a man, he would not have hesitated to bring all committee work to a halt in order to engage in a pissing contest with me. As a butch woman, however, I had a certain power over him; he clearly perceived me as being immune to male feather-ruffling and intimidation. In other words, his usual strategies for getting attention were useless, and all he could do was call me bossy later on.

These three stories illustrate how my butch performance (and I use that word hoping you will attend to the difference between, say *dramatic* performance and *embodied* performance) impacts my various interactions in the academy. Because I am butch, I am visible as a lesbian, I am often asked, for instance, to be the "token dyke" on campus. Students come out to me, or ask me for advice; colleagues want to discuss queer issues with me, or include me on a panel. These responses, plus those from my three stories, indicate that students and faculty see my butchness as powerful, especially as contrasted with femme experience, which is mostly invisible. The power of butch performance seems to me to derive from what I described earlier as "multiple, incongruent identities." I do not see butch as an "identity" per se (although in some ways I could be said always to have been butch, from earliest childhood through marriage to a man to now), but rather as a chosen gender performance. I agree with Patti Smith, who said, "As far as I can tell, being any gender is a drag" (Stein 378, epigram). Judith Butler picks up on this idea: "If gender is drag . . . then gender is a performance that *produces* the illusion of an inner sex or essence or psychic gender core; it *produces* on the skin, through the gesture, the move, the gait (that array of corporeal theatrics understood as gender presentation), the illusion of an inner depth" ("Imitation" 28). What she is saying here is that butch drag looks like, and may even be experienced as, a "psychic gender core." But this essence is far more complex than "what you see is what you get," that is, a woman dressing like a man and appropriating not only the outward signs, but also some of the power and influence, of masculinity. Butler is helpful here again: "the 'identification' with masculinity that appears as butch identity is not a simple assimilation of lesbianism back into the terms of heterosexuality" because "in both butch and femme identities, the very notion of an original or natural identity is put into question" (*Gender Trouble* 156, 157).

This idea of multiple or confusing, simultaneous identities brings me back to the chart I mentioned (Figure 1).[1] Those of you who are familiar with this chart as it appears in women's studies texts will recognize that I have added butch and femme in the "privileged" (top line) and "oppressed" (second line) positions, respectively. As I circle my various identity categories, I notice that I am "privileged" 5 to 4. Right away this complicates the assumption that as a woman and a lesbian, I am uniformly oppressed in the academy. Further, when the identity category "butch" is figured as powerful (as my three stories have shown it can be), even lesbianism can be reconceptualized. In short, these categories must be seen as fluid. Butch was an oppressed identity in the 1950s specifically because butch lesbians were visible and, therefore, targets for harassment, discrimination, and violence. Femme lesbians, precisely because they were *invisible*, had greater access to jobs and relative immunity from harassment (at least, from harassment based on their lesbianism; as women they were just as vulnerable as their straight sisters). Today, however, butch visibility in the academy can provide access to a certain kind of power; the relative invisibility of femmes makes it difficult for them to connect with sources of lesbian community in or out of the academy. Experiences of relative privilege and oppression thus resist consistency.

Figure 1. Multiple, Simultaneous Identities

Male	Middle Class	Heterosexual	White	Young, Middle-Aged	Able-Bodied	Thin	Christian	Butch
Female	Working Class	Lesbian, Gay	Of Color	Old	Disabled	Fat	Non-Christian	Femme
	Impoverished	Bisexual, Trans-Gendered						

Continuing this line of reasoning, I am also led to observe that the very existence of the chart and the commonness of its usage in the academy tend to privilege its "oppressed" categories. Let me tell one final story. I am a member of a listserv for lesbian academics, and recently I "lurked" the list during a discussion of the possible connection between childhood sexual abuse and adult lesbian identity that turned into a flame-throwing exchange about elitism and privilege. The principal flamer is a woman in her final year of graduate school who claims that her identities as working class, Latina, and butch lesbian operate together to deny her privilege in the academy. While I would not venture to claim that she has never been denied privilege on account of her multiple "second row" identities, I would propose that those identities also privilege her, since, as Diana Fuss writes, "in the classroom [and, I would add, in the academy in general] identities are nothing if not commodities" (115). The flamer's chief error is assuming that identity categories are fixed, both in themselves and in the experience of privilege or oppression attached to them. The concept of strategic essentialism holds that an oppressed group may claim its identity as an essence for the purpose of gaining political power — that, for instance, lesbian and gay activists may plead, "We were born this way; we've always been this way; it's not our fault; don't discriminate against us." I see the flamer as adopting a strategic essentialist stance in order to stake out a space for herself as oppressed, and therefore deserving of at least recognition and at most reparations. Fuss acknowledges the utility of this practice, but insists that we in the academy need to interrogate identity and its uses; "we need," she writes, "both to theorize essentialist spaces from which to speak and, simultaneously, to deconstruct these spaces to keep them from solidifying" (118). If it is true, as Judith Butler says, that fixed "identity categories tend to be instruments of regulatory regimes" ("Imitation" 13), then complicating our own multiple identities is a revolutionary act. The stories I have told here have been intended to problematize the simplistic identity schematic represented by the chart. In my classes, in my college, and in the world, I will insist on owning, and performing, all of my incongruent identities; I'll continue being the butch with kids.

Bar Dyke: A Cocktail Waitress Teaches Writing

In *Poisoned Ivy: Lesbian and Gay Academics Confronting Homophobia*, Toni McNaron argues that "remembering one's past . . . constitutes a radical political action. For those of us who have been told, overtly or subtly, that our existence is not quite valid, insisting on having and shaping memories into coherent form constitutes disobedience on a personal level and destabilization on a cultural level" (8). To my mind, McNaron's argument can be taken even a step further. In an academic climate where postmodern theories that focus on the performative nature of identity prevail, political action necessitates not only giving voice to but also performing memory, especially as it relates to the construction of identity. Many academics have memories that can challenge traditional beliefs about who is willing and able to function effectively in the academy, as well as about what it *means* to function effectively in the academy. Those memories help construct nontraditional academic identities that, if performed fully and openly, can deconstruct notions about who university students and faculty are and force the academy to respond more fully to the needs of diverse populations.

One way I make my identities overt is to think like a constructivist but act like an essentialist. Whenever a circumstance allows for it, I perform my identities as a femme lesbian, a survivor of family violence, and a recovering mental patient. One such circumstance arises every couple of years. At the University of Cincinnati, faculty who wish to be reappointed, promoted, or tenured are required to submit dossiers of their work. These dossiers contain evidence of achievement in three areas — professional activity, service, and teaching — as well as self-evaluation statements for each area. The dossier goes through several levels of evaluation, one of which is performed by a college-wide committee. A few years ago, when I was being evaluated for reappointment, that committee returned my dossier to me, saying that while they felt that my work in each of the areas clearly exceeded expectations, they were "disquieted" by my self-evaluation statements. Specifically, the committee believed that I identify too strongly with students and that I should not admit in a professional document that I did not follow a traditional academic path. They suggested that I remove references to my work as a cocktail waitress, refrain from discussing my connections to students who are unfamiliar with academic expectations, and "write tweed" (their phrase).

The return of my dossier with these suggestions reminded me that, though many academics talk about diversity, the academy itself persists in seeing the university as tweed: white, middle class, and heterosexual. This mentality is exactly the mentality that many of my peers in composition studies and I try to subvert when we insist upon speaking our memories and performing our diverse and multifaceted identities. Our colleagues, though, don't always share our enthusiasm for experiential data. For instance, in *Sexing the Self*, sociologist Elspeth Probyn says that when she revealed in an article about anorexia that she was anorexic, a reviewer responded with criticism, arguing that the problem with "postmodern America [is that] the natives are now writing their own ethnography" (12). So when my colleagues on the college committee read my dossier they were responding not only to their individual discomfort with what I had written but also to the disjuncture between my values and the values they have learned as participants in their own academic disciplines.

Here is one of the passages the committee found problematic:

> I do not have a traditional academic background, and I believe that is one of my greatest strengths as a University College faculty member. I just barely graduated from high school, then I muddled around working as a cocktail waitress, selling cars, peddling insurance door-to-door, and living what could be called an aimless existence before I met someone who suggested that I attend college. Only because the "college life" seemed more inviting than the life I had been leading, I began attending a two-year college in my hometown. Then, only because I actually graduated from Hutchinson Community College and someone else suggested that I go on to get my bachelor's degree, I went to a four-year college in Maryland. Then, only because I didn't know what kind of a job I could get with a bachelor's degree in English and someone else suggested that I go to graduate school. I went to Ohio University to get my graduate degrees.

What probably stands out most about this statement is how benign and understated it is. When I wrote this passage I really didn't think much of it. In fact, I was a bit concerned that I had said too little in my general self-evaluation. What seemed as clear to me as what I had said was what I had not said. For instance, even though I was extremely tempted, I didn't write about the fact that the work I did as a cocktail waitress was done at a lesbian bar known for its girl drag shows and for its drag team, which was named for the Village People's song, "Macho Man." I didn't talk about the fact that I believe I got quite a bit of training for being a teacher and running a classroom from my experiences as the emcee for those drag shows, from "working a room." I didn't say that, as emcee, I put my rhetorical skills to great use when I wrote lewd, rhyming introductions for the drag "kings," as we called them. In short, while I knew when I wrote that passage that I was confronting some traditional beliefs about who becomes an academic, my awareness of what I left out of it led me to believe that it was pretty mundane.

And, when a representative of the College Reappointment, Promotion, and Tenure Committee (let's call her Dr. Gatekeeper) called me to set up a meeting to discuss my dossier, I had no idea that she might want to discuss this passage. However, what she told me was that this passage was particularly troubling to the committee, whose members believed it "dangerous" to my professional well-being. She explained that a candidate for reappointment must appear to be "as much like upper-level administrators as possible." The committee, she informed me, was interested in and engaged by my self-evaluation statements, but they believed them "artless" in the sense that passages such as the one above make me sound as if I misunderstand the nature of the university. She said that references to work experience such as cocktail waitressing and admissions that both my existence before I started college and my college career were "aimless" would make me seem to the provost and his peers as if I were not worthy of membership in the academic community.

Had I been more prepared for this kind of reading of my dossier, I might have told Dr. Gatekeeper that Diana Fuss says, "Personal consciousness, individual oppressions, lived experience . . . operate . . . both to authorize and to de-authorize speech" (113). I might have explained that my experience of the academy, both as a student and as a faculty member, had led me to believe that many of my identities — particularly those like the ones I discuss in my self-evaluation statement — are just what Dr. Gatekeeper's comments indicated they are: unauthorized. I might have said that in the four years I spent as an undergraduate I had almost never read any piece of literature that was at all related to my experiences as a lesbian or as a survivor of family violence and institutionalization. I remember no more than two instances in which my teachers discussed issues related to lesbians or represented family life in a way that I recognized. Even in my Psychology of Women course there was no mention of lesbianism, and I was the only person who broached the subject of family violence. In short, my experience was de-authorized not by denial but by silence.

As a faculty member working from a position of relative power, then, I feel a great need to authorize those experiences by giving them voice and by performing them. However, Dr. Gatekeeper's goals (and those of the committee she represented) are clearly different from mine. It's too easy to say that she hoped to protect the status quo; I think her motivations were more complex than that. After all, she honestly believed that she was protecting my interests by instructing me in the ways of the academy. Her relaying of the committee's accusation that my writing was "artless" was her way of sending me the message that she believed I wrote what I did out of naiveté. During our conversation she told me several times that administrators are not creative, that unlike faculty who are also scholars, they reject intellectual complexity in favor of familiarity. Dr. Gatekeeper wanted me to see her as my ally, as one who shares my political consciousness but knows better than I do how to gain power and use it effectively. I, on the other hand, felt at least vaguely confident that I had shown sufficient progress in the three areas under review and wanted to mobilize my confidence into political action.

In performing her function as gatekeeper, my advisor was even more troubled by the following section of my dossier than she had been by the previous one:

> It's 8:10 a.m. on a Wednesday morning and I have just announced that . . . we will . . . sign on to the computers and use them for a classroom activity. Tom, who . . . informs me every day that he probably knows more about computers than I do, is particularly excited. . . . [H]e raises his voice above mine and bellows out instructions that are confusing to everyone in the room. Suddenly, about ten students raise their hands and

wave frantically. I hear things like, "What have I done?" "My computer doesn't work; the screen is blank," and "It's all screwed up!" Tom keeps yelling, I ask everyone to calm down, Tom keeps yelling. Finally, I snap, "Not another word, Tom." While I get everyone else to the same screen, Tom writes an e-mail to me in which he says that I humiliated him. When I am able to return to my computer, I respond that he is absolutely right, that a teacher should never make her students feel humiliated. In his next e-mail to me, he says that he has never been apologized to by a teacher before and says, "You are a great English teacher, my greatest ever."

Mary, student in my 8:00 a.m. English for Effective Communication class, is making her third attempt to pass the course. She is shy; most of the time she looks down at her lap or holds her book in front of her face. During a conference, she tells me she has been hospitalized for depression but that now she is ready to "get back into life and get through college." One day she comes running into class twenty minutes late. Her hands are shaking and she is breathing hard as she takes her seat. After class, she approaches me and explains that she has been in an automobile accident and that it was her fault. She tells me that she was praying and not paying attention to where she was going when she hit a car that was turning in front of her. In a moment of insight, I put my hand on her shoulder and ask, "Were you praying with your eyes closed?" She turns, waves her finger in my direction, and says, "Professor Gibson, *that* was my mistake."

Brian writes an angry journal entry about the paper he has just completed. He says that English teachers are awful people who don't care about their students or about writing. He seems to be challenging me to make negative comments about his paper so that he can characterize me as "just like the rest of them." During a conference, I ask Brian to explain his journal entry, to help me understand its motivation, and to work with me to find a way for us to have productive discussions about his writing. In what turns out to be a fifteen minute soliloquy, he tells me that he grew up in a small town, that his father is in prison for armed robbery, and that his English teacher in high school seemed to blame him for his father's tendency to be a "violent asshole."

Though it is difficult to admit, I strongly identify with Tom, Mary, and Brian. Like Tom, I know what it is like to be insecure, to try to alleviate that insecurity by acting in ways that seem inappropriate and odd to those around me, and to feel humiliated when I am confronted about my behavior. Like Mary, I started college only a short while after being released from a hospital where I was treated for depression; I was frightened and shy, and most of the time I felt like I was driving and praying with my eyes closed. And like Brian, I grew up in a small town where it seemed as though everyone knew about my violent family, considered us "white trash," and treated me accordingly. Tom, Mary, Brian, and I started college believing ourselves uniquely inadequate and fearing that our inadequacies were visible not only to our peers, but also to our teachers.

When I submitted my dossier, I knew that this part of my teaching self-evaluation statement was different from what I had seen in other dossiers. I also knew from listening to hallway chat that the committee was particularly concerned that our self-evaluation statements not make our students look different from, by which they meant inferior to, students in the rest of the university. Many of my colleagues believe that our college, which is the only open admissions unit on the University of Cincinnati's main campus, gets a bad rap because it focuses too much on its underprepared students. I disagree. I believe that our college has a unique opportunity to force the university to rethink its definitions of words like *student, success*, and *access*. Therefore, I was trying to engage in what Fuss calls "trading on" identity and experience. As a constructivist who believes strongly in the multiplicity and liquidity of identity and acknowledges the necessity of problematizing it, I know that identity can be used to "purchase" power. Using the "truth" of my experience, I constructed an identity as a formerly impoverished, scared, and shy student who had no idea how to perform in the academy until I was transformed by education into a rather outspoken middle-class professor of English. By construct, I do not mean that I lied; everything I said about myself in that introduction is true to my experience. What I do mean is that I chose in this instance to use my experience as currency, to use the familiar transformation metaphor to buy from the administrators I knew would read the dossier some understanding of my students' unique situations and potential.

I wanted to perform for those administrators an identity they usually associate with students they characterize as "not college material" and then complicate it with an identity they usually associate with professionals they characterize as "successful." I believed that if I was "out" about some of my experiences, I could mainstream (intellectually speaking) the experiences of students who face similar circumstances. And, because I did not want my students to be further disenfranchised by my attempts to buy them some power, I was extremely careful and thoughtful about the process I used to do that work. In short, I was trying to walk a thin line between using personal experience, or performing memory, to authorize a new kind of discourse and overwhelming my readers with information so unfamiliar that it seemed inappropriate.

In my conversation with Dr. Gatekeeper, and in the notes she gave to me to "guide revision," I was told that the college committee was extremely troubled by my admission that I feel such intense connection to my students. I was informed that, as a faculty member submitting a dossier for reappointment, my task is to identify with administrators, not students. Sitting beside me on the sofa in her office, sipping a cup of tea that she warmed with hot water from the silver pot on her desk, Dr. Gatekeeper explained that I needed to develop a better sense of my place in the academy if I wanted to advance at an appropriate rate. Astonished and perplexed, I finally asked Dr. Gatekeeper what would happen if I did not revise my self-evaluation statements or if I only made small, editorial changes. Her answer was that nothing would happen because my vitae showed sufficient achievement in teaching, service, and scholarship to merit reappointment.

In the end, I made only cosmetic changes to my dossier, and I received a positive letter from the college committee. I was able to follow the old feminist adage "the personal is political" and to disobey in the way McNaron suggests we should by "having and shaping [my] memories into coherent form" (8). And, throughout my discussion of my experiences with Dr. Gatekeeper, I have followed McNaron's lead. After all, I have given the representative from the college committee a rather obvious pseudonym; I have disclosed all kinds of personal information in what Probyn would call an intellectual "striptease"; and I have presented a text that pretty much insists that identity is constructed of memory and experience.

What would happen, though, if I assumed for a moment that Dr. Gatekeeper would be more accurately named Dr. Radical Constructivist and that her motive was to launch a rather leftist interrogation of the essentialist assumptions behind my adoption of identities? Suppose we assume that Dr. Radical Constructivist was asking questions similar to those asked of Probyn's work by feminist critic Laura Marcus:

> How can autobiography's emphasis on the individual, the development of the self and the confluence between author and textual "I," be reconciled with political and theoretical perspectives skeptical of traditional concepts of subjectivity, individualism, and textual authority? (Probyn 13)

Could it be that my attempts to authorize an intellectual discourse for students and faculty whose identities are constructed of memories like mine actually de-authorize that discourse? I know that stories like mine can be used to create silence. Let me give you an example.

I belong to a listserv of colleagues from composition studies. One of the most common strands on the list has to do with issues related to personal power in the academy. Recently, one of the white male members of the list was trying to discuss his feelings of relative powerlessness when compared to other white males. Female members of the list responded angrily, arguing that even when white men are not aware of it or try not to use it, the culture automatically endows them with unearned privilege. The man who had argued his powerlessness responded to those criticisms by explaining that in his dysfunctional family he was expected to take on much of the work and responsibility that would traditionally have been given to his mother. Then he described his family's circumstances in some detail. His disclosures were met with utter silence; no one on the list pursued the power issues originally under discussion; no one responded at all. To my mind, what happened there was that the man whose disclosures stopped the conversation attempted to complicate the issues at hand, but his attempts were so personal that no one knew how to critique his argument or the highly personal disclosure that might have brought us all to a more complex understanding of the way gender functions to empower and disempower in the academy.

If the committee representative is Dr. Radical Constructivist rather than Dr. Gatekeeper, she might have been asking me to reconsider the effectiveness of my approach. She might have been correct when she characterized my self-evaluation statements "artless," if artlessness has to do with not accomplishing my goals. If my intellectual/emotional striptease did nothing to help me create a space in the academy for students and faculty who perform identities such as femme lesbian, survivor of family violence, or recovering mental patient, then all that it did accomplish was to leave me standing buck naked in front of an audience. As is probably obvious, I believe that constructing and performing our nontraditional identities through personal experience is an inherently political act designed to transform the public spaces we inhabit from oppressive realms into inclusive realms. However, I also believe that, without consistent interrogation, over time acts that originate as political resistance can become familiar and institutionalized, thereby losing their power to create change.

Conclusion

Compositionists committed to creating classrooms in which traditional academic power structures are problematized and critiqued must also commit themselves to interrogating their own positions in those classrooms. We must think seriously about the identities we bring with us into the classroom, remain conscious of the way those identities interact with the identities our students bring, and insert ourselves fully into the shifting relationships between ourselves and our students at the same time that we resist the impulse to control those relationships. It is not enough for teachers merely to include in their curricula readings about race, class, gender, and sexuality, for the traditional inclusion model fails to challenge the academic mindset that assumes the centrality of white, middle-class, male, heterosexual values and desires. We must instead make ourselves acutely aware of and constantly responsive to the interplay of identities — both our own and those of our students. The stories we have told here emphasize the shifting nature of our own personal and academic identities. "Bi" presents herself as between comfortably recognizable identities: neither wholly at home among her working-class, neither safely straight nor stereotypically lesbian. "Butch" stresses the paradoxical nature of power in the academy, according to which "dyke" becomes less a liability than a "drag" choice that can be traded on. "Bar Dyke" illustrates the disjuncture among her own need to express herself in an authentic voice, the "tweed" rejection of that voice, and her sense that even what seemed most risky in her self-presentation in fact understated the lived reality. We offer them not as models for teachers, but rather as possibilities for complicating the experience of Otherness in the academy.

Note

1. Note that in the second and third columns I add a third "least privileged" category. Of course, on one level, this third category complicates the relentless binary oppositions that lent the original chart its shape. More than this, however, the sexuality column asserts that even in the context of heterosexual privilege, lesbians and gay men rank higher than bisexual or transgendered people. This ranking is because in our culture "lesbian" and "gay" are assumed to be coherent identities, while bisexuality and transgender are so fluid — and contested — as to resist the consistency of definition and the relative safety of coherence.

Works Cited

Budbill, David. "Roy McInnes." *Working Classics: Poems on Industrial Life*. Ed. Peter Oresick and Nicholas Coles. Chicago: U of Illinois P, 1990. 30.

Butler, Judith. *Gender Trouble: Feminism and the Subversion of Identity*. New York: Routledge, 1990.

———. "Imitation and Gender Insubordination." *Inside/Out: Lesbian Theories, Gay Theories*. Ed. Diana Fuss. New York: Routledge, 1991. 13–31.

Ellsworth, Elizabeth. "Why Doesn't This Feel Empowering? Working Through the Repressive Myths of Critical Pedagogy." *Feminisms and Critical Pedagogy*. Ed. Carmen Luke and Jennifer Gore. New York: Routledge, 1992. 90–119.

Esterburg, Kristin G. "'A Certain Swagger When I Walk': Performing Lesbian Identity." *Queer Theory/Sociology*. Ed. Steven Seidman. Malden, MA: Blackwell, 1996. 259–79.

Fuss, Diana. *Essentially Speaking: Feminism, Nature, and Difference*. New York: Routledge, 1989.

Kennedy, Elizabeth Lapovsky, and Madeline D. Davis. *Boots of Leather, Slippers of Gold: The History of a Lesbian Community*. New York: Penguin, 1994.

Laporte, Rita. "The Butch-Femme Question." *The Persistent Desire: A Femme-Butch Reader*. Ed. Joan Nestle. Boston: Alyson, 1992. 208–19.

McNaron, Toni A. H. *Poisoned Ivy: Lesbian and Gay Academics Confronting Homophobia*. Philadelphia: Temple UP, 1997.

Minh-Ha, Trinh. "Introduction: She, the Inappropriate(d) Other." *Discourse* 8 (1986/1987): 3–9.

Nestle, Joan. "Flamboyance and Fortitude: An Introduction." *The Persistent Desire: A Femme-Butch Reader*. Ed. Joan Nestle. Boston: Alyson, 1992. 13–20.

Oates, Joyce Carol. "Theft." *Ways of Reading*. Ed. David Bartholomae and Anthony Petrosky. 4th ed. Boston: Bedford Books, 1996. 471–507.

Probyn, Elspeth. *Sexing the Self: Gendered Positions in Cultural Studies*. London: Routledge, 1993.

Rich, Adrienne. "When We Dead Awaken: Writing As Re-Vision." *Ways of Reading*. Ed. David Bartholomae and Anthony Petrosky. 4th ed. Boston: Bedford Books, 1996. 549–62.

Stein, Arlene. "All Dressed Up, But No Place to Go? Style Wars and the New Lesbianism." *The Persistent Desire: A Femme-Butch Reader*. Ed. Joan Nestle. Boston: Alyson, 1992. 431–39.

Tracey, Liz, and Sydney Pokorny. *So You Want to Be a Lesbian?* New York: St. Martin's/Griffin, 1996.

Gibson, Marinara, and Meem's Insights as a Resource for Your Reflections

1. Consider the way this essay resonates with the preceding one by Juanita Rodgers Comfort. How does it illustrate or deviate from the vision of personal writing that she sets forth there?

2. Consider how the concepts in Dawn Skorczewski's essay in Chapter 1 might elucidate some of these stories — or how James Slevin's essay (also in Chapter 1) might open up certain complexities here, particularly around the issue of "evidence" and what certain pieces of evidence mean.

Gibson, Marinara, and Meem's Insights as a Resource for Your Writing Classroom

1. How does your own performance in the classroom imitate or depart from some of the potential models you find in this essay? Can you identify moments when you acted or spoke in ways that parallel any of these? If so, how "other" is the Other, and what are we to make of such a term in thinking about the cultural location of our classroom in the university? Can someone teaching a writing course ever really be considered Other, or are all faculty, at a certain level, marginal, even outsider-ish figures vis-à-vis mass culture? Can you think of ways to raise these questions or at least versions of them with your students? At the simplest level, the question you can raise with them is "What is a university?" and thereby circle back to some of the issues raised by Spellmeyer earlier in this chapter as well as by some of the essays in Chapter 1.

Annotated Bibliography

Research and reflection about writers, writing, and our practices of working with writers have proliferated over the last two decades. Ph.D. programs in rhetoric and composition theory have increased. You can find multiple resources to assist you as you teach yourself more about working with writers: Many sourcebooks and introductions to teaching writing are available; journals and NCTE (National Council of Teachers of English, <http://www.ncte.org>) anthologies offer additional theoretical and pedagogical perspectives on the range of topics addressed in this ancillary. Supplementing the works cited in the individual readings, this brief and selective bibliography offers you a starting point for broadening and deepening your thinking about writers and about ways to work with writers.

Entering the Field

Bruffee, Kenneth A. *A Short Course in Writing: Composition, Collaborative Learning, and Constructive Reading*. 4th ed. New York: Harper, 1993. This textbook with prompts for creative and transactional writing can be used in classrooms or by an individual for self-teaching. Bruffee's introduction offers a clear description of the relationships among writing, reading, teaching, and social construction as a needed direction in higher education.

Corbett, Edward P. J., Nancy Myers, and Gary Tate, eds. *The Writing Teacher's Sourcebook*. 4th ed. New York: Oxford UP, 2000. With each edition, the editing team adds new articles to a "canon" of essential discussions. These new articles extend theory and perspective or, as with readings about writers and computers, introduce the teaching strategies that had been considered on the "borders" or not central to teaching practice and have now become necessary strategies.

Ede, Lisa, ed. *On Writing Research: The Braddock Essays, 1975–1998*. Boston: Bedford/St. Martin's, 1999. This book collects nearly twenty-five years of articles that won composition's most prestigious award. It offers not only, then, the best composition scholarship of the last three decades, but a rich historical perspective on the ways the field's interests and methods have evolved.

Enos, Theresa, ed. *A Sourcebook for Basic Writing Teachers*. New York: Random House, 1987. Thirty-nine essays extend the discussion of basic writing. The collection focuses on the sociolinguistic dimensions of literacy and shows the range of contemporary research, theory, and practice, building on the foundation laid by Mina Shaughnessy in *Errors and Expectations*.

Goswami, Dixie, and Peter Stillman, ed. *Reclaiming the Classroom: Teacher Research as an Agency for Change*. Upper Montclair: Boynton-Cook, 1987. This book of essays describes reasons for and methods of conducting research in the classroom. Its scope is impressive, both in variety of research projects and methodologies and in discussions of the effects on instructors and students. The editor has pulled together important — and often original — essays by the leading teacher-scholars in composition and rhetoric.

Graves, Richard. *Rhetoric and Composition: A Sourcebook for Teachers and Writers.* 3rd ed. Portsmouth, NH: Boynton-Cook, 1990. Graves organized this sourcebook for writing teachers of all levels. The thirty-eight selections by well-known theorists and researchers document the energetic growth in the discipline of writing since 1963. Five chapters introduce the novice instructor to and update the veteran instructor about the growth and health of the scholarly discipline; practicing teachers' reports and "lore"; strategies to motivate student writers; questions about style; and "new perspectives, new horizons."

Irmscher, William F. *Teaching Expository Writing.* New York: Holt, 1979. The first text written for teachers of writing, this book poses the central questions every new teacher has. Irmscher writes from all the writer's resources: recall of his decades of teaching writing and his status as the "most senior" director of a composition program; humanistic observation of students as writers; conversation with writers and writing specialists; continuous reading in the discipline; and a lively imagination.

Lindemann, Erika. *A Rhetoric for Writing Teachers.* 3rd ed. New York: Oxford UP, 1995. Lindemann does not supplant Irmscher but enriches the reading about teaching writing. Her text reports both theory and practice.

Myers, Miles. *The Teacher-Researcher: How to Study Writing in the Classroom.* Urbana: NCTE, 1985. An introduction to classroom writing assessment and research into writing processes, this book reviews procedures for teacher research and theoretical frameworks. It shows teachers — from kindergarten through college — ways to study writing in the classroom using specific examples of research.

Pytlik, Betty, and Sarah Liggett, eds. *Preparing College Teachers of Writing: Histories, Theories, Programs, Practices.* New York: Oxford UP, 2002. This book assembles essays from nearly forty teachers from twenty-eight institutions to discuss what new teachers of writing at the college-level need to learn in order to teach well and what sorts of programs are most able to foster the intellectual and professional development of these teachers. It offers rich historical and theoretical contexts for thinking about teacher preparation, as well as insights into institutional, departmental, and programmatic structures, policies, and politics.

Roen, Duane, Veronica Pantoja, Lauren Yena, Susan K. Miller, and Eric Waggoner, eds. *Strategies for Teaching First-Year Composition.* Urbana: NCTE, 2002. An invaluable resource for thinking about the day-to-day workings of the classroom, this book offers several dozen short, practical essays on matters of immediate concern to beginning teachers. Many practical issues that are covered include constructing a syllabus or an assignment, situating the writing course in the context of the wider curriculum, and managing the classroom.

Shaughnessy, Mina P. *Errors and Expectations: A Guide for the Teacher of Basic Writing.* New York: Oxford UP, 1977. Shaughnessy was the first to demonstrate an understanding of the processes that "basic writers" experience. This landmark study helps clarify the philosophy of teaching basic writers and design curriculum and classroom practice to assist these writers to develop into mature writers.

Villanueva, Victor, ed. *Cross Talk in Comp Theory: A Reader.* Urbana: NCTE, 1997. This massive collection of articles represents an overview of the last thirty years of composition theory, a veritable "who's who" of the emerging discipline, and offers a kind of chronology of the field's major interests, as the editor puts it, from "process to cohesion to cognition to social construction to ideology." The book contains forty-one essays, including the major, historical statements by Janet Emig, James Berlin, Mike Rose, Mina Shaughnessy, and others.

Wiener, Harvey S. *The Writing Room: A Resource Book for Teachers of English*. New York: Oxford UP, 1981. Like Irmscher and Lindemann, Wiener offers advice about teaching writing from day one. His focus is the basic writing classroom and his discussion is informed—like Shaughnessy's—by his classroom experiences in an open-door writing program.

Teaching Writing: Key Concepts, Philosophies, Frameworks, and Experiences

Berthoff, Ann E. *Reclaiming the Imagination: Philosophical Perspectives for Writers and Teachers of Writing*. Upper Montclair: Boynton-Cook, 1984. Berthoff's theme of "reclaiming the imagination" reflects her philosophy and practice of encouraging writing as dialectical and reflective action.

Blitz, Michael, and C. Mark Hulbert. *Letters for the Living: Teaching Writing in a Violent Age*. Urbana: NCTE, 1998. By examining closely their students' accounts of life in New York City and in the mining and steel towns of western Pennsylvania, the authors argue that not only is violence a defining feature of many students' experience but that composition can be understood and even taught as an activity of peacemaking. The students in Blitz and Hulbert's classes wrote letters to each other about the diverse circumstances of their lives, and Blitz and Hulbert include this correspondence in the book and accompany it with their own e-mail correspondence to raise difficult questions about the stakes of our mission as teachers of writing.

Bruffee, Kenneth A. "Social Construction, Language, and the Authority of Knowledge: A Bibliographical Essay." *College English* 48 (Dec. 1986): 773–90. This introduction to social constructivist thought in literary criticism and history with its connections to composition studies lays out a foundation of a "social-epistemic" approach to teaching writing. Bruffee provides a bibliography to help other writing teachers explore these philosophical underpinnings.

Emig, Janet. "Writing as a Mode of Learning." *College Composition and Communication* 28.2 (May 1977): 122–27. Emig asserts a "first principle" that informs both contemporary practice in composition classrooms and writing-across-the-curriculum initiatives and programs.

Freire, Paulo. *Pedagogy of the Oppressed*. Trans. Myra Bergman Ramos. New York: Continuum, 2000. Among the most important books written about education in the twentieth century, this book sketches Freire's fundamental insights into the ways classrooms are configured either to alienate students and prepare them for lives of servitude in oppressive regimes or to liberate them through an ongoing practice of critical reflection, dialogue, collaboration, and what he calls "problem-posing." The pedagogy that Freire favors moves beyond the binary opposition of teacher versus student and encourages a more egalitarian dynamic in which everyone plays both roles.

Harris, Joseph. *A Teaching Subject: Composition Since 1966*. Upper Saddle River, NJ: Prentice Hall, 1997. This book is comprised of five elegant essays, each devoted to sorting out the recent history and the different meanings of a key term in the field of composition. The discussions of "Growth," "Voice," "Process," "Error," and "Community" offer one of the best introductions to the key debates within composition theory.

Hillocks, George, Jr. "What Works in Teaching Composition: A Meta-Analysis of Experimental Treatment Studies." *American Journal of Education* 93 (Nov. 1984): 133–70. Hillocks reviews experimental treatment studies of the teaching of composition over twenty years. While assessing effectiveness of different modes and focuses of instruction, he found that a writing-as-process focus within an "environmental mode" was more effective than other approaches to composition. His discussion of the implications of the research is especially useful.

Myers, Miles, and James Gray. *Theory and Practice in the Teaching of Composition*. Urbana: NCTE, 1983. The text has a double audience: It shows teachers how their strategies for teaching writing connect to and reflect an area of research, and it shows researchers that what teachers do intuitively can often be validated by research. The organization of readings by the teaching methods of processing, distancing, and modeling is especially useful.

North, Stephen. *The Making of Knowledge in Composition: Portrait of an Emerging Field*. Upper Montclair: Boynton-Cook, 1987. North discusses the place of "practitioner's lore" and the development of new research methodologies to study questions generated by reflection on the writing experiences of diverse students.

Raymond, James C. "What Good Is All This Heady, Esoteric Theory?" *Teaching English in the Two-Year College* (Feb. 1990): 11–15. Raymond answers this question (often posed by writing teachers who are busy with the daily tasks of working with writers). He "translates" poststructural theory into practical applications.

Smith, Frank. "Myths of Writing." *Language Arts* 58.7 (Oct. 1981): 792–98. Smith describes and clarifies twenty-one misconceptions that students, faculty, and the public hold about what writing is, how it is learned, and who can teach it.

Tate, Gary, Amy Rupiper, and Kurt Schick, eds. *A Guide to Composition Pedagogies*. New York: Oxford UP, 2001. This book surveys today's major approaches to the teaching of writing. Each chapter is devoted to a different approach and is written by a leading figure in the field. For example, Susan Jarratt discusses feminist approaches to teaching writing, and William Covino discusses rhetorical approaches. Other contributors include Chris Burnham on expressivism, Laura Julier on community-oriented pedagogy, and Susan McLeod on writing across the curriculum.

Thinking about the Writing Process

Generating a Draft

Fulwiler, Toby. *The Journal Book*. Portsmouth, NH: Boynton-Cook, 1987. Forty-two essays discuss the use of journals for discovery and invention in writing classrooms and in other disciplines across the curriculum.

Hilbert, Betsy S. "It Was a Dark and Nasty Night It Was a Dark and You Would Not Believe How Dark It Was a Hard Beginning." *College Composition and Communication* 43.1 (Feb. 1992): 75–80. Hilbert writes from lengthy experience as a writing instructor about beginning a new semester with new writers and predictable difficulties. The essay is a tonic and a healthy reminder to us about staying focused on why we teach writing as we enter or return to the classroom.

Johnson, T. R. "School Sucks." *College Composition and Communication* 52.4 (June 2001): 620–50. This essay explores the sources, incarnations, and resistances to pedagogies that emphasize writing as a process. Occasioned by the recent epidemic of school shootings and the author's memory of violent schoolyard rhymes, the essay ranges from rhetoric's historical discussion of the pleasures of writing to composition's more recent interest in academic professionalism to Gilles Deleuze's theory of masochism to the problem of teaching and learning in a consumer culture.

Perl, Sondra. *Landmark Essays on Writing Process*. Davis, CA: Hermagoras, 1994. This volume collects more than a dozen essays as well as a bibliography for further study on the central, even founding insight of contemporary composition — that is, the idea that composing is a process. The book features work by the leading figures in the field, work that articulated, substantiated, and disseminated the crucial new pedagogy that began to capture the attention of many writing teachers in the 1970s and that continues to focus our field in primary, pervasive ways.

Rose, Mike, ed. *When a Writer Can't Write: Studies in Writer's Block and Other Composing-Process Problems*. New York: Guilford, 1985. Eleven essays identify and analyze cognitive and affective dimensions of writing apprehension. The range of discussion emphasizes the effects of the environment and writing situations on the writer: Novice writers, ESL writers, graduate students, and professional writers are all affected by writing apprehension at various times.

———. *Writer's Block: The Cognitive Dimension*. Carbondale: Southern Illinois UP, 1984. This landmark book researching and analyzing writer's block emphasizes that a variety of cognitive difficulties are behind the problem. Case studies and the report of research results offer useful insights about ways to teach writing that will enable writers to get beyond blocks.

Young, Richard, and Yameng Liu, eds. *Landmark Essays on Rhetorical Invention in Writing*. Davis, CA: Hermagoras, 1994. This book offers nineteen classic essays from figures including Wayne Booth, Kenneth Burke, Janet Emig, and Chaim Perelman.

Revising a Draft and Crafting Sentences

Faigley, Lester. "Names in Search of a Concept: Maturity, Fluency, Complexity, and Growth in Written Syntax." *CCC* 31 (Oct. 1980): 291–300. In this article, Faigley argues that sentence combining does not directly correlate with mature and fluent writing style. The relationship between writing fluency and syntactical maturity is more complex than previous research acknowledges.

Flower, Linda, John R. Hayes, Linda Carey, Karen Schriver, and James Stratman. "Detection, Diagnosis, and the Strategies of Revision." *College Composition and Communication* 37 (Feb. 1986): 16–55. This article, produced through collaborative research and writing, describes some of the important intellectual activities that underlie and affect the process of revision. The article presents a working model for revision, for identifying "problems," and for generating solutions.

Harris, Muriel. "Composing Behaviors of One- and Multi-Draft Writers." *College English* 51 (Feb. 1989): 174–91. This study of eight experienced writers who described themselves as one-draft or multidraft writers provides useful materials for individualizing the processes of rewriting for students.

Mlynarczyk, Rebecca Williams. "Finding Grandma's Words: A Case Study in the Art of Revising." *Journal of Basic Writing* 15 (Summer 1996): 3–22. This essay explores how one basic writer's habit of revising for surface features only changed once her teacher's comments shifted from an emphasis on "fixing" the paper to discussing the essay empathetically with the student.

Sommers, Nancy. "Between the Drafts." *College Composition and Communication* 43 (Nov. 1992): 23–31. Nancy Sommers models the use of personal narrative as another kind of "evidence" to support or argue points in academic writing. She suggests that we should encourage and help students to use personal narrative in academic writing when they can. Use of personal narrative along with the traditional sources is a recurring theme in discussions of assisting writers as they rethink purpose, readership, and identity during the process of revising and re-visioning text.

Sudol, Ronald A., ed. *Revising: New Essays for Teachers of Writing*. Urbana: NCTE, 1982. Useful essays describing both the practice and the theory of revising strategies and processes.

Teaching Critical Reading and Writing

Bartholomae, David, and Anthony Petrosky. *Facts, Artifacts, and Counterfacts: Theory and Method for a Reading and Writing Course*. Upper Montclair: Boynton-Cook, 1986. A thorough plan for teaching writing is wholly intertwined with the act of reading critically. This book sets forth a course that is perhaps the complete opposite of the current traditional emphasis on dry exercises as well as the romantic interest in unfettered self-expression. Instead, it locates writing in a rhetorical context comprised of the writing of others. The book is surely one of the most important contributions to the field of composition in the 1980s, and it is yet unsurpassed as a detailed model of how the most recent, major developments in composition theory can be articulated on a day-to-day basis in the classroom.

Berthoff, Ann. "Is Teaching Still Possible? Writing, Meaning, and Higher-Order Reasoning." *College English* 46.6 (Dec. 1984): 743–55. Berthoff surveys and evaluates models of cognitive development and their connections to positivist perspectives on language. She discusses alternative perspectives on language and learning that emphasize reading and writing as interpretation and as the making of meaning.

Elbow, Peter. "Teaching Thinking by Teaching Writing." *Change* 15.6 (Sept. 1983): 37–40. Elbow's argument that "first-order creative, intuitive thinking and second-order critical thinking" can and should be encouraged in writing instruction, could be used for writing-across-the-curriculum initiatives.

Flower, Linda, and John R. Hayes. "The Cognition of Discovery: Defining a Rhetorical Problem." *College Composition and Communication* 31.1 (Feb. 1980): 21–32. The researchers used protocol analysis to study the differences between writers engaged in problem-solving cognitive processes.

Karbach, Joan. "Using Toulmin's Model of Argumentation." *Journal of Teaching Writing* 6.1 (Spring 1987): 81–91. This article illustrates the use of Toulmin's three-part model of argumentation: data, warrant, and claim. While describing heuristic procedures, Karbach proposes this informal logic as a strategy for teaching inductive and deductive logic within any writing assignment.

Kneupper, Charles. "Argument: A Social Constructivist Perspective." *Journal of the American Forensic Association* 17.4 (Spring 1981): 183–89. A communication specialist analyzes argumentation theory from the perspective of social constructionism. He examines uses and connections between argument as structure and argument as process along with their social-epistemic implications.

Lunsford, Andrea. "Cognitive Development and the Basic Writer." *College English* 41 (Sept. 1979): 39–46. After reviewing theories of cognitive development, Lunsford demonstrates that many basic writers operate below the stage of forming concepts and have difficulty in "decentering." She recommends strategies and writing assignments to help basic writers practice and acquire more complex cognitive skills.

Shor, Ira. *Critical Teaching and Everyday Life*. Chicago: U Chicago P, 1987. Influenced by Paulo Freire's pedagogical theories, Shor emphasizes learning through dialogue. His analysis of education is inclusive: open admissions teaching of writing, traditional and nontraditional students and learning environments, elite and nonelite educational missions, and "liberatory" teaching modes that challenge social limits of thought and action and encourage cultural literacy. Cognitive skills are acquired and enhanced through collaborative problem solving and reflection leading to action.

Wink, Joan. *Critical Pedagogy: Notes from the Real World*. 2nd ed. New York: Longman, 2000. This analyzes the often-difficult rhetoric of critical pedagogy to push to new, deeper perspectives on the dynamics of the classroom and the community. The book is rooted in powerful, personal narratives and written in a lively, even informal voice. It brings otherwise abstract ideas to life and constantly tests those ideas against the author's own experience of many years in the classroom.

Teaching Writing with Computers and Teaching Visual Literacy

Blair, Kristine, and Pamela Takayoshi, eds. *Feminist Cyberscapes: Mapping Gendered Academic Spaces*. Stamford, CT: Ablex, 1999. This collection of essays explores varying contexts (virtual and physical, institutional and cultural) that shape electronic space for women. Although issues of gender and cyberspace have most often been relegated to the margins, the editors of this collection hope to bring into the mainstream of composition studies a rich array of concerns about the relationship between women and technology as a way of understanding women's participation in and resistance to systems of inequality. The contributors to the collection rely on materialist feminism, feminist critiques of technology design and its uses, and feminist pedagogy to examine computerized classrooms, Internet technologies (including e-mail, Listservs, and MOOs), and professional development opportunities for women working in computers and composition.

Bolter, Jay David. *Writing Space: The Computer, Hypertext, and the History of Writing*. Hillsdale, NJ: Lawrence Erlbaum, 1991. This book offers a useful contextualization of computer-based writing in the larger history of writing itself, emphasizing the ways computers are at once rooted in familiar technologies and, at the same time, are able to destablize the power-relations and hierarchies that those old technologies support. Bolter provides a useful set of "first principles" for re-imagining rhetoric in the age of the electronic text.

Bruce, Bertram, Joy Kreeft Peyton, and Trent Batson, eds. *Network-Based Classrooms: Promises and Realities*. New York: Cambridge UP, 1993. The collaborative technology of "electronic networks for interaction" accommodates and prompts the social construction of knowledge. The collection ranges from descriptions of "how to" to "effects." Caveat: The rapid development and redesign of the technology and the advent of the World Wide Web may make the nuts and bolts obsolete, so focus on themes, issues, and significance to writing improvement.

Hassett, Michael, and Rachel W. Lott. "Seeing Student Texts." *Composition Studies* 28.1 (2000): 29–47. This article argues for increased attention to document design in composition courses. Centering their discussion on four types of design—intra-textual (fonts), inter-textual (headings), extratextual (tables and charts), and supra-textual (table of contents)—Hassett and Lott offer a pedagogy that focuses students' attention on audience needs.

Hawisher, Gail E., and Charles Moran. "Electronic Mail and the Writing Instructor." *College English* 55.6 (Oct. 1993): 627–43. The writers describe advantages and effects of introducing electronic communication to a composition course. The essay gives practical advice to newcomers.

Hawisher, Gail E., and Cynthia L. Selfe, eds. *Passions, Pedagogies, and 21st Century Technologies*. Logan: Utah State UP; Urbana: NCTE, 1999. This anthology collects twenty-three essays from leaders in the field of computers and composition, including Charles Moran, Anne Frances Wysocki, Patricia Sullivan, and Lester Faigley. The selections in this collection cover such wide-ranging topics as technology and literacy, pedagogical matters, ethical and feminist concerns, and visual rhetoric.

Lanham, Richard. *The Electronic Word: Democracy, Technology, and the Arts.* Chicago: U of Chicago P, 1993. In a reader-based study, rhetorician Lanham analyzes the creative potential of electronic writing for coming closer to these long-standing goals: access, unfettered imagination, and effective communication. He views the electronic word as dramatically and healthily changing the construction and experience of "knowledge."

Responding to and Evaluating Student Writing

Anson, Chris, ed. *Writing and Response: Theory, Practice, and Research.* Urbana: NCTE, 1989. The essays include discussion of responding to student journal writing, responding via electronic media, and responding in conferences. Theoretical perspectives and instructional practice are intermixed.

Belanoff, Patricia, and Marcia Dickson, eds. *Portfolios: Process and Product.* Portsmouth, NH: Boynton-Cook, 1991. In the first comprehensive collection of writings on using portfolios for classroom and portfolio assessment, the editors called for "practitioners' lore" and research. This is the book to start with when considering use of writing portfolios.

Berthoff, Ann. *Forming, Thinking, Writing: The Composing Imagination.* 2nd ed. Portsmouth, NH: Boynton-Cook, 1988. Berthoff focuses on the reading-writing relationship within a course organized around the central task of teaching composition. Insights and practical suggestions abound.

Black, Laurel, Donald Daiker, Jeffrey Sommers, and Gail Stygall, eds. *New Directions in Portfolio Assessment: Reflective Practice, Critical Theory, and Large-Scale Scoring.* Portsmouth, NH: Boynton-Cook, 1994. This collection moves readers beyond the merely introductory discussion of portfolios to critical questions of practice and theory: How do changing notions of literacy intersect with the growing interest in portfolios? How can we apply the portfolio approach to large-scale projects of assessment, involving not simply individual classrooms, but whole programs and schools? How do gender and cultural expectations affect readers of portfolios? This collection addresses these and other challenging questions for the reader already versed in the basics of portfolio assessment.

Brooke, Robert E. *Writing and Sense of Self: Identity Negotiation in Writing Workshops.* Urbana: NCTE, 1991. Brooke describes the effects of responding in the context of writing through workshops: effects on the kinds of writing projects students risked and effects on their processes of negotiating identities as writers.

Cooper, Charles R., and Lee Odell, eds. *Evaluating Writing: Describing, Measuring, Judging.* Urbana: NCTE, 1977. With its comprehensive survey of ways teachers can describe writing and measure the growth of writing, this remains a useful sourcebook. The discussion of involving students in the evaluation of writing includes individual goal setting, self-evaluation, and peer evaluation. Multiple responses to multiple processes and features of the writing are implicitly recommended.

Flower, Linda, and Thomas Hucking. "Reading for Points and Purposes." *Journal of Advanced Composition* 11.2 (Fall 1991): 347–62. By researching how undergraduate and graduate students use point-driven or purpose-driven reading strategies, the authors conclude that readers who use a point-driven strategy tend to stay at a less complex level of interpretation.

Freire, Paulo. *Education for Critical Consciousness.* New York: Continuum, 2002. Freire's argument for educational reform focuses on the need for the development of "critical consciousness" in learners, who thus become the agents rather than the subjects of their education. Freire's focus is congenial with social-epistemic rhetoric and emphasizes the social construction of knowledge through collaborative work.

Hamp-Lyons, Liz, ed. *Assessing Second Language Writing in Academic Contexts*. Norwood, NJ: Ablex, 1991. Twenty-one essays examine the multiple issues of assessing second language writing. Many of the articles focus on assessment design and decision making that affect ESL writers in an assessment program, but the principles of good assessment practices for diverse populations are clearly defined.

Hillocks, George, Jr. "The Interaction of Instruction, Teacher Comment, and Revision in Teaching the Composing Process." *Research in the Teaching of English* 16 (Oct. 1982): 261–82. An early study of the effects of instructor response on student revision and attitudes toward writing. The article points out that helpful commentary or conference discussion promotes a writer's growth.

Huot, Brian, and Michael Williamson, eds. *Validating Holistic Scoring for Writing Assessment: Theoretical and Empirical Foundations*. Cresskill, NJ: Hampton, 1993. While research into composing processes and the cultural contexts that shape them have boomed in recent decades, inquiry into how we assess student writing has proceeded at the same pace. This collection takes up the issue of assessment from diverse angles: the history of holistic scoring, the question of reliability, placement exams, and ESL programs. An important, thorough, expansive set of essays on a much neglected composition issue with which every teacher must grapple.

Newkirk, Thomas, ed. *Only Connect: Uniting Reading and Writing*. Upper Montclair: Boynton-Cook, 1986. The fifteen articles in this collection by major scholars in the discipline of "English" explore the relationships of reading and literary study to composition.

Noguchi, Rei R. *Grammar and the Teaching of Writing: Limits and Possibilities*. Urbana: NCTE, 1991. Beginning with the shared conviction that grammar must be taught within the context and processes of drafting and revising, Noguchi helps writing teachers identify the sites where grammar and writing overlap and suggests productive ways to integrate grammar instruction with issues of meaning, organization, and style.

Odell, Lee. "Defining and Assessing Competence in Writing." *The Nature and Measurement of Competency in English*. Ed. Charles R. Cooper. Urbana: NCTE, 1981. Practical advice about clarifying what an instructor defines as writing competence along with descriptions of holistic and other assessment measures for both classroom and large-scale assessment.

Roseberry, Ann S., Linda Flower, Beth Warren, Betsy Bowen, Bertram Bruce, Margaret Kantz, and Ann M. Penrose. "The Problem-Solving Processes of Writers and Readers." *Collaboration through Writing and Reading: Exploring Possibilities*. Ed. Anne Haas Dyson. Urbana: NCTE, 1989. 136–64.

Welch, Nancy. "One Student's Many Voices: Reading, Writing, and Responding with Bakhtin." *Journal of Advanced Composition* 13.2 (Fall 1993): 493–502. Welch demonstrates a "Bakhtinian" reading of a student text to argue that teachers should respond to the many voices in a student text.

White, Edward M. *Assigning, Responding, Evaluating: A Writing Teacher's Guide*. 3rd ed. New York: Bedford/St. Martin's, 1998. For the "state of the art" in writing assessment, White surveys and evaluates the designs and applications of writing assessments and helps writing instructors use the information garnered through assessment to improve classroom instruction.

———. *Teaching and Assessing Writing*. San Francisco: Jossey-Bass, 1985. The publisher here is significant: In this first major discussion of the symbiosis of writing assessment and classroom teaching, the preeminent publisher of discourse in higher education agreed that this would be an important test. This should be the first book a new writing teacher uses to learn about contemporary research and practice in understanding, evaluating, and improving students' writing performance.

Yancey, Kathleen Blake, ed. *Portfolios in the Writing Classroom: An Introduction.* Urbana: NCTE, 1992. This collection focuses on the use of writing portfolios in secondary and higher education courses across the curriculum. The articles describe objectives and designs for the use of portfolios. This is a very useful introduction to the field.

Issues in Writing Pedagogy

Fostering Literacy

Brandt, Deborah. *Literacy as Involvement: The Acts of Writers, Readers, and Texts.* Carbondale: Southern Illinois UP, 1990. This book explores the ways literacy is commonly understood and criticizes, in particular, the dominant theory that becoming literate hinges on a withdrawal from the immediate social world. Brandt suggests that the move from oral to literate modes of action does not significantly reconfigure the fundamental terms of the interpretive dynamic—context, reference, and meaning.

Cushman, Ellen, Eugene R. Kintgen, Barry M. Kroll, and Mike Rose, eds. *Literacy: A Critical Sourcebook.* Boston: Bedford/St. Martin's, 2001. A useful overview of the contemporary discussion about literacy, this substantial volume of nearly forty lengthy essays considers the topic of literacy in terms of technology and knowledge, cultural history and community involvement, and politics and the workforce.

Dyson, Anne Haas, ed. *Collaboration through Writing and Reading: Exploring Possibilities.* Urbana: NCTE, 1989. The discussion of the interrelationships of reading, writing, and learning was first generated at a conference of researchers and theorists concerned with literacy teaching and training.

Heath, Shirley Brice. "An Annotated Bibliography on Multicultural Writing and Literacy Issues." *Quarterly of the National Writing Project and the Center for the Study of Writing and Literacy* 12.1 (Winter 1990): 22–24. This bibliography lists and annotates sixteen books and articles that focus on multicultural writing and literacy issues, including bilingual education, ESL, writing instruction, literacy, and multicultural education.

Many, Joyce. *Handbook of Instructional Practices for Literacy Teacher-Educators.* Mahwah, NJ: Lawrence Erlbaum, 2001. This book offers accounts by well-known literacy researchers of how they approach literacy instruction and what they have learned from their actual classroom experiences. Divided into specific areas within literary studies, this book offers a strong starting point for those interested in questions of literacy.

Fostering Diversity

Delpit, Lisa. *Other People's Children: Cultural Conflict in the Writing Classroom.* New York: New, 1995. This book develops a powerful, if counterintuitive argument: Much so-called "liberatory" pedagogy actually silences and marginalizes the very minority students it seeks to help. These nine essays explore the particular ways in which the expectations, hopes, and desires that minority students bring to the classroom can diametrically oppose the good intentions of their teachers.

Eichorn, Jill, Sara Farris, Karen Hayes, Adriana Hernandez, Susan C. Jarratt, Karen Powers-Stubbs, and Marian M. Schiachitano. "A Symposium on Feminist Experiences in the Composition Classroom." *College Composition and Communi-*

cation 43 (Oct. 1992): 297–332. In describing their experiences using feminist composition pedagogies, the writers illustrate ways of respecting diversity within a writing community.

Flynn, Elizabeth A. "Feminist Theories/Feminist Composition." *College English* 57.2 (Feb. 1995): 201–12. Flynn reviews four book-length studies in "feminist composition," connecting them to theoretical perspectives and demonstrating the vigorous dialogue from many directions that feminist pedagogues and theorists have engendered.

Herrington, Anne. "Basic Writing: Moving the Voices on the Margin to the Center." *Harvard Educational Review* 60.4 (Nov. 1990): 489–96. Herrington describes the redesign of a basic writing course to give voice to marginalized minority students. After a shift to reading works by mostly nonwhite authors, students were encouraged to reflect in writing on those readings and on their experiences of marginalization.

Rose, Mike. *Lives on the Boundary: The Struggles and Achievements of America's Underprepared*. New York: Free, 1989. Through personal narrative and incisive analysis, Rose describes the underclass of students representing diverse cultures and subcultures who are considered underachieving, remedial, or illiterate. Rose speculates about the nature of literacy and learning curricula that could empower these marginalized writers and learners.

Teaching ESL Students

Carson, Joan G., and Gayle L. Nelson. "Writing Groups: Cross-Cultural Issues." *Journal of Second Language Writing* 3.1 (1994): 17–30. Citing the dearth of research on communication assumptions and behaviors of Asian students in collaborative writing communities, Carson and Nelson call for additional studies of ways in which culturally specific beliefs and behaviors might affect cooperation and interaction in peer response groups and collaborative writing projects.

Connor, Ulla. *Contrastive Rhetoric: Cross Cultural Aspects of Second Language Acquisition*. New York: Cambridge UP, 1996. This excellent survey of the major theories and empirical studies of second-language acquisition pays particular attention to the way a student's first language interferes with the process of learning a second language. A powerful blend of work from a variety of fields, the book combines discourse theory, genre theory, applied and theoretical linguistics, as well as composition studies and rhetoric.

Kasper, Loretta, ed. *Content-Based College ESL Instruction*. Mahwah, NJ: Lawrence Erlbaum, 2000. This book is designed to train teachers in a particular approach to ESL students: pedagogy rooted in actual cultural contents. It offers clear descriptions of classroom practices, as well as for assessing student progress, and even delineates means for incorporating technology.

Leki, Ilona. *Understanding ESL Writers: A Guide for Teachers*. Portsmouth, NH: Boynton-Cook, 1992. This is an excellent handbook for learning about the concerns, expectations, and errors of ESL students. Written for the double audience of ESL instructors and writing teachers, it provides useful advice about responding to the texts of ESL writers.

Reid, Joy, and Barbara Kroll. "Designing and Assessing Effective Writing Assignments for NES and ESL Students." *Journal of Second Language Writing* 3.1 (1995): 17–41. Reid and Kroll emphasize the need to design fair writing assignments that encourage students to learn from writing experiences as they demonstrate what course material they know and understand. They analyze successful and flawed writing prompts and assignments from the perspective of ESL writers; the practical advice they offer is also pertinent to mainstream composition teaching.

Writing across the Curriculum

Anson, Chris, John Schwiebert, and Michael M. Williamson. *Writing across the Curriculum: An Annotated Bibliography*. Westport, CT: Greenwood, 1993. This very useful bibliography describes both scholarship in and pedagogic strategies for extending and using writing across the curriculum, whether the model is "writing as learning" or "writing in the discipline."

Bazerman, Charles, and David Russell, eds. *Landmark Essays on Writing across the Curriculum*. Davis, CA: Hermagoras, 1994. These thirteen essays represent key texts in the development of the writing-across-the-curriculum movement and offer a valuable historical and theoretical synopsis of the field. Included are classic works by Janet Emig, Greg Myers, Susan McLeod, and Toby Fulwiler.

Duke, Charles, and Rebecca Sanchez, eds. *Assessing Writing across the Curriculum*. Durham: Carolina Academic P, 2001. This book offers guidelines for effective assessment of student writing and tools to improve writing in diverse content areas. It also offers ways to rethink particular methods of instructing and grading and ways to craft assignments more effectively.

Fulwiler, Toby, and Art Young, eds. *Language Connections: Writing and Reading across the Curriculum*. Urbana: NCTE, 1982. This text, aimed at all college and university instructors, offers theoretical perspectives and practical activities to prompt writing as learning. The text encourages peer evaluation, conferences between instructors and students, and shared evaluation and includes a bibliography on cross-curricular language and learning.

About the Contributors

Guy Allen is a professor and director of the professional writing and communication program at the University of Toronto at Mississauga. He is currently working at Mount Sinai Hospital in Toronto with Dr. Allan Peterkin, a psychiatrist, and Julie Hahn, an occupational therapist, to explore narrative as a healing tool. The published chronicle of the research will be entitled *A Primer of Narrative Medicine* and coauthored with Allan Peterkin. He is also working on a few books with professional writing and communication students on writing and collections of work by new writers. He works as managing editor for Life Rattle Press and broadcasts new writing on his and Arnie Achtman's sixteen-year-old radio program, Life Rattle (CKLN, 88.1).

David Bartholomae chairs the Department of English at the University of Pittsburgh. His books include *Writing on the Margins: Essays on Composition and Teaching* (winner of the 2005 MLA Mina Shaughnessy Award), *Facts, Artifacts and Counterfacts*, and the textbook *Ways of Reading: An Anthology for Writers*. He is also coeditor of the Pittsburgh Series on Composition, Literacy, and Culture and a former chair of the Conference on College Composition and Communication.

James A. Berlin's *Rhetoric and Reality: Writing Instruction in American Colleges, 1900–1985*, began to exert enormous influence on the field of composition studies immediately after it was published in 1987. *Rhetoric and Reality* was not only the first detailed and powerful study of how the field developed, but it also provided crucial support for what was then an exciting new turn in composition studies—the emergence of rhetorics informed by social-constructionist theory. In his teaching career, Berlin held positions such as director of freshman English at the University of Cincinnati and professor of English at Purdue University. A leading figure in the cultural studies movement in composition, Berlin was writing *Rhetorics, Poetics, and Cultures: Re-Figuring English Studies* when he died quite suddenly at what should have been the midpoint in a long career.

Ann E. Berthoff was among the first scholars to bring rigorous and wide-ranging philosophic depth to our thinking about writing instruction. Her most notable contributions to composition include *Thinking/Forming/Writing: The Composing Imagination* (1978), *The Making of Meaning: Metaphors, Models, and Maxims for Writing Teachers* (1981), *Reclaiming the Imagination: Philosophical Perspectives for Writers and Teachers of Writing* (1984), *The Sense of Learning* (1990), and *The Mysterious Barricades: Language and Its Limits* (1999). She is professor emeritus at the University of Massachusetts Boston.

Wayne C. Booth is a professor emeritus at the University of Chicago. His most well-known books include *A Rhetoric of Fiction* and *The Company We Keep: An Ethics of Fiction*. He is himself the subject of an increasing number of scholarly books, essays, and graduate seminars, for the depth and range of his work in rhetoric in the latter half of the twentieth century may ultimately draw comparison to that giant of the first half of the century, Kenneth Burke. Before his death in 2005, he wrote a memoir, *My Many Selves: The Quest for a Plausible Harmony*, which was published in 2006.

Francis Christensen was a professor of English at the University of Southern California. He began to publish essays about sentence-level pedagogy in the early 1960s, all of which are collected in *Notes Toward a New Rhetoric*. These essays have been widely discussed since his death in 1970, and in 1978, Lester Faigley tested Christensen's ideas in formal, empirical studies. Faigley found that Christensen's program indeed produced student writing that was measurably more mature and received better ratings in blind, holistic scoring.

Juanita Rodgers Comfort is an associate professor of English at West Chester University, where her teaching and scholarship currently focus on the essay traditions of African American women writers. She has published on a range of topics in *College Composition and Communication, WPA Journal, The Relevance of English: Teaching that Matters in Students' Lives, Beyond English, Inc.*, and *Contrastive Rhetoric Revisited and Redefined*.

Robert J. Connors was perhaps the most rigorous historian the field of rhetoric and composition has ever had. He won the Braddock Award in 1982 for his study of the rise and fall of the modes of discourse. He is also the author of *Composition-Rhetoric: Backgrounds, Theory, Pedagogy*, as well as numerous other works. From 1984 through 2000, he taught at the University of New Hampshire, where he served as a professor of English and director of the writing center. At the time of his death in a motorcycle accident in 2000, he was working on a book on the history of process pedagogy.

Lisa Delpit is an eminent scholar and the executive director for the Center of Urban Education and Innovation at Florida International University in Miami, Florida, and former Benjamin E. Mays Professor of Urban Educational Leadership at Georgia State University in Atlanta. In 1993, she received the award for outstanding contribution to education from the Harvard Graduate School of Education. Her published books on education include *Other People's Children: Cultural Conflict in the Classroom* (1995); *The Real Ebonics Debate: Power, Language, and the Education of African-American Children* (coedited with Theresa Perry, 1998); and *The Skin That We Speak: Thoughts on Language and Culture in the Classroom* (coedited with Joanne Kilgour Dowdy, 2002). One of her most recent published articles, "Katrina's Last Victims?" cowritten with Charles Payne, appeared in the January 2007 issue of *The Nation*.

Peter Elbow has been a central figure in the field of composition for more than three decades. His numerous books and articles most often focus on the phenomenology of invention, authorial voice, and teaching. His early books in the 1970s, *Writing without Teachers* and *Writing with Power*, are landmarks of that period. His debate with David Bartholomae in the early to mid-1990s was a focal point of the field in that phase of its development. Elbow is professor emeritus of English at the University of Massachusetts, Amherst, where he directed the writing program. He also taught at Massachusetts Institute of Technology, Franconia College, Evergreen College, and Stony Brook University of the State University of New York (where he also directed the writing program). He recently published "The Believing Game and How to Make Conflicting Opinions More Fruitful" in *Nurturing the Peacemakers in Our Students*.

Michelle Gibson is an associate professor at the University of Cincinnati, where she taught composition for over ten years and where she now serves as director of undergraduate studies for the Women's Studies Department. Along with poetry, she has published work on composition and cultural studies. She and Jonathan Alexander edited a section of *JAC: Journal of Advanced Composition* entitled Queer Compositions. They also continue to edit *QP: Queer Poetry*, an online poetry journal. With Deborah Meem, Gibson coedited *Femme/Butch: New Considerations of the Way We Want to Go* and *Lesbian Academic Couples*. Gibson, Meem, and Alexander are currently writing *Finding Out: LGBT History, Politics, and Culture*, a textbook for introductory lesbian-gay-bisexual-transgender courses to be published by SAGE Press in 2009.

Gerald Graff is a professor of English and education at the University of Illinois at Chicago. He has coedited six books and authored seven, including *Professing Literature: An Institutional History* (1987), *Beyond the Culture Wars* (1993), *Clueless in Academe: How Schooling Obscures the Life of the Mind* (2004), and its sequel, cowritten with his wife Cathy Birkenstein, *They Say / I Say: The Moves That Matter in Academic Writing* (2005). He is also the founder of Teachers for a Democratic Culture and president-elect of the Modern Language Association of America for 2008.

Maxine Hairston was a professor emerita of English at the University of Texas. She was director of freshman English for four years and associate dean for two. She earned her M.A. in European history from the University in 2003 and continued to take courses in history and classics. She was an active member of the National Council of Teachers of English and the Conference on College Composition and Communication, of which she was chair in 1985. She also published many articles in professional journals from 1976 to 1992 and authored five textbooks for teaching college composition. In 2002 several of her former graduate students published a book in her honor entitled *Against the Grain: A Volume in Honor of Maxine Hairston*. Always a writer, she composed her own obituary, which appeared in the *Austin American Statesman* on July 24, 2005.

Joseph Harris is an associate professor of English and director of the Duke University writing program. He served as editor of *College Composition and Communication* from 1994 to 1999, and has authored three books: *A Teaching Subject: Composition since 1966, Rewriting: How to Do Things with Texts*, and *Media Journal: Reading and Writing about Popular Culture*.

Muriel Harris is a professor emerita of English and retired director of the writing center at Purdue University. She has published several books, including two composition textbooks, and numerous articles and book chapters about individualizing instruction in writing and the theory, pedagogy, and administration of writing centers. She has edited the *Writing Lab Newsletter* since 1976, when she first established it. In addition to earlier awards for scholarship and teaching, in 2000 she was the winner of the NCTE Exemplar Award and also the NCTE Rewey Belle Inglis Award.

Patrick Hartwell taught at Indiana University at Pennsylvania and authored a number of works on the teaching of writing, among them *Open to Language: A New College Rhetoric*. He was also known for his development of various games to generate and revise prose. He died in the spring of 2003.

Douglas D. Hesse is founding director of the Marsico Writing Program and professor of English at the University of Denver. He chaired the Conference on College Composition and Communication and was president of the Council of Writing Program Administrators. At Illinois State University, he directed the honors program, the Center for the Advancement of Teaching, the graduate program in English studies, and the writing program. His several dozen articles and chapters focus on creative nonfiction, writing program administration, and writing theory and pedagogy. Coauthor of the *Simon and Schuster Handbook for Writers*, he is currently completing *Creating Nonfiction*, with Becky Bradway, for Bedford/St. Martin's.

Mary E. Hocks is an associate professor of English at Georgia State University, where she teaches courses in writing, composition theory, and digital rhetoric. Her edited collection, *Eloquent Images: Word and Image in the Age of New Media*, appeared in a new paperback edition in 2005 from MIT University Press.

Steven D. Krause is a professor in the Department of English Language and Literature at Eastern Michigan University, where he teaches undergraduate and graduate courses that explore the connections between writing and technology. Among other places, his writings have appeared in *Kairos, College Composition and Communication Online, Computers and Composition*, and *The Chronicle of*

Higher Education. He has given numerous panel presentations, invited addresses, and workshop presentations at conferences and events around the country. Currently, he is working on a book-length research project on blogs as "writerly" spaces. He maintains his own "official" blog at <http://www.stevendkrause.com/academic/blog>.

Martha Marinara is currently codirecting the Information Fluency Initiative at the University of Central Florida, where she is an associate professor in the English department. From August 1998 until August 2006, she directed the first-year writing program at UCF. Marinara received a B.A. and an M.A. in English from Southern Connecticut State University in New Haven, and a Ph.D. in rhetoric from Lehigh University in 1993. She has published two textbooks and several articles on writing pedagogy, feminism, and queer theory. Marinara has also published poetry and fiction, and her first novel, *Street Angel*, was released October 31, 2006.

Deborah Meem is professor of English and women's studies at the University of Cincinnati. Her work has been published in *Journal of the History of Sexuality, College Composition and Communication, Feminist Teacher*, and *Studies in Popular Culture*. Her edition of Eliza Lynn Linton's 1880 novel *The Rebel of the Family* was published in 2002. With Michelle Gibson, she coedited *Femme / Butch: New Considerations of the Way We Want To Go* (2002) and *Lesbian Academic Couples* (2005). With Jonathan Alexander and Michelle Gibson, she is writing *Finding Out*, an introduction to LGBT studies textbook for SAGE Press, which will appear in 2009. She chairs the Lesbian-Gay-Bisexual-Transgender Faculty-Staff Task Force and serves as co-graduate director in the Department of Women's Studies at UC.

Sondra Perl is professor of English at Lehman College and the Graduate Center of the City University of New York. Her works on composing processes and on felt sense have long been benchmarks in composition studies. Her most recent books include *Felt Sense: Writing with the Body* and *On Austrian Soil*, a teaching memoir that focuses on cross-cultural dialogue after the Holocaust.

James P. Purdy is assistant professor of English at Bloomsburg University of Pennsylvania where he teaches writing courses and directs the writing center. He received his Ph.D. from the Center for Writing Studies at the University of Illinois at Urbana-Champaign. His articles have appeared in *Pedagogy: Critical Approaches to Teaching Literature, Language, Composition, and Culture* and *Kairos: A Journal of Rhetoric, Technology, and Pedagogy*, and he is coauthor of a chapter to appear in the forthcoming collection *Reading (and Writing) New Media: A Collection of Essays and New Media*. He also serves on the editorial board of *Computers and Composition: An International Journal*.

Mike Rose is a professor of social research methodology at UCLA. He has published numerous books and articles on teaching writing, most famously *Lives on the Boundary*, a critique of the American school system in which he argues against viewing underprepared students as "remedial" or "deficient." Rose has received awards from the National Academy of Education and the McDonnell Foundation. He has also won a Guggenheim Fellowship, the Grawemeyer Award in Education, and the Commonwealth Club of California Award for Literary Excellence in Non-Fiction. His most recent books are *The Mind at Work: Valuing the Intelligence of the American Worker* and *An Open Language: Selected Writing on Literacy, Learning, and Opportunity*.

Tony Silva is a professor of English at Purdue University, where he teaches classes for ESL students and ESL teachers and directs the ESL writing program. With Ilona Leki, he edits the *Journal of Second Language Writing*; with Paul Kei Matsuda, he hosts the Symposium on Second Language Writing.

Dawn Skorczewski is associate professor of English and American literature and director of university writing at Brandeis University. She is also on faculty at the Massachusetts Psychoanalytic Institute and at the Cincinnati Psychoanalytic Institute. She has served as director of composition at the University of Redlands and Emerson College. Her most recent work includes "Getting Attica Out of Her Mind: A Psychoanalytic Memoir," written in collaboration with Anni Bergman, and *Teaching One Moment at a Time: Disruption and Repair in the Classroom* (2005).

James Slevin was a professor of English, director of the writing program, and director of curriculum and pedagogy for the Center for Social Justice at Georgetown University. He served at the highest levels with all of the major professional organizations, including MLA, CCCC, NCTE, the National Humanities Alliance, and the Council for Basic Education. He published thirty essays in books and journals and served as an outside evaluator or consultant to over twenty English departments and writing programs. At the time of his death in May 2006, he was working on a new project: *For Difficulty: Social Justice and the Intellectual Work of the University.*

Nancy Sommers is the director of the expository writing program at Harvard University. She has won the highly prestigious Braddock Award twice (1983, 1993), and, most recently, she has directed a longitudinal study of the writing abilities of the Harvard class of 2001, from which two films and many articles have emerged.

Kurt Spellmeyer is a professor of English and director of the writing program at Rutgers University, a position he has held for twenty-two years. He has published numerous articles and three books, most recently *Arts of Living: Reinventing the Humanities for the Twenty-First Century.*

John Trimbur is professor of writing and rhetoric and codirector of the professional writing program at Worcester Polytechnic Institute. Since 2001, he has been working in South Africa with the community-based activist organization Asbestos Interest Group and doing research on language policy as a visiting professor at the Centre for Higher Education Development at the University of Cape Town. He is currently working on a book project tentatively titled "Linguistic Memory and Empire: An Essay on the Uneasy Settlement of English in the U.S." Among his many published articles are "Language Policy and Normalization in South Africa: Some Other Lessons"; with Bruce Horner, the Richard Braddock Award-winning "English Only and U.S. College Composition"; and "Linguistic Memory and the Politics of U.S. English."

Nancy Welch is a professor of English at the University of Vermont. She has published scholarly work in *College English, College Composition and Communication*, and *JAC: A Journal of Composition Theory*, as well as fiction in *The Three Penny Review* and *Prairie Schooner*. A collection of her short stories, *The Road from Prosperity*, was published in 2005 by Southern Methodist University Press. Her most recent book is *Living Room: Teaching Public Writing in a Privatized World* (Boynton/Cook 2008).

Acknowledgments (continued from page iv)

James A. Berlin, "Rhetoric and Ideology in the Writing Class," from *College English* (September 1988). Copyright © 1988 by the National Council of Teachers of English. Reprinted with permission.

Ann E. Berthoff, "Learning the Uses of Chaos," originally read at the annual conference of the Canadian Council of Teachers of English, Carlton University (Ottawa), May 1979. Published in *Reinventing the Rhetorical Tradition*, the collection of conference papers. Reprinted with permission of the Canadian Council of Teachers of English Language Arts.

Wayne C. Booth, "The Rhetorical Stance," from *College Composition and Communication* (October 1963). Copyright © 1963 by the National Council of Teachers of English. Reprinted with permission.

Francis Christensen, "A Generative Rhetoric of the Sentence," from *College Composition and Communication* 14 (1963):155–61. Copyright © 1963 by the National Council of Teachers of English. Reprinted with permission.

Juanita Rodgers Comfort, "Becoming a Writerly Self: College Writers Engaging Black Feminist Essays," from *College English* 47:2 (June 2000). Copyright © 2000 by the National Council of Teachers of English. Reprinted with permission.

Robert J. Connors, "The Erasure of the Sentence," from *College Composition and Communication* 52:1 (2000): 96, 28. Copyright © 2000 by the National Council of Teachers of English. Reprinted with permission.

Lisa Delpit, "The Politics of Teaching Literate Discourse," from *Other People's Children: Cultural Conflict in the Classroom*. Copyright © 1995 by Lisa Delpit. Reprinted with permission of Copyright Clearance Center on behalf of the publisher.

Peter Elbow, "Closing My Eyes as I Speak: An Argument for Ignoring Audience," from *College English* (January 1987). Copyright © 1987 by the National Council of Teachers of English. "Ranking, Evaluating, and Liking: Sorting Out Three Forms of Judgment," from *College English* 55:2 (February 1993). Copyright © 1993 by the National Council of Teachers of English. Reprinted with permission.

Michelle Gibson, Martha Marinara, and Deborah Meem, "Bi, Butch, and Bar Dyke: Pedagogical Performances of Class, Gender, and Sexuality," from *College Composition and Communication* 52, 2000: 69–95. Copyright © 2000 by the National Council of Teachers of English. Reprinted with permission.

Gerald Graff, "Introduction: In the Dark All Eggheads Are Gray" and "The Problem Problem and Other Oddities of Academic Discourse," from *Clueless in Academe: How Schooling Obscures the Life of the Mind*, pp. 1–16 and 43–61. Copyright © 2003. Reprinted with permission of Yale University Press.

Maxine Hairston, "Diversity, Ideology, and Teaching Writing," from *College Composition and Communication* 43.2 (May 1992): 179–95. Copyright © 1992 by the National Council of Teachers of English. Reprinted with permission.

Joseph Harris, "Error," first published in *A Teaching Subject: Composition Since 1966*. Copyright © 1997 by Joseph Harris. Reprinted with permission of the author.

Muriel Harris and Tony Silva, "Tutoring ESL Students: Issues and Options," from *College Composition and Communication* (December 1993). Copyright © 1993 by the National Council of Teachers of English. Reprinted with permission.

Patrick Hartwell, "Grammar, Grammars, and the Teaching of Grammar," from *College Composition and Communication* 51:4 (June 2000). Copyright © 2000 by the National Council of Teachers of English. Reprinted with permission.

Douglas D. Hesse, "Portfolio Standards for English 101," from *Strategies for Teaching First-Year English*, edited by Duane Roen, Veronica Pantoja, Lauren Yena, Susan K. Miller, and Eric Waggoner. Copyright © 2002 by the National Council of Teachers of English. Reprinted with permission.

Mary E. Hocks, "Understanding Visual Rhetoric in Digital Writing Environments," from *College Composition and Communication* 54:4 (June 2003). Copyright © by the National Council of Teachers of English. Reprinted with permission. This selection contains screenshots from Anne Frances Wysocki, "Monitoring Order: Visual Desire, the Organization of Web Pages, and Teaching the Rules of Design," *Kairos* 3.2 (Fall 1998), http://english.ttu.edu/kairos/3.2/features/wysocki/bridge.html; Christine Boese, "The Ballad of the Internet Nutball: Chaining Rhetorical Vision Visions from the Margins to the Mainstream in the Xenaverse," Diss. Online 1998 http://www.nutball.com/dissertation/index.htm; and "Colorblind Casting in Shakespearean Works," Spelman College (Web address no longer available). Reprinted with permission.

Steven D. Krause, "When Blogging Goes Bad: A Cautionary Tale about Blogs, Email Lists, Discussion, and Interaction." http://english.ttu.edu/kairos/9.1/praxis/krause/index.html. Reprinted with permission of the author.

Sondra Perl, "Understanding Composing," from *College Composition and Communication* 31:4 (1990). Copyright © 1990 by the National Council of Teachers of English. Reprinted with permission.

James P. Purdy, "Calling off the Hounds: Technology and the Visibility of Plagiarism," from *Pedagogy: Critical Approaches to Teaching Literature, Language, Composition, and Culture*, Vol. 5, No. 2. Copyright © 2005 Duke University Press. Reprinted with permission of the author.

Mike Rose, "Rigid Rules, Inflexible Plans, and the Stifling of Language: A Cognitivist Analysis of Writer's Block," from *College Composition and Communication* 31:4 (1980). Copyright © 1980 by the National Council of Teachers of English. Reprinted with permission.

Dawn Skorczewski, "From Playing the Role to Being Yourself: Becoming the Teacher in the Writing Classroom," from *Teaching One Moment at a Time* by Dawn Skorczewski. Copyright © 2005 University of Massachusetts Press. Reprinted with permission of the publisher.

James Slevin, "A Letter to Maggie," from *Introducing English: Essays in the Intellectual Work of Composition* by James F. Slevin. © 2001. Reprinted with the permission of the University of Pittsburgh Press.

Nancy Sommers, "Revision Strategies of Student Writers and Experienced Adult Writers," from *College Composition and Communication* 31:4 (December 1980). Copyright © 1980 by the National Council of Teachers of English. "Responding to Student Writing," from *College Composition and Communication* 33: 2 (May 1982). Copyright © 1982 by the National Council of Teachers of English. Reprinted with permission.

Kurt Spellmeyer, "Can Teaching, of All Things, Prove to Be Our Salvation?", original title, "The Postscript," from *Arts of Living: Reinventing the Humanities for the Twentieth-Century*. Copyright © 2003 by State University of New York Press. Reprinted with permission of State University of New York Press. All rights reserved.

John Trimbur, "Delivering the Message: Typography and the Materiality of Writing," from *Rhetoric and Composition as Intellectual Work* edited by Gary A. Olson. Copyright © 2002 by the Board of Trustees, Southern Illinois University. Reprinted with permission of the publisher.

Nancy Welch, "Toward an Excess-ive Theory of Revision," from *Getting Restless: Rethinking, Writing, and Revision*. Copyright © 1997 by Nancy Welch. Published by Heinemann, a division of Reed Elsevier Inc., Portsmouth, NH. Reprinted with permission. All Rights Reserved.